6th Edition

CANADIAN MARKETING IN ACTION

Keith J. Tuckwell

St. Lawrence College

www.investopedia.com
www.fool.com

PEARSON

Prentice Hall

Toronto

National Library of Canada Cataloguing in Publication

Tuckwell, Keith J. (Keith John), 1950–
   Canadian marketing in action / Keith J. Tuckwell. 6th ed.

Includes bibliographical references and index.
ISBN 0-13-120091-7

   1. Marketing. 2. Marketing—Canada. I. Title.

HF5415.12.C3T75 2003   658.8   C2003-900214-4

ISBN 0-13-120091-7

Vice President, Editorial Director: Michael Young
Senior Acquisitions Editor: Kelly Torrance
Marketing Manager: Deborah Meredith
Developmental Editor: Pamela Voves
Supervising Production Editor: Avivah Wargon
Copy Editor: Alex Moore
Production Coordinator: Andrea Falkenberg
Page Layout: Carolyn E. Sebestyen
Permissions Research: Lisa Brant
Photo Research: Lisa Brant
Art Director: Mary Opper
Cover Design: Julia Hall
Cover Images: Photonica; Getty Images; PhotoDisc

1 2 3 4 5   08 07 06 05 04

Printed and bound in Canada.

Statistics Canada information is used with the permission of the Minister of Industry, as Minister responsible for Statistics Canada. Information on the availability of the wide range of data from Statistics Canada can be obtained from Statistics Canada's Regional Offices, its World Wide Web site at **http://www.statcan.ca** and its toll-free access number, 1-800-263-1136.

PEARSON
Prentice
Hall

To Esther . . . and our children, Marnie,
Graham, and Gordon.

Contents

[4] Consumer Buying Behaviour   86

[5] Business-to-Business Marketing and Organizational Buying Behaviour   115

PART THREE Marketing Planning   138

[6] Market Segmentation and Target Marketing   139

PART FIVE Price   264

[10] Price Strategy and Determination   265

[11] Price Management   291

PART SIX Distribution   313

[12] Distribution Channels and Physical Distribution   314

[13] Wholesaling and Retailing   344

PART SEVEN Integrated Marketing Communications   371

Preface

When approaching the sixth edition of Canadian Marketing in Action, and after consultation with reviewers, I determined that the flow of the book would be better if the sequence of some chapters was changed. The major change involved the relocation of two chapters: Strategic Marketing Planning and Market Segmentation and Target Marketing. Considerable thought went into this change and I hope that it will make sense to users of the text.

This new edition has been revised based on feedback from current and potential adopters who expressed a desire for a practical marketing textbook that contained new information on several important topics. Among these are customer relationship management (CRM), e-commerce and e-marketing activities, and integrated marketing communications. There is more extensive coverage for each of these topics. Throughout the book, many new examples and illustrations are provided to demonstrate direct application of key concepts. Virtually every illustrative vignette is new. All this has been achieved while maintaining the page count and price point that will be attractive to students.

The original concept of the book has not changed. This book originated because the education market in Canada wanted a good, wholly Canadian resource for teaching marketing. Canadian Marketing in Action provides a careful balance between theory and practice and presents material in a clear, concise style and readable format that students appreciate. It also meets the needs of faculty who face the pressures of time and reduced course hours allocated to introductory marketing courses.

While preparing every new edition I continue to be amazed by how fast the field of marketing is changing. Trends in technology and constantly shifting consumer preferences have immediate impact on marketing strategy and how material is presented in a book of this nature. When reviewing this book you will notice that a significant amount of material has changed—it was an extensive revision process.

Essentially, the organization and presentation of material in Parts 2 and 3 have changed in the new edition. Part 2 is now titled Inputs for Marketing Planning and includes chapters on Marketing Research, Consumer Buying Behaviour, and Business-to-Business Marketing and Organizational Buying Behaviour. These chapters include content relevant for development of a marketing plan and lead directly into Part 3, Marketing Planning. Part 3 includes chapters on Market Segmentation and Target Marketing, and Strategic Marketing Planning.

In addition to meeting the needs stated above, my personal goal was to produce the most up-to-date text in marketing, a text that would not only reflect the state of current marketing practice but also indicate the future direction of marketing in Canada. The key to meeting this challenge was not only having specific chapters on key topics such as electronic marketing but integrating new content on hot topics throughout the book. Customer relationship management, for example, is covered in Chapter 1, Contemporary Marketing; Chapter 5, Business-to-Business Marketing and Organizational Buying Behaviour; Chapter 7, Strategic Marketing Planning; and Chapter 17, Internet Marketing.

The market for an introductory marketing textbook is very competitive: several longstanding and successful books are readily available to teachers and students, and I would like to think that *Canadian Marketing in Action*, now into its sixth edition, is one of those books. When you review the features of the book described in the next sections, I am confident you will find it unique and worthy of consideration.

Critical Issues

This edition focuses on essential issues that are shaping contemporary marketing practice. Among these issues are customer relationship management practices; electronic commerce and Internet-based marketing practices; strategic alliances and partnering among companies; socially responsible marketing; the impact of technology on marketing strategy; database marketing and customer retention strategies; and integrated marketing communications.

New Features

Input from reviewers has resulted in several key changes to the Sixth Edition. Among the more important and exciting changes and additions are the following:

- In Chapter 1 all hot topics are presented briefly to provide an overview of issues that influence the direction of marketing strategies. A subsection on Ethical Practices and Social Responsibility has been expanded. Such expansion is essential considering the rash of negative business and marketing news that has surfaced in recent years. New examples of both good practices and controversial practices are provided.

- Chapter 2, Marketing Environments, includes new examples to demonstrate fundamental aspects of the marketing mix and up-to-date commentary on the latest external trends that influence strategy. Trends are changing so fast it is difficult to keep pace. Special attention is paid to technology, for it is the single most important influence right now.

- Part 2 has been renamed Inputs for Marketing Planning, so content focuses on the collection of research information and data, consumer behaviour, and business buying behaviour. New content about online research is provided, as are new examples demonstrating the application of common consumer and business behaviour concepts. Electronic buying or e-procurement, as it is referred to, is new to Chapter 5.

- Considerable time was spent on Chapter 7, Strategic Marketing Planning. The content is now presented in a sequence that is similar to the flow and presentation of a marketing plan. The influence of corporate plans on marketing plans is presented more simply and clearly. Discussion of content is directly related to the models (presented in figures) included in the chapter.

- Chapters 8 and 9 focus on product-related strategies and decisions. Additional coverage is given to packaging, as packaging now plays a more important role in distinguishing one product from another. The issue of cult brands that appeal to younger generations is included as a new topic.

- Chapters 10 and 11 deal with price-related decisions. While pricing policies are firmly entrenched, several issues have become newsworthy. Among these are the persistent role of price incentives in the automobile industry; price wars in many prominent product categories; and yield pricing strategies in prominent retail organizations.

- Chapters 12 and 13 deal with strategies and decisions related to distribution, wholesaling, and retailing. This section contains expanded coverage of vertical integration concepts and channel conflict and cooperation. As well, there is stronger coverage of the role being played by the Internet and how it is changing distribution strategy. The growing position of American retailers in Canada and the expanding role of electronic retail operations among retailers receive additional coverage.

- Part 7, Integrated Marketing Communications, has been altered so that there is more balanced coverage of the individual components of IMC. In Chapter 14, Integrated Marketing Communications: Advertising and Public Relations, the section on advertising has been streamlined somewhat to afford expanded coverage of public relations: organizations use public relations more frequently and positively today. Chapter 15, Direct Response and Interactive Communications, has been altered to provide better balance between direct response techniques and interactive techniques. Generally, all forms of direct response communications are growing in importance.

- Part 8, Emerging Directions in Marketing, retains its focus on electronic marketing, services and not-for-profit marketing, and global marketing. A stand-alone chapter on Internet marketing (Chapter 17) is essential so that students can quickly grasp and understand the impact electronic marketing techniques are having on the practice of marketing. This chapter can be considered an "essentials" version of electronic marketing practice. Unique characteristics of services, not-for-profit, and global markets, and the corresponding strategies to suit those markets, remain the focus of Chapters 18 and 19.

- Of the 39 Marketing in Action vignettes (an average of 2 per chapter), 30 are new and 5 are updated from the previous edition. These vignettes cover newsworthy stories about key concepts. New companies featured include Procter & Gamble, General Motors, Cisco, A&W, Canadian Tire, Sony, Air Canada, Loblaws, Dell, Grand & Toy, and Four Seasons Hotels, among others.

- Many new illustrations have been added to give the text a fresh, new look. New ads and photographs from 3M, General Motors, Visa International, Volvo, S.C. Johnson, Callaway Golf, Nissan, Shell Oil, and many others aptly demonstrate important marketing concepts.

- Where appropriate, discussion of key topics has been enhanced. Key topics include customer relationship management, the role and influence of technology on marketing practice, lifestyle changes and their effect on marketing, new competition created by the presence of the Internet, the development of new distribution strategies as a means of growth, and the increasing role of direct and individualized communications with customers.

- The new edition retains important elements of the previous ones. The text is presented in a practical, student-oriented style and provides good balance between theory and practice. It is written from a Canadian perspective while considering the influences on marketing from all over the world. No American co-authors influence the direction this book takes or the emphasis it places on the topics covered. All content decisions are based on input from Canadian reviewers and users of the book.

- All the traditional marketing theories are included. Essential topics such as the marketing mix, internal and external influences on marketing, consumer and organizational buying behaviour, market segmentation, target marketing and positioning, strategic planning, and marketing research principles are presented. All these concepts are considered in the context of consumer marketing, business-to-business marketing, services and not-for-profit marketing, and global marketing.

Pedagogy

- **Objective-Based Learning**
  Each chapter starts with a list of learning objectives directly related to the key concepts presented in the chapter. As each objective is covered in the body of the text, a reference in the margin identifies the concepts linked to that objective.

- **Photos, Figures, Charts, and Advertisements**
  Throughout each chapter, key concepts and applications are illustrated with strong visual material. Sample advertisements augment the Canadian perspective.

- **Key Terms**
  Key terms are highlighted within the text and listed at the end of each chapter with page references. Many are defined in the glossary at the end of the text.

- **Weblinks**
  Helpful Internet sites are provided throughout the text and are easily identifiable by the Weblinks icon shown here in the margin.

- **Chapter Summaries**
  The summary at the end of each chapter helps reinforce main points and concepts.

- **Review Questions; Discussion and Application Questions**
  These two sets of questions allow students to review material and apply the concepts learned in the chapter.

- **E-Assignments**
  Each chapter includes one or two exercises that involve the student in using the Internet or evaluating the role of the Internet in developing marketing strategies.

- **Appendices**
  Appendix A, The Financial Implications of Marketing Practice, is a marketing mathematics section, expanding on the content presented in the pricing chapters. Appendix B provides a complete list of the Canadian Marketing Cases: see the description below.

- **Glossary**
  A glossary of the principal key terms and definitions appears at the end of the textbook.

- **Video Cases**
  A new selection of videos is available with the Sixth Edition, on tape and on the Companion Website. These videos were selected from three CBC shows: "Venture," "Undercurrents," and "Marketplace." Also included are segments from "On Location," created specifically for use with Pearson's Marketing texts. Details of how to use the videos in class discussion are included in the Instructor's Manual. Each video illustrates an important element of marketing discussed in the textbook. Each case is described briefly, and a short series of questions is included to stimulate discussion.

Canadian Marketing Cases

Accompanying the textbook, posted at the Companion Website (**www.pearsoned. ca/tuckwell**) and included in the Instructors' Manual are 16 cases, 10 new cases along with 6 that were included with the previous edition. Students access these cases using a code included with each copy of this edition. (Instructors will be able to access the cases through the Instructor Resrouces portion of the site: please see your sales representative for details.) Some of the companies featured in the new cases include Cineplex Odeon Theatres, Country Style Food Services, Hudson's Bay Company, *National Post*, Levi Strauss & Company, and the Toronto Blue Jays. The pricing section includes cases that are quantitative in nature and give the student an opportunity to apply various pricing concepts. All cases are ideal for in-class discussion, presentations, or take-home assignments. A complete list of the cases can be found in Appendix B of the textbook, in the Instructor's Manual, and on the Companion Website.

Supplements

INSTRUCTOR'S MANUAL WITH VIDEO GUIDE AND CANADIAN MARKETING CASES (0-13-120288-X)

Prepared by the author, the manual includes learning objectives, chapter summaries, answers to chapter questions, additional illustrations of key concepts, 16 Canadian marketing cases, guideline answers to case questions, a synopsis of video cases, and an extensive listing of topics suitable for term papers and class presentations.

COMPANION WEBSITE

The Companion Website at **www.pearsoned.ca/tuckwell** is a handy reference for students. The site provides video resources and an online study guide that includes chapter quizzes and application and Internet exercises. The Virtual Marketing Library lists annotated weblinks organized by key areas of marketing, providing a great source of valuable information right at the user's fingertips. A protected area of the site provides access to the Canadian Marketing Cases. Please check your access card for instructions about registering for access to this portion of the site.

TEST ITEM FILE (0-13-120284-7)

More than 1900 questions have been prepared to help test students on the material they have studied. Emphasis in this Sixth Edition is placed on application-oriented multiple-choice questions. Answers, with page references, are given for all objective questions and suggested answers are provided for short answer/essay questions.

PEARSON TESTGEN (0-13-120283-9)

The Pearson TestGen is a special computerized version of the Test Item File that enables instructors to view and edit the existing questions, add questions, generate tests, and print the tests in a variety of formats. Powerful search and sort functions make it easy to locate questions and arrange them in any order desired. TestGen also enables instructors to administer tests on a local area network, have the tests graded electronically, and have the results prepared in electronic or printed reports. Issued on a CD-ROM, the Pearson TestGen is compatible with IBM or Macintosh systems.

CBC/PEARSON EDUCATION CANADA VIDEO LIBRARY (0-13-120281-2)

The videos that accompany the Sixth Edition cover a broad range of marketing topics and feature well-known Canadian and international companies. The problems and opportunities faced by these companies and the strategic direction they might consider can be the focal point of student discussion or assignments.

TELEVISION BUREAU OF CANADA BESSIES (0-13-121422-5)

The Television Bureau of Canada annually recognizes excellence in Canadian television advertising with The Bessies awards program. Copies of the 2001 and 2002 show reels have been made available by the Television Bureau to instructors using this edition of *Canadian Marketing in Action*. These tapes feature the best in recent advertising by Canadian companies for Canadian audiences. Please contact your Pearson Education Canada sales representative for details. These videos are subject to availability. For further information about The Bessies or to inquire about the Television Bureau of Canada's library of nearly 30 000 commercials, please contact the Television Bureau of Canada, 160 Bloor Street East, Suite 1005, Toronto, Ontario, M4W 1B9 (416-923-8813) or visit their website at **www.tvb.ca**

ELECTRONIC TRANSPARENCIES IN POWERPOINT AND AD GALLERY (0-13-120286-3)

A collection of 340 transparencies, culled from the textbook or specifically designed to complement chapter content, is available electronically in PowerPoint software on an Instructor CD-ROM. Selected full-colour ads published in the text are available for viewing in the Ad Gallery included on this CD.

ADVERTISING **AD**VENTURE CD (0-13-140314-1)

This CD-ROM contains a whole host of award-winning ads for use in the classroom. This supplement is available to qualified adopters through your Pearson sales representative.

PEARSON CUSTOM PUBLISHING (WWW.PRENHALL.COM/CUSTOMBUSINESS)

Pearson Custom Publishing can provide you and your students with texts, cases, and articles to enhance your course. Choose material from Darden, Ivey, Harvard Business School Publishing, NACRA, and Thunderbird to create your own custom casebook. Contact your Pearson sales representative for details.

ONLINE LEARNING SOLUTIONS

Pearson Education Canada supports instructors interested in using online course management systems. We provide text-related content in WebCT and Blackboard. To find out more about creating an online course using Pearson content in one of these platforms, contact your Pearson sales representative.

NEW! INSTRUCTOR'S ASSET

Pearson Education is proud to introduce Instructor's ASSET, the Academic Support and Service for Educational Technologies. ASSET is the first integrated Canadian service program committed to meeting the customization, training, and support needs for your course. Ask your Pearson sales representative for details!

YOUR PEARSON SALES REPRESENTATIVE

Your Pearson sales rep is always available to ensure you have everything you need to teach a winning course. Armed with experience, training, and product knowledge, your Pearson rep will support your assessment and adoption of any of the products, services, and technology outlined here to ensure our offerings are tailored to suit your individual needs and the needs of your students. Whether it's getting instructions on TestGen software or specific content files for your new online course, your Pearson sales representative is there to help.

...also available for your students (ask your Pearson sales representative for details!)

MASTERING MARKETING CD-ROM (0-13-046245-4)

This self-paced, interactive software helps reinforce marketing principles by linking theory to practice. It features 12 video episodes, bringing key marketing concepts to life. Students watch as employees at CanGo, a fictional Internet company, are faced with various realistic marketing issues. Interactive exercises accompany each video segment, challenging students to analyze the issue and develop new marketing strategies. Available for a small extra charge in a value-package.

MARKETING PLAN PRO CD-ROM (0-13-065436-1)

Available at a modest extra charge in a value-package, this highly acclaimed software enables students to build a marketing plan from scratch. Marketing Plan Pro also includes sample marketing plans.

THE MARKETING PLAN: A HANDBOOK WITH CD-ROM by Marian Burke Wood (0-13-175947-7)

This brief paperback, which includes Marketing Plan Pro software (described above), is the ideal companion for any course in which students will create a marketing plan.

STRATEGY MAGAZINE

Students can log in to **www.strategymag.com/studentpromo** and receive access for one year to past and current article searches on **www.strategy.com**, a powerful research tool.

Organization of the Text

The book is divided into eight sections:

PART 1 — MARKETING TODAY

The initial section presents an overview of contemporary marketing, its processes, and practices. It introduces the concept of the marketing mix and presents external influences on the planning and implementation of marketing programs. Special topics include ethics and social responsibility, customer relationship management, technology and the role it plays in marketing today, the Internet and e-commerce, and globalization of marketing practice.

PART 2 — INPUTS FOR MARKETING PLANNING

This section examines the inputs a manager considers prior to developing a marketing plan. The emphasis is on various marketing research techniques used to collect information and data, as well as content that demonstrates the nature and application of basic consumer behaviour and business buying behaviour concepts.

PART 3 — MARKETING PLANNING

With appropriate background information available, the marketing manager now shifts attention to identifying and selecting target markets and the development of marketing plans to reach and influence those targets. Marketing plans are influenced by a variety of factors, the main influence being the direction a company wants to take. The links between corporate plans and marketing plans are discussed in detail in this section.

PART 4 — PRODUCT

In this section, the text examines the first element of the marketing mix. How products are developed, marketed, and managed is the focus of the product chapters. This part includes coverage of branding strategy, package design, new product development and innovation, and rejuvenation strategies for established products.

PART 5 — PRICE

This section explores the role of price in the marketing mix. The discussion deals with pricing strategies, the role of pricing in achieving corporate objectives, and methods of determining prices. Also discussed is how the price function is managed in business organizations.

PART 6 — DISTRIBUTION

This section concentrates on the roles of distribution planning and physical distribution, wholesaling, and retailing. The role and impact of the Internet on the distribution of goods and services is a major topic of discussion. Also, emerging trends such as vertical and horizontal integration and electronic retailing are discussed in more detail than in the previous editions.

PART 7 — INTEGRATED MARKETING COMMUNICATIONS

This section has been reorganized to include three distinct chapters dealing with related marketing communications strategies. The initial chapter covers advertising and public relations. The second chapter covers direct response and interactive communications. The third concentrates on sales promotion, personal selling, event marketing, and sponsorships. The intent is to show how communications strategies are integrated in order to achieve marketing objectives. In this edition there is better balance in terms of presenting each component of the marketing communications mix.

PART 8 — EMERGING DIRECTIONS IN MARKETING

The practice of marketing is constantly evolving. With this in mind, this section retains the stand-alone chapter on electronic marketing. While electronic marketing concepts are integrated throughout the text, it is important for a student to understand the fundamentals of electronic marketing while appreciating that it is an addition to, and not a replacement of, traditional marketing practices. The unique considerations of services and not-for-profit marketing and the importance of global marketing are also presented in this section.

ACKNOWLEDGMENTS

Many organizations and individuals have contributed to the development of this textbook. I would like to thank the following organizations sincerely for their cooperation and contribution.

3M Canada Inc.
Accenture
Apple Canada
Bell Canada
BMW Canada
Calloway Golf
Canadian Broadcasting Corporation
Canadian Business
Canadian Geographic
Canadian National Railways
Canadian Tire
Canadian Tourism Commission
Clarica Life Insurance Company
The Clorox Company
Colgate-Palmolive Canada
Del Monte Foods
Dell Computer Corporation
Delta Hotels & Resorts
Ebay.ca
Fidelity Investments
The Ford Motor Company of Canada
    Limited
The Gillette Company
Honda Canada, Acura Division
Kellogg Canada Inc.
Kraft Canada Inc.
L'Oreal Canada

Manulife Financial
NCH Promotional Services Ltd.
Nestlé Canada
Nissan Canada Inc
Pfizer Inc.
Porsche
Preferred Hotels & Resorts
Procter & Gamble
Reckitt Benkeiser Canada Inc.
S.C. Johnson Company
Save.ca
Sears Canada Inc.
Shell Canada Limited
Shoppers Drug Mart
Siemens Canada
Sony Canada
Sprint Canada
Statistics Canada
Tetley Tea Company
Toyota Motor Company of Canada
Unilever Inc.
United Way
VISA Canada Association
Volvo Cars of Canada Ltd.
William J. Wrigley Company
Xerox Canada Ltd.
Yahoo.ca

For undertaking the tedious task of reviewing the textbook at various stages of development, I am indebted to my colleagues. The input provided by each of you was appreciated. I would like to sincerely thank Lily Buchwitz, Wilfrid Laurier University; Brahm Canzer, CEGEP John Abbott College; Martha Cheney, University of Calgary; Bill Corcoran, Grande Prairie Regional College; James Coughlin, Sir Sandford Fleming College; Steve Janisse, St. Clair College; Henry Klaise, Durham College; Shelley M. Rinehart, Univeristy of New Brunswick; and Murray Sang, Concordia University.

For making a contribution to the Canadian marketing cases, I would like to sincerely thank Gary Bissonette, CEO of the Kingston Family Y, Kingston, Ontario. Gary provided the Western Trail and "Fit For Life" cases that appear in this edition and the previous edition.

From Pearson Education Canada, I would like to pass on an a special "thank you" to Kelly Torrance, Senior Acquisitions Editor; Pamela Voves, Developmental Editor; Avivah Wargon, Production Editor; and Alex Moore, freelance copy editor. Finally, I must thank the at-home children of the Tuckwell family for their patience and understanding. You see me working away and wonder why I do it. Thank you, Graham and Gord! A special thank-you to my wife Esther, who has endless patience for what seems like a never-ending process. We deserve a holiday!

Keith J. Tuckwell
2003

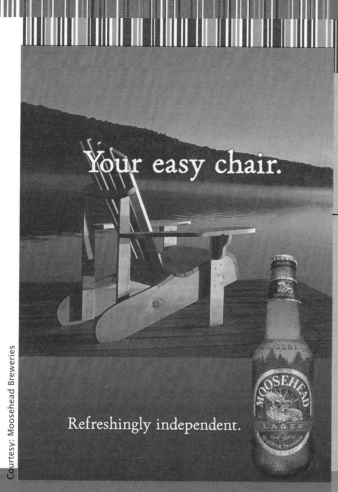

Your easy chair.

Refreshingly independent.

Marketing Today

The purpose of this book is to examine what is involved in the practice and management of marketing. Part 1 presents an overview of contemporary marketing, its processes, and practices.

Chapter 1 shows how marketing has evolved to become the focal point of business activity. Emphasis is placed on the scope of contemporary marketing practice.

Chapter 2 examines the marketing mix and the external variables that managers must consider when developing a marketing strategy.

CP Picture Archive (Mike Ridewood)

Contemporary Marketing

> Learning Objectives

After studying this chapter, you will be able to

1. Define marketing and describe its role and importance in contemporary organizations.
2. Describe how marketing has evolved to become the driving force of business growth.
3. Explain the variety of activities that contemporary marketing practice embraces.
4. Describe the major trends and issues confronting the practice of marketing.
5. Explain the concepts of relationship marketing, social marketing, and database marketing.

The Importance of Marketing

One of the toughest challenges facing a business today is trying to anticipate where the business is going and how it will get there. No company can accurately foresee what the future will bring. What any company does know for sure is that change is occurring rapidly, and if it clings to traditional products and services and traditional practices, it will be heading for failure.

1.
Define marketing and describe its role and importance in contemporary organizations.

Change is occurring everywhere. Technology today is faster, cheaper, and better, and it has changed the way people live and work. Sophisticated notebook computers, cellular phones, and new communications equipment that combines e-mail with voice messaging play key roles in day-to-day business practices. The presence of the Internet and the World Wide Web, allowing businesses to communicate and do business with individual customers, is a testimony to technological advancements. People have changed and businesses have changed. The large group of people that we refer to as "baby boomers" (those born between 1946 and 1964) is more educated and more sophisticated than previous generations. Boomers are more demanding about the products they buy and less loyal to particular brands than in the past. Finally, the economic base of the world is changing. Emerging countries, such as China, Indonesia, and Russia, have large populations and growing middle classes. Their presence on the world stage presents new opportunities for North American-based companies.

Where does marketing fit in all of this? Simply put, marketing is an agent of change. In other words, the role of marketing is twofold. It provides a means for companies to constantly assess changing conditions and then provides the expertise to develop appropriate strategies so that an organization will be able to take advantage of the changes.

Marketing is a vital cog in the corporate wheel! A study conducted by Accenture, a management consulting company, revealed that four of the top five business issues today among senior Canadian executives are marketing related. The issues and their relative importance are as follows:[1]

- Improving customer service (78 percent)
- Increasing customer loyalty (68 percent)
- Attracting new customers (65 percent)
- Reducing costs (62 percent)

Even the biggest companies have been shaken by the speed at which changes are occurring. And, because of their sheer size, such firms find that they cannot respond quickly enough to the changes, and they suffer the consequences. Sam the Record Man, formerly a leading national chain of music stores, for example, faced this dilemma. The presence of fierce competition from rival chains such as HMV Canada Inc. and Wal-Mart Canada Inc., and the growing popularity of music downloads from the Internet, were the key contributing factors in Sam's demise.[2] Simply put, Sam's did not keep pace with the expectations of the modern consumer. New entrants with more aggressive and progressive marketing strategies (e.g., modern-looking stores with lots of space) and new technologies gained the consumer's favour.

To begin understanding the role of marketing, examine any recent purchase you have made, say a new laptop computer. A variety of brands are available: IBM, Compaq, Dell, Apple, and others. Only a few years ago, you would have purchased the computer at an established retailer, such as The Future Shop or Computer City. You more than likely were attracted to certain brands because of advertising, and you probably shopped to find the retailer that offered the best combination of price and service. Today, a similar computer can be purchased directly from companies like Dell who market their products through toll-free 1-800 numbers and the Internet. Dell established an entirely new way of marketing computers to businesses and consumers and, in the process, became a leading brand in the market.

Influencing variables, such as quality, price, availability, advertising, and promotion, are determined by marketers. The marketing organization combines these variables in such a way that they have an impact on the customer. Nike, for example, is a powerful brand name, largely due to its marketing activities. Nike executives speak of their brand as having a "shared set of common values that are intrinsically linked with athletic experience, and which are about performance and innovation."[3] The now-famous marketing phrase "Just Do It" was created to communicate this set of common values to the customer.

Marketing Defined

This brings us to the point where we can try to define marketing, that is, try to explain what this activity involves. Think for a minute-what would your reply be if someone asked you the question, "What is marketing?"

The simplest way of defining marketing would be to call it a process that identifies a need and then offers a means of satisfying it. This definition focuses on two very important steps in the marketing process—identification (on the part of the organization) and satisfaction (on the part of the customer)—and suggests that all marketing activity is focused on a kind of transaction or exchange between the organization and the customer.

American Marketing Association
www.ama.org

marketing

However, in reducing marketing to its bare essentials, a simple definition leaves a great deal unsaid. In an attempt to convey the full complexity of modern marketing activity, the American Marketing Association (AMA), an international association of academics and marketing professionals, has formulated its own definition. **Marketing** is the process of planning and executing the conception, pricing, promotion, and distribution of ideas, goods, and services to create exchanges that satisfy individual and organizational objectives.[4]

exchange

A key word in the definition is exchange. **Exchange** involves the transfer of something of value from the organization in return for something else from the customer so that both parties benefit in the process. Exchange occurs when a customer presents cash, credit card, or debit card for a pair of Nike running shoes at the Bay or Wal-Mart. **Benefit** is based on the discovery and satisfaction of a customer's needs and the building of an ongoing relationship with the customer. Customer satisfaction and relationship marketing are the cornerstones of contemporary marketing and, as such, will be discussed throughout the text.

benefit

The task of marketing today is to collect, analyze, and apply information about customers in order to develop total marketing programs, including products, prices, distribution, and communications, that respond to changing needs and preferences. A truly market-driven company recognizes that being oriented towards the customer is not enough. To grow and prosper, a company requires knowledge of its competitors' products and how customers view them. This is how McDonald's remains number one in fast food retailing, Nike number one in athletic shoes, and Wal-Mart number one in department stores. The goal of the company is to stay one step ahead of the competition by offering goods and services that provide customers with value, all the time.

Marketing Past and Present

We have seen that contemporary marketing is a complex process based on a simple idea: to identify a need and then satisfy it. To understand how a simple thought has grown into such a complex process, it would be helpful to look at the evolution of marketing, for marketing is a philosophy or way of thinking in an organization. Business organizations have moved through several stages of thinking with regard to how they approach customers. Each stage has been marked by a different emphasis in organizational theory, first on production, then on sales, then on marketing. During the 1990s marketing entered a fourth stage, that of societal or socially responsible marketing. It should not be assumed, however, that all companies share the same philosophy about marketing or that they are at the same stage in terms of how they think about it. In fact, all four orientations described below are alive and well.

PRODUCTION ORIENTATION

production orientation

Organizations following a **production orientation** pay little attention to what customers need. Instead, they concentrate on what they are capable of producing. They work on the assumption that customers will purchase the product so long as they can afford it. Businesses realize profits by producing and distributing only a limited variety of products as efficiently as possible. Henry Ford's classic statement "They can have any colour of car as long as it's black" illustrates the philosophy behind the production orientation. Even today, some companies try to survive using this kind of outdated approach.

SELLING ORIENTATION

selling orientation

As manufacturers added new product lines and as more and more competitors entered the market, customers had a greater selection of products. The emphasis shifted from production to selling. The belief behind a **selling orientation** is that the more the company sells, the more profit the company makes. But companies that paid little attention to costs found that this was not always the case. At the same time, consumers became increasingly demanding of a product's quality, performance, and dependability.

This stage was the earliest attempt to match potential customers' needs with products or services. In the automobile industry, competing firms, such as Ford and General Motors, built a variety of models and then searched for a consumer market that would buy those models. The fact that more variety was available meant these companies had to "sell" their goods—their efforts focused on advertising to get customers into the dealer showrooms.

MARKETING ORIENTATION

marketing concept

When a marketing orientation exists, all business planning revolves around the customer. This organizational philosophy has been appropriately coined the **marketing concept** and is expressed as follows: the essential task of the organization is to determine the needs and wants of a target market and then to deliver a set of satisfactions in such a way that the organization's product is perceived to be a better value than a competing product. The resources of the entire firm are directed at determining and satisfying customer needs and building ongoing relationships.

Firms applying the marketing concept realize profits by staying one step ahead of competitors in the delivery of desired satisfactions to customers. In order to do so, they must also concentrate on operating their production, sales, and distribution systems efficiently. There must be a close working relationship among the various departments of a business, and each must contribute to achieve common company goals.

Wal-Mart
www.walmart.com

Wal-Mart, the world's biggest retailer, is a good example of a company that practises the marketing concept. Wal-Mart offers a huge selection of merchandise, reasonable prices, friendly staff, greeters, and a generous product return policy. As well, a sophisticated inventory control system, second to none in the industry, provides for efficient transfer of goods. Wal-Mart's marketing success has had a profound and negative effect on numerous incumbent Canadian retailers. Wal-Mart is now the undisputed leader of discount retailing in Canada.

If there is a lesson to be learned from the Wal-Mart example, it is that business organizations must adopt the marketing concept and reflect it in all their operations. Even Wal-Mart learned this in Canada. Here, it has failed to "Americanize" its Canadian employees, so some changes to operational practices were necessary. Doom is imminent if a company fails to keep pace with change. The demise of such well-known and long-established department stores as Simpson's, Eaton's, and K-Mart prove this. Wal-Mart has now set its sights on becoming the world's largest "e-tailer."

SOCIALLY RESPONSIBLE MARKETING ORIENTATION

socially responsible marketing

The 1990s brought us to a stage where consideration for the environment and social responsibility have come to the forefront of strategic planning and decision making in organizations. This trend will continue. The essence of **socially responsible marketing** is that business should conduct itself in the best interests of consumers and society (Figure 1.1).

Philosophically, conducting business in a socially responsible manner should be natural for all business organizations; after all, the planet's well-being is in everyone's best interests. But pressured business executives in today's hectic environment find it difficult to balance the demands of operating competitively, producing profits, increasing shareholder values, and preserving the environment. The importance of being socially responsible is reinforced by the results of a study conducted by the Canadian Democracy and Corporate

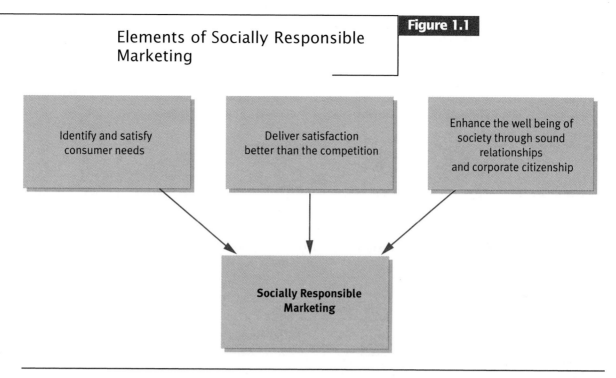

Figure 1.1

Elements of Socially Responsible Marketing

Identify and satisfy consumer needs

Deliver satisfaction better than the competition

Enhance the well being of society through sound relationships and corporate citizenship

Socially Responsible Marketing

Accountability Commission. The study found that 70 percent of consumers felt that business executives have a responsibility to take into consideration the impact their decisions have on employees, local communities, and the country, as well as making profits.[5]

It is certain that consumer and environmental groups do challenge and will continue to challenge companies and industries that market products which are harmful or of questionable value. Such pressure will eventually force all companies to adopt an environmentally minded corporate culture and implement business practices that conform to that culture. For example, Honda Motor Co. introduced a hybrid version of the popular Civic. A hybrid car boosts fuel economy by linking a gasoline engine to an electric motor and battery pack. Environmentalists have touted hybrids as the quickest way to improve vehicle mileage and reduce oil consumption.[6]

Socially responsible marketing can be divided into two main areas: (1) programs designed to conserve, preserve, and protect the environment, and (2) programs designed to support causes of benefit to society (e.g., AIDS research). The latter is referred to as "cause marketing." The growth and interest in socially responsible marketing is a major factor influencing the practice of marketing today. As such, it is discussed in greater detail later in this chapter.

Refer to Figure 1.2 for a summary of the evolution of marketing.

The Marketing Process

2.
Describe how marketing has evolved to become the driving force of business growth.

The fundamental principle on which marketing programs are designed is that an organization anticipates unmet needs in the market and then develops products to meet those needs. It sounds very simple when put into words, yet when put into practice it is a very complex process.

Evolution of Marketing

Figure 1.2

Phase	Characteristics
Production Orientation	• Sell what you can produce • Limited or no choice for customer • Profit from production efficiency
Selling Orientation	• Products matched to customer needs (e.g., quality, variety, etc.) • Choices more readily available • Profits based on expanded sales
Marketing Orientation	• All activity revolves around customers and their satisfaction • Extremely competitive since the customer has a wide choice of goods and services • Profits from efficient production and marketing
Socially Responsible Marketing Orientation	• Fulfill society's expectations (e.g., for a safe environment) • Be a good corporate citizen • Higher short-term costs accepted in return for long-term profit • Both efficient production and marketing to an informed consumer in a rapidly changing environment contribute to profit • Relationship between marketer and customer crucial to profit

market

Before proceeding, the term "market" should be defined. A **market** may be the ultimate consumer, an organizational buyer, or both. In consumer market terms, a market is a group of people who have a *similar need* for a product or service, the *resources* to purchase the product or service, and the *willingness* and *ability* to buy it. In *business-to-business* market terms, a market is an organizational buyer, such as an industry, wholesaler, or retailer, that buys goods and services for its own use or for resale.

So far, we have seen how the marketing concept gradually evolved from several distinct stages of organizational thinking. The obvious question is, why has marketing been so successful in revolutionizing the way business is carried on today? Perhaps the best answer to this question is that the marketing theory has capitalized on a basic psychological truth: people experience pleasure when they are able to satisfy a need. The follow-up to this proposition is that people also seek to repeat pleasurable experiences.

For these reasons, marketing professionals try to design products that are innovative and able to satisfy one or more of their customers' needs. To illustrate, consider a segment of modern day consumers who are pressed for time: households with two working adults.

These families are looking for convenience and ease of use with the products they buy. S.C. Johnson answers this demand with new products like Pledge Grab-It electrostatic dusting cloths or dusting mitts, Pledge Wipes for countertops, and flushable toilet wipes.

Honda Motor Co.
www.honda.ca

The needs that a firm considers can vary from country to country. To illustrate, consider what Honda Motor Co. is doing in North America and Japan. The ultimate reason for Honda's success is the same in both countries: sporty styling with top-notch reputation for quality, especially in engines. In North America, Honda's biggest boost in sales has come from adding the Acura MDX sport utility vehicle to its light-truck line-up. At home in Japan, where the economy is slumping, consumers wanted smaller, cheaper, more fuel-efficient vehicles. Honda reacted by adding new lines of compact cars and small minivans. One of Honda's popular models in Japan is a bubble-shaped subcompact called Fit. It recently zoomed by the larger Toyota Corolla to become the country's best-selling car.[7]

The cost of getting a consumer to make an initial purchase is very high. Some researchers suggest that it is five times more costly to get a new customer to buy than to keep an old one. Therefore, in accordance with the marketing concept, it is in the firm's best financial interests to keep its current customers satisfied. The goods and services provided by a firm must live up to the expectations created by its own marketing efforts; otherwise, the firm will not only lose its credibility but its customer base as well. Toyota believes in this thinking. Every year, two of its models, the Corolla and Camry, are consistently ranked high in customer satisfaction surveys conducted by independent research companies. The Lexus (Toyota's luxury division vehicle) has taken top honours for customer service satisfaction for 9 of the past 10 years, according to a J.D. Power and Associates Customer Service Index Study.[8] Toyota knows that the level of present customer satisfaction can influence decisions by new customers. It is no coincidence that the Corolla and Camry are Toyota's top-selling models. Refer to Figure 1.3 for a visual illustration.

Marketing in Practice

3.
Explain the variety of activities that contemporary marketing practice embraces.

Marketing in practice embraces a host of activities designed to attract, satisfy, and retain customers. The essential elements of this process involve:

1. Assessing customer needs by doing marketing research. The purpose of research is to discover unmet needs among consumers and to determine the potential for new products.
2. Identifying and selecting a target market to pursue.
3. Developing a strategic marketing plan that embraces the various elements of the marketing mix.
4. Evaluating the marketing strategy to ensure that it met its goals effectively.

The following section illustrates the essential elements of the marketing process and provides examples of these activities. Refer to Figure 1.4 for a visual illustration of these elements.

ASSESSING CUSTOMER NEEDS

needs assessment

A needs assessment is the first stage in an organization's marketing planning process. In a **needs assessment**, an organization collects appropriate information about consumer needs to determine if a market is worth pursuing. To do so, the company will use a

Figure 1.3

The Toyota Camry Is Consistently Ranked High in Customer Satisfaction Surveys

Courtesy: Toyota Canada.

market analysis

variety of research techniques and check various sources of information. Typically, a company conducts a market analysis and a consumer analysis. When an organization conducts a **market analysis**, the factors it considers include market demand, sales volume potential, production capabilities, and the availability of the resources necessary to produce and market the product or service. Colgate-Palmolive, an established company

Elements of the Marketing Process

Figure 1.4

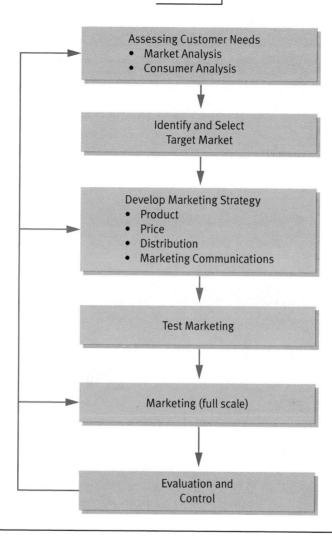

Assessing Customer Needs
- Market Analysis
- Consumer Analysis

Identify and Select
Target Market

Develop Marketing Strategy
- Product
- Price
- Distribution
- Marketing Communications

Test Marketing

Marketing (full scale)

Evaluation and
Control

in the personal care packaged goods market, identified a new opportunity when it introduced Colgate 2in1 Toothpaste & Mouthwash. The product is positioned as a one-stop product to fight both bad breath and cavities. As the ads say, "Toothpaste clean, mouthwash fresh...all in one step."[9] Colgate realized that consumers want convenient solutions. Available in three different flavours, Colgate 2in1 does save a person time. On the basis of the company's expertise in producing and marketing individual lines of toothpaste and mouthwash, the new product line was a natural fit with existing product lines.

consumer analysis   When an organization conducts a **consumer analysis**, it monitors demographic and behaviour changes within Canadian society. Business organizations use marketing research procedures to evaluate changes in consumers' tastes and preferences, attitudes,

LEGO
www.lego.com

and lifestyles so that marketing strategies can be adjusted accordingly. To illustrate the importance of assessing customer needs, consider what Starbucks is doing to market coffee to diverse age groups. Kitty-corner to each other on a busy Vancouver street, Starbucks opened two distinctly different cafés. One café imposes itself on the streetscape in an arc of glass and steel. On a patio sit young people wearing trendy black clothing. The second café nestles tastefully in a brick heritage building. It has a cozy wood interior and is softly lit. The patrons are older, wealthier, and more subdued. One café is for Generation X (19- to 35-year-olds), while the other is for baby boomers (36- to 50-year-olds). By design, the stores are worlds apart—different decor, different atmosphere, different demographics. Starbucks' strategy may seem odd on the surface, but when examined more closely, it demonstrates a way to offer a common grouping of products to diverse targets with different expectations of what a café should be.[10]

For more insight into the importance of assessing customer needs and keeping pace with change, see the Marketing in Action vignette **Toy of the Century**.

IDENTIFYING AND SELECTING A TARGET MARKET

An organization cannot satisfy the needs of all consumers, so it concentrates its efforts on a segment of the population that offers the most promise. That specific segment of the population is referred to as a target market. A **target market** is a group of people to which a company markets its products. Typically, members of a target group have something in common (e.g., they fall within a certain age range, they have similar educational backgrounds or occupations, they live in the same area, or they share a common interest or activity).

To illustrate the concept of targeting, consider that three out of four Canadians drink coffee. Therefore it should be easy to market coffee and coffee-related products. Further examination of the market reveals that half of Canada's coffee drinkers are 35 to 64 years old, and those drinkers who own their own cappuccino/espresso maker are highly educated (college diploma, university degree, and post-graduate degree).[11] Therefore, the target description of potential buyers of cappuccino/espresso makers becomes quite narrow.

In theory, the similarity of the target should mean that all people within the target would respond to a similar marketing strategy. But that is theory. In reality, marketing is extremely competitive, and numerous competitors battle it out for the same set of customers. The competitor with the best strategy, the strategy that has the most impact on the target market, wins the battle!

DEVELOPING A MARKETING STRATEGY

An organization now shifts its focus to devising a marketing strategy or marketing plan. A well-defined strategy includes four key elements that are referred to as the marketing mix. The **marketing mix** refers to a set of strategic elements (product, price, distribution, and marketing communications) that, when combined, appeal to the target market so that its needs are satisfied. Critical decisions are made on each element of the mix. **Product** decisions may involve the setting of quality standards, sizes, brand name, packaging, and level of service. The goal is innovation—to invest considerable sums of money in developing products, resulting in a breakthrough product that will move the company forward. To illustrate, mouthwash products were only available in liquid form prior to the launch of Listerine PocketPaks, a mouthwash on ultra-thin postage-stamp-size strips. According to Pfizer Consumer Healthcare, the manufacturer, sales of

target market

marketing mix

product

Marketing in Action

Toy of the Century

LEGO® toys. It seems that every child has owned a set or at least played with a set. When you think of LEGO toys a picture of small interlocking bricks comes to mind. It is an extraordinary toy. It doesn't break or wear out. Original bricks can be connected with bricks presently being made. What is the key to the success of LEGO toys and will it last in the new era of high-tech, computer-based toys and games?

LEGO products are the world's best-selling toys ever. Global sales exceed 320 billion pieces, or more than 53 bricks for each of the world's 6 billion people. Conventional wisdom suggests that the popularity of the game will wane—kids don't play with that kind of stuff any more. Dead wrong. LEGO bricks have proven to be a versatile toy that changes with the times. For example, the LEGO company has formed an alliance with Electronic Arts Inc., the biggest producer of video games in the United States, to start selling electronic games based on LEGO properties.

In 2002, nothing could be hotter with children than Harry Potter. The LEGO company's response was to market a Harry Potter set that lets children create Hogwarts School of Witchcraft and Wizardry in LEGO bricks and play with their favourite Harry Potter characters in LEGO settings.

Parents have played a role in the success of LEGO toys. They grew up with it, so they appreciate their children playing with it. Parents realize their children shouldn't play video games all of the time. Their imagination and social skills simply would not develop. LEGO bricks provide a solution. They teach children the elements of engineering and design,

enabling them to create entire worlds: castles, towns, bridges, cars, and characters. In a contemporary play world dominated by technology, introversion, and passive watching, LEGO toys are about tactile, hands-on, sociable play. They are good for hand-eye coordination and manual dexterity. The great thing about LEGO bricks is that children can play together, and they can play with their parents.

Not to be outdone by technology, the LEGO company recently launched a robotics line called MindStorms™. It's the only true robotic building system in the world for children. Once the software is loaded in a computer the child can create commands that program "smart bricks." LEGO toys are truly state-of-the-art toys! The company realizes that technology is changing the toy market, but it also realizes what the core strength of the brand is, and that's "playful learning and exploration."

The LEGO company is a privately owned company that is committed to strong core values. It does not make war games or violent games. The design of society, according to the LEGO company, isn't just about construction and urban planning; it's about the values of the people who inhabit it.

Adapted from Brian Hutchinson, "A giraffe, a CEO and a pile of bricks," *Financial Post*, February 23, 2002, pp. FP1, FP8, and Judy Steed, "Lego's leap into the electronic era," *Toronto Star*, December 24, 2001, p. D3.

LEGO, the LEGO logo and the brick configuration are trademarks of the LEGO group. © 2002 The LEGO Group. Used with permission.

PocketPaks are well ahead of schedule and its presence has rekindled interest in the Listerine brand name.[12]

How successful would purple ketchup be in a squeezable bottle? Seven months after launching purple ketchup Heinz reports that 10 million bottles were sold in North America, overall brand sales were up 5.4 percent, and market share increased from 55 percent to 59 percent—this simple yet innovative idea really caught on![13]

price

Marketing organizations are very conscious of the importance of price in today's marketplace. **Price** decisions involve developing a strategy that provides reasonable profit for the firm while making the product or service attractive to the customer. Factors that play a role in price activity include the prices of competing products and how much it costs to make the product. Then, profit has to be added into the price.

distribution

Distribution decisions are concerned, first of all, with transactions between manufacturers, wholesalers, and retailers who ultimately sell the product to the consumer. Food processors such as McCain, Nestlé, and Kraft Canada all market their product lines through a variety of chain stores and independent distributors. Now many companies and industries are bypassing traditional channels of distribution, preferring to market directly to customers. Direct marketing via the Internet is growing by leaps and bounds each year, with growth being fuelled by savvy marketers such as Dell Computer, Amazon.com, and HMV Music. Technology is also spurring the formation of channel relationships—companies in the channel are linking computer systems together to achieve more efficient buying and selling among participants.

marketing communications

Marketing communications decisions involve the development and implementation of media advertising campaigns, consumer and trade promotion activities, events and sponsorships, personal selling programs, and public relations and publicity. This is the most visible area of marketing, and these activities play a major role in creating an image for the product or service. For such consumer products as Coca-Cola and Pepsi-Cola, virtually all forms of communications activity are used to attract consumers. These companies and many others use the traditional mass media (television, radio, newspapers, billboards, and magazines) or specialized media (the Internet) to reach customers with their message.

EVALUATING MARKETING ACTIVITY

test marketing

Products and marketing strategies are usually tested for acceptance in a small area of the market prior to a full-scale launch. **Test marketing** involves placing a product for sale in one or more geographic areas and observing its performance under conditions similar to the ones proposed in the marketing plan. Once the product and the marketing plan have been evaluated, a regional or national "rollout" follows.

To complete the marketing cycle, research is usually conducted periodically so that the organization is certain that the product continues to meet the changing needs (tastes, preferences, habits, and lifestyles) of a volatile marketplace. The organization will also measure the results a product achieves (through its marketing plan) against the objectives that were established. Such objectives usually focus on market share and profit. By constantly staying in touch with customers and adjusting the marketing plans when necessary, an organization will prosper. Research is normally conducted through surveys that are implemented by telephone, personal interview, mail, or online.

The New Realities of Marketing

Moving into the new millennium, it is certain that marketing practice will directly consider the interests of consumers being served, and that more attention will be given to the interests of society. When doing so, a company must consider a host of new developments and issues that, in turn, will affect its attitude towards marketing and how it develops its marketing strategies.

Several key issues and trends will continue to affect marketing practice. Among these trends and issues are the strategic focus on relationship marketing commonly

4.
Describe the major trends and issues confronting the practice of marketing.

referred to as customer relationship management (CRM), the expanding role of database marketing, the sudden and dramatic impact of the Internet and other communications technologies, concern for the environment and other aspects of social responsibility and ethical business practices, the need for and influence of continuous improvement programs, and the pursuit of global marketing opportunities.

CUSTOMER RELATIONSHIP MANAGEMENT

Marketing today is all about relationships, and these relationships go beyond focusing on the ultimate consumer. **Customer relationship management (CRM)** embraces the entire channel—from supplier to producer to distributor to consumer. It looks at activities along this chain and leads to an emphasis on long-term value of customer relationships in addition to short-term sales and profit.

customer relationship management (CRM)

In a marketing context, customer relationship management is the partnering of organizations in a chain of distribution, from the supplier of raw materials to the ultimate consumer who purchases the end product, who then conduct business in such a way that all participants benefit. A relationship, therefore, may involve numerous businesses that cooperatively work together, or it may only involve one company and its consumers. To illustrate, Hudson's Bay Company merged the customer databases for its Bay and Zellers stores as part of a new customer relationship management push. The goal of the program is to identify their best customers and tailor specific product and service offerings to maintain and build upon their loyalty. To implement the program Hudson's Bay partnered with Microsoft, Oracle, and IBM Canada. These partners provide e-commerce supply chain management and CRM components. According to George Heller, CEO of Hudson's Bay Company, retail has traditionally pushed product to the customer. With programs like this the customer pulls the product instead.[14]

5.
Explain the concepts of relationship marketing, social marketing, and database marketing.

Hudson's Bay Company
www.hbc.com

Relationship management is concerned not with individual transactions, but with establishing, maintaining, and enhancing long-term relationships. It's about customer satisfaction, plain and simple. It calls for teamwork and open communication within an organization and among all participants in the chain. It is a flexible system of planning that involves the identification of needs, the establishment of joint objectives, and the breaking down of traditional roles (Figure 1.5).

For relationship marketing to be successful, an organization has to adopt an internal attitude that gives the customer the first and final say. Business organizations exist, above

Relationship Marketing Model

Figure 1.5

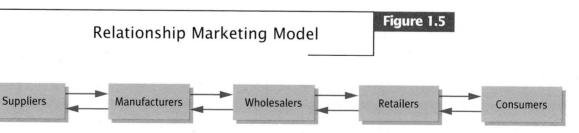

- In establishing partnerships, common needs are identified and joint objectives are established for all members

- Each stakeholder is a partner in a long-term relationship

- Teamwork and cooperation replace competition and conflict to produce desired results for all partners all, to serve their customers, and all employees must recognize that they contribute to this effort. This attitude, often referred to as the **corporate culture**, is defined as the values, norms, and practices shared by all the employees of an organization. Such thinking puts the customer on a pedestal above all others in the organization. A successful business such as 3M thinks "customer" all the time. All employees are part of a marketing team and consider themselves to be in the customer care business. In fact, 3M uses the phrase "From need to...3M Innovation" as its advertising slogan. 3M identifies customer needs and develops innovative products to satisfy those needs. See the illustration in Figure 1.6.

An Innovative Product from an Innovative Company

Figure 1.6

In caring for customers, marketers face two problems all the time: *how to get customers and how to hold on to them.* Traditionally, marketers placed greater emphasis on attracting customers and made much use of the mass media, which is very expensive. Contemporary marketers who believe in relationship marketing strike a balance between attracting and maintaining customers. Loyalty-oriented programs, such as Zeller's Club Z points, Air Miles, and Canadian Tire money, keep current customers coming back. Zellers Canada's Club Z program is one of Canada's most successful loyalty programs. It has amassed 9 million active collectors, a staggering figure given there are only 11 million households in Canada.[15]

strategic alliance

Other types of relationships are forming among companies that are no longer working independently all the time. A new, cooperative attitude between firms has led to the formation of alliances. A **strategic alliance** is a partnering process whereby two firms combine their resources in a marketing venture for the purpose of satisfying the customers they share. Coca-Cola and Procter & Gamble, two large and successful companies, recently announced the formation of a jointly owned company that would marry the breadth of Coke's global distribution network with P&G's research and development skills. The Coca-Cola brands include Minute Maid juices, Hi-C, Five-Alive and Fruitopia. P&G contributed Pringles Chips and Sunny Delight juice drinks. The venture allows both companies to distribute products more quickly by tapping into each other's resources. P&G will get better distribution for Pringles through Coca-Cola, and Coke's juice products will get better distribution and shelf location through Procter & Gamble.[16] For Coca-Cola it's also a new way to compete better with Pepsi-Cola, a company that is a market leader in snack foods through its Frito Lay product line.

Customer relationship management is discussed in more detail in Chapters 3, 4, 5, and 15.

DATABASE MARKETING

database marketing

Only a few decades ago, a mass marketing approach was in vogue—products and messages were mass-produced for the population at large. Today, companies deal directly with customers on an individual basis. This phenomenon is called **database marketing**. Companies collect a mountain of information about customers, analyze it to predict how likely the customer is to buy, and then develop a message precisely designed to meet the individual needs of the customer. Using technological advances in computers, companies can zero in on extremely small segments of the population, often referred to as niches. The ultimate goal is to aim for the smallest segment of all—the individual (Figure 1.7).

In applying the concept of relationship marketing, companies are heading in different directions. Business-to-business marketing organizations, or businesses whose primary customers are other businesses, were the first to embrace relationship marketing. Firms such as IBM, Microsoft, Apple, Procter & Gamble, and Hudson's Bay have successful database programs in place. These firms now use integrated direct marketing strategies (e.g., toll-free 1-800 telephone numbers, telemarketing, and Internet activities) to target messages directly to customers. Direct marketing techniques are explored in more detail in Chapter 15.

Organizations are placing greater emphasis on accountability (e.g., what is the return for the money invested in marketing?). The concept of relationship and integrated direct marketing is based on the belief that it is less expensive and more profitable to hold on to current customers than to attract new ones. Put another way, why invest a lot of money going after those people who aren't likely to become customers?

To illustrate the application of database marketing, consider a situation that Shell Oil faced in Canada. Shell is a member of the Air Miles loyalty program and has access

The Concept of Database Marketing

Figure 1.7

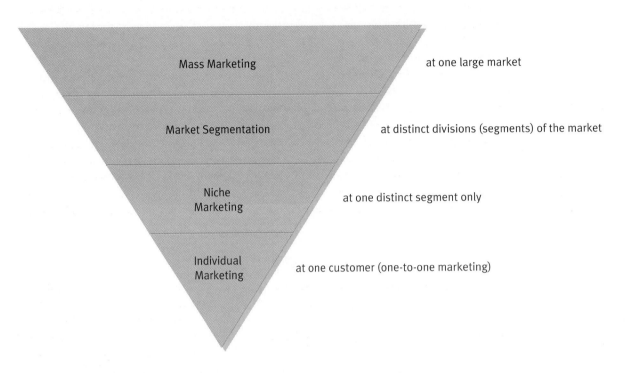

Orientation of Marketing Activity

Mass Marketing — at one large market

Market Segmentation — at distinct divisions (segments) of the market

Niche Marketing — at one distinct segment only

Individual Marketing — at one customer (one-to-one marketing)

Companies now have the capability to approach customers on an individual basis.

to its database. Data mined from the Air Miles program prevented Shell from making a few blunders. When one Shell station was slated for conversion from full-service to self-service, demographic information from Air Miles data suggested the company should proceed with caution. Half of the station's customers were women, and a major reason they used the station was because it offered full service. Shell cancelled the conversion.[17] Relationship marketing recognizes the importance of the value of total volume of sales to a customer over a lifetime of purchases.

database Database marketing and relationship marketing are closely related. A **database** is a customer information file that a company continuously updates. The database is the vehicle that facilitates implementation of customer relationship management programs. Database marketing is explored in more detail in Chapter 3.

TECHNOLOGICAL ADVANCES

Technological advances are having a dramatic impact on marketing, and they will be the single most important influence in the future. From how a company collects and uses information, to the development of new products, to the improvement of production and distribution processes, all are affected by technology. The expanded use of database marketing techniques, and the implementation of relationship management programs, topics just discussed, are a direct result of new computer technology.

New forms of satellite communications are entering Canadian homes. Services are now available that offer hundreds of television channels via satellite. And what about banking via the telephone or the Internet? It seems that banks are obsessed with removing all forms of personal contact as they encourage customers to use electronic technology to conduct normal day-to-day banking transactions.

Wireless devices are bringing together two of the world's fastest-growing industries— the Internet and mobile telecommunications—to create a wireless revolution for electronic business. Business will move from the desktop computer to the street. The vanguard of this revolution is a handful of services that can put the World Wide Web in the palm of your hand by providing access to Internet banking, shopping, and business portals through Web-browsing mobile phones, pagers, or organizers.[18] By 2003, it is estimated that there will be 150 million cell phone subscribers and 40 million wireless subscribers in North America.[19]

Canadian consumers are embracing technology quickly, but marketers should be aware of potential resistance from older age groups. There are significant numbers of people who prefer the "simpler times." This segment of the population may rebel against developments like online shopping and database marketing. Eventually, they will accept and use the new technology, but they want to be reassured that some form of personal service will be retained.

THE INTERNET AND E-COMMERCE

The Internet and the World Wide Web are now vital means of communicating information about goods and services and conducting business transactions with customers. The most recent survey from Statistics Canada (2000) reveals that males and females use the Internet equally, that use increases among younger people in higher-income households; and that geographic location influences usage. For example, people in Western Canada and Ontario use the Internet more frequently than people in Quebec and Atlantic Canada. Overall, 53 percent of Canadians were online in 2000.[20]

Companies are exploring new forms of advertising made available by the Internet, and in many cases, are adding an online component to their traditional media advertising. This new medium is one of the vehicles an organization uses to reach customers on an individual basis (i.e., it's a relationship marketing vehicle). Using the Internet for marketing purposes involves continuous interaction in the pretransaction, transaction, and post-transaction phase of a purchase. It seems to offer unlimited potential.

Presently, organizations are struggling in terms of how to integrate Internet communications with the traditional media mix. "The Internet is substantially different. It's a bit of direct response, it's a bit of broadcast, it's a bit of print, and it's a bit of technology."[21] Some things do appear certain however. First, like television in the 1950s, it will eventually play a major role in communicating information about goods and services, and such communications will result in more electronic purchasing by customers. Second, like television, the Internet will not replace existing media. Instead, it will complement the communications programs that are implemented in the mass media.

In e-commerce, some firms have been very successful, while others have floundered. The Internet offers great potential, but too many companies have had unrealistic expectations. It seems that maintaining a Web site is seen as a kind of "rite of passage to determine whether or not you are a real business in today's marketplace."[22] However, it is wrong to hold the belief, "Create a Web site, they will come, and we will make a fortune."

Companies must first learn how to integrate Web-based activities with other traditional marketing activities, for they are connected. For example, many prominent retailers such as Indigo Books & Music, Canadian Tire, and Future Shop jumped on the e-tail bandwagon only to encounter countless customer relationship problems and fulfillment problems. They discovered that they weren't adding more sales, while sometimes taking sales away from their retail stores. As well, customers who had an unpleasant problem with a firm's online store might consequently shun its entire operation.[23]

La Senza Inc.
www.lasenza.com

With a longer learning curve, companies will figure out how to best to use the Internet for business transactions. La Senza Inc. is an example of a retailer that has combined "bricks and clicks," the combination of traditional retailing with online offerings. According to Laurence Lewin, president of La Senza Inc., handling online orders is not a stress for the lingerie retailer, and consumers know they can trust the brand. "People call up other sites and they don't know who they are or what they are. People will gravitate toward companies that have substance (like La Senza), not ethereal presences floating in cyberspace."[24]

Nonetheless, in ways unimaginable just a few years ago, corporations are using Internet technology to successfully conduct trade over the Internet. Caution is advised however. To illustrate, consider the plight of Amazon.com, perhaps the most well-known online seller. While the famous online seller of books, music, and videos is creating havoc for the traditional bricks-and-mortar bookstores and music stores, and continues to sell more and more books online, it wasn't until 2002 (six years after start-up) that it turned its first dime in profit. This may suggest that the "how to" of Internet marketing has yet to be determined. Internet marketing is discussed in detail in Chapter 17.

ETHICAL PRACTICES AND SOCIAL RESPONSIBILITY

All business organizations are obliged, either legally or morally, to offer for sale safe, ethical, and useful goods and services. They must not deceive customers and must treat all customers fairly. The firm must be concerned with society's well-being. Companies marketing products that are of questionable quality or that are harmful, or who represent products in a deceptive or misleading manner, will come under attack from governments, consumers, and environmental groups.

Ethical behaviour in business organizations cannot be taken for granted. In Canada, the Competition Act governs most general marketing activities. Despite such legislation, business firms have been caught conducting less-than-ethical business and marketing activities. An example of unethical activity is bait-and-switch advertising (enticing consumers to a store for a certain product and then focusing their attention on a more expensive one). It seems that even the biggest and most reputable of companies can be caught doing something unethical. For example, did Bridgestone Corp. (the makers of Firestone tires) knowingly produce and market tires that would self-destruct when installed on a Ford Explorer? Was the Ford Motor Company aware of the potential rollover problem it would encounter with the Ford Explorer? Should both Bridgestone and Ford have taken action sooner than they did to avoid the disasters that occurred? Firestone tires have been linked to 203 traffic deaths. As a result of the problem, Bridgestone absorbed US$1.3 billion in charges in 2000 and 2001 and the company's stock has lost more than half of its value.[25] Ford estimates that settlements involving 5 million vehicles could cost them between US$750 million and $1 billion.[26]

A worldwide study involving 25 000 people conducted by research company Environics International demonstrates the importance of social responsibility. The study revealed that consumers do care and that they avoid products or services of companies they see as not socially responsible. Consumers act on their perceptions of a company. When Canadian participants were asked to name the companies that they respected for being socially responsible, Bombardier Inc. and General Motors Corp. tied for the top spot. Just below that was Bell Canada. Other multinational companies frequently mentioned by Canadians included Microsoft, Toyota, Nortel Networks, Ford, IBM, and McDonald's.[27]

social marketing or cause marketing

Companies are honing their social marketing skills in such a way that public reactions to the company are positive. **Social marketing**, or **cause marketing**, as it is also called, is a methodology for promoting social change. It is used to influence public attitudes and behaviours on such issues as AIDS, literacy, and drug abuse. Social marketing is now an integral component of the marketing effort because it can add value to customer relationships while demonstrating strong corporate leadership. Phillip Watts, chairman of the Royal Dutch/Shell Group of Companies states, "Companies have to behave as an integral part of society. Shell has made a contract for social development. When we take a business decision, we try to strike a balance between economics, the environment and social impacts."[28] Shell Canada Ltd. is presently running an awareness campaign on sustainable development that is careful not to promise too much. The ad says, "solutions won't come easily but you can't find them if you don't keep looking." See Figure 1.8 for the advertisement.

Figure 1.8

Economics, the Environment, and Social Issues Meet in a Social Marketing Message

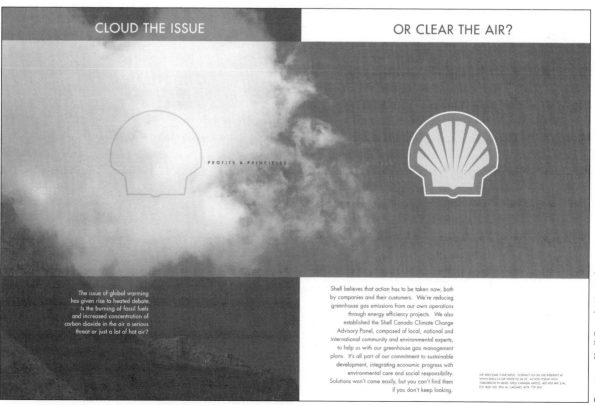

Courtesy: Shell Canada Limited.

Marketing in a socially responsible manner will continue to grow in importance. Progressive-minded business executives realize that what's good for society is also good for a company's bottom line. For more insight into the importance of social marketing, refer to the Marketing in Action vignette **Social Marketing Is Good for Business**.

CONTINUOUS IMPROVEMENT PROGRAMS

Stand still and you are a sitting duck. The competition will eat you alive! Companies spend a small fortune trying to attract customers to their brand. Once the consumer arrives, the product better meet the consumer's expectations. As competition enters the market, and consumers have more choice, products have to improve even further in order to retain customers. That is the concept of continuous improvement. In following such a philosophy a company places emphasis on customer relationships and relies on teamwork and employee input to find new ways of doing things better. Companies that design, build, and market quality products will be profitable companies.

Marketing in Action

Social Marketing Is Good for Business

In the past, leading Canadian companies were well respected for their corporate philanthropy. Typically, they wrote a cheque for a favourite charity, delivered it without much fanfare, and then went back to concentrating on business. Now, that's just not good enough. Companies want to be perceived as socially responsible and to be recognized positively for the contributions they are making to society.

Nike was in a lot of hot water over its labour practices in the mid 1990s, and the experience forced Nike to define its position on corporate responsibility. So negative was the publicity about Nike, individual employees began to wonder what kind of company they were working for and what message was being sent about the people who worked there. Nike had an external and internal marketing problem to deal with.

Nike's response was that if the company was going to approach social responsibility in a meaningful way, it had to be more than just public relations; it would be the core of the company's business and be implemented at every level of the corporation. According to Maria Eitel, vice-president of corporate responsibility at Nike, "As long as companies perceive corporate social responsibility as something 'on the side'—away from the main business decisions-they will continue to be vulnerable."

Conducting business activity in an ethical manner and being socially responsible is a reflection of the attitudes and behaviours of modern-day customers. Customers have put a different slant on how a company views its corporate citizenship. When a company cannot show how its products are distinct from its competitor's products on the basis of traditional marketing strategies, corporate citizenship may be the deciding factor in which brand a customer buys.

Courtesy: RBC Dominion Securities

ISO
www.iso.ch

In contemporary business, companies want to deal with other companies that share a similar philosophy. Such companies may identify themselves by applying for ISO accreditation. The ISO 9000 series of standards is a set of five technical standards designed to offer a uniform way of determining whether manufacturing and service organizations implement and document sound quality procedures. To achieve such a stamp of approval, a company undergoes an audit of its manufacturing and service processes, covering everything from how it designs, produces, and installs its goods to how it inspects, packages, and markets them.[29]

Adopting the ISO standard provides several benefits to an organization. It focuses an organization on identifying and documenting core business processes and services. This leads to process improvement or the identification and correction of weaknesses or flaws in the ways things are done. In Canada, the Quality Institute, a division of the Canadian Standards Association, offers certification, training in ISO 9000, auditor training, and external quality audits.[30]

Today, leading companies recognize that good corporate citizenship goes hand-in-hand with effective marketing, and as a result, cause or social marketing has become an increasingly important part of corporate marketing plans. Marketing surveys over the past few years show that consumers consider social problems to be of concern to society as a whole, including the corporate world, and not just the responsibility of individuals.

At the RBC Financial Group, social responsibility is about a mindset and a corporate culture that see value in interacting with and providing more to society— beyond the bottom line. The cornerstones of social responsibility at the bank are donations, sponsorships, and activities of employees as volunteers in their communities. Through the bank and its subsidiaries, donations of at least 1 percent of a five-year average of net income before taxes are made annually.

In 2000, $26 million was distributed among a variety of worthwhile causes and activities that included education, health, social services, community activities, federated appeals (such as United Way), and the arts. Organizations such as The Canadian Cancer Society, Heart and Stroke Foundation, Canadian Olympic Association, Big Brothers/Big Sisters, local sports associations and amateur athletics, and festival groups, to name just a few, have all benefited from the generosity of the RBC Financial Group. As a result of such involvement, the RBC Financial Group has been designated a "Caring Company" by the Canadian Centre for Philanthropy's "Imagine" program.

Nike Canada is directly involved in a grassroots social marketing program with Canadian Hockey Association (CHA) member organizations. Nike's objectives are to help children across Canada develop hockey skills. Nike provides coaching and training manuals, certificates of achievement, and skills development camps as part of the initiative. It also provides a large but undisclosed amount of cash to the CHA. Nike entered the hockey arena in 1994 with the purchase of Canadian skate-maker Bauer, which it runs as a separate division.

Companies such as these recognize the true benefit of social marketing and good corporate citizenship. If a company is viewed as caring about the community and about issues important to customers, it will definitely help the business develop strong relations and loyalty. In contrast, it can also be said that consumers are quite willing to punish companies they perceive as bad corporate citizens.

Adapted from "Ethics and Corporate Social Responsibility," a supplement to February 2002 *R.O.B. Magazine*, www.royalbank.com/ community/donations and Erica Zlomislic, "Nike gets into social marketing," *Strategy*, October 27, 1997, p. 2.

When quality is put into operation, it is translated into specific product performance characteristics that contribute to customer satisfaction. Therefore, an organization must determine what dimensions of quality are important to its target market, and then deliver exactly what they want, all the time. To illustrate, Grand & Toy, an incumbent Canadian business products supply company, faced stiff competition from Office Depot and Staples Business Depot when they entered the Canadian market. Grand & Toy realized that it could not compete on price. Through market research, Grand & Toy discovered that many customers rated service as being very important. To provide superior service, Grand & Toy revamped its entire distribution system and made a bold promise to deliver goods within 24 hours. They have lived up to that promise and the company continues to prosper. The moral of the story is quite simple: successful companies continuously meet and exceed customer expectations-it gives them competitive advantage.

GLOBALIZATION

globalization

Globalization means that the world as a marketplace is becoming smaller, and progressive-minded companies are pursuing opportunities for growth wherever they may be found. Opportunities in foreign countries often compensate for slow growth or no growth in domestic markets.

A global market already exists for many products, such as automobiles, soft drinks, and credit cards. Companies in these industries recognize that foreign customers and domestic customers are more similar than different. To cite one specific example, Coca-Cola develops worldwide marketing and advertising strategies and then follows through with a consistent message about the product, wherever it is sold, using such advertising slogans as "Always Coca-Cola" or "Enjoy," which are adaptable to all parts of the world. Coca-Cola takes into account any conditions unique to a particular foreign market (e.g., the language and cultural differences). When necessary, strategies are modified to match local market conditions. In describing their marketing actions, it abides by the philosophy of "think globally, act locally." The entire issue of global marketing is discussed in much more detail in Chapter 19.

trading bloc

Another development in the world marketplace is the formation of regional trading blocs. **Trading blocs** are economic alliances between countries in the same area of the world, formed so that all participants will benefit from free and open trade with each other.

The European Union (EU), formed in 1993, is an example of such a bloc. The EU now includes Austria, the United Kingdom, Ireland, Belgium, France, Italy, Denmark, Greece, Germany, Luxembourg, Sweden, Finland, the Netherlands, Spain, Norway, and Portugal.

Closer to home, the North American Free Trade Agreement (NAFTA), a 1992 agreement between Canada, the United States, and Mexico formed a North American trading region. The formation of a free trading region in North America presented new challenges and opportunities for Canadian marketing organizations. Domestically, they face new competition from imported goods, but there are also new export opportunities in the United States and Mexico.

Summary

The text defines marketing as the process of planning and executing the conception, pricing, promotion, and distribution of ideas, goods, and services to create exchanges that satisfy individual and organizational objectives.

In today's competitive marketplace, it is the quality of an organization's marketing activity that determines the success, even the survival, of that organization. Given this situation, businesses are adopting a marketing-oriented corporate culture whereby all the employees of an organization, in every activity they perform, must consider the satisfaction of customer needs as the main priority.

Marketing practice has evolved over time. Early Canadian business development saw much of the organization's profit-making activities centred on creating production efficiency. Gradually, business philosophy shifted to an emphasis on selling, and for the first time, business organizations started to look at the needs of consumers and offered a greater selection of products. Now, the emphasis is on the marketing concept, which is the belief that business must focus directly on satisfying consumer needs. The 1990s brought us to the stage where consideration for the environment and social responsibility were at the forefront of strategic planning. The result has been increased customer service and a more caring business environment. Companies that lag behind in contemporary marketing thinking, or fail to adapt to changes that are occurring in the marketplace, risk financial trouble.

Marketing in practice embraces many activities that culminate in an overall plan to build long-term relationships with customers. These activities include needs assessment, identifying and selecting a target market, developing the marketing strategy by using elements of the marketing mix, and then evaluating the strategy for effectiveness.

In the future, several trends will influence marketing strategy. Among the more important trends are the strategic focus on customer relationship management, the expanding role of database marketing, the influence of technological advances in the area of communications and Internet marketing and e-commerce, concern for the environment and other aspects of ethical practices and social responsibility, global marketing opportunities, and the influence of continuous improvement programs.

Key Terms

benefit 5

consumer analysis 11

corporate culture 16

customer relationship management (CRM) 15

database 18

database marketing 17

distribution 14

exchange 5

globalization 24

market 8

market analysis 10

marketing 4

marketing communications 14

marketing concept 6

marketing mix 12

needs assessment 9

price 14

product 12

production orientation 5

selling orientation 5

social marketing or cause marketing 21

socially responsible marketing 6

strategic alliance 17

target market 12

test marketing 14

trading bloc 24

Review Questions

1. What is the basic premise on which marketing is built?

2. Briefly compare the operating philosophies of companies that have a: production orientation, selling orientation, marketing orientation.

3. A key term in the chapter is "marketing concept." Briefly explain this term and provide an illustration of how it is applied.

4. When a company "assesses customer needs," it conducts a market analysis and consumer analysis. Briefly describe what is involved in each area.

5. What is a target market?

6. Identify the four key elements of the marketing mix.

7. What is relationship marketing, and what role does it play in contemporary marketing?

8. What is database marketing, and what role does it play in contemporary marketing?

9. Briefly explain the importance of social responsibility in the practice of contemporary marketing. Provide some new examples that demonstrate social responsibility marketing.

Discussion and Application Questions

1. How do colleges and universities implement the marketing concept? Cite some examples of marketing activities at your college or university.

2. Coca-Cola is the best-selling soft drink in the world. What marketing factors have contributed to the success of this brand?

3. What elements of the marketing mix are most important to each of the following companies or brands?

    a) Federal Express

    b) Toronto Raptors

    c) Canadian Tire

    d) McDonald's

    e) Pepsi-Cola

4. The text mentions several examples of strategic alliances. Can you identify any other alliances that have made the business news recently? What are the benefits to each company in the alliances you identified?

5. Select a prominent retail, service, or manufacturing organization in your own hometown, and analyze how they have made use of socially responsible marketing practice.

E-Assignment

Visit the Web site of a worldwide brand, such as Coca-Cola or BMW. Analyze the site, and determine how the company uses the Internet to communicate information about relationship marketing, socially responsible marketing, and global marketing. Does the site communicate useful information about the company? Was the site easy to navigate?

Endnotes

1 "Companies throw money at e-commerce without knowing rules of the game," *Financial Post*, May 19, 1999, p. C4.

2 Marina Strauss, "Web business wounded retailer Sams: observers," *Globe and Mail*, November 1/01, p. B5.

3 James Pollack, "Bulletproof brand Nike has no fear of dramatic price increases," *Marketing*, April 7, 1997, p. 5.

4 American Marketing Association, "AMA Board Approves New Definition," *Marketing News*, March 1, 1985, p. 4.

5 Ellen Roseman, "Most want socially responsible companies," *Toronto Star*, February 1, 2002, p. E2.

6 Justin Hyde, "Hybrid Honda sedan sets green standard," *Toronto Star*, February 26, 2002, p. C11.

7 Todd Zaun, "Honda succeeds by having a Fit," *Globe and Mail*, December 31, 2001, p. B4.

8 Justin Hyde, "Lexus, Saturn top service satisfaction survey," *DriverSource*, *Sunday Sun*, July 16, 2000, p. 6.

9 Mercedes M. Cardona, "Colgate expands roster with two new products," *Advertising Age*, July 3, 2000, p. 8.

10 "One café for Yuppies another for Gen-X," *Financial Post*, October 31, 1998, p. D6.

11 "A marketing profile of coffee drinkers," *Marketing*, September 25, 2000, p. 13.

12 Jack Neff, "Building the buzz for PocketPaks," *Advertising Age*, December 31, 2001, pp. 4, 44.

13 "Heinz squeezes out purple ketchup," *Globe and Mail*, August 7, 2001, p. B8.

14 Craig Saunders, "Hudson's Bay plans massive CRM push," *Strategy*, July 17, 2000, p. 9.

15 David Menzies, "Loyalty cards are a mine of data," *Financial Post Magazine*, October 1998, p. 78.

16 Justin Bachman, "Coke joins P&G in new food venture," *Toronto Star*, February 22, 2001, p. C3.

17 David Menzies, pp. 77-78.

18 Kevin Marron, "Unplugged," *Globe and Mail*, March 31, 2000, p. E1.

19 "Unplugging data," *Advertising Age*, March 6, 2000, p. S50.

20 Patrick Brethour, "Women narrow Internet gender gap," *Globe and Mail*, March 27, 2001, pp. B1, B2.

21 Bernadette Johnson, "Advertisers revisiting the Web: Study," *Strategy*, February 12, 2001, pp. 1, 14.

22 Christopher Guly, "Linking web sites and sales requires cash, creativity, help," *Financial Post*, June 20, 1998, p. IT10.

23 Marina Strauss and Patrick Brethour, "Consumers shy away from Web shopping," *Globe and Mail*, December 15, 2001, pp. B1, B4.

24 Mary Gooderham, "Uneasy state of evolution makes e-tailing risky play," *Globe and Mail*, December 20, 2000, p. B13.

25 Carol Wolf, "Tire debacle shreds profit at Bridgestone," *Financial Post*, June 28, 2001, p. C14.

26 Elizabeth Church, "Bad news keeps piling up for Ford," *Globe and Mail*, August 14, 2001, pp. B1, B6.

27 Margot Gibb-Clark, "Consumers value companies based on ethics, survey says," *Globe and Mail*, October 1, 1999, p. B5.

28 Ellen Roseman, "Most want socially responsible companies," *Toronto Star*, February 1, 2002, p. E2.

29 Cyndee Millar, "U.S. firms lag behind in meeting global standards," *Marketing News*, February 15, 1993, p. 1.

30 Sanjiv Purba, "Companies beginning to trade on their ISO certification," *Toronto Star*, August 9, 2000, p. 64.

Dick Hemingway

Marketing Environments

After studying this chapter, you will be able to

1. Explain the concept of the marketing mix.
2. Describe the basic decision-making process associated with marketing mix elements.
3. Identify and explain the impact of external influences on marketing mix strategies.

The environment that marketing operates in is constantly changing. Problems, opportunities, successes, and failures are largely dependent on an organization's ability to adapt to changing conditions. In this regard, a business must anticipate change and how it will affect its operations. To be successful, new strategies must evolve. To foresee and adjust to change, a company reviews and analyzes certain external conditions that influence the nature of its marketing strategies. Trends that occur in the economy, competition, technology, laws and other regulations, and the consumer must be considered when developing a marketing strategy.

The Marketing Mix

marketing mix

1.
Explain the concept of the marketing mix.

2.
Describe the basic decision-making process associated with marketing mix elements.

The **marketing mix** is defined as a combination of the marketing elements that are used to satisfy the needs of a target market and achieve organizational objectives. There are four primary elements in the marketing mix: product, price, marketing communications, and distribution. In planning the marketing strategies for a company, product, or service, decisions are made for each element of the marketing mix (Figure 2.1).

An additional element that has an effect on consumers' purchase decisions is public image. It seems that today's consumers consider the values of a company and its corporate citizenship when deciding what products and services to buy. As discussed in Chapter 1, social responsibility marketing plays a key role in building and maintaining a positive public image. Let us examine the four primary decision areas of the marketing mix along with the influence of public image.

PRODUCT STRATEGY

product strategy

The most critical decision a firm faces is determining what products or services to market. **Product strategy** involves making decisions about product quality, product features, brand name, type and size of packaging, customer service, guarantees, and warranties. Product strategy can be further divided on the basis of *tangibility* (characteristics perceptible by touch, or any of the other senses) and *intangibility* (characteristics not perceptible by the senses). For example, a brand of beer like Molson Canadian is, by and large, not that distinguishable from competing products on the basis of tangible characteristics, such as taste and appearance, or on the basis of price and distribution, which are controlled by government regulation. As a result, product strategy for Molson Canadian will touch on subtle differences in taste (tangibility) but rely heavily on intangible factors, such as heritage or lifestyle associations, to distinguish it from competitive brands. Molson Canadian is a leading brand, the result of effective advertising campaigns that use popular slogans such as "I Am Canadian" to associate the brand to an attractive lifestyle.

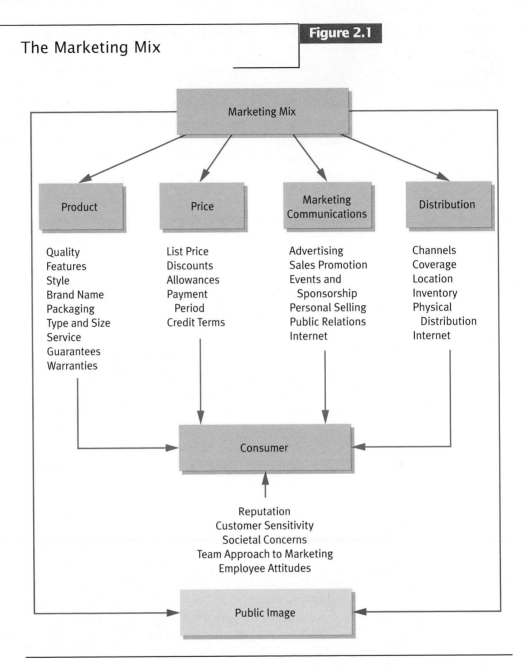

The Marketing Mix

Figure 2.1

Marketing Mix

Product	Price	Marketing Communications	Distribution
Quality	List Price	Advertising	Channels
Features	Discounts	Sales Promotion	Coverage
Style	Allowances	Events and	Location
Brand Name	Payment	Sponsorship	Inventory
Packaging	Period	Personal Selling	Physical
Type and Size	Credit Terms	Public Relations	Distribution
Service		Internet	Internet
Guarantees			
Warranties			

Consumer

Reputation
Customer Sensitivity
Societal Concerns
Team Approach to Marketing
Employee Attitudes

Public Image

**product
differentiation**

VISA
www.visa.com

Product strategy involves **product differentiation**, which is defined as a strategy that focuses marketing practice on unique attributes, or differential advantages of a product that are of value to customers in order to distinguish it from all other brands. For example, the differential advantage of the VISA card is that it can be used in more locations around the world than any other card. The advertising slogan for VISA is "All You Need." Consumption of Becel margarine contributes to a healthy lifestyle, and that is the primary benefit. Recent ads encourage consumers "to take the stairs," "to get some exercise," and "to eat better." See Figure 2.2 for an illustration. In the ketchup market,

Heinz is a brand leader but to add some excitement to a very mature category, it launched purple ketchup in a squeezeable bottle. Market share increased by five points.[1]

PRICE STRATEGY

Price strategy involves the development of a pricing structure that is fair and equitable for the consumer while still profitable for the organization. Since most products are sold in a competitive market, organizations are free to establish prices according to what the market will bear. A host of factors are considered when a price strategy is established,

Figure 2.2

Becel Differentiates Itself by Offering Consumers a Healthier Eating Alternative

Courtesy: Unilever Canada

including the cost of manufacturing the product, the location of the customer, the desired profit level, and the degree of competition. Generally, the less distinguishable a product is among its competitors (a condition referred to as low differential advantage), the less flexibility there is with price, since the product has no outstanding qualities to make it worth spending more on it than on its competitors. It should be pointed out that price is subject to regulation in certain markets and service sectors. In situations where a monopoly or near-monopoly exists, any planned increases in price must be approved by governments or government agencies. For example, prices are controlled for hydroelectric power in some provinces, telephone rates, cable television, and beer, wine, and other alcoholic beverages.

In addition to setting individual product prices, businesses can also establish comprehensive price policies that set company guidelines relating to trade allowances, discount programs, and credit terms. Businesses can provide these additional incentives, and customers can evaluate them while making their purchase decisions. A retailer like Wal-Mart, for example, buys the goods it resells in very large quantities. Therefore it qualifies for larger discounts and allowances from suppliers, and in turn can pass on the savings to its customers. Wal-Mart's price strategy is to offer the lowest possible prices on a regular basis. Wal-Mart's slogan is "We sell for less. Everyday."

Wal-Mart Stores, Inc.
www.walmart.com

MARKETING COMMUNICATIONS STRATEGY

marketing communications strategy

Marketing communications strategy involves another group of mix elements; it is the blending of advertising, public relations, direct response and interactive communications, sales promotion, personal selling, and event marketing and sponsorship. Since there are various methods of communications, it is important that a company or product present a clear and consistent message in each medium to achieve the highest possible impact. This premise is referred to as **integrated marketing communications**.

integrated marketing communications

Advertising is a persuasive form of marketing communications designed to stimulate a positive response (usually a purchase) in a defined target market. In advertising, decisions are made about the content, style, and tone of the message (i.e., what to say and how to say it). For some products a humorous appeal may be used, while in other cases celebrities may be used to endorse the product. Professional golfers, such as Tiger Woods (Nike, Titleist, American Express, and Buick), or Canadian Winter Olympians, such as Catriona LeMay Doan, Jamie Salé, and David Pelletier (Cheerios, Golden Grahams and Honey Nut Chex), for example, play prominent roles in print and broadcast advertising for the products they endorse and use professionally. Companies may also place advertisements focusing on the entire company, rather than just one of its products, to improve their public image (Figure 2.3). Which of the media to use is another strategic decision to be made—should the organization attempt to reach the masses through network television advertising, or should it target a selective audience through a specialized magazine or the Internet?

The Internet is a new medium to send messages through. Unlike traditional print or broadcast media, the Internet is a two-way medium. Experts anticipate that within the next 10 years interactive television, electronic media (e.g., the Internet), and wireless media (e.g., cell phones and personal digital assistants) will play a more important role; and traditional media, such as magazines, newspapers, and commercial television, will have a less important role (refer to the Technology section of this chapter for additional details). Prominent newspapers, magazines, and television networks are already available online and, in most cases, are free of charge to visitors.

Figure 2.3

A Message Communicating Corporate Activity and Corporate Citizenship

Courtesy: Siemens Canada Ltd.

Sales promotion is divided into two areas: consumer promotion and trade promotion. Consumer promotion involves using coupons, cash refunds, contests, and other incentives designed to encourage consumers to make immediate purchases. Trade promotion includes rebates, trade allowances, and performance allowances designed to encourage distributors to carry and resell a product.

Event marketing involves supporting an event with integrated communications. Typically, event marketing is coordinated with advertising and public relations. Event marketing and sponsorships fall into three categories: sports, entertainment, and arts and cultural events. Imperial Tobacco, through brands like du Maurier, is a strong supporter of the

Imperial Tobacco
www.imperial
tobaccocanada.com

arts and theatre, while Molson is a supporter of sports and rock concerts. Both companies recognize the public awareness and public image benefits that these relationships offer.

Personal selling involves face-to-face or other direct forms of communication (e.g., telemarketing) between marketing organizations and potential buyers. Personal selling plays a key role in business-to-business marketing situations (e.g., suppliers of component parts selling to companies producing consumer electronics products or automobiles). Participating in trade shows is another important means of communicating with customers in a personal way.

The linking of various marketing communications efforts is vital for the success of the organization. For example, advertising is designed to create awareness and interest and sales promotion is designed to encourage trial purchases. When both activities are combined, the desired action among consumers may occur faster. In business-to-business marketing, advertising will create company and product awareness but professionally trained sales people create the desire and opportunity to obtain the product; it is the latter activity that "closes deals" or achieves sales. Sales people play a key role in customer relationship management programs.

Public relations concern a firm's relationships and communications with its various publics. These include not only customers but also other groups, such as shareholders, employees, governments, suppliers, and distributors. Generally, public relations are intended to complement an organization's other promotion and marketing strategies. More recently, it has become the main means of communication in times of crisis, and crisis can strike at a moment's notice. The Walkerton water scandal that has been linked to as many as 18 deaths was a nightmare for the municipal government and the Ontario government. More recently, the tire debacle involving Firestone tires and the Ford Explorer had a dramatic and negative effect on two reputable companies. Public relations played a key role in helping each company rebound from the setback.

DISTRIBUTION STRATEGY

distribution strategy

Distribution strategy refers to the selection and management of marketing channels and the physical distribution of products. A marketing channel is a series of firms or individuals that participate in the flow of goods and services from producer to final users or consumers. A product, such as peanut butter, jam, or any similar packaged food product, moves from a manufacturer such as Kraft Canada to a wholesaler such as National Grocers to a retailer such as IGA, who, in turn, sells it to the consumer. These products may also bypass wholesalers entirely and be shipped directly to individual warehouse outlets, such as Costco.

Distribution decisions must be made as to which type of channel to use, the degree of market coverage desired (i.e., how intense the coverage will be), the location and availability of the product, inventory (the amount of product stored at manufacturing or warehousing facilities), and transportation modes (air, rail, water, transport, or pipeline). Developing effective and efficient distribution systems requires that an organization work closely and develop a harmonious relationship with distributors (wholesalers and retailers) who resell a product along the channel. The relationship marketing practices presented in Chapter 1 play a key role in distribution programs.

Progressive-oriented companies are adding direct channels of distribution as they figure out ways to take advantage of Internet business transactions. The Ford Motor Company, for example, has an e-commerce initiative that allows consumers to order cars over the Internet without setting foot inside a dealership. The customer can "spec out" a vehicle and actually have the vehicle delivered without having to haggle about price. Vehicles are custom ordered from the Ford Web site. The e-price that is available is ultimately what the dealer would sell for after the usual buyer-seller negotiations at a dealership.[2]

Operating a distribution system is a complex task, and as a result, companies are turning the task over to external distribution specialists. A specialist analyzes a company's existing distribution and warehousing operation or builds them a new one from scratch, promising to run it better and cheaper, for a fee. Grocery chain Safeway Canada and Wal-Mart Canada, two leaders in their respective markets, each employ a specialist to operate their warehouse and distribution networks.[3]

PUBLIC IMAGE AND ITS INFLUENCE

For any business, large or small, a good reputation is an important asset. Nevertheless, business organizations, particularly large ones, have often neglected their corporate image as they become engrossed in the image of individual brands, product lines, or services. As discussed in Chapter 1, businesses are placing greater emphasis on socially responsible marketing, and as a result, **public image** is now an integral part of an organization's corporate strategy and marketing strategy. A firm's reputation is important enough to require special attention.

public image

In an effort to develop a better public image, many firms are showing greater sensitivity to their customers. As a result, firms have implemented more comprehensive customer service programs and customer relationship management programs. Organizations today recognize that the attitude of all employees towards customers plays a significant role in influencing customer satisfaction and building a better company image.

At the corporate level, companies are enhancing their image by getting involved with issues important to customers. Through **corporate advertising** campaigns they let the public know how they stand on environmental issues and social issues. Corporate advertising is not intended to directly sell a product, but, since the objective is to enhance the image of the company and create goodwill, there could be some long-term and indirect effect on sales. See Figure 2.4 for an illustration and refer to the "Lifestyles and Environmental Concerns" section of this chapter for more details.

corporate advertising

External Influences Affecting the Marketing Mix

3.
Identify and explain the impact of external influences on marketing mix strategies.

As we have mentioned, in developing marketing strategies an organization must consider the external environment in which it operates. It is the unpredictability and the changes that occur beyond the firm that make marketing a dynamic field. For example, if interest rates rise, consumer spending tends to drop. This affects all kinds of industries: housing, automobiles, household appliances, recreation and leisure activities, and others. This causes a ripple effect that extends to the suppliers of these industries. When market planners develop marketing strategies, they must constantly monitor and evaluate the effect of the following external influences: the economy, competition, social and demographic trends, technology, and laws and regulations. See Figure 2.4 for a visual illustration of the external marketing influences.

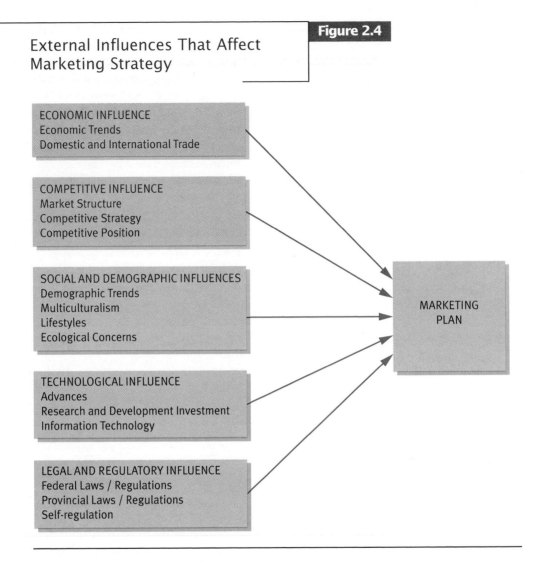

External Influences That Affect Marketing Strategy

Figure 2.4

ECONOMIC INFLUENCE
Economic Trends
Domestic and International Trade

COMPETITIVE INFLUENCE
Market Structure
Competitive Strategy
Competitive Position

SOCIAL AND DEMOGRAPHIC INFLUENCES
Demographic Trends
Multiculturalism
Lifestyles
Ecological Concerns

TECHNOLOGICAL INFLUENCE
Advances
Research and Development Investment
Information Technology

LEGAL AND REGULATORY INFLUENCE
Federal Laws / Regulations
Provincial Laws / Regulations
Self-regulation

MARKETING PLAN

ECONOMIC INFLUENCE

The economy has a significant impact on the marketing activity of an organization. Canada's economic situation is measured by such variables as the gross domestic product (GDP), inflation, unemployment, real income, and interest rates. These indicators determine how conservative or how aggressive an organization's marketing efforts will be. Let us briefly define each of these economic variables:

gross domestic product

1. **Gross Domestic Product** The GDP is the total value of goods and services produced in a country on an annual basis.

inflation

2. **Inflation** Inflation refers to a general rising price level for goods and services, resulting in reduced purchasing power.

unemployment

3. **Unemployment** The unemployed are people who do not have jobs and are actively looking for work.

real income

4. **Real Income** This is income adjusted for inflation over time.

The relationships among these economic variables are dynamic. For example, if during a given period widespread cost increases drive prices up beyond, for instance, the means of lower-income and middle-income groups, the purchasing of goods and services will decrease. The result is reduced purchasing power for consumers and less money available for discretionary or optional purchases. Inflation will slow down the economy, and as fewer workers are required, higher rates of unemployment will prevail. It also shrinks real income. Real income indicates the volume of goods and services that money will buy (e.g., if inflation rises, a $40 000 income in 2004 will be worth less than a $40 000 income in 2003 or previous years because it will purchase less).

disposable income

Disposable income refers to actual income after taxes and other expenses—it is income available for optional purchases. Throughout the 1990s, there was a consistent decline in disposable income. Canadians were working hard but the rising costs of basic necessities and services such as rent, hydro, gas, telephone, and so on meant there was less available for optional purchases such as vacations and sports and recreational activities. Feeling stretched financially, the average Canadian family was concentrating on purchases for necessities only.

The state of the economy also affects the value of the Canadian dollar, which in turn, has a special impact on the activities of Canadian organizations that export internationally. When, for instance, the Canadian dollar is worth less than the American dollar, Canadian-produced goods become more attractive to and marketable among American buyers, since the prices of our goods in their market are lower than those of their own goods. Conversely, if the Canadian dollar were higher in value than the American dollar, our goods would become less attractive because the prices of Canadian goods would be higher than the American ones in their market. In this case, exports to the United States would probably decline. Since the Canadian dollar is presently worth much less than the American dollar, Canada enjoys a favourable balance of trade with the United States. Approximately 85 percent of Canada's exports go to the United States.

Business Cycles

Economic growth in Canada is measured by real growth in gross domestic product from year to year or the percentage increase in the per capita real GDP. Over the long-term Canada has experienced high rates of economic growth. In recent years the percentage rate of growth for GDP has been in the 3 to 3.5 per cent range annually.

The economy of a country either contracts or expands and goes through various stages in the process: recession, depression, recovery, and prosperity. Contraction occurs when an economy reaches a peak—the economy is booming but there is no growth. The future is unknown and often predicted by extending current trends. Therefore, if a downward trend is predicted (e.g., lower GDP) there will be lower spending by consumers. Lower spending then leads to more reductions in output and negative growth in GDP continues in a spiral effect. The longer the period of decline, the more serious the consequences for the economy. A decline in real output that lasts for six months or more

recession
depression

is referred to as a **recession**. A long and harsh period of decline is a **depression**.

Eventually the decline in output (GDP) bottoms out—it is at its lowest value in the business cycle. At this point the economy begins to expand. Initial increases in output and consumer spending lead to optimistic forecasts for growth. Consumers react positively and begin to spend more. Businesses react to the consumer spending and start to

recovery

prosperity

invest more in their operations (i.e., perhaps expand a manufacturing facility or build a new facility). The initial phase of expansion is referred to as **recovery**. When growth is sustained at significant levels for an extended period, the economy is experiencing **prosperity**.

The present state of the Canadian economy is difficult to assess, even for economists. "We know the Canadian economy is in a slowdown. We don't know if it's in a recession," said John McCallum, the former chief economist for the Royal Bank of Canada. "I think what we do know is we're not in the kind of wrenching recession we had in the 1990s."[4] The North American economy was starting to slide before the terrorist attacks of September 11, 2001 on the United States. Since then both Canada and the United States have been undergoing an unusual business cycle in which consumer confidence has remained high (i.e., consumers are still buying new automobiles in record numbers and investing in houses). Consumers have remained optimistic and have been influenced by historically low interest rates between 2000 and 2002.

In contrast, the business sector has retrenched its investment and other activities because of falling profits. In Canada, for example, in 2002, the major domestic automobile manufacturers (General Motors, Ford and DaimlerChrysler) laid off 5000 workers to reduce costs and restore profitability despite the fact that automobile sales reached record levels.

It is expected that the economic effects of the terrorist attacks will wear off and that the business sector of the economy will rebound. The fallout in the short-term has been devastating for companies in the travel industry: airlines, hotels, and car rental companies.

rationalization

When the economy turns sour many companies evaluate the efficiency of their operations and begin a process called rationalization. **Rationalization** is defined as the restructuring, downsizing, and, if necessary, the closing of operations that are not economically justified. With many Canadian companies being owned by companies based in foreign countries, it is sometimes an easy decision to close a Canadian facility. All things being equal, if wages are lower in another country, the decision to reduce production or move production out of Canada makes economic sense. To illustrate, Nike closed a Canadian Bauer skate manufacturing facility that employed 400 people one year after it acquired Canstar Sports Inc. The skates could be made for much less offshore. The automobile industry is presently shifting a lot of vehicle production from Canada to Mexico for the same reason.

Free Trade

NAFTA Secretariat
www.nafta-
sec-alena.org

Canada is part of a North American free trade market that includes the United States and Mexico. The agreement represents an opportunity for Canadian businesses. Companies from all three countries are adjusting to the larger market and are implementing programs to achieve economies in production and marketing. On the positive side, the potential for Canadian industries seems huge. A single market of 360 million people with an annual output of US$10 trillion gives Canada and its free trade partners greater clout in world trading.

A potential negative consequence of free trade is the corporate downsizing that could occur (the process of rationalization just described), especially if the economy in North America were to take a downturn. The lower land costs, taxes, and labour rates in Mexico are attractive to new industries or those industries considering relocation. When all costs are considered, the cost of manufacturing tends to be lower in both the United States and Mexico—a distinct disadvantage for Canada.

COMPETITIVE INFLUENCE

The activity of competitors is probably the most thoroughly analyzed aspect of marketing practice, as competitors are constantly striving to find new and better ways of appealing to similar target markets. The competitive environment that an organization operates in must be defined and analyzed, and the strategies of direct and indirect competitors must be monitored and evaluated.

Market Structures

In Canada, a business operates in one of four different types of market structure: monopoly, oligopoly, monopolistic competition, and pure competition. Each has a different impact on marketing strategy.

monopoly

In a **monopoly**, one firm serves the entire market (there are no close substitutes) and, therefore, theoretically controls most of the marketing mix elements: product, price, marketing communications, and distribution. In Canada, government regulates monopolies so market control is limited. Examples of monopolistic but regulated markets include local-market telephone service, cable television within geographic areas, electricity, and water. Since consumers do not have a choice in matters such as these, governments at all levels must regulate price and service availability, ensuring that customers are treated fairly.

Until very recently, a market situation existed where H.J. Heinz was the only supplier of jars of baby food in Canada. A year earlier, Heinz had persuaded government regulators to slap high anti-dumping duties on Gerber, its main competitor. Gerber subsequently pulled out of the market. But since then, the Competition Bureau found that Heinz abused its position by paying retailers lump sums to agree to carry only Heinz products, signing long-term multi-year contracts with retailers, and giving discounts conditional on exclusive supply of Heinz products. The Competition Bureau ruled that Heinz created a significant additional barrier to entry for competitors, preventing or lessening competition in the marketplace.[5]

The airline industry in Canada is heading towards monopoly as a result of the recent merger of Canadian Airlines with Air Canada. The merged company controls 80 percent of domestic air travel. Via Rail is the only national passenger rail service so it is also a monopoly. Air Canada and Via compete for the same customers, however, even though they operate in different segments of the travel industry.

oligopoly

In an **oligopoly**, a few large firms dominate the market. The beer industry is a good example of an oligopoly in Canada. The two major companies, Molson and Labatt, control about 90 percent of the market with the country's craft brewers splitting the rest. It is very difficult for others to enter the market and be successful, unless they are satisfied with a very small piece of the action. The small breweries simply do not have the marketing budgets to compete in terms of advertising and promotion. In Quebec, small brewers claim that Molson and Labatt are abusing their clout by signing exclusive contracts with grocery stores, pubs, restaurants, and universities. The federal Competition Bureau is investigating the complaint. The small brewers claim the larger brewers are squeezing them out of the market.[6]

In the movie theatre industry, Famous Players and Cineplex Odeon control the distribution of movies. They split new movie releases between themselves, leaving very little for independent theatres. The Competition Bureau is investigating this industry for "abuse of dominance."[7]

In an oligopoly, firms generally compete on the basis of product differentiation and brand image. In the beer industry, subtle differences in taste may not be all that important, but the image of the brand that marketing creates could be a vital factor in the consumer's purchase decision.

monopolistic competition

In a market characterized by **monopolistic competition**, there are many firms, large and small, each offering a unique marketing mix. Marketers use any of the mix elements to differentiate the product or service from competitors. Products are clearly distinguished by brand names. In effect, each competitor is striving to build their market share, but due to the presence of strong competition, there are always substitute products for consumers to turn to.

In the restaurant market, for example, brand names, such as McDonald's, Harvey's, A&W, Burger King, and KFC, compete with each other in the quick-serve segment. A step up from quick-serve are restaurants such as Kelsey's, Jack Astors, Montanas Cookhouse, Shoeless Joes, and so on. When consumers decide to dine out, they must make a decision. Product differences in this industry relate to location, quality, or the image consumers have of each restaurant's product. These variables influence the decision on where to dine.

pure competition

In a market where **pure competition** exists, all firms market a uniform product—no single buyer or seller has much effect on the price. There are many buyers and sellers. In effect, the advantage of one product over another is not that clear to consumers. Pure competition is common in the agriculture industry and in markets for financial assets such as stocks and bonds. Pure competition is not common in other sectors of the economy.

Market structures can change. To illustrate, consider the changes that have occurred in the milk industry. At one time, milk was milk. A 4-litre bag of milk was the same price regardless of brand name. Customers would willingly make substitutions depending on what brand was available. There was pure competition. Demand for milk was falling as consumers showed preference for bottled waters and juices. To fight back, dairies launched innovative milk products such as Natrel Fine Filtre milk. Natrel has a longer shelf life and fresher taste, and is priced higher than regular milk. Other dairies followed suit. Neilson now markets Trutaste and Trucalcium, both of which are positioned as premium brands.[8] The milk industry has moved from pure competition to monopolistic competition. Marketing now plays a key role in determining what brand of milk a consumer will purchase.

New firms can easily enter a purely competitive market, so existing firms, in order to remain competitive, must ensure that there is an adequate supply of products available with a low price and with widespread distribution. Frequently, it is price (low price) that maintains a competitive advantage for any one product.

Most Canadian industries are highly concentrated and best described as oligopolies or as monopolistically competitive.

Competitive Strategies

Once an organization has identified the type of competition it faces, its attention shifts to the strategies of competitors. It must monitor competitors from direct and indirect sources.

direct competition

Direct competition is competition from alternative products and services that satisfy the needs of a common target market. For example, in the deodorant market, Gillette competes directly with Degree, Dry Idea, Arm & Hammer, Mitchum, and others. In the soft drink market, Coca-Cola competes with Pepsi-Cola and a host of private label colas (Z cola, Life cola, etc.), and other branded flavours, such as 7 Up, Crush, and Hires root beer. In the retail marketplace, Wal-Mart competes directly with Zellers. Direct competitors keep a close watch on their competitors' marketing strategies and performance. Success is usually measured in terms of market share and profit. In the retail example just mentioned, Wal-Mart is the leader in the department store market, while all other competitors (Zellers, Sears, Eaton's, and the Bay) have lost ground. The marketing strategy of Wal-Mart, which centres on broad selection and everyday low pricing, has been a hit with Canadian consumers. The established Canadian retailers have tried to respond to the challenge presented by Wal-Mart but, to date, have not been successful.

indirect competition

Firms must also consider indirect competition. **Indirect competition** is competition from substitute products that offer customers the same benefit. For example, when someone is thirsty, they may reach for a soft drink, such as Coca-Cola or Pepsi-Cola, two products that are direct competitors with each other. However, the consumer has a broader choice. They could choose a sparkling water beverage, such as Clearly Canadian (available in a variety of flavours). They could also select a fruit juice, ice tea, or an energy-replacement drink, such as Gatorade or Powerade. When Coca-Cola develops its marketing strategies, it must look beyond traditional soft drinks and consider the activities of other beverages. Coca-Cola is in the beverage business, not just the soft drink business.

The difference between direct and indirect competition is becoming blurred. Pharmacies, such as Shoppers Drug Mart, Jean Coutu, and London Drugs, used to be concerned about each other. Now, Zellers, Wal-Mart, and Loblaws all offer pharmacy services. Wal-Mart is starting to sell groceries and eventually could pose a threat to industry leaders, such as Loblaws, Provigo, and Sobey's. Tim Hortons, at one time, only sold donuts, muffins, and coffee. Now they offer an expanded menu and compete with McDonald's, KFC, Subway, and a host of other fast food restaurants.

Technology is changing the nature of competition in some markets. Book stores such as Chapters and Indigo, and music stores such as HMV have to compete with online retailers such as Amazon.com. Canadian consumers are attracted to the convenience offered by Amazon. Branchless banks, such as the Citizens Bank of Canada and ING Direct, are competitors that the traditional banks now compete with. Today, bank customers conduct a considerable portion of their basic banking, including bill payments, deposits, and withdrawals, through automated teller machines (ATMs), by telephoning centralized call centers, or by doing it online. The Canadian consumers' receptiveness to new banking technology is one reason why the ING Group chose to launch an Internet banking service in this country.[9] Bricks and mortar are no longer a necessity for establishing a presence in the marketplace.

For additional insight into the influence of competition and changes in consumer preferences, see the Marketing in Action vignette **McDonald's Protects Its Lead**.

The Competitive Position

market share

A firm's market share indicates its competitive position in the marketplace. **Market share** is the sales volume of one competing company or product expressed as a percentage of the total market sales volume. Competing products are classified in many ways. Author Philip Kotler describes and classifies competitors as leaders, challengers, followers, and nichers.[10]

Marketing in Action

McDonald's Protects Its Lead

Even though McDonald's is a dominant leader in the quick-serve restaurant market, the company realizes it can never be complacent. Their business, like any other business, must evolve with changes that occur in the economy, the competition, and the consumer. McDonald's excels at what it does because they are usually first to identify change, and by taking appropriate action, they retain a solid leadership position.

In today's fast-paced society the demands of the consumer can be overwhelming. McDonald's is a fast food restaurant and has always prided itself on delivering the goods quickly to customers. But now, McDonald's observes that gratification is becoming increasingly instantaneous—people hardly want to stop their cars to grab their food. Customers in line at a drive-through are increasingly impatient.

How does McDonald's react to such a change? McDonald's generates 50 percent of their sales from drive-through operations. That's up from 40 percent only 3 years ago. Any marketing manager following that kind of sales trends realizes that any improvement in providing more convenience in the drive-through could generate significant profit.

As of April 2002, McDonalds' raised the convenience bar. The company now promotes a 30-second drive-through guarantee. Supported by a national advertising campaign, it's "Thirty seconds from the time you pay till you're on your way." Customers forced to wait longer receive a coupon for a free fries or breakfast sandwich. According to Bill Johnson, "Convenience is now the crucial deciding factor in the marketplace." Convenience also means location (being readily available when needed). That means having restaurants in locations such as malls, hospitals, and entertainment complexes. McDonald's has opened restaurants in all of these places.

In another effort to stay on top of change, McDonald's realized they were losing some customers to coffee houses and other restaurants. McDonald's had to find a way to capture more meal occasions that don't involve burgers. The solution may come in the form of the McCafé, a coffee house concept being test marketed in several Ontario locations. If all goes according to plan, McCafé will woo the Starbuck's crowd with specialty coffees and desserts. The McCafé pilot is just one other way Johnson is trying to reinvent McDonald's in Canada.

McDonald's primary focus remains on its 1200 outlets across Canada that generate an annual sales revenue of $2.4 billion. But the chain—which serves 3 million people or 10 percent of the population daily—must adapt to a new breed of consumers looking for more than just a burger. "We can't be all things to all people," says Johnson. As the uncertain future unfolds, McDonald's must find ways to constantly tweak its menu to offer more choices while still holding true to the fast-food concept. Thus far, McDonald's is doing a very good job at it!

Adapted from Zena Olijnyk, "McLatte with those fries?" *Canadian Business*, March 18, 2002 (online version) and Patrick Allossery, "Fast food in high gear," *Financial Post*, March 4, 2002, p. FP6.

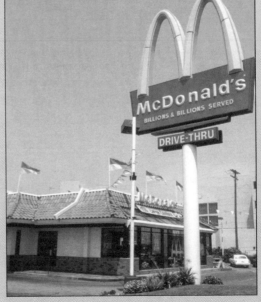

Michael Newman/PhotoEdit

market leader A **market leader** is the largest firm in the industry and is a leader in strategic actions (e.g., new product innovation, pricing and price increases, and aggressive promotion activity). Examples of leaders include Tim Hortons (which controls 67.2 percent of the market among coffee shop chains), Dodge Caravan (which controls 36.6 percent of the minivan market), Colgate (which controls 39.7 percent of the toothpaste market), and McDonald's (which controls about 28.4 percent of the fast food market). McDonald's market share is greater than the sum of Subway, Burger King, A&W, Wendy's, and Dairy Queen.[11] In the soft drink market, Coca-Cola is the undisputed leader worldwide. When Coke says, "Always Coca-Cola," it means it!

market challenger A **market challenger** is a firm or firms (product or products) attempting to gain market leadership through aggressive marketing efforts. Perhaps the best example is the battle between Pepsi-Cola (the challenger) and Coca-Cola (the leader). Coca-Cola still retains leadership in the soft drink business, but Pepsi-Cola, however, uses more aggressive marketing strategies. Its advertising campaigns that use such slogans as "The choice of a new generation" and "Generation Next" grab the attention of the teen market, the heaviest consumers of soft drinks. In the toothpaste market, Crest is a challenger, holding 25 percent of the market.

market follower A **market follower** is generally satisfied with its market share position. Often, it has entered the market late and has not incurred the research and development costs that innovators do. As a result, it is content to follow the leaders on product, price, distribution, and other marketing actions. From the toothpaste market examples cited above, Colgate is the leader and Crest is the challenger. Remaining brands, such as Arm & Hammer, Close Up, Oral-B, Aim, and Macleans, all of which have less than five percent market share, are followers.

market nicher

niche marketing A **market nicher** practises "niche marketing." **Niche marketing** refers to the concentration of resources on one or more distinguishable market segments. Market nichers are the big fish in a small pond, as opposed to the little fish in a big pond. In order to niche market, a firm differentiates itself on the basis of specialization or an area of strength. Examples of market nichers include General Nutrition Cos. GNC stores, a national chain specializing in vitamins and other health supplements, and Pet Value, a chain specializing in pet food. Both of these retailers are cashing in on consumer trends that traditional grocery stores are not. GNC appeals to consumers searching for a healthier lifestyle while Pet Valu attracts shoppers wanting premium brands with quality ingredients not carried by grocers.[12]

The subject of niche marketing is discussed in more detail in the Market Segmentation section of Chapter 4.

SOCIAL AND DEMOGRAPHIC INFLUENCES

Consumers are another of the unpredictable variables that influence marketing strategies. To keep abreast of the changing consumer, market planners analyze demographic and social trends. **Demographics** is the study of the characteristics of a population.

demographics These characteristics include size, growth rates, age, location, gender, income, education, marital status, and ethnic background. Among these characteristics several trends have emerged: the population is aging, household formations are changing, ethnic groups are comprising a larger percentage of the population, and the size of the middle class is shrinking. Let us examine some of these trends.

Size and Age

The age distribution of Canada's population is changing. As of 2001, Canada's population totaled 30 007 0094. The average annual growth rate of the population over the past 25 years has been around 1.3 percent, but in the past 5 years that dropped to 0.8 percent annually, an all-time low.[13] In comparison, the rate of population growth in the United States was 1.0 percent and only 0.4 percent in Europe.

Certain age groups are growing much faster than average. Changes in the age distribution of the population are due to variations in the birth rates in recent years; the baby boom from 1946 to 1964 was followed by a "baby bust" in the late 1960s and the 1970s; a "mini-boom" occurred in the late 1980s. The latter group is often referred to as "echo-boom" generation. Because of the baby boom, the bulk of the Canadian population is maturing. In 2001, it was estimated that 29 percent of the population would be over 50 years. By 2011, the figure increases to 35.4 percent and by 2021 to 40 percent.[14] Baby boomers and seniors will play a dominant role in purchase activity in the next decade and beyond. The aging phenomenon will have an impact on school systems, the labour force, family formation, health care, and the demand for products and services. See Figure 2.5 for details on age trends in Canada.

A good example of how marketing has tapped into the aging market is in breakfast cereals. Most children and teens eat mounds of the stuff, but consumption drops sharply around age 20 years. In their mid-30s, people rediscover the virtues of a regular breakfast. On the basis of this cycle, Kellogg divides the market into three distinct age segments: children, teenagers, and people over 35 years. With the core of the baby boomers in the latter stage, it is plain to see the rationale behind their advertising campaign for Kellogg's Corn Flakes that uses the slogan, "Taste them again for the first time." The ads feature 30-somethings doing just that. Kellogg's also markets directly to people in their 40s and 50s with brands like All Bran—"The drug-free way to regularity."

Location

More Canadians than ever before live in cities. According to the 2001 Census data, 79.4 percent of the population lives in urban areas. Both Ontario and British Columbia

Figure 2.5

Age Trends in Canadian Population (thousands)

Age	1996	%	2006	%	2016	%
0–9	3742.5	12.1	3382.2	10.2	2518.4	9.9
10–19	4157.6	13.4	4038.6	12.1	3688.7	10.4
20–34	6449.8	20.8	6797.9	20.3	6821.1	19.3
35–49	7685.7	24.8	7330.1	22.0	7184.8	20.4
50+	8966.8	28.9	11 812.9	35.4	14 168.7	40.0

Source: Adapted from the Statistics Canada CANSIM II database <http://cansim2.statcan.ca/cgiwin/CNSMCGI.EXE>, tables 051-001 and 052-001.

exceed the national average for urban population. As well, 51 percent of the population lives in four major urban areas: metropolitan Montreal; the Golden Horseshoe area in southern Ontario which includes metropolitan Toronto; the Edmonton-Calgary corridor; and British Columbia's Lower Mainland.[15] A **census metropolitan area (CMA)** encompasses all urban and rural areas that are linked to a city's urban core, either socially or economically. In order for products and services to succeed in the future, there will have to be a greater concentration of marketing strategies in key urban centres. The trend towards urban living is expected to continue.

census metropolitan area (CMA)

Family Formation

The nature of Canadian families is changing. Essentially, families are getting smaller and they are less traditional in structure. The traditional family was a married couple with a few children. Many Canadians now postpone marriage or dispense with it altogether. Common-law unions are increasing, while people who do marry are doing so later in life. Now, married couples comprise 73.7 percent of the population and common-law couples 11.7 percent. The latter is a jump of 4.5 percentage points in the past 10 years. Lone-parent families comprise the remaining 14.6 percent of the population.[16]

More and more children are born and raised outside marriage or experience the breakdown of their parents' marriage. As a result, we are witnessing an evolution in cultural values where there is a difference between younger and older people in their attitudes, values, expectations, and taken-for-granted assumptions. Canadians, many of whom have children, now have relatively high rates of separation and divorce. New forms of cohabitation have produced the **blended family**, where kids move back and forth between parents.

blended family

In the past decade, there was a back-to-the-family unit as baby boomers, who had previously delayed marriage to pursue careers, started forming families. In fact, the baby boomers created a "mini-boom." What has emerged is the so-called **sandwich generation**, in which people are simultaneously trying to assume responsibility for dependent children and care for aging relatives. Such a trend is placing an added burden on family finances.

sandwich generation

The average family size has shrunk to 3.1 members from a high of 3.9 in 1966. The character of the family has changed for economic reasons. With each passing decade there are more women in the work force. Two wage earners per household has become the norm so it is expected that the number of members within each household will remain small. A variety of industries and product categories have responded to these changes. The travel industry and key players such as Club Med have shifted marketing focus away from singles and towards families. The quick-serve restaurant industry (McDonald's and others) has grown significantly while catering to the needs of time-pressed households. A new food category called nutritional portable foods (NPF) that includes products such as Kellogg's Nutri-Grain bars and Harvest Crunch Granola bars meets the needs of consumers that are always on the go.

Spending Power and Wealth

In the past decade, slower productivity growth has meant that prices in Canada have risen faster than incomes. In other words, the spending power of the dollar has shrunk. When other factors such as increases in federal and provincial taxes are considered, the relative wealth or spending power of the middle and lower income groups has dropped. Real wealth is becoming concentrated in the upper income groups. To refer to an old expression, "the rich are getting richer, and the poor are getting poorer." Others refer to this situation as the "disappearing of the middle class."

According to the latest census (2001) young couples with children saw a 30 percent drop in their median wealth between 1984 and 1999. Where the main breadwinner was aged 25 to 34, the family's net wealth was $30 800 in 1999—nearly a third less than it was in the mid-1980s. For most income levels, the share of net wealth dropped. Only in the highest brackets did wealth increase. The top 10 percent of families saw the midpoint of their net wealth jump by 35 percent, rising to an average of $628 100 in 1999.[17]

Wealthy Canadians now form a larger segment of the population than in previous decades, mainly due to the increasing number of dual-income families and to an aging population that is freer of financial obligations, such as children and mortgages. Considering the age variables discussed earlier, the combination of age and wealth really make the 50-year plus market an attractive target. The over-50 group makes up only 12 percent of the population but controls 45 percent of the personal wealth in Canada and 40 percent of the discretionary spending power. They purchase 43 percent of all new domestic cars and 48 percent of all luxury cars. The luxury segment of the automobile industry is reaping the benefits as baby boomers trade in the mini-vans for upscale sports utility vehicles and luxury cars such as Lexus, Infiniti, Jaguar, and BMW. The illustration in Figure 2.6 shows what Infiniti is doing to attract the baby boomer market.

Education

New jobs in North America have higher entry requirements than ever and are largely based on technology. More than ever before, education and training are key issues if Canada is to compete globally. Literacy, numeracy, and problem-solving skills have become increasingly important; the 3 R's have returned in style because they provide the necessary skills for employees to cope with technology. Shortages in the basic skills would adversely affect Canada's ability to compete; in order that we may have a well-trained workforce in the future, it is expected that governments and industries will have to cooperate to increase spending on "quality" education.

The level of education achieved by persons over 15 years of age is increasing. In a 10-year period between 1986 and 1996, the percentage of people with a college diploma increased from 10.4 to 14.1 and those with a university degree increased from 9.6 to 13.3.[18] The result is a more informed shopper. Canadian consumers have accepted innovative electronic products at a much faster pace than those in many other developed countries. Consumers are using the Internet to search for goods and services that provide better value. In fact, Canadians have been quicker to adopt Internet technology than Americans. In 2001, 48 percent of Canadians were connected at home compared to 36 percent of Americans. By 2003 it is projected that 62 percent of Canadian households will be connected.[19] Such acceptance and use of technology is a reflection of an educated society.

Multiculturalism

Canada is emerging as a very culturally diverse country. The population is continuing to shift from one of a predominantly European background. Immigration trends indicate that Asians are becoming a major ethnic group in Canada. Existing within Canadian

Figure 2.6

The Nissan Infiniti Q45 Appeals Directly to Upscale Baby Boomers

subcultures

culture are many diverse **subcultures**—subgroups within a larger cultural context that have distinctive lifestyles based on religious, racial, and geographic differences. Presently, in Canada, about one-third of the population (1996 Census) report an ethnic background other than British or French, up from 25 percent in 1986.

Canada's subcultures are evident in urban and suburban areas of cities where large ethnic populations occupy neighbourhoods. See Figure 2.7 for details regarding the ethnic population of Canada.

Figure 2.7

Canada's Ethnic Population: Ethnic Population of the Top 10 Census Metropolitan Areas

	Ethnic Population	Percentage of Population
Toronto	1772.9	41.6
Montreal	586.4	17.6
Vancouver	633.7	34.6
Ottawa-Hull	161.9	16.0
Edmonton	158.4	18.4
Calgary	170.8	20.8
Quebec City	17.4	2.5
Winnipeg	111.7	16.7
Hamilton	145.6	23.3
London	76.0	19.1

Since 1991, the population has increased in Toronto and Vancouver. Other cities have remained fairly constant in population breakdown.

Source: Adapted from the Statistics Canada Web site <http://www.statcan.ca/english/PGDB/demo28d.htm>.

In the future, successful targeting and meeting of the needs of various ethnic groups promises to be profitable for firms venturing into the sub-markets. Buckley's Mixture, that awful tasting cough syrup, has pursued such an opportunity by targeting the Chinese community. According to David Reiger, director of marketing at Buckley's, "The Chinese people believe in products that taste bad and work: we're a good fit for that attitude." Loosely translated, Buckley's message in Chinese says: "Good medicine tastes awful."[20]

Lifestyles and Environmental Concerns

The 1990s saw a shift in Canadians' attitudes towards work, lifestyles, and consumption. Generally speaking, we are now a society that places a greater emphasis on quality of life rather than work. That said, work is essential to sustain the desired quality of life. There is also a stronger concern for health and welfare. Diet, AIDS, the aging process, and the effects of the environment on health, all became hot topics, creating a widespread desire for general "wellness."

Presently, 45 percent of the population participates regularly in some form of sports activity.[21] As a result, people will continue to spend more for products and services related to a healthy lifestyle. Attitudes about the ingredients in food products are changing, and there is a trend towards natural foods and herbal remedies. Good prospects await low-fat and cholesterol-free food products, natural products, fitness facilities, skin care products, and in-house health-care programs. That said, however, the snack food segment of the market continues to grow. A segment of the population does like to indulge.

To capitalize on healthier lifestyle trends, Sun-Rype introduced a nutrition snack bar that combines the goodness of vegetables with the taste of fruits. The product is easily packed in lunch boxes or brief cases. See Figure 2.8 for an illustration. In the drugstore market, Shoppers Drug Mart has redefined itself on the premise that consumers want to

Shoppers Drug Mart
www.shoppers
drugmart.ca

Figure 2.8

A New Product That Matches Healthier Lifestyles

Courtesy: Sun-Rype Products Ltd.

"feel good." Their new campaign was based on research that revealed peoples' desire to feel good, to have a healthy and productive life. The ads explain that Shoppers provides the products and services to get the most out of life. All of Shoppers' advertising uses the tagline "Take Care of Yourself."[22] In a very competitive market that includes Wal-Mart and Loblaws, Shoppers believes this image campaign will differentiate itself from others.

As discussed in Chapter 1, socially responsible marketing is now in vogue. A shift in consumers' attitudes on social and environmental issues has played a role in changing the way a company views its marketing programs. They are moving towards cause-related marketing programs and are operating on the premise that the emotional attributes associated with cause-linked brands differentiate them from their rivals. If brand cost and quality are perceived as equal, a customer will choose to buy the product associated with the cause.

Kraft Canada (a food company) is fully committed to a worthy cause-hunger. Each year Kraft provides significant amounts of food to Canada's food banks. It also runs an advertising campaign designed to change the stigma associated with using food banks. The Canadian Tire Foundation for Families is a fund-raising program that donates funds received from the purchase of artificial Christmas trees in its stores. Canadian Tire makes the public aware of its commitment through television advertising in the months preceding Christmas. Social marketers say that their efforts are not about giving away money or products to get publicity. Instead it is about building a social identity linked to their company or brands. They believe consumers will buy brands and support companies that reflect their own social values.[23]

TECHNOLOGICAL INFLUENCE

Technology will probably be the greatest single force shaping the Canadian marketplace in the next decade and beyond. Federal and provincial governments, industries, universities, and private non-profit organizations, all fund and perform ventures in science and technology.

The technological environment consists of the discoveries, inventions, and innovations that provide for marketing opportunities. New products, new packaging, cost-reduced materials and substitute materials for existing products, the emergence of e-learning are all the result of technological advancement. In the next decade, advances in electronics, biotechnology, and the information technologies of computing and telecommunications will be the driving force for change and growth. By all accounts, the telecommunications world will be wireless by 2010.

The Internet has had an overwhelming impact on marketing and commerce. So rapid is the pace that it is being measured in "dog years"—or seven years for every human year. In the Internet commerce arena, Canada lags behind the United States. Given that competition comes from all over the world via the Internet, Canadian businesses could lose ground to their American counterparts. Canadian financial institutions are an exception. In this market sector Canada is a leader—Canadians have embraced ATMs and debit cards at an unprecedented rate, and 65 percent of customers already use banks' e-services. Going a step further, five national banks introduced an electronic person-to-person payment system (P2P) in 2002. The service allows money to be transferred instantly by e-mail.[24] By virtue of so many major banks being involved, Canada has the largest P2P penetration of any country in the world.

The Internet has forever changed the speed of business time by eliminating time walls. Evidence that business is moving at an accelerated pace includes the following:[25]

- Companies now develop and market new products in a fraction of the time it took just a few years ago. The rule of thumb a few years ago was seven years from start-up to commercialization.

- Consumers can complete worldwide searches for a product in minutes, compared with months or years before the Internet.

- Manufacturers can distribute products directly to consumers, shrinking time lags by skipping wholesalers and retailers.

- Start-up organizations can become instant and serious threats to long-established businesses. For example, Amazon.com directly affected the book retailing business in North America. The ability to download music from the Internet to personal computers has affected the entire structure of the music industry.

As of this writing, 53 percent of all Canadians are connected to the Internet from one source or another (home, work, and school). A Statistics Canada Survey shows that the Internet is an ideal medium for reaching a target market described as male and female between the ages of 15 and 44, college or university educated, household incomes of $40,000 plus, with slightly urban skew. The Internet reaches a very desirable audience and has the capacity to reach people individually rather than collectively.[26] With each passing year the Internet will play a larger role in marketing and marketing communications.

Information technology is changing the way companies communicate with and do business with customers. It is catching on just as fast as television did in the 1950s, and even faster than the radio in the 1930s. The present pace of growth is actually quicker than that of the telephone. Given the convergence that is taking place between the Internet and traditional channels of communication, such as television and radio, the widespread accessibility that is expected will fuel tremendous growth in Internet commerce. The Internet has great potential to become the focal point for commercial transactions. For more insight into commerce on the Internet, refer to the Marketing in Action vignette **Toad Hall's Internet Success**.

Toad Hall
www.toad
halltoys.com

LEGAL AND REGULATORY INFLUENCE

Yes, Canada is a free enterprise society, but in any society of this nature, the consumer can be subjected to unscrupulous business practices—practices that serve only the needs of the business using them. Consequently, numerous laws and regulations (some voluntary and some involuntary) have been put into place to protect consumer rights and ensure that organizations conduct business in a competitive manner. Ignorance of the law is not a defence for business; companies must act according to the law or face the perils of the judicial system.

The legal environment for marketing and other business practices in Canada is the domain of **Industry Canada**. Its principle responsibility is to administer the **Competition Act**, an act that brought together a number of related laws to help consumers and businesses function in Canada. The purpose of the Competition Act is three-fold:

Industry Canada

Competition Act

1. To maintain and encourage competition in Canada.

2. To ensure that small- and medium-sized businesses have an equitable opportunity to participate in the Canadian economy.

3. To provide consumers with product choice and competitive prices.

Within the Ministry of Industry, there are three distinct bureaus that influence business and marketing activity: the Bureau of Competition Policy, the Bureau of Consumer

Marketing in Action

Toad Hall's Internet Success

When you think of toy retailers, who comes to mind? Toys 'R Us, perhaps. But, have you ever heard of Toad Hall Toys? Likely not. Toad Hall, it seems, is a rather ambitious Winnipeg-based toy retailer that is using the Internet to expand its business. No longer is it just a Canadian company. It presently sells to every continent except Antarctica.

Toad Hall entered cyberspace in 1996 using a toll-free number. Online sales quickly came to represent 1.5 percent of gross sales. When it implemented electronic commercial transaction capability in 1997, the figure jumped to 7.5 percent of sales. Presently, 15 percent of sales are generated online. And where has the business come from? Seventy-five percent of the company's online business comes from the United States, 15 percent percent is international and the remaining 10 percent comes from Canada.

The company's real-world store is located in the picturesque Exchange District of Winnipeg. It specializes in high-end toys that encourage children to think, learn, and be creative. Playmobil and Brio are among the store's internationally known lines. Toad Hall sees its Web site as a marketing tool and a second store.

What prompted the move to Web marketing was pure economics. Company management viewed print catalogues and an interactive site as the same thing. But the cost of printing and distributing a catalogue, and then paying for a 24-hour toll-free order line, would have been hundreds of thousands of dollars. The initial cost of the Web site, which was self-developed, was $50 a month.

Toad Hall registered its site with all the search engines, and its pages are stuffed with "meta-tags," the keywords that search engines use to identify the relevance of sites they will return in response to a searcher's query. The company offers 2000 of its 25 000 lines online.

Internet success is traced to the fact that Toad Hall's customers are generally financially well-off individuals looking for creative, well-made, and constructive toys. Even better, these customers were comfortable with computers. The company also believes that privacy issues have long since faded. People now understand that sending your credit card number over the Internet can be more secure than giving it to a waiter or store clerk.

Toad Hall has not spent money on banner advertising, believing that such an investment would not yield any appreciable return. Perhaps they are right. E-Toys, an online toy store based in California, spends anywhere from $13 million to $19 million a year on advertising, and they do not turn a profit. Toad Hall did spend money subcontracting the e-commerce functions of its site to a specialist. Once a customer clicks onto the ordering area, they are in nGage-operated online territory. nGage is a transaction service that handles every aspect of the credit card transaction and files full financial online marketing reports to Toad Hall and the other companies it represents. Once the consumer hits the "buy" button, nGage takes over invisibly.

What is the moral of the story? Very simply, technology is levelling the playing field so that small companies can effectively compete with big companies. Small, progressive-minded companies can act much more quickly than large bureaucratic companies; hence, the competitive advantage that larger companies normally enjoy disappears. Perhaps the big companies can learn some marketing lessons from the small ones!

Adapted from **www.e-com.ic.gc.ca/english/stories/toadsucc** and Judy Waytiuk, "How a toy store became a global exporter for a couple of hundred bucks a month," *Marketing*, May 24, 1999, p. 29.

Courtesy: Toad Hall Toys

Affairs, and the Bureau of Corporate Affairs. Presently the federal government and numerous provincial governments are revamping consumer protection laws to reflect the explosive growth in e-commerce and the surge of complaints by people and small businesses doing business on the Internet. According to Bob Runciman, Consumer Affairs Minister in Ontario, "The times have left the law behind the marketplace."[27]

Bureau of Competition Policy

This bureau enforces the rules that govern and promote the efficiency of a competitive Canadian marketplace. Its chief instrument for carrying out these functions is the Competition Act. Among the trade practices that it routinely reviews are mergers and acquisitions. The bureau seeks to ensure that monopolies are not created, that competition is not affected negatively, that no price fixing or other pricing infractions occur, and that advertising does not misrepresent a product or mislead the consumer. Its role was illustrated in a July 2000 decision whereby Coca-Cola was not allowed to acquire the Cadbury Schweppes beverage brands (Crush, Dr. Pepper, and Canada Dry) in Canada. Such a deal would have concentrated too much of the market in the hands of one company. Coca-Cola's market share would have increased to 48 percent. Coca-Cola presently controls about 38 percent of the market.[28] Companies can contact the Bureau for information about the regulations and interpretation of the Act.

Bureau of Consumer Affairs

This bureau promotes a safe, orderly, and fair marketplace for consumers and businesses. In consultation with other government agencies and organizations that represent business groups, it establishes and enforces regulations and programs that protect the interests of consumers. The bureau also ensures that dangerous products are identified and that certain products that cause injury are removed from the market. The legislation under the jurisdiction of Consumer Affairs Canada includes the Canadian Packaging and Labelling Act, the National Trademark and Labelling Act, and the Weights and Measures Act.

Bureau of Corporate Affairs

This bureau provides a regulatory framework for the business community in Canada. Its intent is to ensure orderly conduct among businesses across the country, to encourage economic development, and to promote creativity, innovation, and the exploitation of technology. It is also responsible for laws governing copyright, industrial design, patents, and trademarks. Legislation administered by Corporate Affairs includes the Bankruptcy Act, the Canada Corporations Act, the Patent Act, and the Copyright Act.

Companies must understand and operate within the legal and regulatory environment, or face the perils of the court system. The Federal Court of Canada recently fined F. Hoffmann-LaRoche Ltd. of Switzerland a record $50.9 million after the firm and four other drug companies pleaded guilty to price-fixing. All companies involved fixed prices for vitamins and additives, inflating the cost of such products as cereal, hamburgers, and bulk vitamins. The other firms were fined a total of $37.5 million.[29]

Laws and regulations are not uniform across Canada. For this reason, a company may find it necessary to be knowledgeable about any provincial legislation that may affect it. Regulations governing the marketing of securities, insurance and liquor, for example,

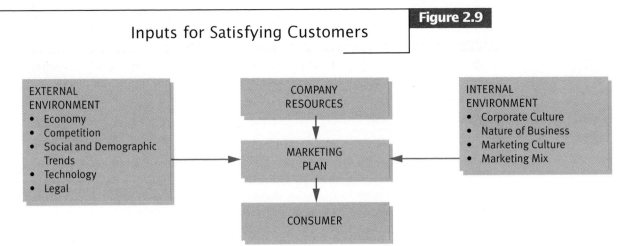

Figure 2.9

Inputs for Satisfying Customers

vary from province to province. A product like margarine cannot be the same colour as butter in the province of Quebec. In all other provinces, colour is not an issue. Therefore Unilever, a maker of margarine, has to produce and market separate product lines for the Quebec market. Unilever is presently battling the Quebec law in court claiming that it contravenes interprovincial and international trade laws.[30]

self-regulation

Self-regulation is an alternative to government regulation. In the advertising industry, the Advertising Standards Canada (a group that represents advertisers and advertising agencies) established the Canadian Code of Advertising Standards for its members to follow. Within this code are specific guidelines governing such issues as how the genders are portrayed in advertising, accuracy and clarity of product claims, price claims, comparative advertising, and advertising to children, to name a few. Organizations such as the Canadian Marketing Association (CMA) and Canadian Banker's Association have established policies and guidelines that their member companies agree to follow.

As a conclusion to this chapter, refer to Figure 2.9. This chart provides a visual summary of the various elements that must be considered in an organization's quest to satisfy consumers.

Summary

The environment that marketing operates in is dynamic, and organizations must therefore constantly anticipate and react to change. How an organization handles change is a key factor in its success or failure in the marketplace.

From a management viewpoint, there are certain elements that marketing can control. These elements are referred to as the marketing mix. The marketing mix consists of strategic decisions for four variables: product, price, marketing communications, and distribution. When the variables are combined, a company will have a marketing strategy for each of its products. It should be noted, however, that public image plays a major role in whether or not consumers accept or reject a company and its products.

Marketing communications embraces another mix of five variables: advertising, sales promotion, personal selling, public relations, and event marketing and sponsorship. The efficient distribution and utilization of information is crucial to the decision-making process and a company's competitive position in the marketplace.

Decisions about the marketing mix are influenced by conditions that exist beyond the company. When devising marketing strategies, a company must consider the economy, competition, social and demographic trends, technology, and laws and regulations. When analyzed, the conditions that are present, though beyond the control of the organization, have a significant influence on the direction of its marketing practice.

Key Terms

blended family 45
census metropolitan area (CMA) 45
Competition Act 51
corporate advertising 35
demographics 43
depression 37
direct competition 40
disposable income 37
distribution strategy 34
gross domestic product 36
indirect competition 41
Industry Canada 51
inflation 36
integrated marketing communications 32
market challenger 43
market follower 43
market leader 43
market nicher (niche marketing) 43
market share 41

marketing mix 29
monopolistic competition 40
monopoly 39
oligopoly 39
price strategy 31
product strategy 29
product differentiation 30
prosperity 38
public image 35
pure competition 40
rationalization 38
real income 36
recession 37
recovery 38
sandwich generation 45
self-regulation 54
subcultures 47
unemployment 36

Review Questions

1. Identify and briefly describe the elements that comprise the marketing mix.

2. What is the differential advantage for the following organizations or products?

   a) Wendy's

   b) Mennen Speed Stick Deodorant

   c) Comfort Inn Motels

   d) Amazon.com

   e) Gatorade

   f) Nike

3. Describe the basic characteristics of the following markets and identify a new example of each:

   a) Monopoly

   b) Oligopoly

   c) Monopolistic competition

   d) Pure competition

4. Briefly describe the four classifications of competitors.

5. What is the difference between direct competition and indirect competition? Provide a new example to demonstrate

the difference between the two forms of competition.

6. Explain what niche marketing is and briefly describe two examples of the concept in practice.

7. Briefly explain how social and demographic trends affect marketing activity. What demographic trends will become more important in the future?

8. How important is technology, and what impact will it have on marketing organizations in the future?

9. Briefly explain the roles of the Bureau of Competition Policy and the Bureau of Consumer Affairs.

Discussion and Application Questions

1. Canadian Tire remains a highly successful company despite competition from American retailers. Analyze the marketing mix of Canadian Tire. Which elements of the marketing mix have contributed to the success of this company? Be specific.

2. Provide some examples of companies that have a good corporate image. What marketing activities have helped these companies achieve their image?

3. Identify a company or product (good or service) that you would characterize as a market leader. Briefly describe the nature of its marketing practice. Identify the challenger in the same market and briefly describe their marketing practice. What makes the leader the leader?

4. With reference to the vignette "McDonald's Protects Its Lead," what new marketing strategies can you recommend to McDonald's in order to fend off competitors and keep it in the forefront of the fast food marketplace? Consider the bigger picture when analyzing who McDonald's competitors really are.

E-Assignment

1. Conduct some Internet-based secondary research to compile some recent statistics about Internet growth. Identify the variables that are considered when determining growth (e.g., number of Web sites, number of users, value of transactions, etc.).

2. Visit the Statistics Canada Web site (www.statcan.ca) and determine the following:
   - What are the components of population growth, and what are the basic trends in each area for the past five years?
   - What five areas from around the world comprise the largest source of immigrants entering Canada?
   - What percentage of the Canadian population has a university degree? What percentage has some form of postsecondary education?
   - How many households are there in Canada and what is the average expenditure per household?

Endnotes

1 Stephanie Thompson, "EZ being green: Kids line is latest Heinz innovation," *Advertising Age*, July 10, 2000, pp. 3, 50.

2 Keith McArthur, "Ford gears up online buying project," *Globe and Mail*, May 13, 2000, pp. B1, B2.

3 Casey Mahood, "Firm delivers cost-saving solution," *Globe and Mail*, July 30, 1996, p. B9.

4 Alan Toulin, "Prime rate tumbles to record low," *Financial Post*, January 16, 2002, p. FP1.

5 Heather Scoffield, "Heinz's baby food fight comes to an end," *Globe and Mail*, August 2, 2000, p. B3.

6 Stuart Laidlaw, "Brewers' marketing moves probed," *Toronto Star*, January 6, 2001, p. E3.

7 Susan Pigg, "Independent movie chains say probe is too late," *Toronto Star*, December 20, 2000, pp. E1, E12.

8 Lara Mills, "Playing with perfection," *Marketing*, June 1, 1998, p. 13.

9 John Schofield, "Virtual competitors," *Maclean's*, " July 7, 1997, pp. 52-53.

10 Philip Kotler, *Principles of Marketing*, 3rd Canadian edition (Scarborough, Ontario: Prentice-Hall Canada Inc. 1997), p. 51.

11 "Report on Market Shares," *Marketing*, May 27, 2002 2001, pp. 9-14.

12 Marina Strauss, "Niche sellers fin Rx for success," *Globe and Mail*, February 15, 2001, p. B11.

13 Jane Armstrong, "Canada is 30 million, but will that last?" *Globe and Mail*, March 13, 2002, www.globeandmail.ca

14 Statistics Canada, CANSIM, Matrix 6900.

15 Statistics Canada, *Daily*, March 12, 2002, www.statcan.ca/english/dai-quo

16 Statistics Canada, 1996 Census *Nation* tables.

17 Sandra Cordon, "Gap between rich an poor widens," *Kingston Whig-Standard*, March 16, 2002, p. 16.

18 Statistics Canada, 1996 Census *Nation* tables.

19 *Canadian Internet Advertising 2000: A Message for the Medium*, A Report Prepared by Multimediator Strategy Group, Toronto, p. 7.

20 "Buckley targets Chinese on their own terms," *Marketing*, December 12, 1994, p. 3.

21 Statistics Canada, Catalogue No. 87-211-XPB.

22 Heidi Staseson, "Shoppers returns to image strategy," *Strategy*, May 21, 2001, p. 7.

23 S. Phineas Upham, "Packaging values," *Financial Post*, July 17, 1999, p. D6.

24 Tyler Hamilton, "Cash is in the e-mail," *Toronto Star*, February 11, 2002, pp. E1, E2.

25 Claudia Cattaneo, "Wake-up call for e-commerce," *Financial Post*, May 31, 1999, pp. C1, C13.

26 Patrick Brethour, "Women narrow Internet gender gap," *Globe and Mail*, March 27, 2001, pp. B1, B2.

27 Colin Perkel, "Consumer laws to be revamped," *Toronto Star*, August 11, 2001, p. E5.

28 John Greenwood, "Coke's deal for brands from Cadbury fizzles," *Financial Post*, July 27, 2000, pp. C1, C9.

29 "Record fine for company," *Maclean's* October 4, 1999, p. 49.

30 Konrad Yakabusli, "Unilever loses Quebec margarine case," *Globe and Mail*, May 27, 1999, p. B3.

Inputs for Marketing Planning

This section presents topics that are classified as inputs for marketing planning. Prior to striking a marketing plan, the marketing manager must have a thorough understanding of the customer, be it a consumer or business organization. Understanding customers frequently involves the collection of data and information through marketing research. Chapter 3 examines in detail the role and process of marketing research and shows how organizations collect information that assists in the planning of their marketing activities.

Chapter 4 presents the elements of consumer behaviour, the purchase decision process, and the factors that influence it. Chapter 5 focuses on the behavioural tendencies of business, industry, and governments, and the steps involved in their decisions to purchase goods and services.

Bruce Ayres/Stone

Marketing Research

After studying this chapter, you will be able to

1. Define the role and scope of marketing research in contemporary marketing organizations.
2. Outline the basic stages in the marketing research process.
3. Describe the methodologies for collecting secondary and primary research data.
4. Explain what uses are made of secondary and primary research data in resolving marketing problems.

Since a considerable amount of money is invested in the design, development, and marketing of goods and services, a marketing organization is very concerned about protecting its investment. In addition, its desire to remain competitive and be knowledgeable about consumers' changing needs makes it necessary to collect appropriate information before and after critical decisions are made. Carefully planned marketing research is the tool that provides organizations with the insight necessary to take advantage of new opportunities. This chapter will discuss the marketing research process and the impact it has on making business decisions and planning marketing strategies.

Marketing Research: Role and Scope

1.
Define the role and scope of marketing research in contemporary marketing organizations.

Molson
www.molson.com

marketing research

Research provides an organization with data. The data do not guarantee that the firm will take proper decisions and actions since data are always open to interpretation. The old saying that "some information is better than no information" puts the role of marketing research into perspective. A vital marketing tool, it is used to help reduce or eliminate the uncertainty and risk associated with making business decisions.

In many ways, marketing research is a form of insurance—it ensures that the action a company might take is the right action. To demonstrate, consider the case of Molson Canadian. When Vice-President of Marketing Brett Marchand first showed senior executives a commercial called the "Rant," it wasn't greeted with overwhelming applause. The ad showed a young guy working himself into a feverish pitch over what it means to be a Canadian. More specifically, the ad zeros in on things that separate Canadians from Americans. From marketing research, Molson discovered a pent up sense of patriotism among young Canadians. The "Rant" ended up touching a nerve with Canadians who related to "this proud Canadian message," says Marchand.[1] The ad generated a great deal of publicity, even in the United States, and helped Canadian recover some degree of lost market share. The moral of the story is simple: research provides useful information to develop an effective marketing strategy.

The American Marketing Association defines **marketing research** as the function which links the consumer/customer/public to the marketer through information—information used to define marketing opportunities and problems; to generate, refine, and evaluate marketing actions; to monitor marketing performance; and to improve the understanding of marketing as a process.

Marketing research specifies the information required to address these issues; designs the method for collecting information; manages and implements the information collection process; analyzes the results; and communicates the findings and their implications.[2]

THE SCOPE OF MARKETING RESEARCH

Marketing research focuses on markets and the marketing mix, and its scope seems endless. The testing of new product concepts is the single-most common task asked of market research firms by their customers. Other uses of marketing research include: testing advertising for impact and effectiveness; conducting surveys to measure customer satisfaction; tracking brand awareness versus the competition; pre-testing of advertising strategies; and measuring the influence of pricing tests. Regardless of the nature of the research study, the information obtained will assist managers in their decision-making.

Making informed business decisions is easier, and more profitable, when you have the right information. When Tetley first entered the Canadian market, it relied on marketing research to help understand the Canadian tea drinker. According to Jim Balmer, Tetley Canada's marketing manager, "Marketing research helped Tetley move from last place in the Canadian market to first place in 15 years."[3] The challenge for marketers is to sift through available data to detect patterns that will positively influence marketing decisions.

How do managers go about collecting information? Prudent marketing decision makers combine their intuition and judgment with all other information sources available. They use the scientific method, which implies that the data generated are reliable and valid.

reliability

validity

scientific method

Reliability refers to similar results being achieved if another study were undertaken under similar conditions. **Validity** refers to the research procedure's ability to actually measure what it was intended to. The key elements of the **scientific method** are:

1. The awareness of a problem is reached through exploratory investigations.

2. Information sources and methodologies of collecting information are implemented properly.

3. Alternative solutions are thoroughly evaluated.

4. Data are properly analyzed and interpreted.

5. Specific actions taken are based on research findings.

The Marketing Research Process

2.

Outline the basic stages in the marketing research process.

The research process is a systematic one with many steps: problem awareness, exploratory research, secondary data collection, primary research, data transfer and processing, data analysis and interpretation, and recommendations (Figure 3.1).

PROBLEM AWARENESS

In the problem awareness stage, an attempt is made to specify the nature of the difficulty. For example, a company or product may be experiencing declining sales, but the decline itself is not the problem. Instead, it is a symptom that makes people aware that there is a deeper problem within the organization that must be identified. Many practitioners of marketing research state that the proper identification of a problem is the first step in finding its solution. Therefore, it is essential that a problem be precisely defined. After all, a business organization does not want to waste valuable time and money collecting information that will not lead to action. Currently, market research projects are usually commissioned to address a specific decision that has to be made, and good research projects are designed to address that decision alone. Once such data are available, they may be linked to other research projects at a later date.

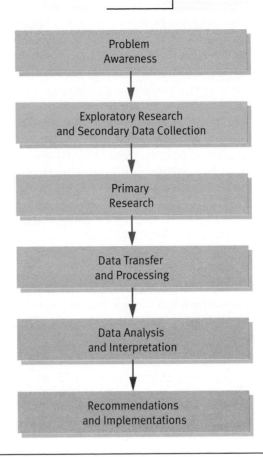

Marketing Research Process

Figure 3.1

Defining a problem involves developing a clearly worded statement that provides direction for further research on the topic to be investigated. To define a problem precisely, a company usually performs some form of exploratory research.

EXPLORATORY RESEARCH

exploratory research

funnelling

situation analysis

Exploratory research is research that helps define the precise nature of a problem through the use of informal analysis. This informal analysis is often referred to as the funnelling process. **Funnelling** is the process of dividing a subject into manageable variables and thereby narrowing down the field so that specifically directed research can be conducted. Funnelling is accomplished by means of a thorough situation analysis. In a **situation analysis**, the researcher collects information from knowledgeable people inside and outside the organization and from secondary sources, such as government reports, studies on related issues, and census data. Many variables are analyzed as potential problem areas, and through the funnelling process, areas that appear to be unrelated are eliminated.

Figure 3.2 illustrates exploratory research and the funnelling process. Let us assume that the sales of a product are declining. This indicates that there is a problem. To find the cause of the decline would be to identify the problem. Identifying the true nature of the problem is the task of exploratory research. As the diagram demonstrates, the company could follow several routes in order to pinpoint the problem. The researcher investigates a number of matters: product and product quality issues, marketing communication strategies, pricing strategies, availability, and distribution. In this case, the problem is narrowed down to marketing communications. From there, the researcher looks into possible areas of marketing communications where the real problem might be, rejects some, and further pursues others—advertising, in our example. As this analysis unfolds, it should become apparent which elements are contributing to the sales decline. The eventual isolation of a "creative" problem in this illustration (a problem with the advertising message) assumes that other areas have been evaluated, at least informally, and rejected as the source of the problem.

Exploratory Research and Funnelling Process

Figure 3.2

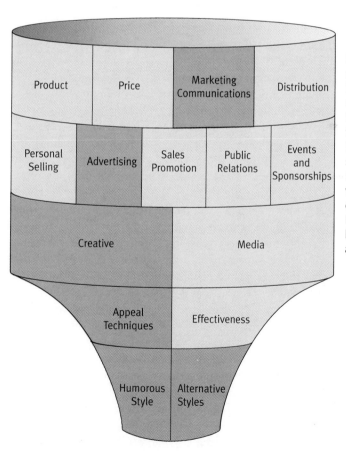

Exploratory research narrows the scope of an investigation until a specific problem is identified. In this example, a problem has been traced to the style of advertising. Potential problem areas were explored and discarded along the way. Primary research would be conducted on styles of advertising.

Sometimes the problem is both pinpointed and resolved through discussions held with people knowledgeable in the area of concern or through the collection and consideration of secondary data. Or, new information may be uncovered that changes the focus of the issue under investigation. If it turns out that primary research is required (that is, if the problem is not resolved through secondary research), it can only be conducted if the problem is specific in nature or narrow in scope. The exploratory process narrows the scope of the problem until it becomes resolvable.

SECONDARY DATA

secondary data

Exploratory research usually involves the use of secondary data. **Secondary data** are data that have been compiled and published for purposes unrelated to the specific problem under investigation, yet they may have some significance in its resolve. They are available from sources both internal and external to the company.

Internal Data Sources

Internal data sources are those that are available within the organization. Such information includes customer profiles (e.g., size and frequency of purchase), sales analysis reports (e.g., sales by region, nation, customer, or product), inventory analysis, production reports, cost analysis, marketing budgets (e.g., actual spending versus planned spending), profit-and-loss statements, and accounts receivable and payable. This information is incorporated into a company's database and is updated continuously for use in planning and decision-making.

management information system (MIS) or database management system

A database system, or management information system, is a vital tool for marketing. A **management information system (MIS)** or **database management system** consists of people and equipment organized to provide a continuous, orderly collection and exchange of information (internal and external) needed in a firm's decision-making process.[4] Refer to Figure 3.3 for a sample model of a management information system. With so much information now available, the emphasis has shifted from the generation of information to the shaping and evaluation of information to make it useful to the decision maker. What has evolved is the decision support system. A **decision support**

decision support system (DSS)

system (DSS) is an interactive, personalized marketing information system designed in such a manner that it can be initiated and controlled by individual decision makers.[5]

Marketing research information contained in a decision support system is useful for both control purposes and planning purposes. Control information includes routine reports that indicate what has happened in an organization, such as sales reports, inventory reports, budget reports, and cost reports. Such information is continuously updated and distributed to managers through the management information system and will influence the marketing strategy during the course of an operating year. For example, if raw material costs or packaging costs rise unexpectedly, a price increase will have to go into effect if profit levels are to be maintained.

The decision support systems that exist today are interactive, flexible, discovery oriented, and easy to learn and use. A good decision support system not only allows managers to ask "what if" questions but also enables them to manipulate the data any way they want. It is a useful tool for sales forecasting, planning marketing budgets, and financial analysis.

The information collected by marketing research on such matters as economic, demographic, psychographic, and geographic patterns is valuable for planning purposes. When such data are integrated into the firm's database with actual performance data (e.g., sales volume and market share data), they form a solid foundation for developing

Sample Model of a Management Information System

Figure 3.3

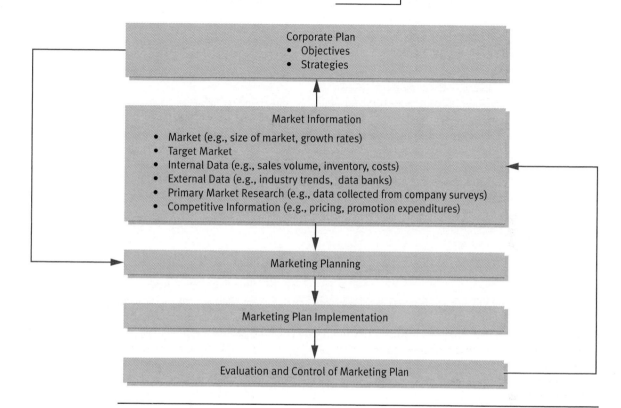

Corporate Plan
- Objectives
- Strategies

Market Information
- Market (e.g., size of market, growth rates)
- Target Market
- Internal Data (e.g., sales volume, inventory, costs)
- External Data (e.g., industry trends, data banks)
- Primary Market Research (e.g., data collected from company surveys)
- Competitive Information (e.g., pricing, promotion expenditures)

Marketing Planning

Marketing Plan Implementation

Evaluation and Control of Marketing Plan

annual marketing plans. Procter & Gamble, for example, maintains a database of 50 000 studies and conducts 4000 to 5000 consumer studies a year in North America.[6]

data mining

The electronic era has resulted in an information explosion that now allows for the storage and transfer of great amounts of business data in a short time. What has emerged is a new concept called data mining. In a marketing context, **data mining** is the analysis of information that establishes relationships between pieces of information so that more effective marketing strategies can be identified and implemented. Rather than looking at an entire data set, data mining techniques attempt to locate informational patterns and nuggets within that database.[7]

Air Miles
www.airmiles.ca

The goal of data mining is to produce lower marketing costs and increased efficiency by identifying prospects most likely to buy or buy in large volume. Banks are always seeking ways to increase revenues from credit card operations, mainly through more interest earned and reduced administrative costs. CIBC uses data mining software to stay a step ahead of its competitors. "In today's competitive market, the window of opportunity with any customer is very small. Our target marketing and campaign management methods help us get through that window more quickly," says Julio Tavares, director of database marketing for CIBC Card Services.[8] Such a system could, for example, identify customers that require features available on other cards offered by CIBC.

For more insight into data mining and its impact on marketing, see the Marketing in Action vignette **Data Mining: Data—Information—Action.**

Marketing in Action

Data Mining: Data—Information—Action

Like it or not, we are being observed. From "Net Nanny" software tracking programs to friendly corporations that make life easier for consumers through such things as credit and debit cards, loyalty programs, and the Internet, there is a myriad of vehicles designed to provide a corporation with the means of collecting, storing, and analyzing information about you. If this sounds frightening, maybe it is!

Technology is spearheading an electronic information revolution. The availability of smarter software programs allows an organization to sift through mountains of information to uncover patterns of consumer behaviour that most marketing professionals would never even think to ask about.

The goal of data mining is what IBM executives call "mass customization." IBM believes that companies must evaluate a variety of information sources in order to create dossiers on individuals. By doing so, they can determine if someone is a likely customer and how to encourage that person's patronage. Consequently, IBM established a separate company to develop and market products that will help clients manage their customer relationships.

Wal-Mart is a company adept at data mining. Don't be fooled by the folksy greeters. Wal-Mart controls one of the largest data collection systems anywhere in the world and claim they can reconstruct customer behaviour from cash register tapes. They can trace the exact route each customer has taken through each store, based on what he or she has purchased. It is amazing what information can be derived from electronic scanners at the point of sale. Wal-Mart's electronic tracking system identifies fast moving lines and automatically reorders goods when needed.

Invasion of privacy is an issue associated with data mining. Should companies be allowed to sell information about customers to other companies? Take Air Miles, for example. Why do people have these cards? Do they actually think this program is about giving away free plane trips? Air Miles, which was started by the Loyalty Management Group, has the ability to keep an electronic record of everything a person purchases. Presently, 7.2 million Canadian households belong to

Air Miles, and there are 134 corporate sponsors, including the Bank of Montreal, Shell Canada, the Bay, and the LCBO in Ontario. The customer does earn free air travel and other incentives but the key to the program is the accumulation of data regarding customer preferences and spending habits.

At sign-up, an individual divulges age, household size, and income. Such information is a treasure trove for any and all Air Miles participants. Company participants are encouraged to run cross-promotions as a means of collecting and sharing information with other members. Sponsors can pay extra for a separate peek at another's data. Holt Renfrew, for example, might want the names of Bank of Montreal's Gold MasterCard holders for a special promotion. It does not require much imagination to determine that other Air Miles participants are exchanging information. Air Miles is a data miner, an outsourcer of marketing information.

Now, factor in all of the transactions handled by Interac, a co-operative owned by financial institutions that processes electronic banking transactions (debit cards and credit cards). Nearly 47 percent of all consumer transactions (2.24 billion transactions in 2001) are handled this way, all leaving an electronic trail. The banks are sitting on a mother lode of data: who went shopping, at what time, where, how often, what they bought, and how much they spent. It is only a matter of time. Yes, you are being watched!

Adapted from David Steinhart, "Popularity of direct payment making money obsolete," *Financial Post*, February 1, 2002, p. FP7. David Eggleston, "We've come a long way, baby," *Strategy Direct Response*, November 8, 1999, p. D13; and Kimberley Noble, "The data game," *Maclean's*, August 17, 1998, pp. 14–19.

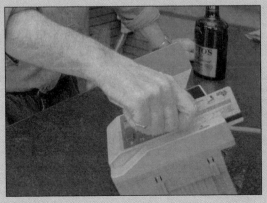

CP/Tony Bock

External Data Sources

An organization refers to external sources when internal information does not resolve the problem at hand. The primary sources of external data are government, business, and academia. As well, the Internet can provide a wealth of valuable information to marketing organizations.

Federal, provincial, and municipal governments have an abundance of information that marketing organizations can examine. The major source of government information is Statistics Canada, which provides census information (population and household trends, income, education, and occupation trends) and information on all aspects of the economy (employment, inflation, interest rates, domestic production, and international trade, to name a few) for free or a small fee. Much of this information is published in *The Market Research Handbook,* and *The Canada Yearbook,* and it is readily available in summary form online from the Statistics Canada Web site. At the federal and provincial levels, the department or ministry involved with industry, trade, and commerce is the most common source of business information. At the municipal level, the departments of economic development publish reports relevant to their municipalities.

Basic data can also be obtained from a variety of commercial sources:

Newspapers and Business Periodicals These focus specifically on business and commerce and include such publications as *The Globe and Mail's Report on Business* and *Report on Business Magazine, Canadian Business, The National Post (Financial Post section)* and *The National Post Business Magazine.*

Handbooks and Surveys These sources usually provide information on consumer income and expenditure, employment, occupation, and other relevant demographic data. Sources include *The Handbook of Canadian Consumer Markets,* published by the Conference Board in Canada, and *FP Markets—Canadian Demographics.*

Other Surveys and Directories A variety of information is included in this category, such as company history and financial information, surveys on various industry sectors, and annual reports published by publicly held companies. Specific examples include Dun & Bradstreet's financial and credit information on businesses operating in Canada and their trade directories, such as *The Canadian Key Business Directory* and *The Guide to Canadian Manufacturers.* These directories provide statistical information and classification of companies by industry and by type of product manufactured.

Industry and Trade Journals Most Canadian industries have trade journals that provide information on particular industries. Information on the grocery trade can be found in journals, such as *Canadian Grocer, Grocer Today*, and *L'épicier.* Typically, such journals contain information on industry trends and articles on topical issues affecting the industry.

Commercial Research Houses These firms conduct periodic and ongoing studies that are helpful to marketing organizations. The cost of obtaining information from these sources can be high, depending on the nature of the information. But, since competitors also have access to the same information, the costs are shared by all purchasers and remain reasonable. Nielsen Marketing Research is an example of a company that sells information on a subscription basis. Its consumer index provides manufacturers of packaged consumer goods with information on market share trends, sales volume, inventory, distribution, pricing, media expenditures, and more.

Its television index provides relevant data on viewing trends (e.g., what people watch and how long they watch).

scanner

More recent and innovative research services offered by Nielsen include in-store and in-home scanning. A **scanner** is a device that reads the universal product code (UPC) on items and produces instantaneous information on sales. Electronic check-out counters now in most supermarket chains allow for easy collection of information about the public's shopping habits. Nielsen's in-store scanning service tracks the purchases of thousands of consumers at the checkout counter by scanning the product codes.

Nielsen also offers a service called Scan Track, an in-home tracking system where consumers electronically scan the UPCs of their own purchases when they return from a shopping trip. As Nielsen banks more consumer-purchase data, it will be able to develop demographic profiles of buyers of specific products, a valuable commodity for brand manufacturers and retailers. The electronic information is transferred to the Nielsen computer by telephone.

Environics is a Canadian research company that conducts an annual survey of 2600 Canadians aged 15 years and older. In-home interviews consist of more than 250 questions probing social values and beliefs. The results reveal the strength and direction of social trends in Canada. Marketers can participate in the survey for $26 000 each and have proprietary questions included for another $2500 each.[9] The answers are cross-tabulated with social and cultural questions, and the survey provides a customized analysis of the values and beliefs of the clients' customers, the customers of their competitors, and the public at large. The availability of this information plays a key role in shaping a company's marketing strategy as it combines demographic data (the characteristics of a population) with lifestyle information (attitudes, interests, activities, etc.). Information such as this helped shape the advertising strategy for Molson Canadian that was discussed earlier in this chapter.

Industry Associations Associations serve as the promotional arm of a particular industry and provide useful information to marketing organizations. To illustrate, Canadian media consumption data (showing the public's level of exposure to different media) is available from associations, such as the Television Bureau of Canada (TVB), the Print Measurement Bureau (a databank for magazine information), and NADbank Inc. (newspaper research and data). Information available from these sources shows how effective these media are in reaching the Canadian consumer. Such information is useful when an organization is developing an advertising strategy.

Online Databases

online database

In the past, collecting information from the external data sources listed above was a time-consuming and tedious task. The rapid development of online databases means that information now can be transferred almost instantaneously. An **online database** is a public information database accessible to anyone with proper communication facilities.

Online databases are available from public and commercial sources. Among public sources available electronically is the federal government's census data (Statistics Canada). Census data is collected every five years. The information collected is very detailed and covers dozens of demographic and socioeconomic topics, such as family and household structures, occupation, income, education, ethnicity, age, marital status, and so on.

Under an agreement with Canada Customs and Revenue Agency, Statistics Canada produces detailed statistics culled from the annual federal tax returns. For marketing databases, data are available for over 22 000 urban and 5000 rural postal codes. The variables include statistics on average income, distributions of tax filers by income categories, investments to various retirement programs, sources of income, donations to charitable organizations, and combined incomes for multiple tax returns in the same household. These are just a few of the public database sources available to marketing organizations.

directory databases

From commercial sources, such as Dun & Bradstreet, organizations can access **directory databases**. These databases provide a quick picture of a company and its products and services. Typical information includes: ownership, size (dollar sales), and location of the company; number of employees; identification of key management personnel and officers; and basic profit data. Examples of directories that are available electronically include *The Canadian Key Business Directory* and *The Canadian Trade Index*. Dun & Bradstreet also provides direct mail lists and telemarketing lists to companies that want to reach companies with specific characteristics.

Many Canadian publications are now available on the Internet. Among the more popular sources for information are *Maclean's* magazine, *The Globe and Mail*, *The National Post*, and other daily newspapers. With *Maclean's*, the entire magazine can be read on screen. The online version gives subscribers the ability to talk to each other and to the magazine's writers and editors via the interactive *Maclean's* Forum.

Secondary data offer the marketing organization numerous advantages and disadvantages. For a list of these advantages and disadvantages, see Figure 3.4.

Secondary Data and Online Database Information

Figure 3.4

Secondary Data

Advantages

1. Information is inexpensive or obtainable at no cost.
2. Information is readily available.
3. Possibly the only source of information (e.g., census data).
4. Useful in exploratory research stage where information is assessed to identify a problem.

Disadvantages

1. The data do not resolve the specific problem under investigation (e.g., data were compiled for another problem or purpose).
2. Reliability and accuracy of data are questionable.
3. Information can be outdated, even obsolete, for the intended situation.

Information From an Online Database

Advantages

1. Data are available very quickly (on the spot).
2. Identification of relevant data occurs quickly.

Disadvantages

1. Amount of data available is overwhelming (discourages use of data).
2. Hidden costs associated with retrieval and distribution of data (e.g., cost per hour for computer time).

Primary Research

3.
Describe the methodologies for collecting secondary and primary research data.

primary research

research objectives

hypotheses

If secondary research does not resolve the problem, the research process moves to another stage: the collection of primary data. **Primary research** refers to the process of collecting and recording new data, called primary data, in order to resolve a specific problem, usually at a high cost to the sponsoring organization. Primary research is custom designed and focuses on resolving a particular question or obtaining specified information. A procedure is developed and a research instrument designed to perform the specific task. In directing the primary research, the marketing organization identifies the precise nature of the problem, the objectives of the study, and the hypotheses associated with it. **Research objectives** are statements that outline what the research is to accomplish, while **hypotheses**, which are statements of predicted outcomes, are confirmed or refuted by the data collected. The outcome of the research often leads to certain actions by the marketing organization. Refer to Figure 3.5 for a summary of the steps involved in primary research.

Conducting a marketing research study is beyond the scope and expertise of most marketing organizations in Canada. Consequently, independent market research firms are hired to perform the task. Usually, a marketing research manager from the sponsoring organization is responsible for supervising the research study and works directly with the marketing research firm in designing the project.

Figure 3.5

Primary Research Steps

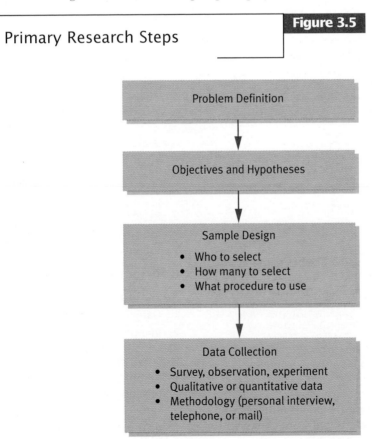

Problem Definition

Objectives and Hypotheses

Sample Design
- Who to select
- How many to select
- What procedure to use

Data Collection
- Survey, observation, experiment
- Qualitative or quantitative data
- Methodology (personal interview, telephone, or mail)

SAMPLE DESIGN

4.
Explain what uses are made of secondary and primary research data in resolving marketing problems.

sample

population

sampling frame

probability sample

non-probability sample

Prior to implementing a research study, the researchers identify the characteristics of the people they would like to participate in the study. This process is referred to as sample designing. A **sample** is defined as a representative portion of an entire population that is used to obtain information about that population. A sample must form an accurate representation of the population if the information gathered is to be considered reliable. Some basic steps have to be taken to develop a representative sample:

1. ***Define the Population*** (*Universe*) It should be first pointed out that the terms "population" and "universe" are interchangeable in research terminology. A **population** is a group of people with certain specific age, gender, or other demographic characteristics. Defining a population involves identifying its basic characteristics. For the purposes of primary research, a description of a population might be "male golfers between the ages of 21 and 45 years living in cities with over 500 000 residents." A proper research procedure will screen potential respondents for these characteristics.

2. ***Identifying the Sampling Frame*** The **sampling frame** refers to a listing that can be used for reaching a population. The telephone directory could be used as a sampling frame for the golf population described above, as could a subscription list from *Score* or *Golf* magazines. If Sears wanted to conduct research among its current customers, it could use its credit card account holder list as a means of access. Membership lists from various associations are often useful for identifying potential respondents.

3. ***Determining the Type of Sample*** The researcher has the option of using a probability sample or a non-probability sample. If a **probability sample** is used, the respondents have a known or equal chance of selection and are randomly selected from across the population. For example, the researcher may use a pre-determined and systematic procedure for picking respondents through a telephone directory. The known chance of selection enables statistical procedures to be used in the results to estimate sampling errors.

   In a **non-probability sample**, the respondents have an unknown chance of selection, and their being chosen is based on such factors as convenience for the researcher or the judgment of the researcher. The researcher uses his or her experience to determine who would be most appropriate. For example, an independent retailer may conduct a survey by approaching potential customers who visit the store. Factors such as cost and timing are other reasons for using non-probability samples.

4. ***Determining the Sample Size*** Generally, the larger the sample, the greater is the accuracy of the data collected and the higher the cost. The nature of the research study is a determining factor in the number of participants required. Some researchers use a 1 percent rule (1 percent of the defined population or universe), while others state absolute minimums of 200 respondents. To illustrate the concept of sample size consider the Environics Social Monitor research study referred to earlier in the chapter. This study collects data on social values and trends in Canada each year using a sample of 2600 households, but the data gathered is projected across the entire population. The accuracy of the sample is usually calculated statistically and stated in the research report. Therefore, a researcher takes into consideration the margin of error that is acceptable and the degree of certainty required.

Environics
erg.environics.net

DATA COLLECTION METHODS

There are three primary methods a researcher can use to collect data: surveys, observation, and experiments (Figure 3.6), and the data collected can be either qualitative or quantitative in nature (see pp. 75–77).

Survey Research

survey research

For **survey research**, data are collected systematically through some form of communication with a representative sample by means of a questionnaire that records responses. Most surveys include pre-determined questions and a selection of responses that are easily filled in by the respondent, the interviewer. This technique is referred to as **fixed-response questioning**. Survey research is conducted by personal interview, telephone, and mail and online through company Web sites.

fixed-response questioning

A survey is usually designed to be structured or unstructured. In a structured survey, the questionnaire follows a planned format: screening questions at the beginning, central issue questions (those dealing with the nature of the research) in the middle, and classification (demographic) questions at the end. In the case of questions dealing with the specific nature of the issue, a funnelling technique is used. **Funnelling** (of questions) refers to the use of general questions initially, progressing to more specific questions as the respondent proceeds through the questionnaire. Closed-ended or fixed-response questions—those that include a list of possible answers (e.g., tick-off or multiple-choice questions)—are the most popular. They permit the data to be easily transferred to a computer for tabulation and subsequent analysis. Some sample questions used in survey research are included in Figure 3.7.

funnelling

Observation Research

observation research

In **observation research**, the behaviour of the respondent is observed and recorded. In this form of research, participants do not have to be recruited; they can participate in a

---

Data Collection Methods	**Figure 3.6**

Survey

- A systematic collection of data made by communicating with a representative sample, usually by using a questionnaire
- Disguised or undisguised, structured or unstructured formats are used

Observation

- Behaviour of respondent is observed by personal, mechanical, or electronic means

Experiments

- The manipulation of variables under controlled conditions to observe respondents' reactions
- Good for testing marketing influences (e.g., product formula changes, package design alternatives, advertising copy tests)

A Survey Using Fixed-Response and Open-Response Questions

Figure 3.7

SWISS CHALET
ROTISSERIE & GRILL

Since 1954, Swiss Chalet has been famous for its unique rotisserie chicken.

Our tasty "Quzzy" chicken is slowly basted in its own juices so it's always crispy golden on the outside, tender and juicy on the inside. While we are proud of our famous chicken, we are equally proud of our "Fall Off the Bone" ribs and "Best Anywhere" french fries.

Our Goal is to be your first choice in comfort dining. We promise you the comfort of family, good friends, at home hospitality and a welcoming environment.

How well are we delivering on our promises to you of Terrific Food, At-Home Hospitality and Intensive Caring?

	Poor	Adequate	Very Good	Excellent
Courtesy: You were greeted with a friendly smile upon arrival, made to feel comfortable and always valued with first-class service and respect throughout your stay.				
Appearance: Our staff are well-groomed and always present a neat, clean and professional look for you.				
Knowledge: Our servers were skilled, professional and knowledgeable.				
Food Quality: You were "Thankful" for the quality, freshness and presentation of our Terrific Food.				
Décor & Atmosphere: You found the décor and atmosphere warm, inviting and comfortable.				
Value: You think we offer good value.				

Have you dined with us before?   No ☐   Yes ☐

Would you recommend us to friends?   No ☐   Yes ☐

Overall, did you feel the restaurant delivered on our promise of Terrific Food, At-Home Hospitality & Intensive Caring?   No ☐   Yes ☐

How often do you visit Swiss Chalet?   Once a month ☐   Less often ☐   First time ever ☐

Additional comments: _____

Name: _____ Phone: _____

Address: _____

City: _____ Prov: _____ Postal code: _____

MAIL POSTE

0347097099

03470970994MSS1TB-BR01

VALERIE E. MCILROY
VICE PRESIDENT MARKETING
6303 AIRPORT ROAD
MISSISSAUGA ON L4V 1R8

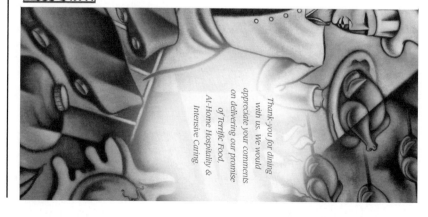

Thank-you for dining with us. We would appreciate your comments on delivering our promise of Terrific Food, At-Home Hospitality & Intensive Caring.

study without knowing it. To illustrate, the purchase behaviour of people in a supermarket can be observed in person or by electronic means. The behaviour of a shopper accepting or rejecting a product could be the focus of such a study. In other situations, respondents are usually aware of being observed, perhaps through a two-way mirror, by a hidden camera while being interviewed, or by electronic measurement of impulses.

The "people meter," an innovation developed by Nielsen Marketing Research, is an example of observation research. The people meter is an electronic device attached to Canadian television sets (a sample group of sets) that records who is watching television, what is being watched, and for how long. The collection of such information is of vital importance to television networks and to advertisers placing commercials on those networks.

cookie

Electronic observation on the Internet tracks the surfing behaviour and purchase behaviour of people. Electronic observation is achieved through cookies. A **cookie** is a file that Web sites are permitted to store in a user's computer. The contents of those files can contain information about a user's preferences—and that information is a valuable resource to marketers. The code tracks the computer, not the individual user (as several people in a household may use the same computer). Cookies help companies personalize Web pages by applying the user's name or by listing previous purchases, thus building a relationship with users, one at a time.

Procter & Gamble
www.pg.com

Observation research is growing in popularity. In fact, Procter & Gamble has gone as far as to take video cameras into households to examine behaviours as consumers go about their daily routines. The goal of such an effort is to uncover potential new product ideas. For more insight into the role of observation research and how it can influence marketing decisions, see the Marketing in Action vignette **Procter & Gamble Pays a Visit**.

Experimental Research

experimental research

In **experimental research**, one or more factors are manipulated under controlled conditions, while other elements remain constant so that respondents' reactions can be evaluated. With this type of research, the test market is the acid test for a new product or service. **Test marketing** involves placing a product for sale in one or more limited markets, representative of the whole, in order to observe the product's performance under a proposed marketing plan. Good test marketing provides a marketing organization with three main benefits: it allows the marketing organization to observe the reactions of consumers to the product; it enables alternative marketing strategies to be evaluated (e.g., different strategies can be tested in different geographic markets); and it provides experience prior to an expensive regional or national launch.

test marketing

Information gained from test marketing is useful for planning. For example, actual trend data for sales and market share can be used to forecast similar data should a product be launched regionally or nationally. As well, the effect that a new product will have on the sales of current similar products can be considered. Such an effect is often referred to as **cannibalization** or **cannibalization rate**—the rate at which a new product reduces the sales of an existing product. Finally, a company can determine the characteristics of consumers who will buy the product (i.e., knowledge of demographic and psychographic characteristics will help define pricing and promotion strategies).

cannibalization (rate)

In contemporary marketing, there are those who believe test marketing is absolutely essential and those who believe it is a stage that can be skipped. Information Resources

Marketing in Action

PROCTER & GAMBLE PAYS A VISIT

One of the world's largest packaged goods companies is experimenting with video observation as a means of discovering potential new product ideas. The initial step involved sending video crews and cameras to 80 households in Britain, Italy, Germany, and China.

Procter & Gamble thinks the exercise in voyeurism will result in a mountain of priceless insights into consumer behaviour that more traditional methods—focus groups, interviews, home visits—may have missed. They could be right since most forms of research ask consumers for feedback, and their memories can be selective. With a video the behaviour is observed. A person either did something or did not do something.

After a family agrees to participate, filmmakers arrive at the home when the alarm goes off and stay until bedtime, usually for a four-day stretch. Obviously, there are certain ground rules. People are not followed into the bathroom or bedroom and any kind of romantic activity is off limits to the cameras. A London-based research firm called Everyday Lives is implementing the research on behalf of P&G. Families are recruited and financial incentives are offered to encourage participation.

P&G is hoping to learn about the lifestyles and local habits of young couples, families with children, and empty nesters in foreign markets where major growth opportunities exist. Even though P&G is a large multinational company, only one-third of the world's population buys P&G products compared to 98 percent of US households.

Through observational research the company hopes to develop products that solve problems shoppers didn't even know they had. In a Chinese household, for example, a mother was observed multitasking—cooking at the stove and watching television—while feeding a baby. Such knowledge could inspire product and package design in ways that give the company an edge over rivals.

Adapted from Emily Nelson, "P&G wants the truth: Did you really brush your teeth?" *Globe and Mail*, June 1, 2001, p. M2.

Information Resources Inc.
www.infores.com

Inc., a large provider of test market services, recommends that at least two markets be tested, not only to compare the impact of different demographics but also to cancel out the potential effects of natural disasters, plant closings, or other purely local factors.[10] The opposite view is that competition is so intense today that a test market tips off the competition as to what a company is doing and gives them time to react. As well, advancing technology is shortening the life cycles of many products. If a product stays too long in the test market, a competitor could launch its product first. The product in the test market would then look like a follower rather than a leader.

A company is well advised to assess the pros and cons of test marketing and make a decision to use it or not on a case-by-case basis. For example, products that involve a high financial risk should be tested initially. Products considered to be fads would not have time to be tested before the financial opportunity would be lost.

QUALITATIVE DATA VERSUS QUANTITATIVE DATA

According to the nature of the information sought, research data are classified as qualitative or quantitative. There are significant differences between these classifications.

Qualitative Data

qualitative data

focus group

Qualitative data are usually collected from small samples in a controlled environment. They result from questions concerned with "why" and from in-depth probing of the participants. Typically, such data are gathered from focus group interviews. A **focus group** is a small group of people (8 to 10) with common characteristics (e.g., a target market profile), brought together to discuss issues related to the marketing of a product or service. A typical qualitative project consists of four to six groups representing various regions or urban areas of Canada (e.g., Toronto, Montreal, Vancouver, and Halifax).

The word "focus" implies that the discussion concentrates on one topic or concept. A trained moderator usually conducts the interview over a period of a few hours. The role of the moderator is to get the participants to interact fairly freely in order to uncover the reasons and motivations underlying their remarks. Probing uncovers the hidden interplay of psychological factors that drive a consumer to buy one brand rather than another. The major drawback of using focus groups concerns the reliability of the data. The sample size is too small to be representative of the entire population, and most people in a focus group do not like to show disagreement with a prevailing opinion. For that reason interviews are held in several locations.

Marketing decisions involving considerable sums of money are very risky if based on such limited research. One of the most spectacular focus group failures, the launch of New Coke in the 1980s, came about because the soft drink maker was not asking the right questions. Worried that archrival PepsiCo had a better-tasting product, Coca-Cola asked consumers if they liked its new formulation without ever asking if they wanted its tried-and-true beverage changed.[11] New Coke failed miserably when it was launched, and the public backlash was so significant that Coca-Cola had to re-introduce the original Coke as Coca-Cola Classic.

The Coca-Cola example shows the weakness of focus groups—they are exploratory in nature. A follow-up quantitative survey is required to establish numbers, which costs organizations additional money and time. On the positive side, attitudes that are revealed in a focus group can be used as a foundation for formulating questions and questionnaires if and when quantitative research is required. The attitudes uncovered can be expressed as answers for closed-ended questions in a questionnaire.

Qualitative research also reinforces the beliefs, attitudes, and convictions of marketing managers. For example, unsubstantiated beliefs or attitudes that a marketing manager may have had prior to the research (e.g., that the perceived quality of the product is not as high as expected) can be confirmed in the discussion among participants. Hearing responses in a focus group has greater impact than an impersonal and voluminous statistical study. Qualitative research is best applied to exploratory topics—detailing processes, building hypotheses, and refining ideas. It can be used to set the direction for further in-depth studies.[12]

Quantitative Data

quantitative data

Quantitative data provide answers to questions concerned with "what," "when," "who," "how many," and "how often." This research attempts to put feelings, attitudes, and opinions into numbers and percentages. The data are gathered from structured questionnaires and a large sample to ensure accuracy and reliability. The interpretation of results is based on the numbers compiled, not on the judgment of the researcher. For this reason, it is a tool that is used for measuring and evaluating rather than investigating and exploring. A brief comparison of qualitative and quantitative research is contained in Figure 3.8.

In today's marketplace, the respective roles of qualitative research and quantitative research are changing. There is a tendency for companies to do more qualitative research. Not to diminish the value of quantitative research, the numbers are included in a report to support the actions taken by marketers. At Molson, for example, there is a vice-president accountable for marketing research. Molson does focus groups and qualitative research but it also does quantitative research on all television ads before production of the ad takes place. Each ad must hit a specific persuasion level. "We do not shoot ads until we know they will persuade beer drinkers to drink that brand," says Michael Downey, Molson senior vice-president, global marketing.[13]

SURVEY METHODOLOGY

personal interviews

telephone interviews

There are four primary means of contacting consumers when conducting surveys to collect quantitative data: telephone, personal interview, mail, and the Internet. **Personal interviews** involve face-to-face communication with groups (e.g., focus groups) or with individuals and are usually done through quantitative questionnaires. Popular locations for interviews are busy street corners, shopping malls, and the homes of respondents. **Telephone interviews** involve communication with individuals via the telephone. Usually, the interviews are conducted from central locations (e.g., one central location can reach all Canadian markets), and consequently there is supervised control over the interview process.

Technology is having an impact on telephone survey methodology to the point where human interviewers are no longer needed. A system known as Totally Automated Television Interviewing (TATI), developed by PinPoint Research of California, actually eliminates the need for the physical presence of an interviewer. The system incorporates digitized voice technology, touch-tone data capture, and voice recognition capabilities that allow a computer to walk callers through a survey.[14] So much for the

Pinpoint Research
www.pinpoint
research.com

Comparing Qualitative and Quantitative Research

Figure 3.8

Qualitative Research

- Collected from a small sample group
- Question format is unstructured
- Questions deal with why people act, do, purchase, etc.
- Small sample poses reliability (of data) problems

Quantitative Research

- Collected data from a truly representative sample (e.g., 200–300 people who represent a specified target market)
- Structured format (e.g., questionnaire with pre-determined responses) is common
- Questions deal with what, when, who, how many, and how often
- Data are statistically reliable; degree of error can be calculated

benefits of human interaction! Modern technology also allows data to be transferred from the telephone directly to a computer.

mail interviews   **Mail interviews** are a silent process of collecting information. Using the mail to distribute a survey means that a highly dispersed sample is reached in a cost-efficient manner. The main drawbacks are the lack of control and the amount of time required to implement and retrieve the surveys.

online surveys   **Online surveys** on the Internet allow an organization to be much less invasive in collecting information. Some companies have actually found that consumers seem more willing to divulge information over the Internet, compared with the more traditional means of surveying. As well, it takes less time to get results. Procter & Gamble is experimenting with online research for new product concept testing. In a paper environment P&G would spend $25 000 and get results in 2 months. Online the same test costs $2500 and results are available in 2 weeks.[15]

In the future, online research could become the backbone of consumer research activity. It provides quality information and it's immediate. For companies searching for and testing new product concepts it could produce better ideas, faster.

On the downside, recruiting participation can be a lot like fishing—participation is left up to the fish. Therefore, the validity of the information is questionable.[16] The fact that more than 53 percent of Canadians aged 15 and over presently have access to the Internet at home, at work, or at some other location, with that number increasing each year, bodes well for the future of online research.

The decision about which of these survey techniques to use is based on three primary factors:

1. *Nature of Information Sought* The amount of information to be collected and the time it will take to complete the survey are considerations. For example, if discussion is necessary to get the answers needed, personal interviews in a focus group may be best. If large amounts of information are required, the best option may be the mail.

2. *Cost and Time* When time is critical, certain options are eliminated. The telephone and the Internet are the best means of obtaining quick, cost-efficient information. Costs must also be weighed against benefits. The net financial gains expected to result from the research may determine which method is to be used.

3. *Respondent* The selection of a survey method can be influenced by the location of the respondents and how easily they can be reached. For example, if the participant is to be reached at home, any method—personal interview, telephone, mail, or online—can be used. Responding online is very convenient for people. In contrast, if the participant has to be reached in a central location, such as a shopping mall, a personal interview is the only choice.

Refer to Figure 3.9 for a summary of the advantages and disadvantages of each survey method.

Data Transfer and Processing

editing   Once the data have been collected, editing, data transfer, and tabulation take place. In the **editing** stage, completed questionnaires are reviewed for consistency and completeness. Whether to include questionnaires with incomplete or seemingly contradictory

data transfer   answers is left to the discretion of the researcher. In the **data transfer** stage, answers

Survey Methodology for Collecting Quantitative Data

Figure 3.9

PERSONAL INTERVIEW

Advantages

- Higher rates of participation
- Visual observations possible by interviewer
- Flexibility (e.g., inclusion of visuals possible)
- Large amounts of data collected

Disadvantages

- Higher cost (time needed)
- Reluctance to respond to certain questions
- Interviewer bias is possible

TELEPHONE INTERVIEW

Advantages

- Convenience and control
- Costs less
- Timely responses
- Geographic flexibility

Disadvantages

- Lack of observation
- Short questions and questionnaire
- Can be viewed as an invasion of privacy

MAIL SURVEYS

Advantages

- Geographic flexibility in selecting target
- Cost-efficient
- Large sample obtainable
- Respondent in relaxed environment
- Impersonality results in more accurate responses

Disadvantages

- Lack of control
- The time between distribution and return is long
- Potential for misinterpretation by respondent
- Low response rates

ONLINE RESEARCH

Advantages

- Efficient and inexpensive reach (elimination of telephone and humans)
- Less intrusive than traditional methods
- Convenient for respondent
- Fast turnaround of information (2–3 days versus 4–5 weeks)

Disadvantages

- Immature medium (low penetration compared with telephone)
- Limited sample frame (Internet users only)
- Research via bulk e-mail associated with SPAM (Internet junk mail)
- Reliability of information is questionable

---

to questions are transferred to a computer. On quantitative questionnaires, most questions are closed ended (require fixed-response answers), and all answers are pre-coded to facilitate the transfer. In the case of telephone surveys, it is now common to enter the responses directly into the computer as the questions are being asked.

Once the survey results have been entered into a computer, the results are tabulated. **Tabulation** is the process of counting the various responses for each question and

tabulation

frequency distribution

arriving at a frequency distribution. A **frequency distribution** shows the number of times each answer was chosen for a question. Numerous cross-tabulations are also made.

cross-tabulation

Cross-tabulation is the comparison and contrasting of the answers of various subgroups or of particular subgroups and the total response group. For example, a question dealing with brand awareness could be analyzed by the age, gender, or income of respondents. Computer software is used to produce tabulated results in a presentable format (rows and columns of numbers).

Data Analysis and Interpretation

data analysis

Data analysis refers to the evaluation of responses on a question-by-question basis, a process that gives meaning to the data. At this point, the statistical data for each question is reviewed, and the researcher makes observations about it. Typically, a researcher makes comparisons between responses of subgroups on a percentage or ratio basis.

data interpretation

Data interpretation, on the other hand, involves relating the accumulated data to the problem under review and to the objectives and hypotheses of the research study. The process of interpretation uncovers solutions to the problem. The researcher draws conclusions that state the data's implications for managers. For additional insight into the role of research, analysis and interpretation, read the Marketing in Action vignette **Positive Perceptions Lead to Effective Saturn Campaign**.

Positive Perceptions Lead to Saturn Campaign

If you know anything about the Saturn automobile it's that it is a "different kind of car and a different kind of company." Past advertising campaigns have instilled that message in our minds. Saturn Canada wanted to develop a new way of expressing the Saturn difference. Marketing research would play a key role.

The research started with a series of workshops with Saturn owners. There, the buyers' "superior ownership experience" surpassed all other observations. The workshops were followed by focus groups. Many participants could easily recall past commercials, so there was a high level of awareness of what Saturn was about. In the focus groups, brand attributes were expressed as rational or emotional statements and tested by the "Benefits Explosion" methodology, a system in which consumers rank specific benefit statements

about a product. The relationships that customers had with the car and the dealer topped the list.

The research provided input for a new ad campaign that demonstrates the personal nature of the Saturn buying and ownership experience, while reinforcing Saturn's offerings and its commitment to "do things differently." One new commercial explains the benefits of the 30-day or 2500 km money-back guarantee. A young woman loses her job shortly after buying a Saturn. Regrettably, she returns the car, but the Saturn dealer is there to help when she gets a new job. Another new commercial gives car buyers the option of buying a Saturn online from any location. It features a woman named Susan, whose face lights up when her Saturn dealer meets her at the airport with the keys to her new car. These ads were based on Saturn customers' actual experiences.

Viewers were emotionally touched by the ads in the campaign and an unprecedented number of positive comments were received from consumers.

Recommendations and Implementation

The recommendations outline suggested courses of action that the sponsoring organization should take in view of the data collected. Once a research project is complete, the research company will present its findings in a written report. Frequently, an oral presentation of the key findings is also made to the client. Very often senior management is informed of the data as it becomes known, so that the managers are better prepared for possible actions or changes in strategic direction. Preparing senior managers in this way is important, particularly if the proposed actions are in conflict with their personal views and feelings. The managers most likely to implement research findings are those who participate in research design, have the flexibility to make decisions, and see research findings that confirm their intentions.

These days, thanks to changing technology and faster turnaround times, market research is more streamlined, with clients expecting solid decision-making results—yesterday. Voluminous research reports, often referred to as "doorstoppers" are now being replaced by personal presentations, using PowerPoint or the like to display succinct objectives and results, rather than extensive tables and numbers.

For a more complete look at how marketing research influences the direction of marketing strategy refer to Figure 3.10. The figure identifies a problem faced by Kraft Dinner, outlines the research procedures used to obtain information, and shows the actions taken as a result of the information.

Saturn used research effectively—the data provided a lead on how to get to the heart of Saturn customers and intenders.

Saturn used qualitative and quantitative research to test the relevance of the commercials. Once they were on air they were measured for appreciation, wear-out (whether the target is tiring of the message), brand measures (how the target views the brand character), brand linkage, message comprehension, reach, and likeability.

By doing research at various stages of the advertising development process, Saturn is enjoying the benefits of an effective advertising campaign.

Adapted from Eric Leblanc and Kate Tutlys, "The Heart of the Matter," *Marketing*, July 16, 2001, p. 10.

Rhoda Sidney/PhotoEdit

Figure 3.10

Psychological Profiling Leads to New Advertising for Kraft Dinner

Advantages

Kraft Dinner is the country's number-one-selling grocery item with a 75 percent share of its category and Kraft Canada's biggest volume business. Despite such a lofty status sales were flat and had been for some time.

Problem

To discover just what was ailing this powerhouse brand. It was hypothesized that erosion in brand confidence among consumers was due to the fact there was no communication with people to find out what they love about Kraft Dinner.

Marketing Research Procedure

A methodology was employed that would create a personality profile for the brand. There would be an exclusive focus on the emotional aura around the brand. The notion of a brand carrying human traits is nearly as old as advertising itself, but it is only lately that psychiatric profiling has been gaining momentum.

To determine Kraft dinner's personality profile, two specific exercises were undertaken by research participants:

1. "Kraft Dinner has died. You have to write the obituary that goes in your local newspaper."

2. "You're a psychiatrist and Kraft Dinner has come to see you. Analyze the problem and tell him a solution."

Research Findings

From the obituary pages

- "Tragically yesterday the hero of many a Canadian meal died accidentally."

- "He was affectionately known as KD by his many friends."

- "There was an easy way about him that was both knowing and comforting."

- "KD valued his time with friends."

From the psychiatrist's couch

- "Kraft has low self-esteem and insecurity."

- "Kraft Dinner is feeling guilt and anxiety about his image."

- "Kraft has low self-esteem, is old, lethargic, and withdrawn."

Analysis and Interpretation

Kraft Dinner is

- Dependable
- Comfortable
- A friend
- Nonjudgmental
- Easy-going
- Unpretentious
- Trustworthy
- Loved by all

Recommended Therapy

- Build self-confidence
- Remember and promote the immortal place he holds in our hearts
- Raise self-esteem
- Get across the point that you are worth more

Actions Taken

Kraft raised the price of Kraft Dinner, redesigned the packaging, launched a new KD Web site and created a series of television commercials targeting young people who grew up eating the product. The ads touched on a person's relationships with Kraft Dinner.

Results

Testing of the commercials revealed that the spots outperformed all others in the category in North America. Already the biggest seller on the grocery shelves, Kraft Dinner experienced a significant increase in base brand sales.

Source: Adapted from Peter Vamos, "Psychological profiling gets inside a brand's head," *Strategy,* August 27, 2000, p. 2.

Summary

Marketing research must be viewed as a tool that assists the manager in the decision-making process. It is a systematic procedure that, if used properly, will produce reliable and valid data.

The research process begins with a firm's becoming aware of a problem situation. From there, exploratory research is conducted to narrow the scope of the investigation. To do so requires the consultation of knowledgeable people and secondary data sources. Advancing computer technology and the availability of online database information now provide a company with the information it needs, quickly. A database is the nucleus of the organization's management information system. This system ensures the continuous and orderly flow of information to the decision makers, who use the information to develop marketing strategies.

The integration of interactive decision support systems now allows managers to evaluate "what if" situations. Progressive-minded companies are now involved in a new procedure called data mining. Data mining provides an organization with a means of converting raw data into useful information that can be used to identify and implement more effective marketing strategies. Information for the database is collected from in-house sources, external secondary sources, and online database sources.

If the problem is not resolved at this stage, the next step is primary research. Primary research is the gathering of new data from a representative sample. The process requires the determination of who and how many should participate in the sample. These decisions are part of the sample design process.

Primary data are collected from surveys, observation, and experiments. Survey data are qualitative or quantitative in nature. Qualitative data are collected by focus group interviews or by one-on-one interviews and answers the question "why." Quantitative data are obtained by questionnaires through personal interview, telephone, and mail or online and involves translating thoughts and feelings into measurable numbers. Once the data are secured, they are computer processed for analysis and interpretation by the researcher.

Experimental research involves testing a marketing mix activity within a controlled situation in order to measure the effectiveness of the activity. Test marketing is an example of experimental research. In a test market, a product is placed in a representative market so that its performance under a proposed marketing plan can be observed.

Key Terms

- cannibalization (rate) 74
- cookie 74
- cross-tabulation 80
- data analysis 80
- data interpretation 80
- data mining 65
- data transfer 78
- decision support system (DSS) 64
- directory databases 69
- editing 78
- experimental research 74
- exploratory research 62
- fixed-response questioning 72
- focus group 76
- frequency distribution 80
- funnelling 62
- funnelling (of questions) 72
- hypotheses 70

Review Questions

1. In the context of marketing research, what is the relationship between the following sets of terms?

   Secondary data and primary data

   Research objectives and hypotheses

   Observational and experimental techniques

   Population and sampling frame

   Qualitative data and quantitative data

   Probability sample and non-probability sample

   Frequency distribution and cross-tabulation

   Tabulation and cross-tabulation

   Data analysis and data interpretation

2. What is the "problem awareness" stage of the marketing research process?

3. What is the difference between fun-

   nelling and situation analysis in the exploratory research stage?

4. What is a decision support system? What are its uses?

5. What is data mining, and what advantages does it offer a marketing organization?

6. What are the advantages and disadvantages of secondary data sources?

7. Briefly explain the four steps in the sample design process.

8. What purpose does a test market serve?

9. What is a "focus group?" What are the benefits of focus group research?

10. Under what circumstances would you use the telephone for collecting survey data? When would you use the personal interview?

Discussion and Application Questions

1. Visit the reference section of a library. Select any Canadian-based trade index and outline the nature and usefulness of the directory's content.

2. "Decisions based on qualitative data are not risky." Discuss this statement by examining the nature of informa-

   tion collected by qualitative research. Also refer to the vignette "Procter & Gamble Pays a Visit," before arriving at an opinion.

3. With reference to the vignette "Data Mining: Data—Information—Action," what is your opinion about the avail-

ability of purchase information to participating sponsors in loyalty programs? Is it an invasion of privacy? Should the practice be allowed? Explain.

4. You are about to devise a new advertising strategy (a message strategy) for the Porsche Boxster. You do not know how to present the automobile to potential customers and would like to find out more about them. What information would you like to obtain, and what procedure would you recommend to obtain it?

E-Assignment

1. Visit the Molson "I AM" Web site (www.IAM.ca). Proceed through the registration procedure. In terms of marketing research, what is the value of the information that Molson is requesting? How do you think Molson will use this information? Reassess the situation over a period of time, that is, after you have received some communications from this Web site.
2. Select a market where there is a clear brand leader and brand challenger (e.g., Colgate and Crest toothpastes, Coca-Cola and Pepsi-Cola, Molson Canadian and Labatt Blue). By visiting the Web site for each brand, your objective is to document relevant marketing information about the brand. Is the Web site a useful source of competitive information? What is your opinion? Do any of the sites attempt to collect information about you? What is the value of the information they are collecting?

Endnotes

1 Chris Daniels, "Canuck vs Yanks," *Marketing*, May 22, 2000, p. 26.

2 "New definition for marketing research approved," *Marketing News*, January 22, 1987, p. 1.

3 Ken Deal, "The eyes and ears of business," *Marketing*, May 17, 1999, p. 18.

4 George Kress, *Marketing Research*, 3rd Edition (Englewood Cliffs, NJ: Prentice-Hall, 1988), pp. 1320–133.

5 Carl McDaniel and Roger Gates, *Marketing Research Essentials* (St. Paul, MN: West Publishing Company, 1995), p. 89.

6 Emily Nelson, "P&G wants the truth: Did you really brush your teeth," *Globe and Mail*, June 1, 2001, p. M2.

7 Ross Waring, "The promise and reality of data mining," *Strategy*, June 7, 1999, p. D9.

8 Burke Campbell and Murray Conron, "Data under the scope," *Financial Post*, January 14, 2002, p. IT1.

9 Chris Daniels, "Cashing in on the new nationalism," *Marketing*, May 22, 2000, p. 26.

10 Jack Neff, "Whit Bread, USA," *Advertising Age*, July 9, 2001, pp. 1, 12.

11 "Managers should rethink the power and limitations of focus groups," *Financial Post*, December 14, 1999, p. C4.

12 George Stalk and Jill Black, "Consistent mistakes plague customer research," *Globe and Mail*, July 24, 1998, p. B21.

13 Wendy Cuthbert, "Hold the numbers," *Strategy*, June 4, 2001, pp. B6, B7.

14 Tim Triplett, "Survey system has human touch without humans," *Marketing News*, October 24, 1994. p. 16.

15 Jack Neff, "P&G weds data, sales," *Advertising Age*, October 23, 2000, pp. 76, 80.

16 Perry Vanier, "Polling online," *Marketing*, June 25, 1999, p. 22.

Canadian Press/CP

Consumer Buying Behaviour

two

> **> Learning Objectives**

After studying this chapter, you will be able to

1. Describe the steps in the consumer purchase decision process.
2. Describe the influences that affect consumer behaviour and lifestyle choices.
3. Explain the role and importance of consumer behaviour with respect to the development of marketing strategies.
4. Outline the various behavioural influences that affect consumer purchase decisions.

The behaviour of Canadian consumers is in a constant state of flux. The expression "the only constant in life is change" holds true here. It is this change that marketing organizations must recognize and act on. Organizations must anticipate changes among consumers and develop the appropriate marketing strategies to meet the challenges of a dynamic marketplace. To keep abreast of change, an organization will implement many of the research procedures that were discussed in the previous chapter. Many factors affect behaviour change in the consumer. Among them are:

1. The aging population and the change in lifestyle associated with aging
2. The growth in dual-income families
3. The formation of different sorts of households
4. The emphasis placed by some people on achieving a higher standard of living, while others retreat to more practical values and simpler lifestyles
5. The growth of various ethnic groups in large urban centres
6. The role of advancing technology and the way it shapes buying behaviour
7. The cyclical nature of the economy

This chapter will discuss the dynamics of consumer behaviour and illustrate how marketing organizations use information about behaviour to develop marketing strategies.

What Is Consumer Behaviour?

consumer behaviour

Consumer behaviour is defined as "the acts of individuals in obtaining goods and services, including the decision processes that precede and determine these acts."[1] An organization must have a firm understanding of how and why consumers make purchase decisions so that appropriate marketing strategies are planned and implemented.

From a purely competitive viewpoint, marketers must have access to information on consumer buying motivation in order to develop persuasive strategies for getting consumers to buy or use a product. Consequently, large sums of money are allocated to marketing research in order to determine who makes the buying decision and what factors play a role in making the decision.

Prior to examining the factors that influence buying decisions, one should appreciate the steps involved in the decision-making process.

The Consumer Purchase Decision Process

1.
Describe the steps in the consumer purchase decision process.

Knowing exactly how purchase decisions are made is difficult. While we know that certain variables influence behaviour, there are so many contributing variables that we cannot be certain which ones actually trigger a response. The purchase of a particular brand of product could be the result of an endorsement by a celebrity or a friend; it could be based on past experience with the product; or it could be due to the delivery of a free sample. Every purchase situation is unique. Sometimes, too, a consumer may be governed by rational (logical) behaviour for one purchase and at other times by irrational (emotional) behaviour.

Despite these difficulties, a generic model of the buying decision process may be offered. Essentially, there are five steps in the consumer purchase decision process (Figure 4.1). These steps are problem recognition, information search, evaluating alternatives, purchase decision, and post-purchase evaluation.

Let us examine each step in the decision-making process in detail.

PROBLEM RECOGNITION

problem recognition

The process begins with **problem recognition**. At this stage, a consumer discovers a need or an unfulfilled desire; for example, the muffler on the family station wagon goes, the engine of a 10-year-old automobile finally gives out, or a child outgrows a pair of ice

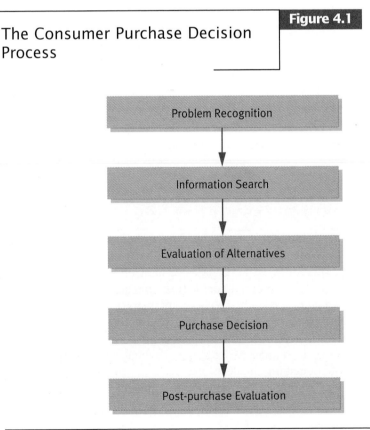

Figure 4.1

The Consumer Purchase Decision Process

skates. In each case, there is a need to replace the product. A person could also simply decide they want something, like a new colour television or a cell phone. In this case the purchase process is based more on impulse.

INFORMATION SEARCH

information search

Once the problem or need has been defined, the individual conducts an **information search** to solve the problem. The extent of the search varies with the nature of the purchase. If it is a routine purchase, no information may be sought. If it is a complex decision, numerous sources of information may be investigated. Generally, as the risk increases (i.e., as the price increases), the extent of the search for information also increases.

Sources of information may be internal or external. For example, your personal experiences with a product may be sufficient to make a new decision. A person will spend little time on the decision to replace a tube of toothpaste or bottle of mouthwash. However, if a person wanted to buy a new car, numerous external sources would be consulted. The primary external sources of information include personal sources (e.g., relatives and friends), public sources (e.g., ratings organizations, such as Consumer Reports or the Canadian Automobile Association), and commercial sources (e.g., the marketing activities of companies).

Prior to making an important buying decision, consumers will also surf the Internet in order to secure product information. The General Social Survey conducted by Statistics Canada (2001) demonstrated that 79 percent of men and 70 percent of women searched the Internet for information on goods and services, by far the most popular activity reported after e-mailing.[2] Another study conducted by Ernst & Young and Maritz Automotive Research Group shows that 25 percent of people who are in the market to buy a new car use the Internet in their buying process. A majority (83 percent) of this group will use it to search out information, and 13 percent will conduct the transaction online. The research report suggests that automakers and dealers need to ensure that their sites are full of information and easy to navigate.[3] Such factors influence perceptions of companies and their products.

The importance of the purchase plays a key role in the time and effort a consumer will spend searching the marketplace for information. Purchase decisions are classified as routine, limited, or complex. *Routine* purchases do not involve much money and take little time. Products that are routinely purchased include items subject to brand preference, such as toothpaste, coffee, cigarettes, and deodorant. In contrast, *complex* purchase decisions require a lot of time, effort, money and a proper evaluation of alternatives. In this case, consumers are more receptive to advertising information and as indicated above will visit Web sites to track down information that may assist them. Products that fall into this category are housing, automobiles, televisions, audio-video equipment, and major household appliances. For example, a student's search for a suitable computer system calls for complex decisions: does the student purchase a PC or a Mac-based operating system? At one time, the decision to buy a PC was almost a given, but in the late 1990s, Apple bounced back and had much success marketing the iMac (in a variety of colours) and the G3 and G4 series of computers. In 2002 Apple launched the flat screen iMac with even greater success. A lot of first time buyers opted for the Apple products. Refer to Figure 4.2 for an illustration of the purchase decision continuum.

With information in hand, the consumer will move to the next stage.

The Purchase Decision Continuum

Figure 4.2

Factors	Routine Decision	Limited Decision	Complex Decision
Time	Low	Limited	Extensive (Rigid Process)
Evaluation	Minimal	Some	Significant
Preference	Existing Product	Open to New Product	Very Open to New Product Information
Purchase Frequency	Frequent	Moderate	Low
Risk	Low	Moderate	High
Experience	High	Some	Low

EVALUATION OF ALTERNATIVES

3.
Explain the role and importance of consumer behaviour with respect to the development of marketing strategies.

evaluation

Let us pursue the example of the purchase of a new automobile. At this stage, a consumer will establish some kind of criteria against which the attributes of the automobile will be evaluated. For a marketer, this is a crucial stage, since the quality of a marketing strategy is being tested. Will the advertising deliver the right message? Will the message be convincing and actually motivate an individual to act on it?

To illustrate the concept of **evaluation**, let us assume that someone is contemplating the purchase of an entry-level luxury car. With such a car, they are looking for a certain amount of value along with prestige, an interesting combination. On the value side, the criteria may include safety, comfort, durability, and price. On the prestige side, the criteria may include the look of the car and its trendy image, performance, and responsiveness. The criteria place the makes of cars in the consumer's evoked set. The **evoked set** is a group of brands that a person would consider acceptable among competing brands in a class of products. In this case, the evoked set may include a moderately priced BMW, Mercedes-Benz, Jaguar X-Type, Infiniti I35 and the Cadillac Catera. Manufacturers refer to these cars as downscale luxury cars and price them in the $35 000 to $45 000 range.

evoked set

PURCHASE DECISION

purchase decision

Once the best alternative has been selected, a consumer is ready to make the **purchase decision**. In the case of the car purchase, the consumer will visit a few dealers and more than likely test-drive the model that is under consideration.

Now, the consumer will go through another decision-making process, as he or she must decide who to buy the car from and when to buy it. These decisions will be based

4.
Outline the various behavioural influences that affect consumer purchase decisions.

on such factors as price, availability of credit, the level and quality of service, and dealer reputation.

The simultaneous evaluation of the car and the dealer influences the final decision. For example, the customer may forego his or her first choice, say the BMW, to take advantage of an extended warranty, better service, and maintenance package offered by the Mercedes dealer.

The decision on when to purchase the car could be based on such circumstances as personal financial situation, the offer of a rebate by a manufacturer, or low financing rates. The latter two are intended to stimulate a more immediate purchase and are usually offered on a seasonal basis or when the economic situation dictates such programs.

POST-PURCHASE EVALUATION

Purchases involve risk, and the higher the cost of the purchase, the greater is the risk for the consumer. Once the decision to purchase has been made, the delivery order signed, and the bank loan secured, certain common questions arise. Did I make the right decision? Do I feel good, bad, or indifferent about the purchase?

cognitive dissonance

The purchase of routine items is based on past experience and satisfaction; therefore, there is a positive, secure feeling after the purchase that says, "I trust this product." Conversely, other purchases may result in dissatisfaction leading to brand switching, a process involving more purchases and evaluations. Such dissatisfaction is the result of **cognitive dissonance**, which is defined as the unsettled state of mind experienced by an individual after he or she has taken action. Its presence suggests that the consumer is not confident that he or she has made the right decision. The customer may begin to wish that another alternative had been chosen as the mind goes through numerous "what if" scenarios.

The consumer can overcome cognitive dissonance by taking certain actions. In the example of the automobile purchase, a person could re-read favourable consumer reports, get out the brochures again and review all the positive attributes, or perhaps talk to a friend about the purchase.

From a marketing perspective, the organization should initiate appropriate follow-up activities to put the consumer's mind at ease. In the automobile purchase decision, simply keeping in touch through service reminder notices may be all that is required. Progressive companies understand the importance of satisfaction and realize that the sale is simply the first step in what they hope will be a long-term relationship.

Influences on Consumer Behaviour

2.
Describe the influences that affect consumer behaviour and lifestyle choices.

The purchase decisions of Canadian consumers are influenced by psychological, social, cultural, and economic factors. These influences cannot be controlled by the marketing organization. They simply occur and interact to form the dynamics involved in the consumer purchasing decision process. Knowledge of these influences, however, is essential, since an organization can use this knowledge to maximize the effectiveness of the marketing strategies it devises and implements (Figure 4.3). Variables, such as product, price, availability, and various forms of marketing communication activities, are manipulated in such a way that collectively and positively they have an influence on consumers.

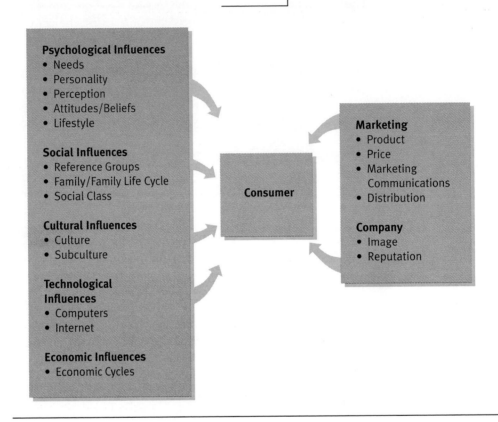

Figure 4.3

Influences on Consumer Behaviour

Psychological Influences
- Needs
- Personality
- Perception
- Attitudes/Beliefs
- Lifestyle

Social Influences
- Reference Groups
- Family/Family Life Cycle
- Social Class

Cultural Influences
- Culture
- Subculture

Technological Influences
- Computers
- Internet

Economic Influences
- Economic Cycles

Consumer

Marketing
- Product
- Price
- Marketing Communications
- Distribution

Company
- Image
- Reputation

PSYCHOLOGICAL INFLUENCES

The primary psychological characteristics that influence consumer behaviour and purchase decisions are needs, motives, personality, perceptions, perceived risk, attitudes and beliefs, and lifestyles.

Needs and Motives

needs

motives

Let us clearly distinguish between needs and motives. The term **needs** suggests a state of deprivation or the absence of something useful, whereas **motives** are the conditions that prompt the action necessary to satisfy a need (the action stimulated by marketing activities). The relationship between needs and motives is direct in terms of marketing activities. Needs are developed or brought to the foreground of consumers' minds when products' benefits are presented to them in an interesting manner (e.g., in conjunction with a lifestyle that the targeted people associate themselves with) so that they are motivated to purchase the product or service.

Needs are classified in an ascending order, from lower level to higher level (Figure 4.4).

hierarchy of needs

In this **hierarchy of needs**, an individual progresses through five levels:

1. *Physiological Needs* Food, water, sex, and air (basic survival needs)

2. *Safety Needs* Security, protection, and comfort

3. *Social Needs* A sense of belonging; love from family and friends
4. *Esteem Needs* Recognition, achievement, and status; the need to excel
5. *Self-Actualization Needs* Fulfillment; realization of your potential (achieving what you believe you can do)

There are two principles at work in this hierarchy:[4]

1. When lower-level needs are satisfied, a person moves up to higher-level needs.
2. Satisfied needs do not motivate. Instead, needs yet to be satisfied influence behaviour.

Understanding consumers' needs is essential for a marketing organization. Consider the following example in which a marketer calls attention to safety needs in order to motivate people to purchase automobiles. Customers perceive Volvo to be a safe automobile largely based on advertising over time that has stressed the safety features of the automobile. See Figure 4.5 for an illustration. The desire to be accepted by peers (that is, the need for social satisfaction) is commonly appealed to in advertising for personal care products and clothing. For example, the images presented by Calvin Klein or Tommy Hilfiger have an impact on style-conscious youth and people aged 20 to 29.

The Hierarchy of Needs

Figure 4.4

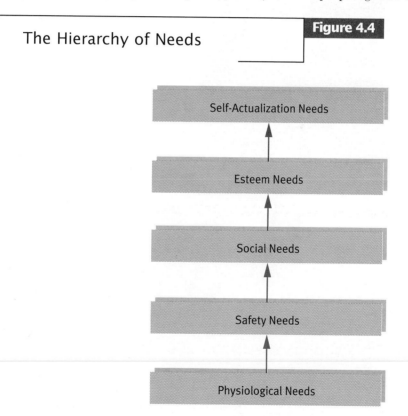

Basic premise of needs satisfaction: satisfaction leads to needs at a higher level; behaviour is influenced by needs yet to be satisfied.

Source: *Motivation and Personality* 3rd edition by Maslow, © Adapted by permission of Pearson Education Inc., Upper Saddle River, NJ.

Figure 4.5

Volvo Integrates Safety Features With Contemporary Styling to Influence Customers

Courtesy: Volvo Cars of Canada and Sharpe Blackmore Euro RSCG

Esteem needs are addressed in messages that portray people in successful business roles and occupations; a senior executive is shown travelling first class on an airline or driving an automobile symbolic of success, such as a Mercedes-Benz, Porsche, or Jaguar. Showing someone as being attractive to the opposite sex or having lots of friends targets social and esteem needs.

Personality and Self-Concept

personality

Personality refers to a person's distinguishing psychological characteristics, those features that lead to relatively consistent and enduring responses to the environment in which that person lives. It is influenced by self-perceptions, which, in turn, are influenced by physiological and psychological needs, family, culture, and reference groups. Why would someone pay $85 000 for a Porsche, when a less expensive automobile will perform the same task? Why do people buy designer-label clothing at high prices and in upscale boutiques, when low-priced items performing the same functions are available? Such purchases are based on the image we desire to have of ourselves. To appreciate this principle, one must understand the self-concept theory.

self-concept theory

Self-concept theory states that the self has four components: real self, self-image, looking-glass self, and ideal self.[5]

1. *Real Self* The real self is seen through an objective evaluation of the individual—it is you as you really are. One's perception of the real self is often distorted by the influence of the other selves.

2. *Self-Image* This is how you see yourself. You might, for example, see yourself as being hip, or being an intellectual, even though you may be neither.

3. *Looking-Glass Self* This concept derives from the way you think others see you.

4. *Ideal Self* This is how you would like to be. It is what you aspire to be.

Marketers use this self-concept theory to their advantage. They know that, human nature being what it is, many important decisions are based on the looking-glass self and the ideal self. Goods and services that help to fulfill the ideal self are appealing to the consumer.

The importance of self-image in buying and marketing is illustrated by the "wellness" trend that surfaced in the mid to late 1990s and continues to the present. People are increasingly conscious of what they are eating and what they are doing recreationally—their lifestyle patterns are changing. As a result, consumers are investing in health club memberships and personal workout equipment, such as exercise bikes and rowing machines. Such purchases are based on the desire to improve one's image—to look and feel better.

On the eating side of the lifestyle equation, Kellogg recently launched Vive, a new soy-based cereal. Soy by itself doesn't tempt the taste pallet, so Vive features a cinnamon flavour, crunchy flaked cereal with granola clusters. It is perfectly positioned to capitalize on the health claim that a daily intake of soy protein can help reduce the risk of heart disease, stroke, and several forms of cancer.[6]

Baby boomers are leading the charge in terms of lifestyle change. According to Christine Lowry, vice-president nutrition and corporate affairs at Kellogg Canada, boomers are becoming increasingly "literate" when it comes to healthy eating. "They're looking for products that put the health need into context for them; they want something that tastes good but also meets their health and nutrition needs." Coca-Cola has also reacted to this trend. Now, they place more emphasis on their Fruitopia juices and Dasani water product lines than they do on soft drinks.[7]

Marketers must stay abreast of such changes among consumers. A shift in emphasis with regard to the various elements of the self should result in different marketing strategies.

Perception

perception

Perception refers to how individuals receive and interpret messages. Marketers know that different individuals perceive the same product differently. A variety of marketing actions influence consumer perceptions—advertising, pricing, packaging, and place of purchase—but perceptions differ because consumers are quite selective about the messages they receive. Selectivity is based on their level of interest and their needs. There are three levels of selectivity:

1. *Selective Exposure* Our eyes and minds only notice information that is of interest.
2. *Selective Perception* We screen out messages and information that are in conflict with previously learned attitudes and beliefs.
3. *Selective Retention* We remember only what we want to remember.

Generally speaking, consumers do not recall much from the advertising messages they are exposed to. But, if a consumer is considering a purchase of, say, an expensive digital camera or personal computer system, that consumer will be interested in learning about the various products available so that an informed decision can be made. He or she becomes receptive to messages about cameras and personal computers, while screening out other messages. This selective nature of perception helps explain why only some people respond to marketing activities; others quite simply do not notice them. The challenge for marketers is to penetrate the perceptual barriers—they must design messages and strategies that will command attention and compel the reader, listener, or viewer to take action. In an increasingly fragmented media environment this challenge is now more difficult.

Perceived Risk

perceived risk

Closely associated with perception is the **perceived risk** associated with the purchase of a good or service. The risk factor is generally higher for first-time purchases or when the price of any purchase increases. Will the purchase cause embarrassment or social rejection rather than acceptance? For example, children between the ages of 10 and 15 are very aware of the status associated with brands and brand names, and they make definite brand choices. To show up at school wearing just a plain T-shirt could be socially destructive. What they must have are shirts bearing brand names such as Old Navy, Tommy Hilfiger, La Senza Girl, Roots, Nike, and other logos, so they can be part of the "cool" crowd.

Marketers recognize the importance of perceived risk and develop strategies to help reduce risk. A celebrity endorsement from Wayne Gretzky will tempt people of all ages to buy Post Cereal, visit McDonald's for a meal, or perhaps buy a casual sweater at the Bay (he endorses a line of clothing). When a new food product is introduced, coupons and free samples are often distributed to help reduce the risk in making the first purchase. Securing an endorsement from a professional body gives a brand instant credibility. Crest and Colgate toothpastes, for example, are both endorsed by the Canadian Dental Association.

Attitudes and Beliefs

attitudes

Let us make the distinction between attitudes and beliefs. **Attitudes** are an individual's feelings, favourable or unfavourable, towards an idea or object (the product or service).

beliefs

Beliefs are the strongly held convictions on which an individual's actions are based. Generally speaking, marketing organizations present their products to consumers in a way that agrees with prevailing attitudes. Marketers have found that it is expensive to try to change attitudes.

The importance of attitudes can be quickly illustrated by the change in shopping patterns taking place in North America. People are now oriented more toward the home and family, and as a result the incidence of home shopping, either by catalogue, telephone, or online, is growing while traditional retail shopping is starting to decline. This will benefit marketers who make it convenient for buyers to respond to appeals from their kitchen counter or office chair.

Sometimes, a company's own worst enemy is its success in the past. For example, the Gap met with overwhelming success through the 1980s and 1990s based on its "fashion basics with an edge" image. Their marketing strategy was tailored toward teenagers and people in their twenties and thirties—a rather broad target market. The Gap image clicked with the attitudes of its audience and the fashions offered were almost goof-proof. Inevitably though, Gap, like Nike and Levi's, fell victim to "brand fatigue" as its image became too familiar. They also made mistakes in the kind of clothes they were selling. Instead of sticking to basics like cool jeans and T-shirts they started offering eccentric styles and offbeat colours that were out of touch with the needs, wants and attitudes of its most precious young customers.[8] Teenage shoppers, the most trend-conscious consumers, began to desert the store in 2001, resulting in a sharp decline in sales and profits. Teens and young adults shifted their allegiance to stores like American Eagle Outfitters and Abercrombie & Fitch.

The Gap
www.gap.com

While it is difficult for a marketing organization to change attitudes, it must be prepared to act when consumers' attitudes do change. Now that consumers are looking for healthier foods, many established brands are benefiting by emphasizing product attributes formerly ignored. A simple change in packaging did the trick for Campbell's Ready to Serve soups. The brand was experiencing depressed sales despite the growth in health-associated foods. On the package the words "Healthy Request" were isolated and made larger. "By making it simpler for the consumer to find the healthier choice, the Healthy Request lines have growing at a rate of 30 percent in the last 6 months."[9]

The moral in these illustrations is simple: products must first be aligned with the psyche of the consumers before they will consider buying a particular product. Further, if a company decides to launch a new product, it must consider consumers' loyalty, attitudes, and perceptions before proceeding too far with a project.

Lifestyle

lifestyle

Lifestyle is a "person's pattern of living as expressed in his or her activities, interests, opinions, and values."[10] Marketing organizations try to determine who buys their product on the basis of demographic variables, such as age, income, gender, and education. Nevertheless, individuals with these variables in common, who even look alike and live side by side, can be entirely different in their lifestyle. It is the psychographic profile, obtained through research, that indicates differences between people and why different people buy the products they do. Psychographic research determines the activities, interests, and opinions of consumers (commonly referred to as their AIOs). The compilation of data places people in descriptive classifications (descriptions of people with similar tendencies). In Canada, Goldfarb Consultants conduct lifestyle research, and they have divided the population into two classifications: traditionalists and non-traditionalists. For a summary of these classifications, see Figure 4.6.

Psychographic information shows how an individual's interest in a particular product depends on his or her lifestyle. Automakers produce and market a range of vehicles to satisfy the requirements of various lifestyle groups. Trendy sports cars with European or Japanese styling appeal to *bold achievers* (aggressive and confident individuals who are success- and responsibility-oriented; they are motivated by status and prestige). Refer to Figure 4.7 for an illustration. In contrast, a family minivan made by Ford or Chrysler appeals to a *day-to-day watcher* (someone motivated by familiarity, loyalty, and security, and influenced by quality, brand name, and authority figures). Psychographic jargon embraces an array of terms to describe people. Those just mentioned are only a few of them.

Lifestyle Segments in Canada

Figure 4.6

Segment	Percent of	Characteristics
Traditionalists		
Day-to-Day Watchers	24	Represent the status quo; don't like the fast pace; motivated by familiarity, loyalty and security; influenced by quality, brand name, and authority figures.
Old-Fashioned Puritans	18	Prefer simpler times; express conservative values; motivated by price and quality; influenced by value-oriented messages; motivated by sales and other forms of discounts.
Responsible Survivors	12	Frugal shoppers who look for best price; have money but do not like to spend it; motivated by price; shop at low-end stores; heavy television viewers, so it is a good medium to reach them with.
Non-traditionalists		
Joiner Activists	16	Idealists; liberal-minded; careful decision makers; willing to spend; motivated by information, therefore receptive to advertising messages; rational appeals have influence (quality, service, dependability, etc.).
Bold Achievers	15	Aggressive and confident individuals; success- and responsibility-oriented; innovators who lead in attitude and purchase decision; motivated by status, prestige, and success; products purchased reflect success; want higher-priced goods and exclusivity.
Self-indulgents	14	Resent authority; motivated by self-gratification, therefore often buy impulsively (even on major purchases); price not a factor; want easy road to success; messages should stress gratification as source of motivation.

A Lifestyle Advertising Message Using Excitement, Status, and Prestige Appeals

Figure 4.7

Psychographics allow the marketing organization to position its products effectively in the marketplace. The beer industry in Canada is laden with lifestyle advertising based on psychographic research. Budweiser appeals to a blue-collar, rugged outdoors type of male; Carlsberg appeals to socially active and sexually active 30-something, single males and females. According to the beer company, these people are entering their "Carlsberg Years." Potential users of a brand who identify with the particular lifestyle portrayed in an advertising campaign are apt to view the brand favourably. With sufficient motivation, the likelihood of purchase is stronger.

Many organizations have capitalized on a lifestyle trend that involves healthier eating. For example, Kraft Canada launched Very Very Cherry, one of three flavours of a portable mixed fruit snack eaten directly from a plastic container. The unique selling point is that the convenience of the product meets the portable fruit snack needs of consumers (see Figure 4.8).

Canadian Grocer
www.cdngrocer.com

Figure 4.8

Very Very Cherry Appeals to Consumers Wanting Convenient, Portable Food Products

Courtesy: KraftCanada Inc.

For more insight into how lifestyle changes are affecting marketing practice read the Marketing in Action vignette **Hectic Lifestyles are Driving Change**.

Marketing in Action

Hectic Lifestyles are Driving Change

Restaurants and bars are wondering where their customers have gone. Consumers are eating fewer meals in restaurants like McDonald's—in fact, sales are flat at McDonald's on a year-to-year basis, and there are concerns about growth in the years ahead.

In today's health-conscious, time-strapped culture, the days of heavy drinking and long hours at the pub with colleagues are also diminishing, Now, people are more interested in beating the traffic and just getting home. And they have good reason to do so. Right now a third of middle-aged Canadians consider themselves workaholics and claim they don't have enough time to spend with their family and friends. Moreover, a growing number of Canadians claim severe "time stress." To alleviate the stress, many Canadians are exercising at the gym rather than drinking at the pub.

These trends are good news to food marketers, especially those that offer convenience foods. However, in today's culture, convenience also means healthy-consumers are looking for quick, tasty, and healthy food alternatives that fit their lifestyle.

A recent study conducted by *Canadian Grocer* magazine revealed that consumers wait until the last minute to decide what's for dinner. The decision is made on the way home from work or at preparation time. With 70 percent of meals eaten at home, there's an opportunity for marketers to slip in quick and simple meal solutions. One-dish meal solutions are all of a sudden very popular. Pop it in the microwave and presto! You have a meal.

What has emerged is a new food market referred to as the "home meal replacement market." It is a small but growing segment of Canada's $96 billion a year food industry, designed to meet time-crunched families' needs for fast, efficient meals. Rather than picking up a pizza or going to McDonald's, moms want to go through the motions of cooking, even if it is just a quick meal.

At the supermarket, packaged frozen boxed meats, traditional frozen dinners, and frozen pizzas are all doing a brisk business. A relatively new brand of packaged refrigerated entrees called 44th Street that started from scratch only a few years ago is now generating sales of $20 million annually. Priced at $9.99, 44th Street offers six different entrees, including two kinds of chicken, a roast pork loin, roast beef sirloin, and meat loaf. They are distributed in stores such as Loblaws, A&P, Sobey's, and Dominion.

44th Street is a new concept that required consumer education. The idea of selling pre-cooked meat from a refrigerator is so new that the grocery retailers didn't know where to position it in stores. The product is cooked in the bag it's sold in, so the risk of contamination is eliminated, and shelf life is quite long. Although 44th Street is designed for microwave preparation, many consumers opt for the alternate cooking instructions—for many it fits the need to partially cook the meal even though time is precious.

One of the marketers behind 44th Street looked at her situation and sees exactly why the product is successful. "I work full time, I have two daughters, and I go to school. You want to provide a healthy, wholesome meal but you also want something that's efficient. A 10-minute pot roast just makes sense."

Adapted from Dana Flavelle, "Just like your mother's Sunday roast—only faster," *Toronto Star*, January 2, 2002, pp. E1, E7, Tavia Grant, "Hearth & Home replaces bars and booze," *Globe and Mail*, January 25, 2002, p. C1 and "A grocery gold mine," *Marketing*, July 16, 2001, p. 22.

© Ted Horowitz/CORBIS/MAGMA

SOCIAL INFLUENCES

The social factors that influence the purchase decision process include reference groups, the family, and social class.

Reference Groups

reference group

A **reference group** is a group of people with a common interest that influences its members' attitudes and behaviour. Reference groups that people are commonly associated with include fellow students in a class, co-workers, sports teams, hobby clubs, civic and recreational associations, and fraternal organizations. It can also be your immediate *peer group*—the friends you hang with. A member of a group experiences considerable pressure to conform to the standards of the group, to "fit in." The desire to fit in influences the type of products a member will purchase.

The influence of reference groups is quite strong among younger people. For example, children and teens share a desire to wear the latest fashions, to shop at the trendiest stores, or to have parts of their body pierced. They like to set trends, not follow trends. As indicated earlier in the chapter, The Gap was once their stomping ground, now its Old Navy and American Eagle Outfitters.

Because of young people's fickle nature it is difficult to develop an effective marketing strategy that will have an influence on them. But, by pinpointing the reference groups that affect young people, or any other group for that matter, a marketing organization can develop appropriate strategies for reaching them. Television commercials that show certain groups using specific products and services—sports teams (beer), successful professionals (automobiles, clothing, and accessories), or college students (casual clothing, entertainment, and travel)—are suggesting that these groups can be joined if such purchases are made.

Trying to get back into favour with the youth market and to take some steam out of Nike's popularity, Reebok went directly after the hip-hop generation with a new brand called RBK. RBK is the moniker for a street inspired collection of young men's fashions that include long shorts, T-shirts, athletic-style jerseys, tank tops, and shoes. The brand is associating itself with a hip-hop, urban basketball scene and includes an endorsement from NBA star Alan Iverson.[11] Once a few kids buy in, the wave of acceptance is sure to follow—at least that's the thinking at Reebok.

Reebok
www.reebok.com

Family

Various members of a family think and act as individuals and the decisions they make can influence household purchases. The actual impact each member has on the decision depends on the type of product or service under consideration. In the past, the impact each person had on the purchase decision was related to the traditional roles of household members. For example, fathers were in charge of cars and household repairs and mothers in charge of groceries. Traditionally, purchase decisions were classified as husband-dominant, wife-dominant, or shared equally.

Today, the lines are blurring between the sexes, and the decision makers are not who they once were. Companies must be aware that women buy or influence 70 percent of all new car purchase decisions, 50 percent of computers, and 53 percent of stocks. Around the house, women influence 40 percent of home improvement projects.[12] Among the elements contributing to the role changes are the increasing numbers of two-income families and of women working outside the home, as well as the growth of single-parent families.

double targeting

Changing roles and responsibilities among male and female heads of households are changing how marketers view target marketing. Consequently, some marketers are double targeting. **Double targeting** involves devising a single marketing strategy for both sexes or devising separate strategies to appeal to the different sexes. In its simplest form, a product would have one strategy for females and another for males. The risk of such an undertaking is in the confusion it may cause among females and males. They may ask: for whom is this product intended?

The Chrysler Sebring automobile employs a dual targeting strategy that is implemented through careful placement of advertising messages. The Sebring uses the same advertising strategy to appeal to career-minded males and females between the ages of 30 and 40. The print ads include a beauty shot of the car with a successful-looking male or female standing beside it. The copy in the ad extols the pleasure and excitement of driving such a car. From Chrysler's perspective, the issue is this: would a male and female drive the same kind of sporty-looking car? Carefully planned placement of the ads resolves the problem. Chrysler reaches males through specific-interest magazines such as *National Post Business* and reaches females through specific-interest magazines such as *Elm Street* or *Chatelaine*. Chrysler can place either ad (at separate times) in a general-interest magazine like *Maclean's*.

Canadian Tire has also adopted a dual targeting strategy. Forever known as the domain of male shoppers on a Saturday, Canadian Tire embarked on an expansion and renovation program that includes bigger stores, wider aisles, improved displays, brighter lighting, and in-store boutiques. A new line of Martha Stewart paint was added to draw in more female shoppers. Female shoppers were identified as a priority target—they make up a growing proportion of hardware and home decorating shoppers. As a result of a more pleasant shopping experience for all customers, sales have increased by $1 billion since 1996, and the company remains very profitable.[13]

As indicated in the lifestyle section of the chapter, families are working longer and harder, and in families where both heads of household work there is a constant need for goods and services that provide convenience. These consumers also look for more convenient ways to access information and to shop. Therefore, smart marketers are shifting their focus from mass marketing toward targeted marketing strategies. There has to be more emphasis on direct marketing techniques such as direct response advertising and Internet communications. While the transition has been slow, it will pick up speed as consumers adapt to the technology that is available to them.

The rush to convenience is best demonstrated in the cell phone market. Cell phone usage is growing between 20 and 30 percent a year and usage is expected to hit 16.6 million subscribers in Canada by 2003.[14] The cell phone of the future will allow consumers to handle information and communications in a host of different ways that was not previously possible.

The *role of children* also has to be considered by the marketer. Children often influence purchase decisions in three areas: items for themselves, items for the home, and family vacations. A recent research study conducted by YTV among tweens (kids 9 to 14) and their parents, revealed that 9 out of 10 tweens influence the purchase of their own clothes; 8 out of 10 tweens get a say in what games, toys, snack foods, and restaurants the family chooses; and 3 of 10 influence the purchase of a family car. The report estimates that today's tweens represent almost $1.8 billion worth of spending power and that "kidfluence" or influence over their parents' spending is worth 10 times what they spend on themselves.[15]

From what cereal is on the breakfast table to the type of vehicle the family drives, Canada's 8 million kids, dubbed Generation Y, are making their voices heard in a way that earlier generations wouldn't have dared. Speaking personally, I can't imagine my parents coming to me and saying, "What kind of TV should we buy?" That would never have happened. But the times are changing fast; it is the tweens and teens of today that will kick Internet buying into high gear. Marketers recognize that activity directed at children now will help form impressions and habits that will influence their buying patterns as adults.

From a marketing viewpoint, it is essential to determine who has the most influence within a family situation. Once this is known, strategies containing an appropriate message and using suitable media can be directed at the decision maker and the influencer. In spite of these changes, it is still generally safe to say that in households headed by an adult male and an adult female, or a same sex household for that matter, the more expensive a product or service, the greater is the likelihood of a shared decision in order to make the right decision.

Family Life Cycle

family life cycle

The **family life cycle** is a series of stages a person undergoes, starting with being a young single adult, progressing to marriage and parenthood, and ending as an older single individual. Understanding the stages in the life cycle offers insight into household purchase decisions. The family life cycle theory is based on the changing needs of a family as it progresses through the various stages. Such theory can be used by an organization to develop better target marketing strategies. The number of households in each stage can be determined through the study of demographic data.

Needs change in each stage according to variables, such as age, income, marital status, and the presence of children. The purchase priorities of a young working family with children will be quite different from those of an older married couple with no children living at home. Different types of buying occur in each stage. Generally, as individuals grow older and as incomes rise, the overall financial burden eases.

Figure 4.9 is a flowchart of the family life cycle. While the cycle itself may not change, the circumstances that families face in each stage do change. Social and demographic trends have a direct influence on family formations. For example, families in the first decade of the 21st century will be different from the families of the 1990s, and so on. The new family is smaller in size (3.1 members), and two working adults is the norm. The trend to smaller families is expected to continue in what was once referred to as the "traditional" household. The "Leave It to Beaver" family (working father and stay-at-home mother) that was portrayed on television in the 1950s and 1960s now represents only a small portion of Canadian households.

With birth rates declining, divorce rates rising, and the baby boom generation aging, the population is getting older and household formations are changing. In terms of the life cycle concept, the key groups in the first two decades of the new millennium are the older cohort, Generation X, and those in the middle. Companies will launch new products geared specifically to mature targets, and reposition existing products to make them appeal to older people. At the same time they must also attract new, younger customers— a real marketing dilemma. Oldsmobile, for example, an automobile for the 50-plus crowd, launched new cars and new advertising to attract a younger audience but was unsuccessful. Perceptions held by young people about Oldsmobile were too difficult to overcome.

The Modernized Family Life Cycle

Figure 4.9

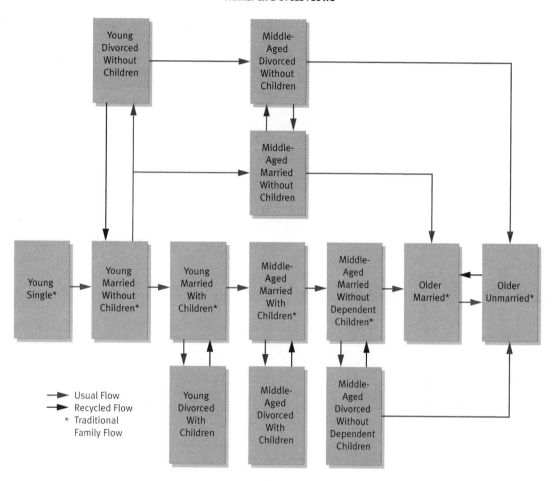

FAMILY LIFE CYCLE FLOWS

Source: Family Life Cycle Flows from Patrick E. Murphy and William Staples, "The Modernized Family Life Cycle," *Journal of Consumer Research*, June 1979, p. 17. Reprinted by permission of The University of Chicago Press.

Toyota
www.toyota.com

Some companies are concerned that their image will age with boomers if they neglect younger generations. In other words, the "geezer" status could be harmful. Boomers have helped make Toyota Camry the top-selling car in North America, but now the carmaker feels trapped by the relationship. In fact, the average age of a Toyota customer is 47 compared to Honda at 40 and Volkswagen at 38. In order to appeal to younger customers Toyota launched the Echo, a compact car aimed at first-time buyers, and the MR2 Spyder aimed at Generation X bold achievers.[16]

Social Class

social class

A person's social class derives from a system that ranks or classifies people within a society. **Social class** is the division of people into ordered groups based on similar values, lifestyles, and social history. This division into groups is based on such variables as income, occupation, education, and inherited wealth. In Western society, class groups are divided as follows: upper-upper, lower-upper, upper-middle, lower-middle, upper-lower, and lower-lower. Individuals can move in and out of the various social classes as they go through life. As an example, the young business executive on the rise in the corporate world could move rapidly from, say, a lower-middle class background to a lower-upper class level as he or she gains more power, responsibility, and income in an organization. Conversely, a senior executive accustomed to a certain style of living and a certain social circle could suffer socially if he or she suffered a job loss. The fallout would affect the social position of the entire family.

A person's place in the class structure influences his or her purchases of housing, automobiles, clothing, travel, and entertainment. The lower-upper class executive, if single, is likely to live downtown, drive a trendy automobile that reflects achievement, wear custom-designed suits, and dine out frequently at the "in" spots. Such purchases help create or maintain the image that goes with the corporate position.

CULTURAL INFLUENCES

culture

Culture refers to behaviour learned from external sources, such as the family, the workplace and education that help form the value systems that hold strong sway over every individual. Over time, people's values can change. North America's value system is largely shaped by a demographic phenomenon—the baby boom generation. These people were the "hippies" of the 1960s, the "me generation" of the 1970s, and the "yuppies" of the 1980s. In the 1990s, these middle-aged boomers adopted an environmentally conscious orientation (e.g., conserve, preserve, protect).

As each decade passes, individuals' values change; they acquire different needs, different responsibilities, and different attitudes. In the 1980s, materialism prevailed, and individuals constantly strove to possess—a larger house in comparison with those owned by their parents and grandparents or a prestigious automobile that suggested success. By contrast, the 1990s saw boomers looking for relaxation; they wanted to work less and were willing to accept less financial reward. A sense of equilibrium and simplicity had set in. In purchasing goods, strategic consumption had replaced conspicuous consumption.

These examples show how the values of the Canadian society can change from decade to decade. Marketers monitor the changing values of society and of sub-groups in society in order to identify the new needs that the change produces. A firm's ability to adapt marketing strategies to the changing personality of the Canadian marketplace ultimately determines success or failure.

Subculture

subculture

Many diverse subcultures exist within the Canadian culture. A **subculture** is a subgroup of a culture, which has distinctive attitudes and values that set it apart from the national culture. Canada's subcultures are evident in cities, where parts of urban and suburban neighbourhoods contain large populations of one ethnic group. Very often, these ethnic groups are served by their own media, which provide marketers with an effective means of reaching them.

Prudent marketers are recognizing the opportunities that these markets represent. Experts forecast that by 2011 45 percent of Toronto's population will consist of members of ethnic minorities.[17] Such a number suggests the full marketing implications for mainstream marketers that are currently ignoring the language markets. To reach Toronto, a company will have to turn to ethnic marketing sooner or later. Vancouver is another major urban market with a high ethnic concentration. In both markets, Chinese-Canadians and South-Asians are the largest visible minorities.

Because of their unique characteristics and attitudes, **adolescents** can generally be said to belong to a subculture. Some adolescent groups differentiate themselves from the main culture more obviously than other groups do. The "punks" of the 1980s, the "skin-heads" of the 1990s, and the "Goths" of the early 2000s differentiated themselves from the more traditional teenage groups through their taste in music, the style of their clothing and accessories, and their physical appearance. The products they purchased and the activities they participated in were different from those of the mainstream teenagers.

Generally speaking, the adolescent market is status conscious and brand name oriented. They buy what is "in," what is "right," and what is needed to be "cool." As indicated earlier in the chapter, they are subject to a high degree of peer pressure. Teens—by their significant numbers and substantial buying power—are among marketers' most coveted demographic groups. They are volatile and switch allegiances fast, so marketers have to be ready to react to rapid changes in tastes and preferences.

Nike
www.nike.com

Marketers have to understand the mindset of teens to be successful. A saturation campaign may generate brand awareness, but youth are going to recognize this as a massive effort to get money out of their wallets.[18] Real success today comes from different campaigns directed at different niches of the youth market. Brands such as Nike and Hilfiger are successful because they appeal to a variety of different youth targets. These brands target different youth with different messages and advertise in special interest publications that reach unique youth target audiences.

To attract this market, marketing communications must be fun and exciting; they must be in line with the lifestyle teenagers lead and can relate to, representing the image that the market wants. To illustrate, the advertising for such products as Mountain Dew ("Do the Dew") appeals directly to the needs of active young people. The ads show social situations and leisure activities that teenagers are typically involved in, or would like to be involved in, and they appeal to the adolescent belief that social acceptance follows from using a given product.

In assessing cultures and subcultures, marketers must decide if a national marketing strategy is suited to everyone or if subcultures should be isolated and appropriate strategies developed for them. A prudent manager may conclude that consumers across the country need the same products, but the way in which products are presented will vary. This concept is discussed in greater detail in the next section.

Staying abreast of all of the changes in the consumer marketplace is a constant challenge for marketers. For more precise details on what marketers can expect in the new millennium, see the Marketing in Action vignette **Shifting Behaviour and Customer Relationship Management.**

Consumer Behaviour in Regional Canadian Markets

Are regional cultural differences in Canada significant enough to warrant unique marketing strategies? The most obvious differences are the ones between English-speaking Canada and French-speaking Canada. A common strategy in the past was to adapt English advertising for the French Canadian market, but such strategies produced only limited success and, often, failure. French Canadians do not respond to the same cues

Marketing in Action

Shifting Behaviour and Customer Relationship Management

n her book *Harness the Future*, Shirley Roberts identifies nine traits of tomorrow's consumer. She states that consumers will be

- Far less homogeneous
- Independent thinkers who seek control over their lives
- More educated and sophisticated
- Pursuers of higher quality of life
- Extremely demanding
- Optimistic, but well grounded in reality
- Seekers of new experiences and innovation
- Pursuers of wellness and environmentalism
- Aging, but more active

Given these traits, it is imperative that companies shift from managing a brand or company to managing a customer, a customer who will proceed through different life stages, lifestyles, and income levels. In doing so, the emphasis that has already been placed on targeted marketing strategies will continue, but at a more rapid pace and a more individualistic way.

How a company communicates with customers will continue to change. Rather than rely solely on mass advertising campaigns, greater emphasis will be placed on targeted media that reach narrowly defined audiences and on the Internet, since it reaches customers one at a time. Kraft Canada is one company that is capitalizing on database marketing techniques and Internet communications to bond better with its customers.

Kraft prides itself on being a provider of simple food solutions; its products (Kraft Dinner, Miracle Whip, Shake 'n Bake and Minute Rice to name only a few) are ideally suited for a time-pressed society. As well, Kraft is a service provider—it provides information to customers on how to use its products when preparing meals. Consumers watch TV specials featuring Kraft kitchen experts to learn how to cook basic recipes and nearly a million Canadians get its *What's Cooking* magazine in the mail. The magazine is full of suggestions, includes obvious plugs for Kraft brands, and features the kitchen experts at Kraft who develop the recipes. Hundreds of thousands receive recipes weekly via e-mail, as well as visiting Canada's number-one food Web site (www.kraftcanada.com).

Consumers buy Kraft brands because they've talked to someone there, because Kraft listens, and

and triggers as do English-speaking Canadians, nor do they watch the average Canadian television programming. As consumers, Francophone Quebecers, as a whole, tend to be characterized by: (1) their positive cultural values of family loyalty and pride; (2) their emotional rather than rational decision-making behaviour; and (3) their unique social- and community-driven leisure behaviour.[19] Marketers must recognize such differences and develop marketing programs that lend themselves to the Quebecers' value structure. For additional information about the uniqueness of the French Quebec market refer to Figure 4.10.

In the context of marketing, francophone Quebecers, by and large, tend to be more emotional than English Canadians and to respond to different stimuli. Brand, service, and selection are decided on an emotional basis more than on a purely rational one. Marketers who understand that the values of Quebecers are different recognize that these consumers seek different benefits from a product. Therefore, a solid advantage must be established first, and then, to maintain loyalty, the advantage must

because Kraft "gets me." Such a tight relationship with customers is the result of a recently implemented direct marketing strategy. It wanted to understand its customers better, to engage them in one-to-one dialogue, and build loyalty. According to Carl Nanni, executive vice-president marketing services at Kraft (pictured below), "Customers are crying out for closer relationships so that is what we're providing." Current technology allows Kraft to get at its consumers' needs and wants better, and deliver more individual solutions quicker and cheaper.

Kraft isn't neglecting mass advertising but sees the CRM program and brand advertising as complementary. The strengths of the brands and their corporate name (being synonymous with food) are built into the customer relationship management program. The unifying strategy across all media is "Family, Food. Simple." Kraft consistently delivers on their promises so customers know exactly what to expect.

Kraft is a leader in this area while other packaged goods companies are struggling with how to integrate the Internet and other direct marketing techniques. Kraft has found a way to align itself with an increasingly sophisticated consumer who has a greater need for knowledge, simplicity, improved quality of life, and individualized attention.

Kraft's implementation of direct marketing programs and customer relationship management programs reflects an innovative philosophy for such a big organization. The company clearly recognized a need to change its ways of doing business if it was to continue to be successful. Many of Kraft's direct competitors will have to play catch up if they are to survive in the packaged-goods marketing jungle.

Adapted from Leslie Young, "One Bite at a Time," Marketing Direct, November 5, 2001, pp. 10, 11, Eun-Mi (Liz) Adams, "The big piece of the mosaic," *Marketing*, June 21, 1999, p. 16; and Shirley Roberts, "The new consumer," *Marketing*, April 13, 1998, pp. 12-13.

Photograph of Carl Nanni courtesy of Kraft Canada Inc.

be communicated in a manner that will have an impact on the francophone Quebec consumer. Quebecers want products that are like them and that respect the fact that they are different.

Recognizing the importance of humour in the lives of Quebecers paid huge dividends for Pepsi-Cola. Pepsi has employed French comedian Claude Meunier in a long-running advertising campaign that sends Quebecers laughing all the way to the Pepsi cooler. One recent television ad shows Meunier in a convenience store stocked with nothing but Pepsi-Cola. The Meunier campaign is unique in the Pepsi system, and it is the longest-standing campaign and longest-standing celebrity endorsement in the history of the brand. As a result of the campaign, Pepsi has gone from a number two position in Quebec to outselling Coke by two to one.[20]

Quebec, it seems, is a society that thrives on local heroes, whether they are from the world of sports, arts, business, or even politics. Quebecers will elevate to hero status anyone who is seen as contributing in a big way to their uniqueness. Therefore, marketing

Figure 4.10

The Uniqueness of the French Quebec Market

A decision that many marketing executives must make is whether or not to develop unique marketing strategies for the Quebec market. Are the language and cultural differences significant enough to justify such an investment? Here are just a few of the unique characteristics of the French Quebec market.

Attitudes and Opinions

	French Quebec %	Rest of Canada %
I enjoy keeping fit	59	48
I prefer low-fat or light foods	43	33
I consider myself to be a risk-adverse investor	42	18
I like to dine at fine restaurants as often as possible	41	26
I seldom make a financial move without expert advice	31	22
I am more of a spender than a saver	22	32
A career should be an individual's first priority	20	34
Health-related issues are given too much attention these days	39	27

Personal Consumption

	French Quebec %	Rest of Canada %
Buy lottery tickets	68	56
Drink wine	60	47
Own personal life insurance	49	27
Shop at specialty stores for fruit and vegetables	45	23
Ride a bike	44	28
Use a cell phone	11	23
Own a swimming pool	13	4
Eat snack cakes	55	20

Based only on the above statistics, it can be observed that French Quebecers probably enjoy a higher level of fitness than the rest of Canada, are conservative investors, like to save rather than spend, place family ahead of career, like to indulge in fine foods, wines, and snacks, and are less likely to use a cell phone. You be the judge. Should unique marketing strategies be devised for this market?

Source: Adapted from Andrea Haman, "Quebecers snub diets and compacts for port and luxury cars," *Strategy*, April 9, 2001, figures cited from PMB 2000 (two-year database).

managers who, from the outset, plan strategies with Quebec in mind and who implement programs that are culturally relevant will garner success.

What about the rest of Canada? Is Western Canada different than Central Canada and Eastern Canada? There are differences but it's the significance of the differences that dictate the need for unique regional marketing strategies. From an annual survey conducted by the Print Measurement Bureau it appears that Westerners are closer to Torontonians than either group would like to admit, but what distinctions there are seem to hark back to pioneer stereotypes.

To illustrate, consider the nature of alcohol and beer consumption. In Western Canada more rye whiskey (21 percent of population) is consumed compared to Toronto (16 percent of population). Slightly more Westerners partake of beer, but what they drink beer from is revealing. In the West the sheer practicality of canned beer is embraced by 30 percent of the population compared to only 12 percent in Toronto. Such knowledge could play a role in the development of new advertising campaigns for beer brands, at least in terms of the type of container displayed in the ads.

The spending habits of the two regions tend to mirror consumer behaviour. Toronto households spend more on food, clothing, and personal care products than those in Calgary or Vancouver. Westerners make up for the shortfall by spending more on recreation, alcohol, and tobacco.[21]

TECHNOLOGICAL INFLUENCES

Several factors are combining to make dramatic changes in the way in which consumers buy goods and services. These factors include the growing numbers of time-pressed consumers, the availability of information through the Internet, and transaction convenience offered by retailers and banks.

To illustrate, consider the role of plastic cards in the purchasing process. According to a recent study, 67 percent of people prefer to use debit or credit cards to make purchases rather than cash or cheques. Interac has had a profound and positive impact on the daily lives of Canadians. People can leave home with their keys and their bank card, and know that they don't have to worry about anything else. A decade ago, a consumer would go to a bank and withdraw $500 to spend over two weeks. When ABMs were introduced in the early 1980s, the $500 transaction was replaced by five $100 withdrawals. Today, consumers will make several debit card purchases rather than going to the ABM. It is technology that is changing our purchasing behaviour.

Data compiled by the financial industry verify these changes. In Canada, in 2001, there were 2.24 billion debit card transactions worth $94.9 billion, compared with 185 million transactions worth $9.4 billion in 1994. The preference for using plastic is expected to continue in the next decade as the availability of automatic banking machines expands—they are available at convenience stores, gas stations, hockey rinks, and restaurants. Canadians continue to be world leaders in debit and ABM usage.[22] Consumers' excessive use of debit cards is somewhat bewildering as they work to the advantage of the banks. With credit cards at least there is a grace period before interest rates kick in. We have yet to embrace smart cards—plastic cards with an embedded microchip that can be programmed to carry electronic cash—but their acceptance is only a matter of time and convenience.

ECONOMIC INFLUENCES

The economy directly or indirectly influences the attitudes, values, and lifestyles of Canadian society. There is little doubt that the cyclical nature of the economy shapes the purchase decisions of consumers. When the economy is in recession, for example, a situation where inflation, unemployment, and interest rates may be on the rise, the discretionary income of consumers may be low. Consequently, major purchases will be delayed, and consumers will make products they do have last longer; new purchases of items, such as a larger house, a renovation, a car, or a major appliance, may be placed on hold. Marketing organizations must be prepared to adjust their marketing strategies as the economy enters various cyclical stages (refer to Chapter 2) and as consumers' attitudes and perceptions change.

Conversely, if the economy is booming, consumers are more likely to purchase more goods and services. The construction and housing industries are good examples of markets that accommodate Canada's economic shifts. When mortgage rates decline, the cost of carrying a mortgage drops; therefore, there is a frenzy as first-time buyers enter the market, and current homeowners consider trading up to larger accommodations, even though the steady demand forces the price of housing up. Generally, business organizations remain conservative in hard times and are aggressive in good times.

Summary

Consumers, through their decision to purchase a product or service, determine an organization's success. Since organizations cannot control consumers, it is essential that they understand them so that they can adapt their strategies to consumers' thinking and behaviour.

The consumer decision-making process involves five distinct stages. These stages include problem recognition, information search, evaluation of alternatives, the purchase decision, and post-purchase behaviour.

This chapter discussed the dynamics of consumer behaviour and illustrated how marketing organizations can use behavioural information to advantage when developing marketing strategies. The study of consumer behaviour deals with why people buy the products and services they do and explains why two or more people behave differently or similarly. It has shown that purchase decisions are primarily based on four major influences: cultural, social, personal, and psychological. As well, external influences, such as technology and the economy, play a role in shaping consumers' buying behaviour. Marketing organizations possessing knowledge of the influences on behaviour are adept at developing target market profiles and at using these profiles to prepare marketing strategies that trigger a response from the target markets.

Key Terms

attitudes 96

beliefs 97

cognitive dissonance 91

consumer behaviour 87

culture 106

double targeting 103

evaluation 90

evoked set 90

family life cycle 104

hierarchy of needs 92

information search 89

lifestyle 97

motives 92

needs 92

perceived risk 96

perception 96

personality 95

problem recognition 88

Review Questions

1. Briefly explain the steps in the consumer decision process.

2. Briefly explain what cognitive dissonance is.

3. Identify the five levels of the hierarchy of needs. What is the essence of Maslow's theory of needs and motivation? Provide two new examples that demonstrate the application of needs and motivation theory.

4. Briefly explain the four components of the self-concept theory and illustrate how they have an influence on marketing strategy. Provide two new examples that demonstrate the application of this theory.

5. Explain the difference between selective exposure, selective perception, and selective retention.

6. Explain how an understanding of consumer attitudes is essential before developing a marketing strategy. Provide an example that has considered the importance of understanding consumer attitudes.

7. What is double targeting? Provide a new example of a brand or company that practises double targeting.

8. What role does the family life cycle play in the development of a marketing strategy?

9. What is the difference between culture and subculture? What are the implications of culture and subculture on marketing activity?

Discussion And Application Questions

1. Compare and contrast your own behaviour when making the following purchase decisions:
   a) A new business suit for an important job interview
   b) An audio component set
   c) A case of beer

2. "Marketing strategies that appeal to our desires are more effective than those appealing to current needs." Discuss. Provide some examples to justify your viewpoint.

3. Examine the role of reference groups in the purchase of the following products:
   a) Blue jeans
   b) Personal computers
   c) Chocolate bars
   d) Cosmetics

4. On the basis of your knowledge of the hierarchy of needs and the theory of motivation, what level of needs do the following products appeal to? (Consider the slogan and anything you may know about the product's advertising.)
   a) Molson Canadian "I AM Canadian"
   b) Nike "Just Do It"
   c) Apple "Think Different"
   d) Harley-Davidson "Things Are Different on a Harley"
   e) Lexus "The relentless pursuit of perfection"
   f) Gatorade "Is it In You"

5. Assess some of the points raised in the chapter regarding regional Canadian markets. Conduct some secondary research on this issue and determine

the practicality of implementing regional marketing strategies in Canada. Is it worthwhile or not?

6. Refer to the vignette "Shifting Behaviour and Customer Relationship Management." The vignette suggests that future consumers will be more educated, sophisticated, intelligent, and demanding. If you were responsible for marketing any one of the following products: Coca-Cola, Mazda Miata, or Zellers, what strategies would you recommend to attract and retain customers?

E-Assignment

1. Assume you have made a decision to purchase a laptop computer. Gathering information about the various brands will be an important first step before you decide what make and model to buy. Using only the Internet (e.g., search engines, company Web sites and online publications), compare and contrast three different brands. Once you have completed your investigation, identify the advantages and disadvantages of using the Internet for information-gathering purposes.

2. Find the Goldfarb Consultants Web site on the Internet. At the site, go to the Interactive page and accurately fill in the psychographic profile survey. When you have completed the survey, ask for the results. You should receive a summary psychographic profile of yourself. Also, refer to the textbook (see Figure 4.7) for a summary profile. Is this how you perceive yourself? Comment briefly on what you think of the survey.

Endnotes

1 James F. Engel, David T. Kollatt, and Roger D. Blackwell, *Consumer Behaviour*, 2nd Edition (New York: Holt Rinehart and Winston, 1973), p. 5.

2 "General Social Survey: Internet Use, *Daily*, Statistics Canada, March 26, 2001.

3 "e-Tire kickers," *Marketing*, March 27, 2000, p. 30.

4 Abraham H. Maslow, *Personality & Motivation* (New York: Harper & Row Publishers, 1954), p. 370.

5 John Douglas, George Field, and Lawrence Tarpey, *Human Behaviour in Marketing* (Columbus, OH: Charles E. Merrill Publishing, 1987), p. 5.

6 Peter Vamos, "Manufacturers push boomers' health buttons," *Strategy*, February 12, 2001, pp. 1, 12.

7 Ibid.

8 David Olive, "Gap's Mickey Drexler: Fashion victim," *Toronto Star*, December 19, 2001, pp. E1, E11.

9 Peter Vamos, "Manufacturers push boomers' health buttons," *Strategy*, February 12, 2001, pp. 1, 12.

10 Philip Kotler, Gordon McDougall, and Gary Armstrong, *Marketing*, Canadian Edition (Scarborough, ON: Prentice-Hall Inc., 1988), p. 142.

11 Richard Linnett, "Reebok re-brands for hip-hop crowd," *Advertising Age*, January 28, 2002, pp. 3, 27.

12 Astrid Van Den Broek, "What women really want," *Marketing*, July 19/26, 1999, p. 18.

13 Sean Silcoff, "Winners take everything," *Canadian Business*, September 24, 1999, pp. 47-50.

14 Tyler Hamilton, "Mobile phone use to skyrocket: Study," *Globe and Mail*, September 16, 1999, p. B5.

15 Julie Look, "Tweens are media hogs," *Strategy*, January 1, 2001, p. 28.

16 "The end of the boom," *Marketing*, February 5, 2000, p. 40.

17 Malcolm Dunlop and Christine Comi, "Multicultural explosion," *Strategy*, February 11, 2002, p. 25.

18 David Showcroft and Mike Farrell, "Peer pressure a huge factor in success of brands," *Strategy*, January 3, 1998, p. 34.

19 "What Quebec wants," *Sales and Marketing Management in Canada*, July 1991, p. 16.

20 Lara Mills, "Campaign with Legs," *Marketing*, May 15, 2000, pp. 12, 13.

21 "Getting to know Western Canada," *Strategy*, October 8, 2001, p. 21.

22 David Steinhart, "Popularity of direct payment making money obsolete," www.financialpost.com, February 12, 2002.

CHAPTER

5

Business-to-Business Marketing and Organizational Buying Behaviour

After studying this chapter, you will be able to

1. Identify the types of customers comprising the business-to-business marketplace.
2. Describe the unique characteristics of organizational buying behaviour.
3. Explain the role that partnerships play in business-to-business marketing.
4. Describe the influence of e-procurement practices on business-to-business markets.
5. Identify the various types of organizational buying decisions.
6. Identify the steps involved in the organizational decision process.
7. Describe the unique characteristics of the government market.

In business marketing, organizations market goods and services to other organizations. Marketing strategies used in the business-to-business market are quite different from strategies used in the consumer market. Firms succeed in the business-to-business market when they fully understand the complex buying process that is involved and the criteria that are used to evaluate purchase decisions. Today, suppliers in business-to-business marketing must also embrace the e-commerce model as more and more buying organizations continue to adopt automated and collaborative purchasing models. By doing so, they are able to reduce costs and improve customer service.

The business-to-business market comprises business as well as industrial, government, institutional, and professional segments. In serving these diverse markets, organizations must identify the unique demands and needs of each, and then develop responsive marketing strategies showing how their products or services will resolve a special problem or satisfy a particular need.

This chapter illustrates the characteristics that influence organizational buying behaviour.

The Business-to-Business Market

business-to-business market

1.
Identify the types of customers comprising the business-to-business marketplace.

The **business-to-business market** comprises individuals in an organization who are responsible for purchasing goods and services that the organization needs to produce a product or service, promote an idea, or produce an income. The business-to-business (or B2B) market can be divided into five distinct buying groups: business and industry, governments, institutions, wholesalers and retailers, and professions.

BUSINESS AND INDUSTRY

Much of Canada's economic progress in the 20th century was due to growth in manufacturing. However, since the 1960s, services have contributed an increasing share of total output and employment. Presently, service-producing industries represent about 70 percent of economic production and goods producing industries the remaining 30 percent. Among service industries the largest in terms of size are financial services (finance and insurance, real estate and renting and leasing) wholesale and retail trade, public administration, and educational services. Manufacturing makes up more than half the goods producing sector. Other goods producers include agriculture, mining, and oil and construction industries.[1]

outsourcing

Growth in service-related jobs is a reflection of a strong investment in technology in industries, such as trade, finance, and business services (e.g., computer services, communications services, and engineering and scientific services). Also, a shift among manufacturers towards outsourcing has created growth in services. **Outsourcing** is defined as the contracting of services or functions previously done in-house. For example, most companies at one time purchased photocopying machines. Employees would do their own copying or, if large quantities were required on a continuous basis, a separate department would be responsible for printing needs. This is a service that a specialist like Xerox Canada Ltd. provides, for a fee. Xerox has positioned itself as a document services specialist (Figure 5.1). Other services that can be contracted out include data processing, advertising, legal services, and e-business transaction services. The demand for specialists in these and other service areas has grown immensely.

Figure 5.1

Xerox Communicates Its Document Services to Companies Interested in Outsourcing

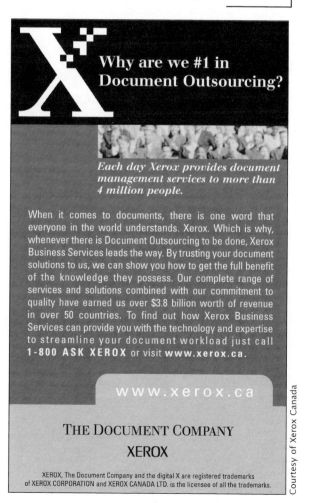

Courtesy of Xerox Canada

Business and industrial organizations are grouped under the categories of users, original equipment manufacturers, wholesalers and retailers, and service businesses. For a brief description of these categories, see Figure 5.2.

GOVERNMENTS

Collectively, the federal, provincial, and municipal governments form Canada's largest buying group. Governments tend to have a specialized buying procedure involving detailed order specifications and tender submissions from potential suppliers. The government market is discussed in greater detail later in the chapter.

INSTITUTIONAL MARKETS

The third major buying group is the institutional market, which includes hospitals, restaurants, and educational establishments. These customers require a variety of products and services from potential suppliers. The government funds hospitals and educational establishments, so operating objectives are not based on profit. Their motivation for buying is based on improving health care or quality of life. That said, budgets in this sector are not what they used to be so buyers actively search for lower cost alternatives. The restaurant segment represents opportunity for manufacturers to develop private label products.

WHOLESALERS AND RETAILERS

Business organizations use wholesalers and retailers to resell their goods and services. Typically, a wholesaler purchases finished products (e.g., a grocery wholesaler, such as

Figure 5.2

Categories of Business and Industry Organizations

Users

Organizations that purchase products to produce other products (e.g., a firm purchases capital equipment, such as machinery, in order to manufacture products on an assembly line).

Original Equipment Manufacturers (OEMs)

Companies purchasing industrial products that are incorporated directly into other products (e.g., General Motors is an OEM because it purchases finished radios, spark plugs, tires, and other products to install in its automobiles).

Wholesalers and Retailers

Intermediaries that purchase products to sell to other intermediaries or to final users (Safeway, The Bay, Canadian Tire).

Service Businesses

A variety of businesses including leisure and personal services, food and beverage services, accommodation services, and business services (e.g., Royal Bank, London Life, McDonald's, Sheraton Hotels, Air Canada). Collectively, these organizations need a variety of goods and services in order to conduct their business operations.

National Grocers, will purchase goods from suppliers, such as Kraft, General Mills, and Procter & Gamble), hold those goods in inventory in their warehouse, and then ship them to retailers (e.g., IGA) as demand dictates. In the grocery industry, it is quite common for national marketing organizations, such as Kraft or Procter & Gamble, to present a sales plan to their key account customers (e.g., Loblaws, Safeway, Sobeys) at the start of a year. At that time, marketing support from the selling organization and volume commitments from the customers are negotiated and agreed to.

PROFESSIONS

The professional market consists of doctors, lawyers, accountants, architects, engineers, and so on. The products that professionals buy usually improve the efficiency of their practice; for example, the purchase of microcomputers and other communications equipment enhances productivity in an accounting office or law office.

It should be recognized that these four buying groups (business and industry, governments, institutions, and professionals) may require the same or similar products and services, but their needs and reasons why they buy are quite different. For this reason, marketing organizations must develop precise marketing strategies for each segment of the market.

The Characteristics of Organizational Buying Behaviour

organizational buying

2.
Describe the unique characteristics of organizational buying behaviour.

When a marketing firm develops a marketing mix that it can use to approach business customers, it should understand the elements that influence the decision-making process in organizations. **Organizational buying** may be defined as the decision-making process by which firms establish what products they need to purchase and then identify, evaluate, and select a brand and a supplier for those products.

Business markets are quite different from consumer markets (Figure 5.3). Their principal distinctions are that they have fewer buyers than consumer markets; the buyers tend to be concentrated near each other; the market presents different kinds of demand; the buying criteria are practical; and a formal buying process is used. Organizations involved in business-to-business marketing have accepted the concept of relationship marketing more quickly than have consumer goods companies. Through cooperation and the implementation of intranets and extranets that link separate businesses together by computer, efficiencies in buying and selling are being achieved. The concept of e-procurement (discussed later in this chapter) is growing rapidly. Let us examine the characteristics of organizational buying behaviour in detail.

NUMBER OF BUYERS

There are fewer buyers or customers in the business-to-business market than there are in consumer markets, but the few buyers have immense buying power. To illustrate, the "Big Three" domestic automobile manufacturers (General Motors, Ford, and Chrysler) dominate their industry, just as two large Canadian breweries (Molson and Labatt) dominate the beer industry. Firms like these are few in number but purchase incredible quantities of products (e.g., the new tires required by the automakers and beer bottles required by the breweries). In the business market, the dollar value of individual purchases is much larger than it is in the consumer market (e.g., the value of a capital good, such as a computer, compared with a consumer shopping good, such as a dress shirt). For this reason, marketing organizations will spend more on marketing communications, particularly personal selling, to reach these customers.

Figure 5.3

Some Differences between Consumer and Business-to-Business Marketing

Consumer Marketing	Business-to-Business Marketing
Product	
Products are standardized, purchased frequently, and marketed by brand name.	Products are complex and marketed on the basis of a combination of price, quality, and service. Products are purchased less frequently.
Price	
Distributors are offered a list price and a series of discounts. Savings are passed on to consumers.	The same as consumer marketing, plus extensive price negotiation or contract bidding.
Marketing Communications	
Mainly advertising, with support from sales promotion and direct marketing techniques. Personal selling used in the channel of distribution.	Mainly personal selling, with support from sales promotion and direct marketing techniques. Mass advertising is now more common than in previous times.
Distribution	
Mainly traditional channels—manufacturer to wholesaler to retailer to consumer.	Short, direct channels due to need for personal selling and high dollar value of transaction.
Purchase Decision	
Made by an individual or household members.	Made by influence centres (users and non-users) and buying committees.
Buying Behaviour	
Consumers more subject to emotional appeals that play on concerns about image, status, prestige.	Organizational buyers are more rational due to the formality of the purchase decision process.

Due to restructuring in many large organizations, a phenomenon caused by the poor economy in the early 1990s, small business customers now represent greater opportunity. Small businesses are actually creating the majority of new jobs in Canada. Recognizing this trend along with the fact that small business represented 25 to 30 percent of PC sales in Canada, Compaq gave the market special attention. Compaq tailored certain product lines for small business and developed a distinct promotional campaign aimed at that segment.[2]

LOCATION OF BUYERS

Business markets tend to concentrate by area; the Quebec City to Windsor corridor is a popular location for manufacturers. Ontario and Quebec account for 70 percent of the nation's manufacturing establishments, 76 percent of the value of goods manufactured, and 76 percent of people employed in manufacturing industries.[3] This area is also the centre of banking and financial services in Canada. Resource-based industries, such as agriculture, forestry, and fishing, dominate other regions.

To identify and locate potential target markets, marketing firms utilize the **Standard Industrial Classification (SIC)** system. The SIC is a numbering system, originally established by the federal governments of Canada and the United States. It has been modified due to the free trade agreement that now includes Mexico and has been renamed the **North American Industry Classification System (NAICS)**. Data mining techniques allow a supplier to track down key prospects who can utilize its goods and services (customers with buying potential) within an industry category.

The standard industrial classification system subdivides the main classifications into major industry segments; for example, a major classification may be retail trade, of which there are 163 270 businesses. The system then subdivides retail trade into categories such as general merchandise stores, department stores, variety stores, and miscellaneous general merchandise stores. Further subdivision will identify firms by sales volume and number of employees. The major benefit of the SIC system is that by providing lists of the customers within a target market, it makes it easier for the marketer to develop strategies for reaching the target market.

North American
Industry
Classification
System (NAICS)
www.statcan.ca/
english/Subjects/
Standard

The combination of fewer buyers, with higher dollar value, and geographic concentration makes personal selling an attractive and practical way to market goods and services to these markets despite the high costs of such an activity. However, other promotional techniques, such as direct mail, telemarketing, and the Internet, now play an expanding role in helping firms penetrate the business-to-business marketplace. The e-commerce business-to-business marketplace (as compared to business-to-consumer transactions) presently dominates online purchase transactions. As of 2001, B2B e-commerce amounted to $30 billion, which is five times as much as the business-to consumer e-commerce.[4]

DEMAND CHARACTERISTICS

There are two types of demand in the business-to-business market: derived demand and joint (shared) demand. **Derived demand** is a concept that states that the demand for products sold in the business-to-business market is actually derived from consumer demand, that is, from demand ultimately created by the final user. To illustrate this relationship, consider what happens when soft drink manufacturers switched from steel cans to aluminum cans. As beverage manufacturers, such as Coca-Cola, Pepsi-Cola, and Molson, moved to widespread use of the aluminum can, which consumers wanted, the manufacturer's demand for products produced by aluminum manufacturers increased dramatically. At the same time demand fell for glass and steel containers so manufacturers of these products were affected negatively.

derived demand

Pepsi
www.pepsi.com

**joint (shared)
demand**

Joint or **shared demand** occurs when industrial products can only be used in conjunction with others—when the production and marketing of one product is dependent on another. This happens when the various parts needed for a finished product may arrive from various sources to be assembled at one central location. To manufacture Maxwell House coffee, for example, Kraft Canada would need coffee beans (probably imported from South America), plastic lids (from a plastics manufacturer who produces the lids to Kraft's specifications), glass or plastic jars (from a glass manufacturer or plastics manufacturer), paper labels (from a printing shop), and a cardboard shipping case (from another paper products supplier).

If any of these components is unavailable, demand for the other components will decrease, and the production and marketing of Maxwell House coffee will be adversely affected. Phenomena such as strikes and natural disasters that make certain items scarce can also lessen demand for other items. For this reason, business marketers often have alternative sources of supply available. The use of electronic ordering systems (customer relationship management programs) also helps ensure a steady flow of inventory through the channel of distribution.

THE BUYING CRITERIA ARE PRACTICAL

In business and industry, the buying criteria tend to be practical and rationally pursued. Although impractical or irrational motives may sometimes be present, they generally play a small role. Quality, price, and service form the basis for buying decisions in business and industry.

vendor analysis

Central to the buying procedures of organizations is a vendor analysis. A **vendor analysis** entails an evaluation of potential suppliers. They are assessed based on their technological ability, consistency in meeting product specifications, overall quality, on-time delivery, their ability to provide needed quantity, and their reputation in their industry. How well a supplier rates in these areas affects its chances of selection, but price also plays a key role in the decision. Before signing a deal, the buyer may request bids based on predetermined specifications or negotiate an acceptable price from a supplier that the vendor analysis indicates is acceptable.

Let us examine these criteria in more detail:

1. *Price* Price is usually evaluated in conjunction with other buying goals. The lowest price is not always accepted. A company will consider the differential advantages offered by vendors and evaluate price in the context of other purchase criteria. Where the cash outlay is significant, cost is viewed from a long-term perspective. Potential long-term savings as a result of the purchase are weighed against the high purchase cost in the short term.

2. *Quality* Business customers look for sources of supply that can provide the same unvarying quality with each order. Since a supplier's product becomes part of a new product during manufacturing, it could affect the quality of the final product if the supplier's product were inconsistent in quality. Generally, when business customers assess price-quality relationships, they do not sacrifice quality for price.

3. *Service and Services Offered* Customers frequently review a supplier's reputation for keeping its current customers satisfied. They do so by contacting other customers to see how well the supplier performs the service function. The primary concern of the buying organization is that repair and replacement services be readily available when needed. The sales representative will play a key role in managing the customer relationship.

4. *Continuity of Supply* Customers are concerned about the long-term availability of a product or service. They want to know how reliable the supplier is in meeting customer demand. To maintain a steady source of supply, customers often deal with numerous suppliers, knowing that such factors as strikes could halt the flow of a product from any one supplier. Further, the location of potential suppliers is now less important in the decision-making process. Companies now search the world for suppliers who can best combine the qualities of price, quality, and delivery. In the automobile industry, North American suppliers must compete for contracts with

suppliers from the Far East and Europe. The presence and use of the Internet has facilitated the ongoing search for new, better and less costly suppliers. Refer to the section on e-procurement for more details.

The advertisement in Figure 5.4 shows how Clarica appeals to business customers. Clarica, a leading insurance company, delivers a message about leadership and reputation. Its position of leadership is reinforced when it says, "Your clear choice for group benefits." It leaves an impression regarding product and service quality.

Clarica Communicates Its Leadership Position and Reputation

Figure 5.4

It's about relationships

Our benefits solutions start with one simple ingredient – clear dialogue with our customers.

Through dialogue we learn and understand our customers' needs.
And our customers get to know and understand what we can deliver.

It's all about relationships. Relationships built on listening,
understanding each other, and working closely together.

Together we'll find solutions to your benefits needs.
Contact Jeff Kinch, National Marketing, at 1-888-588-5650 or e-mail jeff.kinch@clarica.com

Clarica. Your clear choice for group benefits.

Investment and insurance solutions - Since 1870

™ Trademark of Clarica Life Insurance Company

www.clarica.com

A FORMAL BUYING PROCESS IS FOLLOWED

In many business organizations, one individual has the authority to sign the purchase order, but many other individuals may influence the purchase decision. There are two primary causes of this situation in modern business. First, businesses today often utilize **buying committees**, which bring individuals together to share the responsibility of making the purchase decision. Second, businesses may hold meetings of various informed groups of people in order to arrive at a purchase decision. This informal approach, involving several people in the organization, is called a **buying centre**.

buying committees

buying centre

1. *Buying Committees* To illustrate the concept of a buying committee, we will assume that a firm is considering the purchase of a million-dollar piece of production-line equipment. Since the financial ramifications are significant, it is imperative that the best possible decision is made. Consequently, the firm appoints a committee consisting of key personnel from Production, Engineering, Finance, Marketing, and Purchasing so that the decision can be evaluated from a variety of angles. Theoretically, such a decision-making process is very rational, and the participants are comforted to know that a costly purchase decision is a shared one.

2. *Buying Centres* In buying centres, which are more informal than buying committees, the individuals involved have certain roles. Researchers have identified five specific roles:

   Users—those who use the product (e.g., laptop computers or cell phones used by traveling business people)

   Influencers—those who assist in defining specifications for what is needed (e.g., an engineer designs a production line)

   Buyers—those with the authority and responsibility to select suppliers and negotiate with them (e.g., a purchasing agent)

   Deciders—those with formal or informal power to select the actual supplier (e.g., a high-dollar-value purchase of technical equipment may ultimately be the responsibility of a vice-president of manufacturing)

   Gatekeepers—those who control the flow of information to others in the centre (e.g., a purchasing agent may block certain information from reaching influencers and deciders).

   From a marketing perspective, it must be determined who on the committee or within the buying centre has the most influence. Once that is known, the best means of communicating with the influence centre must be determined. What role should personal selling, sales promotion, advertising, and direct marketing have in the overall strategy, and what priority should each have?

CENTRALIZED PURCHASING

In today's economic environment, buying organizations are looking for the best possible prices and value for dollars spent. Consequently, many firms have developed centralized purchasing systems in order to secure better price discounts based on volume purchases. For example, the Bay, Zellers, and Home Outfitters, all owned by Hudson's Bay Company, have formed one large buying division that purchases for each retail division. In these situations, marketers must deal with just a few buyers, all at a high level of management. Hudson's Bay also links hundreds of Bay, Zellers, and Home Outfitters vendors to buying groups for the interchange of electronic procurement documents.

assortment

Retailers are concerned with offering consumers a balanced assortment of merchandise. **Assortment** refers to the variety of products—the types, models, and styles of product that meet a retailer's target market needs. Assortment decisions are based on how well the supplier's product "fits in" with the merchandise mix. Decisions on what product lines to carry and how much inventory to stock are made easier by sophisticated computer-controlled systems. Working from the electronic cash register at the point-of-sale, a retail buyer can track the movement of goods in all retail outlets on a daily basis. For many retail organizations, automatic computer ordering is now the standard practice. Such systems consider product movement, desired inventory levels, and delivery time. Where relationship management models exist, an order request from a buyer will automatically trigger delivery from a supplier.

PERSONAL CHARACTERISTICS

Business buyers are just as human as other consumers; thus, the more knowledge a marketer has about the specific buyer, the more impact the marketing message can have. To address the needs of certain personalities, emotional appeals centred on status and prestige may be included in overall marketing strategies, along with ordinary rational appeals. Marketers also recognize that many business decisions are influenced or made in social settings such as on the golf course, over a drink after a squash match, or at a sports or theatre event of some kind. Entertaining customers is an essential aspect of business-to-business marketing.

RELATIONSHIPS ARE SOUGHT

In today's marketplace, organizations that deal directly with one another (suppliers, manufacturers, and distributors) are doing so in a more cooperative, less competitive way. Programs are being established to evaluate the flow and use of goods and services through the channel of distribution. The aim of a partnership is to devise and implement strategies that will produce mutual benefits for all participants. The concept of building relationships is discussed in detail in the next section.

Integration and Partnering in Business-to-Business Marketing

customer relation-ship management (CRM)

3.
Explain the role that partnerships play in business-to-business marketing.

The manner in which business-to-business organizations do business with each other is changing. What is becoming increasingly more common is the trend towards buyer-seller cooperation and the formation of partnerships. Earlier in the text, this partnering was referred to as **customer relationship management (CRM)**. There are numerous other expressions used to describe CRM-relationship marketing, strategic alliances, partnerships, and value-added marketing. Movement towards the formation of partnerships is due, in part, to the rationalizing and restructuring of operations that firms have gone through in recent times. In the process of evaluating business practices, firms have discovered newer and more efficient methods. As well, the increasing level of competition between similar products has contributed to the partnership concept, since it can give an otherwise undistinguished product an edge in the marketplace.

Acceptance of this concept has created a fundamental change in the seller-buyer relationship. The essential ingredient is an integrated tie between customers and their suppliers. This means that members of a channel of distribution create closer links among themselves (Figure 5.5). When partnering is applied to marketing a business or industrial product, the marketer must acquire more detailed information about its customers and their operations. The marketer must be more familiar with the role its product plays in the customer's operation. Therefore, collecting information about the customer and their operations is an essential element in the marketing process.

Partnering is also changing the nature of communications with customers. Salespeople still play a key role, but rather than calling on customers individually, **project teams** are being formed to deal with customers' needs more effectively. Under the leadership of an Account Manager (sales representative) the team may include customer service people, engineers, traffic specialists, information systems specialists, and so on. Essentially, a team from the marketing organization is dealing with a team (buying committee) of the customer. The two teams work together to achieve common goals. They devise programs that are compatible so that all parties benefit. As an example, consider that Federal Express' core business is the delivery of orders for many companies. Now, it will go one step further by offering to take over a client's entire logistics system, from warehousing and inventory management to order processing and customer billing. In effect, it assumes responsibility for managing a component of the customer's business (this is the concept of outsourcing, discussed earlier).

In the partnership process, companies seek partners anywhere in the world. General Motors was the first automobile manufacturer to adopt a global-supply sourcing policy to strengthen its worldwide buying power. GM's goal is to obtain components at the best possible price from suppliers. Such a relationship calls for long-term contracts—some for the life of the model—so that suppliers are guaranteed the necessary volume to support their capital investments that will reduce costs and improve quality. For General Motors and their suppliers, the goal is to design, produce, and market a better-quality car in a shorter space of time.[6] If the goal is achieved, the partners prosper financially.

Another form of partnering is frequently referred to as reverse marketing. **Reverse marketing** is an effort by organizational buyers to build relationships that shape suppliers' goods and services to fit the buyer's needs and those of its customers. The generic-label products and President's Choice (PC label) products marketed by Loblaws, Super

project teams

General Motors
www.gm.com

reverse marketing

Figure 5.5

Relationship Marketing Model-Business-to-Business Marketing Application

Suppliers ⇄ Manufacturer ⇄ Distributors ⇄ Consumers

- All parties collaborate to achieve common goals and satisfy the consumer
- Common goals include: inspiring brand loyalty
  developing new products
  efficient delivery
  parts and supplies cost savings
  service excellence
- A team approach is best; cooperation instead of competition in the channel of distribution

Valu, and other retailers in the Loblaws chain are an example of reverse marketing. Each of these products is designed to meet quality standards established by Loblaws. To retain the business, source manufacturers must maintain standards at all times. In other cases, companies request that suppliers constantly strive to improve the quality of products they market. Buying organizations will go as far as to monitor suppliers to ensure that continuous improvement programs are in place. Suppliers who fail to maintain the desired standards set by manufacturers could lose the supply contract.

Advancing technology and the ability to conduct the buying-selling process online are affecting the nature of supplier-buyer relationships in the business-to-business market. See the Marketing in Action vignette **Big 3 Automakers Form Internet Supply Chain** for insight into the partnership practices in the automobile industry.

Marketing in Action

Big 3 Automakers Form Internet Supply Chain

The potential applications of e-commerce extend to every facet of a business, from selling products and services to communicating with partners and suppliers, to providing training to employees. Quite simply, e-commerce is transforming the way in which business is conducted. The automobile industry, typically a slow moving industry, and the biggest member of the old economy, has embraced the Internet and is taking advantage of the cost efficiencies it offers.

The Big Three automakers, General Motors, Ford, and DaimlerChrysler AG, formed a worldwide parts-sourcing operation that involves $240 billion in annual spending. The buying system operates from one Internet portal and is the world's largest virtual market. Using the latest technology, this transaction system helps each company source its parts and supplies at the most favourable price and in a timely manner, leading to improved efficiency and cost savings. Essentially, these companies will operate better and faster, as will their suppliers, if they wish to retain the business. What is transpiring is a complete change in the way these companies do business.

The primary advantage of the system is that it gives the industry a powerful tool to buy and sell everything from hubcaps to paper clips, as well as collaborate on building automotive components. The venture will cut costs substantially and potentially generate billions of dollars in transaction fees. GM's Japanese partners-Isuzu, Subaru, and Suzuki, as well as Ford's Japanese affiliate, Mazda, are expected to join the network.

While it might seem that the industry is going soft in terms of competition, each company still has to sell its cars to consumers. The battle for market share and consumer preference will continue and perhaps even intensify as companies start offering better value. This unified supply system is designed to reduce costs. If it does, the consumer will benefit.

From a parts supplier's point of view, a company will have to be up to speed technologically, or it will be completely out of the loop. This is either an opportunity or a threat for automobile industry participants. There are about 60 000 suppliers that will have to re-invent their own business models if they wish to survive.

Adapted from "Big 3 automakers merge online supplier exchanges," *Toronto Star*, February 26, 2000, p. D5.

Courtesy: General Motors of Canada

E-PROCUREMENT

e-procurement

4.
Describe the influence of e-procurement practices on business-to-business markets.

Ariba Inc.
www.ariba.com

The Internet has spawned e-procurement buying opportunities. **E-procurement** is an Internet-based business-to-business marketplace through which participants are able to purchase supplies and services from each other. With improved efficiency, businesses can access procurement sites and services to get multiple bids, issue purchase orders and make payments. E-procurement has been growing as major companies, often in the same industry, seek to slash purchasing costs. The concept of e-procurement is the future for business-to business marketing organizations. As Robert Lent, senior vice-president and co-founder of Ariba Inc. suggests, "You'll either buy on a B2B market, sell on a B2B market, create a B2B market or be killed by a B2B market." He could be right when you consider what the telecommunications industry is doing. Nortel Networks and IBM Corp. and six other international technology companies banded together and established such a marketplace to buy and sell electronic equipment to and from one another.[7] Such a relationship shuts out other sources of supply.

Combining customer relationship management practices with e-procurement models fosters long-term relationships with buyers and sellers and presents a situation where participants are directly influenced by the decisions and actions of other participants.

The size of the e-commerce business-to-business market is presently $30 billion but that the market is expected to expand to as much as $275 billion by 2004.[8] Companies will either be part of the system or they will watch it unfold from the sidelines. Companies that have not joined in do so for valid reasons. Barriers to entry include suppliers being rooted in the Old Economy, the cost of adopting new technologies, e-security concerns, and the fact that purchasing managers aren't that knowledgeable about e-commerce. They feel submerged under a flood of new technologies and online solutions and simply don't know how to proceed. Companies classified as followers may not be able to catch up to the leaders who have quickly embraced technology.

As a way of easing into e-commerce practice most organizations use the Web as a search tool for finding out more about products and identifying suppliers, but to survive in the future active participation via online partnerships is essential.

Types of Buying Decisions

5.
Identify the various types of organizational buying decisions.

The types of buying decisions that business and industrial organizations face are classified according to *time* needed to make the decision, the *cost* (and risk associated with high cost decisions), and the *complexity* of the product. There are basically three types of buying situations: new task, modified rebuy, and straight or full rebuy.

NEW TASK PURCHASE

new task purchase

What is called a **new task purchase** occurs when a business buys a product, usually an expensive one, for the first time. The organization lacks familiarity with the item, so it seeks information that will assist it in making the best decision. Since the product represents a high risk because of its great costs, numerous individuals often participate in the evaluation and decision, sometimes, for example, through a buying committee. Capital equipment such as new buildings, custom-designed production equipment and communications equipment are examples of new task purchases.

MODIFIED REBUY

modified rebuy

In a **modified rebuy**, an organization purchases a product, usually of medium price, that it purchases infrequently. Typically, the organization is less than satisfied with the product it currently uses and so searches the marketplace for a substitute that will perform better, one that will, for example, operate more efficiently and save the firm money. Savings in the long-term can be measured against any short-term cost increases. Replacing power tools or photocopier equipment in an office are modified rebuy situations.

STRAIGHT (OR FULL) REBUY

straight or full rebuy

Straight or full rebuys are used for inexpensive items bought on a regular basis. Essentially, they are routine reorders requiring no modification, since the needs they fulfill remain relatively constant. Because the risks are low, the decision is a simple one, much like the routine purchase made by a consumer. The ongoing purchase of office supplies qualifies as a straight rebuy.

A summary of the key differences between the types of buying decisions is included in Figure 5.6.

Steps in the Buying Decision Process

6.
Identify the steps involved in the organizational decision process.

Since business organizations and similar groups generally exhibit rational buying behaviour, the decision-making process tends to be clearly defined. The typical buying model has eight stages (Figure 5.7). Let us examine each of these stages.

PROBLEM RECOGNITION

problem recognition

As the initial stage, **problem recognition** describes the fact that a change has occurred in the organizational environment, which reveals a problem or a new need that must be

---

Figure 5.6

Types of Buying Decisions in Busines-to-Business Marketing

Type	Price	Risk	Knowledge	Involvement
New Task	High	High	Limited. Must seek information on best alternatives	Buying committee
Modified	Medium Rebuy	Some	Good. Seek out new information for better products	Buying committee, buying centre influence, or purchasing agent
Straight Rebuy	Low	Minimal	Good. Product considered acceptable	Low. Routine order by purchasing manager

A Typical Buying Decision Model in Business Organizations

Figure 5.7

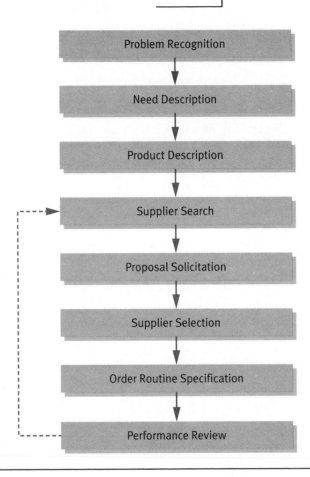

resolved. For example, a computerized inventory system signals that it is time to reorder; plant personnel become dissatisfied with production capacity; purchasing is not satisfied with some of the current suppliers because of their slow, unreliable delivery and lack of sufficient supplies; or marketing determines that an internal information and communications system more efficient than the present one is needed.

NEED DESCRIPTION

need description

For the **need description**, the buying organization identifies the general characteristics and qualities of the needed item or service. In effect, it starts to look at potential solutions by reviewing alternatives that have been successful in the past.

PRODUCT DESCRIPTION

product descriptions or **specifications**

With a general solution in mind, the buying organization now establishes precise **product descriptions** or **specifications** of the item needed. The process of formally describing the characteristics of the product ensures that needs are clearly communicated both within the organization and to potential suppliers. The quantity required is usually stipulated at this time, which assists suppliers in submitting bids. Specifications may consist of blueprints for a new production line, documented copy quality, and maximum run length for a photocopier, or stipulations on temperature tolerances for a machine tool. The specifications are key criteria against which a potential supplier's products are evaluated. At this stage, too, the buying organization usually determines who will be responsible for deciding on the purchase. Will the responsibility remain with the purchasing manager, or will a buying committee be formed? The marketing organization must be ready to identify those with the most influence and direct its communications appropriately.

SUPPLIER SEARCH

supplier search

During the **supplier search** stage, the buying organization looks for potential suppliers. Usually, two key decisions need to be made in the purchase process: first, which product or service the organization should buy and, second, from what particular supplier it should buy. Buying organizations, at this point, search for and qualify acceptable suppliers, using the *vendor analysis* discussed earlier in this chapter. To qualify a supplier means that the buying organization determines that the supplier can provide the product in a steady, reliable manner.

The Canadian Trade Index
www.ctidirectory.com
Frasers Trade Index
www.frasers.com

At the same time, marketing organizations evaluate the prospective buyers. Potential sources of information for both organizations include trade indexes, internal records of any past dealings with the other organization, trade advertising journals, and sales representatives. Trade indexes referred to frequently in Canada include *The Canadian Trade Index*, *Scott's Industrial Index*, *Canadian Key Business Directory*, *Frasers Trade Index*, and Standard Industrial Classification codes (SIC codes).

To ensure that they are seriously considered, potential suppliers must make themselves known to buyers. They must be listed in trade indexes for the products and services they provide, and they must actively communicate with potential customers through some combination of promotional programs. As discussed in the marketing research chapter, most business directories are now online or available on CD-ROM so that access to company information about potential suppliers is more convenient than in the past. A company's reputation (as communicated across an industry by positive word of mouth) also plays a role in the supplier selection process.

PROPOSAL SOLICITATION

proposal solicitation

In **proposal solicitation**, the buying organization seeks and evaluates detailed written proposals from acceptable suppliers. Depending on the complexity of the purchase, the proposal could consist of a formal bid, a written quotation, or a price catalogue reference.

bid

1. *Formal Bid* A **bid** is a written tender submitted in a sealed envelope by a specified deadline. There are two forms of bids:

closed bid

A **closed bid** is a written, sealed bid submitted by a supplier for review and evaluation by the purchaser on a particular date. The bid is based on specifications, or precise descriptions of what are required, published by the purchaser. Usually, the bid from the lowest "responsible" supplier is accepted, that is, one who is reputed to be dependable and stable.

open bid

An **open bid** is less formal and may only involve a written or oral price quotation from a potential supplier. The quotation usually specifies how long the price is in effect. Typically, during an open bidding process, buyers and sellers negotiate a price.

quotation

2. *Quotation* A **quotation** consists of a written document, usually from a sales representative, that states the terms of the price quoted.

3. *Price Catalogue Reference* In this situation, the price is obtained by referring to a catalogue where all prices are listed. Buyers usually maintain current supplier catalogues on file. This procedure is common for routine orders of standardized products and supplies.

SUPPLIER SELECTION

supplier selection

At the **supplier selection** stage, the buying organization evaluates the proposals of qualified suppliers and selects the one that matches its needs. Each proposal is assessed with reference to the purchase criteria. In a complex buying situation, the supplier's proposal might be judged on such factors as price, quality, delivery, technical support service, warranties, and trade-in policies.

While weighing these many variables, buyers usually attempt to negotiate a better price with the shortlisted suppliers. The bargaining process between buyers and sellers is now at its peak. The influence of buying centres (informal) or buying committees (formal) must be considered and their members addressed by the marketing organization during this phase. Another option for the buying organization is to select several sources of supply for its own protection, assuming there are equal alternatives to choose from.

For routine purchases, there is not much distinction between the solicitation and the selection stages. Where costs and risks are low, solicitation and selection can occur simultaneously.

ORDER ROUTINE SPECIFICATION

order and reorder routine

After the supplier has been selected, the buying organization and marketing organization (the successful supplier or suppliers) agree on an **order and reorder routine** stipulating such matters as the procedure for accepting orders, delivery times, return policies, quantities to be ordered, repair and service policies, and any other factors judged important by the buyer.

This document constitutes a written contract or agreement between the buying and marketing organizations. In large businesses and retailing organizations today, order routines are left to electronic technology. Sophisticated point-of-sale equipment automatically triggers a company's inventory control and reordering system.

PERFORMANCE REVIEW

performance reviews

Since businesses are constantly looking for products and services to improve the efficiency of their operations, there is no guarantee that the relationship between a buyer and seller will be a lasting one. In fact, the relationship may only last as long as the last price quotation. Once the purchaser receives a lower quotation, a new supplier may replace the existing one even if the current supplier has been satisfactory. To ensure that their operations remain as efficient as possible, businesses implement **performance reviews**.

Thus, as the final step in the buying process, the buying organization establishes a system of obtaining and evaluating feedback on the performance of the supplier's products. The purchasing manager will design an internal system for securing responses from user groups. Depending on whether the feedback is positive or negative, a decision to continue with or to drop a supplier is made. New price negotiations could also occur at this stage.

To marketers, this procedure demonstrates that the sale is never over. To avoid being dropped as a supplier, marketing organizations must accept criticisms and adapt their strategies, when necessary, to ensure that customers' needs are continuously satisfied. It has been shown that strong personal and business relationships develop when marketing organizations take fast, corrective action to resolve customer problems.

The steps involved in buying business and industrial goods is complex and requires considerable attention on both the buying and selling sides as companies today are constantly searching for better value. As discussed in the previous section, e-procurement practices are now more common and partnerships are forming between members of the supply chain. For additional insight into the benefits of e-procurement business practices see the Marketing in Action vignette **Teamwork Pays Dividends**.

Special Considerations for the Government Market

7.
Describe the unique characteristics of the government market.

The government market is divided into three categories: federal, provincial, and municipal. Collectively, these governments represent tremendous opportunity for Canadian firms that are eager to have a piece of the government business. Government purchases range from food to military equipment to office buildings to office supplies.

HOW DO GOVERNMENTS BUY?

Governments create the law in Canada, and by law, all Canadian governments must solicit competitive bids before making their purchase decisions. The bids, usually submitted in writing, are based on specifications established by government buyers. In the federal government, the Ministry of Supply and Services is responsible for choosing among the bids on most brand-name products for all federal agencies. As in the business-to-business market in general, such factors as price, availability, quality, and performance play key roles in the selection process. Because of the need for fiscal restraint, the government is more price sensitive than in the past and, as a result, will source products from any country or location. The goal is to secure the best mixture of price and quality, wherever that source may be. The Ministry of Supply and Services operates out of its Hull, Quebec, headquarters and from regional offices strategically located across Canada. Provincial governments operate in a similarly centralized fashion.

source list

Canadian businesses in pursuit of government contracts must have themselves placed on a source list kept by the Ministry of Supply and Services. A **source list** includes the names, products, and services of all those companies that have expressed an interest in dealing with the federal government. To be considered as a potential source of supply, a firm should contact the ministry office in Hull or a regional office.

Despite the business potential that government markets represent, the red tape commonly associated with dealing with governments often keeps potential suppliers away. For example, the government stresses price (low price). Consequently, some suppliers are reluctant to bid as the venture could be unprofitable. This is a critical factor for small suppliers who cannot compete with larger suppliers that can produce greater quantities at lower cost. As well, government purchases typically involve extensive paperwork, even for routine reorders. The problem is compounded for custom-designed products and complex decisions.

On the positive side, the federal government, in particular, favours buying from small Canadian enterprises and from businesses located in economically depressed areas, even

Marketing in Action

Teamwork Pays Dividends

The Internet, combined with a new set of common standards, tools, and Web-based services, has provided businesses with new ways of working with partners, suppliers and customers to cut costs, share information, pool resources, and respond more quickly to changing circumstances.

Some people refer to the new way of doing business as *"collaborative commerce."* With collaborative commerce, technology is being used to link business processes and information systems of different companies together so closely that they can anticipate one another's needs and act almost in unison to achieve a common goal. Financial and resource management software that automates companies' internal operations is now routinely Web-enabled and can be patched up with networks of other companies.

Cisco Systems Inc. is a pioneer of collaborative commerce. Cisco estimates they save as much as $700 million (US) a year by managing their supply chain over the Internet. The system is efficient, it requires fewer people and traditional order processing tasks are eliminated. Cisco also estimates savings of several hundred million dollars in getting products to market more quickly.

Cisco's system starts with the customer. Forecasts of customer demand are posted online in a private electronic marketplace so that Cisco suppliers get advance notice of what they need to build in order to support customers. As customers' requirements change, that information is immediately available to suppliers. The end result is that customers' demand and suppliers' supply match up exactly. The system lowers costs and allows for customization of products.

The Cisco procurement system points out the difference between the old way and the new way of doing business. In the old way, a manufacturer figured out what supplies were needed in order to fulfill an order and then purchased the raw materials. The same manufacturer using a collaborative commerce model provides suppliers with a forecast of their sales and an understanding of how their manufacturing process works. They leave it to suppliers to figure out what raw materials will be needed and when they should be delivered.

The use of a collaborative model requires a fundamental change in operational culture in an organization. It must divulge information that used to be considered private. It also involves trusting outsiders to make important decisions that were previously made in-house. Relinquishing some control has been an adjustment for companies and is a stumbling block for many companies contemplating entry into e-procurement.

Adapted from Kevin Marron, "The technology of teamwork," *Globe and Mail*, November 9, 2001, p. E1.

though the costs of these purchases may be higher. In this regard, the government has a variety of purchase objectives. While it strives for efficiency by choosing the lowest bid most of the time, it is also concerned with social and economic issues. Its policies try to encourage employment in depressed areas and foster growth in the small-business sector, an important sector for Canadian employment now and in the future.

Summary

The business-to-business market comprises four primary buying groups: business and industry, governments, institutions, and the professions, all of which require a vast array of products and services. This market has fewer buyers but larger buyers than the consumer market and is concentrated in certain geographic areas.

Business markets are quite different from consumer markets. The principal distinctions are that they have fewer buyers than consumer markets; the buyers tend to be concentrated near each other; the market presents different types of demand; the buying criteria are practical; and a formal buying process is used. Relationship marketing practices are also more prevalent in business marketing than in consumer marketing. The business-to-business economy has embraced the Internet, and many companies are forming cooperative ventures to achieve more cost efficiency in their respective operations. For many industries, the entire supply chain is automated, using buyer-seller customer relationship management programs and the introduction of e-procurement purchasing models.

The types of buying decisions that business organizations face are classified according to time needed to make the decision, the cost, and the complexity of the product. New task, modified rebuy, and straight (full) rebuy are the different types of purchases made by organizational customers.

The basic buying process is a series of eight steps: problem recognition, need description, product description, supplier search, proposal solicitation, supplier selection, routine order specification, and performance review.

The challenge for marketers in approaching the business market is to consider the different buying behaviours in each of the major segments and then develop effective and efficient marketing mixes that will satisfy them. The approaches taken will vary from one segment to another. As well, they may have to tailor their strategies to specific companies because the unique needs and problems of one company will vary from another.

Key Terms

assortment 125
bid 131
business-to-business market 116
buying centre 124
buying committees 124
closed bid 131
customer relationship management (CRM) 125
derived demand 121

e-procurement 128
joint or shared demand 121
modified rebuy 129
need description 130
new task purchase 128
North American Industry Classification System (NAICS) 121
open bid 132
order and reorder routine 132

Review Questions

1. What are the four major buying groups comprising the business-to-business market?

2. How is buying behaviour different in the business market from that in the consumer market?

3. Explain the influence the following characteristics have on organizational buying behaviour:

   a) Number of buyers

   b) Location of buyers

   c) Derived demand and joint demand

   d) Centralized purchasing

4. Briefly describe the primary buying criteria in business-to-business buying situations.

5. Distinguish between a buying committee and a buying centre.

6. Explain the concept of e-procurement. What benefits does the e-procurement model offer a participating company?

7. What is the difference between a new task purchase and a modified rebuy?

8. Briefly describe the steps in the decision-making process that organizations follow to make purchases.

Discussion and Application Questions

1. If interest rates and inflation were to rise and consumer demand for colour television sets declined, how would demand be affected in industries other than television production? Provide examples to illustrate your viewpoint.

2. "Developing partnerships with suppliers and customers is crucial to the success of business-to-business marketing organizations." Do you agree or disagree with this statement? Justify your position.

3. Review the vignettes "Teamwork Pays Dividends" and "Big 3 Automakers Form Internet Supply Chain." Identify the benefits of this type of relationship marketing system. Do you see any potential drawbacks with such a system? Conduct some secondary research to determine how e-procurement practices are being implemented in other industries.

E-Assignment

Visit the purchasing manager of a local market manufacturing company or service-based organization (e.g., a hotel, hospital, or college). Discuss with him or her the procedures that the organization uses for a modified rebuy or new task purchase (perhaps examine a recent purchase in detail). What factors were most important in arriving at the purchase decision? How has this company integrated the Internet into its buying operations? What advantages has the Internet provided? Report your findings to the class.

Endnotes

1 Statistics Canada, CANSIM II, tables 379-0019 and 379-0022, modified March 14, 2002.

2 Ken Deal, "The eyes and ears of business," *Marketing*, May 17, 1999, p. 18.

3 *Marketing Research Handbook*, 1999, p. 180.

4 "Number Crunching," Buying and Selling Online, supplement to *Profit* magazine, September 2001.

5 Adapted from Frederick E. Webster and Yoram Wind, *Organizational Buying Behaviour* (Englewood Cliffs NJ: Prentice-Hall, 1972), pp. 78-80.

6 Timothy Pritchard, "GM speeding ahead with changes," *Globe and Mail*, June 13, 1992, p. B6.

7 John Partridge, "Two banks, Bell part of big e-commerce venture," *Globe and Mail*, September 7, 2000, pp. B1, B11.

8 Rachel Ross, "E-commerce forecast to swell," *Toronto Star*, February 1, 2001, p. E4.

Courtesy of Superstock

Marketing Planning

This section concentrates on two essential elements of strategic marketing planning. First it discusses the concept of market segmentation and the identification of target markets. The focus then shifts to the strategic planning process where links are drawn between various types of plans in an organization.

Chapter 6 illustrates how organizations use information about consumers to identify market segments and pursue target markets where profitable opportunities exist. The concept of product positioning is introduced. Chapter 7 draws relationships between planning at the corporate level and planning at the operational or marketing level of an organization.

General Motors Canada

Market Segmentation and Target Marketing

After studying this chapter, you will be able to

1. Describe the differences between mass marketing and market segmentation.
2. Describe the process used and information needed to identify and select target markets.
3. Describe the various types of segmentation strategies commonly used in contemporary marketing practice.
4. Explain the concept of positioning and its role in contemporary marketing practice.

What Is a Market?

market

1.
Describe the differences between mass marketing and market segmentation.

Before discussing market segmentation, let us review what a market is. A **market** is a group of people who have a similar need for a product or service, the resources to purchase the product or service, and the willingness and ability to buy it. The reality of this explanation is that most products and services are marketed to smaller groups (called segments) that fall within the larger mass market. This practice is referred to as market segmentation.

Essentially, a firm adopts a strategy of mass marketing, or it uses some variation of market segmentation to its advantage. As briefly discussed in Chapter 1, organizations now have the ability to reach individual consumers with direct marketing strategies. This is the ultimate form of market segmentation, a concept that will be discussed in detail in this chapter. Let us start by distinguishing between mass marketing and market segmentation.

MASS MARKETING

mass marketing

When an organization practises **mass marketing**, it implements one basic marketing strategy to appeal to a broad range of consumers, not addressing any distinct characteristics among the consumers. In effect, the nature of the product or service is such that it enjoys widespread acceptance. In contemporary practice, this type of marketing is the exception rather than the rule, but certain products and services are suited to this approach.

In bygone eras, firms had a much stronger production orientation than marketing orientation. Where a production orientation existed, mass marketing was appropriate because consumers were offered a limited choice. Products came in one form for everybody; they did not cater to different tastes and desires. Marketing made a general appeal. In today's environment, where great competition exists, firms are striving to differentiate their products in order to make them more attractive to potential users. Using marketing research information to advantage, the firm identifies different segments in need of specialized products and services. Consequently, mass marketing is used less.

Firms that hold onto the mass marketing concept suffer the consequences. Perhaps the Canadian retailing market best demonstrates this principle, for traditional mass marketers like Hudson's Bay and Sears are struggling. In retailing today two types of retailers have emerged in healthy positions. First, there are the top-end retailers such as Holt-Renfrew and Harry Rosen that appeal to higher-income groups and older age groups. The status and prestige they offer has appeal and they continue to prosper—

Harry Rosen
www.harryrosen.com

customers willingly pay higher prices for their fashions. At the other end of the scale, discount stores such as Wal-Mart and Zellers have prospered. These stores appeal to value-conscious consumers in low- to middle-income ranges. The problem area is in the middle. Stores such as the Bay and Sears are being squeezed between the high-end specialties and the discounters. As well, they face stiff competition from specialty stores that appeal to the mid-market customer. The Bay and Sears have a hard time distinguishing themselves from one another and from the discounters and specialty stores. Their customers have been exiting to the low end and the top end.

The middle-range stores recognize that they cannot be all things to all people, anymore, and are making changes. Sears, for example, moved furniture and appliances into a separate specialty retailing operation and focused on soft goods and fashion in its department stores. To make customers aware of the changes, Sears implemented an advertising strategy that encouraged consumers to investigate "the softer side of Sears." Once this was established the tagline changed to "The many sides of Sears" and more recently "For the many sides of you." The Sears strategy is evolving and working.

In contrast, the Bay tried to move upscale in 2000 by focusing on a select grouping of company brand names that would appeal to their primary customer—females 35 to 55 years old, middle income, homemaker to career woman. Stores were remodelled to provide the customer a more pleasant shopping experience. That strategy failed to work. In 2001 the Bay introduced a low-priced "value" program to win back customers. It was like a Wal-Mart strategy but at a higher price point—the Bay promoted "everyday low prices."[1] In department store marketing nothing seems to be working for the Bay. The Bay has launched Home Outfitters and it has been reasonably successful; the new chain is not influenced by the Bay's brand name.

MARKET SEGMENTATION

market segmentation

Market segmentation is the division of a large market (mass market) into smaller homogeneous markets (segments or targets) on the basis of common needs and/or similar lifestyles. Segmentation strategies are based on the premise that it is preferable to tailor marketing strategies to distinct user groups, where the degree of competition may be less. The firm specializes by concentrating on segments of the population. In this regard, organizations will pursue segments where opportunities are the greatest (e.g., where competition is less or where their product can be clearly distinguished from the competition that does exist). For example, the Four Seasons Hotel chain is very successful in the upscale (high quality, good service, and high price) segment of the lodging industry. Its marketing efforts are directed at segments of the population that can afford the amenities it offers. In contrast, a hotel chain such as Choice Hotels Canada, which operates under the names Comfort Inn, Quality Inn, Clarion, Rodeway, and Econo Lodge is also successful, but in a different segment. Its strategy is to provide good quality at a much lower price. Its marketing effort is directed at the price-conscious traveller.

To maximize profits, a firm commonly has to operate in many different segments. A successful segmentation strategy enables a firm to control marketing costs, allowing it to make profits. As well, the organization may be able to develop a distinct niche for itself or for a product line or brand that it markets. For example, Gatorade established the sports drink segment of the beverage market and, to this day, dominates the category in terms of market share. Niche marketing is discussed in detail later in this chapter.

On the downside, organizations employing market segmentation must be alert to shifting consumer trends and the cyclical patterns of the economy. For example, in the

Gatorade
www.gatorade.com

lodging segments described above, all hotels would be affected by a recession. However, Choice Hotels might not be affected as much as the Four Seasons because its prices are lower. In fact, Choice Hotels may even experience some growth as cost-conscious travellers from other segments come looking for better value. For this reason many organizations operate in a variety of market segments in order to protect overall profitability.

Identifying and Selecting Target Markets

2.
Describe the process used and information needed to identify and select target markets.

Segmentation involves three steps: identifying market segments, selecting the market segments that offer the most potential (e.g., profit or future competitive position), and positioning the product so that it appeals to the target market. Once these steps have been taken, an organization shifts its attention to developing a marketing mix strategy. Typically, a company pursues those target markets that offer the greatest profit potential. When identifying target markets, an organization will use marketing research to learn the demographic, geographic, psychographic, and behaviour-response characteristics of the market (Figure 6.1). Let us examine each one of these segmentation variables.

Figure 6.1

The Elements of Market Segmentation: Variables Used to Identify Target Markets

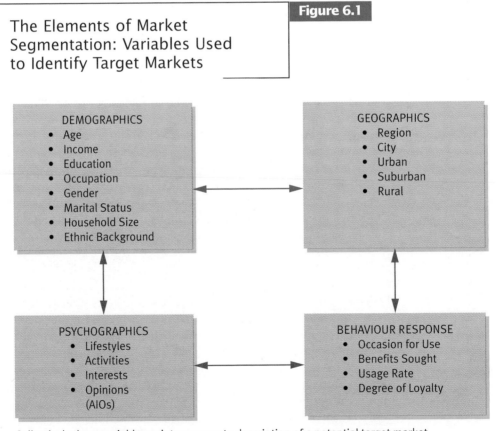

Collectively these variables paint an accurate description of a potential target market.

DEMOGRAPHIC SEGMENTATION

demographic segmentation

Demographic segmentation is defined as the division of a large market into smaller segments on the basis of combinations of age, gender, income, occupation, education, marital status, household formation, and ethnic background. Marketers monitor trends among these demographic characteristics and adjust their marketing strategies accordingly. As discussed in Chapter 2 and 4, two major demographic trends will influence the direction of marketing activities in the future: the aging population and the evolving ethnic mix. Refer to Figure 6.2 for a look at the state of Canada's population by age in 2004.

Age

Looking specifically at *age*, the Canadian market can be classified and described according to age ranges: *millennials* describe those 1–19 years; *Generation Y* describes young adults between 20 and 26 years of age-they are a subset of *Generation X* (people aged between 21 and 37); *baby boomers* are 38–56 years; and *Grey* means 55+ years. For different reasons, each of these age segments presents unique challenges for marketers in the future. Let us examine a few examples.

Canada's Estimated Population Structure in 2004

Figure 6.2

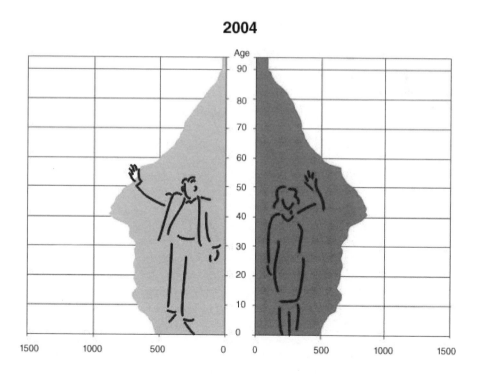

Source: From Statistics Canada publication, "Annual Demographic Statistics," Catalogue 91-213, 2000.

The **youth** market is very important to companies because brand loyalties are just in their formative stages. The youth market can be segmented further: children 1–9 years, tweens 9–13 years, and teens 13–19 years. The Canadian tween market alone numbers 2.5 million and spends $1.8 billion annually on items such as candy, shoes, clothes, and music.[2] There are 3.3 million Canadian teenagers who are heavily influenced by the music scene, so that's where marketing organizations want to be.

The youth market is a hard market to reach and it is influenced less by traditional mass media advertising. Brands like Levi's, Frito Lay, Nike, and Mountain Dew are venturing into grassroots initiatives to reach teens in their own environment. Frito Lay, for example, sponsors the EdgeFest alternative-music concert tour and Mountain Dew sponsors Canada's Ultimate Street Beat Video Dance Party. This event tours hundreds of high schools each year, providing teens with a video dance party while allowing them to interact with marketers.[3] These brands see the value of one-to-one interaction with their consumers.

Since youth are the most avid users of the Internet—spending at least 12 hours a week online—companies are changing their communications strategies to reach them. Frito-Lay Doritos brand has reduced its investment in TV advertising and increased investment online. Their effort included a revamp of the Web site **doritos.com**, the formation of partnerships with other hot teen sites such as **mtv.com**; and the creation of an unbranded "underground" Web site, **fortheboldanddaring.com** (which, as this text went to print, remained under construction).[4]

Generation X, or the **Nexus generation** as some refer to them, were born in the sixties and seventies and are between the ages of 21 and 37. Some general characteristics of this generation include the following: they live in the present, like to experiment, and look for immediate results. They are selfish, cynical, quick to blame others for their mistakes, and dependant upon their parents. More than 40 percent of them still live with their parents or have left home only to return to their parents.[5] Generation X has learned from their parent's mistakes. They are marrying later, having kids later, and want to spend more time with their family.

d-Code, a Canadian market research company that specializes in analyzing Generation X, offers some additional perspectives on Generation X. They are very different from the preceding generations. "They want to succeed, and they are resourceful, adaptable, and optimistic. They are not that loyal and have a penchant for job-hopping. This generation is entrepreneurial by nature; about a quarter of them expect to be self-employed."

With such knowledge in hand, the Volkswagen focused its Jetta marketing efforts on the 20-something market. There was opportunity because Generation X was just entering their car buying years and had not formed an opinion about the Volkswagen name. Volkswagen had been advertising its German heritage and sales were floundering. A new advertising campaign in which young people could recognize their attitudes, yearnings, expectations, and disappointments had a profound and positive effect on sales. Ads were supported by the now famous "Drivers Wanted" slogan. The Jetta built a new brand image by connecting emotionally with young, urban car buyers.[6]

Boomers are entering middle age or are beyond middle age, falling into the 36- to 54-year-old category. They are by far the largest age segment (see Figure 6.2). They will be the major buying influence over the next 20 years. Baby boomers will continue to shape the car market. Boomers launched the truck market into orbit when the minivan became the family taxicab. That was followed by an infatuation with sport utility vehicles. When the kids leave the nest, the next stage will be luxury cars and sports cars.

Automobile manufacturers have to respond quickly to the changing tastes of this age segment. A new segment called entry-level luxury has emerged and includes automobiles such as the Volkswagen Passat, Jaguar X-Type, Volvo V60, Lexus IS300, and the Mercedes C-Class. All vehicles are in the $35 000 to $50 000 range. The growth in this segment is driven by a change in demographics. Baby boomers have reached the right age category and earning power to buy luxury automobiles. It's pure marketing-luxury models are being produced in response to the increase in buyers looking for them. Sales of entry-level luxury cars in Canada tripled (from 13 000 units to 37 000 units) between 1995 and 2000.[7]

The **grey market**—people that are 55 years of age and older—is expected to be quite different than past generations. The current emphasis on health and physical well being suggests that they will not be "old," either physically or in outlook. They are also expected to retain the spending patterns of their younger days. Consequently, marketers' perceptions of older consumers will have to change. Many organizations perceive older consumers to be duds. They don't buy anything, they're too brand loyal, too cheap, they are focused on keeping what they have, they're old—no fun.

Prudent marketers have a different perspective. They realize that the 55-plus market controls most of Canada's wealth (80 percent) and discretionary spending power (55 percent) and by 2006 they will represent 35 percent of Canada's population.[8] Smart companies are altering their marketing strategies accordingly. Members of the new grey segment are different than their predecessors. They spend more on entertainment, jewelry, sports cars, and cosmetics than any other age group and they purchase experiences such as exotic vacations and cosmetic surgery. Buying tendencies like these caught Sears' attention. Sears has bridged the boomer and grey generations and offers a "Mature Outlook" program—a rewards program for customers over the age of 50.

The 55-plus group are anything but consumer duds! New products will have to be positioned to appeal to the needs of older targets, and existing products will have to be repositioned in order to survive. Reaching this target is also an issue. Recent statistics show older people to be the fastest growing segment among users of the Internet.

Demographic trends pose a conundrum to marketers. For example, how does a brand become attractive to young people without alienating its older core users? They know that if they do not attract new customers while they are young, chances are they may never get them at all. When managers see the average age of their core user getting progressively rising, they know they have a problem on their hands.

Gender

Gender has always been a primary means of distinguishing product categories: personal care products, magazines, athletic equipment, and fashion goods are categorized according to the gender of the buyer. With more and more women in the workforce outside the home each year (a significant change from earlier generations) and the changing roles of men and women in Canadian households, the marketing orientation will become increasingly "unisex," as both sexes will buy and use similar products. Women play an important role in purchase decisions. They make up 42 percent of Canada's 4.5 million RRSP contributors and provide 34 percent of the $12.1 billion in contributions. They are responsible for 50 percent of the computers sold in North America, 65 percent of new car sales, and influence 50 percent of all household renovation decisions. Clearly, organizations have to be more aware of the importance of gender segmentation.

Companies are just starting to effectively pursue the women's market. Canadian Tire is a leader in this area. They discovered that women were much more discriminating than men when shopping. Consequently, Canadian Tire altered its style of merchandise presentation so that women could touch the products and try them out. They even built in-store boutiques with displays that offer detailed information about the products in question.[9]

When communicating with such an empowered woman, an organization must be very careful not to portray women in stereotypical situations, or be ready to suffer the consequences if they do. A message will have impact if it communicates to a woman based on how she sees herself or wants to see herself. It should speak to her as an individual, one who defines her individuality today differently from how she will define it tomorrow. It understands that women are different from men. Special K's advertising campaign "Look good on your own terms" met this challenge. It acknowledged that women resent being portrayed as effortlessly slim and continuously glamorous. They reject being victimized by impossible standards.[10]

Fidelity Investments
www.fidelity.com

Recognizing opportunity, investment firms, such as Fidelity Investments, are targeting women. As can be seen in Figure 6.3, Fidelity markets a financial product to young, working women who want to save for the education of their children. By portraying women in contemporary roles, Fidelity is demonstrating a progressive approach to implementing marketing strategy.

While marketers are slowly waking up to the potential that lies in marketing to women, both women and men are suspicious of any product that is marketed purely as a "woman's product." Certainly, women do not want products that they perceive as inferior to men's products.[11] Degree deodorant, long known for its body-heat-activated proposition, has always been a gender-neutral brand but more females than males buy it. Degree sales got a boost in the form of a clear gel product line extension that appeals directly to young males. Degree gel was launched in three scents—Exhilaration, Cool Rush, and Stamina. The advertising message was delivered in a tone and manner that appeals to young males. Degree was not worried about alienating females. In fact, their research shows that women are attracted to the idea that the brand works well for men.[12]

Ethnic Background

Canada's **ethnic diversity** will present new opportunities for Canadian marketers. People within the Canadian culture represent many diverse subcultures (subgroups of a larger population) that have distinctive lifestyles based on religious, racial, and geographic differences. As of 2001, Canada's visible minorities totaled 5.7 million or about 18 percent of the population. The largest minority groups are Chinese (23 percent of ethnic population), South Asians (21 percent), blacks (19 percent), and West Asian/Arabs (13 percent). Canada's subcultures tend to be concentrated in three key regions: Ontario, Quebec, and British Columbia and a whopping 75 percent of visible minorities live in four cities: Toronto (37 percent), Vancouver (15 percent), Montreal (14 percent), and Calgary/Edmonton (9 percent).[13]

Since ethnic communities are concentrated by location, they are accessible market niches for marketing organizations to pursue. Burger King chanced onto ethnic marketing when it introduced the BK veggie burger (a beef-free, vegetable-friendly soy burger). It reached an audience beyond the health-conscious. Veggie burgers took off among Toronto East Indians whose religious beliefs forbid beef consumption. That led to an

Gender Segmentation: An Advertisement Directed at Working Female Adults

Figure 6.3

"A global network of dedicated professionals, that's a lot of expertise."

The strength of more than 520 dedicated Fidelity portfolio managers, analysts, and traders worldwide. The flexibility to respond to market changes through research offices located in North America, Europe and Asia. Fidelity provides you with the resources and proven investment discipline that only the world's largest mutual fund company can offer. To help you reach your investment objectives with confidence.

Speak with your investment professional about Fidelity, or call us at

1 800 263-4077   www.fidelity.ca

Read the important information contained in a fund's prospectus before investing.

WHERE 15 MILLION INVESTORS PUT THEIR TRUST™

1999 ad courtesy of Fidelity Investments

original advertising campaign that promoted the veggie burger on a broader scale to East Indians. The ads aired on East Indian TV programs in Toronto and Vancouver.[14]

Procter & Gamble, a large packaged-goods company, entered the multicultural marketing arena in a different way. They saw opportunity in the sponsorship of community festivals. They have sponsored New Year festivals and dragon boat festivals in Toronto and Vancouver. With sponsorship came exposure in the local communities along with an opportunity to create in-store promotions around the events.[15]

GEOGRAPHIC SEGMENTATION

geographic segmentation

Geographic segmentation refers to the division of a large geographic market into smaller geographic or regional units. The Canadian market can be divided into five distinct areas: the Maritimes, Quebec, Ontario, the Prairies, and British Columbia. Geographic considerations used in conjunction with demographics provide the marketer with a clear description of the target market, and from this description, marketing strategies can be developed. As discussed in Chapter 4, different strategies may be required for different regions, providing those differences are significant and the potential returns profitable. The most obvious difference is in Quebec, where the language and cultural characteristics require the use of original marketing strategies. Several regional trends are emerging in Canada. One trend is that Quebec's proportion of the total population is dropping and is likely to continue to do so. Such declines are due to the political climate in the province, lower birth rates, and the fact that Quebec does not attract its share of Canada's immigrants. Another trend is that only three provinces, Ontario, Alberta, and British Columbia, exceed the national average in population growth.

Geographic regions are subdivided into *urban* and *rural* areas. Within urban metropolitan areas, the market can be divided further on the basis of location: urban downtown, suburban, and regional municipalities that surround large cities. More Canadians than ever before are living in urban metropolitan areas. In fact, 79 percent of Canadians live in urban areas. There is also a concentration of population in four broad urban regions: the extended Golden Horseshoe area of southern Ontario; Montreal and environs; British Columbia's lower mainland, and southern Vancouver Island. Fifty-one percent of Canada's population lives in these areas.[16]

Considering the distribution of Canada's regional and urban populations, it is not surprising that successful marketing strategies have an urban orientation. These strategies may also differ according to location within the urban area. The attitudes, opinions, and lifestyles of a downtown urban dweller may be quite different from those of the suburban dweller. Similar comparisons can be made between the urban dweller and the rural dweller. The differences in need, attitude, and outlook on life create constant challenges for marketing organizations. A retailer like the Bay, for example will plan its downtown stores differently than its suburban stores. Different lines of merchandise are carried because different kinds of shoppers visit the stores.

geodemographic segmentation

The combination of geographic and demographic segmentation has spawned the use of the term "geodemographics." **Geodemographic segmentation** is the isolating of dwelling areas (e.g., areas within a city) according to geography and demographics, on the basis of the assumption that people seek out residential neighbourhoods in which to cluster with their lifestyle peers. For example, younger, higher-income households clustering in re-developed downtown areas, and dual-income, traditional families concentrating in suburbia are applications of the geodemographic concept. Applying the same principle on a regional basis, practitioners refer to regional marketing strategies as micro-marketing.

micro-marketing

Micro-marketing involves the development of marketing strategies on a regional basis, giving consideration to the unique needs and geodemographics of different regions.

Many Canadian marketing organizations are moving away from "broadstroke" national marketing strategies towards strategies based on regional considerations and opportunities. Other companies are proceeding in the opposite direction and developing universal strategies that are appropriate for all of North America, or even for the global marketplace. The phrase "thinking globally and acting locally" is a common theme among marketing organizations today.

PSYCHOGRAPHIC SEGMENTATION

psychographic segmentation

The combination of demography and geography has been the traditional way to segment Canadian markets, but in today's competitive marketplace, marketing organizations have added a more sophisticated variable: psychographics. **Psychographic segmentation** is market segmentation on the basis of the activities, interests, and opinions (the lifestyles) of consumers. Psychographic segmentation is multi-dimensional: it considers a variety of factors that affect a person's purchase decision. Such information is advantageous to marketers because it tells them not only who buys but also why they buy.

Psychographics examines lifestyles, on the basis of observed activities, values, attitudes, interests, and beliefs. Many of these variables were discussed in Chapter 4—Consumer Buying Behaviour. Such examination helps marketers understand why two people who are demographically identical behave in very different ways and purchase different types of products and services. When organizations target psychographically, they present products in line with the lifestyle of the target market so that the personality of the product matches the personality of the target. The beer industry in Canada is a heavy user of psychographics-based advertising. The Molson Canadian advertising campaign that uses the slogan "I AM" is a good example. The campaign was launched in March 2000 using a now very famous commercial titled "The Rant." In the commercial, Joe (an average Canadian male) dismisses American stereotypes about Canadians in a rousing speech. As Joe states his case for Canadian patriotism, images of Canada appear on the screen. His speech starts slowly but builds to a feverish pitch and ends with the line, "My name is Joe, and I am Canadian."

Research conducted by Molson showed that the 19- to 25-year-old target market was becoming "overt" in their Canadian pride. It was a bit like a dormant volcano, something ready to erupt. The initial spot focused squarely on the idea of being Canadian and being proud to say you are Canadian. It connected with the target audience on an emotional level. Such a direct approach increases the likelihood that the ad will leave its brand mark on consumers, and it did. In live versions of the commercial in theatres, people stood up and cheered![17] Molson Canadian extended the campaign by introducing additional commercials that focused on stereotypical differences between Canadians and Americans.

In Canada, numerous psychographic research studies have been conducted, resulting in a variety of descriptive classifications of the Canadian population. One such company, Goldfarb Consultants of Toronto, has classified Canadians into six psychographic cells within two broad segments: traditionalists and non-traditionalists. The Goldfarb segments were presented in Chapter 4.

Psychographic information shows how an individual's interest in a product depends on his or her lifestyle. Automakers produce and market a range of vehicles to satisfy the lifestyle requirements of the Canadian lifestyle groups. Trendy sports cars with European styling appeal to bold achievers, while a family station wagon or a minivan appeals to old-fashioned puritans. See the illustration in Figure 6.4.

A Lifestyle Message Directed at Bold Achievers

Figure 6.4

In the fashion retailing business, Harry Rosen and other upscale boutiques appeal to bold achievers and self-indulgers. The middle-of-the-road groups, such as old-fashioned puritans, are likely to shop for clothing in established department stores, such as the Bay and Sears, and in national chains, such as Fairweather and Tip Top. In contrast, responsible survivors are likely to purchase clothing in discount departments stores, such as Wal-Mart and Zellers, and in low-end retail chains.

**behaviour
response
segmentation**

BEHAVIOUR RESPONSE SEGMENTATION

Behaviour response segmentation involves dividing buyers into groups according to their occasions for using a product, the benefits they require in a product, the frequency with which they use it, and their degree of brand loyalty. It is used in conjunction with other segmentation variables.

Occasion for Use

In order to increase the consumption of the product, marketers using the occasion-for-use segmentation strategy show how the product can be used on various occasions. For example, advertisers show such products as eggs, breakfast cereals, and orange juice being consumed at times other than their traditional mealtimes. Other products are associated with special occasions and are promoted heavily at these times. Flowers and chocolates, for example, are associated with Valentine's Day, Mother's Day, Easter, and Christmas.

Benefits Sought

Benefit segmentation is based on the premise that different consumers try to gratify different needs when they purchase a product. For example, a car buyer may place greater emphasis on style and road-handling ability; a shampoo buyer may want conditioning or dandruff control. If the target market is rational in nature, marketers will focus on quality, price, efficiency, and dependability. If the target is influenced by emotions, different forms of presentation that play on feelings (sex, fear, love, status, etc.) can be used. To see the difference, consider a product such as blue jeans. An inexpensive, private-label brand purchased at a discount department store will perform the same function as a high-priced, designer-label brand purchased at a high-end fashion retailer. The reason people buy one brand of jeans instead of another derives from a combination of demographic (age, income, education, and occupation) and psychographic (activities, interests, and opinions) variables.

Usage Rate

Frequency of use is an important segmentation variable. Marketers will conduct research to distinguish the characteristics of a heavy user from those of a medium or light user. Very often, an 80/20 rule applies, that is, 80 percent of a product's sales volume and profits comes from 20 percent of its users (heavy users). To attract more heavy users, the heavy user demographic and psychographic profiles can be used to determine the best way to present the product. The benefits of the product are communicated in a manner that will attract those potential users.

Loyalty Response

The degree of brand loyalty a customer has also influences segmentation strategy. As with usage-rate segmentation, the marketing organization should conduct research to determine the characteristics of brand-loyal users. Strategies would then be developed to attract users with similar profiles and behaviour tendencies. From a marketing viewpoint, consideration must be given to users with varying degrees of loyalty. For example, defensive activities (for defending or retaining market share) are directed at medium and heavy users to maintain their loyalty. Distributing coupons on the package for use on the next purchase is an example of a defensive activity. Offensive tactics, such as trial coupons delivered by the media, are employed to attract new users and users of competitive brands. Because brand switching does occur, marketers must be conscious of customers at both ends of the loyalty spectrum.

Consumers can be divided into three categories according to loyalty:[18]

1. ***Brand-Loyal*** These consumers gravitate consistently towards the same brand or pool of brands (alternatives that are perceived to be equal in terms of quality, value, price, availability, and so on). For example, Nike and Adidas running shoes may be perceived as being equal, as are soft drinks Coca-Cola and Pepsi-Cola. A competitive product that offers superior benefits can sway the purchase decision of these consumers. For example, the image of Energizer batteries lasting longer (as advertised by that pink bunny that "keeps on going, and going, and going...") helps maintain loyalty; this brand is seen as being more dependable than competing products.

2. ***Inertia-Driven*** Although these consumers are brand loyal, their loyalty is based on habit rather than reason. They do not know why they buy the same brand all the time; they simply do it. It is difficult for competing brands to attract this type of customer. If they try to attract this group, price and promotion incentives would be part of the marketing incentives arsenal.

3. ***Brand-Promiscuous*** These consumers are irrepressibly mobile. They are always switching and are up for grabs with each purchase. They, too, are influenced by price and promotion incentives, but they always look for the best deal available at the time of purchase.

A new study from Grey Canada shows Canadian consumers to be promiscuous—in that they are willing to carry on affairs with multiple brands. A majority of Canadians revealed that price is the deciding factor when choosing brands in consumer goods categories.[19] With so much brand choice available, marketers must change their way of thinking. They have to get beyond features, benefits, and performance. They must focus on relationship issues and communicate with customers more directly and continuously to build patronage. Companies that listen to and interact with current and prospective customers through effective personal selling strategies, online marketing communications, and online buying are developing more loyal customer bases.

Market Segmentation Strategies

3.
Describe the various types of segmentation strategies commonly used in contemporary marketing practice.

Assuming that the marketing organization has identified and selected the target markets it wishes to pursue, the next decision deals with the degree of coverage and activity in the various segments. This section will focus on specific segmentation strategies: market differentiation, niche marketing or market concentration, market integration, and relationship marketing.

MARKET DIFFERENTIATION

market differentiation

Market differentiation involves targeting several market segments with several different products and marketing plans (different marketing strategies for each product and segment).

To illustrate the use of market differentiation, consider the following examples. Procter & Gamble is a large, diversified, consumer packaged-goods company that operates in many segments: household cleaning products, consumer food products, and personal care products, to name a few. In the shampoo, conditioner, and hair care market they dominate with brands such as Pantene, Pert Plus, Head & Shoulders, Physique, Inner Science, Infusium, and Vidal Sassoon. Laundry products include Bounce, Cheer, Downey, Era, Gain, and Tide. They market hair care products with different formulations and fragrances and laundry products in powdered and liquid forms to satisfy the different needs of the targets they pursue.

A company such as Kraft Canada participates in numerous food categories. Their main meal preparations include Kraft Dinner, Delissio Rising Crust Pizza, and Stove Top stuffing mixes. Dessert and snack items include Jell-O jellies and puddings, Dad's cookies, Oreo cookies, Ritz crackers, and Toblerone chocolate. It can all be washed down with Maxwell House Coffee, Tang flavour crystals, or Crystal Light low calorie drink mix. Most, if not all, consumer packaged-goods companies practise market differentiation: they are multi-product companies operating in a variety of market segments.

The main advantages of market differentiation are that sales are maximized by participation in numerous segments and that profits increase if the company has adequately differentiated its product from competitive offerings. On the risk side, the costs of differentiation can be high, since the company offers a number of product variations, operates in new distribution channels, and promotes a multitude of brands. Since financial resources for marketing are usually scarce, companies generally evaluate potential revenues carefully against the costs of obtaining them to ensure that adequate profits will be achieved.

NICHE MARKETING

niche marketing or market concentration

Niche marketing, or **market concentration**, is defined as targeting a product line to one particular segment and committing all marketing resources to the satisfaction of that segment. Niche marketing is a good strategy for small companies that have limited resources and for large companies wanting to target specific segments with specialized products. Often, the segments pursued are quite small, so the key to success is in finding opportunities that do not require large economies of scale in production and distribution. Attractive niches have the following characteristics:

1. The niche is sufficiently large and has enough purchasing power to be profitable.
2. It is of negligible interest to major competitors so that there is little threat from these firms.
3. The firm has the required skills and resources to serve the segment effectively.
4. The firm can defend itself from an attacking competitor.

To successfully implement a niche marketing strategy, an organization should consider four basic steps: identifying the niche, exploiting the niche, expanding the niche, and defending the niche.[20]

Identifying the Niche

Some good examples of niche marketers include Porsche and Jaguar, which appeal strictly to an upscale, status-conscious segment of the automobile market. They offer modes tailored to entry-level luxury buyers up to top-end luxury buyers. Microbrewers such as Sleeman's Breweries Limited offer unique-tasting beers to customers searching for something different from the mainstream beers offered by Labatt and Molson.

Toni Plus
www.toniplus.com

When identifying market niches, an organization evaluates market opportunities to determine ways of differentiating product offerings or finding target groups that are dissatisfied with current product offerings. As an example, consider the fashion retailing business. Most stores offer product lines that fit slim people. If a young person is overweight the shopping experience can be very frustrating—and being overweight is a growing problem among young males and females. Seeing a real niche opportunity, a relatively new store called Toni Plus (four stores in Toronto and one in Calgary) started offering 14-plus sizes in styles fit for the youth market. Established retailers such as Reitman's and Penningtons Superstore followed by opening junior sections offering plus-size fashions.[21]

Exploiting the Niche

Once the niche is identified and the entry made, the organization must decide how to exploit the niche. It must assess the threat of competition (will the idea be easy to duplicate?) and the length of time the new opportunity will last (will consumer preferences and tastes change quickly, or will technology outdate the idea?).

In the plus-size retailing example cited above, certain decisions had to be made to exploit the niche. Should new sections be opened up in existing stores? Should existing sections be expanded? Should new standalone stores be opened? What is the best way to communicate with the teen market to generate awareness and build traffic in the stores?

The experience of a US retailer demonstrates an appropriate strategy. California-based Hot Topic, which attracts women 15 to 30 years old, unveiled Torrid, an operation that would meet the fashion needs of plus-size women in the same age bracket. Hot Topic could have simply added the plus-size merchandise to its existing stores but opted for standalone stores and a new banner based on customer feedback. From e-mail, Web site questionnaires, and in-store response cards, customers overwhelmingly stated they wanted their own stores. Hot Topic opted for small stores in mall locations. It offers its own line of private label products along with popular brands like Paris Blues. In Canada, Penningtons chose to expand its plus-size sections, and uses college and university newspapers and YM magazine to communicate a new image to a younger target audience.

Firms using a niche strategy must mobilize rapidly. Otherwise, opportunities will be missed. They must be able to enter and withdraw from a market quickly, if necessary. Competitors who decide to enter late (too late) often suffer financially. The plus-size fashion retailing market has room for more participants.

Expanding the Niche

Once a firm has entered a segment, it must decide on ways to broaden the customer base. In the luxury automobile market, companies such as BMW, Jaguar, Lexus, and Porsche saw opportunity with a younger target audience. Most Porsche buyers, for example, are between 45 and 55 and in upper income brackets. Porsche launched the Boxster to appeal to younger buyers who wanted the sporty image along with the lower price point. Since the launch of the Boxster, sales of Porsches in North America have doubled.[22] Jaguar is attempting to do the same with its Jaguar X-Type, an entry-level luxury model priced around $45 000. This niche is expanding rapidly as all domestic and foreign manufacturers are bringing out entry-level luxury cars.

In the plus-size fashion retail market there will be more entries. Tommy Hilfiger recently announced it would enter this segment. Other designer labels will follow. Accordingly, plus-size fashions are now readily available in major department stores such as Sears and the Bay, a true reflection of how a niche expands.

Defending the Niche

Profitable market niches do not go unnoticed by competitors. Being the first to get into a niche does create an advantage, but if competition enters, the opportunities begin to level off. Usually, a firm will defend a segment as long as it is profitable; otherwise it moves to more attractive situations. To defend a position necessitates a shift in marketing strategy. The firm can improve or modify the product, lower its price, seek out new channels of distribution, or experiment with new forms of advertising. As an example, Japanese carmakers, who at one time marketed only small, economy models, have gradually moved their product line upward to compete effectively with domestic manufacturers in virtually every price segment of the North American market. Toyota has been so successful, it is on the verge of passing Daimler Chrysler to become the third largest automobile company in North America.

For a summary of the key elements of niche marketing strategies, refer to Figure 6.5.

Key Elements in Niche Marketing Strategies

Figure 6.5

Step and Strategy

1. Identify the Niche

Market research reveals
- New ways to differentiate products
- Dissatisfied or untapped segments

Concentrate on company strength and careful use of resources

2. Exploit the Niche

Tactical selection of segment to enter
- Avoid segments easy for competition to enter
- Determine how long it will last
- Be mobile in entering or withdrawing

Step and Strategy

3. Expand the Niche

Protect current position while expanding the niche
- Efficient use of marketing mix
- Expand customer base
- Meet changing needs
- New channels of distribution
- Offer added value to differentiate

4. Defend the Niche

Defensive orientation in marketing mix
- Improve product
- Lower price
- New channels of distribution
- New forms of advertising pursue new opportunities at right time

MARKET INTEGRATION

market integration

Market integration is an expansion from a single segment into other similar segments. Market integration is followed for several reasons. First, the needs of consumers change; as consumers mature, their needs, attitudes, and outlook are altered. Second, new competition enters a particular segment, posing a threat to firms already there; in other words, the segment becomes more fragmented. Third, products and markets reach the maturity stage of the product life cycle and are threatened by new technology, which results in new, innovative products. To survive, a company must alter its marketing mix to stay in tune with current customer demands. The quick-service restaurant industry faces all these challenges. Therefore, a company such as McDonald's has to react positively with new marketing strategies in order to retain its position as a market leader. The following actions show how McDonald's continuously responds to change and how market integration works:

- McDonald's opens as a hamburger chain that appeals directly to children and teens.
- Target market expands to include young adults (original target market is getting older).
- A family restaurant concept is adopted so that the restaurant is presented as an informal place to enjoy a family meal.
- The menu is expanded to include items that will have broader market appeal; fish, chicken, pizza, ribs, and salads are added over a period of time. Healthier lifestyles and changing food preferences necessitate product changes. New products meet with varying degrees of success and failure.
- The hours of operation expand to appeal to different users and reflect changing demographics and lifestyle trends; "drive-thrus" open to appeal to late-night customers and time-pressed customers. Breakfast menus cater to early morning customers.
- The restaurants appeal to a senior segment (meal economy and social opportunity).
- Seasonal restaurants are opened at Wasaga Beach, Ontario and Montreal's La Ronde Amusement Park.
- Added-value services, such as birthday parties and play areas, are offered to complete the appeal to all age groups. Marketing strategies for segments complement each other.
- An agreement is signed with Wal-Mart to open up satellite restaurant locations across Canada.
- The McFlurry, a tempting dessert item, is launched.
- In response to shifting taste preferences, McDonald's launches the Arch Deluxe hamburger and chicken meals to appeal directly to the adult segment. The kids and teens segments were shrinking in size, and adults preferred the products offered by Wendy's and Burger King. Arch Deluxe products are eventually pulled from the market due to poor sales and replaced with the Big Extra, another adult-style burger.
- McDonald's test markets half-size stores in small towns.
- Breakfast Bagels are introduced in four delicious flavours.
- McDonald's launches the McValue Menu-special pricing on select menu items on certain days and everyday low prices on Extra Value Meal combinations.
- More emphasis is placed on the drive thru (accounts for 50 percent of sales). The company experiments with 2-lane service and a 30-second service guarantee.

- McDonald's test markets the McCafé, a coffee-shop concept in Burlington, Ontario. McCafé offers specialty coffees and baked goods in a café environment. It will compete with Starbucks, Second Cup and other cafés.

- McDonald's launches Boston Market in select locations in Canada. Boston Market is a wholly owned subsidiary offering home-style cooking in a unique environment. It will add sales to McDonald's existing business.

This example illustrates how changes in marketing occur over time. Marketing organizations realize that standing still results in competitive disadvantage and ultimately the demise of the product or company. In effect, market integration is a strategy that lies between market differentiation and mass marketing. It is based on the premise that one way to expand volume and market share is to appeal to users of similar products in other market segments. Appealing to new user segments usually involves a marketing strategy that is different from the original strategy. When a company departs from its original concept, one that was successful and profitable, uncertainty and risk prevail.

RELATIONSHIP MARKETING (ONE-TO-ONE MARKETING)

The concept of relationship marketing, a marketing strategy based on database marketing techniques, was presented in Chapters 1 and 3. The significance of relationship marketing should now have more meaning in the context of market segmentation.

Today, organizations have access to advanced information technology that involves the development and management of sophisticated computer and communication systems. Such systems collect information internally and externally and meet the companies' new requirements for information processing.

relationship marketing or **database marketing**

In **relationship marketing** or **database marketing**, as it is often called, an organization collects demographic, psychographic, media, and consumption information on customers in order to target them more effectively. Such information is available from the home (electronic meters that detect television viewing), businesses (scanners at retail checkout counters), online/CD-ROM databases (indexes to business publications and statistical data on firms and households), and from interactive online communications with customers. The availability of such information is changing the way marketers communicate with potential customers. For example, marketers are turning from the traditional media (television, radio, newspaper, magazines, and outdoor) towards a direct approach (telemarketing, direct mail, direct response television, and a variety of interactive media alternatives: CD-ROM, kiosks, and the Internet).

Because of advancing technology, progressive marketers can now reach what was once thought of as an unobtainable goal: a personal, one-to-one relationship with prospective customers. Such is not the case for many other marketing organizations, as the jump to true database marketing and Internet commerce is a difficult one. Lack of corporate commitment, limited internal expertise, and a lack of proper assessment of marketing needs have delayed movement.

In spite of entry barriers to Internet commerce, it is imperative that Canadian companies adopt an e-commerce model and e-marketing strategies. A US-based study reveals that Web-savvy consumers are younger and more affluent than those not familiar with the Web. They lead more active lives and because they have integrated the Internet into their lives it has changed the way they live, work and buy. They are active buyers online and they are more active buyers at retail stores.[23] Online consumers are no longer a vanguard group of trendsetters, but a cohesive, powerful, and growing consumer force that is dramatically reshaping the marketing landscape. From a business and marketing perspective, a company is either on the technology steamroller or under it.

Canadian statistics reveal the Internet's potential. Presently 53 percent of Canadians 15 and older use the Internet regularly. Three-quarters of Internet users search for goods and services online (they do their product homework there) and 25 percent have made a purchase online.[24] Once the purchase rate reaches critical mass, the Internet market will be enormous. From a consumers' perspective the biggest barrier to online shopping is transferring financial information (credit card numbers) online.

Canadian firms will continue to grapple with technology, and the progressive-minded will discover new, cost-efficient ways to reach their customers. Through traditional forms of advertising, the Ford Motor Company encourages potential customers to visit their Web site for information about their products. The customer can actually build and price a new car while at the site. See the illustration in Figure 6.6.

Multi-channel retailers—companies with bricks-and-mortar stores, online services and/or catalogue services, like Sears Canada Ltd.—have taken the lead in Internet sales. Other successful online retailers include Chapters.ca, tsc.ca (the Shopping Channel) and Staples.ca. By connecting with and transacting business with consumers online these firms are collecting valuable database information that will ultimately lead to more effective and efficient marketing strategies regardless of the means of communications with customers.

Involvement in database marketing shows the direction that marketing is heading in. Access to more precise information has shifted the focus of marketing from conquest (attracting a new customer) to retention (keeping a current customer). The benefit of database marketing is in building a lifetime relationship with a customer. The database is the vehicle for forming that relationship. For more insight into relationship marketing practices, refer to the Marketing in Action vignette **Kraft and Via Target Directly.**

Additional discussions of database marketing applications are included in Chapter 3 (marketing research), Chapter 14 (advertising), Chapter 15 (direct response and interactive communications), and Chapter 17 (e-marketing). Figure 6.7 provides a summary of the various market segmentation strategies.

Market Positioning Concepts

positioning

4.
Explain the concept of positioning and its role in contemporary marketing practice.

Once a target market has been identified and a product developed to meet the needs of the target, the next step is to position the product. **Positioning** refers to the place a product occupies in the customer's mind in relation to competing products. It involves (1) designing and marketing a product to meet the needs of a target market, and (2) creating the appropriate appeals to make the product stand out from the competition in the minds of the target market (through marketing mix activities). How a consumer perceives a product is influenced by image initially (pre-purchase stage) and actual experience with a product (post-purchase stage).

Positioning involves assessing consumer needs and competitive marketing activity to determine new opportunities. For any successful brand, whether it is Coca-Cola, Sears, or McDonald's the success of the brand lies in having a stable positioning. It means staying in touch with today's consumers and altering marketing executions to continually connect with them. To illustrate, consider the message that McDonald's communicates to Canadians. Over the years it has used a variety of slogans to capture

Customers Can Build Their Own
Car and Determine the Price at
Ford's Web site

Provided by Ford Motor Company of Canada

Figure 6.6

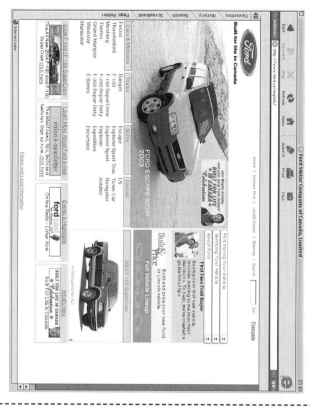

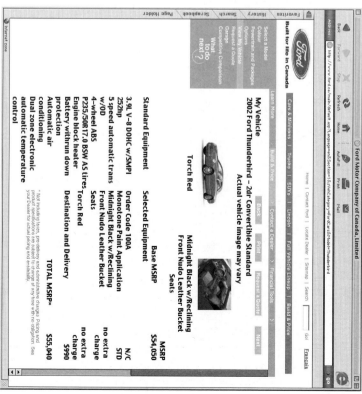

The Market Segmentation Continuum

Figure 6.7

Mass Marketing	Market Integration	Market Differentiation	Niche Marketing	Database (Relationship) Marketing
Resources, product, and plan appeal to one large market	Resources, products, and plans appeal to new user segments while protecting current segments	Resources, products, and marketing plans are aimed at distinct segments (multiple segments)	All resources and plans are allocated to one market segment	Resources tailored to and directed at customers on one-to-one basis

Marketing in Action

Kraft and VIA Target Directly

From packaged goods to services, it seems that everyone is joining the relationship marketing bandwagon. Companies have been doing research for years to determine customer profiles; they would use these profiles to develop marketing strategies to reach the most attractive targets. Now they go a step further. They are taking steps to build their own databases and then devising programs that target actual customers—where they live!

In packaged goods, Kraft saw the light when it realized mass advertising simply wasn't paying off. Kraft determined that their investment in advertising, estimated at more than $100 million in the US alone was actually yielding a negative return on investment. The company's goal was to be more efficient in how they spent advertising dollars. Hence, Kraft decided to assess the potential of direct and database marketing programs.

Kraft tested Web promotions (e.g., coupons online), direct mail, custom publishing, and televi-

sion sponsorships, and the financial results were positive. The company and many of its brands have Internet sites, and the sites are a means of collecting data about customers. Simply put, the Web provides an excellent opportunity to add "stickiness" to an existing relationship between Kraft and its customers.

VIA Rail Canada is also moving into customer relationship marketing. For several years VIA Rail has operated a program called VIA Preference—a program that awards a customer points based on kilometres travelled and can be redeemed for free travel or free services at a later date.

Only three years ago, VIA could not identify who its primary customers were—they had no idea who was boarding their trains. Now they understand exactly who the frequent travellers are, they know the routes they travel, and what classes of service they are using. That's valuable information that can be used to encourage even more train travel.

VIA Preference evolved over three years. Year one was dedicated to acquiring new members. Year two was dedicated to collecting information about the members, in particular a history of their travel pat-the essence of what the company offers. The restaurant recently introduced a new tagline "There's a little McDonald's in everyone." What does it mean? In terms of positioning it is an attempt to focus on customers and the way that McDonald's touches their lives. "It's a rallying cry that allows us to build strategically everything we do around it, from marketing to in-store training," says Rem Langan, vice-president of marketing at McDonald's.[25] McDonald's brings its positioning strategy to life in television commercials that show a cross-section of customers—kids, teens, working adults, and seniors—in wholesome images enjoying the various product offerings.

The positioning that a company desires and the perceived positioning of a product by consumers are often quite different. In positioning a product, organizations collect information about a brand's attributes and about the attributes of competing brands. From the data collected, marketers can plot all brands on a perceptual map. Once plotted, a marketer can see where changes in marketing strategy are necessary if a brand is to improve or alter its image with consumers. As well, gaps on the map (places not occupied by any existing brands) may show where new marketing opportunities exist.

terns and lifestyle interests. The information was gathered from initial application forms, periodic mail surveys, Web site surveys and ongoing communications with customers through the VIA call centre. VIA can now identify who their most valuable customers are: 58 percent are male living in households with $75 000 plus incomes; 47 percent are business travellers; they read the *Globe and Mail*; and the CBC is their favourite television network.

In year three, VIA Rail turned its focus to putting the information to work through targeted marketing ventures and advertising campaigns. For example, an offer for reduced-rate summer travel for a family vacation could be sent only to their most valuable customers—say the top 20 percent by volume travelled. The offer is mailed directly to the customer. No waste in delivering the message!

Kraft and VIA Rail Canada are looking at ways of being more efficient. Senior executives want their managers to be more accountable for what is spent— they want to see results. Relationship marketing is heading the companies in the right direction.

Adapted from David Bosworth, "Better late than never," *Strategy Direct + Interactive*, January 29, 2001, p. D12 and Laura Pratt, "Via puts focus on customer recognition," *Strategy Direct Response*, July 19, 1999, p. D11.

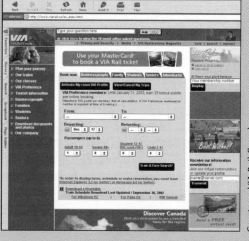

Courtesy: VIA Rail Canada

To illustrate the concept of positioning and perceptual mapping, consider the Canadian retailing market, with a focus on fashion retailers. In this market, department stores compete with specialty stores. For the sake of the illustration, let us assume that stores can be classified into three broad categories: top-end (high price and quality), middle-of-the-road (average price and quality), and low-end (lower price and quality). Competing stores will be plotted on a two-dimensional axis that considers the attributes of price and quality. With reference to Figure 6.8, the map shows that discounters, such as Wal-Mart and Zellers, are positioned in the lower-price and lower-quality quadrant, while a store such as Holt Renfrew and Harry Rosen are in the higher-price and higher-quality quadrant. Department stores such as Sears and the Bay are in the middle along with a battery of specialty retailers selling clothing, electronics goods and appliances, and home furnishings. As indicated in an earlier discussion of department stores, the stores in the middle are suffering. Customers' shopping patterns are shifting to stores at the higher and lower ends of the spectrum. Such a trend is the result of economic and

A Perceptual Map That Positions Three Classifications of Stores

Figure 6.8

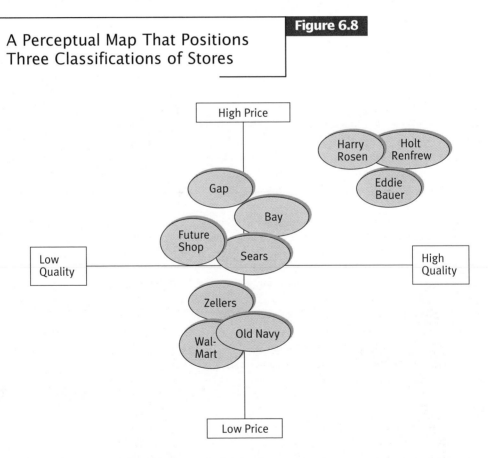

Competitors are clustered on a positioning map. Here Sears is positioned in the middle as the goods they sell are in the mid-price and mid-quality range. Sears competes with similar stores like The Bay (similar lines and prices) and Future Shop (similar lines and prices for electronics goods). Sears must also be concerned with the strategies of stores above and below their price–quality range. Wal-Mart offers general merchandise and clothing at lower prices and quality while Harry Rosen offers trendy men's fashions at high prices. Many more stores could have been added to this positioning map.

income circumstances along with miscues in marketing strategy. The Gap, for example, suffered severe financial consequences in 2001 when it began offering styles that were not in sync with core customer needs. Customers switched to other stores for what they were looking for.

When developing a marketing strategy, positioning strategy is really the foundation. All marketing activities revolve around what a company or brand wants the customer to understand about itself. For more insight into this important concept, see the Marketing in Action vignette **Positioning Strategy: A Key Decision for A&W**.

Marketing in Action

Positioning Strategy: A Key Decision for A&W

When so many marketing organizations are obsessed with attracting new and younger customers, A&W has opted for a completely different strategy. Are baby boomers still interested in fast food or do they prefer the ambiance of a more upscale restaurant? A&W is banking on the former.

A&W is repositioning itself around the needs of baby boomers and they are hoping that everything nostalgic will woo back the customers. A&W wants to get boomers thinking about their younger years where burgers, rings, and root beer ruled. According to Jeff Mooney, CEO of A&W Foodservices of Canada Inc., "Everything we do is focused on the baby boom. It's just like military strategy, concentrate your troops, take your hill, and then take the next one. When you cluster and focus, you win."

A&W has always been a strong force in western Canada but it is now marching eastward and is being lead by a familiar product, A&W Root Beer. But A&W has been here before, in fact, they dominated the fast food market between 1956 and 1972. McDonald's had something to do with their demise! Until McDonald's arrived A&W had its way with the baby boomers. But, as boomers got older and had their own children, A&W's fortunes waned, since the growing tide of children wanted McDonald's Happy Meals and action figures. Business at A&W fizzled.

A&W is not about to give up. Knowing that about one third of Canada's population are boomers (9.3 million), A&W looked around, examined the trends and concluded that virtually every marketing

success in recent memory was tied to the baby boom generation—minivans, RRSPs, sports utility vehicles, and so on. A&W wanted a piece of the action. In its move eastward, they opened 6 standalone restaurants in 2000 and are planning on 15 more in 2002. The restaurants are adorned with black-and-white pictures from the fifties and sixties and there's music playing: the Rolling Stones, the Beach Boys, and the Beatles. It's enough to make a boomer feel right at home!

A&W is pinning its future on boomers. They are older but their taste for the past hasn't dimmed. Currently A&W gets about 46 percent of its business from boomers while competitors average about 36 percent. Mooney expects an even brighter future since parents will soon be free of children. "Boomers will be free to make their own fast food choices. The next 15 years will be ours," he says.

Adapted from Christian Cortroneo, "It's back to the future for A&W's marketing strategy," *Toronto Star*, February 22, 2002, p. E4.

Eyewire.

TYPES OF POSITIONING

The impression or perception a consumer holds about a product is directly influenced by the impact of the marketing strategy. For example, how consumers perceive and interpret advertising messages are one influence. Other factors, such as price, quality, and where a product is purchased, combine to make an impression in the consumer's mind. In the implementation stage, there are several common strategies used to position a product. Here are a few of them.

Head-On Positioning

head-on positioning

In **head-on positioning**, one brand is presented as an alternative equal to or better than another brand. This strategy is usually initiated by a brand challenger, typically the number two brand in the market. The strategy is to show people who declare they regularly use one brand actually choosing another product. The "Pepsi Challenge" is now a classic example of such head-on positioning. In the television commercials for this campaign, non-believers were challenged in a taste test. Once they experienced the taste of Pepsi, their conclusion was rather obvious. In one famous television commercial, the driver of a Coke truck is seen secretly taking out a Pepsi from a store cooler. The remaining cans tumble out of the cooler, drawing attention to the driver.

Other examples of head-on positioning include the battle between Duracell and Energizer. Confusing messages for both brands imply that one lasts longer than the other. In the case of Energizer, the "it keeps on going and going," campaign featuring the famous bunny has made a lasting impression on consumers.

Head-on positioning requires financial commitment, since the brand leader is likely to react with increased marketing spending. In the past, a direct counterattack by the brand leader was unlikely. A brand leader preferred to let its number one position and product benefits speak for it. In many markets today, the level of competition is so intense, even brand leaders resort to using head-on strategies.

Brand Leadership Positioning

Brands that are market leaders can use their large market share to help position themselves in the minds of consumers. Their marketing communications are designed to state clearly that the product is successful, a market leader, and highly acceptable to a majority of users. Coca-Cola has successfully used this approach to build the world's most recognized brand. "Coke is it," "Can't beat the real thing," "Always Coca-Cola," and more recently "Enjoy" are examples of universally recognizable signatures. The brand name, unique bottle, and popular slogan are a deadly combination for Coca-Cola—they are instantly recognizable by consumers everywhere.

Visa portrays its leadership positioning strategy by focusing on transactions and acceptance virtually everywhere in the world. The Visa advertising slogan "All you need" confirms their leadership position in the customer's mind (Figure 6.9).

Product Differentiation

Product differentiation is a strategy that focuses on the unique attributes or benefits of a product—those features that distinguish one brand from another. Gillette's Mach3 razor is a good example of differentiation. The Mach3 is the world's first three-blade system

An Illustration of Brand Leadership Positioning

Figure 6.9

Visa Canada Association

(see Figure 6.10). The three-blade system shaves closer in a single stroke, offering consumers the benefit of less irritation. The Mach3 lives up to the reputation established by its predecessors. Gillette razors really are "the best a man can get." The Mach3 was the leading brand in North America two months after it was introduced.

In the tea market, Tetley is the market leader and its positioning strategy has always been based on product differentiation. According to Glynne Jones, president of Tetley Canada, "it is the simple things that make a big difference."[26] The introduction of round

The Mach3 Razor Uses a Product Differentiation Strategy: It Is the Only Three-Blade System on the Market

Figure 6.10

Courtesy: The Gillette Company

tea bags, with 2000 perforations to ensure free-flowing flavour, gave Tetley a point-of-difference over its competitors—and a 25 percent market share. Another visible aspect of Tetley's consistent positioning strategy are the Tetley Tea Folk, those friendly little animated characters—Sydney, Clarence, and the Head Gaffer—who talk up the virtues of Tetley tea and who have been busy working their way into tea drinkers' hearts for almost 25 years.

Technical Innovation Positioning

Technical innovation is often more important for a company as a whole than for individual products. Companies seeking to project an image of continued technical leadership will use this strategy to position themselves as representing the leading edge of technology. Such a position, if firmly established in the minds of customers, will benefit new products when they are introduced to the market. At the product level, technology can create an advantage that will set one product apart from the others and make it more appealing to the customer. Motorola prides itself on technological advancements in communications equipment. It uses the slogan "What you never thought possible" in its advertising. 3M does the same. 3M is a company that invests heavily in research and development and they are constantly bringing new products to market. Regardless of the product, 3M ties all of its communications together with the slogan *"from need to…3M innovation"*.

Lifestyle Positioning

In crowded markets where product attributes are perceived as similar by the target market, firms must look for alternative ways of positioning their products. The addition of psychographic information has allowed marketers to develop marketing communications on the basis of the lifestyle of the target market. Essentially, the product is positioned to "fit in" or match the lifestyle of the user. Products in categories such as beer, alcohol, perfume, automobiles, and travel frequently use this strategy, as do brands that want to attract a youthful customer.

Lifestyle positioning uses emotional appeals, such as love, fear, sex, and adventure in order to elicit a response from the target. To illustrate, consider what Mountain Dew is doing in the soft drink beverage market. Mountain Dew has become a cutting-edge brand in recent years based on the image it projects. Mountain Dew's image, as projected in wild and crazy advertising through the "Do the Dew" campaign, has created a tight link with thirst-quenching teens. These are teens who enjoy having an outrageous time with the brand outdoors and who identify with the extreme sports that Mountain Dew is associated with. Among teens, the brand is seen as energetic, upscale, and youthful, exactly the image that Pepsi-Cola wants it to have (Mountain Dew is a Pepsi-Cola brand).

Refer to Figure 6.11 for a summary of the steps involved in market segmentation and positioning. Once the target market has been identified and the positioning strategy established, attention is shifted to the development of a marketing strategy using the elements of the marketing mix.

REPOSITIONING

In a competitive marketplace, marketing organizations must be ready to alter their positioning strategies. It is unrealistic to assume that the positioning strategy that is adopted initially will be appropriate throughout the life cycle of a product. Therefore, products will be repositioned on the basis of the prevailing environment in the marketplace. **Repositioning** is defined as changing the place that a product occupies in the consumer's mind in relation to competitive products. There are two primary reasons for repositioning or adapting a product. One, the marketing activities of a direct competitor may change, and, two, the preferences of the target market may change.

repositioning

Steps Involved in Marketing Segmentation and Positioning

Figure 6.11

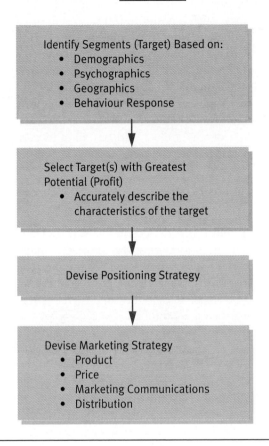

Identify Segments (Target) Based on:
- Demographics
- Psychographics
- Geographics
- Behaviour Response

Select Target(s) with Greatest Potential (Profit)
- Accurately describe the characteristics of the target

Devise Positioning Strategy

Devise Marketing Strategy
- Product
- Price
- Marketing Communications
- Distribution

The process of repositioning is based on a brand's continuous monitoring of such changes. Companies that do not monitor change often lose touch with their customer and suffer in terms of lower sales and declining market share. Nowhere was this more evident than in the Canadian beer market, a product category that is synonymous with lifestyle positioning strategies. Coors traditionally appealed to a professional crowd while Molson Export appealed to macho males. Both brands were losing market share and sales from year-to-year were in decline. Attempts were made by both brands to broaden their appeal to a wider cross-section of the beer-drinking population but they were unsuccessful.

Export finally broke out of the doldrums in 2001 with the launch of the "Had Ex Today" ad campaign. The new ads featured a completely different type of guy-rather than being macho they are somewhat vulnerable and insecure. The TV spots emphasized an age-old male dilemma: spending time with your girlfriend versus spending time with your friends. The initial spot showed a guy named Bob fooling around with his girlfriend only to be interrupted by another guy who (thankfully) saves him from having all that sex. Other similarly themed commercials followed.[27] The new image has repositioned the brand in the minds of male beer drinkers between 19 and 25 years of age. Molson reports that sales and market share for Export have increased as a result of the campaign. Export's image today isn't what it used to be—a repositioning success.

The concepts of positioning and repositioning are important to understand. Potential marketers must realize that marketers do not position brands, consumers do. Once a brand's basic positioning has become set in the customer's mind, there is little marketers can do to influence it, and any change that can be effected tends to happen extremely slowly. Therefore, if a positioning strategy is working, a company should avoid the temptation to change things.

Tetley tea has faced that temptation on numerous occasions. Tetley's advertising agencies have often recommended they dump the Tea Folk, mentioned above. They would argue that fresher, newer approaches were needed. Tetley management stood firm because they know the value of the characters—they were recognized by 80 percent of Canadian consumers. Equity like that is not easily tossed aside. The characters are part of the brand and what it stands for in the minds of consumers.[28] With regard to positioning strategy perhaps the old expression should apply: "If it ain't broke, don't fix it."

Summary

This chapter discussed the key concepts associated with marketing strategy and market segmentation. A market was defined as a group of people having a similar need for a product or service, the resources to purchase the product or service, and the willingness and ability to buy it.

In terms of market segmentation, organizations must identify their target markets as precisely as possible. They do so by making good use of information provided by demographics (age, gender, income, education, occupation, and so on), geographics (regional location and location within a region), and psychographics (activities, interests, and opinions). The organization will constantly monitor trends in these areas so that it can adapt its marketing strategies accordingly.

Behaviour response segmentation is another variable which can be used to develop more effective marketing strategies. This type of segmentation deals with the occasion for using a product, the benefits sought by consumers, the frequency of use, and the degree of brand loyalty. Once the organization has identified and selected the target markets to pursue, the next decision deals with the degree of coverage and activity in each segment. It can choose between mass marketing and the various types of market segmentation strategies, including product differentiation, niche marketing, market integration, and one-to-one (relationship) marketing, Any combination of strategies could be used, and such combinations are common in larger organizations operating in many different types of markets.

Positioning involves designing a product or service to meet the needs of a target market, and then creating the appropriate marketing appeals so that the product stands out in the minds of consumers. Some common positioning strategies include head-on comparisons with competitors, product differentiation, technical innovation, brand dominance, and lifestyle approaches. As a product matures, such factors as competitive activity and changing consumer preferences will force the re-evaluation of positioning strategies.

Key Terms

- behaviour response segmentation 151
- demographic segmentation 143
- geodemographic segmentation 148
- geographic segmentation 148
- head-on positioning 164
- market 140
- market differentiation 152
- market integration 156
- market segmentation 141

- mass marketing 140
- micro-marketing 148
- niche marketing (market concentration) 153
- positioning 158 LED loyalty, Equity, Differentiation
- psychographic segmentation 149
- relationship marketing (database marketing) 157
- repositioning 167

Review Questions

1. Identify the four conditions that must be present for a market to exist.

2. Explain the difference between mass marketing and market segmentation.

3. What is the difference between demographic segmentation, geographic segmentation, and psychographic segmentation?

4. Explain why it is important for marketing organizations to monitor demographic trends in Canada.

5. Briefly describe the four types of behaviour response segmentation and provide an example of each.

6. Explain the concept of niche marketing. What are the risks associated with being a niche marketer?

7. Explain the relevance of positioning and repositioning in marketing practice.

Discussion and Application Questions

1. Cite some examples of niche marketing in your community. Briefly explain the strategies used by these companies.

2. Can one product be successfully positioned to be attractive to several different target markets (e.g., 20-somethings and baby boomers) at the same time? Discuss and provide examples to verify your position.

3. Divide the following markets into segments on the basis of categories of products within the market. Identify three major brands in each subcategory and the differential advantage of each.

    a) Coffee
    b) Deodorant
    c) Laundry detergent
    d) Soft drinks
    e) Cereal

4. Refer to the vignette "Positioning Strategy: A Key Decision for A&W." What is your opinion of the strategy that A&W is implementing? Does it make sense to focus specifically on the baby boom segment? Do you think that other fast food restaurants will follow A&W's lead?

5. Provide two new examples of companies or products (goods or services) that segment their market according to the following:

    a) Age
    b) Ethnic mix
    c) Income
    d) Marital status
    e) Lifestyle

E-Assignment

1. Assume that you are the brand manager for an existing chocolate bar (pick one). You would like to reposition the bar so that is attractive to the tween market in Canada. You lack information on this market segment. Conduct an Internet search to uncover relevant demographic and psychographic information about tweens. On the basis of this information, how will you reposition the chocolate bar? What strategies will you recommend?

2. Assume you are the director of marketing for Mazda Canada. Your immediate objective is to develop a positioning strategy for the Mazda Miata so that is more appealing to the 20-something crowd. Presently, the Miata is popular with the 35-plus age group who like to buy older models of the car rather than new models. Mazda's business goal is to sell more new models. What will the positioning strategy be and how will you implement it?

Endnotes

1. Marina Strauss, "Bay launches low-price program," *Globe and Mail*, October 18, 2001, p. B3.

2. John Heinzl, "Kids: Don't believe everything you're sold," *Globe and Mail*, Friday December 7, 2001, p. M1.

3. Marlene Milczarek, "Where the kids are," *Marketing*, August 6, 2001, p. 13.

4. Stephanie Thompson, "Doritos to net teens," *Advertising Age*, January 12, 2002, p. 8.

5. www.cc.colorado.edu/Dept/EC/generationx96/genx/genx3.html.

6. Patrick Allossery, "Generation X the right target for Volkswagen," *Financial Post*, February 8, 1999, p. C4.

7. Neil Dunlop, "Pinnacles of pleasure," *Financial Post*, April 21, 2001, pp. F1, F6.

8. Klaus Rohrich, "Life after 49," *Marketing*, February 3, 1998, p. 18.

9. Hollie Shaw, "Who's calling the shots?" *Financial Post*, July 31, 2001, p. C1, C6.

10. Marlene Hore, "Just like a woman," *Marketing*, July 19/26, 1999, p. 3.

11. John Gray, "Experts say stop the lip service and start marketing to women," *Strategy*, February 15, 1999, p. 21.

12. Jack Neff, "Male mystique rises a Degree," *Advertising Age*, December 31, 2001, pp. 3, 29.

13. Jo Marney, "Counting ethnic Canadians in," *Marketing*, June 4, 2001, p. 24.

14. Patrick Lejtenyi, "Call in the specialists," *Marketing*, June 4, 2001, pp. 19, 22.

15. "P&G steps up multicultural commitment," *Strategy*, August 14, 2000, p. 24.

16. Statistics Canada, *The Daily*, March 12, 2002, www.statcan.ca/english/dai-quo.

17. Lare Mills, "Bud Light, Canadian get big ad push," *Marketing*, March 27, 2000, p.2 and Patrick Allossery, "Molson gets Canadian," *Financial Post*, April 10, 2000, p. C5.

18. Marion Chankowski, "Segmentation strategy will get you around the promotion clutter," *Marketing*, October 3, 1988, pp. 22-24.

19. Patti Summerfield, "New study reveals demise of brand loyalty," *Strategy*, December 7, 1998, p. 11.

20. Alan J. Magrath, "Niche marketing: finding a safe warm cave," *Sales and Marketing Management in Canada*, May 1987, p. 40.

21. Simon Ashdown, "Fashion retailers reach out to plus-size teens," *Strategy*, October 8, 2001, p. 7.

22. Jean Halliday, "Porsche goes beyond status as a niche player," *Advertising Age*, December 1, 1997, p. 50.

23. "Study finds web-savvy are young, affluent consumers," *Toronto Star*, March 13, 2001, p. D4.

24. Josh Rubin, "Web shoppers wary, StatsCan study finds," *Toronto Star*, March 27, 2001, p. D5.

25. "McDonald's new rallying cry," *Marketing*, July 16, 2001, p. 1.

26. Nadia Molinari, "Mister Tea," *Marketing*, March 25, 1999, pp. 17, 18.

27. Astrid Van Den Broek, "Molson backs Ex over too much sex," *Marketing*, October 2, 2000, p. 3.

28. Nadia Molinari, "Mister Tea," *Marketing*, March 25, 1999, pp. 17, 18.

Courtesy of Brewsters Brew Pub

Strategic Marketing Planning

After studying this chapter, you will be able to

1. Identify the distinctions and relationships between corporate planning and marketing planning.
2. Distinguish between strategic planning and tactical planning.
3. Describe the relationships between the various stages of the planning process.
4. Identify the role and influence of corporate plans and their influence on marketing plans.
5. Describe the various types of strategies used by the company as a whole, and by the marketing departments, for marketing goods and services.
6. Outline the stages of the marketing planning process.
7. Explain the control procedures used in marketing planning.

marketing plan

Before developing a **marketing plan**—a document that outlines the direction and activities of an organization, product, or service—a marketer must consider the plan for the rest of the organization. Marketing strategies are directly influenced by the overall business plan or corporate plan. A corporate plan provides direction to all the operational areas of a business, from marketing and production to human resources and information systems. To understand marketing planning, therefore, it is imperative that we know the planning process of an organization and appreciate the interaction of plans at different levels of the organization.

The Business Planning Process

Strategic business planning involves making decisions about three variables: objectives, strategies, and execution or tactics. Let us first define these planning variables:

objectives

1. **Objectives** are statements that outline what is to be accomplished in the corporate plan or marketing plan. For instance, they outline how much profit or market share is to be achieved over a one-year period. Objectives are specific, measurable and time based.

strategies

2. **Strategies** are statements that outline how the objectives will be achieved. Strategies usually identify the resources necessary to achieve objectives, such as money, time, people, and type of activity.

execution or **tactics**

3. **Execution**, or **tactics**, refers to the plan of action that outlines in specific detail how the strategies are to be implemented. Tactical plans usually provide details of an activity's cost and timing.

A diagram of the business planning process as it applies to marketing is provided in Figure 7.1.

PLANNING VERSUS STRATEGIC PLANNING

When a company embarks on a plan, it anticipates the future business environment and determines the courses of action it will take in that environment. For example, a firm

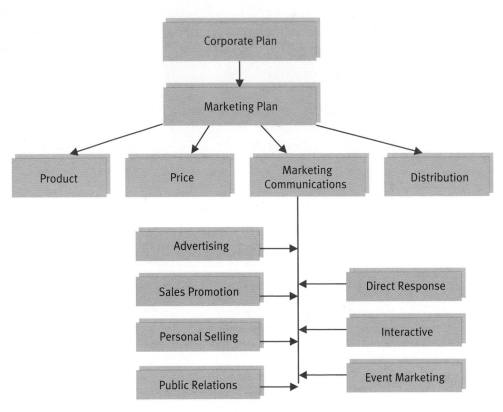

Business Planning Process— Marketing and Marketing Communications Orientation

Figure 7.1

The corporate plan provides guidance to the marketing plan and the marketing plan provides guidance to the marketing communications plan. Corporate plans are strategic in nature, while marketing plans and marketing communications plans are strategic and tactical in nature.

will look at trends in the areas of the economy, demography, culture, and technology and then develop a plan that will provide for growth in such changing times. A typical plan considers the long-term (three to five years) and the short-term (one year) situations. For example, a firm devises a five-year plan that sets the guidelines and the direction the company will take. This is the long-term plan. Each year, the plan will be evaluated and, where necessary, revisions made on the basis of economic and competitive circumstances. This is the short-term plan.

strategic planning

Strategic planning is the process of determining objectives (stating goals) and identifying strategies (ways to achieve the goals) and tactics (specific action plans) that will help achieve the objectives. It is a comprehensive process done at most levels of an organization. A **corporate plan** originates at the top of the organization and is largely based on input from senior executives, such as the president and the vice-presidents.

corporate plan

Such plans are usually not elaborate documents, since their purpose is to identify the corporate objectives to be achieved over a specified period. The corporate plan acts as a guideline for planning in the various operational areas of the company.

Business planning throughout the organization begins and ends at the corporate or senior management level. The senior management formulates the overall strategic direction for the organization and establishes the financial objectives the company should aspire to (sales, profits, return on investment). Then, in accordance with the objectives and directions passed down from the senior management level, the marketing department develops marketing plans that embrace objectives, strategies, and tactics for individual products, divisions, or target markets.

Marketing plans consider such matters as the marketing mix (product, price, distribution, marketing communications), target market characteristics, and control and evaluation mechanisms that determine the effectiveness of the strategies that are implemented. Marketing plans are very specific. As we can see in Figure 7.1, specific objectives, strategies, and tactics are developed for most of the elements of the marketing mix. These elements can then be further subdivided, and individual plans written for each of its divisions. Figure 7.1 shows how marketing communications can be divided into advertising, direct response and interactive communications, public relations, sales promotion, personal selling, and event marketing.

As this planning process indicates, each plan is related to another. The phrase "a chain is only as strong as its weakest link" is an appropriate description of these relationships. Strategic planning attempts to coordinate all the activities so that the various elements work harmoniously. For example, in the case of marketing and advertising, all the activities must present a consistent message for the company about its products in order to create a favourable impression in the minds of consumers. One weak link in the chain can create conflict or confuse the target market. For example, a product's selling price could be set too high in relation to the customer's perception of quality. Or, the product fails to live up to the promises made in advertising. Inconsistent activities spread over numerous company products could seriously disrupt attempts to achieve marketing and corporate objectives.

Corporate Planning

In Figure 7.1, business planning is divided into two distinct categories: (1) corporate planning, and (2) operational planning, which includes marketing planning. Corporate planning is the planning done by the top management and usually includes three variables: a mission statement, a statement of corporate objectives, and a statement of corporate strategies.

Since the corporate plans provide direction for all the functional areas of the company, including marketing, they tend to be long-term in nature and broad in scope, and consider the overall well-being of the organization.

MISSION STATEMENT

mission statement

A **mission statement** is the foundation of the corporate plan; it is a statement of the organization's purpose. It reflects the operating philosophy of the organization and the direction the organization is to take. Such statements are related to the opportunities the company seeks in the marketplace. They are marketing oriented and only work if the company's products and services are designed and marketed to fit the demands of the customers. Stemming from the marketing concept, mission statements recognize customer needs, and consider the competition, as well as the need to build long-term customer relationships. They may be quite detailed or very brief in their content. To illustrate, the mission statement for PepsiCo is as follows:[1]

> Our mission is to be the world's premier consumer products company focused on convenience foods and beverages. We seek to produce healthy financial rewards to investors as we provide opportunities for growth and enrichment to our employees, our business partners and the communities in which we operate. And in everything we do, we strive for honesty, fairness and integrity.

PepsiCo is a multi-division, multi-product company. Its operating divisions include Pepsi-Cola North America and PepsiCo Beverages International, Frito-Lay North America and Frito-Lay International, Gatorade/Tropicana North America, and Quaker Foods North America.

vision statement

Some companies include a vision statement in the corporate plan. A **vision statement** defines future plans, what the company is and does, and where it is headed. If a vision statement is used, the mission statement tends to focus more on the present condition of the company and what it wants to accomplish. To illustrate the combined vision statement and mission statement concept, consider the following statements from VIA Rail Canada:[2]

> *Our Vision*
> To be the best passenger transportation company in Canada.
>
> *Our Mission*
> To provide high quality, low-cost passenger rail service.

CORPORATE OBJECTIVES

corporate objectives

4.
Identify the role and influence of corporate plans and their influence on marketing plans.

Corporate objectives are statements of a company's overall goals and take their direction from the mission statement. They may state how much return on investment or what level of sales or market share is desired of a particular market segment. Objectives may also include statements about where the company might diversify, what businesses to acquire, and other goals. Good objective statements are written in quantifiable terms so that they can be measured for attainment. Consider the following examples:

- To increase total company sales revenue from $500 000 000 to 550 000 000 in 200X.
- To increase market share from 25 percent in 200X to 30 percent in 200X.
- To increase return on investment from 10 percent in 200X to 13 percent in 200X.
- To recycle at least 70 percent of our waste paper.

Objectives like these provide the framework for the development of detailed plans in the operational areas of the organization, with marketing being one of those areas. While not divulging precise quantitative objectives, the overriding corporate objective at PepsiCo is "To increase the value of our shareholder's investment through integrated operating, investing, and financing activities."[3] Specific financial targets would be established for each operating division.

CORPORATE STRATEGIES

corporate strategies

After the corporate objectives are confirmed, the organization identifies **corporate strategies**, which are plans outlining how the objectives are to be achieved. The factors considered when strategies are being developed are marketing strength; degree of competition in markets the company operates in; financial resources (e.g., the availability of investment capital or the ability to borrow required funds); research and development capabilities; and commitment (i.e., the priority the company has placed on a particular goal). PepsiCo's corporate strategy is to concentrate resources on growing businesses, through internal growth and carefully selected acquisitions. Their strategy is continually fine-tuned to address the opportunities and risks of the global marketplace.

Assuming growth is the corporate objective, corporations could proceed in an endless range of strategic directions to achieve it. A company could achieve growth through any one of, or combinations of, the following avenues.

Penetration Strategy

penetration strategy

A **penetration strategy** calls for aggressive and progressive action on the part of an organization. Growth is achieved by building existing businesses (company divisions or product lines). A company like Coca-Cola, for example, wants to build its leadership position in the world's beverage market. To do so it focuses its financial and marketing resources on improving the sales of its soft drink, juice, sports drink and water beverages. Among its product lines are well known brands such as Coca-Cola Classic, Diet Coke, Fruitopia, PowerAde and Dasani. A brand like Coca-Cola Classic faces stiff competition from Pepsi-Cola as well as generic (no name) brands. To stay a step ahead of competitors and to maintain a presence among consumers, Coca-Coal invests a significant amount of money in advertising and promotion each year.

Acquisition Strategy

acquisition strategy

Strategies based on **acquisition**, or the purchase of another company, have become prominent in the past decade. For many companies, it is preferable to buy their way in to an attractive market rather than spend money developing a presence in that market. Assuming the financial resources are available for an acquisition, a company can take advantage of attractive opportunities quickly.

Nestle SA, a Switzerland-based global company well known for its chocolate products, is a company in acquisition mode. In 2001, Nestle acquired Ralston Purina to create the world's largest pet food company (Nestle was already in the pet food business). In the same year, Nestle bought Haagen-Dazs ice cream (Nestle was already in the ice cream business). The acquisition gave Nestle 11 percent of the global ice cream market, ranking them second behind Unilever PLC, a company with 17 percent market share.

Nestle justifies these acquisitions based on future profit potential, noting that pet food sales are growing by about 6.5 percent annually, about double that for human food. Ralston Purina is a dominant brand in the United States, controlling about one-third of the pet food market. Nestle hopes to leverage the Purina brand name through its worldwide distribution system.[4] Haagen-Dazs is a leading brand in the US "out-of-home" ice cream market and dominates the more profitable "scooping" segment that accounts for about 40 percent of the market. Nestle's objective is to become the world's biggest seller of ice cream so more acquisitions are on the horizon.[5]

Nestle
www.nestle.com

PepsiCo exercised its selective acquisition strategy in 2001 when it purchased the Quaker Oats Company for $13.4 billion.[6] The motivation for acquiring Quaker was to pick up the Gatorade brand, the leading sports-beverage drink. The acquisition strengthens Pepsi's position in its war with Coca-Cola.

For more insight into acquisition strategies see the Marketing in Action vignette **Canadian Tire Buys Mark's Work Wearhouse.**

Marketing in Action

Canadian Tire Buys Mark's Work Wearhouse

What does an auto parts, sporting goods, and tool retailer want with a company that peddles pajamas and khaki pants? At first glance the acquisition of Mark's Work Wearhouse by Canadian Tire doesn't seem like a strategic fit. Wayne Sales, president and CEO of Canadian Tire, thinks otherwise.

Canadian Tire was sitting on a huge pile of cash reserves and felt that its existing business was running out of room to grow sales. Canadian Tire operates 450 locations coast-to-coast generating sales revenue of $5.2 billion. Latest year profits were $148 million. Acquiring Mark's adds $500 million to sales but only $8.2 million to profits. The price tag to acquire Mark's was $116 million.

Clear and quantitative corporate objectives that were established by the sales department forced the company to adopt an acquisition strategy. The objective between 2002 and 2005 is to increase annual sales by 10 percent and profit by as much as 15 percent.

Canadian Tire justifies the acquisition by pointing out several benefits. First, there will be annual savings of $7 million by combining administrative expenses. Second, both retailers have the same core customers: their average age is 25 to 59, with household incomes of $55 000 plus. These customers seek basic, durable products for everyday use. Third, there is a good opportunity for cross-merchandising and advertising. Mark's shoppers, for instance, may eventually get Canadian Tire money stuffed into the pockets of the blue jeans they buy. Having more Canadian Tire money in circulation drives people back to Canadian Tire.

The financial clout of Canadian Tire also gives Mark's access to resources to open new stores more quickly than before or to acquire other clothing retailers they previously couldn't afford. Canadian Tire is not interested in pursuing fashion-forward soft line retailers whose sales and profits are subject to economic cycles. Canadian Tire prides itself on being fairly recession-proof, focusing on everyday needs. It believes that Mark's focus on workwear, a product line that accounts for about 40 percent of sales, and casual clothing makes it less susceptible to economic slumps.

Some industry analysts question Canadian Tire's move into soft goods saying it is an awkward fit rather than a strategic fit. Cynthia Rose-Martel, an analyst at Harris Partners Ltd. in Toronto, stated, "It's more of an investment than a marriage of common interests and there weren't any operational synergies beyond the obvious real estate and marketing cost savings." Keith Howlett, an analyst at Desjardins Securities, expected Canadian Tire to pursue growth by building its core categories of auto parts, sporting goods, or even outdoor furniture, rather than embarking on a whole new line of business.

You be the judge. Does this acquisition make sense or should Canadian Tire stick to the business it knows best?

Adapted from Marina Strauss and Elizabeth Church, "Canadian Tire makes surprise Mark's Work Wearhouse bid," *Globe and Mail*, Thursday December 20, 2001, p. B1 and Steven Theobald, "Canadian Tire swallows Mark's Work Wearhouse," *Toronto Star*, December 20, 2001, pp. C1, C12.

Dick Hemingway

New Products Strategy

new product
strategy

A **new product strategy** requires considerable investment in research and development. Such a strategy also requires financial commitment over an extended period, as it takes considerable time to develop a new product. Procter & Gamble hadn't launched a really new product in 15 years and the company wasn't growing financially. In 1999, however, P&G introduced three breakthrough products: Dryel, a product that cleans clothes at home that would usually be dropped off at the cleaners; Febreeze, a spray that removes smells from fabrics; and Swiffer (cloths that remove dust and dirt from dry household places). Truly new products like these create new revenue streams for organizations. Such a strategy is proving more effective than simply expanding existing products.

Good product ideas don't go unnoticed. SCJohnson, a family-owned company firmly established in the household cleaning products category, launched Oust fabric refresher and Pledge Grab-It cloths to address consumer needs and offer innovative choices in the marketplace. See Figure 7.2 for an illustration.

Vertical Integration Strategy

vertical integra-
tion strategy

In a **vertical integration strategy**, one organization in the channel of distribution owns and operates organizations in other levels of the channel. For example, a prominent wholesaler may own retailers that are supplied by the wholesaler. George Weston Limited, for example, is Canada's largest wholesale food distributor. Its warehouses supply retail chains such as Loblaws, Provigo, and Zehrs, among others.

George Weston Ltd.
www.weston.com

Dofasco, a large Canadian steel company followed the vertical integration strategy in 2001. It purchased a laser-technology company from a subsidiary of Magna International, one of Canada's leading parts manufacturers for the automobile industry. The deal makes Dofasco more than just a supplier of steel—ownership at different levels of the distribution channel puts it closer to the value-added technologies that turn steel into auto parts.[7]

Strategic Alliance Strategy

strategic alliance

Strategic alliances are now very popular among companies wanting to find ways of reducing costs or improving operating efficiencies. A **strategic alliance** is a relationship between two or more companies who decide to work cooperatively to achieve common goals. Imperial Oil Limited and Tim Hortons recently formed a strategic alliance that calls for Tim Hortons food kiosks in 300 Esso stations across Canada. Both firms are trying to transform the neighbourhood gas station into a lunch destination and have dubbed the concept "dashboard dining."

In forming the alliance, Imperial Oil hopes to wean itself from its dependence on the slim profit margins of retail gas sales. They already generate much better margins on the convenience store items they sell. The alliance allows Tim Hortons to expand at an unprecedented rate and at much lower cost. Once completed, the kiosks will account for 1 in 10 of all Tim Hortons locations. The two firms hope to attract a walk-in lunch business, a real departure from the roots of a service station. Esso is turning into a convenience retailer who just happens to sell gasoline.[8]

Golf club operator ClubLink formed an alliance with Delta Hotels to build a 250-room hotel and conference centre at the Glen Abbey Golf Club just west of Toronto. It's a marriage that makes sense. According to Bruce Simmonds, president and CEO of

Figure 7.2

New Products Like Grab-It Mitts Bring New Revenue

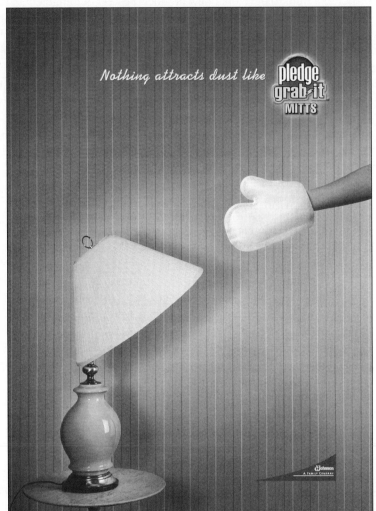

Courtesy: SCJohnson

ClubLink
www.clublink.com

ClubLink, "The development of a hotel and conference centre will make Canada's number one premium daily fee course more attractive to the travelling golfer seeking a high-quality golf experience. We are joining Canada's largest owner and developer of high-quality golf courses with the largest first class hotel company in Canada."[9] Delta also manages ClubLink's four golf resorts in the Muskoka region north of Toronto.

Divestment Strategy

divestment strategy

Bigger is not always better! Rather than expanding some companies are consolidating their operations by **divesting** themselves of operations that are not profitable. Divestment alternatives include downsizing, closing, or selling parts of a company.

**diversification
strategy**

In the 1980s and early 1990s Molson followed a **diversification strategy**—they acquired businesses in completely new areas, areas where their management expertise was stretched to the limits (chemical manufacturing and retailing). Facing financial pressure in the mid-1990s, Molson switched directions and adopted a reversification strategy. **Reversification** refers to a firm's retreat to its core business by selling off divisions that are unprofitable or not suited to its future direction. Molson sold all of its divisions except beer—the objective was to focus on what the company does best: brew and sell beer. It seems odd that Molson would sell the Montreal Canadiens, but economic realities outweighed the emotional attachment between the two company divisions. As an indication of Molson's commitment to beer, the company recently acquired Kaiser Brewing, Brazil's second largest beer company.

reversification

**strategic business
unit (SBU)**

The examples cited throughout the corporate strategy section illustrate the concept of strategic business units. A **strategic business unit (SBU)** is a unit of a company that has a separate mission and objectives and can be planned independently of the other businesses of the company. At PepsiCo for example, the operating divisions include Pepsi-Cola, Frito-Lay, Gatorade/Tropicana, and Quaker. The growth potential of each business unit determines the level of marketing support (time, money, and human resources) it receives. The parent company is responsible for establishing strategic business unit priorities. By analyzing consumption trends, PepsiCo may realize that sales of soft drink beverages are flat and that sports drink beverages are growing in popularity. Therefore, to grow the overall PepsiCo business, additional financial resources could be provided Gatorade and Tropicana products and less provided for Pepsi-Cola products.

portfolio analysis

When a company analyzes its business units, it assesses the strengths and weaknesses of each unit, recommends additions and deletions when necessary, and allocates resources according to growth potential opportunities. In marketing terms the company is conducting a **portfolio analysis**.

Cross-Marketing

cross-marketing

Cross-marketing is a strategy in which two independent or seemingly independent organizations share facilities and/or resources to market their goods and services to similar types of customers. Maple Leaf Sports & Entertainment Ltd. introduced a cross-marketing campaign in 2000 to convince Leaf fans to take in more Raptors basketball games. The company, owners of both the Leafs and the Raptors and their Air Canada Centre home, does not want to convert fans from one sport to another, but have them watch both. Targeted mainly at adults, the Raptors are convinced that the best way to invite people into the game of basketball is through hockey. Television ads feature Raptor team members talking about the Leafs and vice versa.[10]

Some corporations practise cross-marketing by combining several of their operating divisions under one roof. Such a practice provides savings in terms of capital and operating costs. Cara Operations combines Swiss Chalet and Harvey's in one location. Tricon Global combines KFC and Taco Bell, and Wendy's International combines Wendy's and Tim Hortons. The restaurants share the cost of land, and building and site work while maintaining separate kitchens, counters, drive-thru windows and crews. Each restaurant expects to get crossover business from the other restaurant. What makes these concepts work is the similarity of their customers' needs—quality products, competitive prices, and quick service.

Marketing Planning

6.
Outline the stages of
the marketing plan-
ning process.

The marketing department operates under the direction of a chief marketing officer (or similar title) within the guidelines established by the senior management or executive branch of the organization. The objectives, strategies, and action plans developed by marketing are designed to help achieve the overall company objectives. Where planning is concerned, the major areas of marketing responsibility include:

1. Identifying and selecting target markets
2. Establishing marketing objectives, strategies, and tactics
3. Evaluating and controlling marketing activities

**marketing
planning**

Marketing planning is the analysis, planning, implementation, evaluation, and control of marketing initiatives in order to satisfy target market needs and achieve organizational objectives. It involves the analysis of relevant background information and historical trend data, and the development of marketing objectives and strategies for all products and services within the company. The integration of the various elements of the marketing mix is outlined in the marketing plan of each product. Other elements of marketing planning include target market identification, budgeting, and control mechanisms. In contrast to strategic corporate plans, marketing plans are short-term in nature (one year), specific in scope (they deal with one product and outline precise actions), and combine both strategy and tactics (they are action oriented). They are also subject to change on short notice, as a result of economic shifts or competitive activity. Figure 7.3 summarizes the stages of marketing planning. The following is a description of the various elements of marketing planning. For an illustration of a real-world marketing plan visit the Web site that accompanies this text book: www.pearsoned.ca/tuckwell

While there is no typical format for a marketing plan (i.e., the content and structure varies from company to company) it is usually subdivided into major sections based on background content and planning content. In terms of background the company conducts a **situation analysis** (sometimes called environmental analysis) in which data and information about external and internal influences are compiled. External considerations include economic trends, social and demographic trends, and technology trends. As well, information is compiled about the market, competition, and customers.

situation analysis

SWOT analysis

Using this information, a **SWOT analysis** (an evaluation of a brand's strengths, weaknesses, opportunities, and threats) is undertaken. The SWOT provides guidance for developing marketing strategies. In the **marketing plan**, the objectives, strategies, and tactics for the brand or company are clearly delineated. The following is a description of the various elements of a marketing plan.

marketing plan

MARKETING PLAN BACKGROUND—SITUATION ANALYSIS

As a preliminary step to marketing planning, a variety of information is compiled and analyzed. Often referred to as an **environmental scan**, the information collected includes some or all of the following:

**environmental
scan**

External Influences

1. *Economic Trends* Basic economic trends dictate the nature of marketing activity (e.g., if the economy is healthy and growing, more resources are allocated to marketing

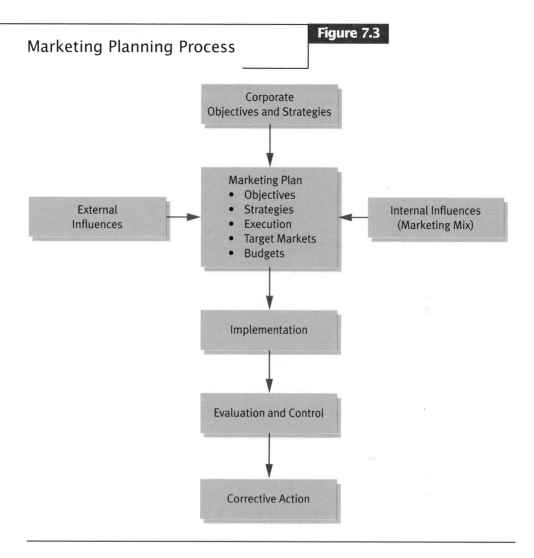

Figure 7.3

Marketing Planning Process

Corporate
Objectives and Strategies

↓

Marketing Plan
• Objectives
• Strategies
• Execution
• Target Markets
• Budgets

External
Influences → ← Internal Influences
(Marketing Mix)

↓

Implementation

↓

Evaluation and Control

↓

Corrective Action

activity; if the economy is in a recession, a more conservative approach is often adopted).

2. **Social and Demographic Trends** Basic trends in age, income, immigration, and lifestyle influence decisions on what target markets to pursue. For example, the Canadian population is aging and there is a steady migration of the population to urban areas. These factors necessitate a change in marketing strategy.

3. **Technology Trends** The rapid pace of change (e.g., in computers and communications equipment) influences the development of new products, shortens product life cycles, and influences the communications strategies used to reach customers.

4. **Market Size and Growth** A review is made of trends in the marketplace over a period. Is the market growing, remaining stable, or declining?

5. **Regional Market Importance** Market trends and sales volume trends are analyzed by region to determine areas of strength or weakness, and areas to concentrate on in the future.

6. *Market Segment Analysis* The sales volume for a total market and for segments within a market are reviewed. For example, the coffee market is analyzed in terms of regular ground coffee, instant coffee, decaffeinated coffee, and flavoured coffee.

7. *Seasonal Analysis* An examination is conducted of seasonal or cyclical trends during the course of a year. For example, special holidays, such as Christmas, Thanksgiving, Hallowe'en, and others, often have an impact on sales volume.

8. *Consumer Data* Current users of a product are profiled according to such factors as age, income, gender, lifestyle, and location.

9. *Consumer Behaviour* A review is made of the degree of loyalty customers exhibit towards a product or brand. Are customers loyal, or do they switch brands often? Other factors considered are benefits consumers seek in the product and how frequent their purchases are.

10. *Other Factors* Factors such as pack size trends (regular size, single size, family size, etc.), colours, scents or flavour; analysis of products sold; or other relevant areas play a role in the planning process.

11. *Media* Trends in competitive spending on media advertising will influence marketing communications decisions and budgeting.

Product (Brand) Analysis

An assessment of a brand's marketing mix strategy is reviewed at this stage. An attempt is made to link marketing activities undertaken in the past year with the sales volume and market share that was achieved—did the plan work? Is the brand meeting consumers' expectations?

1. *Sales Volume* Historical sales tends are plotted to forecast future growth

2. *Market Share* Market share success is the clearest indicator of how well a brand is performing. Market share is examined nationally and regionally in order to identify areas of strength and weakness.

3. *New Product Activity* The success or failure of new product lines introduced in recent years is highlighted (e.g., new pack sizes, flavours, product formats, and so on).

4. *Distribution* The availability of a product nationally or regionally is reviewed. Distribution is also assessed based on type of customer (e.g., chains versus independents and the successes or failures of online distribution initiatives).

5. *Marketing Communications* An assessment of current activities will determine if strategies are to be maintained or if new strategies are needed. A review of media spending and utilization (e.g., television, newspaper, magazines, outdoor, Web sites, events and promotions, and so on) is used to assess their impact on brand performance, nationally and regionally.

Competitive Analysis

Major competitors are identified and their performance is analyzed. Essentially, a competitive product is reviewed much like a company's own brand. A manager will want to know a competitor's sales volume trends and market share trends and what marketing activities they have undertaken to produce those trends. This calls for a review of their marketing mix activities.

SWOT ANALYSIS

Once the market, product and competitor information is assembled, the next step is an appraisal of it. Such an appraisal is referred to as a SWOT analysis. The acronym SWOT stands for strengths, weaknesses, opportunities, and threats. A SWOT analysis examines critical factors that have an impact on the nature and direction of a marketing strategy. Strengths and weaknesses are internal factors (e.g., resources available, research and development capability, production capability, and management expertise), while opportunities and threats are external factors (e.g., economic trends, competitive activity, and social and demographic trends).

The end result of a SWOT analysis should be the matching of potential opportunities with resource capabilities. The goal is to capitalize on strengths while overcoming weaknesses. A SWOT analysis can be conducted at any level of an organization—product, division, or company.

POSITIONING STRATEGY STATEMENT

The concept of positioning strategy was discussed in Chapter 6. There, it was stated that positioning attempts to place a desirable image about a product, service or company in the minds of customers. In the context of the marketing plan, a positioning strategy statement acts as a focal point for the development of marketing strategies and the utilization of the marketing mix.

Effective positioning strategy statements are realistic, specific, uncomplicated, and they clearly distinguish what the brand has to offer. To illustrate, consider the positioning statement for VISA Canada.

VISA gives you the confidence that you are able to do anything.

The benefits of having and using a VISA card are successfully portrayed in advertising campaigns that says your VISA card is "All You Need." In one television ad, a young couple is driving to the airport. Sensing his wife's frustration, the husband says, "It will be my last trip for a while." Her expression suggests otherwise. When they arrive at the airport, he opens the trunk to reveal two suitcases. The phrase, "When you need a one-way ticket out of the doghouse" appears on screen. As the now happy and excited couple embrace, the tagline "VISA. All you need" appears. A print ad that also executes VISA Canada's positioning strategy appears in Figure 7.4.

MARKETING OBJECTIVES

marketing objectives

Marketing objectives are statements identifying what a product or service will accomplish over a one-year period. Typically, marketing objectives concentrate on sales volume, market share, and profit (net profit or return on investment), all of which are quantitative (as opposed to qualitative) in nature and measurable at the end of the period. Objectives that are qualitative in nature could include new product introductions, new additions to current product lines, product improvements, and packaging innovations. To illustrate the concept of marketing objectives, consider the following sample statements:

Sales Volume: To achieve a unit volume of 200 000 units by the end of the year, an increase of 10 percent over the current year sales.

Market Share: To achieve a market share of 30 percent in 12 months, an increase of four share points over the current position.

Figure 7.4

A Print Execution Demonstrating VISA Canada's Leadership Positioning Strategy

Courtesy: VISA Canada Association

Profit: To generate an after-budget profit of $600 000 in the next 12 months.

Product: To launch a new package design in the fourth quarter of this year.

Objectives should be written in a manner that allows for measurement at the end of the year. Were the objectives achieved or not?

MARKETING STRATEGIES

**marketing
strategies**

Marketing strategies are the "master plans" for achieving marketing objectives. Marketing strategies usually include four main elements: a positioning strategy statement, a description of the target market, discussion about how the various elements of the marketing mix will be used, and a budget.

Target Market

target market

When developing a marketing plan, the planner identifies, or targets, markets that represent the greatest profit potential for the firm. A **target market** is a group of customers who have certain characteristics in common: similar needs, habits, and lifestyles. The planner must ask what these are, and if there is one primary user group or several user segments which have a need for the product or service. After gathering this information, the manager will define the target market in terms of demographic (age, income, gender, education, and occupation), psychographic (lifestyle), and geographic (location) characteristics. To demonstrate, the following profile might represent the *primary target market* for an upscale automobile or someone interested in the services of a financial planning company:

Age: 25 to 49 years old
Gender: male or female
Income: $75 000 plus annually
Occupation: Managers, owners, professionals, executives (referred to as MOPEs)
Education: College or university
Location: Cities of 200 000 plus population
Lifestyle: Progressive thinkers and risk takers who like to experiment with new products and who are interested in the arts, entertainment, and vacation travel.

Additional targets or *secondary targets* as they are referred to, will have a different profile.

Marketing Mix

At this stage of the planning process, the role and importance of each element in the marketing mix and those activities that comprise each element of the mix are identified. The task is to develop a plan of attack so that all the elements combine to achieve the marketing objectives. For example, in the soft drink business, both Coca-Cola and PepsiCo offer products of comparable quality and price. Therefore, it is the strength of their advertising (a marketing communications strategy) and their availability (distribution strategy) that determines competitive advantage. Both brands will invest heavily in these two areas. Different brands facing different situations may utilize the various elements of the marketing mix a different way.

Budget

The corporate plan has already identified a total marketing budget for the company, giving consideration to the overall profit concerns for the forthcoming year. The budget must be allocated across all company products on the basis of the firm's analysis of current priorities or profit potential. Managers responsible for product planning must develop and justify a budget that allows enough funds to implement the strategies identified in their marketing plan and to achieve the financial objectives identified for the product. The final stage of the budgeting process is the allocation of funds among the activity areas in the plan (product development, advertising, sales promotion, personal selling, event marketing, and direct marketing). It should be recognized that there is much competition internally among brand managers for budget resources.

Marketing Execution

Marketing execution or **marketing tactics**, as they are often referred to, focus on specific details of activities that were identified in the strategy section of the plan. In general terms, a tactical plan outlines the activity, how much it will cost, what the timing will be, and who will be responsible for implementation. Detailed tactical plans for all components of the plan-product improvement, advertising, sales promotion, and marketing research, and so on, are included here.

For a summary of the information that is usually included in a marketing plan, refer to Figure 7.5. Also, visit the Web site that accompanies this textbook to view an illustration of an actual marketing plan: www.pearsoned.ca/tuckwell

MARKETING CONTROL AND EVALUATION

Since clearly defined and measurable objectives have been established by the organization and by the marketing department, it is important that results be evaluated against the plans and against past performance. This evaluation indicates whether current strategies need to be modified or whether new strategies should be considered. **Marketing control** is the process of measuring and evaluating the results of marketing strategies and plans and taking corrective action to ensure that the marketing objectives are attained. Marketing control involves three basic elements:

1. Establishing standards of marketing performance expressed in the form of marketing objectives
2. Periodically measuring actual performance (of the company, division, or product) and comparing it to with the established objectives
3. Taking corrective action (e.g., developing new strategies) in those areas where performance does not meet the objectives

Refer to Figure 7.6 for a diagram of the control process. The nature of an organization's control process can vary and the frequency of evaluation is left to the discretion of the management. For evaluating the effectiveness of marketing strategies, there are three primary measures or indicators: *marketing strategy reviews*, *financial reviews*, and *strategic control reviews*.

Marketing Activity Reviews

The effectiveness of a marketing plan is measured against a few key indicators: *sales volume*, *market share*, and *profit*. Activity reviews typically occur on a quarterly basis and often involves a gathering of brand managers, sales managers and some senior marketing executives. Planning cycles that have activity reviews built in give an organization the opportunity to make strategic adjustments during the course of a year.

For any of the three indicators (sales, market share, and profit) the managers will compare *actual results* versus *planned results* and *actual results* versus *results for the same period a year ago*. Understanding why sales are up or down is the responsibility of the sales managers and brand managers, so naturally there is much discussion among these managers to figure out the results and agree on how to proceed. By reviewing per-

Content of a Marketing Plan

Figure 7.5

MARKETING BACKGROUND— SITUATION ANALYSIS

External Influences

Economic trends
Social and demographic trends
Technology trends

Market Analysis

Market size and growth rate
Regional market importance
Market segment analysis
Seasonal analysis
Consumer data (target user)
Consumer behaviour (category and
  brand loyalty)
Product trends
Media expenditures

Product Analysis

Sales volume trends
Market share trends
Distribution trends
New product activity
Marketing communications activity

Competitive Analysis

Market share trends
Marketing activity assessment
Competitive innovations

SWOT Analysis

Strengths
Weaknesses
Opportunities
Threats

MARKETING PLAN

Positioning Statement

Marketing Objectives

Sales volume
Market share
Profit
Other

Marketing Strategies

Target market description
Marketing mix strategies
  - Product
  - Price
  - Marketing Communications
  - Distribution
  - Marketing Research
  - Budget

Marketing Execution

Action plans
  - Product
  - Price
  - Marketing communications
  - Distribution
  - Marketing research
  - Profit improvement

Financial Summary

Brand profit & loss statement

Marketing Budget

Allocation by activity
Allocation by time (month, quarter, etc.)

Marketing Calendar

Activity schedule by month

---

formance and customer feedback together they can mutually agree on revised figures and marketing activities for the balance of the year. Collectively, any revised figures to which the managers agree have an impact on the financial well-being of the company and affect the activities of the other operational areas of the company.

Part of the marketing activity review should also include a review of competitor activity. What are the competitors doing? Are they gaining or losing market share? Such

Marketing Control Process

Figure 7.6

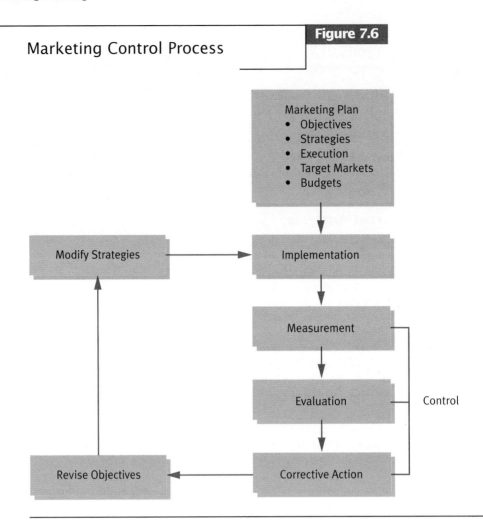

analysis attempts to link marketing activities to share performance in an effort to determine which activities are effective and which are ineffective.

Financial Reviews

As part of the organization's marketing control process, periodic profit reviews are conducted for all product lines and divisions. Key variables in a profit review are up-to-date *sales forecasts*, *costs*, and *marketing budgets*.

Since senior executives are largely evaluated on profit the organization generates and the value of a company's stock, the financial review process can be challenging for the marketing department. For example, if it is forecast that profit will fall short of expectations by the end of the fiscal year, marketing budgets will have to be trimmed. Such reductions could occur by product, by division, or by region. For example, the advertising budget could be slashed in order to protect other marketing activities. A financial review forces managers to establish priorities and withdraw funds from those activities that will feel the effects the least.

Strategic Control

Strategic control is more long term in nature than marketing control. Since conditions in the marketplace (economy, technology, competition, and governments) change rapidly, marketing strategies soon become outdated. An organization must be ready for change! Therefore, strategic reviews are intensive and are conducted every three to five years. Within this framework, marketers reassess marketing strategies for all products annually, during the preparation of the marketing plan.

marketing audit

The primary instrument for evaluating strategic direction and overall effectiveness of marketing activities is a marketing audit. A **marketing audit** is a systematic, critical, and unbiased review and appraisal of the marketing department's basic objectives and policies, and of the organization, methods, procedures, and people employed to implement the policies.[11] An external consultant often conducts the marketing audit in order to eliminate any political bias that may exist in an organization. The task of the auditor is to evaluate plans and the quality of the marketing effort as objectively as possible.

Keeping Pace with Change

In contemporary marketing, an organization must be flexible in order to take advantage of new developments in the marketplace. Throughout the planning cycle, a firm is presented with new threats and opportunities that can make a plan obsolete rather quickly. Consequently, the wise marketing manager builds a contingency plan into a master plan. A contingency is the possibility of something happening that poses a threat to the organization. A **contingency plan** involves the identification of alternative courses of action that can be used to modify an original plan if and when new circumstances arise.

contingency plan

A contingency plan is based on "what if" or "worst-case" situations. If these situations develop, the organization is ready to implement alternative strategies. Some events that would require alternative action would be:

1. The competition unexpectedly increases its level of media advertising.
2. The competition reduces its price to build market share.
3. A new competitor enters the market.
4. A strike in your own plant halts production of your product.

Such situations add a dimension of foresight to strategic marketing planning and force the manager to plan for the unexpected at all times.

Linking Marketing Strategies to Corporate Strategies

As discussed earlier in the chapter, corporate strategies plot the basic direction an organization will take for an extended period—it may follow an acquisition strategy, a penetration strategy, or a new product development strategy, among many potential alternatives.

Once the basic direction is established, individual products must develop their own marketing strategies that will be implemented over a one-year period. If it is a retail operation, a marketing plan is struck for the entire organization. The collective success or failure of the products influences the overall health of the organization and whether or not corporate objectives are achieved. Some of the more common marketing strategies have labels similar to the corporate strategies discussed earlier. Refer to Figure 7.7 for a visual illustration of these strategies.

MARKET PENETRATION

market penetration

Strategies that focus on **market penetration** are aimed at improving the market position of an existing product in existing markets. Essentially, these strategies attempt to increase sales to current users while stealing market share from competitors. In this respect, the marketing mix elements are modified to develop a better formula for getting current and new customers to buy. Among the options are: improving the product, lowering the price, changing the style of advertising, or any combination of these.

In the computer market, Dell Computer effectively implements a penetration strategy. Dell passes on cost savings to consumers and because the cost of component parts has been dropping in recent years the savings have been significant. Second, Dell uses a just-in-time inventory system—it only brings together enough parts to make a computer when it has already sold the computer. Dell moves a computer out the door in an average of 3 days, while other companies take as long as 60 days. Selling directly to consumers and business customers, rather than through retail distributors, also keeps costs down. This combination of low price (based on low costs) and direct distribution has made Dell the leading brand of microcomputer in North America.[12] Competitors have not been able to duplicate Dell's strategy successfully.

MARKET DEVELOPMENT

market development

A company pursuing a strategy based on **market development** attempts to market existing products to new target markets. Such strategies attempt to attract consumers of different demographic categories, different lifestyles, or different geographic areas. To illustrate, a hotel chain, such as Westin or Sheraton, may generate most of its business from business travellers during the week. To spur weekend business, these hotels assemble and market family package plans (weekend holidays) at very reasonable prices. Instead of having vacant rooms, the hotel generates incremental revenue to cover the costs of operating the hotel.

Common Marketing Strategies

Figure 7.7

	EXISTING PRODUCT	NEW PRODUCT
EXISTING MARKET	Market Penetration	Product Development
NEW MARKET	Market Development	Diversification

Other businesses may grow by taking a successful product in Canada and marketing it in a foreign country. If the market growth is flat in Canada, a foreign market may offer greater growth potential. Roots, for example, is planning to expand operations in the United States. Roots is well known in Canada for its unique merchandise—its own outdoorsy yet stylish private label fashions. Presently, Roots only has seven locations in the US but many more are on the horizon. Compared to other Canadian retailers, Roots is in an enviable position to attack the US market. It received a healthy dose of recognition thanks to the publicity from its Canadian and American team uniforms at the 2002 Winter Olympics in Salt Lake City.[13]

Toyota used a market development strategy when it redesigned the Matrix model to entice a younger target audience. The more stylish and sporty look is illustrated in Figure 7.8. For additional insight into market development strategies and product development strategies see the Marketing in Action vignette **Toyota Pursues Younger Customers**.

Toyota Matrix

Figure 7.8

Courtesy: Toyota Canada

Toyota Pursues Younger Customers

Toyota is a successful automobile company. In fact, it is on the verge of surpassing Chrysler to become the third-largest seller of cars in North America. General Motors and Ford lead the pack. Sometimes you become a victim of your own success, however, and that's exactly the dilemma that Toyota finds itself in.

The average age of a Toyota customer is 50. Toyota's older average age is due to its success at getting loyal younger buyers from the past to trade up to more expensive Toyota models as they get older. The Corolla, for example, is their number one selling car in Canada, while Camry is one of the leaders in overall car sales in North America.

Toyota's corporate objective is to attract a younger buyer and to do so will require a combination of new product lines and the restyling and reimaging of some existing car lines. Demographic trends strongly suggest that Toyota make the move toward a younger customer. The population group referred to as Generation Y, echo boomer, or millennial (late teens and early twenties right now) is going to be huge and they are just entering their car-buying years. Toyota estimates there will be 4 million of them a year until 2010. That's a market worth pursuing!

Some initial steps taken by Toyota include the restyling of the Celica model. The sportier look of the Celica has dropped the average age of the Celica owner to 36 years from 44 years. The Echo was launched in 2000 to attract young first-time buyers, but surprisingly the concept was so popular that the average age was 44 years. Half of the buyers were new to Toyota, however, so that's incremental business that would have gone elsewhere. With the Echo, Toyota might have misread the market but they were very happy with the results.

Toyota also unveiled the Matrix, a 5-door wagon aimed at the 20-something target market. The Matrix is a hybrid of a sports car and an SUV, with compact-car pricing. It is ideally positioned to meet the needs of new, young buyers.

The Matrix was launched using a strategy that combined media, events, and promotions that would associate Matrix with the younger target's lifestyle. Entertainment, socializing, and sports and fitness are important to the target market so media opportunities were chosen that would reach the target while they were enjoying those activities. Media advertising included full-motion cinema ads, health club posters, and restro-bar posters. The Internet was used to develop a relationship with the target. A contest, "The Toyota Matrix—Drive It, Win It," called for entries online. Participants had to write a short essay on how they would use a Matrix for a month during the summer of 2002. Close to 11,000 entries were submitted.

The Matrix also sponsored Snow Jam in five geographic markets and the FIVB Beach Volleyball stop in Montreal. These events associated Matrix with customers interested in extreme sports.

Longer term it is expected that Toyota will do for youth what it did for luxury car buyers. To attract affluent customers a separate brand called Lexus was introduced. That strategy was very successful. Considering the sheer size and potential of the Generation Y target, a completely new brand tailored specifically to them is not out of the question.

Adapted from information provided by Toyota Canada; Kae Inoue, "Toyota covets young buyers," *Financial Post*, January 9, 2002, p. FP6; Tobi Elkin and Jean Halliday, "Toyota launches Corolla campaign," *Advertising Age*, February 25, 2002, pp. 4, 29; and News Line, *Marketing*, February 25, 2002, p. 3.

Christopher Bissell/Getty Images

PRODUCT DEVELOPMENT

product development

In the case of a strategy involving **product development**, new products are offered to current target markets, or existing products are modified and marketed to current users. Such initiatives may include the introduction of new sizes, colours, and flavours. Expansion of a product line by extending the line is quite common. This involves the use of the same brand name on new products or related products (a family of products).

Pfizer Canada used a product development strategy when it introduced Benylin First Defense and Benylin Energy Boosting Lozenges. Benylin is the leading brand in the cough and cold remedy market in Canada. Benylin First Defense helps boost the immune system to treat the early signs of a cold. Benylin Energy Boosting Lozenges are designed to treat fatigue, one of the top three symptoms of a cold. Both products offer consumers an additional benefit—they contain recognized herbal compounds (herbal remedies are the fastest growing segment among over-the-counter pharmaceutical products). Benylin First Defense contains echinacea, menthol, and is sweetened with honey. Energy Boosting Lozenges contain ginseng, an ingredient traditionally known as an invigorator or energy booster.[14] Benylin now has a unique and complete line of cough and cold remedy product for consumers to choose from.

DIVERSIFICATION

diversification

Diversification, as it applies to products, refers to the introduction of a new product to a completely new market. In effect, the company is entering unfamiliar territory when it uses this strategy. Such a strategy requires substantial resources for research and development, initially high marketing expenses, and a strong commitment to building market share. To illustrate, consider Unilever Canada's venture into the cosmetics and perfume market. Unilever is one of the world's largest consumer products companies and is best known for brands such as Becel and Imperial margarine, Lipton soup and dinner mixes, Ragu sauces, Dove and Lever 2000 soap, Degree deodorant, and Sunlight detergent. Unilever has strong distribution in grocery and drug store outlets.

Only a decade ago Unilever ventured into new territory when it started marketing prestige fragrances and body products under the brand names Obsession, Eternity, Escape, Contradiction, and cK. These brands fall under the umbrella of the designer label Calvin Klein. Unilever was marketing new product lines in a new market in a new channel of distribution—department stores were new to the packaged goods company. The venture represented risk, but Unilever was successful. Calvin Klein is presently the leading brand of fragrance with 20 percent market share.[15]

Apple computer, always a niche player in the computer market, and always a company that does things differently, opted for diversification when it decided to open up its own retail stores. There was irony in the decision because competitors like IBM and Gateway were in the process of closing their retail operations. The market was soft and customers preferred to buy directly. Apple's main selling points are that its products are cool and sexy—not the same kind of bland, generic-looking PCs that everyone else has. Apple believes its loyal customers will be more than willing to visit their retail locations. Some analysts believe this is misguided, and that it will prove to be simply a time-consuming way to lose a lot of money.[16]

Summary

The quality of marketing planning in an organization is influenced by the business planning process itself. In terms of marketing, two different but related plans are important: the corporate plan and the marketing plan. Each plan is based on the development of objectives, strategies, and tactics. A corporate plan provides direction to a marketing plan; a marketing plan provides direction to the various components of marketing, such as product strategy and marketing communications strategy.

Business planning is a problem-solving and decision-making effort that forces management to look at the future and to set clear objectives and strategies.

Business planning is divided into two broad areas: corporate planning, and operational planning, which marketing is a part of. Corporate planning starts with the development of a mission statement, followed by corporate objectives and strategies. These plans consider both the short term and the long term. Some of the more common corporate strategic alternatives include: penetration strategies that focus on more aggressive marketing, acquisition strategies, entering and developing new markets, new product development programs, forming strategic alliances, vertical integration strategies, diversification and reversification strategies, and cross-marketing.

Strategic marketing planning involves reviewing and analyzing relevant background information and conducting a SWOT analysis, establishing appropriate marketing objectives, devising a positioning strategy, identifying target markets, devising marketing strategies (utilization of the marketing mix) and marketing executions (specific action plans to implement the strategies), accessing budget support, and control procedures. The more commonly used marketing strategies include: market penetration, market development, product development, and diversification. Once the strategies are implemented, they are subject to evaluation. The evaluation and control process attempts to draw relationships between strategic activities and results. The organization determines which activities are effective or ineffective and then alters its strategy as needed. Due to uncertainty in the marketplace, wise marketing planners build in contingency plans into the overall marketing plan. Such plans force planners to consider in detail the environments that influence marketing activities.

Key Terms

acquisition strategy 177
contingency plan 191
corporate objectives 176
corporate plan 174
corporate strategies 176
cross-marketing 181
diversification 195
diversification strategy 181
divestment strategy 180
environmental scan 182
execution (tactics) 173
market development 192
market penetration 192
marketing audit 191

marketing control 188
marketing execution (marketing tactics) 188
marketing objectives 185
marketing plan 173
marketing planning 182
mission statement 175
marketing strategies 186
new product strategy 179
objectives 173, 182
penetration strategy 177
portfolio analysis 181
product development 195
reversification 181
situation analysis 182

strategic alliance 179
strategic business unit (SBU) 181
strategic planning 174
strategies 173

SWOT analysis 182
target market 187
vertical integration strategy 179
vision statement 176

Review Questions

1. In planning, what are the basic differences among objectives, strategies, and tactics?

2. What is a mission statement and what role does it play in terms of corporate and operational planning?

3. What is the relationship between a corporate plan and a marketing plan?

4. At the corporate planning level, what is the difference between an acquisition strategy and a strategic alliance strategy?

5. What is the difference between a diversification strategy and a reversification strategy?

6. What is a SWOT analysis?

7. What is the relationship between a positioning strategy statement and the marketing strategies and executions of a brand or company?

8. In this chapter, marketing strategies are described as the "master plans" for achieving marketing objectives. What does this mean?

9. What is the difference between a marketing activity review and a financial review?

10. What is a contingency plan and why is such a plan necessary?

11. At the product planning level what is the difference between a market development strategy and new product development strategy?

Discussion and Application Questions

1. Has the concept of relationship marketing (Chapter 1) had an influence on strategic planning? What is your opinion?

2. Provide additional examples of the following corporate strategies:
   a) Strategic alliance
   b) Acquisition
   c) Diversification
   d) Cross-marketing
   e) Divestment
   f) Reversification

3. Identify a product (a good or a service) that uses the following marketing strategy:

   a) Market penetration
   b) Market development
   c) Product development
   d) Diversification (product)

4. Marketing evaluation and control procedures tend to be quantitative in nature. Is this the best approach for measuring the effectiveness of marketing strategies? Can you suggest any alternatives?

5. Refer to the vignette "Canadian Tire Buys Mark's Work Wearhouse." Provide a response to the question posed in the last paragraph of the vignette.

6. Refer to the vignette "Toyota Pursues Younger Customers." Conduct some secondary research to see what other companies are doing. Are they after the same target audience? Have they introduced new models and new advertising strategies to entice a younger customer into the fold? Provide examples to illustrate what is going on.

E-Assignment

The purpose of this assignment is to determine how and why companies use different corporate strategies to achieve growth. Conduct some secondary research on the Internet to determine the type of corporate strategy being implemented by the following firms. What conditions are prompting the use of these strategies?

a) London Drugs
b) Colgate-Palmolive
c) Bombardier Inc.
d) Four Seasons Hotels

You may find that these companies use several different strategies at the same time. Provide examples of their activities to verify the strategies they employ.

Endnotes

1. www.pepsico.com/corp/contnet.shtml.

2. www.viarail.ca/corporate/en_entr_viar.html.

3. www.pepsico.com/corp/overview.shtml.

4. Peter Kaplan, "U.S. allows Nestle to acquire Ralston," *Globe and Mail*, December 12, 2001, p. B10 and Marcel Michelson, " Nestle purchase creates largest pet-food maker," *Toronto Star*, January 3, 2001, p. B2.

5. Mark Deen, "Nestle swallows Haagen-Dazs in North America," *Financial Post*, December 28, 2001, p. FP 12.

6. Brad Foss, "Pepsi seals Quaker deal," *Globe and Mail*, December 5, 2000, p. B4.

7. Mike Petapiece, "Dofasco buys auto parts firm," *Toronto Star*, May 6, 2000, p. E3.

8. "Esso to serve up Tim Hortons," *Globe and Mail*, March 27, 2002, p. B8.

9. "Hotel complex to be built at Glen Abbey," *Toronto Star*, September 21, 2000, p. C4.

10. Brenda Bouw, "Watch me, watch my friends," *Financial Post*, April 29, 1999, p. C8.

11. E. Jerome McCarthy, Stanley J. Shapiro, and William D. Perrault, *Basic Marketing* (Homewood, Illinois: Irwin, 1986), p. 742.

12. Mathew Ingram, "Dell should remember: Winning isn't everything," *Globe and Mail*, November 17, 2001, p. B9.

13. Lisa D'Innocenzo, "Niche marketing key to successful stateside retail expansion," *Strategy*, March 11, 2002, pp. 1, 10.

14. Patti Summerfield, "Drug brands boost offerings with after-pills," *Strategy*, February 25, 2002, p. 10.

15. www.unilever.ca.

16. Mathew Ingram, "Apple Computer takes the road less travelled," *Globe and Mail*, October 27, 2001, p. B7.

Dave Starrett

Product

This section discusses the first element of the marketing mix: the product. Chapter 8 examines product strategy and includes such topics as branding and brand name strategies, packaging and labelling strategies, and the concept of customer satisfaction programs. Chapter 9 takes a management viewpoint and discusses how products are managed throughout their life cycle.

Dick Hemingway

Product Strategy

four

> Learning Objectives

After studying this chapter, you will be able to

1. Define the total product concept and explain the concept of the product mix.
2. Outline the classifications and sub-classifications of consumer goods and industrial (business) goods.
3. Explain the role and importance of branding and brand names in the development of product strategy.
4. Characterize the various stages of brand loyalty.
5. Explain the role of packaging decisions in the development of product strategy.

Product strategy is but one element of the marketing mix. This chapter presents the key decision-making areas for marketers when they are developing a product strategy. The key elements discussed in this chapter include the product mix, product classifications, brand name and packaging considerations, and brand loyalty.

The Total Product Concept

product

1.
Define the total product concept and explain the concept of the product mix.

A **product** is "a bundle of tangible and intangible benefits that a buyer receives in exchange for money and other considerations."[1] In effect, the consumer purchases much more than the actual object. To demonstrate, consider the purchase of a luxury automobile like a Porsche. The decision to purchase is not based on transportation needs. This is a car you do not really need; you buy it in order to display your achievements and success. Such a purchase is bound up with the intangibles of prestige, status, and image.

This example illustrates that a product is more than the actual physical object. There are several elements that a marketer can emphasize when attempting to attract consumers; those elements comprise the benefits that a buyer receives. This package of benefits is referred to as the **total product concept**. It includes the physical item, as well as the package, brand name, label, service guarantee, warranty, and image presented by the product.

total product concept

THE PRODUCT MIX

product mix

The **product mix** is the total range of products offered for sale by a company. It is the collection of product items and product lines that a firm tries to market. Each of the products or product items in the mix appeals to a particular segment, and in a way that makes it distinct from the offerings of the competition. Most, if not all, large consumer packaged-goods companies have a complete product mix, that is, they offer for sale a variety of different products that appeal to different user segments.

product item

A **product item** is defined as a unique product offered for sale by an organization. The key word in this definition is unique. Marketers refer to the distinguishing product characteristic or primary benefit of a product or service, the one feature that distinguishes a product from competing products, as the **unique selling point (USP)**. These features may include the format of the product, the sizes and variety available, or the ingredients contained in the product. To illustrate, let us examine the following innovation in new product development.

unique selling point (USP)

When one thinks of mouthwash, a brand such as Scope and Listerine may come to mind. Further, one would think about these brands in a liquid form. Pfizer Healthcare recognized a new need when it launched Listerine PocketPaks—postage-stamp-size strips that contain the same germ killing ingredients as Listerine mouthwash. PocketPaks appeal to people that are on the go throughout the day and are looking for discreet and portable answers.

In the toothpaste market, Procter & Gamble introduced Crest Dual Action whitening toothpaste, a relatively new member of the Crest family of toothpastes. That was followed with Crest Whitestrips—thin flexible strips coated with a tooth-whitening gel that contains peroxide (a whitening agent used by dentists). The strips are applied to one's teeth for 30 minutes each day. Crest promises a whiter smile within 14 days. Crest Whitestrips offers an easy and convenient solution for people wanting to feel good about their appearance. For more details about unique selling points see the illustration in Figure 8.1.

Figure 8.1

Crest Whitestrips Offer Some Unique Selling Points

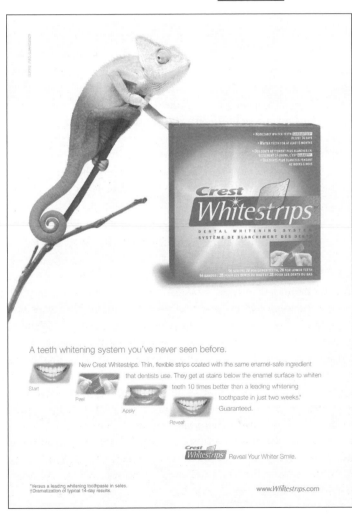

© The Procter & Gamble Company. Used by permission.

product line

A **product line** is a grouping of product items that share major attributes but may differ in terms of, for example, size, form, or flavour. For example, Gatorade is available in several different package sizes and in both liquid and powder forms. In the liquid form, there are two separate lines: regular and frost. The various flavours are available in eye-catching colours that attract the teen target market. A popular brand of cereal such as Cheerios was once a standalone product in a few different package sizes. Now Cheerios offers several flavours, including Frosted Cheerios, Honey Nut Cheerios, Multi Grain Cheerios, and Apple Cinnamon Cheerios. Cheerios appeals to the taste needs of all family members regardless of age.

product line width

product line depth

A firm's product line is described in terms of width and depth. **Product line width** is the number of lines in the mix. **Product line depth**, on the other hand, refers to the number of items in the line. All items and lines collectively form a firm's product mix. Unilever Canada is the largest seller of margarine in Canada. In terms of *width* it offers Becel, Imperial, Blue Bonnet, Country Crock, Fleischmann's, and Monarch brands. The various product sizes and format variations (e.g., regular and light varieties) for each brand would comprise the depth of the line.

The width and depth of a product mix depend on the firm's overall marketing strategy. Packaged-goods firms, such as Unilever and industrial-product companies, such as General Electric, have large product mixes that are both wide and deep. They want to balance risks, offset seasonal sales fluctuations, and address the various needs of customers.

Product Classifications

2.

Outline the classifications and sub-classifications of consumer goods and industrial (business) goods.

consumer goods

industrial (business) goods

Goodyear
www.goodyear.com

nondurable goods

durable goods

services

Products are divided in two basic ways. First, and most important, a product is classified according to the target market it is intended for. Second, it is classified according to the durability and tangibility it offers.

Products are also broadly classified into two groups on the basis of who buys them and why; these groups are called consumer goods and industrial (business) goods. **Consumer goods** are products and services purchased by consumers for their own personal use or benefit. **Industrial (business) goods** are those products and services purchased by businesses, industries, institutions, and governments that are used directly or indirectly in the production of another good or service that is resold, in turn, to another user (possibly a consumer). In the classification of products, it is the intended use by the customer that distinguishes consumer goods from industrial (business) goods, but a product can be both. For example, a tire manufactured by Goodyear is a consumer good if sold by a retail outlet to a consumer. It is an industrial good if purchased by the Ford Motor Company for installation on the assembly of an automobile.

A **nondurable good** is a tangible good normally consumed after one or a few uses. Examples include everyday products, such as toothpaste, beer, coffee, milk, and detergent. These products are replenished frequently. A **durable good** is a tangible good that survives many uses. Examples include automobiles, appliances, personal computers, VCR and DVD equipment, and athletic equipment. These items are purchased infrequently. **Services** are intangible; they are activities and benefits we take advantage of but do not take possession of. Examples include banking and financial services, hotels, household-care services (lawn and garden maintenance or painting and decorating), and repair services. Service industry marketing strategies are discussed in Chapter 18.

CONSUMER GOODS

Consumer goods are commonly classified into four categories: convenience goods, shopping goods, specialty goods, and unsought goods (Figure 8.2). This classification is based on consumer buying behaviour.

Convenience Goods

convenience goods

Convenience goods are those goods purchased frequently, with a minimum of effort and evaluation. Typical examples include food items like bread, milk, cookies, and chocolate bars, and personal care products such as soap, deodorant, and shampoo. Convenience goods fall into the "routine" decision-making process discussed in Chapter 4.

staple good

impulse good

emergency good

Convenience goods are subdivided into three categories: staples, impulse goods, and emergency goods. A **staple good** is one that is regularly needed or used, such as milk, bread, deodorant, and headache medicine. People buy many of these items by brand, remaining loyal to such names as Gillette, Secret, Tylenol, and Advil. An **impulse good** is a good purchased on the spur of the moment: certain items purchased in a supermarket, such as candy bars, chewing gum, and magazines, are examples of impulse goods. Availability is a key issue; thus impulse items are often found at checkout counters. An **emergency good** is purchased suddenly when a crisis or urgency arises; a snow shovel purchased at the first snowstorm of the season or a tensor bandage purchased when a muscle becomes strained are examples of emergency goods.

Generally, consumers do not spend much time purchasing convenience goods (e.g., price comparisons from store to store are unlikely). Therefore, it is in the best interests of the marketing organization to inform the consumer of the merits of the product through advertising and promotion and to make sure that the product has an attractive, eye-catching package and is readily available when consumers need it.

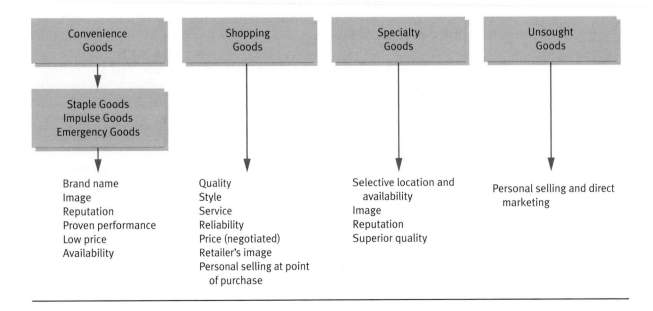

Figure 8.2

Marketing Considerations for Consumer Goods

Convenience Goods	Shopping Goods	Specialty Goods	Unsought Goods

Staple Goods
Impulse Goods
Emergency Goods

Brand name	Quality	Selective location and	Personal selling and direct
Image	Style	availability	marketing
Reputation	Service	Image	
Proven performance	Reliability	Reputation	
Low price	Price (negotiated)	Superior quality	
Availability	Retailer's image		
	Personal selling at point		
	of purchase		

Shopping Goods

shopping goods

Shopping goods are goods that the consumer compares on such bases as suitability, quality, price, and style before making a selection. Other factors of concern to the shopper include dependability, service, functionality, guarantees, and warranties. Examples of shopping goods include automobiles, clothing, major appliances, household furnishings, decoration services, and major repairs around the house. The price of shopping goods tends to be higher than for convenience goods, therefore, buying behaviour tends to be more rational in nature.

Marketing considerations deemed important for shopping goods include being located near competitors where comparisons can be easily made; having a consistent and attractive image (proven performance has advantage over little-known brands); and having effective communications so that awareness among consumers is high when their need for the product arises.

To illustrate these principles, the "idle repairman" gives Maytag a competitive advantage in the appliance market. Maytag's marketing strategy emphasizes quality, and all its advertisements are variations of the same theme: a bored repairman, dressed and ready to go to his job, but no opportunity to do so.[2] Such a consistent message over time has given Maytag an excellent reputation and customers a basis for comparison with other brands.

Specialty Goods

specialty goods

Specialty goods are goods that consumers make an effort to find and purchase because the goods possess some unique or important characteristic. In effect, the consumer has already decided what item to buy. It is simply a matter of making the shopping excursion to buy it. Generally speaking, the marketing considerations that are important for specialty goods include the image and reputation resulting from communications and product quality, and the availability of goods in the appropriate stores, that is, the few specialty retailers that carry special lines or represent manufacturers that consumers will look for. The price, usually a high one in keeping with the product quality and the prestigious image created by other marketing activities, is also a consideration in marketing specialty goods. A Cartier watch, for example, could be classified as a specialty good on the basis of these criteria.

Whether an item is a specialty good, a shopping good, or a convenience good depends on the behaviour of the consumer; a specialty good for one may be a shopping good for another. For instance, an individual who insists on wearing athletic shoes that display a brand name, such as Nike or Adidas, looks for a store that sells the cherished brand and will travel anywhere to purchase it. To this person, these shoes are a specialty good. Others may simply drop into a nearby store, compare the merchandise with other brands they have seen, and then decide to purchase a pair of shoes. In this case, the shoes are a shopping good. One good is distinguished from the other on the basis of how much effort consumers put into the purchase.

Unsought Goods

unsought goods

Unsought goods are goods that consumers are unaware they need or that they lack knowledge about. Essentially, an unsought good is an item that, although useful or valuable, is of such a nature that the consumer lacks interest in purchasing it. Encyclopedias are the most widely cited example of unsought goods. While the product has a clear educational value, its availability in a library or online via the Internet means that there is little incentive to purchase it. Life insurance is another example, as it is a product many consumers are uncomfortable discussing. It is a product many people postpone considering and purchasing.

Given the nature of unsought goods, the primary influence on decisions to purchase is personal selling. Advertising will create awareness, but it is a consistent and persistent sales message that precipitates action by consumers.

INDUSTRIAL (BUSINESS) GOODS

industrial (business) goods

By definition, **industrial (or business) goods** are products and services that have a direct or indirect role in the manufacture of other products and services. These goods are classified not on the basis of consumer behaviour but by the function the good has in the production of another good. The major marketing considerations for industrial goods are price (low price based on price negotiation and bidding), personal selling, ability to meet customer specifications, and the reliability of supply when direct channels of distribution are used.

Typically, industrial (business) goods are subdivided into three categories: capital items, parts and materials, and supplies and services (Figure 8.3).

Capital Items

capital items

Capital items are expensive goods with a long life span that are used directly in the production of another good or service. Whether an item has a direct or indirect role in the production process determines which of the two types of capital item it is.

installations

Installations are major capital items used directly in the production of another product. Examples of installations include buildings, production line equipment (e.g., robots in assembly plants), and computer systems. These goods are characterized by their high price, long life, reliance on strong personal selling programs to gain customer acceptance, technical sales and support service, and direct channels of distribution. A lengthy and complex decision-making process confronts the marketer of installations.

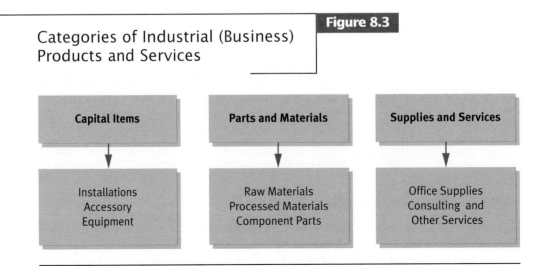

Figure 8.3

Categories of Industrial (Business) Products and Services

Capital Items	Parts and Materials	Supplies and Services
Installations Accessory Equipment	Raw Materials Processed Materials Component Parts	Office Supplies Consulting and Other Services

**accessory
equipment**

Accessory equipment refers to items that are usually not part of a finished product but that do facilitate a firm's overall operations, that is, their role is indirect. Typically, these goods are much less expensive than installations and include such products as microcomputers, photocopier machines, power tools, and office furnishings. These goods are characterized by their reasonably long life, the significance of price negotiation in the marketing process, and the unique features of the product that appeal to rational buying motives.

Parts and Materials

**parts and
materials**

Parts and materials are less expensive goods that directly enter another manufacturer's production process. These goods are an integral part of the customer's product and affect its quality. Parts and materials are subdivided into three categories: raw materials, processed materials, and component parts.

raw materials

Farm goods and other materials derived directly from natural resources are **raw materials**. Raw materials from natural resources include crude oil, lumber, and iron ore. Farm goods include wheat, livestock, fruits, vegetables, and milk, all of which are used by food processors in the manufacture of packaged consumer food products, such as bread, cheese, and jams.

**processed
materials**

DuPont
www.dupont.com

component parts

Processed materials are materials used in the production of another product, but which are not readily identifiable with the product. Examples include DuPont Nylon, a synthetic fibre used in clothing and other fabrics, and other yarns that become part of cloth fabrics. In each example, the original material is further processed or fabricated in the manufacturing process of another good so that it changes form.

Component parts are goods that are used in the production of another product but do not change form as a result of the manufacturing process. Typically, these items are part of an assembly-line process. Imagine the construction of an automobile: various components of the car are fitted together in sequence as the product automatically moves along a line. The tires, steel frame, seats, dashboards, engines, steering columns, doors, glass windows, radios, and other parts are classified as components to an automobile manufacturer. They arrive at a manufacturing facility ready for assembly. Price negotiation is an important consideration in the purchase of component parts. A buyer usually commits to buying large quantities if the source of supply is reliable. The contract states the length of the purchase period, usually one or more years.

Supplies and Services

Supplies and services are those goods purchased by businesses and industries that do not enter the production process but facilitate other operations of the organization.

supplies

Supplies are standardized products that are routinely purchased with a minimum of effort. Typically, they are divided into three categories: maintenance, repair, and operating supplies. Paint is an example of a maintenance supply; bearings and gears are examples of repair supplies; writing instruments, paper and stationery, toner cartridges, and fastening devices are examples of operating supplies. Customers of such items look for quality at a good price. Purchasing agents also perceive service by the supplier's sales representatives to be important.

services

Services are the intangible offerings required to operate a business efficiently. Services are diverse, both in nature and in cost. For example, repair services or ongoing maintenance contracts, such as grounds keeping or janitorial services, may be relatively inexpensive. By contrast, a management consulting service employed to analyze the management practices of a firm is expensive, as are specialized services, such as advertising or information processing. In the case of ongoing services, such variables as price and service reliability are important to the buyer; for specialized, complex services, the reputation and quality of the people performing the service are important. The growth in outsourcing, a concept discussed earlier in the textbook, has resulted in a much higher profile for the marketing of services. For example, companies that lack expertise in technology are actively pursuing software development specialists and Internet marketing specialists to assist them in establishing an online marketing presence.

Branding and Brand Names

3.
Explain the role and importance of branding and brand names in the development of product strategy.

Just what is a brand? This very question was asked of several marketing professionals and the responses varied considerably:

> "A promise that is publicly conveyed by everything a customer can observe: the brand name, logo, advertising, signage, storefront, billing statements, displays, and shopping environment (this explanation considers retailers to be brands)."

> "A name, logo, and/or symbol that evokes in customers a perception of 'added value' for which they will pay a premium price."

> "A product with a personality."[3]

It seems that a brand is more than the tangible product. How a consumer perceives a product largely depends on the brand name and what it stands for, that is, on the image that marketing has developed for it over an extended period. For example, such names as Porsche or Jaguar suggest a certain quality and status. Obsession, a brand of perfume, projects a mysterious, sexual image. Maxwell House coffee is known for being "good to the last drop." While customers are accustomed to seeing brands and take them for granted, for the marketing organization, branding decisions are quite difficult.

Some key terms associated with branding decisions are as follows:[4]

brand

1. A **brand** is a name, term, symbol, or design (or some combination of the four) that identifies the goods and services of an organization so that they can be differentiated from those of the competition. Brand is a comprehensive term that includes all brand names and trademarks.

brand name

2. A **brand name** is that part of the brand that can be spoken. It may consist of a word, letter, or group of words and letters. Examples include such names as Nike, Colgate, Hertz, Kellogg's, Lexus, Listerine, Roots, Yahoo!, and eBay.

brandmark (logo)

3. A **brandmark (logo)** is a unique design, symbol, or other special representation of a company name or brand name. Examples include the blue Ford oval that appears on the front or back of the cars, on dealer signs, and in advertising and promotional literature; Nike's famous swoosh that appears on all its shoes, or Apple Computer's famous apple with a bite taken out of it. Figure 8.4 includes a selection of brandmarks.

trademark

4. A **trademark** is that part of a brand which is granted legal protection so that only the owner can use it. The symbol ® is the designation of a registered trademark. Trademarks include the brand names and symbols described above. Coke and Coca-Cola are registered trademarks of the Coca-Cola Company. The Nike swoosh is a trademark of Nike. The swoosh is so well known that it can stand alone in advertisements and communicate a message about the brand. In some cases, trademarks

become so well known that they become household words. When this happens, the trademark holder is a victim of its own success because the trademark loses its distinct nature. Such is the case of famous trademarks like Xerox and Kleenex.

copyright

5. **Copyright** is the exclusive right of the author to reproduce, sell, or publish the matter and form of a dramatic, literary, musical, or artistic work. Copyright protection is automatic, but copyrights are often designated by the symbol ©, indicating the work is a registered copyright.

patent

6. A **patent** protects a manufacturing process or product design from being copied by competitors. It gives a manufacturer the sole right to develop and market a new product, process, or material as it sees fit. An industrial design registration protects appearance, while a true patent protects function. Under Canada's Patent Act, the maximum life of a Canadian patent is 20 years from the date on which the application is filed.

BRANDING STRATEGY

Many types of brands exist and they can be distinguished according to who names them. Most of the brands mentioned in this section so far are manufacturer's brands or national brands. These brands are usually supported with their own marketing strategies to make them competitive and distinctive in the marketplace.

National Brands

A national brand organization has two brand name options: an individual brand strategy or a family brand strategy, both of which offer advantages and disadvantages.

individual brand

Individual Brands An **individual brand** is a means of identifying each product in a company's product mix with its own name. This brand name strategy is common among large grocery products manufacturers, such as Procter & Gamble and Kraft Canada. Some

---

A Selection of Brandmarks

Figure 8.4

Courtesy: Petro-Canada Inc., Nissan Automobile Company (Canada) Ltd., Honda Canada, Infiniti

Procter & Gamble names include Scope (mouthwash), Secret (deodorant), and Pampers (disposable diapers). Kraft names include Minute Rice (long-grain rice), Dream Whip (dessert topping), Shake 'n Bake (coating mix), and Stove Top (stuffing mix).

multibrand strategy

Very often, a marketing organization operates in several market segments of a product category. In this case, a multibrand strategy is used. The term **multibrand strategy** refers to the use of a different brand name for each item a company offers in the same product category. To illustrate, Unilever Canada makes and markets tea under a variety of brands—Red Rose, Salada, PG Tips, and Lipton Tea. Through advertising, each brand has acquired a different image among consumers. In effect, the brands compete against one another, but the revenues they generate all return to the same source.

An individual brand name is sometimes extended to an innovation in the market. For example, when Pfizer Healthcare launched a new mouthwash in a dry format the product was called Listerine PocketPaks. When Procter & Gamble launched Whitestrips, a gel-coated strip that whitens teeth, the Crest name was added. The product is known as Crest Whitestrips. Such marketing decisions give a brand instant credibility among distributors and consumers.

family brand

Family Brands A **family brand** exists when the same brand name is used for a group of related products. Family brand names are usually steeped in tradition and quickly come to mind because they have been on the market for a long time. Examples include such names as Heinz, Campbell's, Quaker, Jell-O, Christie, and Del Monte. These brand families take three different forms:

1. *Product Family* In this case, a group of products holds its own family name. Jell-O dessert products, Post cereals, Aunt Jemima pancake and syrup mixes, and Tylenol cough and cold remedies are a few examples.

2. *Company Family* Here, the brand name is also the company name. Heinz (ketchup, juices, sauces, baby food, and other food products) and Nike (footwear, hockey equipment, golf equipment and sportswear) are two examples. Other popular company brand names include Kodak, Sony, and Kraft.

3. *Company and Product Family* In this case, the marketing organization combines both variables. The company name makes up part of the brand name, with another brand name making up the other part. Examples include:

Company	Product
Kellogg	Corn Flakes, Frosted Flakes, Special K, Eggo, Pop Tarts
Gillette	Right Guard, Foamy, Silkience, Sensor, Mach3
Nissan	Infiniti, Pathfinder, Extera, Altima, Maxima, Sentra, Murana

Volvo Cars
www.volvocars.com

A family brand strategy offers two *advantages* to a marketing organization. First, promotional expenditures for one product will benefit the rest of the family by creating an awareness of the brand name, and, second, new products become accepted readily, since they capitalize on the success and reputation of the existing family products. For example, Nike stands for empowerment and Mercedes for excellence in engineering; and for Volvo, it is safety. Retailers and wholesalers like such new products because they come with additional promotion support and result in increased demand for the family of products. Consumers accept the product because of the reputation and performance of related products under the same brand name.

A family brand strategy has a *disadvantage* as well. The failure or poor quality of a new product could tarnish the image of a family of products; for that reason, such products are usually removed from the market quickly by the marketing organization.

In deciding what brand strategy to use, a company analyzes its own situation in relation to its corporate and marketing strategies. It may also stumble upon a brand name. Such was the case of an American shoe company founded by Phil Knight. He had only 24 hours to come up with a brand name and symbol. An executive of the company casually suggested Nike—the winged Greek goddess of victory. None of the company executives knew who Nike was, they did not like the name, and they could not pronounce it very well, but the 24-hour limit was up, so the name stuck. The swoosh was designed by a Portland, Oregon, design student for a mere $35. It was her first job. Now the name and swoosh stand for "Just Do It," one of the most potent and resilient advertising slogans of all time. A $35 investment now has extraordinary meaning and influence in the marketplace.[5]

Co-branding

co-branding

A brand strategy now gaining popularity among national brand manufacturers is co-branding. **Co-branding** occurs when a company uses the equity in another brand name to help market its own brand name product or service. The marketer feels that using multiple brand names in conjunction with a single product or service offering provides greater value to demanding customers. In a competitive marketing environment, co-branding is being used as a means of preventing customers from switching to lower-cost non-branded equivalents.[6] An example of a co-branding strategy is the launch by Neilson Dairies of Crispy Crunch, Jersey Milk, Caramilk, and Malted Milk milkshake products sold in single-serve plastic containers. The exterior of the container resembles the chocolate bar wrapper. Dairy competitor Nestle uses the same strategy on its ice cream lines. Rather than just using the Nestle brand name, it's Nestle Rolo ice cream, Nestle Coffee Crisp ice cream, and Nestle Mackintosh's creamy toffee ice cream. Rolo, Coffee Crisp, and Mackintosh are brand names owned by Nestle that compete in the confectionary market. See Figure 8.5 for an illustration.

When using a co-branding strategy, a key issue to consider is "fit." It is essential for both brands to complement each other. The transfer of chocolate bar brand names into such categories as cereal and ice cream is a good fit (e.g., Neilson Cadbury's Mr. Big ice cream bars or Oreo cookie ice cream sandwiches and Nestle Rolo ice cream).

Private Label Brands

private label brand

A **private label brand** is a brand produced to the specifications of the distributor (wholesaler or retailer), usually by national brand manufacturers that make similar products under their own brand names. Some examples of these brands are:

Company	Brand Name
Canadian Tire	Mastercraft, Motomaster, Persona
Sears	Kenmore, DieHard, Craftsman
Zellers	Cherokee, Truly
Shoppers Drug Mart	Life, Rialto, Quo
Loblaws	President's Choice

Figure 8.5

An Example of a Co-Branding Strategy

Courtesy: Nestlé Canada

The private label brand was originally conceived as a means by which a retailer could provide the price-conscious consumer with a product of reasonable quality as an alternative to national brands. Loblaws is a leader in private label branding with its President's Choice (PC) brand. It is marketed in all Loblaws-owned outlets (Loblaws, Provigo, Zehrs, Super Value, and others). Research conducted by Loblaws reveals that people shop at Loblaws because of the President's Choice brand. It's that popular! More recently, Loblaws has extended the PC brand into financial services (PC Financial). In the longer term, the name could be associated with insurance and travel.

Canadian Tire recently launched the Persona brand name for its appliance, linen, china, and silverware lines. The new label will help Canadian Tire gain ground in a category where it has been at a disadvantage against competitors with their own private labels like Sears and the Bay.[7]

Private label brands have taken business away from national brands. Their popularity peaked in 1996 when they accounted for 24.1 percent of grocery sales. Presently, they account for between 22 and 23 percent of grocery store sales. At Loblaws, the combination of PC and No Name (generic products) products accounts for about one-third of customer spending.[8]

Generic Brands

generic brand

A **generic brand** is a product without a brand name or identifying features. The packaging is kept simple; a minimum of colour is used, and words simply identify the contents, for example, "Corn Flakes" or "Peanut Butter." Generic brands are common in such product categories as cereals, paper products, canned goods (fruits, vegetables, and juices), and pet foods, among others. Consumers who purchase generic brands may sacrifice a little in quality but appreciate the savings they offer. In Canada, it was Loblaws and its related supermarkets (Super Value and Zehrs, to name two) that popularized the use of generic brands. Through corporate advertising campaigns, the grocery chain encouraged consumers to look for its "yellow label" products in stores. Other chains, such as Safeway and A&P, quickly followed the lead of Loblaws.

Private label and generic brands intensify competition. Shelf space is limited, so it is more difficult for national brands to compete for space. As well, computer technology allows retailers to eliminate quickly any national brand product lines that are not moving at a desired rate. To fend off the growth of private label and generic brands, national brand manufacturers have responded with various forms of price discounting and have introduced new brands in lower-price segments. To protect its position in the cookie market, Dare Foods now markets Dare Premium cookies (high price and quality), Dare Classic cookies (medium price), and Dare cookies (lower price). Such a strategy is becoming more common in many consumer packaged-goods segments.

Licensed Brands

licensed brand

Brand image is a powerful marketing tool and a valuable asset to marketing organizations. The use of one firm's established brand name or symbol on another firm's products can benefit both firms financially. To make such an arrangement, the owner of the brand name or symbol enters into a licensing agreement with a second party. Licensing is a way of legally allowing another firm to use a brand name or trademark for a certain period (the duration of the contractual agreement). The licensee usually pays a royalty to the company owning the trademark. When a brand name or trademark is used in this manner, it is called a **licensed brand**. Clothing lines often adopt well-known brand names. Brand names such as Molson, Coca-Cola, Nike, and Adidas appear on T-shirts and sweatshirts. Sports leagues, such as the NHL, NBA, and Major League Baseball, also market the rights to their team logos and trademarks to clothing manufacturers. Putting brand names on clothing provides moving advertisements for the owners of the brand name or trademark and ready-made promotion for the owners of the licensed product.

Limited Edition Brands

limited edition brand

As the name suggests, a **limited edition brand** is a brand only intended to be on the market for a short period of time, as it capitalizes on the popularity of an event or individual. Perhaps the best example of a limited edition brand was the phenomenal success of Flutie Flakes in northeastern United States and Southern Ontario. Flutie Flakes was named to take advantage of the popularity of Doug Flutie, the former star quarterback of the Buffalo Bills. Capitalizing on the success of Flutie and the rise of the Buffalo Bills from the football cellar to playoff contender, PLB Sports, the manufacturer of the cereal, could not keep up with demand for the product. Wegmans, a New York supermarket chain, was selling 14 500 boxes a week, more than 4 times its previous top-selling cereal.[9]

Companies possessing the foresight to market limited edition brands must do so effectively in the short term, if profits are to be made. Should the popularity of the star fade, the brand could face a quick exit from the market. Doug Flutie is long gone from Buffalo!

Cult Brands

cult brand

Unique in the world of branding is the cult brand. A **cult brand** is a brand that captures the imagination of a small group who spread the word, make converts, and help turn a fringe product into a mainstream name. Cult brands are not fads; instead they start out small and build a steady following, sometimes over many years. Many cult brands decide to stay small, for that is the key to their success; they are hard to get. In contrast, other cult brands opt for growth and eventually become leading national brands. Such brands include Krispy Kreme, Apple, Mazda Miata and L.L. Bean, to name a few. There is an irony associated with growth of a cult brand. Once a brand goes mainstream, the core customers that established the cult image lose interest. Jeep, for example, was once a unique vehicle with a utilitarian design and purpose. Now it is simply another sports utility vehicle owned by urban warriors.

For more insight into the nature of branding and the associations between customers and brands, see the Marketing in Action vignette **Brands That Stir Passions**.

THE BENEFITS OF BRANDS

Branding offers consumers and marketing organizations several benefits. Some of the benefits for the consumer are as follows:

1. Over time, the brand name suggests a certain level of quality. Consumers know what to expect; they trust and have confidence in a brand.

2. There can be psychological rewards for possessing certain brands. For example, purchasing a BMW automobile might suggest achievement for the owner while wearing a suit with a designer label may make one feel stylish.

3. Brands distinguish competitive offerings, allowing consumers to make informed decisions. Such names as Minute Rice, Lipton Cup-A-Soup, and Post Fruit & Fibre suggest clear messages or benefits about the product.

The marketing organization also enjoys benefits:

1. Branding enables the marketer to create and develop an image for a product or service. In the automobile market, the name Lexus is associated with "excitement," while in the tea market Tetley Tea is well known for its round perforated teabag that offers a better tasting tea. The brand image is partially created through advertising. In most advertising, a close relationship exists between a brand and its slogan. In the case of Tetley the slogan is: "Tetley. Good things all round." See Figure 8.6 for an illustration. Collectively, they help form an impression in the consumer's mind. Here are a few examples:

   Tetley—"Tetley. Good things all round."

   VISA—"All you need."
   Nike—"Just Do It."
   3M—"from need…to 3M Innovation."
   Apple—"Think Different."

Marketing in Action

Brands That Stir Passions

Why is it that some consumers adopt an almost religious association with a particular brand? And why do they promote it to others with the conviction that others will share the same feelings? That is the mystery of cult brands.

If you doubt the existence of cult brands that stir strange passions try attending the opening of a Krispy Kreme outlet (many will be opening across Canada in the next few years). Throngs of people, some camping overnight will queue up for that first bite of a soft, sugary donut. And then there's Apple, the computer with the sexy image that attracts 85 000 users to MacWorld Expo, an annual 4-day convention in San Francisco. There, devotees can "touch" Steve Jobs, co-founder and CEO of Apple, their God—they cheer his every word!

A cult brand seizes the imagination of a small group who spread the word and help turn a fringe brand into a mainstream name. It is not a fad; a fad takes off like a rocket, peaks, and fizzles quickly as it passes through a large population. Cult brands usually start out small and build a steady following, sometimes over years.

People are drawn to cult brands because they want to belong to something. That explains why Harley-Davidson is the archetypal cult brand. Its most loyal consumers formed an organization named for the 303rd Bombardment Group (from World War II) who flew missions to France and Germany—Hell's Angels. The outlaw group boosted the bike's exposure and occasionally popped up in the news for criminal activity. The group's bad-boy image resonated with Middle America. Today with sales of $2.9 billion and a 25 percent market share in the US, Harley is one of the few brands to have maintained a cult status as it developed the mass market.

Apple wasted a lot of time and money trying to compete with other personal computer companies. The launch of the now famous "Think Different" advertising campaign sparked a revival—among cult followers. Mac users consist of a minority of home users plus a clutch of creative people in advertising, publishing, and Hollywood. Apple has to be satisfied with a six percent share of the desktop and laptop market.

The irony of a cult brand is that it is not created—it just happens. That doesn't sound like good marketing but a company owning a cult brand can certainly reap the financial rewards or suffer severe financial fallout once it goes mainstream. Snapple, a brand, owned by Quaker Oats, was a cult brand possessing a quirky personality. Wanting to expand the brand, Quaker introduced a silly ad campaign that positioned Snapple as an alternative to Coke and Pepsi. Quaker diluted the quirkiness and consumers felt cheated. Sales plunged 23 percent. Quaker later sold off the Snapple division and lost $1.4 billion on the deal.

A golden rule of marketing is to keep the core customer happy. But what does a company do when it grows? Can they afford to cut loose some of their devotees? Krispy Kreme is in that predicament. With sales rising rapidly and new outlets being opened at a rapid pace, does Krispy Kreme stick to donuts and coffee or does it add cappuccino and latte to be more like Starbucks? That's a marketing dilemma!

Adapted from Melanie Wells, "Cult Brands," *Forbes*, April 16, 2001, www.forbes.com/forbes/2001/0416.

Dick Loek/CP Photo Archive

Figure 8.6

Tetley's Slogan (bottom of ad) Reinforces a Unique Selling Point— The Round Tea Bag

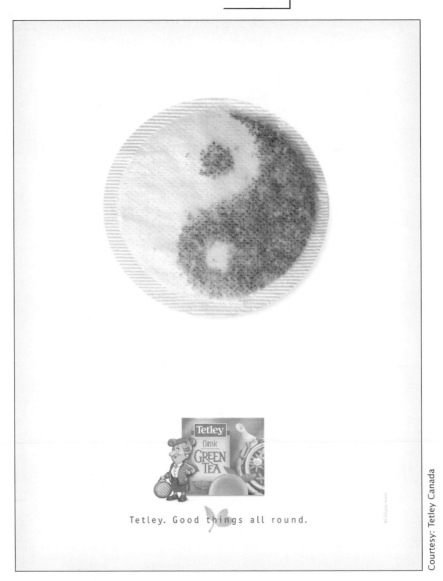

Tetley. Good things all round.

Courtesy: Tetley Canada

2. Satisfied customers will make repeat purchases and hopefully remain loyal to a brand. This loyalty stabilizes market share and provides for certain efficiencies in production and marketing.

3. A good brand name will communicate the point of difference (USP) and highlight the distinctive value added. For example, the name Lean Cuisine addresses two strategic issues: lean communicates the low-calorie benefit, and cuisine implies that it tastes good. The name is meaningful and pleasant sounding. Household goods

tend to have names that communicate what they do (e.g., Ziploc, Spray 'n Wash, Liquid Plumr, S.O.S., and Mr. Clean).

Creating and using brand names is a crucial aspect of product strategy, since the attributes of a brand—its package and logo and its image—influence other marketing activities, specifically pricing and promotion. Given the cost of marketing activities, a brand (name and trademark) must be more than just a tool for distinguishing one brand from another. It must communicate the key point of difference and highlight the distinctive value added.

BRAND LOYALTY

4.
Characterize the various stages of brand loyalty.

brand loyalty is defined as the degree of consumer attachment to a particular brand of product or service. This degree of attachment can be weak or strong and varies from one product category to another. Brand loyalty is measured in three stages: brand recognition, brand preference, and brand insistence.[10]

brand loyalty
brand recognition

In the early stages of a product's life, the marketing objective is to create **brand recognition**, which is customer awareness of the brand name and package. Once awareness is achieved, a brand may offer customers free samples or coupons to tempt them to make the first (trial) purchase.

brand preference

In the **brand preference** stage of a product's life, the brand is in the ballpark—that is, it is an acceptable alternative and will be purchased if it is available when needed. If it is unavailable, the consumer will switch to an equal, competitive alternative. For example, if Pepsi-Cola is requested at McDonald's and the order cannot be filled because the product is unavailable there, the consumer will usually accept the substitute, in this case, Coca-Cola.

brand insistence

At the **brand insistence** stage, a consumer will search the market extensively for the brand he or she wants. No alternatives are acceptable, and if the brand is unavailable, the consumer is likely to postpone purchase until it is. Such a situation is a marketer's dream, a dream rarely achieved. Some critics insist that the original Coca-Cola product (now called Coke Classic) reached a level beyond brand insistence. So strong was the attachment that the product could not be changed. When it was, the backlash from the consumer franchise was so strong that the company had no alternative but to bring the original product back.

The task of the marketer is to keep customers loyal. Study after study has shown that it is many times more difficult and expensive to convert a new customer than it is to retain a current customer. In preserving loyalty, companies cannot take their customers for granted. Many brands are instituting customer relationship management (CRM) programs that are specifically designed to keep a customer a customer. The concept of CRM was discussed earlier in the textbook.

Nabisco, Inc.
www.nabisco.com

To illustrate how fast loyalty can fade, consider the case of Chips Ahoy, a prominent cookie product marketed by Nabisco. At one time, it was the market leader with strong brand loyalty. Its primary benefit was a chip content of 20 to 25 percent. But along came President's Choice Decadent Chocolate Chip Cookies offering 39 percent chip content. President's Choice became the best-selling cookie nationally, even though it is only sold in 20 percent of grocery stores, while Chips Ahoy's national market share dropped below 2 percent.[11] This illustration shows that premium private label brands can be a major force in consumer goods.

brand equity

The benefits of brands and the various levels of brand loyalty are what marketers refer to as brand equity. **Brand equity** is defined as the value a consumer derives from a product over and above the value derived from the physical attributes, those characteristics and associations that are linked to a brand that can add value to it. Brand equity consists of four variables: name awareness, a loyal customer base, perceived quality, and the brand's association with a certain attribute. For example, consumers' attitudes and feelings about a product, as in the above-mentioned case of Coca-Cola, help establish brand equity. Much research has been done on brand equity and its importance in marketing.

Brand Power: What Makes a Great Brand?

Brand names, trademarks, logos, and advertising slogans all play a major role in creating an image with consumers. Whether it applies to a product or service or to a company itself, the right name can produce customer loyalty, recognition in the marketplace, and money at the bottom line. The opposite is also true. A bad brand name can bury a company in obscurity or sink a new product faster than you can say Edsel.

To illustrate, consider the case of Nike. Scott Bedbury, the man who gave the world "Just Do It," started working for Nike in 1987, when it was a $750-million company. Seven years later, Nike was a $4-billion business. In between, Bedbury directed Nike's worldwide advertising efforts and broke the "Just Do It" branding campaign. According to Bedbury, building a great brand depends on knowing the right principles. Among these principles are the following:

1. **A great brand is in it for the long haul** Thinking long term, a great brand can travel worldwide, transcend cultural barriers, speak to multiple audiences, and let you operate at the higher end of the positioning spectrum—where you can earn solid margins over the long term.

2. **A great brand can be anything** Anything is brandable. Nike, for example, leverages the deep emotional connection that people have with sports and fitness. In computers, most people do not know how processors work or why they are superior to the competition. But what they want is a computer with "Intel inside." Intel is a classic case in branding strategy.

3. **A great brand knows itself** The real starting point is to go out to customers and find out what they like or dislike about the brand and what they associate as the very core of the brand concept. The customer's view of a brand can be very different from that of company executives.

4. **A great brand invents or re-invents an entire category** Such brands as Apple, Nike, and Starbucks made it an explicit goal to be protagonists for each of their product categories. Apple was a protagonist for an individual: anyone wanting to be more productive, informed, and contemporary. At Nike, Phil Knight (company founder and CEO) is the consummate protagonist for sports and athletes.

5. **A great brand taps into emotions** The common ground for great brands is not performance. They recognize that consumers live in an emotional world. Emotions drive most, if not all, of our decisions.

6. **A great brand has design consistency** They have a consistent look and feel and a high level of design integrity. Consider such brands as McDonald's, Coca-Cola and Disney. They refuse to follow any fashion trend that does not fit their vision.

7. **A great brand is relevant** Many brands try to position themselves as "cool." More often than not, brands that try to be cool fail. Being cool is not enough to sustain a brand. A brand has to be relevant—it provides what people want, and it performs the way people want it to. Consumers are looking for something that has lasting value.

Brands also have monetary value and that value reflects the status of a brand on a global scale. There are not that many truly global brands but the top five are well known names: Coca-Cola (valued at $68.9 billion), Microsoft ($65.1 billion), IBM ($52.8 billion), GE ($42.4 billion), and Nokia ($35.0 billion).[12] There are no Canadian brands in the latest ranking of the top 100 global brands.

For more information on the importance of brand names and the impact that they have on consumers, refer to the Marketing in Action vignette **Brand Power: What Makes a Great Brand?**

These principles are fine, but there are no guarantees for success. Brands are subject to the whims of consumers, a fluctuating economy where uncertainty prevails, and the rapid pace of technological change. A brand could come out of nowhere and become a billion dollar brand or it could be humbled quickly by a changing economy.

Interbrand, a management consulting company in the United States, analyzes global brands and reports that Coca-Cola is the number one brand valued at US$68.9 billion in 2001. It is a steady performer from year to year and is not subject to the ravages of economic cycles like many other brands. Brands such as Amazon.com and Yahoo! rose to prominence with the dot.com wave but when the dot.com bubble burst, the value of these brands dropped considerably. In 2001 the value of the Ford brand name dropped 17 percent from $36.4 billion to 30.1 billion. It was literally run over by the Firestone tire controversy. In spite of the fall, the Ford brand name still ranked 8th among the world's leading brands.

Even the powerful Nike brand (which ranks 34th in global value) has had its share of problems due to bad publicity associated with production practices in the Far East. It has fallen out of favour with some, perhaps due to an over-saturation of marketing hype. For many consumers "Just Do It" has become "Just Cool It." Too much of anything may not be a good thing. Competitors, such as Adidas, are quietly taking market share from Nike. In sharp contrast, a brand like Starbucks experienced a huge increase in value, moving from $1.3 billion to $1.8 billion, an increase of 32 percent in 2001. Firmly established brands such as IBM, Microsoft, GE, Disney, and McDonald's tend to retain their top-10 status from year to year.

Do these stories imply that all brands, however big, are eventually doomed to fade? The answer is no, but it depends on the quality of marketing behind the brand. It seems that brands such as Nike, Disney, and Coca-Cola, which are often referred to as "philosophy brands," have an advantage. These brands express an attitude toward life, which can be extended into a variety of different areas. Therefore, a true brand transcends product format and has a relationship with the consumer that has more to do with the beliefs the brand expresses than the product itself. As markets change, the brand has to use the power of that relationship to expand and evolve into new formats and markets. Those that do not are destined to fail.

Adapted from "The World's 10 Most Valuable Brands," *Business Week*, August 6, 2001, www.businessweek.com/magazine/content, Richard Tomkins, "Fading stars of the global stage," *Financial Post*, March 8, 1999, p. C4; and Scott Bedbury, "What great brands do," www.fastcompany.com/10.bedbury.html.

Courtesy of Nike Inc.

Packaging and Labelling Strategies

5.
Explain the role of packaging decisions in the development of product strategy.

How important is a package? Very important! Packaging has become an essential element in building a brand's image. Packages have to change with the times, but they must not lose touch with the identity that gave them their special appeal. Coca-Cola, for example, has kept its signature alive by using the original handwriting of a company accountant from nearly a century ago. Today's white-on-red logo is recognizable even in other alphabets. Coke has not had to change. But, then, other brands do not have the same stature as Coca-Cola.

Package designers understand that 40 percent of communications is visual, and 80 percent of visual communications is conveyed through colours and shapes. Further, they know that when they design a package they must capture the attention of consumers in the blink of an eye. Such knowledge aided L'Oreal Canada when it launched L'Oreal Kids shampoo. The package has a fish eye as its main graphic element, and the brightly coloured bottle is shaped like a fish, with the eye and a mouth formed to dispense product (see Figure 8.7). The squeezable bottle also floats in water, so the package is a toy as well as a hair-cleaning product. The package also contained a less obvious marketing element—the bottle is made of low-density polyethylene that lets the product's fragrance actually come through the packaging. When the customers are in the aisle, they can actually smell the fragrances. L'Oreal Kids captured 49.5 percent of the children's hair care market within three months of its launch.[13] Sales results like this verify the importance of an attention-getting package in a cluttered retail shelf environment.

L'Oreal Canada
www.lorealparis.ca

A Unique Package Design That Attracts Attention

Figure 8.7

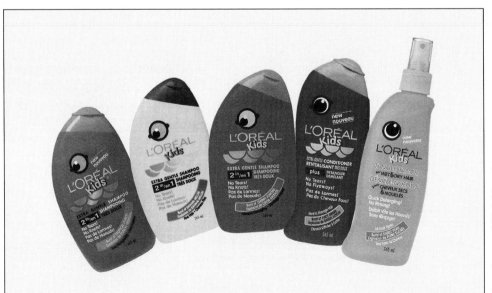

Compliments of L'Oréal Canada

THE ROLE AND INFLUENCE OF PACKAGING

packaging

Packaging is defined as those activities related to the design and production of the container or wrapper of a product. But more than that, it is the combination of the package (which attracts the consumers' attention), the product (the quality inside the package), and the brand name that contributes to the image held by consumers. It is an integral part of product strategy.

Some recent statistics reveal how important packaging is in the marketing of a product. More than 80 percent of purchase decisions at a supermarket are made within the store, and 60 percent of those are made on impulse. In the average 22-minute shopping trip, a consumer only spends 12 seconds in front of any product category and views an average of 20 products per second.[14] A product's marketing life is thus reduced to seconds. The package is of utmost importance! It must work hard to make the product appeal to the senses in a convincing way.

The design of a package contributes to brand equity—those characteristics and associations linked to a brand that can add value to it. Such factors as shape, size, and colour contribute to the personality of a brand. For example, when you think of Coca-Cola, a particular shape of bottle probably comes to mind along with the colour red. Research shows that a large size of cereal box gives the consumer a feeling of bounty, of expansive, energy-giving food (e.g., a Kellogg's Special K package). In contrast, small cereal packages make cereals seem heavy or solid (e.g., a Post Grape Nuts package).[15]

The power of colour cannot be underestimated. The colour of the Kodak film box is so well known that that particular hue is often called "Kodak yellow." As they are emotional triggers, and consequently powerful marketing tools, colours are carefully selected. Hot colours—reds, oranges, and yellows—are associated with fast foods, for example. Red demands attention and is a sign of power. Dark colours project richness, while white denotes purity and freshness.

Colour is so important, a company may not be able to change if it wanted to. Take the case of Tetley Tea. When Tetley redesigned the package, consumer research was undertaken. The existing package was blue and the face panel included images such as a wooden table, a carnation, some cookies, and a teapot. It was not clear—even to the company—what the core elements of the design were. Research, however, suggested that Tetley "owned" the colour blue. So strong was the association that to change it would be self-sabotage. The colour blue dominated the new design (see Figure 8.8) but all other elements were dropped except for a cup and saucer, and teapot.[16]

In devising packaging strategies, package shapes and textures, colours, brandmarks, symbols, personalities, illustrations, photography, and type styles are all considered. Used correctly, they can trigger instant recognition of a brand—think of Tide's swirl of orange and yellow; Campbell Soup's red-and-white can; and Quaker Oats' kindly-looking Quaker man.

COMPONENTS OF A PACKAGE

The package is what consumers look for when they are thinking of a purchase; marketers, therefore, spend considerable time and money developing effective, functional, and eye-catching designs. There are four basic components to a package. The **primary package** contains the actual product (e.g., the jar containing the jam, the tube of toothpaste, and the plastic bottle holding shampoo or liquid soap).

primary package

secondary package

The **secondary package** is the outer wrapper that protects the product, often discarded once the product is used the first time. The box that tubes of toothpaste are

Figure 8.8

The Redesigned Package for Tetley Tea—Bold Blue Colour and Fewer Elements on the Front of the Package

Dick Hemingway

packed in is an example. Even though these outer packages are discarded, they are important to the marketer, as it is their design that attracts the customer's eye to the product.

labels

Labels are printed sheets of information affixed to a package container. A label can be wrapped around a jar of coffee, a can, or a cardboard canister or glued to a flat surface at the front or back of a rigid surface. Labelling is discussed in detail in a following section.

shipping carton

Packages are packed in cartons, usually corrugated cardboard cartons, to facilitate movement from one destination to another. The **shipping carton** is marked with product codes to facilitate storage and transportation of merchandise. Today, more products are being shrink-wrapped, a process of putting a plastic wrap on the product packed on cardboard trays (e.g., fruit juices and soft drinks).

FUNCTIONS OF A PACKAGE

Essentially, a package has three basic functions. It must protect the product, market the product, and offer convenience to the consumer.

Protect the Product

Since a product may pass through many warehouses on its way to the consumer, even those products that are not fragile require protection. The degree of protection needed depends on how long the products will be in storage, how they will be transported, what kind of handling they will experience, and how much protection from heat, light, and moisture they will need.

Market the Product

A retailer is concerned about the size and shape of the package, since shelf space is limited, and whether or not enough information is on the package to resell the product. For example, will it provide adequate information for consumers who examine products in a self-serve store environment?

In its communications function, the package does everything a medium, such as television or a magazine, should do. For this reason, a package design should be researched with consumers because the package is loaded with psychological implications. It is the "look" of the package that helps the consumer form opinions about quality, value, and performance.

Studies have shown that a change in colours, graphic, or configuration can dramatically alter the consumer's perception of the product. To illustrate, consider the case of Nabisco Bits & Bites. Initially packed in a cracker-style box, sales were stagnating. Analysis revealed the package was counterintuitive to the social image of a snack. Nabisco needed a package as convenient as a potato chip bag. The solution was the doyne pouch (named after its inventor). The package is a standup foil bag with a resealable Ziploc-like mouth (see Figure 8.9). Between 1996 and 2000 sales of Bits & Bites tripled. So pleased were they with the results, Nabisco extended the pouch pack to other product lines.[17]

Provide Convenience to Consumers

A package should be easy to carry, open, handle, and reseal. For example, if it is a liquid, it should pour without spills or drips (e.g., squirt tops on dish detergent containers and no-drip spouts on liquid laundry detergent containers). If the product is heavy or bulky, handles of packages often become an important aspect of the design. Examples of convenience in packaging include resealable plastic lids for jars and cans, twist-off caps, straws on fruit juice cartons, and canned goods with molded metal bottoms that allow stacking.

PACKAGING AND THE ENVIRONMENT

With regards to packaging, social and environmental issues have forced manufacturers to think more creatively. Product safety is a major concern of consumer groups and governments. Unforeseen scares, such as the notorious Tylenol incident in the mid-1980s, in which deaths were temporarily linked to packages of Tylenol, must be avoided at all costs. As a result of such scares, the pharmaceutical industry brought to market the concept of tamper-proof packaging. Most drug products now have extra seals on the inner and outer packages, and consumers are advised by manufacturers not to purchase a product if either of those seals is broken. In the soft drink industry, there was once a problem of exploding glass pop bottles. For that matter, any large bottle that could tip from a store shelf presents danger to consumers. Safer plastic bottles are now the norm in the beverage industry.

Consumers are also concerned about unnecessary and extravagant packaging that adds to the cost of the product and waste at landfill sites. As well, the excessive use of

Figure 8.9

The Change to a Standup Pouch Pack Increased Sales Dramatically for Bits & Bites

Dick Hemingway

raw materials is depleting Canada's natural resources. Many companies have taken this concern to heart. The Bits & Bites example cited earlier also applies here. By going to the resealable pouch pack, Nabisco eliminated a layer of packaging, the cardboard container. The result was less expensive but more attractive packaging along with less waste for landfills. Nabisco effectively combined environmental issues with marketing issues.

LABELLING

Labels are those parts of a package that contain information. A label serves three functions: it identifies the brand name and the owner of the brand; it provides essential information to the buyer; and it satisfies legal requirements where applicable. In the case of food products, labels may also communicate nutritional information. The typical components of a label include the brand name, usually in a distinctive font, an illustration that represents the product (e.g., a cup of steaming coffee on a coffee jar), directions for use, a universal product code, and information that is mandated by law. The universal product code, or the UPC as it is commonly referred to, is a series of black lines that appear on virtually all consumer packaged-goods. These bars identify the manufacturer and product item (brand, size, variety, and so on). Electronic scanners at the point of sale read these codes. For retailers, the UPC symbol offers several benefits, namely, reduced labour costs, better records on product turnover (allowing quicker and better informed decisions on what items to carry), and greater inventory control (automatic reorder points are established).

The mandatory information includes the volume or weight of the product and the company name and address. With new legislation coming into effect for food products, Canadian marketers will soon be able to trumpet health benefits of their products in three areas: nutrition labelling, nutrient content claims and health claims. The legislation makes nutrition labelling mandatory on most pre-packaged foods. The information will be included in a Nutrition Facts box on the package.[18]

Sometimes, promotional information is included on a package temporarily. For example, a brand of cereal may run a contest for a free trip and include a phrase, such as "Win a trip to a Walt Disney World Resort…see side panel for details" in a flash on the front of the package. Refer to the Kellogg's cereal example in Figure 8.10 for an illustration of promotion-oriented package. Packages flashes like this only appear during the promotion period.

Figure 8.10

A Package That Includes a Promotional Offer to Grab Attention

Dick Hemingway

Summary

A product is a combination of tangible and intangible benefits offered to consumers. Marketing organizations develop and market a total product concept. This concept includes the physical item, the image, the brand name, the level of sales support, and other activities.

The total range of products offered for sale is referred to as the product mix. Products are classified according to characteristics such as durability and tangibility. Products are also classified either as consumer goods or industrial (business) goods. Consumer goods are intended for the personal use of the customer, while industrial goods are generally used in the production of other goods and services. It is the use by the customer that distinguishes consumer goods from industrial goods.

Consumer goods are further subdivided into convenience goods, shopping goods, and specialty goods. These types are generally distinguished by price and by the time taken to purchase the item. Industrial goods are subdivided into three categories: capital items, parts and materials, and supplies and services.

How a customer perceives a product largely depends on the brand. Marketing organizations use branding as a means of identifying products and developing an image. Branding involves a number of decisions in the areas of brand name, brandmark (logo) and trademarks. Broadly speaking, an organization has two branding options: individual brands or family brands. Recently, some packaged goods manufacturers have introduced a co-branding concept, in which two brand names share equal billing on one product. Private label brands and generic brands are other strategies used by distributors of consumer goods. Their presence and popularity with consumers has negatively impacted the sale of national brands. Consumers come to trust what the brand name stands for and, if they derive satisfaction from the brand, to develop certain levels of brand loyalty. Loyalty is expressed in terms of recognition, preference, and insistence.

Packaging plays an integral part in the product mix. Decisions that must be made about packaging concern the type and nature of package to use, when to alter the package design, and the labelling and shipping requirements. Packages selected must fulfill four basic functions. A good package protects the product, markets the product, provides the consumer with convenience in handling and using the product, and is environmentally safe.

Key Terms

accessory equipment 207

brand 208

brand equity 217

brand insistence 217

brand loyalty 217

brand name 208

brand preference 217

brand recognition 217

brandmark (logo) 208

capital items 206

co-branding 211

component parts 207

consumer goods 203

convenience goods 204

copyright 209

cult brand 214 *harley davidson*

durable goods 203

emergency goods 204

family brand 210

generic brand 213

impulse goods 204

individual brand 209

industrial (business) goods 203, 206

installations 206

Review Questions

1. Explain what is meant by the "total product concept."

2. What is the difference between product line depth and product line width? Provide some examples other than those in the text to illustrate the difference.

3. What is the difference between a durable good and a nondurable good?

4. Describe the characteristics of the following goods:
   a) Convenience goods
   b) Shopping goods
   c) Specialty goods
   e) Unsought goods

5. There are three categories of convenience goods. Identify and briefly explain each category.

6. What are the three classifications of industrial (business) goods?

7. What is the difference between a brandmark and a trademark?

8. What is the difference between an individual brand strategy and a family brand strategy?

9. Explain the concept of co-branding. Can you identify any benefits in using such a strategy? Provide some new examples of co-branding to dramatize the benefits the strategy offers.

10. What is the difference between a private label brand and a generic brand?

11. Distinguish between brand recognition, brand preference, and brand insistence.

12. What is brand equity? How is it determined?

13. Briefly describe the basic functions of a package.

Discussion and Application Questions

1. Provide two examples of each of the following types of industrial (business) goods:
   a) Installation
   b) Accessory equipment
   c) Component part
   d) Processed material

2. Provide examples of five different private label brands other than those mentioned in the chapter. Conduct some secondary research on a few of these brands to determine how popular they are.

3. Review the vignette "Brands That Stir Passions." Consider the dilemma that

Krispy Kreme faces. Should Krispy Kreme expand its menu and move more into the mainstream or should it continue to do what it does best—make and sell donuts? Conduct some secondary research on this brand before finalizing your position.

4. Examine the vignette "Brand Power: What Makes a Great Brand?" Using the criteria identified in the vignette, select a great brand name (in your opinion) and provide an explanation as to why it enjoys such status.

5. Select any two packages on the market. Choose one you think is good and one you believe is not so good. Discuss the marketability of each package.

E-Assignment

Evaluate the following brand names in terms of the desirable characteristics a good name should possess (refer to the Marketing in Action vignette "Brand Power: What Makes a Great Brand Name"). Visit the Web site for each name and explore a few pages at each site. Does the Web site project a good image for the brand? Examine how colour is used at each Web site. Does colour influence your perception of the brand (positively or negatively)? Explain. Use other brand names and Web sites, if you wish. The brands:

Coca-Cola **www.coca-cola.com**
Nike **www.nike.com**
Starbucks **www.starbucks.com**
Apple **www.apple.com**
McDonald's **www.mcdonalds.com**

Endnotes

1. Lawrence Reny et al., *Decisions in Marketing* (Plano, TX: Business Publications Inc., 1984), p. 20.

2. Marina Strauss, "Maytag makes no. 1 out of loneliness," *Globe and Mail*, June 18, 1991, p. B4.

3. John Heinzl, "The attack of the brand flakes," *Globe and Mail*, November 24, 2000, p. E1.

4. *Dictionary of Marketing Terms*, 2nd Edition, (Hauppauge, NY: Barron's Educational Series Inc., 1994).

5. Eric Young, "Harnessing the power of a brand," *Marketing*, May 8, 1985, 1995, p. 37.

6. S. Carpenter, "Some co-branding caveats to obey," *Marketing News*, November 7, 1994, p. 4.

7. Lisa D'Innocenzo, "Canadian Tire hopes to nail kitchenware category with private label," *Strategy*, May 6, 2002, p. 6.

8. Marina Strauss, "Loblaws looks to expand President's Choice brand," *Globe and Mail*, January 25, 2000, pp. B1, B11.

9. Lawrence Carrell, "Bills are out but Flutie's still scoring with flakes," *Globe and Mail*, January 7, 1999, p. B7.

10. Dale Beckman, David Kurtz and Louis Boone, *Foundations of Marketing* (Toronto, ON: Holt, Rinehart and Winston, 1988), pp. 316-317.

11. Jeff Pappone, "Loblaws' private label the choice of Harvard," *Financial Post*, June 4, 1999, p. C4.

12. "The World's 10 Most Valuable Brands," *Business Week*, August 6, 2001, www.businessweek.com/magazine/content.

13. Astrid Van Den Broek, "Message in a bottle," *Marketing*, May 11, 1998, pp. 16-17.

14. Jo Marney, "More than a pretty face," *Marketing*, April 10, 1995, p. 25.

15. *Off the Shelf*, a publication of Design Partners Inc., vol. 2 No. 1, n.d.

16. Wendy Cuthbert, "Between the concept and the shelf," *Strategy*, March 13, 2000, p. 31.

17. Carey Toane, "Success is in the bag," *Marketing*, October 9, 2000, p. 25.

18. Leslie Young, "New health claims rules applauded," *Marketing*, June 25, 2001, p. 3.

Dave Starrett

Product Management

After studying this chapter, you will be able to

1. Describe the organizational systems for developing and managing products.
2. Describe the nature of product-related decisions.
3. Explain the impact the product life cycle has on the development of marketing strategies at each stage of the cycle.
4. Describe the alternatives available to an organization for developing new products.
5. Identify and explain the steps in the new product development process.

Product management concerns three key areas: (1) the internal organization structure for managing current products; (2) the allocation of resources for the development of new products; and (3) dealing with changing market needs, especially as products progress through their life cycles. In this third area, the firm must be aware of the need to change marketing strategies during the various stages of the product's life cycle. Organizations realize that demand for the products they offer for sale now will not last forever.

The influence of technology is changing the way a company thinks about new product development and how it manages existing products. In a nutshell, every decision has to be made more quickly. Standing still means a company could lose a step to a competitor—the financial impact could be costly. Difficult decisions must be made about what new products to introduce and when, and what existing products should be dropped and when. This chapter will look at the key areas involved in product management.

Organization Systems for Managing Products

1.
Describe the organizational systems for developing and managing products.

The trend in contemporary marketing practice is to combine various organizational structures so that products may be developed and marketed more efficiently than before. In packaged-goods companies, an organizational structure called the *brand management system* has traditionally been the norm, but, more recently, it has given way to category management and *geographical management systems*. Companies in business-to-business marketing are moving toward target market management systems. For example, business-to-business organizations develop new products and manage existing products to meet the needs of particular market segments (e.g., communications, health, transportation, and so on) or particular industries (e.g., chemicals, banking, and so on). The type of management system used often depends on three factors: the size of an organization, the growth objectives established by an organization, and the resources possessed by an organization.

BRAND MANAGEMENT

brand manager

A **brand manager** (product manager) is an individual who is assigned the responsibility for the development and implementation of marketing programs for a specific product or group of products. In a brand management system, all company brands are divided up so that managers are responsible for the marketing activity of one brand or group of brands. The brand manager works closely with others in the organization and with external suppliers in such areas as advertising and promotion, package design, and marketing research. For multi-product companies, this system ensures that all products receive equal attention in planning, even though some products may have a higher marketing profile when plans are implemented. A diagram of the brand management system is presented in Figure 9.1. In this system, it is assumed that the manager is ultimately responsible for all marketing mix elements. In many organizations, the manager may also be responsible for the profitability of the brand.

CATEGORY MANAGEMENT

category manager

A **category manager** is an individual who is assigned the responsibility for developing and implementing the marketing activity for all products grouped in the category. The category management system is a management structure that groups products according to their similarity to one another. Naturally, products in the same category are closely related. A large multi-product packaged-goods company, such as Unilever, has categories such as margarine (Becel, Imperial, Blue Bonnet, Monarch and others), tea-based beverages (Red Rose, Salada, Lipton), culinary products (Lipton Soup Mix, Lipton Cup-a-Soup, Lipton SoupWorks) and side dishes (Lipton Noodles & Sauce, Lipton Side Kicks, Lipton Homestyle Potatoes).

In this system, the category manager adopts a more generalized view of the business than would an individual brand manager in the brand management system (Figure 9.1).

In Canada, the system has become popular as manufacturers realize they must work more closely and cooperatively with retailers (relationship marketing), who have significant buying power and who organize their shelves according to the sales volume of brands within each product category.

Supermarkets such as Loblaws, Sobeys, and Safeway use category management systems (space management systems). They work with suppliers cooperatively and manage categories of products instead of individual brands. Buyers at these and other chain stores deal with all suppliers within a category (e.g., pet food, snack food, soft drinks, juice beverages, and so on). Electronic scanning determines which products are moving well. This information determines which products to carry, and which ones to delete as new products come along. The goal of space-management programs is to improve sales in each category. Manufacturers that market brand leaders in a category have leverage with retailers that can be detrimental to slower moving brands.

Pepsi-Cola and several supermarkets are experimenting with a concept dubbed the "power aisle." It is an aisle dedicated to PepsiCo's food (Frito-Lay products) and drink products (Pepsi-Cola, Mountain Dew, and others). The strategy of the power aisle is straightforward: both categories located together should build sales volume for both. If the experiment is successful, Pepsi will have a unique advantage over Coke, since Coca-Cola does not have a snack food division. Test market results are positive: sales of Frito-Lay products increased 21 percent and sales of all soft drinks, not just Pepsi, increased modestly.[1]

REGIONAL MANAGEMENT

regional marketing management system

Geography plays a key role in a **regional marketing management system**. In this management structure, decision-making is decentralized. Instead of an organization being

Figure 9.1

Alternative Product Management Systems

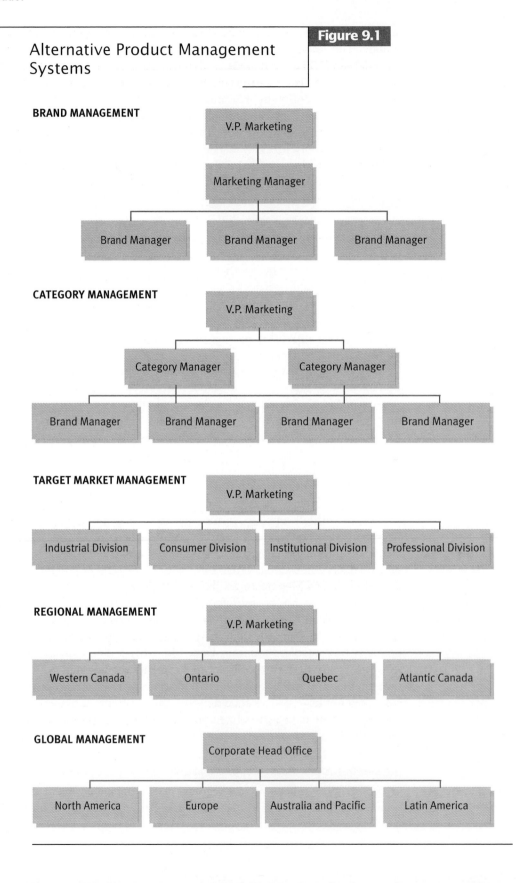

BRAND MANAGEMENT

V.P. Marketing

Marketing Manager

Brand Manager | Brand Manager | Brand Manager

CATEGORY MANAGEMENT

V.P. Marketing

Category Manager | Category Manager

Brand Manager | Brand Manager | Brand Manager | Brand Manager

TARGET MARKET MANAGEMENT

V.P. Marketing

Industrial Division | Consumer Division | Institutional Division | Professional Division

REGIONAL MANAGEMENT

V.P. Marketing

Western Canada | Ontario | Quebec | Atlantic Canada

GLOBAL MANAGEMENT

Corporate Head Office

North America | Europe | Australia and Pacific | Latin America divided up into production, marketing, finance, and by division of products, a country is divided up geographically into regions. Molson Breweries, for example, has established separate companies to manage three regions: Western Canada, Ontario/Atlantic, and Quebec. A national marketing team manages a group of brands referred to as "strategic national brands." Canadian and Export are in this group. Each region has a staff of marketing, sales, and promotion personnel who develop marketing strategies and implement programs for "strategic regional brands." As well, regional teams execute national brand strategies. According to Molson, such a system allows a company to build on its strengths and chip away at its weaknesses. The closer the decision makers are to the action, the quicker is the response time for planning and implementing new marketing strategies.[2]

MARKETING SERVICES MANAGEMENT

marketing services management system

In a **marketing services management system**, an effort is made to shift some of the brand manager's responsibility to marketing services (see Figure 9.1). There is a partnership between brand managers and/or category managers and marketing services personnel. Division of responsibility is different in this system, as some activities that could be assigned to a brand manager instead become the responsibility of marketing services. In other words, some brand manager responsibilities shift to marketing services. It is quite common for marketing services to be the contact point for external suppliers such as advertising agencies, sales promotion companies, and marketing research companies. It is common for both management groups (marketing services and the brand managers) to collaborate in planning, implementing, and evaluating marketing strategies.

A second alternative involves the elimination of the brand manager. Here, the organization separates brands and categories according to strategic (long-term) planning and tactical (short-term) planning. One group evaluates strategic brand direction while the other thinks and manages activities on a day-to-day basis. The marketing services group offers assistance to the planning managers by providing information from external specialists such as ad agencies and research companies. This system works best when the group does all of the planning for a category of products—it provides efficiency in planning and allows for multi-brand promotions.

TARGET MARKET MANAGEMENT

target market management system

In a **target market management system**, the organization recognizes that different customer classes with different needs require different marketing strategies (see Figure 9.1). Such a strategy makes sense for multi-divisional companies dealing with diverse target markets. A company with both industrial and consumer customer bases would utilize different strategies when communicating with those targets. For example, Ericsson, a participant in the global telecom industry, recently divided its management system into three business segments on customers instead of products. The three divisions are network operations (wireless and fixed solutions for data and telecommunications), consumer products (mobile phones being the core product), and enterprise solutions (permanent and mobile business communications systems).[3]

Ericsson
www.ericsson.com]

Sony Electronics is in the midst of a sweeping reorganization of its marketing management system. Its new system manages according to consumers' life stages. For insight into how their system works, read the Marketing in Action vignette **Sony Manages by Lifestyle**.

GLOBAL MANAGEMENT

global management structure

Companies with growth aspirations now view the world as one market. What has emerged is a **global management structure**. In this system, ideas that are developed in one country may be considered for another so that economies of scale are achieved. The often-used expression "Think globally, act locally" is now a common salute among multinational marketers. In other words, while brand managers and marketing managers in Canada are responsible for marketing in Canada, they are also influenced by the decisions of managers elsewhere. In extreme cases managers in small countries can be eliminated entirely.

Procter & Gamble's management philosophy is global where possible and local where necessary. It wants its successful brands to be marketed in as many countries as possible even if it jeopardizes the position of successful local market brands. To illustrate, P&G recently phased out the Royale brand name (paper products) in Canada and replaced it with the global Charmin brand in bathroom tissues and the Puffs brand in facial tissues. Such a change was not dramatic; it involved transition so that current customers would not be alienated. The first step involved the shrinking of the Canadian brand names on the box while magnifying the Charmin and Puffs brand. Eventually the Royale name was dropped.

Sony Corp.
www.sony.com

Mothballing the Royale brand fits with P&G's worldwide management directive where the focus is on profitable brands that allow it to leverage the scale of its manufacturing and marketing resources. In a manner similar to a domestic company looking at a regional management system, P&G is managing brands geographically but on a global scale.[4]

A Closer Look at Product Decisions

2.
Describe the nature of product-related decisions.

A brand manager (product manager or category manager) is responsible for all areas of the marketing mix. A brand manager must establish profitable and fair prices; decide on the use of promotional elements, such as advertising, sales promotion, and event marketing; and decide on where the product should be available to customers.

Being more specific about the product, decisions occur in several key areas: modifying the product, altering the product mix, introducing a new package design, and maintaining and withdrawing a product from the market.

PRODUCT MODIFICATIONS

Products are modified in many ways and for many reasons. Changes in style are often implemented to give a product a contemporary look; automobiles are redesigned to appeal to changing consumer tastes and preferences. The home appliance industry recently introduced brighter, technologically innovative products (refrigerators, stoves, washers, and dryers) in vibrant or translucent colours (blues, yellows, and reds), retro contours, and commercial sizes. The addition of a fashion aspect to appliances (something that may seem odd) added some enthusiasm to a stagnant industry and gave manufacturers a niche in which to position their products uniquely. The success of the colourful iMac computers influenced product decisions for appliances. Apparently, consumers were just plain tired of white rectangular boxes. The timing was perfect![5]

Functional modifications make a package easier or safer to use. A no-mess-pour spout to a container for a liquid product is an example of a functional modification.

Marketing in Action

Sony Manages by Lifestyle

In an attempt to more effectively market its consumer electronics product lines, Sony Corp. is restructuring its marketing management system to target consumers by lifestyle stages. A new internal management unit under the title Consumer Segment Marketing division will radically change the way Sony markets its products.

In the past Sony used the traditional brand management structure; now managers will be assigned to champion various demographic and lifestyle segments. This will affect all aspects of strategic marketing planning—everything from product development and advertising to retail merchandising and consumer loyalty programs. Sony North America generates about $8 billion in consumer electronic sales each year. From now on sales and profits will be reported by consumer segments.

The mission of the Consumer Segment marketing division is "to develop an intimate understanding of Sony's end consumers...from cradle to grave." Sony has identified the following segments:

Affluent
CE Alphas (early adopters of technology at any age)
Zoomers (55+)
SoHo (small office/home office)
Families (35 to 54 years)

Young Professionals/DINKS (double income, no kids, 25 to 34)
Gen Y (under 25)

Sony continuously strives to find a better way of doing things. Its present goal is to get closer to the consumer, to understand their unique needs and how their needs change as they age.

Under the new management structure Generation Y and its various sub-segments—tweens, teens, college students—are of critical importance. Like many other marketing organizations, Sony wants to establish some brand loyalty early, build a comprehensive database, and then initiate frequent contact through relationship marketing.

Adapted from Tobi Elkin, "Sony marketing aims at lifestyle segments," *Advertising Age*, March 18, 2002, pp. 3, 72.

Bill Lai/MaXx Images Inc.

Quality modifications include improvements, such as making the product more durable (e.g., floor wax or furniture polish), improving the taste (a beverage or food product), and improving the speed (a personal computer). Golf is an industry that relies on subtle product improvements in club design or ball technology to sustain growth and differentiate products. Refer to Figure 9.2 for an illustration.

PRODUCT MIX

As discussed in the previous chapter, product mix decisions concern the *depth* and *width* of a product line. The addition of new products and the creation of extended versions of existing products are the lifeline of growth-oriented marketing organizations. To foster growth, a manager looks for gaps in the marketplace (perceived opportunities) and recommends developing products for the opportunities with the highest potential. This procedure is referred to as **product stretching** and is defined as the

product stretching

sequential addition of products to a product line so that its depth or width is increased. Stretching can occur in several ways. Colgate-Palmolive makes 19 types of Colgate toothpaste in various sizes (that's a lot of choice!) and they do so for good reason. While meeting the unique needs of different customers, new items drive sales growth. In 2001, 38 percent of Colgate's $9.4 billion (US) sales came from products introduced in the past 5 years.[6]

Figure 9.2

Modifications in Design Are Crucial in Order to Continuously Improve a Product

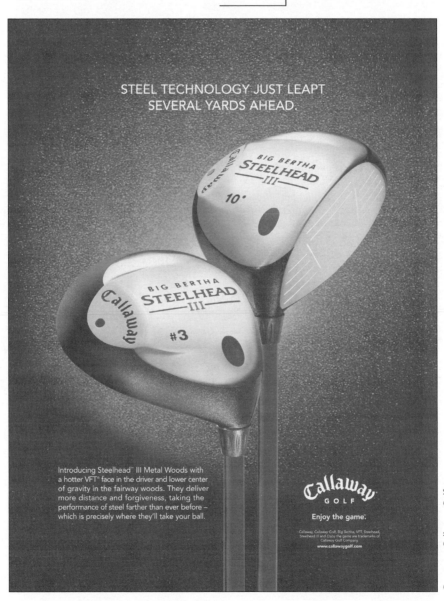

Courtesy: Callaway Golf

In the household cleaner market, Mr. Clean expanded its product line by adding four new scents-a scent for each season-spring garden, summer citrus, sparkling apple, and invigorating breeze (see Figure 9.3).

PACKAGING DECISIONS

Packaging is an integral part of product strategy. It is common for consumer goods to undergo several package-design changes throughout their lives. Similar to the periodic redesign of an automobile, package changes are intended to bolster the image of the

Figure 9.3

Stretching a Product Line by Adding New Scents

The freshness of the seasons. The strength of Mr. Clean.

Mr. Clean now brings you Seasons' Freshness". An antibacterial cleaner with four great scents.
Spring Garden, Summer Citrus, Sparkling Apple and Invigorating Breeze.
They'll remind you of your favourite season. Any time of the year.

product, provide a contemporary appearance, or fulfill some other product and marketing objective. For example, when Campbell's Soup wanted to redesign the label for its Habitant brand soup, the designers clearly understood that such phrases as "warm and homemade" were the mantra for the project. As well, the yellow and blue colours had to be maintained. The objective of the new design was to portray existing brand character while upgrading appetite appeal (Figure 9.4). Habitant is positioned as a wholesome, good homemade soup, and its brand character is warm, caring, uncomplicated, and traditionally Canadian.[7]

MAINTENANCE OR WITHDRAWAL

One of the toughest decisions facing a manager is whether or not to cut the lifeline of a product. Such a decision should be based on profit or loss and strategic fit, but other factors, such as sentiment and emotion (attachment to long-established products), enter into the decision as well. It is unrealistic to think that products will remain profitable indefinitely, particularly in the fast-paced marketplace of today. For example, Anglo-Dutch food giant Unilever recently sold 15 North American brands so it could concentrate on a smaller collection of core brands. By selling the brands Unilever gave up $400 million in annual sales. Canadian brands that were sold included St. Lawrence corn oil and Crown and Beehive corn syrups. According to Patrick Cescau, Unilever's foods director, "The brands sold represent an attractive portfolio but fall outside our strategy to focus on leading brands such as Ragu, Hellman's, and Lipton."[8]

The Product Life Cycle

product life cycle   Products go through a series of phases known as the **product life cycle**. The term refers to the stages a product goes through from its introduction to the market to its eventual

Figure 9.4

Redesigning Packages and Labels Is an Important Product Decision

Courtesy: The Habitant Soup Company

3.
Explain the impact the product life cycle has on the development of marketing strategies at each stage of the cycle.

withdrawal (Figure 9.5). According to the life cycle theory, a product starts with slow sales in the introduction stage; experiences rapid sales increases in the second (growth) stage; undergoes only marginal growth or even some decline when it reaches maturity; and then enters the decline stage, where sales drop off at a much faster rate each year. The variables of *time*, *sales*, and *profits* are the determinants of a product's stage in the life cycle. The life cycle concept is popular in strategic marketing planning. Since the conditions of each stage are quite different, the life cycle suggests that different strategies, or marketing mixes, should be used in each phase. This section of the chapter examines the four stages of the life cycle and discusses some of the marketing implications that each stage presents to the manager.

Although profit and time affect what stage an item is perceived to be in, sales is the primary indicator of what stage of the cycle a product has reached. Thus, the degree to which a market accepts and then rejects a product determines how long the life cycle of that product will be. All products do not have the same life cycles; some are quite long (Wrigley's Gum and Quaker Oatmeal), while others are quite short (Crystal Pepsi).

INTRODUCTION STAGE

introduction stage

As its name suggests, a product's **introduction stage** is the period after it has been introduced into the marketplace and before significant growth begins, during which the company tries to create demand for the product. It is a period of slow sales growth, since the product is new and not yet widely known. Losses are frequently incurred in this stage because research and development expenses must be recovered and a heavy investment in marketing is needed to establish an awareness of the brand. This marketing investment is a reflection of the company's commitment to building a viable market position.

The immediate objective during the introduction stage is to build demand and create brand name awareness. A sizable budget is allocated to marketing communications

Product Life Cycle

Figure 9.5

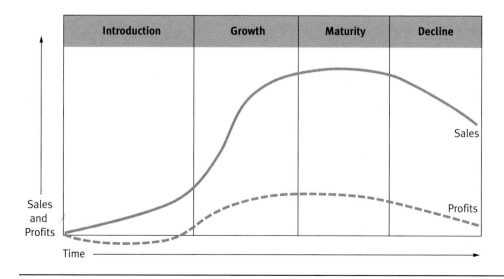

BMW Canada
www.bmw.ca

to create awareness of the item and to tempt people to try it. It is common for advertising to include incentives, such as coupons, which reduce the consumer's financial risk in making the first purchase. Widespread media coverage is also commonly used to communicate the product's benefits to the target market. Establishing an Internet presence is now very important for new products. By doing so, information about the product can be communicated well before the actual introduction of the product and create a pent up demand for it. BMW Canada used an Internet strategy effectively when it introduced consumers to the new Mini, a sporty, retro-looking vehicle formerly known as the Mini Cooper. Demand was so high that there were waiting lists for the product when it was launched. Canada was only allotted 2000 so the new dealer network had no problem selling them. Granted, the revival of the Mini garnered lots of unsolicited and positive publicity.

Setting prices high is common at the introduction stage, since it is easier to lower prices later on than to increase them, should such a need arise. Such a strategy is designed to offset development costs as quickly as possible. Also at this stage, the firm attempts to secure as great a distribution as possible by offering distributors allowances and discounts. Obtaining widespread distribution is difficult for new, unproven products.

The length of time a product stays in the introduction stage depends on the rate of adoption by consumers or on the degree to which sales increase annually.

GROWTH STAGE

growth stage

As indicated by the sales curve in Figure 9.5, the **growth stage** is a period of rapid consumer acceptance. Sales rise rapidly, as do profits. Several competitive brands generally enter the market at this stage, each seeking for itself a piece of the action; this means that aggressive marketing activity for the original product must continue in order to protect and build its market share.

The emphasis of the activity in this stage shifts from merely generating awareness to include creating preference. Many of the activities implemented are designed to encourage consumers to prefer a particular product or brand. Depending on the degree of competition, the organization maintains or perhaps increases its marketing investment at this point. Advertising messages focus on product differentiation (unique selling points) and are intended to give consumers a sound reason why they should buy a particular product. Since more information about the target market is known at this point, messages and media selection become better suited to the target; therefore, the marketing activities tend to be more efficient at this stage. A greater variety of promotion incentives are also used, since it is important to get people to make both trial purchases (by continuing to generate awareness of the product) and repeat purchases (by encouraging preference and loyalty). In addition to coupons, refund offers and contests are commonly used, since they encourage multiple purchases by interested consumers.

Price strategies at this stage remain flexible, that is, they are often determined by competitive prices. The consumer's perception of a product and of the benefits it offers also play a role in pricing strategy. Since consumer demand is higher in the growth stage than it is during the introduction stage, distribution is now easier to obtain. In effect, the combination of consumer demand and trade incentives offered by the manufacturer makes the product attractive to new distributors and helps move the product through the channel of distribution.

MATURE STAGE

mature stage

In the **mature stage** of a product's life cycle, the product has been widely adopted by consumers; sales growth slows, becoming marginal; and eventually, a slight decline develops. Profits stabilize and begin to decline because of the expenses incurred in defending a brand's market share position.

When a product is in the mature stage, advertising tends to give way to other forms of marketing communications—funds formerly allocated to advertising may be shifted into other areas such as sales promotion and price discounting. In the mature stage the objective is to conserve money rather than spend it. The goal is to generate profits from mature products that can be reinvested in the development of new products (Figure 9.6). There are exceptions to every rule, however, since this is a period where the only way to grow is to steal business from the competitor. In Canada's soft drink market, for example, sales are relatively flat from year to year. Both Coca-Cola and Pepsi-Cola are leading brands with similar spending patterns in marketing communications. If one company were to reduce its investment in advertising, what might happen to its market share? It is the nature of the competition that will determine how much is spent on marketing communications.

Generally, most products remain in the mature stage for a long period of time, so product managers are accustomed to implementing marketing strategies for mature brands. In maturity, a brand faces a choice. Does it adopt a defensive strategy and try to maintain market share, or does it adopt an offensive strategy and try to rejuvenate the brand (see the section on extending the product life cycle for details about rejuvenation strategies)?

Should a defensive strategy be adopted, budgets are established at a level that will protect market share. Since maintenance of present customers (loyalty) is a priority,

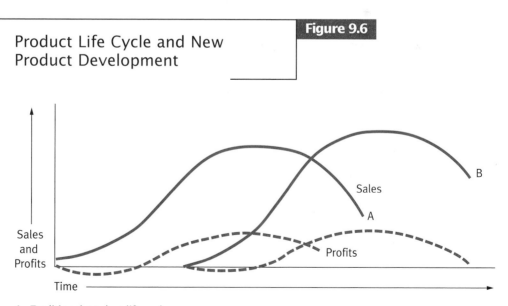

Figure 9.6

Product Life Cycle and New Product Development

A: Traditional product life cycle
B: New product, traditional life cycle
Product A generates profits to support the development and marketing of product B.

there is often greater spending on promotion activity rather than on media advertising. Promotions that encourage brand loyalty include cash refunds, contests, and giveaways with the purchase of a brand. Such offers are designed to encourage repeat purchase or multiple purchases at one time.

The New Beetle from Volkswagen is an example of a product that reached maturity rather quickly. Introduced in 1998, it was initially a "pay-anything-to-get-it, can't-keep-it-on-the-lot" success story. Nostalgic consumers willingly paid the sticker price and dealers drew up lengthy waiting lists. The Beetle was a success and it helped revive a stagnant brand (Volkswagen) in North America. By 2000 however, sales slumped by 23 percent and Beetles were in plentiful supply on dealers' lots in Canada and the United States. Now the emphasis is on price (low price), incentive packages, and cut-rate financing, much like any other vehicle on the market. An automotive star is suddenly an also-ran.[9]

The dilemma that the Beetle faces is much like any other mature product. What does the brand do once the initial euphoria fades? In the automobile market, most cars go through a style change, but with the Beetle its distinctive style is its defining characteristic, so style changes are not an option. Alternatives that involve other elements of the marketing mix will have to be explored.

To protect market share in the packaged goods industry, prices are often dropped, which reduces profits. Distribution will remain reasonably stable if the organization continues to offer trade discounts and allowances to wholesalers and retailers. However, as sales move from a slight growth to an actual decrease, distributors start to eliminate slower moving products and replace them with exciting new product innovations.

DECLINE STAGE

decline stage

In the **decline stage** of the product life cycle, sales begin to drop rapidly, and profits are eroded. Products become obsolete as many consumers shift to innovative products entering the market. Price cuts are a common marketing strategy in a declining market, as competing brands attempt to protect market share.

Because the costs of maintaining a product in decline are quite high, marketing objectives in the decline stage focus on planning and implementing the withdrawal of a product from the market. Marketers cut advertising and promotion expenditures to maximize profit or minimize potential losses and generate funds that can be invested in new products with greater profit potential. Since companies do not have the resources to support all products equally, the wise ones have products at various stages of the product life cycle so that the marketing strategies can be effectively managed within financial constraints (see Figure 9.6).

A summary of the key marketing influences on the product life cycle is included in Figure 9.7. Although the product life cycle theory commonly forms a basis for the development of marketing strategies, it has certain limitations. "If you assume a business will inevitably mature, and then decline, rest assured that's exactly what will happen."[10] This statement is a reflection of a company's attitude: those companies that follow life cycle planning too closely encourage a defeatist attitude among managers. Instead of assuming that maturity and decline are inevitable, managers should strive for innovation and generally play an aggressive role in ensuring future success—acting in the market rather than reacting to the market. The video game market provides a good illustration. In the early 1990s, Nintendo became complacent. It was the dominant brand controlling about 80 percent of the game market. Sega was in hot pursuit. Sega's strategy was to aggressively develop new and better products and then support new product introductions with exciting advertising. Now there is even more competition as Sony and Microsoft (Xbox) are both aggressively marketing their own hardware and software lines. Market share is split between four major brands, each trying to outdo the other with new technology.

EXTENDING THE PRODUCT LIFE CYCLE

Many product managers attempt to rejuvenate their brands and extend their life cycles for as long as possible by employing a more offensive strategy in the mature stage. The three most commonly used strategies for extending the life cycle of a brand are to look for new markets, to alter the product in some way, and to experiment with new marketing mixes. The effect of life cycle extensions is illustrated in Figure 9.8. Let us examine each of these options in more detail.

Figure 9.7

Product Life Cycle Characteristics and Strategic Marketing Focus

Stage	Characteristics	Strategy
Introduction	• Low sales • Negligible profits, even losses • No or few competitors • Innovative customers	• Large budget needed to create awareness for new product • Build distribution and expand market • Usually a high price is established • Promotion incentives for trial
Growth	• Rapid sales growth • Profits grow rapidly and peak • Mass market customers • More competitors enter	• Market penetration • Brand preference encouraged through advertising and repeat-purchase incentives • Product differentiation • Large budget needed due to competition • Intensive distribution • Possibly lower price
Mature	• Marginal growth and then decline in sales • Profits start to decline • Mass market • Many competitors	• A sustained budget needed to protect current share position • Emphasis on promotion instead of on advertising • Repeat purchase incentives • Intensive distribution • Product improvements • Possible price decrease
Decline	• Rapid decline in sales • Product obsolete • Low profit; potential loss • Competition drops out • Laggards purchase	• Cut marketing support • Allocate profits to new products • Price cuts common • Eventual withdrawal

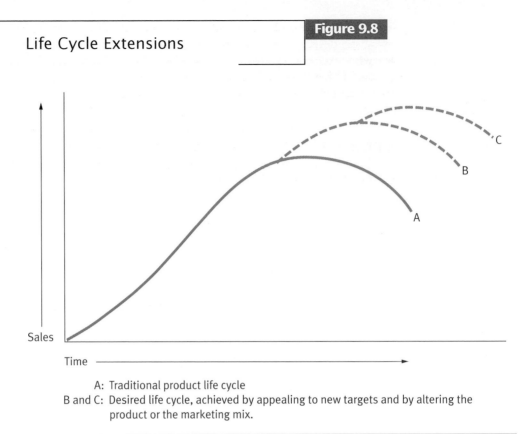

Figure 9.8

Life Cycle Extensions

A: Traditional product life cycle
B and C: Desired life cycle, achieved by appealing to new targets and by altering the product or the marketing mix.

Tap New Markets

Increasing the number of product users can be accomplished in three ways: by attracting competitors' customers, by entering new segments, and by converting non-users to users.

Attract Competitors' Customers This strategy is common in packaged goods markets. For example, Pepsi-Cola constantly strives to attract Coca-Cola drinkers by using the Pepsi "Taste Patrol" campaign. In taste tests, Coke drinkers are convinced that Pepsi tastes better than Coke. In the stagnant beer market, Blue, Coors, Canadian, and others battle head-to-head to get established and to get loyal drinkers to switch brands. The only way a brand can build share in a stagnant market is to attract users of other brands while keeping its current customers loyal.

Enter New Market Segments This approach could involve geographic expansions (e.g., a regional brand expanding into other regions) or going after new demographic target markets (e.g., different age and income groups) with the same or different versions of a product. Johnson & Johnson is the most widely cited example of a company that has used such a strategy; the company successfully repositioned its baby shampoo as a shampoo suitable for adults. The "gentle" characteristics of the product have proven to be an effective and unique selling point among adults. Mennen deodorant does it by offering Speed Stick for men and Lady Speed Stick for women.

Convert Non-Users It is not too late to attract new users at this point. Perhaps it is users of other products and services that provide the key to extended growth. For example, an individual may be persuaded to deal with more than one bank, in the search for the best interest rates for investments or loans. The business customer who has always relied on the postal service to deliver packages may be an attractive prospect for airfreight and overnight-courier-service companies. Many PC computer users purchased their first Apple computer when the iMac was launched. Perhaps their curiosity was piqued by all the marketing hype that supported the iMac. The iMac brought Apple back to life.

Apple
www.apple.com

Alter the Product

In a product alteration strategy, the marketing organization changes certain characteristics of the product to attract new users. Some rejuvenation strategies include making improvements in quality, features, and style in order to encourage customers to purchase more of the product.

Quality Improvement The marketing organization improves the primary benefit of a product and presents the product as "new and improved." For example, the product is made more durable than before, offers better colour than before, tastes better, or rides more smoothly along rough roads. A good example is Hostess Frito-Lay, a company that reformulated several of its popular brands, including Dorito's nacho-flavoured chips, Ruffles potato chips, and Lay's potato chips. Even though Frito-Lay controls about 40 percent of the snack-food market, it feared for its leadership position because of overcrowding (new product entries from current and new competitors). The new chips were processed with cottonseed oil and were fried using new technologies. The result was a better-tasting, crispier, and crunchier chip-benefits other competitors were not offering. Lays chips were packed in bags that said, "New! Tastier and Crispier." Staying a step ahead of the competition is the name of the game. Stand still and the competitor will take business away from you!

Feature Improvements The product is offered in new sizes, such as bonus packs, which give more of the product for the same price (e.g., information such as "25 percent more" appears on the package); or in new formats (e.g., laundry detergents are introduced in liquid formats under existing brand names, or bleach is added to the powdered formula). Another option is to modify the container to offer improvement or convenience in serving. See the illustration of French's mustard in Figure 9.9.

Binney & Smith, makers of Crayola products, followed a feature improvement strategy when it introduced washable crayons, which allow children to use their surroundings as a canvas without sending their parents to the cleaners. Masterpieces drawn on walls with the washable crayon are easily removed with mild soap and water from most surfaces. Research conducted by Binney & Smith revealed parents' concerns about how to remove unwanted marks on walls. Washable crayons meet that concern head-on.

Style Improvement This strategy is appropriate for durable goods, such as major appliances, home entertainment products, and automobiles. In the automobile industry, familiar names, such as Cadillac, Lincoln, and Corvette, remain, but the style and appearance of these cars change from time to time. General Motors completely

Figure 9.9

A Squeezable Container and a Stay Clean Cap Make Serving French's Mustard More Convenient

Courtesy: Reckitt Benckiser

redesigned the Cadillac in 2002 to give it a younger, sportier appearance. The goal was to attract a younger customer—someone who would typically buy a BMW or Audi. Small kitchen appliances such as coffee pots, kettles, and toasters have been redesigned recently to incorporate a "retro-look." Typically the designs have a contoured shape (rounded edges). Internally, the mechanics remain the same, but the body is altered for a statement in style.[11] See Figure 9.10 for an illustration.

Add New Product Lines In this situation the product is offered in different flavours (e.g., for soft drinks or mouthwash) or scents (e.g., for cologne or deodorant) to entice

Figure 9.10

A Change in Style Often Rejuvenates a Product—
Canadian Tire Launched the Persona Private Label
Line with a Retro Look

a different user to try the product. The objective of the product line extension is to provide increased sales to the brand by meeting an unfulfilled need in the market. For example, market research conducted by Nestlé in 2001 revealed that the flavour orange was one of the hottest new food trends. Orange was being featured in cooking shows on television. Armed with such knowledge, Nestlé introduced Nestlé's Legend Gold Edition Mandarin Chocolate ice cream. So popular was the flavour that it became one of the top three flavours sold in Canada. According to Graham Lute, Nestlé's senior vice-president of consumer marketing communications, "Everyone's into layered combinations now, and that's what's providing the appeal."[12]

The addition of "light" products is another means of extending an existing line. Nestlé, for example, introduced Taster's Choice "Lite," and Kraft Canada introduced Maxwell House "Lite," products that contain 50 percent regular coffee and 50 percent decaffeinated coffee. Both brands are trying to cash in on the image and reputation of their core brand by bringing new users with different needs to the extended product.

Change Other Marketing Mix Elements

Pricing Since products usually enter the market with a high price, the mature stage is the time to reduce price. The practice of price discounting encourages consumers to try different products. Instead of having its price lowered permanently, a product might frequently be offered to distributors at a discount and with allowances so that they can, in turn, offer price specials to consumers on a temporary basis. Earlier in the chapter it was mentioned that the Volkswagen Beetle was offering price incentives such as low financing rates and manufacturer rebates in an effort to reverse declining sales trends.

Advertising Since sales volume in the mature stage is stable, marketers are prudent about expenditures, particularly where advertising is concerned. Emphasis is placed on controlling product costs and spending only enough on advertising to maintain the current market position. Copy (message) changes are made in line with product improvements, new features, or style changes. There are exceptions to this fundamental principle (see the discussion about Coca-Cola and Pepsi-Cola that appeared in the product life cycle section of this chapter).

Sales Promotion As stated earlier, the mature stage sees greater stress placed on sales promotion than on advertising. The use of promotions to get current customers to increase their purchases is crucial at this stage. Such promotions include cash refunds, contests, and premium offers (e.g., bonus items packed in a product, as when free toys are included in cereal boxes).

Distribution The combination of product improvements and lower prices makes the product more attractive to distributors that have not yet carried the product. Because of this, the marketer seeks non-traditional channels of distribution. For example, marketers of food and snack food now sell some product lines through discount department stores, such as Wal-Mart and Zellers. Harvey's has established in-house restaurants in Home Depot stores. Tim Hortons has established a relationship with Imperial Oil and will be selling a full menu of products through Esso stations coast-to-coast in Canada. Strategies like these get customers into the retail outlets, and once they are there, they spend money on other items.

How a company manages mature products is a continuous challenge. For a look at how Lever Ponds breathed new life into Q-tips, refer to the Marketing in Action vignette **Q-tips Re-invents Itself.**

CONSUMERS INFLUENCE THE PRODUCT LIFE CYCLE

The degree to which consumers accept or reject a product is the measure of its success or failure. Product acceptance is concerned with two areas: adoption or individual acceptance, and diffusion or market acceptance.

adoption

Adoption is defined as a series of stages a consumer passes through on the way to purchasing a product on a regular basis. The adoption process has up to five distinct

Marketing in Action

Q-tips Re-invents Itself

C otton swabs are not exactly an exciting product. And, cleaning one's ears is not usually at the top of the list of things to do. This is a problem for Q-tips cotton swabs. For a product that has been on the market for 75 years, how do you build market share?

The solution is simple: if people are not going to spend more time cleaning their ears than they already do, then you have got to let them know that Q-tips are good for a lot more than just cleaning ears.

Q-tips is a strong and established brand but sales were languishing. The company established the goal of increasing sales and market share. According to Philip George, account director at Ogilvy & Mather, the advertising agency responsible for Q-tips, "We wanted to expand our share by getting users to use more Q-tips. And one way to do that was to expand the range of uses for the brand." When it embarked on the new approach, Q-tips was not floundering. The brand held 67 percent market share and enjoyed high levels of consumer trust and confidence. So popular was the brand name that there was a danger of it becoming a generic term for any cotton swab.

To fend off cheaper competitors and private label brands, Q-tips wanted a stronger positioning for the brand, and it had to be accomplished on a modest budget. In the past, Q-tips positioned itself as a product for mothers and babies, but research showed that only 10 percent of mothers actually use the product on their babies. Research also showed that people use Q-tips for all kinds of things: applying makeup, dusting, touching up a paint job, or cleaning the heads of a VCR. Ogilvy & Mather would take advantage of this knowledge.

The first step was to reassert the superiority of the product and help consumers understand why they should pay a premium price for it. That campaign was followed with one that highlighted alternative uses. Says George, "First you get people nodding their heads that Q-tips are a better product. Once you do that, then it is easier to go into the 'extended use' phase of the campaign."

The superiority campaign ran in Canadian consumer magazines and featured cutouts in the distinctive shape of a Q-tip, behind which appeared images of roses and clouds—each intended to denote one of the product's attributes: gentleness, softness, and so on. The tag was "so if you want a Q-tip, buy a Q-tip."

The extended use campaign relied mainly on billboard posters and transit ads. The ads featured split images designed to resemble a flipbook (i.e., small spiral-bound pad with a cover). The end of a Q-tip appears on one side of each board, paired on the other by a variety of household implements: a makeup brush, a feather duster, a paintbrush, and so on. The ads relied on visual illustrations and were a bit like puzzles, letting consumers use their imagination to get the message. The copy reads, "All purpose Q-tips." The strategy was to communicate the message in a very simple way.

A sampling program provided additional support to the new strategy. Samples of other company products, such as Vaseline Intensive Care lotion and Thermasilk shampoo, were included in Q-tip packages. And, for the 75th anniversary of the brand, a special commemorative tin was packed with large-sized boxes to encourage incremental consumption.

The marketing strategy was a success. Q-tips sales have increased by 60 percent since Lever Ponds made the initial shift to the new strategy four years ago. Impressed by the results, the American division decided to use the advertising campaign. The challenge now facing the Canadian division is how to keep the creative approach fresh. How do you surprise the consumer again?

Adapted from David Todd, "Q-tips cottons on to extended use strategy," *Strategy*, January 17, 2000, p. 28.

ALL PURPOSE Q-tips

Courtesy: Ogilvy & Mather Canada

steps: awareness, interest, evaluation, trial, and adoption (Figure 9.11). Not all consumers accept products at the same rate (e.g., the numbers buying in maturity are greater than growth). The gradual acceptance of a product from introduction to market saturation is referred to as the **diffusion of innovation**. Everett M. Rogers has conducted intensive research into the diffusion process, and he makes three conclusions. First, individuals require different amounts of time to decide to adopt a product; second, consumers can be classified on the basis of how quickly or how slowly they adopt a product; and, third, there are five categories of adopters.[13]

diffusion of innovation

Refer to Figure 9.12 for an illustration of the adopter categories and the proportion of the target market population that each represents.

innovators

The **innovators** are the first group of consumers to accept a product. They are risk takers, ambitious, aggressive trendsetters who like to be apart from the mainstream. Eager to try new products, they represent only 2.5 percent of a target market.

early adopters

Early adopters are more discreet but are a larger group of opinion leaders who like to try new products when they are new. They are strongly affected by the status and prestige of having a new item early. This group represents 13.5 percent of a target market.

early majority

The **early majority** represents the initial phase of mass-market acceptance. They follow the lead of early adopters and buy a proven commodity. This group represents 34 percent of a target market.

The Adoption Process

Figure 9.11

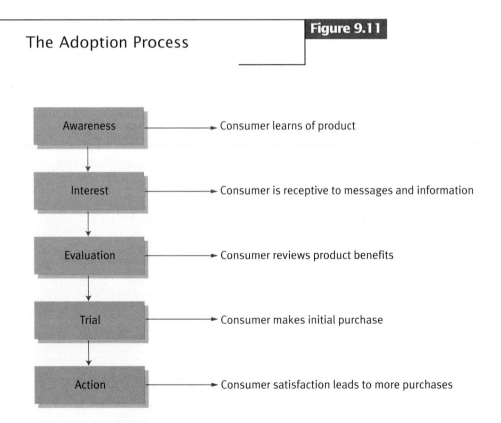

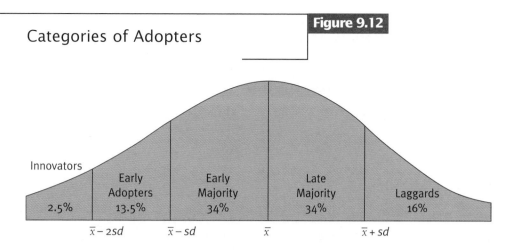

Figure 9.12

Categories of Adopters

Innovators 2.5% | Early Adopters 13.5% | Early Majority 34% | Late Majority 34% | Laggards 16%

$\bar{x} - 2sd$ $\bar{x} - sd$ $\bar{x}$ $\bar{x} + sd$

Source: Reprinted with the permission of The Free Press, a Division of Simon & Shuster, Inc., from *Diffusion of Innovations,* 4th edition by Everett M. Rogers. Copyright 1995 by Everett M. Rogers. Copyright 1962, 1971, 1983 by The Free Press.

late majority

The **late majority** is the remainder of the mass market. This group is usually lower in social and economic status and tends to be older and only willing to try products that have been around for a while. They comprise 34 percent of a target market.

laggards

Laggards are the last to purchase and represent 16 percent of a market. Typically, they buy the same old things, that is, they do not like change. They are not influenced by advertising and brand image but are influenced by price and reference groups.

It should be noted that innovators and early adopters have moved on to new innovations by the time that the mass market starts buying a product. In technology markets, such as hand-held organizers, DVDs, cell phones, and satellite dishes, sales trends suggest that there are many more early adopters adopting new products earlier than ever before. Electronic gadgets are enjoying record sales. Over a 4-year period between 1997 and 2000, 10.8 million DVD players have been sold. By comparison, the VCR only sold 2 million in its first 4 years and the CD player, 3.8 million.[14] Technology is now a big part of people's lives.

THE LENGTH OF THE PRODUCT LIFE CYCLE

All products do not follow the same life cycle. So far, this chapter has presented what may be called the traditional product life cycle so that marketing strategies associated with each stage can be described. Let us examine some of the common variations in the length and shape of the product life (Figure 9.13 for a visual illustration).

instant bust

1. The term **instant bust** applies to a product that a firm had high expectations of and perhaps launched with a lot of marketing fanfare but that, for whatever reason, was rejected by consumers very quickly. A prime example is the Edsel, Ford's classic blunder of the 1950s. When New Coke was launched in 1985 to replace the old Coca-Cola, regular Coca-Cola customers went crazy. So strong was the public backlash the product was withdrawn after only 79 days on the market and replaced with the original flavour now called Coca-Cola Classic. The *Washington Post* called the Coke fiasco "a marketing blunder of Edsel magnitude." Not to be outdone, Pepsi

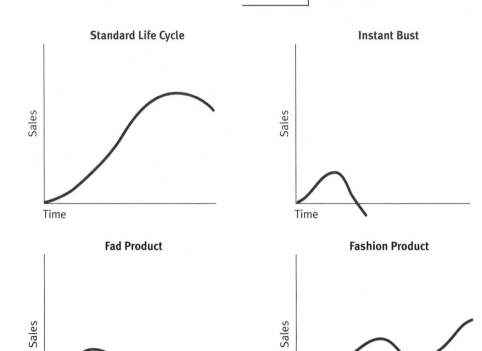

Variations of a Product Life Cycle

Figure 9.13

A.M., a breakfast cola that offered more caffeine and less carbonation was a financial disaster for PepsiCo.

fad

2. The cycle of the **fad** is reasonably short, perhaps one selling season or a few seasons, and usually financially successful for the organization. The toy industry is one where fads are common. Competing companies such as Hasbro and Mattel invest heavily in many products in the hope of developing that one big seller. Over the years, products such as Cabbage Patch Dolls, Pogs, and Pokemon enjoyed overwhelming success, but just as quick as they were popular, they became unpopular. Companies cannot rely too heavily on fads. To illustrate, the Coleco Toy Company went into receivership a few years after the Cabbage Patch success. Overhead costs created by Cabbage Patch were very high, and the company did not have any successful products to follow the Cabbage Patch craze.

fashion

3. The cycle of a **fashion** is a recurring one. What is in style now will be out of style later and, perhaps, back in style at an even later date. Product categories that are subject to fashion cycles include clothing (items such as business suits, skirts, and

bathing suits), cosmetics, and automobiles. In the fashion industry, casual clothing (business casual) is now popular all days of the business week. As a result, the sales of dress shirts, ties, and suits have been falling. But recently, business and industry have been slowly moving back to more formal dress codes. In the words of the old saying, "What goes around comes around."

4. These variations indicate that marketers must not be satisfied with passing through the various stages of the conventional product life cycle. Instead, strategies must be implemented that will initiate growth as the product matures. In this regard, many of the product and marketing mix decisions discussed in this chapter will come into play.

brand acceptance wall (BAW)

In the context of product acceptance by consumers, marketing experts now think that products face what is called the **brand acceptance wall (BAW)**. The BAW is a barrier that stops most products from further consumer acceptance.[15] The obstacle is caused by a combination of lack of customer acceptance and an uncoordinated marketing communication strategy. Those brands that pass the wall become major market players. Gatorade, for example, started as a niche product, but its integrated and coordinated marketing strategy made it a major market brand. In contrast, Snapple, a product with broad market appeal, never generated sufficient brand acceptance to become a serious contender in the beverage market. Snapple has since retreated to regional markets, where it may not survive.

In the athletic shoe market, Nike has done a great job of building a strong customer brand based on loyalty. In contrast, Reebok, once a strong competitor of Nike, only met with limited success. Market share for Reebok shoes today is nowhere near what it was 15 years ago. Leveraging a brand is another way of breaking through the BAW. Nike leveraged its name by getting into clothing and accessories. Microsoft, initially a software developer, leveraged its brand into all types of partially related categories, such as cable TV, the Internet, and magazine publishing.

New Products vs. Rejuvenated Products

4.
Describe the alternatives available to an organization for developing new products.

Some of the biggest decisions a company makes deal with new product activity. Should a company invest considerable sums in developing a completely new product from scratch, or should it, at much lower cost, repackage and reposition existing products to extend their life cycle?

A brand name has built-in equity from the millions of dollars invested in it over time—there is an image tucked away in the consumer's brain, ready for recall. It is easy to take this image out and breathe new life into it. Reviving a tired image saves time, money, and the hassles associated with new product development. Considering the failure rate of new products—as many as 8 out of 10 new products fail—it is easy to see why many manufacturers now prefer to reposition or revive an image. To draw a comparison between the two approaches, consider the Frito-Lay examples cited earlier in this chapter. Reformulating Dorito's nacho chips took 6 months from conception to store shelves, while development of Sun Chips, a totally new product line, took 10 years and millions of dollars.[16]

Finding out what the customer really wants reduces the product development cycle and helps reduce the risk of new product failures. Marketers are rejuvenating mature brands, giving them fresh starts by selling consumers on new uses for the product without substantially changing the product or its packaging, using brand extensions, or overhauling the brand's image.

Procter & Gamble followed a new product strategy in the late 1990s when it introduced Febreze (a product that removes odours from carpets and furniture) and Swiffer (an electrostatic mop that collects dust, dirt, and other objects from floors and walls). These were entirely new product categories. It had been 15 years since P&G had launched a completely new product. More recently, Procter & Gamble launched two more new products: Crest Whitestrips (a dental whitening system) and Crest SpinBrush (a battery-operated brush with a spinning head). The Crest brand name now goes well beyond toothpaste (see Figure 9.14). Truly new products like these create new revenue streams for marketers, especially if they are competing alone in a new category.

line extensions

The key to successful **line extensions** is the brand name. What the company must consider is, how far can it extend the name? A brand extension must fit in with the

Figure 9.14

Extending a Brand Name into New Product Categories

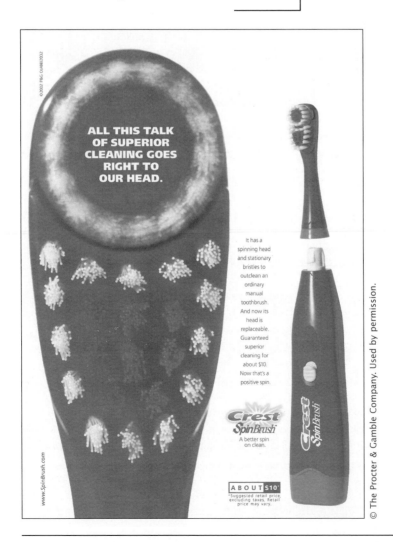

brand's parent, and it should reinforce the positive impression that potential consumers have of the brand. Simply tinkering with an existing brand name and trying to tie it into another product does not guarantee success. Manufacturers must study the elasticities and boundaries of a brand. Clorox is an established name and brand leader in the bleach business, but as a detergent, it was a dismal failure. In contrast, Church & Dwight, makers of Arm & Hammer Baking soda, extended the chemical mix into a variety of higher-margin products—toothpaste, soap pads, and flavoured gum. There is a peril associated with line extensions. If a brand extends itself too far, the customer gets confused about what the brand really stands for.

The Arm & Hammer example cited above shows that extensions work if they are planned properly. You be the judge on the following example. Nike has been very successful marketing shoes and clothing. It is building on that success by marketing hockey equipment and golf balls under the Nike name. Soon to be added are watches and eyewear, where Nike will compete with successful brands such as Swatch, Ray-Ban, and Oakley. What are Nike's chances of success?

New Product Development

new product

5.
Identify and explain the steps in the new product development process.

In the truest sense of the word, a **new product** is a product that is truly unique and that meets needs that have previously been unsatisfied. Personal digital assistants (PDAs) such as the PalmPilot or BlackBerry are truly new products. Advances in microcomputer technology, for example, are occurring so rapidly that the word "new" in this industry is relatively meaningless. Nonetheless, the major players, such as IBM, Compaq, and Apple, to name a few, continue to invest heavily as they search for breakthrough products in this rapidly growing market segment. Apple Computer Inc. for example, virtually reinvented itself when it launched the iMac computer and iBook laptop computer. Three years later, in 2001, Apple unveiled a radical new design for the iMac desktop computer—a dome-shaped base containing the guts of the computer that sprouts a futuristic flat-screen monitor. Steve Jobs, the CEO of Apple, sees the new iMac as the "ultimate digital hub" to listen to music, watch videos, and edit photographs.[17]

One may ask, do we need a gum that relieves irritated throats when a product like Halls lozenges serves the market effectively? Like any consumer packaged goods company, Wrigley's was looking for a way to grow. They launched a completely new product in a different format into an established category—a real marketing challenge. The product, called Alpine, contains menthol and eucalyptus and claims to relieve sore throats and coughs (see Figure 9.15). In the research phase when consumers were asked about the concept, their response was, "We have never thought about it, but if there was a gum that actually soothed sore throats we would buy it." Prior to launch, Halls owned 75 percent of the market. Wrigley's has made an impact as Halls share has dropped to 66 percent since Alpine was launched.[18]

Line extensions of existing brands are also classified as a form of new product. A well-known brand such as Crest toothpaste was originally marketed as a standalone product. Now there is Crest Complete, Crest Kids, Crest Sensitivity Protection, Crest Multicare, Crest Dual Action Whitening, and Crest Tartar Protection. The consumers' need for a nice smile has become very sophisticated. The illustration in Figure 9.9 shows the various line extensions for French's mustard.

In Canada, new innovations can be protected by patent if the innovation is registered in accordance with the Patent Act, administered by Consumer and Corporate

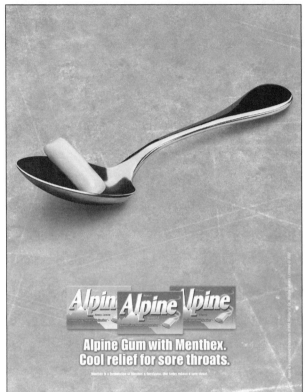

Figure 9.15

Wrigley's Launched a New Product in a New Format in an Established Product Category

Courtesy: Wm. WRIGLEY Jr. Company

knock-offs

Affairs Canada. Some organizations choose to ignore patent protection laws and produce and market copies of patented products, though doing so is illegal. These look-alike products are referred to as **knock-offs**. Technological products are especially prone to this practice, and it is a major concern. The presence of knock-offs shortens the innovation's life cycle. Consequently, there is less opportunity to recover development costs associated with the innovation.

THE NEW PRODUCT DEVELOPMENT PROCESS

The development of innovative products involves seven steps: idea generation, screening, concept development and testing, business analysis, product development, test marketing and marketing planning, and commercialization (Figure 9.16). In the 1960s, it took about 60 product ideas to produce 1 successful new product. Today however, the odds are much better. Companies are doing a better job of generating new ideas because they are catching more bad ideas earlier, they are using more formal and sophisticated development processes, and they are employing multi-functional teams to generate and develop concepts. Let us examine each step in the development process.

Idea Generation

All products stem from a good idea. Where do these ideas come from? Contemporary organizations are receptive to ideas from any source—customers, suppliers, employees, or marketing intelligence about competitors. Internally, a company may have a research and development department in place, with the sole responsibility for researching and developing ideas. Other companies may schedule regular meetings of executives and cross-sections of employees to brainstorm for potential opportunities.

Employees at Kellogg's work in cross-functional teams, with market researchers alongside food technologists and engineers. This organizational approach to new product development is paying dividends. One recent idea that met with success is Raisin Bran Crunch. The product offers thicker, coated flakes that do not get soggy in milk. Raisin Bran Crunch captured 1 percent of the cereal market without eroding the business of other Kellogg's bran cereals. Equally popular has been Special K with Red Berries (crunch flakes with slices of real strawberries). "Our research showed that 30 percent of consumers add fruit to Special K. Adding real strawberries in the box adds an incredible sensory experience and makes it convenient for women wanting a breakfast that helps them stay fit."[19]

Screening

screening

The elimination of ideas begins with product **screening**. The purpose of screening is to quickly eliminate ideas that do not appear to offer financial promise for the company. Such a screening process is the responsibility of senior management, who must decide if the new idea is in line with the overall company strategy. For new ideas to be compared, a rating checklist or scale might be used in screening ideas. Such a checklist would include criteria important to the company, such as patent protection, sales potential, threat of competition, compatibility with current products, marketing investment required, anticipated life cycle, degree of uniqueness, expertise in production, and capital

Figure 9.16

The Process of Developing a New Product

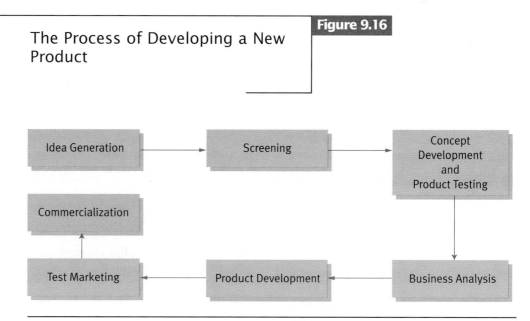

investment required. An examination of these criteria allows a company to gauge the compatibility of each new product idea with the overall company strategy.

Concept Development and Testing

concept test

A **concept test** involves the presentation of a product idea in some visual form (usually a drawing or photograph) with a description of the basic product characteristics and benefits. The purpose of a concept test is to find out early how consumers react to the product idea. Typically, a consumer is provided with the product's picture, description, and price and is then asked questions to determine his or her level of interest and the likelihood of the person purchasing the product. Such a step is a crucial one, since this feedback determines whether the firm invests in prototype product development, an expensive proposition. Companies only proceed with ideas consumers perceive to be of high interest. To gauge the level of acceptability, a firm may show different information about the same concept. It may, for example, test different prices in order to determine how price influences the level of interest in the concept and to see at what point the concept becomes uninteresting. Such information is important for the sales and profit projections in the next stage.

Business Analysis

business analysis

A **business analysis** entails a formal review of some of the ideas accepted in the screening stage, the purpose of which is again to rank potential ideas and eliminate those judged to have low financial promise. By this time, the company is dealing only with product ideas that have been judged positively by potential customers. Consequently, the company must determine the market demand for the product and the costs of project production and marketing and estimate revenue and profit. Such a review includes a thorough evaluation of competitive offerings and their marketing strengths and weaknesses.

Product Development

prototype

In this stage, the idea or concept is converted to a physical product. The purpose is to develop a prototype or several prototype models for evaluation by consumers. The **prototype** is a physical version of a potential product, that is, a product designed and developed to meet the needs of potential customers. New video games, for example, are thoroughly tested with young males to quickly determine which ideas offer the greatest potential. Many games exit the development process at this stage. The prototype is refined on the basis of feedback obtained in consumer research. In effect, the research and development department experiments with design and production capability to determine what type of product can be produced within the financial constraints established in the business analysis stage.

At Kellogg's R&D facilities, a pilot plant one-tenth the scale of an actual manufacturing facility runs test batches of cereals and snacks. Issues that must be resolved at this stage include: the type and quality of materials available to use for manufacturing; the method of production and any additional capital requirements; the package configuration and its influence on production, shipping, and handling; and the time required for start-up (the time needed to have all equipment and materials in place, ready for production).

At this stage, various functional areas of the firm must cooperate to ensure that the product is what the customer wants. What Production and Engineering can provide may not be what Marketing wants. Therefore, these departments work together to coordinate their plans.

Product development is a very expensive phase of the development process. In addition to pure research costs, the firm has to pay to have the prototypes constantly tested for consumer reaction. Marketers develop brand names, identify the key benefits, develop a price, and perhaps provide consumers with samples of the prototype for their perusal and use. Many of the research techniques presented in Chapter 3 are used to collect this information.

Test Marketing and Marketing Planning

test market

At this point, the company develops an introductory marketing plan to support test marketing. The **test market** is the first real acid test for the product. It is the stage at which consumers actually have the opportunity to purchase the product instead of simply indicating that they would purchase it. The test market allows the company to gain feedback in a relatively inexpensive way. Many marketers view the test market stage as mandatory; without it, a significant financial risk is faced. It tells the company whether a product should be launched regionally or whether it should be launched nationally, in which case the loss to the company would be great in the event the product fails. The test market evaluates the product and the marketing plan so that further modifications can be made to both, if necessary, prior to an expensive full-scale launch. Others feel the test market stage could be bypassed, since it tips off competitors about a firm's activity. It gives competitors time to react and develop imitations or plan defensive strategies for products already on the market.

A firm may conduct several test markets in order to generate conclusive information to assist in the planning for market expansion. Even then, the results may mislead a company. Pepsi-Cola, for example, test marketed and then launched Crystal Pepsi (a clear version of Pepsi-Cola), but the product failed miserably. In contrast, Pepsi One, a product with one-third the calories of regular Pepsi, has been a success. Coca-Cola spent time test marketing Mello-Yello before it was launched. Mello-Yello contains orange, lemon, lime, grapefruit, and tangerine flavours and is positioned as a high-energy, intense-flavour beverage. It will compete directly with PepsiCo's Mountain Dew.

Commercialization

commercialization

Commercialization is the concluding step in the new-product development process; the company puts together a full-scale production and marketing plan for launching a product on a regional or national scale. All the refining, adjusting, and tinkering with product design characteristics, production considerations, and marketing strategies is over at this point. The product, at this point, should meet the needs and expectations of the target market. Marketing communications acquaint distributors and consumers with the product and what it offers. The product has now entered the introduction stage of the product life cycle described earlier in this chapter and is now subject to the costs and activities normally associated with that stage. The product will find future success only if the organization modifies its strategies as the product and market segment mature.

Current Issues in New Product Development

Given the pace of technological change and the hypercompetitive nature of many markets today, a new criterion is appearing on the product development landscape. That criterion is the speed at which the new product gets to the market. As well, technology is shortening the traditional product life cycle for many products. Products are introduced, reach maturity, and disappear from the market in an incredibly short period of time. Computer software products are a good example of a condensed life cycle. The cycle of introduction to decline may only last a few months to a year. In that short period of time, a software product may be replicated or improved. Consequently, the ability to identify, coordinate, and build brand value becomes critical in the early stages of introduction.

Shortening the time frame offers two advantages. First, it is a way of staying ahead of competitors. The pioneer (first company into a market) acquires customers first and those customers often become attached to the brand and resist offers to switch to a second or third entry. Brand preference can actually be established prior to the arrival of competition. Second, a quick entry into a market will produce revenues more quickly and reduce the amount of costs associated with managerial evaluation of the product concept, countless test markets, and the education process that must take place among consumers.

Design technology and online transmission of product designs to interested stakeholders is a means by which product development programs can be shortened. Product design drawings on paper, for example, can be all but eliminated, 3-D design techniques on computer screens can be sent to decision makers immediately online. Such practice can cut days and weeks from the development cycle. "If a car manufacturer can significantly cut the new product development cycle-from 48 to 36 months or even 24 months—they may be able to get an innovative new product to market first and fill a niche before competitors even get wind of it."[20]

Summary

Product management concerns three key areas: the organization structure for managing products and services, the development of new products to stimulate growth in the organization, and the management of marketing strategies for products throughout their life cycles. The brand management system is most typical of packaged-goods companies and business-goods companies, although organizations are moving towards category management, marketing services management, target market management, and global management organization structures. The key decisions in product management concern the development of new products and the rejuvenation of current products. Regarding current products, decisions revolve around product modifications, alterations to marketing mix strategies, and whether to keep a product in the market or withdraw it.

The product life cycle refers to the stages a product passes through from its introduction to its withdrawal from the market. The life cycle involves four stages: introduction, growth, maturity, and decline. The marketing strategies employed by the firm vary considerably from stage to stage. Generally, products remain in the mature stage for the longest period; the variables of time, sales, and profit are the indicators of what stage a product is in. The length of the life cycle varies from one product or product category to another. Some cycles are short (fads), while others are long (fashions). Regardless of the length of the cycle, the primary objective of the organization is to generate profits. Profits are maximized in the late growth and mature stages of the product life cycle; hence, organizations initiate strategies for extending these phases. These strategies include tapping into new markets by attracting new segments (competitors' users or non-users); altering the product by making quality, feature, or style improvements; or changing the marketing mix.

The degree to which consumers accept a new product determines its success or failure. Product adoption is concerned with a product's being accepted by individual consumers, whereas diffusion is concerned with acceptance by a market. People are categorized according to how quickly or how slowly they adopt a product. There are five categories of adopters: innovators, early adopters, early majority, late majority, and laggards.

There are seven steps in the research and development process for new products: idea generation, screening, concept development and testing, business analysis, product development, test marketing and marketing planning, and commercialization.

Key Terms

adoption 248
brand acceptance wall (BAW) 253
brand manager 230
business analysis 258
category manager 231
commercialization 259
concept test 258
decline stage 242
diffusion of innovation 250
early adopters 250
early majority 250
fad 252
fashion 252
global management structure 234
growth stage 240
— innovators 250

instant bust 251
introduction stage 239
knock-offs 256
— laggards 251
late majority 251
line extension 254
marketing services management system 233
mature stage 241
new product 255
product life cycle 238
product stretching 235
prototype 258
regional marketing management system 231
screening 257
target market management system 233
test market 259

Review Questions

1. Briefly describe the role and responsibility of the brand manager.

2. Briefly describe the following marketing management systems.

   a) Brand management

   b) Category management

   c) Regional management

   d) Target market management

   e) Global management

3. Identify and briefly describe the four key areas of product decision making.

4. Briefly describe the characteristics and conditions that exist at each stage of the product life cycle. How do marketing objectives vary at each stage?

5. What factors determine the stage a product is at in the life cycle?

6. Briefly describe the marketing strategies an organization uses to extend the life cycles of its products.

7. What is the difference between adoption and diffusion of innovation?

8. What are the various stages in the consumer adoption process?

9. Identify and briefly describe the adopter categories.

10. Describe the differences between an instant bust, fad, and fashion.

11. What is a knock-off?

12. Briefly describe the seven steps in the new product development process.

Discussion and Application Questions

1. "The decision to withdraw a product from the market should be based on profitability only." Discuss the merits of this statement.

2. Provide examples of brands or companies that are using the following strategies to extend their life cycle: (a) entering new market segments, (b) altering the product, and (c) adding new lines. Explain the strategy in each case.

3. "The speed at which technology is advancing means that product life cycles will be much shorter." Is this statement true or false? If true, what are the implications for a company dealing with this situation? Provide some specific company or product examples.

4. Review the vignette "Sony Manages by Lifestyle." Will such a management system produce more effective marketing programs? Is it a system other companies should consider? What is your opinion?

E-Assignment

In this assignment, you will conduct a product life cycle analysis. Select one of the categories of products listed below and visit the Web sites for each product or company. Then, answer the questions. Use alternative product categories and two leading brands, if you wish.

Soft Drinks	Coca-Cola and Pepsi-Cola
Toothpaste	Colgate and Crest
Delivery Service	FedEx and UPS
Coffee Shops	Starbucks and Second Cup

1. What stage of the product life cycle is each product in? What conditions are these brands facing? Explain your position on the basis of information gathered from Web sites.

2. What strategies are these products using to build sales volume and increase market share? Are their marketing strategies similar to or different from what you have learned about strategies employed at the various stages of the product life cycle? Explain.

Endnotes

1. Constance Hays, "PepsiCo takes marketing to the aisles," *Globe and Mail*, August 3, 1999, p. B7.

2. Lara Mills, "Molson overhauls marketing team," *Marketing*, September 20, 1999, p. 3.

3. Abigail Schmelz, "Ericsson realigning to focus on markets," *Financial Post*, July 20, 1999, p. C8.

4. Angela Kryhul, "Global where possible, local where necessary," *Marketing*, October 22, 2001, p. 8.

5. Sarah Smith, "New Colour in white goods," *Marketing*, May 28, 2001, pp. 12-16.

6. Emily Nelson, "Is so much choice really better?" *Globe and Mail*, April 20, 2001, p. B7.

7. Astrid Van Den Broek, "Souped-up design," *Marketing*, October 26, 1998, p. 14.

8. Alan Clendenning, "Unilever selling off 15 brands," *Globe and Mail*, June 1, 2001, p. B10.

9. Greg Keenan, "Beetle-mania dies as car's sales slow," *Globe and Mail*, December 6, 2000, p. B5.

10. William Band, "Achieving success in mature markets requires careful approach," *Sales & Marketing Management in Canada*, March 1987, p. 16.

11. Sarah Smith, "New Colour in white goods," *Marketing*, May 28, 2001, pp. 12-14.

12. Lesley Young, "Nestlé jumps on orange's appeal," *Marketing*, March 25, 2002, p. 4.

13. Everett M. Rogers, *Diffusion of Innovations*, 3rd Edition (New York: Free Press, 1982), p. 246.

14. Mike Snider, "Inspecting Gadgets," *Ottawa Sunday Sun*, January 9, 2000, p. 46.

15. Don Shultz, "IMC in the hyper-competitive marketplace," *Marketing News*, July 21, 1997, p. 37.

16. Gary Strauss, "Companies freshen old product lines," *USA Today*, March 20, 1992, pp, B1, B2.

17. Mark Evans and Robert Thompson, "Apple turns up the heat in living room tech wars," *Financial Post*, January 8, 2002, pp. FP1, FP6.

18. Lisa D'Innocenzo, "Gum 'knocks the snot' out of lozenge category," *Strategy*, April 8, 2002, p. 6.

19. "Kellogg puts the 'power of red' into breakfast," www.prnewsire.com, April 16, 2001.

20. Gerry Blackwell, "Industrial design of the times," *Globe and Mail*, February 28, 2002, p. B13.

Sun Media Corp.

Price

The role of price in the marketing mix is the focal point of this section. Chapter 10 examines the factors that influence pricing decisions, the pricing objectives of an organization, and the methods used to determine price. Chapter 11 dwells on management-related pricing decisions. Pricing policies are established, and then discussion centres on discounts and allowances, new-product pricing, and the role of leasing as a pricing option.

Price Strategy and Determination

After studying this chapter, you will be able to

1. Explain the importance of price in marketing strategy.
2. Describe the various types of economic markets that Canadian firms operate in and their influence on pricing strategy.
3. Describe the influences that various external and internal forces have on pricing strategy.
4. Differentiate among profit, sales, and competitive pricing objectives.
5. Calculate basic prices, using a variety of pricing methodologies.
6. Describe a variety of legal issues that affect pricing strategy.

This chapter introduces some of the basic pricing concepts used in marketing strategy. The discussion initially focuses on the variety of markets that Canadian firms operate in and the implications these different markets have for pricing strategy. The external and internal factors influencing pricing strategy are then discussed. Finally, the issues of how pricing strategy is used to achieve marketing objectives and what specific methods are available for determining prices are addressed.

The Definition and Role of Price

price

1.
Explain the importance of price in marketing strategy.

Price is defined as the exchange value of a good or service in the marketplace. The key word in this definition is "value." The value of a good or service is derived from its *tangible* and *intangible* benefits and from the perception a consumer has of it once he or she has been subjected to other marketing influences. Let us use an example to explain what tangible and intangible benefits are. A household decides to buy an expensive, top-of-the-line vacuum cleaner because of the product's superior capacity for and speed in picking up dirt from a rug. This is tangibility, a characteristic that can be experienced by the senses—in this case, something that can be seen. The vacuum cleaner is also purchased at a large, reputable department store where the service and warranty are better than those offered by a small, independent dealer. This is an intangible benefit, one that cannot be seen and so will go unnoticed until the vacuum cleaner breaks down.

Prices take many forms and terms. Consider the following examples of price:

- Your college tuition fee
- A club membership
- The rate of interest on a loan
- Admission charged at a theatre
- A donation to a charity
- Rent charged for an apartment
- A fare charged on a bus or train
- A bid at an online auction site

Harry Rosen
www.harryrosen.com

From a marketing organization's perspective, price is the factor that contributes to revenues and profits. In planning price strategy, the firm must consider a multitude of variables in order to arrive at fair and competitive prices in the marketplace while providing reasonable revenues and profits internally. It is only one element of the marketing mix, but it can be the most important. For example, a prominent retailer like Wal-Mart relies on price to establish and maintain its image with consumers. Being a discount department store, Wal-Mart's objective is to offer customers good value at reasonable price levels. Wal-Mart uses the advertising slogan "Everyday low prices. Always." to make its point with consumers. At the opposite end of the scale are specialty retailers such as Harry Rosen, an upscale men's emporium. Customers of Harry Rosen view price as an unimportant variable in the purchase decision. Instead, it is the image created by the high prices that attracts the upscale clientele.

In a relatively free market economy like Canada's, price is also a mechanism for ensuring adequate levels of competition. In a free and open market, where competition is strong, supply and demand factors influence price. Thus, when demand for a good increases, marketing organizations have the flexibility to increase price. When demand for a product drops, organizations tend to lower prices in order to entice consumers to continue to buy the product. To illustrate, consider what happens if the economy falls into a recession. Consumers spend less and retailers and manufacturers who provide goods to retailers suffer the financial consequences. To gain back customers, retailers will lower prices across the board or offer discounts more frequently. An automobile manufacturer will offer price incentives (e.g., cash back offers to entice buyers to take action). Low demand or slow sales at the retail level will affect the pricing strategy of all members of a channel of distribution. It is this freedom to set prices in response to the marketplace that ensures competition will occur.

Influences on Price

2.
Describe the various types of economic markets that Canadian firms operate in and their influence on pricing strategy.

Several major influences are considered when establishing the price of a product: the nature of the market the product competes in, the nature of consumer demand for the product, production and marketing costs incurred by the firm, and the markups and profit margins expected by distributors. With the exception of production and marketing costs, all other influences are external to the firm.

NATURE OF THE MARKET

3.
Describe the influences that various external and internal forces have on pricing strategy.

A firm's ability to establish price depends on the type of market it operates in. In the Canadian economy, there are several different types of markets: pure competition, monopolistic competition, oligopoly, and monopoly (Figure 10.1).

In a market environment of **pure competition**, there are many small firms marketing the same basic product; therefore, no single firm can dictate or offset the market. The firm has no choice but to charge the going market price. The firm's primary decision then is limited to determining how much to produce.[1]

pure competition

law of supply and demand

The market in this situation controls the selling price. The basic **law of supply and demand** applies: an abundant supply and low demand lead to a low price, while a high demand and limited supply lead to a high price. Often, it is simply expectations about supply or demand that have an impact on price. For example, if the supply of gasoline

Figure 10.1

Canadian Markets and Their Price Implications

Factor	Pure Competition	Monopolistic Competition	Oligopoly	Monopoly
Competition and Product	Many sellers with same or similar product.	Many sellers with differentiated product.	Few large sellers with some product differentiation.	Single seller with unique product.
Price Decision Criteria	Price based on open market. How much should be produced?	Price based on competition and brand loyalty. How much should be produced and invested in marketing?	Price based on competition. Quick reaction to price changes. How much should be invested in marketing?	Price based on fair and reasonable profit for supplier.
Controls	None. Dictated by market dynamics.	Some.	Some (e.g., uniform beer pricing in retail outlets in some provinces).	By government or other regulatory body (e.g., CRTC).

were expected to dwindle below normal demand, there would be a rush to buy the resource and its price would be driven up, at least temporarily. In other cases, it is the actual supply and demand that influences prices. The demand for stocks on the stock market influences the rate at which they are traded.

monopolistic competition

If a market is characterized as **monopolistic competition**, there are many competitors selling products that, though similar, are perceived to be different by consumers.[2] Marketing strategy, particularly product strategy, in these circumstances is to try to distinguish one's own brand from the others. Such variables as service, style, function, and packaging are used to convey a difference to the consumer. The use of such elements is referred to as non-price competition, and it is their use that explains why leading brands, such as Crest and Colgate (toothpaste) and Sony (consumer electronics products), are perceived to be better than other brands.

If the consumer thinks there are differences between the brands, brand loyalty can be created. Traditionally, consumers who are brand loyal are less likely to be influenced by price; that is, they are willing to pay a little more for the brand of their choice than for other brands. Consumers typically identify a few brands in a product category to which they remain loyal. At the point of purchase, they select the brand with the lowest price (e.g., if Colgate is priced lower than Crest, they purchase Colgate).

Generally, if a firm wishes to attract the users of its competitors' products on the basis of price savings, those savings must be more important than the other reasons consumers buy products: reasons having to do with quality, image, and good service. In today's economy, disposable income is shrinking from year to year for a majority of people. Consequently, price has become a primary source of buying motivation. The customer is looking at price, establishing a range or price ceiling first, and then assessing the product alternatives on the basis of features (quality, service, image) within that range.

oligopolistic market

Petro-Canada
www.petro-canada.ca

In an **oligopolistic market**, there are a few large sellers of a particular good or service. Industries traditionally associated with oligopolies are the brewing industry, dominated in Canada by Molson and Labatt, and the gasoline industry, dominated by Petro-Canada, Imperial Oil, and Shell.

In an oligopoly, a competitor's actions are monitored closely. The competition is so intense that if one firm raises or drops its price, other firms will quickly do the same. For example, if a bank like the Bank of Montreal drops or raises its prime rate a quarter of a percent, within a day or two, other national banks will follow suit. This reaction is especially pronounced in markets where the products are basically the same. To illustrate, gasoline is gasoline. If Esso raises its prices, Petro-Canada and Shell are likely to follow quickly. In fact, in a matter of hours, usually overnight, the price at every gas station in a city will increase to exactly the same figure. To many consumers, this practice hints at collusion and price fixing, though independent investigations by Industry Canada (Bureau of Consumer Affairs) have never proven this to be so. Sometimes, price wars erupt in the gasoline business, and consumers temporarily enjoy bargain basement prices. In a price war, the consumer is the only winner. Very often, the price war places financial hardship on the companies involved.

monopoly

In a **monopoly** a single seller of a good or service for which there are no close substitutes serves the market. With so much control, a company can manipulate supply and demand for the good or service and influence prices to the detriment of the public. In Canada, monopolies are not common, but they do exist in the service industry sector. For example, in the airline industry there is only one large national airline (Air Canada recently acquired Canadian Airlines) so the rates charged on long-haul routes are at the discretion of Air Canada. When two airlines were competing for customers there was pressure to keep prices down. Air Canada does face some competition from regional air carriers, so on short-haul routes within regions (e.g., within the Atlantic provinces) it has to offer customers more competitive prices.

Other examples of monopolies include provincial power corporations like SaskPower and Hydro-Quebec. Cable television companies such as Shaw Cable and Rogers Cable that have protected market areas (e.g., the local communities that each serve) are also monopolies. A customer wanting cable television pays the going rate or looks at alternatives such as a satellite dish offered by Bell ExpressVu.

Canadian Radio-Television Communications Commission
www.crtc.gc.ca

In Canada, monopolies cannot charge whatever they wish. Regulations are in place and are governed by agencies that report to the government. For example, the CRTC must approve price increases in the cable television industry and long-distance telephone service market. Price changes are only allowed if the monopolist (a Rogers or a Bell) can justify the increase to the regulating body.

Brandon is a poopy pants with poop in his pants

CONSUMER DEMAND FOR THE PRODUCT

The number of consumers in a target market and the demand they have for a product has a bearing on price. Essentially, there are two common principles at work. First, consumers usually purchase greater quantities at lower prices. Second, the effects of a price change on volume demanded by consumers must be factored into the pricing strategy. To illustrate, if price is increased and demand drops significantly, the objective of the price increase (higher sales revenue or profit) will not be achieved. This principle is referred to as **price elasticity of demand**.

price elasticity of demand

elastic demand

There are two types of demand: elastic demand and inelastic demand. **Elastic demand** describes a situation in which a small change in price results in a large change

inelastic demand

in volume (e.g., price increases by 5 percent and volume drops by 15 percent). If demand is elastic, the firm's total revenues go up as price goes down, and revenues go down when price goes up. **Inelastic demand** is a situation in which a price change does not have a significant impact on the quantity purchased. In this case, total revenues go up when prices are increased and go down when prices are reduced. For example, the Toronto Maple Leafs raise ticket prices every year. Every ticket for every game is always sold regardless of how well the team performs. These demand concepts are represented in Figure 10.2.

In Canada's two most common markets, monopolistic competition and oligopoly, demand is based on the need in the marketplace and the availability of substitute products. If need (demand) for a product category is high, all competing firms can maintain high prices and reap the financial benefits. However, once a major competitor changes prices—say, lowers the price significantly—demand in the market can change. Such would be the case if a prominent brand like Dell Computer dropped its prices for an extended period. Being a leader in the PC market, such a move could put pressure on Compaq, Toshiba, Apple, and others to respond. Such an action could occur if an economy slows down and sales of all computer brands start to stagnate.

The Difference between Elastic and Inelastic Demand

Figure 10.2

If demand is elastic, consumers are price sensitive. When price increases, demand goes down significantly.

In the illustration, when price increase from $500 to $750, revenue declined from $400 000 (800 units × $500) to $150 000 (200 units × $750).

If a demand is inelastic, consumers are not price sensitive. A large increase in price has a limited effect on sales volume.

In the illustration, when price increased from $750 to $1500, revenue increased from $225 000 ($750 × 300 units) to $300 000 ($1500 × 200 units).

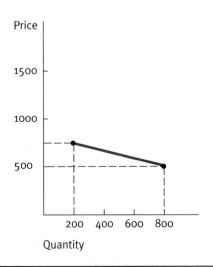

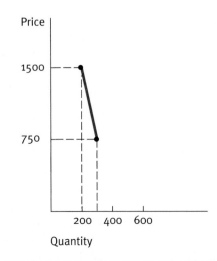

Consumer behaviour also has an impact on pricing strategy. A consumer may compare the price and quality of one product with other similar products; to other consumers, such matters as image, status, and prestige may be so important that the actual price of the product is ignored (a product such as a Rolex watch would be in this category). In the first case, the consumer behaves rationally, so the price of the product is important. In the second case, the consumer acts less rationally and is influenced by other factors, so price is less important. Thus, products aimed at status-seekers are apt to be priced high to convey prestige, while products targeted to the price-conscious would logically be priced low.

PRODUCTION AND MARKETING COSTS

Costs that have a direct effect on price include the costs of labour, raw materials, processed materials, capital requirements, transportation, marketing, and administration. A common practice among manufacturing firms is to establish a total product cost, taking into consideration these elements, as well as a desirable and fair gross profit margin. The addition of the profit margin to the cost becomes the selling price to distributors. Such a practice is based on the assumption that the resulting retail price will be acceptable to consumers. See Figure 10.3 for an illustration.

Figure 10.3

An Illustration Showing the Cost Components of a Packaged Goods Product

	Cost Items	Actual Cost
	Ingredients	$15.75
	Packaging (inner/outer)	1.79
	Shipping Case	0.68
	Labour	1.48
	Manufacturing	0.20
	Warehousing	0.34
	Total Plant Cost	20.24
Add:	Freight Cost	1.36
	Total Product Cost	21.60
Add:	Gross Profit Margin (40%)	8.64
	List Price	30.24
Add:	Retail Profit Margin (25%)	7.56
	Retail Price (per case of 24)	37.80
	Selling Price at Retail	1.57

This example assumes a desired profit margin of 40% for the manufacturer of the product and a 25% markup at retail. The manufactured item is a case good that contains 24 packages in a shipping case. After all costs and profit margins are considered for the manufacturer and distributor, the price at retail is $1.57.

The pricing decisions of an organization become increasingly difficult as costs rise. If cost increases are gradual and the amounts are marginal, a firm can usually plan its strategy effectively; it can build prices around projected cost increases for a period of time, using, say, a one-year planning cycle. Unforeseen increases (those that happen quickly and unexpectedly) are a different matter. In such cases, a firm may choose to absorb the cost increases and accept lower profit margins, at least for the short term, in the hope that the situation will correct itself. If it does not, there is little choice but to pass the increase to channel members in order to ensure long-term profitability.

To illustrate, consider a situation that Consumers Packaging Inc. faces. Consumers Packaging is the largest supplier of glass jars and bottles in Canada, controlling 85 percent of the market (a near monopoly). The company had been absorbing significant cost increases in natural gas, but when the price of gas tripled, they had no alternative but to pass a portion of the increase on to companies that buy jars and bottles. Several buyers dug their heels in and refused to pay the higher prices because they had a contract agreement with Consumers that stipulated a lower price. In some industries the bottle accounts for about 25 percent of product cost. For a company like Heinz, a maker of baby food, the jar could represent 15 cents of an 80-cent item.[3] Higher jar prices would have to be passed on to consumers. This example shows cost increases have a rippling effect on the price of a good at all levels of the channel of distribution.

cost reductions

Another option available to the organization is to search for and implement **cost reductions**, which are reductions of the costs involved in the production process. Examples of some cost reduction measures include improving production efficiency (e.g., achieving lower long-term costs by adding automation), using less expensive materials (e.g., lower-priced ingredients and packaging materials), shrinking the size of a product (e.g., baking smaller cookies while maintaining the same pricing), and relocating manufacturing facilities to a region where production costs are lower (e.g., the migration of production from Canada to Mexico or the Far East).

To illustrate the cost reduction principle, consider a recent program implemented by Hostess Frito-Lay. The bag size of chips was reduced from 170 grams to 150 grams and the actual size of the package was made smaller. Retail prices dropped accordingly. In the US the weight of the package was reduced a further 7 percent with no corresponding drop in price. A small change in packaging can make a huge difference to a company's bottom line. Frito-Lay sells an estimated 1.18 billion kilograms of snack food each year. The 7 percent cut in package size will save the company $154.7 million (US) a year.[4]

Generally, a firm tries to combine cost reductions with reasonable price increases. It will remain competitive and move prices, when necessary, to protect the profitability of the firm. Should costs actually decline, the company has the option of lowering prices or taking advantage of higher profit margins. An example of an industry in which cost reduction has resulted in lower prices is the computer industry. The advancing technology of microcomputers and ancillary products has lowered prices within the industry. The lower prices, in turn, have resulted in expansion of the entire market so that all competitors have benefited.

CONSIDERATION OF CHANNEL MEMBERS

The ultimate price a consumer pays for a product is influenced by markups in the channel of distribution. Once the title to the product changes hands, pricing is determined at the discretion of the new owner. Like manufacturers, however, the distributors (wholesaler and retailer) who resell products usually have competition. They are concerned about moving the merchandise. Hence, their markup usually conforms to some standard in the industry that provides a reasonable profit margin.

To encourage channel members to charge prices that are in agreement with a manufacturer's overall marketing strategy, a manufacturer considers several factors. They provide for an adequate profit margin (e.g., they consider the distributor's operating and marketing costs), they treat all customers fairly (e.g., all distributors are offered the same list price), and they offer discounts to encourage volume buying or marketing support (e.g., a portion of a discount offered by a manufacturer is passed on to the consumer by the distributor). In the latter case, the objective of the discount is to influence consumer demand during the discount period. Some examples of distributor markups are included in the Pricing Methods section of this chapter.

Pricing Objectives

4.
Differentiate among profit, sales, and competitive pricing objectives.

In a pure business environment, the primary goal of the organization is to produce the highest possible rate of return to the owner (shareholder, partners, sole proprietor, and so on). Pricing strategies are part of a marketing strategy that must be in line with this overall company strategy.

A firm is not locked into one particular pricing strategy. In fact, each product or product line (market) will be assessed independently, and appropriate objectives will be established for the product in question. Organizations strive to achieve three basic objectives in pricing: profit maximization, sales volume maximization, and establishing a competitive position. Pricing objectives are often influenced by the stage of the product life cycle a product is in.

PROFIT MAXIMIZATION

profit maximization

The goal of **profit maximization** is to achieve a high profit margin, a high return on investment, and a recovery of any capital invested. In this case, a company sets some type of measurable and attainable profit objective based on its situation in the market. Consider the following example:

> Objective: To achieve a net profit contribution of $2 000 000 and a return on investment (ROI) of 30 percent in fiscal year 200x.

While we cannot assess how conservative or how aggressive this objective is, it is certain that the organization will implement a marketing strategy to accomplish it. At the end of the year, the degree of success can be measured by comparing actual return to planned return. The profits obtained are redirected into new product development projects, which facilitate the organization's expansion into new markets. Historical trends pertaining to such ratios as a firm's return on investment or return on sales are also a factor in attracting potential new investors to the firm.

SALES VOLUME MAXIMIZATION

sales volume maximization

The objective of **sales volume maximization** is to increase the volume of sales each year. A firm strives for a growth in sales that exceeds the growth in the size of the total market so that its market share increases. An example of a sales volume objective follows:

> Objective: To increase sales volume from $15 000 000 to $16 500 000, an increase of 10 percent, in 200–. To increase market share from 25 percent to 27.5 percent in 200–.

Sales levels, as we have seen, are affected by price; an increase in price can result in a decrease in demand and, therefore, a reduction in the quantity sold. In Figure 10.4, we see that when price goes down (P1 to P2), volume (quantity) goes up (Q1 to Q2); when prices go up, volume goes down.

An organization also develops the appropriate marketing strategies, including price strategy, for achieving sales objectives. In establishing these objectives, a firm considers the type of market it operates in and its elasticity of demand. Generally, brand leaders have the most flexibility in establishing sales and market share objectives. Brands with a small share of the market tend to follow the trend established by the leader. To achieve market share objectives, a firm often sacrifices profit, at least temporarily.

ESTABLISHING A COMPETITIVE POSITION

competitive pricing

The aim in this case is to minimize the effect of competitors' actions and provide channel members with reasonable profit margins. To attain such an objective, an organization assesses the competitive situation, including its own position in the market, and adopts a strategy termed *status quo pricing*, or simply **competitive pricing**, that puts its prices above, equal to, or below those of competitors. In effect, each competitor uses a pricing strategy to position itself in the consumer's mind.

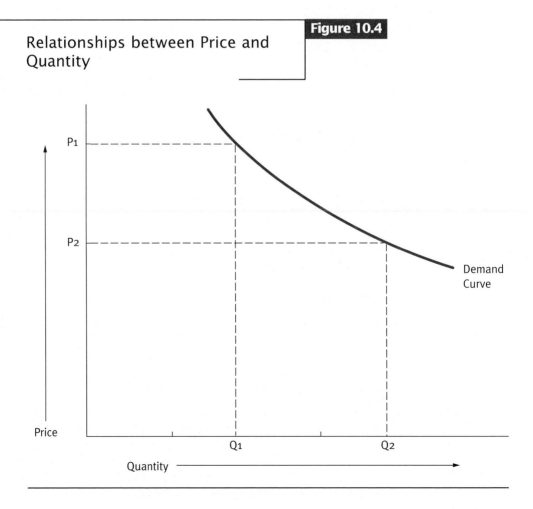

Figure 10.4

Relationships between Price and Quantity

Above Competition

To set a price above a competitor, a product must be perceived as being of higher quality than the competitors' products or must offer customers an intangible benefit, such as prestige or status, or it will fail. Such a strategy provides a higher profit margin on each unit sold and is usually reserved for market leaders in a product category. Q-tips, for example, controls about 65 percent of the cotton swab market. Consumers' perceive the brand with a high level of trust and confidence. As a result, Q-tips can charge more than its competing brands do.

Equal to Competition

A firm that uses this strategy adopts a conservative position because it does not want to be caught in price wars. In effect, the company is satisfied with its volume, market share, and profit margin and is content to follow the lead of others.

Below Competition

Here, a firm uses price to secure and hold a certain position in the market. To accomplish this objective, the company must accept lower profit margins (unless it is producing so efficiently that profit margins are maintained despite the reduction in price). If the volume of sales rises significantly because of the low prices, production efficiency will increase, which will produce, in turn, lower costs and better profit margins.

Wal-Mart effectively demonstrates how a low price strategy can work. Wal-Mart's combination of everyday low prices and good product selection has produced a leadership position in Canada's department store market. While other elements of their marketing mix have also played a role, the focus on price (low price) is what drives traffic to the stores. Zellers, an established Canadian retailer who once led the discount segment, has been forced to respond and is implementing strategies that emphasize marketing mix elements other than just price.

Pricing Methods

5.
Calculate basic prices, using a variety of pricing methodologies.

A firm may use one or any combination of three basic methods in calculating prices for the products and services it markets: cost-based pricing, demand-based pricing, and competitive-based pricing (Figure 10.5).

COST-BASED PRICING

cost-based pricing

In the case of **cost-based pricing**, a company arrives at a list price for the product by calculating its total costs and then adding a desired profit margin.

The costs usually included in this calculation are as follows:

fixed costs

1. **Fixed costs** are those costs that do not vary with different quantities of output (e.g., equipment and other fixed assets, such as light, heat, and power).

variable costs

2. **Variable costs** are costs that do change according to the level of output (e.g., labour and raw materials). Variable costs rise and fall, depending on the production level—up to a point, per-unit variable costs frequently remain constant over a given range of volume. Generally, the more a firm is producing, the greater the quantities of raw materials and parts it buys, and this increased volume leads to lower unit costs; therefore, the variable costs should be lower.

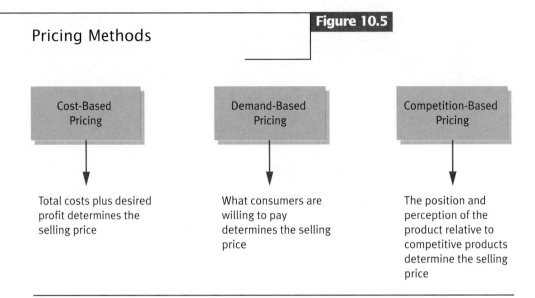

Pricing Methods

Figure 10.5

| Cost-Based Pricing | Demand-Based Pricing | Competition-Based Pricing |

Total costs plus desired profit determines the selling price

What consumers are willing to pay determines the selling price

The position and perception of the product relative to competitive products determine the selling price

For an illustration of these cost concepts, refer to Figure 10.6, which shows how fixed, variable, and total costs vary with production output. In the long term, the firm must establish prices that recover total costs (i.e., fixed costs plus variable costs). An organization that is using cost-based pricing to do so has a few options: *full-cost pricing, target pricing,* and *break-even pricing (break-even analysis).* All three consider the variables of costs, revenues, and profits. Refer to Figure 10.7 for the mathematical formulas and an example of each pricing method.

Full-cost Pricing

full-cost pricing

In **full-cost pricing**, or cost-plus pricing, a desired profit margin is added to the full cost of producing a product. In such a system, profits are based on costs rather than on revenue or demand for the product. When a firm establishes a desired level of profit that must be adhered to, the profit goal could be interpreted as a fixed cost (see Figure 10.7).

Target Pricing

target pricing

Target pricing is designed to generate a desirable rate of return on investment (ROI) and is based on the full costs of producing a product. For this method to be effective, the firm must have the ability to sell as much as it produces. The major drawback of this method is that demand is not considered. If the quantity produced is not sold at the target price, the objective of the strategy, to achieve a desired level of ROI, is defeated (see Figure 10.7).

Break-even Analysis

break-even analysis

Break-even analysis has a greater emphasis on sales than do the other methods, and it allows a firm to assess profit at alternative price levels. Break-even analysis determines the sales in units or dollars that are necessary for total revenue (price x quantity sold)

The Concept of Fixed, Variable, and Total Costs

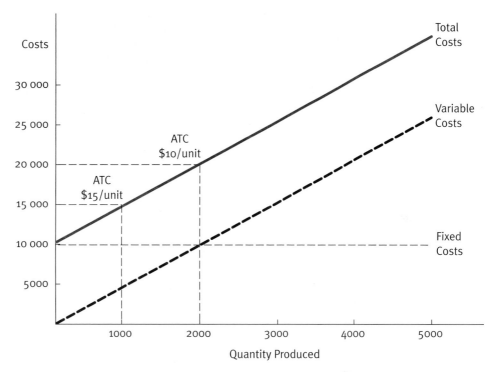

The total cost per unit declines as the quantity produced increases. At 1000 units of production, the average total cost (ATC) is $15/unit. At 2000 units of production, the average total cost (ATC) is $10/unit.

to equal total costs (fixed plus variable costs) at a certain price. The concept is quite simple. If sales are greater than the *break-even point (BEP)*, the firm yields a profit; if the sales are below the *BEP*, a loss results (see Figures 10.7 and 10.8).

DEMAND-BASED PRICING

demand-based pricing

demand-minus (backward) pricing

chain markup pricing

As the name suggests, this is the price that customers will pay that influences demand-based pricing the most. In **demand-based pricing**, the firm has a choice of two basic options. If it uses **demand-minus (backward) pricing**, an organization determines the optimum retail selling price that consumers are willing to accept and then subtracts the desired profit margin and marketing expenses (markup) of distributors to arrive at the costs for which the product should be produced. Very often, the product cannot be produced for the costs determined using this method. Many new product projects are cancelled at an early stage because of this cost-analysis process.

If the firm uses **chain markup pricing**, it establishes all costs and then considers the profit margins of its distributors. The markup that each channel member takes is incorporated into the calculation. In this case, it is presumed that the ultimate selling price

Pricing Methods: Examples

Figure 10.7

1. Cost-plus pricing

A manufacturer of colour televisions has fixed costs of $100 000 and variable costs of $300 for every unit produced. The profit objective is to achieve $10 000 based on a production of 150 televisions. What is the selling price?

$$\text{Price} = \frac{\text{Total Fixed Costs} + \text{Total Variable Costs} + \text{Projected Profit}}{\text{Quantity Produced}}$$

$$= \frac{\$100\ 000 + (\$300 \times 150) + \$10\ 000}{150}$$

$$= \frac{\$155\ 000}{150}$$

$$= \$1033.33$$

2. Target Pricing

A manufacturer has just built a new plant at a cost of $75 000 000. The target return on investment is 10 percent. The standard volume of production for the year is estimated at 15 000 units. The average total cost for each unit is $5000 based on the standard volume of 15 000 units. What is the selling price?

$$\text{Price} = \frac{\text{Investment Costs} \times \text{Target Return on Investment \%}}{\text{Standard Volume}}$$

$$+ \text{Average Total Costs (at Standard Volume/Unit)}$$

$$= \frac{\$75\ 000\ 000 \times .10}{15\ 000} + \$5000$$

$$= \$5500$$

3. Break-even Pricing

A manufacturer incurs total fixed costs of $180 000. Variable costs are $0.20 per unit. The product sells for $0.80. What is the break-even point in units? In dollars?

$$\text{Break-Even in Units} = \frac{\text{Total Fixed Costs}}{\text{Price} - \text{Variable Costs (per unit)}}$$

$$= \frac{\$210\ 000}{\$0.80 - \$0.20}$$

$$= 350\ 000$$

$$\text{Break-Even in Dollars} = \frac{\text{Total Fixed Costs}}{1 - \dfrac{\text{Variable Costs (per unit)}}{\text{Price}}}$$

$$= \frac{\$180\ 000}{1 - \dfrac{\$0.20}{\$0.80}}$$

$$= \$240\ 000$$

Standard Break-Even Chart

Figure 10.8

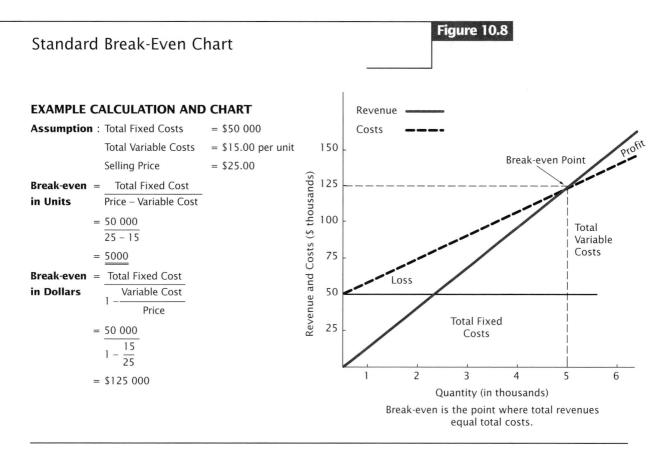

EXAMPLE CALCULATION AND CHART

Assumption : Total Fixed Costs   = $50 000

Total Variable Costs = $15.00 per unit

Selling Price   = $25.00

$$\text{Break-even in Units} = \frac{\text{Total Fixed Cost}}{\text{Price} - \text{Variable Cost}}$$

$$= \frac{50\ 000}{25 - 15}$$

$$= \underline{5000}$$

$$\text{Break-even in Dollars} = \frac{\text{Total Fixed Cost}}{1 - \dfrac{\text{Variable Cost}}{\text{Price}}}$$

$$= \frac{50\ 000}{1 - \dfrac{15}{25}}$$

$$= \$125\ 000$$

Break-even is the point where total revenues equal total costs.

is acceptable to consumers. Examples of these demand-based price calculations are included in Figure 10.9.

COMPETITIVE BIDDING

competitive bidding

Competitive bidding involves two or more firms submitting to a purchaser written price quotations based on specifications established by the purchaser.

Due to the dynamics of competitive bidding and the size, resources, and objectives of potential bidders, it is difficult to explain how costs and price quotations are arrived at. For example, let us assume that several firms are submitting bids for the opportunity to construct a new building. There could be great variation among price quotations if one firm considers all its costs and then adds a profit margin, while another firm sets its price at the break-even point. The objectives of firms submitting bids differ: some businesses simply want to win the contract, while others expect to earn a certain profit. Thus, if a firm builds a high profit margin into its bid, the likelihood of its being accepted by the purchaser diminishes.

Demand-Based Pricing Methods

Figure 10.9

1. Demand-Minus (Backward) Pricing (Markup on Sales)

A CD and tape distributor has determined that people are willing to spend $30.00 for a three- CD/tape set of classic rock 'n' roll tunes. The company estimates that marketing expenses and profits will be 40 percent of the selling price. How much can the firm spend producing the CDs and tapes?

Product Cost
= Price × [(100 − Markup %)/100]
= $30.00 × [(100 − 40)/100]
= $30.00 × (60/100)
= $18.00

2. Chain Markup Pricing (Markup on Costs)

A manufacturer of blue jeans has determined that their total costs are $20.00 per pair of jeans. The company sells the jeans through wholesalers who in turn sell to retailers. The wholesaler requires a markup of 20 percent and the retailer requires 40 percent. The manufacturer needs a markup of 25 percent. What price will the wholesaler and retailer pay? What is the selling price at retail?

a) Manufacturer's Cost and Selling Price
= $20.00 + 25% Markup
= $20.00 + $5.00
= $25.00

b) Wholesaler's Cost and Selling Price
= Manufacturer's Selling Price + 20% Markup
= $25.00 + $5.00
= $30.00

c) Retailer's Cost and Selling Price
= Wholesaler's Selling Price + 40%
= $30.00 + $12.00
= $42.00

Pricing and the Law

6.
Describe a variety of legal issues that affect pricing strategy.

The federal government oversees price activity in Canada through the Competition Act. The act covers many important areas that organizations must be aware of. Ignorance of the law is not a defence in a court of law should a firm find itself violating any rules and regulations. Some of the key legal issues are discussed in this section.

ORDINARY PRICE CLAIMS

A common practice among retailers is to quote sale prices using comparisons with the ordinary selling price of an article. For example, "Save up to 50 percent off the regular price." For the purposes of the law, no person or business shall

> make a materially misleading representation to the public concerning the price at which a product or like products have been, are, or will be ordinarily sold.[5]

The following general test can be used to determine whether an expression is in violation of the law:

> Would the use of the expression lead a reasonable shopper to conclude that the comparison price quoted is that at which the product has been ordinarily sold?[6]

When a comparison price is used to communicate the offer, it should be a recent and relevant price, that is, the price at which the product has normally been sold over an extended period of time. According to the law, a sale price is only legal if at least 51 percent of the annual sales of the product were gained through regular price positioning. Many prominent retailers have violated this law and have faced severe penalties: Suzy Shier was fined $300 000 and Color Your World $225 000. In each case, the companies were deficient in offering (a product) for a sufficient period of time, or having achieved sales in a sufficient volume at regular price, in order to make a claim that (the advertised price) was a sale price.

Hudson's Bay Co. was recently fined $600 000 for advertising that bicycles were on sale when they were not. The Federal Competition Bureau found that the Bay misled consumers by stating in its flyers and newspaper ads that bicycles were on sale for a short time. In fact, the "sale prices" were in effect for a much longer time.[7] By law, consumers cannot be mislead by sales promotions that create a general impression of urgency, when there is no urgency.

Retail Council of Canada
www.retailcouncil.org

The Retail Council of Canada is lobbying to have this law changed. They would like to see a law based on time limits rather than sales volume. Their argument is based on the hyper-competitive nature of the current retail market (e.g., the law was written in much less competitive times). As well, consumers are now more accustomed to looking at sale prices than regular prices. The regular price is largely irrelevant to consumers.

For further details about problems associated with retail price strategies see the Marketing in Action vignette **New Software Pushes New Price Strategy**.

MANUFACTURER'S SUGGESTED LIST PRICE

manufacturer's suggested list price (MSLP)

It is common for manufacturers to suggest that retailers charge a certain price for their products; this amount is called the **manufacturer's suggested list price (MSLP)**. Such prices usually allow retailers adequate profit margins, but retailers can charge more or less if they want to. The laws on MSLP are somewhat vague. However, if a retailer has never charged the MSLP but uses it to suggest that a sale price offers a greater saving than it actually does, that retailer has broken the law. In this case, the message is misleading because the retailer has customarily sold the product at another price, a lower price. If both the regular selling price and the MSLP are quoted in a sales message, the intent to mislead is less pronounced.

DOUBLE TICKETING AND BAR CODE PRICE VARIANCES

double ticketing

Double ticketing occurs when more than one price tag appears on an item. When this situation occurs, the product must be sold at the lower price. This provision of the law does not prohibit the practice but requires that the lower of the two prices be collected from consumers.

Double ticketing is now less of a problem as retailers in many industries have moved to bar code pricing and price scanning at the point of sale. Electronic price scanning is efficient, since the labour costs associated with tagging items are eliminated. Incorrect price scanning is now a complaint from customers. A study by the Quebec Office of

Marketing in Action

New Software Pushes New Price Strategy

Consumers are so accustomed to sale pricing that they don't want to buy an item at regular price. Why do consumers have such an attitude? It has a lot to do with the amount and frequency of sale prices offered by department stores such as Sears, the Bay, and Zellers. To please customers and make a profit, departments stores must find a better way of managing markdowns. Otherwise, they will suffer the financial consequences.

Some major retailers are experimenting with sophisticated new software programs to test principles similar to "yield management" pricing, a price strategy that airlines have mastered. For the record, yield management involves charging different prices in order to maximize revenue for a set amount of capacity at any given time. Capacity could mean the number of seats in an airline, theatre, or sports arena. Not everyone pays the same price to attend a hockey game—the trick is to optimize price for each level of seating based on proximity to the ice surface. In the case of an airline, the next time you are on a flight ask the person next to you what they paid for their seat. You'll be amazed at what the difference might be. One of you received a bargain!

With the new software programs, retailers are trying to do the same thing. An item such as a bikini is only in demand for a limited time; as the end of the season approaches, its value to customers plummets. The challenge for the retailer is how to outfox customers who have been willing to wait and wait for a bargain.

Technology is fuelling a new price revolution and it is producing a system that involves highly flexible prices—for everything from mortgages to eBay merchandise. Instead of taking a one price fits all approach, buyers and sellers are meeting in customized marketplaces transformed by technology. Bricks and mortar stores are finding they have to drop prices to match what's available to customers online.

With exploding competition from discounters, specialty stores, and the Internet, department store markdowns are soaring. Twenty years ago, marked-down goods accounted for about 8 percent of departments store sales. Today that figure is closer to 40 percent.

Truthfully, retailers hate markdowns. Discount an item too late, and stores are stuck with truckloads of inventory. Too early, and they lose profits as people snap up bargains prematurely.

The technology, still fairly new and untested, requires detailed and accurate sales data to work well. It involves a highly sophisticated look at historical sales data in order to pinpoint just how long to hold out before a retailer needs to cut a price—and by just how much.

Retailers certainly hope the software programs will solve the markdown problem, but they must realize that it can't solve other retailing problems that are affecting profitability, such as poorly chosen merchandise, intense competition, or a weak economy. It is not the saviour but simply another tool in the war chest.

Adapted from Amy Merrick, "Retailers add markdowns to flexible pricing trend," *Globe and Mail*, August 7, 2001, p. B11.

Elena Rooraid/PhotoEdit

Consumer Protection, an arm of the provincial government, found that 15.5 percent of items purchased were scanned incorrectly, and virtually all errors were made in favour of retailers. Stores in the study included Canadian Tire, Eaton's, the Bay, Sears, Wal-Mart, and Zellers.[8]

BAIT AND SWITCH

bait and switch

Bait and switch selling is the practice of advertising a bargain price for a product that is not available in reasonable quantity. A customer arrives at a store expecting to buy one product but is directed to another, often at a higher price. If the lack of supplies is beyond the control of the store or agent and this can be proven if challenged, the firm running this advertisement is not liable for penalty. Offering rain cheques is a way to avoid liability. A **rain cheque** guarantees the supply of the original product or a product of comparable quality within a reasonable time to those consumers requesting the product.

rain cheque

PREDATORY PRICING

predatory pricing

Periodically, an organization employs a pricing strategy that is judged to be unfair because it violates the spirit of competition. One such negative practice is **predatory pricing**, which occurs when a large firm sets an artificially low price in an attempt to undercut all other competitors and place them in a difficult financial position.

The ultimate goal of predatory pricing is to drive the competition out of business; then the predator can increase its prices. To illustrate, consider an allegation launched by the now defunct Roots Air against Air Canada. Roots Air claimed Air Canada engaged in predatory pricing when it reduced the price of a Toronto to Calgary fare to $909. Roots was charging $1998 for a full-fare and $1526 for an economy fare for the same route. Air Canada's fare for the Toronto to Edmonton route (a route that Roots did not have) was $1903. Roots asked why such a discrepancy in Air Canada fares, given the distances to Calgary and Edmonton from Toronto are about the same. Roots claimed it was a deliberate strike at a new air carrier and requested the Competition Bureau to investigate the issue.[9]

This case points out the dilemma the government (the Federal Bureau of Competition Policy) faces when investigating predatory pricing cases. Predatory pricing is one of the most difficult anti-trust offences to prove. Recent statistics show that 550 complaints lodged by Canadian businesses resulted in only 23 formal investigations, 3 cases going to court, and 1 conviction. To get a conviction, the Competition Bureau must establish that prices are unreasonably low, as well as prove that the company had an explicit policy of using predatory pricing to eliminate competition. While the law acts as a deterrent, it does not shield companies from competitors able to set lower prices because they are genuinely more efficient.[10]

Predatory pricing laws date back to the early 1900s. Critics of the legislation feel that it is time for change because conditions in the marketplace are different now. Today, many feel that attempts to monopolize should not be illegal. In effect, all companies attempt to monopolize (the goal is always to get more and more of something, to take away from competitors). Companies that fail to compete soon fall by the wayside. Price, like quality, is simply one of the levels on which businesses compete. Canada is a free market. Shouldn't companies be able to price their products wherever they want?

For more insight into the effect of predatory pricing, see the Marketing in Action vignette **Is Air Canada a Predator?**

 **Marketing in Action**

Is Air Canada a Predator?

Offering a low price shouldn't mean that a company is a predator—a predator is a company whose primary objective is to run another company out of business. The goal of any business is to excel at what they do, to make a better offer to a customer, to build a business. In doing so, price strategy is bound to play a key role. If so, competitors must find a way to match prices, or suffer the consequences.

Examine the facts presented in this vignette and decide for yourself if Air Canada is a predator. CanJet Airlines is a small regional air carrier based in Halifax, Nova Scotia. It began flying in Eastern Canada in September 2000. The cost of CanJet's one-way fare from Halifax to Ottawa is $96. Air Canada was charging $605 for the same route. Unexpectedly, Air Canada dropped its fare to $109 for selected flights on this route.

CanJet lodged a complaint with the Federal Competition Bureau stating, "It looks to us that their intention is to stop us from succeeding, and you have to ask how long would those low fares (Air Canada) last if we weren't operating?" The complaint further stated that Air Canada is specifically targeting CanJet because the low prices are only available for times when CanJet is also flying. In response, Air Canada claims they cut prices as part of a long-standing policy of remaining competitive in all markets. They were matching a competitor's price.

Roots Air charges just under $1000 to fly between Toronto and Vancouver. Air Canada lowered its rates for the same route to $909. Air Canada charges $1388 for a flight between Winnipeg and Vancouver, a route of much shorter distance.

Shouldn't the Toronto to Vancouver fare be higher? Roots Air claims, "There's no other imaginable reason for dropping this fare other than to deliberately strike at a new player that's a real threat to their market dominance."

Air Canada dismisses the Roots Air complaint. "The notion that Air Canada is engaging in predatory behaviour by offering an economy fare with restricted conditions between Toronto and Vancouver at $909 defies common sense. This type of posturing can't be taken seriously."

Clearly all the facts in this case are not available for you to consider. However, it is possible that Air Canada is attempting to hit new competitors where it hurts the most—in the pocketbook! What do you think? Is Air Canada a price predator or is it simply implementing pricing strategies to protect its position in the market?

Adapted from Peter Fitzpatrick, "Air Canada predatory: CanJet," *Financial Post*, September 8, 2001, p. C8 and Robert Meinbardis, "Air Canada accused of predatory pricing," *Toronto Star*, March 9, 2001, p. E2.

Chuck Stoody/CP Photo Archive

PRICE FIXING

price fixing

Price fixing refers to competitors banding together (conspiring) to raise, lower, or stabilize prices. While such a practice is common and relatively easy to implement, it is illegal under the Competition Act. Price fixing usually occurs in markets where price is the most important variable in the marketing mix. When implemented, there is an agreement between the participants, which, if followed, will result in benefit for them all. As mentioned earlier in the chapter, oil and gasoline companies are often accused of price fixing as prices at the pump are perceived to increase by all firms simultaneously. Despite the perception, such charges have not been found to be true.

To discourage price fixing, the anti-conspiracy provisions of the Competition Act are clear—companies and their executives are accountable for illegal actions and face stiff fines and jail terms if charged and found guilty. To illustrate the severity of the penalties associated with price fixing, the Competition Bureau recently ordered 4 international drug companies operating in Canada to pay $7.7 million for fixing prices of a food additive. The lawsuit had accused the companies of fixing the price of citric acid from 1991 to 1995. Citric acid is a common food additive that is used to control acidity in food products. Hoffman-LaRoche, Jungbunzlauer, Archer Daniels Midland, Haarmann & Reimer, and a subsidiary of Bayer AG are the firms paying out the damages.[11] Fines of this nature are necessary to deter anti-competitive behaviour.

Alternative Pricing Strategies

BARTERING

Barter Business Exchange
www.ncbarter.com

bartering

A growing practice among many companies is the use of bartering. While bartering has been around for a long time, companies are beginning to realize that there are other ways of exchanging goods and services. Bartering is the practice of exchanging goods and services for other goods and services rather than for money. **Bartering** involves reciprocal agreements between two or more companies in the exchange of goods and services they provide each other. Companies prominent in the bartering business include Barter Business Exchange, Barter Connection Inc., and Nationwide Barter Corp. These companies act as commissioned brokers for thousands of companies that want to exchange goods by bartering.

Companies involved in bartering see numerous advantages: it conserves cash flow, increases market exposure, and offers an opportunity to enhance sales with clients who would not otherwise purchase products. For small businesses, where cash flow is a concern, bartering represents great opportunity. Essentially, there are two types of bartering systems: retail barter exchanges and corporate barter companies. In a retail **barter exchange**, small companies trade products and services among themselves, with each company paying the barter exchange a transaction fee. In contrast, a **corporate barter company** takes possession of the goods and attempts to redistribute them among exchange members.

In a bartering environment, companies pay an initiation fee to sign on with an exchange, at which point they are granted access to the range of offerings being tendered by other members. Trades need not be direct—instead, a company buys something with barter dollars—the currency of bartering. Members use either barter dollars that have accumulated in their barter bank account as a result of other members buying their products, or if they have not amassed any barter dollars, the exchange may extend a line of credit. The barter exchange takes a commission between 3 and 5 percent, generally from both the buyer and the seller.[12]

retail barter exchange

corporate barter company

ONLINE AUCTIONS

auction

The Internet is the new arena for auctions. An **auction** is a method of sale whereby an object for sale is secured by the highest bidder. On the Internet, the online auction operates on the same principle. Online auctions are operated in several environments: business-to-business, business-to-consumer, and consumer-to-consumer.

In business-to-business situations, online bidding has the effect of widening the supplier pool for a good or service. In bidding for contracts, the lowest price is often the winning price. So, in theory, if there is lots of bidding, prices should be lower. In business-to-consumer markets and consumer-to-consumer markets, consumers compete against one another to drive up the price for the auctioned item—in some cases, above the fair market value. Consumers should be aware of regular retail pricing before getting involved with online bidding. ebay.ca is an example of an online auction company (see Figure 10.10).

More details about online pricing are included in Chapter 17.

The Home Page of an Online Auction

Figure 10.10

Summary

Price refers to the exchange value of a good or service in the marketplace. Prices are offered in many different forms, including fares, commissions, interest rates, and fees. In the Canadian economy, an organization's control over price is influenced by the nature of the market it operates in. The four basic markets are pure competition (where no control exists, since prices are controlled by the market), monopolistic competition (where firms have some control, but are mainly directed by the competition), oligopoly (where organizations also have some control but where pricing is directed even more by competition—a sort of follow-the-leader type of approach), and monopoly (where pricing is controlled by governments or some government-designated body).

Three major variables affect a firm's pricing activities: consumer demand for a product; channel members, whose profit margins are considered in a firm's estimation of the final price; and finally, costs, which affect the ability of a company to produce and market a product that will yield an adequate and reasonable profit margin for the firm and fair prices for customers.

The prices established by an organization are part of an overall marketing strategy that is designed to achieve specific objectives. The three basic pricing objectives are profit maximization (improving owners' return on investment), sales volume maximization (improving growth rates and market share), and establishing competitive position (maintaining adequate profit margins so that all companies that sell the product remain satisfied).

Specific methods for calculating price include cost-based pricing, demand-based pricing, and competition-based pricing. The method a firm uses is chosen according to the nature and degree of competition in the markets it operates in.

Companies must be aware of the laws that affect pricing strategy. Any violation of laws could lead to serious financial consequences. Some areas that are cause for concern include bait and switch tactics, improper quoting of sales prices, bid rigging and price fixing, double ticketing and bar code price variances, and predatory pricing practices.

A company may also barter its goods and services with goods and services from another company. In the case of bartering, a value is placed on the product or service provided in the exchange. Another new pricing alternative is to offer items for sale by auction. In online auctions, consumers bid against each other and drive the price of the auctioned item up—sometimes higher than its fair value.

Key Terms

auction 286
bait and switch 283
bartering 285
break-even analysis 276
chain markup pricing 277
competitive bidding 279
competitive pricing 274
corporate barter company 285
cost reductions 272

cost-based pricing 275
demand-based pricing 277
demand-minus (backward) pricing 277
double ticketing 281
elastic demand 269
fixed costs 275
full-cost pricing 276
inelastic demand 270
law of supply and demand 267

Review Questions

1. Briefly explain how operating in (a) an oligopoly and (b) a monopolistic competition market affects the pricing activity of an organization.

2. What are the differences between elastic demand and inelastic demand?

3. What is the difference between a profit maximization pricing objective and a sales volume maximization pricing objective?

4. Briefly describe the importance of the competition to a firm's pricing strategy.

5. Explain the concept of competitive pricing. Provide some new examples of companies or brands that practise "above competitor" pricing and "below competitor" pricing.

6. Explain the difference between fixed and variable costs.

7. What is the difference between demand-minus (backward) pricing and chain markup pricing?

8. Briefly explain the usefulness of break-even analysis.

9. In terms of pricing, explain the tactics of bait and switch.

10. What is predatory pricing?

11. Briefly explain the concept of bartering.

Discussion and Application Questions

1. Given the following information, calculate the unit price, using the cost-plus pricing method:

   Fixed Costs = $350 000
   Variable Costs = $65.00 per unit of production
   Profit Objective = $29 500 based on a production level of 600 units

2. Calculate the break-even point in units and dollars, given the following information:

   Fixed Costs = $300 000
   Variable Costs = $0.75 per unit
   Selling Price = $2.50 per unit

3. A book publisher determines that the consumer will pay $29.95 for a reprint of a classic bestseller. It estimates that marketing expenses and profit margin will consume 60 percent of the selling price. Using the demand-minus pricing method, calculate how much the publisher can spend on producing the book.

4. Visit a few fast food restaurants in your area (e.g., McDonald's, Burger King, Wendy's) and assess from the menu the pricing strategies that each restaurant offers. Briefly analyze the pricing strategies for effectiveness. Are their strategies appropriate? Are there other pricing strategies that they should consider?

5. Ace Manufacturing produces refrigerators. The fixed costs amount to $250 000, and the variable costs are $175 for each unit produced. The company would like to make a profit of $20 000 on the production of 200 units. What selling price must the company charge?

6. A manufacturer has total fixed costs of $54 000. Variable costs are $2.50 per unit. The product sells for $8.00. What is the break-even point in units?

7. A manufacturer of dress belts estimates that consumers will pay $22.00 for its belts. The company sells the belts through wholesalers, who, in turn, sell to retailers. The manufacturer takes a markup of 25 percent in selling to wholesalers, and the wholesalers take a markup of 15 percent in selling to retailers. What price will the wholesalers and retailers pay for the belts? Use the chain markup pricing method to arrive at a solution.

8. A manufacturer produces blank videotapes for $1.50. It adds a 60 percent markup on cost to establish a selling price to wholesalers. Wholesalers then add a 40 percent markup in setting the price that retailers will pay. If the retailer charges consumers $4.99 for the blank videotapes, what will its markup be?

9. The Baltic Manufacturing Company built a new plant at a cost of $12 500 000. Its target return on investment is 15 percent. The standard volume of production for the year is 25 000 units. The average total cost of each unit is $500, based on the standard volume of 25 000 units. What is the selling price? Use the target pricing formula to arrive at a solution.

10. Review the vignette "Is Air Canada a Predator?" Assess the information presented in this vignette and offer a position about Air Canada's status as a predator. You may wish to conduct some additional research on this subject prior to arriving at a conclusion.

11. Rather than increase prices year after year, many firms are evaluating cost reduction alternatives. Conduct some secondary research and provide some new examples of companies and brands that are following a cost reduction strategy. What are the risks associated with this strategy?

E-Assignment

In this assignment, you will be doing some comparative shopping. Your goal is to make a rational buying decision based on all the information you uncover. You have decided that you would like to buy a new car in the $15 000 to $20 000 price range—some kind of entry-level car. You have also decided that you want a Japanese car. From the Yahoo! Web site, request a search for online auctions. When you arrive at the auction page, click on the "automotive auction." On the next page, click on "Yahoo! Autos." Now you can begin to compare some makes and models. Plug in the makes from the menu and select the price range. On the basis of the information you have found, what car will you buy? Why? What are the benefits and drawbacks of buying a car online? If you wish, repeat the exercise using another online service.

Endnotes

1. Alexander MacMillan and Bohunmir Pazderka, *Microeconomics*, 3rd Edition (Scarborough: Prentice-Hall Canada Inc, 1989), p. 107.

2. Ibid. p. 181.

3. Oliver Bertin, "Bottle prices expected to rise," *Globe and Mail*, February 2, 2001, p. B. 5.

4. Stuart Laidlaw, "Makers shrinking products to expand their bottom line," *Toronto Star*, December 4, 2001, pp. D1, D11.

5. Practices Branch, Consumer and Corporate Affairs Canada, *Misleading Advertising Bulletin*, 1984, p. 34.

6. Ibid.

7. "Hudson's Bay fined for misleading ads," *Financial Post*, May 5, 1998, p. 20.

8. Zena Olijnyk, "Wal-Mart finishes first in scanner test," *Financial Post*, November 26, 1998, p. C1.

9. Robert Meinbardis, "Air Canada accused of predatory pricing," *Toronto Star*, March 9, 2001, p. E2.

10. John Geddes, "The dilemma of predatory pricing," *Financial Post*, September 23, 1991, p. 3.

11. "$7.7 million payout in vitamin price fixing lawsuit," *CBC News*, www.cbc.ca/stories/2002/02/28.

12. Laura Pratt, "Trading places," *Financial Post Magazine*, March 1998, p. 97.

Price Management

After studying this chapter, you will be able to

1. Describe the various pricing policies practised by Canadian marketing organizations.
2. Outline the various discounts and allowances offered to customers by marketing organizations.
3. Characterize the alternative pricing strategies used in the course of the product life cycle.
4. Explain what the role and benefits of leasing are as a pricing strategy in the marketplace.

This chapter will focus on the management of pricing activity. The various pricing policies a firm may adopt are discussed, and the types of discounts that are commonly offered in the marketplace are explained. The influence of the product life cycle on price management is also presented. Discussion in this area centres on the pricing of new products and the pricing changes that are implemented throughout the product life cycle. Finally, the use of leasing as an alternative to selling goods is examined.

Pricing Policies

1.
Describe the various pricing policies practised by Canadian marketing organizations.

Pricing policies are the basic rules about pricing that enable a firm to achieve its marketing objectives. The policy options available are classified into four primary categories: psychological pricing, promotional pricing, geographic pricing, and flexible pricing. A firm may use one or any combination of these price policies, depending on the objectives established for the product or the nature of the market that the product competes in.

PSYCHOLOGICAL PRICING

psychological pricing

In the case of **psychological pricing**, the organization appeals to tendencies in consumer behaviour other than rational ones. It is a practice used more often by retailers than by manufacturers. Psychological pricing influences the purchasing patterns of the final consumer. There are several types of psychological pricing strategies, as described below.

Prestige Pricing

prestige pricing

Prestige pricing is the practice of setting prices high to give the impression that the product is of high quality. This practice is strongly associated with luxury goods. The fact that the price is high contributes to the image of the product and the status of the buyer. Refer to Figure 11.1 for an illustration. For example, a mink coat that sells for $10 000 carries prestige that is inherited by whoever buys it. The price of the mink has been set high enough to create the image of quality and status. A consumer seeking such prestige may be attracted to a very expensive perfume, forgetting that the scent of the perfume should probably be the primary consideration. When prestige pricing has been effective in creating the desired image, demand for certain products actually decreases if the price is reduced.

An Illustration of Prestige Pricing

Figure 11.1

© AFP/CORBIS/MAGMA

Odd-Even Pricing

For psychological reasons, an odd number is more effective with consumers than a rounded-off number. Thus, a colour television is priced at $499.00 because it is then not seen as costing $500.00. Research has shown that consumers register and remember the first digit more clearly than they do subsequent ones (in this case the 4, which puts the price in the $400 range).[1] Setting prices below even-dollar amounts is called **odd-even pricing**. It is popular with retailers and explains the widespread use of such prices as

odd-even pricing

$19.95, $99.95, and $199.95. The sales tax in most provinces and the Goods and Services Tax (GST) put the price into the next range, over the "even barrier," but do not have a major influence on purchases because consumers are accustomed to these mandatory additions to most of the items they purchase.

The number 9 seems to play a key role in odd-even pricing. To illustrate its strength consider the case of an association that was marketing a book but didn't know the exact price to charge. Price points of $23, $25, $27, and $29 were tested. To the delight of the association the $29 price point got the highest response. Consumers simply didn't perceive a difference between $23 and $29. Studies have shown that prices ending in "9" can be more attractive to buyers than lower numbers within the same range.[2]

Price Lining

price lining

Price lining refers to the adoption of price points for the various lines of merchandise a retailer carries. Thus, in the case of a clothing store, the retailer establishes a limited number of prices for selected lines of products rather than pricing the items individually. For instance, price ranges for business suits could be set in the $300 range ($399), the $500 range ($599), and the $700 range ($799). Customers entering the store are directed to the assortment of suits that fall within their price range, once it is known. In each range, the retailer may have purchased suits from different suppliers at different costs but is satisfied with an average markup within each price range because it saves the consumer any confusion over price. Assuming the retailer understands the needs and expectations of its customers and how much they are willing to pay, it can establish its price lines (price ranges) accordingly.

Customary Pricing

customary pricing

Customary pricing is the strategy of matching prices to a buyer's expectations; the price reflects tradition or is a price that people are accustomed to paying. For example, chocolate bars of average size and weight are expected to have the same price, regardless of the different brand names. Other examples are the prices of daily newspapers, which increase only marginally from time to time, and transit fares for buses and subways. In the candy business, consumers started some years ago to balk at the continual price increases of chocolate bars, and the industry was faced with flat sales. As an alternative to increasing price, manufacturers decided to shrink the product by reducing the weight of the bars. This option was more acceptable than raising the price—and less fattening! The concept of cost reductions was discussed in Chapter 10.

Unit Pricing

unit pricing

Unit pricing is a policy adopted by retailers, particularly grocery retailers, of listing the cost per standard unit of a product to let shoppers compare the prices of similar products packaged in different quantities. Typically, posting bar code price tags on shelf facings does this. The bar codes allow consumers to determine per-gram prices in different-sized containers. In the case of food items, a shelf sticker states the retail price, the size or weight of the item, and the cost per unit of measurement (e.g., cost per gram, cost per millilitre). Although unit prices were originally designed to assist low-income groups, research has shown that well-educated income groups of the middle and upper-middle classes refer to them most often.[3]

Technology has eliminated the need for price tags on individual items in many retail operations. Instead, bar code tags that match individual product bar codes are placed on shelf strips. While such a system is good for the retailer, it can cause confusion among shoppers. For example, the price charged at the checkout could be different from that displayed on shelf bar codes. Retailers are now obligated to provide scanners so that shoppers can verify prices at any time in the store. To protect consumers, the province of Quebec has instituted a new law governing checkout transactions that are less than 98 percent accurate. Shoppers who are overcharged by more than 2 percent will get any item worth $10 or less free. On items worth more than $10, a $10 cash payment is made to the customer.[4] Such a law encourages retailers to have an accurate pricing system in place.

Promotional Pricing

promotional pricing

Promotional pricing is defined as the lowering of prices temporarily to attract customers (i.e., offering sale prices). In a retail environment, the objective of this practice is to attract people to (build consumer traffic in) the store; retailers know that while the customers are in the store, they could purchase other merchandise at regular prices. In a manufacturing environment, companies offer a variety of promotional incentives to attract new users (often users who purchase competing brands). Common types of promotional pricing used by retailers include loss leaders and multiple-unit pricing strategies.

loss leaders

Loss leaders are products offered for sale at or slightly below cost. The consumer recognizes the item as a true bargain and is attracted to a store by the offer. Honest Ed's department store in downtown Toronto is famous for daily "door-crasher" specials. So successful are these door crashers that people line up hours before the store opens to get a shot at the specials, a phenomenon that occurs with unusual regularity.

multiple-unit pricing

A&P
www.aptea.com

When **multiple-unit pricing** is followed, items are offered for sale in multiples (pairs are quite common), usually at a price below the combined regular price of each item. Such a practice is quite common in food retailing. Stores such as Safeway, Loblaws, Super Value, Sobeys, and A&P offer such deals in their weekly flyers (e.g., soup at 2/$0.99). Other variations include such deals as "two for the price of one" specials or "buy one get one free" or "buy one at regular price and get the second at half price." These types of offers are more frequent in other segments of the retailing industry, such as clothing and hardware stores.

Low sale prices for national brands in supermarkets and drug stores receive financial support from the manufacturer. The manufacturer offers a variety of trade discounts in order to lower the price for the consumer and sell a greater volume of product in the short term (for more information, see the section on Source Pricing and Offering Discounts in this chapter).

GEOGRAPHIC PRICING

geographic pricing

Geographic pricing is a pricing strategy based on the answer to the question, "Who is paying the freight?" Does the seller pay the freight costs of delivering the merchandise to the buyer, or does the buyer absorb these charges? Are freight charges averaged to all customers and included in the price? These are geographic pricing questions, and their answers are largely based on the practices of the industry in which the firm operates. In some industries, the seller customarily pays, while in others the buyer generally pays. A choice by a seller not to pay the costs in an industry where the sellers usually do pay would have an adverse effect on sales, even though the product might otherwise be the preferred choice. Several geographic pricing possibilities exist, including F.O.B. pricing (free-on-board pricing), uniform delivered pricing, and zone pricing (Figure 11.2).

F.O.B. Pricing

Under this classification are two subcategories for pricing based on who pays the freight.

F.O.B. origin

F.O.B. Origin (Plant) In an **F.O.B. origin** arrangement, the seller quotes a price that does not include freight charges. The buyer pays the freight and assumes title (ownership) of the merchandise when it is loaded onto a common carrier—a truck, a train, or an airplane. This practice is satisfactory to local customers, but distant customers are disadvantaged. Under such a pricing system, a customer in Vancouver would pay much more for merchandise shipped from Montreal than would a customer in Toronto.

F.O.B. destination

F.O.B. Destination (Freight Absorption) To counter the impression that distant customers are being penalized, the seller under the terms of **F.O.B. destination** agrees to pay all freight charges. How much of the charges the seller actually absorbs is questionable, however, since the freight costs are built into the price that the buyer is charged. In any event, the title does not transfer to the buyer until the goods arrive at their destination—the buyer's warehouse. Such a strategy is effective in attracting new customers in distant locations.

Uniform Delivered Pricing

uniform delivered pricing

In the case of **uniform delivered pricing**, the price includes an average freight charge for all customers, regardless of their location. To develop a uniform delivered price, a firm calculates the average freight cost of sending goods to the various locations of its customers. This practice is more attractive to distant customers than to nearby customers, who pay more than they would under a different pricing system. Local customers pay **phantom freight**, or the amount by which average transportation charges exceed the actual cost of shipping for customers near the source of supply.[5]

phantom freight

"Who Pays the Freight?"

Figure 11.2

F.O.B. Origin, or Plant	*Buyer*	The buyer takes title when the product is on a common carrier (e.g., a truck).
F.O.B. Destination, or Freight Absorption	*Seller*	The seller pays all freight necessary to reach a stated destination.
Uniform Delivered Price	*Buyer*	The buyer's price includes an average freight cost that all customers pay regardless of location.
Zone Pricing	*Buyer*	All customers within a designated geographic area pay the same freight cost.

Zone Pricing

zone pricing

In the case of **zone pricing**, the market is divided into geographic zones and a uniform delivered price is established for each zone. For these purposes, the Canadian market is easily divided into geographic zones: the Atlantic Provinces, Quebec, Ontario, the Prairies, British Columbia, and the Territories. Each of these zones may be subdivided further. The Ontario zone could be divided into Northern Ontario, Eastern Ontario, South-central Ontario, and Southwestern Ontario. For an illustration of geographic pricing strategies and calculations, see Figure 11.3. Air freight carriers, such as Federal Express and UPS, use zone pricing. The distance a parcel travels determines the rate charged. For example, one price is charged for 0 to 599 miles, another for 600 to 1199, and so on.

FLEXIBLE PRICING

flexible pricing

Flexible pricing means charging different customers different prices. While such a practice initially seems unfair, its actual effect is to allow buyers to negotiate a lower price

---

Geographic Pricing Strategies

Figure 11.3

F.O.B.	Maritimes	Quebec	Ontario	Prairies	B.C.
F.O.B. Origin (Toronto)	$10.00	$10.00	$10.00	$10.00	$10.00
Add: Profit Margin and					
Freight to Each Customer	2.75	1.75	1.10	2.00	3.25
Customer Pays	12.75	11.75	11.10	12.00	13.25
Uniform Delivered Price:					
Zone Price	16.50	15.50	15.00	16.50	17.00
Multiply by:					
Volume Importance of					
Each Region	5%	25%	40%	15%	15%
Uniform Delivered Price			$15.72		
Zone Price:					
F.O.B. Origin (Toronto)	$10.00	$10.00	$10.00	$10.00	$10.00
Add: Profit Margin (40%)	4.00	4.00	4.00	4.00	4.00
	14.00	14.00	14.00	14.00	14.00
Add: Average Freight to					
Each Region	2.50	1.50	1.00	2.50	3.00
Zone Price for Each					
Customer	16.50	15.50	15.00	16.50	17.00

than that asked by the sellers. It means that the price is open to negotiation. Such negotiations are typical in the purchase of something expensive, say a house or an automobile. In the case of a purchase of a car, negotiations are commonly referred to as "dickering." The salesperson and the buyer dicker back and forth until a mutually agreeable price is arrived at, usually a price well below the sticker price.

According to the Automobile Protection Association, price dickering is one of the most hated aspects of buying a new car. It is an unpleasant experience and a major reason why people resist buying. Both manufacturers and car dealers are taking steps to remedy the situation. The Saturn subsidiary of General Motors, for example, does not negotiate prices. Consumers are also finding a higher level of comfort by buying an automobile online.

Product Mix Pricing

When a product is part of a larger product mix, setting prices is more difficult. The goal in this situation is to set prices so that profits are maximized for the total mix. Some products may be priced low while others are high. On balance, profit objectives are achieved and customers are generally satisfied with the price they pay.

Product mix pricing embraces the following situations.

Optional-feature Pricing This involves offering additional products, features, and services along with the main product. Specific option packages are often offered with local phone plans. As more options are added, the price of the plan will increase (see Figure 11.4).

Product-line Pricing Companies normally develop product lines rather than single products. For example, Sony offers flat screen televisions in various sizes: 27", 31," 35" and so on. Corresponding prices might be $899, $1299, and $1799.

Captive-product Pricing Some products require the use of ancillary, or captive products. If so, a company must price the captive product appropriately in order to encourage use. Microsoft and Sony, manufacturers of electronic game sets (hardware) and games (software) must carefully price each product.

Fixed-variable Pricing Service firms commonly offer two-part pricing consisting of a fixed fee plus a variable usage fee. Fees charged for basic and long distance telephone service by firms such as Bell and Rogers AT&T work this way as do fees for companies providing Internet access. In the case of Internet access the base fee is for a certain number of hours with additional charges for extra hours.

Product-bundling Pricing In this situation the seller bundles their products and features at a set price. Rogers Communications practises this option when it sells cellular telephones. Various long-distance packages are available at set fees. Typically, the price of the phone is set low to attract customers. Rogers makes its profit in the long-term based on the monthly fees it charges and how frequently the customer uses the telephone.

Source Pricing and Offering Discounts

list price

Part of price management involves offering discounts to customers. The firm first establishes a **list price**, which is the rate normally quoted to potential buyers. Then, a host of discounts and allowances, which provide savings off the list price, are commonly offered

Figure 11.4

An Illustration of Optional-Feature Pricing; Price and Discounts Increase As Features Are Added

Courtesy: Sprint Canada

to customers. In effect, price discounts and allowances become part of the firm's promotional plans for dealing with trade customers—wholesalers, for example—who, in turn, pass on all or some of the savings to the retailers they supply. Very often, it is the combination of allowances that convinces customers to buy in large volumes. In business buying situations, the buyer rarely pays the list price. Typically, a buyer is eligible for some of the discounts given by a manufacturer. Various types of discounts exist.

CASH DISCOUNTS

2.

Outline the various discounts and allowances offered to customers by marketing organizations.

cash discounts

Canadian Tire
www.canadiantire.ca

quantity discounts

Cash discounts are granted when a bill is paid promptly, within a stated period. An example is 2/10, net 30. In this case, the buyer may deduct 2 percent from the invoice price if the charge is paid within 10 days of receipt of the invoice. The account is due and payable within 30 days at invoice price. While this discount appears to be small, it adds up to considerable savings for such mass merchandisers as Canadian Tire, Safeway, and the Bay.

QUANTITY DISCOUNTS

Quantity discounts are offered on the basis of volume purchased in units or dollars and can be offered non-cumulatively (i.e., during a special sale period only) or cumulatively (i.e., so that they apply to all purchases over an extended period, say, a year). Normally, eligible purchases are recorded in an invoicing system, and a cheque from the supplier is issued to cover the value of the discounts earned by the buyer at the end of the discount period. Refer to Figure 11.5 for an illustration of a quantity discount schedule.

The supplier establishes quantity discounts. However, depending on the circumstance, quantity discount schedules can be negotiated. If, for example, an industry is in the middle of an economic slump (e.g., hotels and airlines in a weak economy), a supplier may be amenable to higher discounts to attract corporate customers. Holiday Inn Canada offers a 25 percent discount to corporate clients who guarantee 5000 room nights a year, but only 72 Canadian corporations are eligible for this discount. Consequently, Holiday Inn will negotiate room limits in order to secure new business.[6] To secure better rates, buyers must be knowledgeable of suppliers' travel volume. To ensure higher discounts through higher travel volume, corporations are now pooling the travel of employees of all their subsidiaries.

TRADE OR FUNCTIONAL DISCOUNTS

There are several types of trade discounts.

Slotting Allowances

slotting allowance

A **slotting allowance** is a discount offered by a supplier to a retail distributor, for the purpose of securing shelf space in retail outlets. These allowances are commonly offered

A Quantity Discount Schedule

Figure 11.5

Schedule Based on Volume Purchased over One Year

Volume		Discount
Units	Dollars	
100–1000	200 000–2 000 000	10%
1001–2000	2 000 001–4 000 000	15%
2001–3000	4 000 001–6 000 000	20%
3001–4000	6 000 001–8 000 000	25%

with the introduction of new products. Since shelf space is scarce, it is often difficult to motivate distributors to carry new products. Given the number of new products that are introduced each year, retailers can be selective and are more receptive to suppliers who offer discounts to help defray the costs associated with getting a new product into their system (e.g., warehousing costs, computer costs, and redesigning store shelf sections).

The practice of offering and accepting slotting allowances is a controversial issue. Critics argue that such a practice puts small suppliers at a disadvantage, since they cannot afford them, and therefore getting a new product into distribution is difficult for them. Large suppliers do not necessarily like to offer these allowances, but since retailers have control in most markets (oligopolies exist in most cases) over the channel of distribution, the alternatives are few if guaranteed distribution is the goal.

Off-Invoice Trade Allowances

off-invoice allowance

An **off-invoice allowance** is a temporary allowance, applicable during a specified time period and is deducted from the invoice at the time of customer billing. The invoice indicates the regular list price, the amount of the discount, and the volume purchased. Consider the following example:

Product (24 units in case)	$36.00 per case
Off-Invoice Allowance	$7.20 per case
Net Price	$28.80 per case
Volume Purchased	10 cases
Amount Due	$288.00
Terms:	2/10, Net 30

Manufacturers offer an off-invoice allowance to distributors as an incentive to purchase in greater volume in the short term, and to encourage distributors to pass on the savings to their customers. In the example above, as much as $0.30 per unit ($7.20/24 units) could be passed on. Instead of allowing for such discounts on the invoice, a manufacturer sometimes offers them on the basis of a **bill-back**, in which case the manufacturer keeps a record of the volume purchased by each customer and issues cheques at a later date to cover the allowances earned over the term of the offer.

bill-back

Performance (Promotional) Allowances

performance allowance

A **performance allowance** is a price discount given by a manufacturer to a distributor that performs a promotional function on the manufacturer's behalf. These discounts are frequently made available in conjunction with off-invoice allowances. When the discounts are combined, a wholesaler that purchases in larger volumes will achieve greater savings. The performances that qualify for the allowances may take some or all of the following forms:

1. There is guaranteed product distribution to all stores served by the distributor (e.g., Canadian Tire or Loblaws agrees to ship a certain quantity of the product to each of its stores in a certain region), rather than a system whereby the distributor waits for individual stores to place orders.

2. In-store displays are set in a prominent location.

3. The product is mentioned in retail advertising flyers or in newspaper advertisements that announce weekly specials.

Performance allowances are usually negotiated between a manufacturer and a distributor, and an agreement is signed. The distributor is paid on proof of performance at the end of the term of the offer. Refer to Figure 11.6 for an illustration of promotional discount calculations that a manufacturer may use to promote its product and of their effect on the price customers pay.

SEASONAL DISCOUNTS

seasonal discounts

Seasonal discounts apply to off-season or pre-season purchases. They are typical of products and services that sell strongly only in a certain season or during certain times. For example, downtown hotels are busy during the week with business travellers but require family package plans to attract customers on weekends. Summer resorts and vacation retreats often offer 20 to 30 percent discounts before and after their prime season. Television viewing is much lower in the summer months. Therefore, networks such as CTV and CBC offer discounted rates to advertisers during this period.

REBATES

rebates

Rebates are temporary price discounts that take the form of a cash return made directly to a consumer, usually by a manufacturer. Periodically, car and appliance manufacturers offer cash rebates to customers who buy their models. Frequently, the rebate program becomes the focal point of advertising campaigns. Such programs are commonly used to reduce inventories or to stimulate sales in traditionally slow selling seasons, or at times when the economy is weak. For more insight into rebates, read the Marketing in Action vignette **Price Incentives Stimulate Sales, Hurt Profits.**

List Price and Discount Calculations

Figure 11.6

Information:

Cost of Product	$40.00 per case
Trade Discount	$4.00 per case
Quantity Discount	2% for each 100 cases
Performance Allowance	5%
Cash Discount	2/10, n30
Customer Purchases	500 cases

Calculation of Price to Customer:

List Price	$40.00
Less: Trade Discount (10%)	4.00
	36.00
Less: Quantity Discount (2% × 5)	3.60
	32.40
Less: Performance Allowance (5%)	1.62
	30.78
Less: Cash Discount (2%)	.62
Net Price	30.16
Total Discount	9.84
Total Percentage Discount ($9.84/40)	= 24.6 %

rather than selling goods. Reducing the level and frequency of trade discounts places the responsibility for success where it ought to be—on the shoulders of skill and creativity, not on tricks of the trade.[7] Any savings on the trade side of the budget could be put into brand-building activities such as advertising and consumer promotions.

Some retail markets in Canada are classified as oligopolies (e.g., supermarkets, hardware stores, and department stores). Store leaders in each category have a lot of control over their suppliers and they pressure suppliers for deeper and more frequent discounts. **forward buying** Retailers purchase products under a system known as forward buying. **Forward buying** is the practice of buying deal merchandise in quantities sufficient to carry a retailer through to the next deal period offered by the manufacturer. In effect, the retailer never buys goods at the regular price. According to the Grocery Products Manufacturers of Canada, more than 67 percent of all commodity volume sold to retail distributors in Canada is bought on deal.[8]

Pricing and the Product Life Cycle

3.
Characterize the alternative pricing strategies used in the course of the product life cycle.

Pricing a new product presents unique challenges for a marketer. Equally as challenging is how to adjust prices throughout the life cycle of a product. There are basically two strategies for pricing a new product: skimming and penetration. Which strategy is used depends on the objectives established by the firm at the introduction stage and at subsequent stages of the product life cycle. Generally, higher prices are associated with the early stages, when the firm is trying to recover product-development costs quickly; lower prices are associated with the latter stages, when more competition exists (Figure 11.7). These generalizations are simply guidelines, however. Throughout any given product's life cycle, there could be a lot of experimentation with price.

PRICE SKIMMING

price skimming
A **price-skimming** strategy involves the use of a high price when a product enters the market, which enables a firm to maximize its revenue early. Some of the conditions that encourage the use of a skimming strategy are on the following page:

New Product Pricing Strategy

Figure 11.7

Price	Skimming	Price Penetration
Strategy	High entry price	Low entry price
Objective	Maximize revenue, and recover research, development, and marketing costs quickly	Gain market acceptance fast, expand the market, and build market share
Suitable Market Characteristics	Inelastic demand and markets where customers are less price sensitive	Elastic demand and markets where customers are price sensitive

1. The product is an innovation or is perceived to be significantly better than competing products. Such a situation justifies a higher price.

2. If competing products exist, they are few in number and are generally weak. New products that carry strong and popular brand names face little risk in using a skimming strategy.

3. The product is protected by patent; the resulting lack of direct competition allows a product to recover its development costs quickly by using this strategy.

A skimming strategy should only be used in cases where the marketing organization has a thorough understanding of the target market's behaviour. If price is an important consideration for consumers, a skimming strategy will not encourage new buyers to try a product, and the adoption and diffusion process will be slow. A possible hazard of skimming is that competitors who see a product enjoying high profit margins, mainly due to the lack of competition and a skimming pricing strategy, are likely to bring similar products to the market very quickly. Users of a skimming strategy recognize that it is easier to lower prices than it is to raise prices during the life cycle of a product.

To illustrate the concept of price skimming, consider Gillette's launch of the Mach3 razor system. Mach3 was priced at a greater than 50 percent premium over Gillette's own Sensor brand (the leading brand on the market). Gillette believed that the benefits offered through product innovation justified the price. Apparently Gillette was right. Since Mach3 was launched, Gillette's total sales have increased by 30 percent.[9]

When it comes to pricing the latest gizmos in the electronic technology world, price skimming is the strategy used. Take for example, HDTV (high definition television sets). A customer will pay outrageous prices for a HDTV for the advantages it will offer and its prestige. Innovators and early adopters buy for these reasons. As HDTV progresses through its life cycle, the price will change to successfully reach larger market segments (e.g., groups classified as early majority and late majority). The same can be said of DVD players. Initial versions launched by Sony and Panasonic were priced very high but as more and more manufacturers and brands entered the market, the prices for all brands were reduced.

PRICE PENETRATION

price penetration

A **price penetration** strategy establishes a low entry price in order to gain wide market acceptance for the product quickly. The objective of price penetration is to create demand in a market quickly, to build market share, and to discourage competitors from entering. Generally, low prices are attractive to a larger number of customers, so demand and market-share objectives are achieved more rapidly. Potential competitors who analyze the market situation may think twice about entering it if they see that the profit margins of existing competitors are low and their market shares large. Under such circumstances, the opportunity to recover development costs, especially in a short time, diminishes. Certain conditions are favourable to the use of a penetration strategy:

1. The market or market segment is characterized by elastic demand, that is, demand that goes up if prices are low—buyers tend to be price sensitive.

2. The marketing organization has the ability to keep production costs down. Either costs are low initially, allowing a satisfactory profit margin to be achieved with the low-price strategy, or the firm banks on improved production efficiency—resulting from the volume selling encouraged by the strategy—to reduce costs.

3. The market is clearly divided into segments on the basis of price, and the low price or economy segment is large enough to justify entrance or accommodate competition among several brands.

The shortcoming of a penetration strategy is that it generally takes a long time to recover the costs of development and marketing, including the high costs of introducing products because a high volume of sales is necessary in order to do so. If volume sales are not produced as quickly as anticipated, the realization of any profit may be delayed.

To illustrate the concept of penetration pricing, consider the success of generic and private label products in Canada. What helps make private label brands and generic brands successful is their low price in relation to the national brands they compete against. In Canada, the number-one-selling brand of refrigerator, oven, washer, and dryer is Kenmore, a private label brand marketed by Sears. Kenmore's price advantage, as well as the fact that its products are perceived to be of good quality by consumers, enables it to compete successfully against well-known national brand names, such as Maytag, Hotpoint, LG, and others, in these product categories. In the airline industry, Air Canada is using a penetration strategy with the launch of two new discount airline brands, Zip (in Western Canada) and Tango (in Eastern Canada). According to the CEO, Robert Milton, "Consumers want low fares on a year-round basis. These carriers provide an attractive and affordable option with convenient connections to Air Canada's worldwide network."[10]

For more insight into the intricacies of pricing policies, refer to the Marketing in Action vignette **Coke and Mazda Rethink Price Policies.**

Zip
www.4321zip.com
Tango
www.flytango.com

Leasing As a Pricing Option

lease

A **lease** is a contractual agreement whereby a lessor (owner), for a fee, agrees to rent an item (e.g., equipment, house, land) to a lessee over a specified period. In recent years, certain industries have increasingly used leasing in place of buying and selling. When considering the purchase of expensive capital equipment, buyers now frequently assess the lease option.

4.
Explain what the role and benefits of leasing are as a pricing strategy in the marketplace.

Expensive capital equipment such as computers, office equipment and furnishings, and automobiles are often purchased on a lease agreement. Colleges and universities, for example, often lease computer equipment so that they have access to the latest technology when a lease expires. The leasing industry in Canada has grown significantly in the past few years. Estimates of its size are as high as $22 billion for the equipment lessor market annually.[11] Generally, the more "high-tech" a piece of equipment is, the more likely it is that companies will lease it. Another standard rule-of-thumb is: if it appreciates, buy it; if it depreciates, lease it.

In the consumer market, it is estimated that 50 percent of new-car owners lease instead of buying. Most print ads you see in magazines and newspapers today actively promote the lease option. The main advantage of the car lease is that one pays only for the use of the vehicle versus the entire car. This can mean payments of 20 to 30 percent less than bank financing payments. This is due to an equity benefit remaining in the car belonging to the leaseholder at the end of the term.

operating lease

There are two types of leases. An **operating lease** is usually short term and involves monthly payments for the use of the equipment, which is returned to the lessor after a specified period. The lessee does not pay the full value on the equipment, so after the

Marketing in Action

Coke and Mazda Rethink Price Policies

Marketing managers often adjust prices to achieve short-term increases in sales volume. In some markets today, however, consumers are so accustomed to lower prices that it is difficult for manufacturers to maintain any sense of regular prices. To illustrate, the soft drink market is a hard-fought battleground between Coca-Cola and Pepsi-Cola. One week Coke is on special, the next week it is Pepsi. In special seasons, such as Christmas, they are both offering low prices to encourage multiple purchases. What effect does this practice have on profits?

In a nutshell, profit margins shrink. For the past five years, Coca-Cola has pursued volume by offering steep discounts in North American supermarkets. Supermarkets account for 50 percent of Coke's sales volume. The result was 8 percent average growth on volume each year, but profits were falling. This trend was unsatisfactory for Coca-Cola and its bottlers.

In a move to restore better profitability, Coke changed its pricing strategy: It would charge more and presumably sell less. In 1999, bottlers in Canada and the United States were charged 2 to 3 percent more, and they, in turn, charged their customers about 5 percent more. The result was a higher price at retail.

A shift in price strategy forces change in other areas of marketing. The repositioning of Coke at a premium price point would require new advertising. Coke developed a new campaign that was designed to connect the brand with consumers and raise brand value. By making the changes, Coca-Cola only expects a volume growth of 1 percent, a much lower level than before, but profits will be much higher. Ultimately, success will depend on how consumers respond to the new marketing initiatives.

In another illustration, it could be said that pricing policy had a significant impact on the rise and fall of Mazda Miata's popularity. When first introduced, the Miata was so popular that there were huge waiting lists for it. In the first 6 months in Canada, Mazda sold 2827 Miatas at a price of $16 985. Consumers perceived the price to be fair for an entry-level sports car. The following year, the price climbed slightly to $17 510, and sales blossomed to 3906. But by the next year, sales started to slip, and the trend continued until 1996 when national sales were only 558 cars.

Nowadays, the most basic Miata lists at $26 025. This price represents a 53 percent price increase over a decade that has seen the consumer price index only rise by 22 percent. Why would Mazda raise the prices so high? Rising prices and falling sales is a trap that Japanese sports cars have fallen into before. The Honda Civic CRX, known in its later years as the Honda del Sol, and the Toyota Supra were cars that suffered a similar fate.

Did Mazda misread the Canadian market? In explaining things, one industry analyst stated, "Customers' expectations evolve. In the sports car segment, return customers wanted more and more bells and whistles. That costs money. For a manufacturer like Mazda, it's possible to decrease sales volume, and maintain or increase profit because of a higher price." That explanation sounds great in theory, but it misfires in practice.

The Miata started out as a simple sports car. It had nice lines, a peppy engine, and very basic appointments. While it was aimed at the 20-something crowd, the car was more popular with an older age group that wanted to recapture some of its lost youth. Rather than add the bells and whistles and increase the price, perhaps Mazda should have kept things simple—they might have attracted the next generation of 35- to 45-year-olds who were chasing the same dream. Today, a fully-loaded Miata is priced as high as $35 000. Is the Miata's future in doubt?

Adapted from Betsy McKay, "Coca-Cola sets prices at premium," *Globe and Mail*, November 16, 1999, p. B.18; Jeff Jackson, "Two seater sticker shock," *Financial Post Magazine*, August 1999, pp. 60-61.

Courtesy: Mazda Canada

full pay-out lease

lease term is up, the residual value belongs to the lessor. This is a standard arrangement if a consumer is leasing an automobile. A **full pay-out lease** is a longer-term lease, and the lessor recovers the full value of the equipment's purchase price through monthly payments. It operates much like a bank loan, with the leased goods as collateral. In effect, it is like 100 percent financing with no down payment. This type of lease is more common for items classified as capital goods (e.g., heavy construction equipment, manufacturing equipment).

Leases provide advantages for buying organizations and marketing organizations. For the buying organization, a lease preserves working capital for other ventures, and it allows the company to keep pace with technology (e.g., trade up to new equipment at the end of the lease period). This is a good option for companies that want to keep pace with computer technology, a market in which products become obsolete quickly. Payment schedules are usually lower than those financed by a standard bank loan. For the marketing organization, a lease provides a sale that otherwise would have been lost if the purchaser had to buy it. Financially, the same amount of money is collected but over a longer period. This helps the cash flow in the marketing organization.

Summary

The pricing policies of an organization are the rules it establishes for setting prices that will enable it to achieve marketing objectives. Price policies are generally divided into four categories: psychological pricing (pricing concerned with tendencies in consumer behaviour), geographic pricing (pricing that takes into account freight and shipping costs and whether the seller or the buyer is to absorb such costs), promotional pricing (pricing concerned with the availability of discounts and allowances for attracting potential customers), flexible pricing (charging different prices to different customers), and product-mix pricing (establishing low and high prices for various combinations of product offerings so that on balance profits are maximized).

In managing price strategy, an organization starts with a list price and then offers discounts and allowances to potential buyers. The discounts commonly offered to distributors include cash discounts for prompt payment; slotting allowances for securing distribution of new products; quantity discounts, which are meant to encourage volume purchases; performance allowances that are paid to customers for performing a promotional function; seasonal discounts; rebates, which are temporary discounts intended to stimulate demand; and trade-in allowances.

As an alternative to offering discounts, some firms are moving to value pricing, whereby everyday low prices become the norm instead of the cyclical system of offering regular prices followed by sale prices.

When a firm introduces a product, it chooses between price skimming and price penetration. Price skimming involves the use of a high entry price, which maximizes revenue and recovers development costs as quickly as possible. It is a strategy suitable for innovative products or for products perceived as offering better value. In the case of price penetration, the organization employs a low price in order to gain wide market acceptance for a product and to discourage potential competitors from entering the market.

Implementing price strategies can be a problem for an organization, which must be careful to stay within the laws. In advertising price, an organization must make fair and reasonable representations or suffer the consequences of court decisions. All discounts offered must be made available to all competing distributors and must be offered, where applicable, on a proportionate basis, that is, distributors must be treated fairly in accordance with their size.

Finally, leasing is becoming a popular pricing strategy in the Canadian marketplace. Certain industries—computer, automobile, and aircraft, for example—now frequently use leasing in order to generate new business. For the marketer, the primary advantage of leasing is that it preserves a sale that would have been lost had the lease option not been available. Leasing enables the lessee to avoid the debt load that would result from buying.

Key Terms

bill-back 301
cash discounts 300
customary pricing 294
F.O.B. destination 296
F.O.B. origin 296
flexible pricing 297
forward buying 305
full pay-out lease 309
geographic pricing 295
lease 307
list price 298
loss leaders 295
multiple-unit pricing 295
odd-even pricing 293
off-invoice allowance 301
operating lease 307
performance allowance 301

phantom freight 296
prestige pricing 292
price lining 294
price penetration 306
price skimming 305
promotional pricing 295
psychological pricing 292
quantity discounts 300
rebates 302
seasonal discounts 302
slotting allowance 300
trade-in allowance 304
uniform delivered pricing 296
unit pricing 294
value pricing (everyday low pricing) 304
zone pricing 297

Review Questions

1. Identify and briefly explain the various types of psychological pricing.
2. What is a loss leader, and what role does it play in pricing strategy?
3. Briefly explain the difference between uniform delivered pricing and zone pricing. Under what conditions is one option better than the other?
4. Briefly explain the nature of the following product-mix price policies
   a) Optional-feature pricing
   b) Captive-product pricing
   c) Fixed-variable pricing
   d) Product-bundling pricing
5. Briefly explain the nature and role of (a) quantity discounts, (b) trade discounts, and (c) performance allowances.
6. Briefly contrast a price-skimming strategy with a price-penetration strategy. Under what conditions is one option better than the other?
7. Explain the concept of price lining. What are the advantages of this type of pricing strategy?
8. What objectives do the following types of allowances achieve: (a) slotting allowance, (b) off-invoice allowance, and (c) performance allowance?

9. Briefly explain the concept of value pricing.

10. What is the difference between an operating lease and a full pay-out lease?

Discussion and Application Questions

1. Visit a car dealer in your area. Select a particular model of car and examine the pros and cons of leasing the car versus buying the car. Which method is best, and why?

2. Refer to the Marketing in Action vignette "Price Incentives Stimulate Sales, Hurt Profits." Evaluate the dilemma that automobile manufacturers find themselves in. Are there other marketing solutions that you can offer?

3. Is it fair to charge different customers different prices? Discuss.

4. Which pricing strategy (penetration or skimming) is best suited to the following new product introductions?

   a) A new line of deodorant and antiperspirant (brand name: Trust) for the unisex market

   b) A new HDTV (high-definition television) set from Sony

   c) A new, low-cholesterol margarine that looks and tastes just like butter

   d) A new tire whose tread design repels water, keeping it away from the tire in rainy conditions.

5. Review the Marketing in Action vignette "Coke and Mazda Rethink Price Policies." What price strategy is best for a brand like Coca-Cola? How frequently should the brand go on sale? Is advertising a brand image more important than price? Discuss.

6. Conduct some secondary research on Everyday Low Pricing (EDLP). How is it being implemented in Canada and what companies are involved with it? What effect has EDLP had on the sales and profits of the companies involved? Have consumers reacted positively to it?

E-Assignment

In this assignment, you will assess the discount programs offered by various rental car companies. Visit the Web sites of at least two companies in this industry. Select from Hertz, Budget, Thrifty, or another popular brand name. Surf the sites to determine the nature and extent of the discounts that each company offers. Very often, price incentives of the car rental company are tied in with incentives from other travel companies. This marketing strategy may influence a rental decision. At each site, take the steps indicated to secure rates for a typical reservation (e.g., a weekend rental). Which site offers the best rate? (Beware of hidden charges or charges contained in fine print.) Are prices and price incentives clearly communicated to the customer? Is there a reason why you might rent a vehicle from one company and not from the other? Is your decision based on price, or is some other aspect of marketing more important? State your position on the basis of your experience in visiting the Web sites.

Endnotes

1. Gabrielle A. Brenner and Rauven Brenner, "Memory and markets, or why you pay $2.99 for a widget," *Journal of Business*, vol. 55, no. 1, 1982, pp. 147-158.

2. Paul Hunt, "Analyzing the psychology of pricing," *Marketing*, February 25, 2002, p. 27.

3. Bruce McIlroy and David A. Hacker, "Unit pricing six years after introduction," *Journal of Retailing*, Fall 1979, pp. 45-47.

4. Conway Daly, "Quebec plans to ease price-tag rules for big retailers," *Globe and Mail*, September 6, 1999, p. B4.

5. Dale Beckman, David Kurtz, and Louis Boone, *Foundations of Marketing* (Toronto: HBJ Holt Canada Limited, 1988), p. 865.

6. Carolyn Green, "No more free lunches for corporate suppliers," *Financial Post*, April 21, 1991, p. 34.

7. Mike Sleeper, "Changing roles for manufacturers/brokers in the retail equation," www.imperialdist.com/articles.

8. James Pollack, "GPMS head calls for straight-forward pricing," *Marketing*, May 10, 1993, p. 4.

9. Mercedes Cardona and Jack Neff, "Everything's at a premium," *Advertising Age*, August 2, 1999, p. 12.

10. "Air Canada unveils 'Zip': new western discount airline, *CBC News*, April 19, 2002, www.cbc.ca/stories.

11. David Powell, *Canadian Market Review & Outlook World Leasing Yearbook 2002*, Canadian Finance & Leasing Association, www.cfla.ca/yearbook2002.

PhotoDisc

P A R T

6

Distribution

This section shows the role of distribution in the marketing mix. Key topics include distribution planning, physical distribution and marketing logistics, wholesaling, and retailing. Chapter 12 presents the structure of distribution channels and how they are managed, the concept of integrated marketing systems, and the nature of physical distribution and logistics management.

Chapter 13 describes the various types of wholesalers and retailers and the functions they perform. Emphasis is placed on new forms of retailing on the Canadian scene.

CP Picture Archive (Rene Johnston)

Distribution Channels
and Physical Distribution

six

After studying this chapter, you will be able to

1. Define distribution planning and describe the different types of channels and functions of channel members.
2. Describe the factors considered in selecting channels of distribution.
3. Outline the conflicts present in a channel and the strategies used to reduce conflict.
4. Explain the concept of integrated marketing systems.
5. Explain the various components of logistics management.

distribution

The third element of the marketing mix is place or distribution. **Distribution** involves all the functions and activities related to the transfer of goods and services from one business to another or from a business to a consumer. Given the competitive nature of the market today, business organizations constantly strive to improve the efficiency of their distribution systems. Very often, the goal of an organization is to reduce the costs of distribution to improve profit margins or to find new channels of distribution to gain competitive advantage.

Distribution Planning

1.
Define distribution planning and describe the different types of channels and functions of channel members.

distribution planning

Distribution planning is "a systematic decision-making process regarding the physical movement and transfer of ownership of goods and services from producers to consumers."[1] The physical movement and transfer of ownership include activities such as order processing, transportation, and inventory management. These activities are carried out among members of the channel of distribution, which comprises organizations and people commonly referred to as wholesalers, retailers, agents, and brokers. In marketing terminology, these organizations are called channel members, intermediaries, or middlemen.

BASIC ROLE OF INTERMEDIARIES

intermediary

An **intermediary** offers producers the advantage of being able to make goods and services readily available to target markets. A manufacturer located in Winnipeg, Manitoba, would have difficulty contacting retail customers in all parts of Canada if it did not have a direct sales force of its own, and even if it did have such a sales force, it would not be able to contact its customers frequently. To address this difficulty, the manufacturer sells to a wholesaler that, in turn, contacts retail customers and supplies the product to them (Figure 12.1). In option A of this figure, 16 transactions occur when four different manufacturers attempt to reach four consumers. In option B, where an intermediary is used, the transactions are reduced to eight. Option B provides a more economical transfer of goods.

Intermediaries provide assistance to manufacturers in the sorting process. The **sorting process** includes the accumulation, allocation, sorting, and assorting of merchandise. Sorting is necessary because manufacturers and consumers have different objectives. Manufacturers like to produce and market limited variety in large quantities, whereas

sorting process

Economies of a Distribution System

Figure 12.1

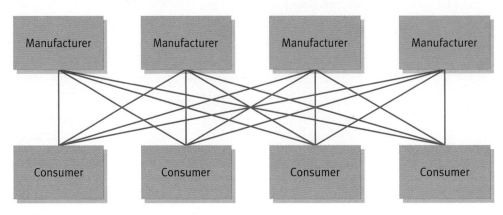

Option A. With no distributor, 16 transactions occur.

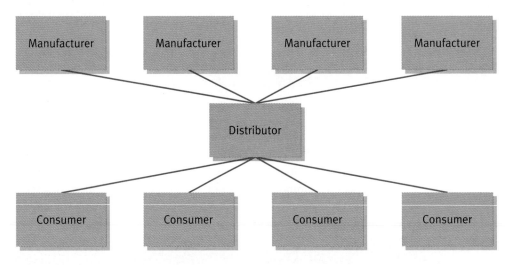

Option B. The inclusion of a distributor reduces the number of transactions to eight.

consumers want a large selection of brands, colours, sizes, and price ranges. Sorting reconciles these basic differences. Let us examine each stage of the sorting process.

accumulation

Accumulation involves wholesalers purchasing and storing quantities of merchandise that come from many producers. The wholesalers re-distribute the merchandise in small quantities among the retailers they serve.

allocation

Allocation is a function provided by wholesalers and retailers that involves dividing the goods available from a producer among the various wholesale and retail customers. In times of great supply, customers can order the quantity they need and be confident of receiving the required amount. In times of high demand and short supply, a producer would have to allocate goods among its various wholesalers, who, in turn, would do the same for the retail customers. This situation could occur during a labour strike, when goods may not be readily available, or when there is unprecedented demand for a product (e.g., a fad item such as a hot toy product).

sorting

Sorting involves separating merchandise into grades, colours, and sizes. For example, fruit is graded "choice" or "fancy" for the purposes of labelling canned goods. Eggs are graded as "grade A small," "medium," "large," and "extra large." The function of **assorting** involves making sure that the merchandise is available to consumers in an adequate variety of brand names, features, and price ranges.

assorting

The Structure of Distribution Systems

TYPES OF DISTRIBUTION CHANNELS

direct channel

Channels of distribution are either direct or indirect. A **direct channel** is a short channel, one in which goods move from producers to consumers without the use of intermediaries. Organizations that use the Internet to market goods are employing a direct channel. An **indirect channel** is a long channel, one in which goods are moved through a series of intermediaries before reaching the final customer (Figure 12.2).

indirect channel

Manufacturer to Consumer

The manufacturer-to-consumer channel of distribution is a *direct* channel, in which manufacturers themselves contact and distribute to the final users. It may take the form

The Channels of Distribution

Figure 12.2

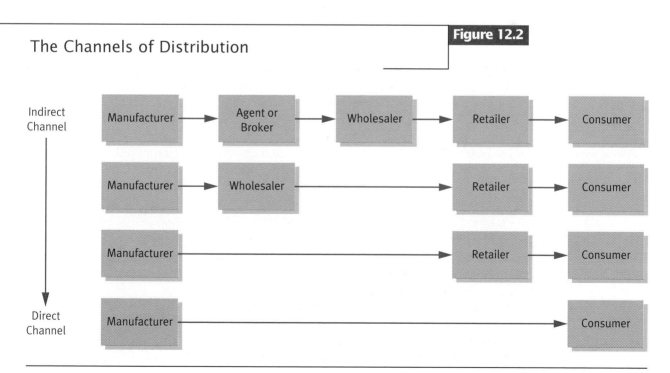

of a business-to-business transaction or a transaction in which a business sells directly to a consumer. Software companies, for example, can sell their products directly to consumers online and then distribute the products electronically. Financial services companies, such as Canada Life and London Life, sell directly through their head office or regional branch offices to consumers, using their own sales force.

The growth of online marketing is changing the nature of direct distribution. Organizations that traditionally did not sell directly to consumers are finding ways to do so via the Internet. Dell Computers is an innovator in this area. Dell built its entire business on direct distribution strategies initially through toll free 1-800 numbers. For Dell, the Internet was simply a logical extension to this strategy. Today, Dell operates one of the highest volume Internet commerce sites in the world. Dell generates more than $50 million per day in revenue over the Internet, and the Internet accounts for slightly over half of its total annual business.[2]

Manufacturer to Retailer to Consumer

The inclusion of a retailer makes the channel somewhat indirect. The retailer provides consumers with convenient access to goods. Apparel manufacturers, such as Levi Strauss (blue jeans and leisure wear), Nike (sport shoes and leisure clothing), and Tan Jay (ladies' fashions), sell directly to retail buyers of department stores and corporate chain stores. Retailers often store the merchandise in their own central warehouses so that it can be distributed to retail stores at a later time. Sometimes the manufacturer will open their own stores to sell goods. Sony, for example, operates a chain of Sony Stores to sell its consumer electronics products.

Direct channels are employed when a company wants to maintain control of its marketing programs and have close contact with customers.

Manufacturer to Wholesaler to Retailer to Consumer

Colgate-Palmolive
www.colgate.com

The addition of channel members increases the number of transactions and makes the channel indirect. The addition of a wholesaler is common in industries where products are ultimately sold through numerous types of retail outlets—convenience goods, such as food, household cleaning products, personal care products and pharmaceuticals, fall into this category (Figure 12.3). A manufacturer, such as Colgate-Palmolive (personal-care products) or S. C. Johnson (waxes and household cleaning products), ships its goods to wholesalers, who in turn ship to retailers they serve. Sobeys Inc., for example, operates its own wholesaling division in the form of four distribution centres strategically located across Canada. The wholesaling division is responsible for the redistribution of products to all Sobeys' retailers that include Sobeys, IGA, Price Chopper, Bonichoix, and Foodland, among many others.

Channels That Include Agents and Brokers

The inclusion of agents and brokers makes the channel very long. Typically, an agent or a broker represents a host of small manufacturers who do not have the resources to sell through the channel themselves. In this system, the agent or broker represents the manufacturer to the wholesale and retail trade or to the final consumer and earns a commission based on the sales generated. Independent general insurance brokers, for

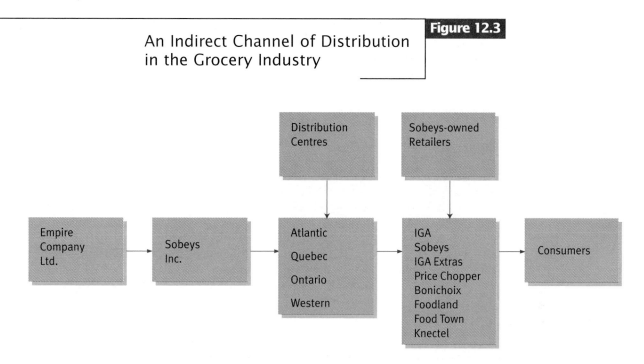

An Indirect Channel of Distribution in the Grocery Industry

Figure 12.3

Empire Company Ltd. → Sobeys Inc. → Atlantic / Quebec / Ontario / Western → IGA / Sobeys / IGA Extras / Price Chopper / Bonichoix / Foodland / Food Town / Knectel → Consumers

Distribution Centres

Sobeys-owned Retailers

Products ordered by Sobeys Inc. from suppliers are delivered to regional distribution centres. The distribution centres perform the wholesaling function and redistribute products to company-owned and -operated retail outlets. This is an example of corporate vertical marketing integration.

example, represent numerous companies when they are selling automobile insurance. On the basis of their customers' needs, these brokers search among their insurance providers for the best price. Since the manufacturer is not in direct contact with the customer, it has less control in marketing its product.

Figure 12.2 illustrates the channels available to marketing organizations. Generally speaking, consumer goods tend to use indirect channels, while industrial goods tend to use shorter channels. Industrial marketers use shorter channels because of the geographic concentration of customers, the limited numbers of customers, and the specific design of products to suit unique customer needs. Service channels tend to be shorter due to the intangibility of services and the need for personal relationships in the marketing process.

Traditional models, such as those just mentioned, are changing. Both business-to-business companies and manufacturers of consumer goods are evaluating the Internet as a means of generating customer contact and ultimately as a means of distributing goods. Therefore, such factors as the numbers of customers and location of customers may be less important now when determining which type of channel to use. Companies that are embracing electronic commerce technology prefer to do business with similar companies. Consequently, companies are open to new sources of supply based on the technological needs of their organization.

FACTORS CONSIDERED IN DEVELOPING A CHANNEL

2.
Describe the factors considered in selecting channels of distribution.

Which type of channel a firm uses depends on which markets it would like to reach and what objectives are to be achieved. A number of questions must be answered: What levels of customer satisfaction are necessary? What functions will intermediaries perform? What degree of coverage is desired? Organizations consider the following characteristics when making channel decisions.[3]

Customer Location

Autobytel, Inc.
www.autobytel.com

A manufacturer that wants to reach a large, geographically dispersed customer group requires indirect channels; the costs would be excessive if they were to contact widely dispersed customers directly and transport goods to them. In contrast, to reach a few customers that need lots of service requires short channels. The potential of the Internet to sell goods to distant customers is altering traditional thinking on this matter. Until recently, customers always purchased new cars at car dealerships. Now, Ford and GM, in response to competition online from such companies as Autobytel, are examining streamlined dealer networks and the Internet as a means of retaining customers.

Product Characteristics

Perishable goods like fruits and vegetables require direct channels or channels whereby the goods are transferred quickly to avoid spoilage. Products requiring installation and frequent maintenance, such as photocopiers and plant machinery, also require direct channels. Companies such as IBM, Compaq, and Xerox use a variety of channels, but they ship directly to other business organizations. The technical information communicated by their sales force to potential buyers necessitates the direct approach. For frequently purchased, inexpensive convenience goods, such as confectionery products and household cleaning supplies, indirect channels are used.

Trends and conditions in the marketplace are reshaping distribution decisions in organizations. IBM, Compaq, Canon, and a host of their competitors are experimenting with the Internet to market and distribute goods. In developing online marketing systems, all these companies have encountered glitches, and they are generally dissatisfied with the result they have achieved. The root of the problem is customer service, one of the cornerstones of direct channel distribution. Research survey after research survey indicates that online marketing companies neglect service and follow-up to a certain degree. The result is a high level of dissatisfaction in customers. This demonstrates that the buying process is complex and if a company does not cater to human factors in the selling and buying process, it will fail.[4]

Competition

It is appropriate to employ the same channels as competitors and to employ channels that are common to a particular industry, but a firm gains a competitive advantage by developing a new channel of distribution. Having a product available in a non-traditional environment results in new purchases by consumers. For example, well-known retailers, such as Tim Hortons, Second Cup, and Starbucks, and manufacturers, such as Campbell's Soup, Sara Lee, and Nestlé, are expanding into hospital and school cafeterias.[5] In Britain, Nestlé is experimenting with Nescafé Coffee Houses. Their goal is to tap into the trend of more people eating and drinking outside the home more often.

Nestlé established a corporate objective of finding ways of interacting with and delivering products to consumers more directly, rather than relying solely on retailers.[6]

To gain a competitive edge in the battle for soft drink supremacy, Pepsi-Cola recently sealed a contract agreement with United Airlines whereby Pepsi controls all pouring rights on all United Airline flights worldwide. The Pepsi-Cola Company is a major corporate customer of United Airlines.[7] Contract distribution is discussed in more detail later in the chapter.

Due to competitive pressure and changing consumer buying patterns, IBM Canada has decided to shut down its retail operation. The company finds that more customers are buying their personal computers at IBM's Web site and small businesses are buying from resellers (other dealers who assist with installation). Canada was the only country where IBM had its own stores.[8]

Company Resources

**Thomas, Large &
Singer Inc.**
www.thomas
largesinger.com

Size and financial resources determine which marketing functions a firm can or cannot handle. Small firms with customers located from coast to coast generally need to transfer the distribution function to intermediaries, who can perform the task with greater efficiency. Small manufacturers of food products, for example, that do not have their own sales force, rely on food brokers to contact wholesalers and retailers on their behalf. Thomas, Large & Singer Inc. is an example of a broker that calls on retail grocery stores, food service establishments, and industrial buyers. This broker serves these market segments through their own sales force and a full-service warehouse.

Large companies have more flexibility and can employ their own direct sales force or use a combination of direct and indirect channels, depending on the customer segments they are going after. The Internet is proving to be a cost-efficient way for small and large businesses to reach customers efficiently. For small businesses, the Internet has levelled the playing field.

Stage in the Product Life Cycle

The stage a product has reached in the product life cycle also affects what channel is used. An attempt is made to use a channel that offers the service and adds the value suitable for the particular stage a product has reached and for the rate of growth in the overall market. The service and value provided by channel members (wholesalers and retailers) before, during, and after a transaction occurs are taken into account. Considered are such factors as warehousing (e.g., the ability to maintain adequate inventory) and selling (e.g., customer contact and after-sales service).

In the *introduction* stage, when innovators and early adopters comprise the market, distribution is usually difficult to achieve. Products, therefore, are sold through retail specialists who spot trends, screen and select the best new products, and act as a communication link between manufacturers and leading-edge consumers (those who like to try new products when they first arrive on the scene). To illustrate, when the Internet was in its early years, service providers were small local companies—then along came Bell Sympatico, Rogers Communications, and several other cable companies. These larger companies now dominate the market. New dot-com companies such as Amazon.com decided to deal directly with customers online right away—there is no need for a storefront in today's business environment.

In the *growth* stage, buyers come from the early majority segment, and market growth is rapid. The producer requires new channels of distribution to reach a broader range of consumers. The channel must now be able to handle the tremendous increase in volume. Typically, mass merchandisers—large wholesaling and retailing operations, such as Sears and the Bay—enter the distribution picture at this stage to capitalize on a popular product trend.

In the *mature* stage, a market segment referred to as the late majority start buying the product. Market growth is marginal or flat. Generally, the motivation for making a purchase is low price. Discount retailers, such as Zellers and Wal-Mart, will play a more prominent role in the marketing and merchandising of the product.

In today's competitive marketplace, the distinction between department stores and discount department stores has blurred as consumers search for the best value. Both types of stores appeal to the early adopters and early and late majority adopters, and hence they are all useful distributors in the growth and mature stages.

In the *decline* stage, a product will lose distribution as existing retailers move onto newer products. Volume is declining rapidly. Therefore, channels adding little value to the product start to dominate. Direct marketing through direct-mail programs is a good example of the type of channel used. Mail programs simply communicate that a product is available and that it can be distributed directly to the customer at a certain price. Services normally associated with retailing are not important.

Throughout the life cycle of a product, firms constantly evaluate new distribution options. Distribution makes the product available, and the more readily available a product is, the greater is the likelihood of purchase. Sometimes consumers can find a product where they would least expect to. Starbucks coffee is now available in Chapters Bookstores and on Via Rail trains. Second Cup coffee is available on Air Canada flights. As mentioned above, Pepsi-Cola products are the only soft drink beverages served on United Airlines, and full-serve McDonald's restaurants exist in Wal-Mart stores. Having a product available in a non-traditional location prompts impulse purchases and is a good way of reaching first-time customers via a trial purchase of the product.

CHANNEL LENGTH AND WIDTH

channel length

When trying to develop an appropriate channel, a producer must consider two characteristics: length and width. **Channel length** refers to the number of intermediaries or levels in the channel of distribution. As indicated earlier, channels are direct (short) or indirect (long). As products increase in price, sell less frequently, and require more direct forms of communication to keep customers informed, the channels become shorter and contain fewer intermediaries. The direct communication of accurate, often technical, product information between a seller and a buyer is more important under these conditions.

As channels become longer, control shifts from the producer to others in the channel. When this situation occurs, the producer implements "pull" strategies (advertising and promotional messages directed at final users) to assist in moving a product through the channel.

channel width

Channel width refers to the number of intermediaries at any one level of the channel of distribution. The width of the channel depends on how widely available a producer wants its product to be. Convenience goods, such as milk, bread, tobacco, candy and gum, toothpaste, and deodorant have wide channels of distribution at both wholesale and retail levels. Shopping goods, such as clothing, furniture, and appliances, require a narrower or more selective list of retailers to sell to consumers. Wholesalers may or may not be used in these markets. Specialty goods are generally available in only a limited number of locations for any particular geographic market. For example, a market the size of Regina (Saskatchewan) or Kitchener (Ontario) would only need one Mercedes-Benz dealer. A market the size of Vancouver has six dealers.

Manufacturers and other suppliers of goods and services are not restricted to any one channel. Xerox, Microsoft, and IBM all market high-tech goods and services to industrial, institutional, professional, dealer, and consumer markets, using different channels to reach these targets. In effect, these firms use multiple channels (Figure 12.4). A **multiple channel** is a type of distribution for which different kinds of intermediaries are used at the same level in the channel of distribution. Microsoft can ship its software directly to dealers who, in turn, sell the product to consumers and business customers, or Microsoft can market and distribute software directly to consumers or business customers online. In this case, two different channels are used to reach the same end user.

multiple channel

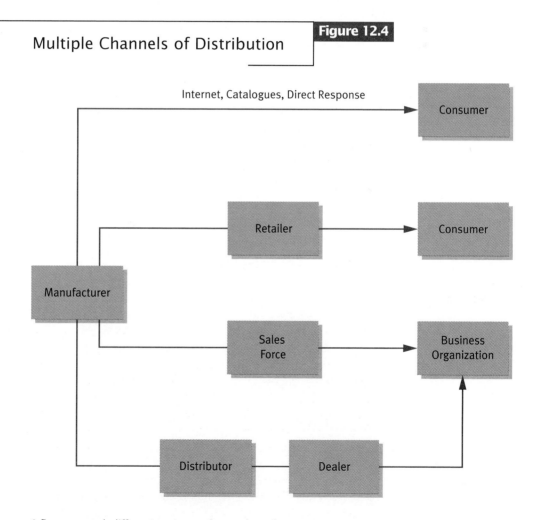

Multiple Channels of Distribution

Figure 12.4

A firm can reach different customers in a variety of ways.

INTENSITY OF DISTRIBUTION

In planning distribution and developing an appropriate type of channel with the proper length and width, a producer has to consider what sort of coverage of the market is needed. The degree of market coverage or the availability of a product can be intensive, selective, or exclusive (Figure 12.5).

intensive distribution

1. An **intensive distribution** strategy is used by a company that wants to reach as much of the population as possible. This usually applies to low-priced, frequently purchased, branded, convenience goods requiring no service or limited service. Producers continually search for new wholesale and retail outlets to sell through so that the product is convenient for the customer to purchase. It is a strategy directed at the largest number of consumers. Part of Tim Hortons' success is attributed to distribution. At one time in Kingston, Ontario there were only 3 Tim Hortons serving a population of 115 000. Today there are 11 locations strategically located to serve the same population. Competitor establishments are few and far between.

selective distribution

2. A **selective distribution** strategy is suitable for medium-priced shopping goods that are purchased less frequently. With this type of distribution, the product is available in only a few outlets in a particular market. Selective distribution is often appropriate for consumer shopping goods and for industrial accessory equipment, where consumers may have preferences for particular brand names. In this situation, limiting the number of retailers allows the marketing organization to reduce total marketing costs while establishing better relationships with channel members. The number of Ford or GM dealerships in a city is an example of selective distribution.

exclusive distribution

3. An **exclusive distribution** strategy is sought for high-priced shopping or specialty goods that offer the purchaser a unique value. Typically, the product is purchased infrequently and is associated with prestige and status. In any given geographic area, only one dealer or retail outlet exists, a circumstance which helps protect the pro-

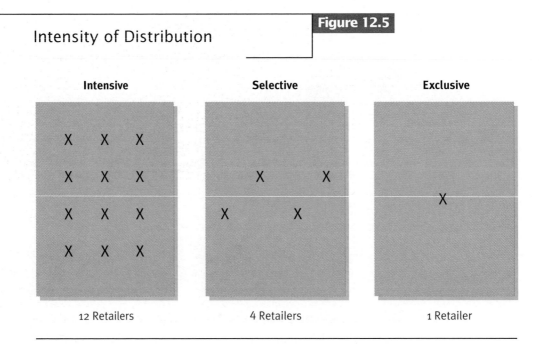

Figure 12.5

Intensity of Distribution

Intensive	Selective	Exclusive

12 Retailers   4 Retailers   1 Retailer

ducer's image. Typically, the producers and retailers cooperate closely in decisions regarding advertising, promotion, inventory carried by the retailers, and prices. The producer's goals are to present a prestigious image and maintain channel control. High profit margins on every unit sold compensate for lower volume sales.

Channel Conflict and Cooperation

All channel members have the same basic objectives of making a profit, providing efficient distribution, and keeping customers satisfied. However, the strategies used by the different members in a channel often lead to problems or conflict between members. Potential sources of conflict often revolve around disagreements on distributor functions or a desire to retain control by a particular member of the channel.

In today's Canadian marketplace, the balance of control or power in some markets has shifted from manufacturers to retailers due to the convergence and consolidation of retailing empires. In Canada right now, 5 large grocery distributors led by Loblaw Companies control about 80 percent of food store sales and, therefore, they control the most valuable commodity in retail marketing—shelf space. If your product is not available in their stores, you're dead! "Manufacturers will tell you the big grocery retailers have them by the short and curlies," says the president of one company.[9] Such control breeds conflict.

TYPES OF CONFLICT

3.
Outline the conflicts present in a channel and the strategies used to reduce conflict.

The most common types of conflict are horizontal conflict and vertical conflict.

Horizontal Conflict

horizontal conflict

Horizontal conflict stems from competition between similar organizations at the same level in the channel of distribution. For example, if Sears and the Bay are selling the same make and model of camera, each store may strive to have the better or more attractive price policy. But if one store constantly has the lower price, the store with the higher price may begin to question the manufacturer, inquiring whether the other retailer is receiving preferential treatment. Were better discounts offered to the store with the lower price? Such competition between similar firms is an example of horizontal conflict, which can flare into frustration and resentment.

Vertical Conflict

vertical conflict

Vertical conflict occurs when a channel member feels that another member at a different level is engaging in inappropriate conduct. For example, if wholesalers do not pass on discounts that are offered by manufacturers to retailers, friction between the wholesaler and retailer will develop. A manufacturer may pressure a wholesaler or retailer to keep prices at a certain level, but the action desired by the manufacturer may be contrary to the profit objectives of the distributors; conflict is the result.

Conflict is common between suppliers and retailers in situations where retailers have control of the channel. Zellers recently requested that a Montreal-based swimwear manufacturer increase its rebates from 16 to 19 percent if it wanted to retain the business. The swimwear company did not like the situation but said, "As the number of retailers you can sell to in Canada decreases, you have to deal with it." A spokesperson for Hudson's Bay, the owner of Zellers, said, "There's nothing wrong with such a request. It's just how things are done."[10] That may be so, but it does little to foster supplier–distributor relations.

Similarly, manufacturers who establish their own retail stores (e.g., Original Levi's Store and Sony Store) or set up their own Internet store to deal with consumers directly risk conflict with other independent retailers that sell their merchandise. The question remains: should manufacturers own and operate their own retail stores in direct competition with dealers that also distribute the same products? For more insight into this issue and the conflict it can create refer to the Marketing in Action vignette, **Should Manufacturers Be Retailers?**

ACHIEVING COOPERATION IN THE CHANNEL

channel captain

Securing cooperation in the channel of distribution is the task of the channel captain. A **channel captain** is a leader that integrates and coordinates the objectives and policies of all other members. The manufacturer is usually the first link in the channel but is not always the one that controls the channel. Depending on the circumstances, leadership and control may be held by the manufacturer, the wholesaler, or the retailer.

Manufacturer Control

Autonation, Inc.
www.autonation.com

When the manufacturer is in control, the channel is usually a direct one. Goods are distributed directly to the industrial user or to consumers, or they are distributed through a company-owned or -sponsored retail outlet (e.g., a dealer). Microsoft controls the sale and distribution of its computer operating systems. General Motors and Ford control the distribution of their automobiles through a dealer network in which each dealer must meet and maintain certain standards of operation. Both companies are in the process of streamlining their North American dealer networks to achieve greater efficiency and better pricing policies for consumers. They realize that their distribution systems are outdated and with new competition from mega-sized car dealers, such as Car Canada and AutoNation, and online distributors, such as Autobytel, they are at a competitive disadvantage. Changes are necessary. The goal for both companies is to regain control of the channel by having fewer super dealerships replace smaller local market dealerships.

Wholesaler Control

When a group of wholesalers controls the channel, the only way for manufacturers to gain access to retailers is through the wholesaling operation. For any product to be sold in Loblaws, Zehrs, No Frills, Your Independent Grocer, Valumart, Fresh Mart, Fortino's, Atlantic SaveEasy, Atlantic Superstore, or Atlantic SuperValue, it must pass through one wholesaling operation-Loblaw Companies East Distribution. Loblaws Companies Limited owns all these retail distributors. For a manufacturer to obtain distribution in any particular retail outlet, it must market its lines to Loblaws central buying office. Once the product is listed and approved for sale, the wholesaler acts as a coordinating body and service operation for the retailers it supplies. All merchandising and promotion activity is funnelled through the wholesaler. Figure 12.3 portrays visually the control held by wholesalers in the Canadian grocery trade. Sobeys Inc. is one of five wholesaler/retailer

Marketing in Action

Should Manufacturers Be Retailers?

John Forzani, the CEO of one of Canada's largest sports retailing companies, doesn't favour suppliers that set up retail operations. Given his position, perhaps his view is a bit biased! As an indication of his beliefs, Forzani recently bought a $3 500, 30-inch Sony television at Sounds Around, a local consumer electronics store—he avoided the Sony Store.

In justifying his position Forzani states, "It's a conflict. It makes it extremely difficult to compete with them." This point of view is shared by many a retailer. In the worldwide Sony system, Canada is unique. Canada is one of the few countries where Sony operates a national chain of stores, 72 outlets and counting. Its flagship store in the Toronto Eaton Centre is a haven for gadget-seekers who see interactivity as a key influence in the buying decision.

The degree and nature of competition is the real issue. The existing dealer network represents Sony effectively and does a good job selling its goods. When a supplier becomes a retailer, existing dealers stand to sell less of the same products. Sporting goods manufacturer Nike Inc. is the latest company to join the retail fray. As an added threat to existing retailers, Sony, Nike, and other companies are setting up Web sites to sell their goods directly to consumers.

In defending their position, Sony says, "We're not about stealing market share from our dealers. The Sony stores are a showcase for the brand, and in most cases, shoppers compare prices elsewhere before they buy." To their credit, Sony does not undercut dealers' prices.

Dealers seem resigned to competing with Sony. The Future Shop is one of those dealers. Future Shop sees a benefit to Sony's retail presence: they display products so well that it's a kind of advertisement for the goods. The stores have a polished look and that has pushed Future Shop to sharpen its merchandising, display, and pricing practices.

Sony stores have not always been profitable. In fact, they lost money until 1999. Their turnaround was helped by the consumers' rush in recent years for the latest home electronics toys. Stores are being relocated to more fashionable malls and revamped to blend entertainment with technology. It's quite a shopping experience.

Sony uses database marketing to build its business. It recently mailed out $10 gift certificates to its 60 000 best customers and ran a contest that offered prize values up to $10 000 on Sony merchandise in Sony stores. Now that's marketing that would scare the heck out of the existing dealer network!

Adapted from Marina Strauss, "Competition heats up as suppliers become retailers," *Globe and Mail*, November 3, 2000, p. M1.

Dick Hemingway

companies that control 80 percent of grocery store sales in Canada. It is also an example of vertical market integration, a concept discussed later in this chapter.

Retailer Control

Sometimes one retailer or a select group of retailers controls the process of selling to consumers a wide variety of manufacturers' products. Leading retailers with significant market share fall into this category. In the home hardware market and automotive supply market, a retailer like Canadian Tire has control. In the department store market Wal-Mart dominates. Among grocery retailers, Loblaws and its related retailers that were mentioned earlier are dominant. In the drugstore sector, Shoppers Drug Mart exercises considerable control. A few chains like these control a major portion the volume of merchandise sold through retail outlets in their market segment.

Some of the examples described under wholesaler control and retailer control appear to be similar. This is done intentionally to demonstrate that if true control is the goal, a company will operate on several levels of the channel of distribution. In the grocery business in Canada, the dominant wholesalers and the dominant retailers are one and the same.

In all the above situations, it is a marketing organization of some kind that is in control. It should be noted that online marketing and e-commerce have changed the power equation. Now, consumers have unprecedented access to information about products, competitive pricing, and sourcing options. If they are not satisfied with what one e-business offers, a competitor is just a mouse click away. Attracting e-shoppers and then retaining them requires a different mindset for traditional marketing organizations that are moving online.

Controlling the channel is a battle over who owns the consumer. If you're Wal-Mart (a retailer), you have a certain amount of control. If you're Coca-Cola (manufacturer), you have control. The truth is, no manufacturer, wholesaler or retailer has control. It works the other way around. If consumers aren't getting what they want, they will take their business somewhere else.

ENCOURAGING COOPERATION IN THE CHANNEL

To illustrate how cooperation is achieved, let us consider a situation in which the manufacturer is the channel captain. The channel captain motivates channel members to accomplish specific objectives or perform certain tasks by providing good service, attractive pricing policies, advertising and promotional support, and sales training (Figure 12.6). Another factor that has helped establish cooperation in the channel of distribution is the adoption of relationship marketing practices.

Figure 12.6

Conflict and Cooperation in Channels

Types of Channel Conflict

Horizontal

Conflict and competition between similar organizations at the same level of the channel

Vertical

Conflict between channel members at different levels of the distribution system

Channel Cooperation

A manufacturer encourages cooperation by:

1. Providing distributors with adequate and proper service in all facets of marketing and distribution support.

2. Providing fair and equitable pricing policies to all distributors.

3. Providing advertising and promotional support to encourage reselling and merchandising support.

4. Providing all dealers and retailers with adequate sales training so that all will benefit.

Service

To provide good service, to ensure dealers' orders can be filled quickly, the manufacturer maintains adequate inventory. In many cases, for example, car dealers in Canada can obtain original replacement parts within one day of the request. Advancing computer technology has certainly assisted in processing orders; they can now be accepted, processed, and delivered much more quickly than before.

Pricing Policies

Manufacturers recognize that every member of the channel must maintain a fair and competitive profit margin. Therefore, they establish list prices and offer discounts and allowances that permit members to make a reasonable profit. Movement of merchandise is a concern to middlemen; therefore, manufacturers must allow for higher margins on slow-moving items and lower margins on fast-moving items so that, on balance, the intermediary maintains a reasonable level of profit.

Advertising and Promotion

Another way to coordinate the different objectives of channel members is through cooperative advertising, which involves sharing of advertising expenses between manufacturers and distributors and the manufacturer providing copy and illustrations to be integrated into the distributor's advertising. This arrangement allows the manufacturer to promote its product while giving the distributor the opportunity to promote itself. Incentives, such as sales contests and dealer premiums, can also spark interest in a manufacturer's products, at least temporarily, and help gain distributors' support in increasing sales or in acquiring new accounts.

Sales Training

Manufacturers who train their distributors how to sell the product gain the interest of their distributors. Any training provided, particularly to the distributor's sales staff, encourages cooperation. Companies such as Compaq and Apple spend time training the sales staff of dealers' computer stores. Detailed training in hardware and software, which provides crucial product knowledge, is the key to success at this stage in the distribution process. The training is mutually beneficial; without it, dealers might be unable to persuade consumers or businesses to buy, and the dealer and the manufacturer would both suffer.

Adoption of the Relationship Marketing Concept

supply chain

supply chain management

As discussed in Chapters 1 and 5, relationship marketing involves the partnering of organizations in a chain of distribution, from supplier of raw materials to the ultimate consumer who purchases the end product, who then conduct business in such a way that all participants benefit. In the context of distribution strategy this relationship is often referred to as supply chain management. A **supply chain** is a sequence of companies that perform activities related to the creation and delivery of a good or service to consumers or business customers. **Supply chain management** refers to the integration of information among members of the supply chain to facilitate efficient production and delivery of goods to customers. Electronic commerce technology is fuelling the rise in sophisticated supply chain management programs in all kinds of industries. It is creating a seamless system between the original source of supply and the end user (see Figure 12.7).

The formation of electronic online relationships between distributors and suppliers is a means of improving efficiency and reducing conflict. It is a flexible system that advocates teamwork and cooperation among all organizations. The implementation of relationship marketing in distributing goods is discussed in more detail in the section on Physical Distribution in this chapter.

For more insight into the complex nature of relationships in the channel of distribution refer to the Marketing in Action vignette **War and Peace Between Ford, Ford Dealers**.

A Seamless Supply Chain

Figure 12.7

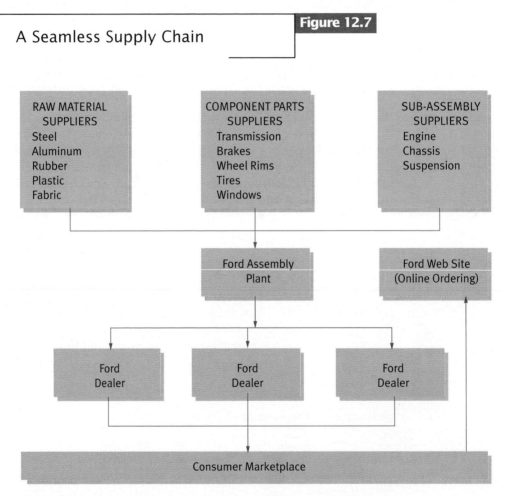

Numerous materials, component parts, and assembled parts must be available at the assembly plant at the right time. This indicates the importance of just-in-time inventory management practices and electronic order processing and delivery procedures. All partners in the channel of distribution must work toward the same goal.

 **Marketing in Action**

War and Peace Between Ford, Ford Dealers

After decades of maintaining a bloated, costly system of franchised dealers, Ford is moving rapidly to modernize the way they distribute and sell their cars and trucks. Ford is in the process of buying out some dealers, consolidating others, and experimenting with new ways to make the distribution and sale of vehicles more efficient.

Due to new competitive pressures from big, publicly owned dealer groups and the Internet, Ford is trying to squeeze costs out of a distribution system that has remained isolated from the massive streamlining that has been going on in the manufacturing and parts supply sectors of the industry.

A related distribution problem is location. Many Ford dealerships are located in downtown areas that made sense in the 1940s and 1950s. They are too small and too far off the beaten path to attract many consumers today. The planned restructuring calls for larger locations closer to where people live, work, and shop.

Ford's actions in Quebec City are indicative of what lies ahead, and that action has many dealers upset. There, Ford bought out four dealers and reduced the number of dealerships to three from five. Eventually, the plan is to have just one dealership with satellite service centres elsewhere in the city. Bobby Gaunt, the president of Ford, justifies the change, saying, "If one thinks they can continue to manage the business in the same way they always have, then they are being naive, and Quebec City is a good example of that." Another factor justifying the move is Ford's low market share in Quebec City. Here, it is only 12.5 percent, compared with the national average of 21 percent.

Manufacturer–dealer relations suffered another blow when Ford announced it was eliminating its separate Lincoln-Mercury dealerships. These dealers were to become Ford dealers. That would create a situation where a number of Ford dealers would be located less than one kilometre apart, leaving them to compete with each other rather than the real competition. To say the least, this decision caused lots of friction (vertical conflict) between the dealers and the manufacturer, and among the dealers themselves (horizontal conflict). Four Ford dealers subsequently launched a class-action lawsuit against the company, claiming their business has suffered since being converted to a Ford dealership.

Ford's position on all issues is very simple. The goal of the plan is to sell more cars, more efficiently, and to be a leader in customer service by 2004. It simply could not retain an archaic distribution system in such a rapidly changing marketplace.

A couple of years have passed since the changes were implemented and peace appears to have broken out between Ford and its dealers. Both parties agreed to embrace electronic commerce, and possibly reduce the number of dealers in some markets while increasing the number in others, changing the way customers are greeted and cutting the amount of time it takes to deliver a new vehicle from factory to consumer.

Ford has put on hold the concept of Ford Auto Collections. The auto collection idea involves dealers and Ford sharing ownership in one company that owns all dealers outlets in a city. This concept is used in several cities in the United States and, as described above, is being test marketed in Quebec City. The class-action lawsuit remains before the courts despite the fact that 22 Lincoln-Mercury dealers have settled their differences with Ford.

One would think there would be harmony between Ford and its dealers. After all, they are selling the same product. This case demonstrates that new policies and change in structure can create discord. Steps must be taken to mend fences in order to achieve the common goal—to sell more vehicles!

Adapted from Thomas Watson, "No plans to shut dealerships, Ford Canada says," *Financial Post*, June 28, 2001, p. C7; Greg Keenan, "Ford makes peace with dealers," *Globe and Mail*, September 14, 2000, p. B11; Greg White, "Ford plans to purchase dealerships," *Globe and Mail*, November 22, 1999, p. B12; and Greg Keenan, "Ford cutting dealerships to one in Quebec City," *Globe and Mail*, June 24, 1998, pp. B1, B11.

Dick Hemingway

Integrated Marketing Systems

4.
Explain the concept of integrated marketing systems.

In order to gain control of a channel of distribution or to foster cooperation among its members, a firm develops a planned integrated marketing system. There are two categories of integrated marketing systems: vertical marketing systems (or vertical integration) and horizontal marketing systems (or horizontal integration).

VERTICAL MARKETING SYSTEM

vertical marketing system (VMS)

In a **vertical marketing system (VMS)**, channel members are linked at different levels in the marketing process to form a centrally controlled marketing system in which one member dominates the channel. A channel captain has control in a vertical marketing system, whether the captain is the manufacturer, the wholesaler, or the retailer. There are three types of vertical marketing systems: administered, contractual, and corporate.

Administered VMS

administered VMS

In an **administered VMS**, the organization with the greatest economic influence has control. This firm plans the marketing program, and identifies and coordinates the responsibilities of each member. For example, category management systems implemented by grocery distributors (e.g., Safeway, Sobeys and Loblaws) puts the wholesaler/retailer in control of the channel. Suppliers such as Procter & Gamble and Kraft have to manage their brands within the shelf space they are allocated. As discussed in the pricing chapters, these retailers can place undue pressure of suppliers for discounts—a form of control. Companies like Wal-Mart and Canadian Tire also have control, since they contract with suppliers for a large portion of the suppliers' output. Canadian Tire, for example, arranges marketing agreements with manufacturers to supply its Mastercraft and Motomaster product lines.

Contractual VMS

As implied by the name, this VMS is governed by a legal agreement that binds the members in the channel. Three forms of contractual vertical marketing systems are possible: retail cooperatives, wholesale-sponsored voluntary chains, and franchises.

retail cooperatives

Retail cooperatives are composed of independent retailers that join together to establish a wholesaling operation (e.g., a large distribution centre). It is a system that is initiated by retailers and is designed to allow them to compete successfully with chain stores. Each retailer owns a share of the operations and benefits from the economies of scale in terms of buying and marketing goods. For example, lower prices are available to members in the form of discounts and allowances due to the higher volume of goods purchased collectively. Home Hardware is an example of a retail cooperative.

voluntary chain

**Independent Grocers
Alliance, Inc.**
www.igainc.com

A **voluntary chain** is initiated by the wholesaler and consists of a group of independent retailers organized into a centrally controlled system. Retailers agree to buy from the designated wholesaler. As in the case of the retail cooperative, the increased buying power results in lower prices for all retailers. IGA (Independent Grocers Alliance) and Western Auto are examples of voluntary chains. The voluntary chain implements inventory management programs, and merchandising and advertising programs that benefit all members.

franchise agreement

In a **franchise agreement**, the franchisee (retailer), in exchange for a fee, uses the franchiser's name and operating methods in conducting business. The success of franchises is based on the marketing of a unique product or service concept and on the principle of uniformity, according to which franchisees conduct business in a manner consistent with the policies and procedures established by the franchiser. Typically, franchise dealers receive a variety of marketing, management, technical, and financial services support in return for a fee. Regardless of their location, franchise operations, such as McDonald's, KFC, Second Cup, Budget Rent-A-Car, and Midas Muffler, offer goods and services as well as a quality level that customers are familiar with.

Corporate VMS

corporate VMS

A **corporate VMS** is a tightly controlled arrangement in which a single corporation owns and operates each level of the channel. The ownership and control of the channel can be located at either end, that is, manufacturers may own wholesalers and retailers, or retailers may own the source of supply. In Canada, George Weston Limited (one of Canada's largest bread and dairy products producers) is at the helm of a corporate VMS using forward integration. Weston is both a manufacturer and distributor of the products it makes. Its various manufacturing divisions include Weston Bakeries (makers of Wonder, D'Italiano, Country Harvest, and Weston breads) and Neilson Dairy (the largest milk producer in Ontario under the Neilson and Neilson Trutaste brand names). Weston also operates seafood and frozen food divisions. The products produced by these companies are readily available in all the distribution outlets owned by Weston. Among the retail distributors are Loblaws, No Frills, Atlantic Superstore, Provigo, Atlantic SaveEasy, and Your Independent Grocer.

forward integration

backward integration

Regardless of the type of vertical marketing system, the direction of control is forwards or backwards. In **forward integration**, manufacturers have control; in **backward integration**, retailers have control. Wholesalers can integrate either forwards or backwards.

To illustrate the forward integration concept, Coca-Cola licenses bottlers (wholesalers) in various markets to buy Coca-Cola syrup concentrate, who then carbonate, bottle, and sell the finished product to retailers in local markets. Production and marketing of the beverage must meet the specifications established by Coca-Cola. As indicated earlier in the chapter, the grocery industry is controlled by a small number of companies that operate a multitude of retail stores across Canada. This is an example of backward integration (refer to Figure 12.3).

Manufacturers must constantly meet the demands of these few retailers or they may incur losses in distribution.

HORIZONTAL MARKETING SYSTEMS

horizontal marketing system

In a **horizontal marketing system**, many channel members at one level in the channel have the same owner. In the Canadian hotel business, Choice Hotels operates under a variety of banners: Comfort, Quality, Sleep, Clarion, Rodeway, Econo Lodge, and Mainstay Suites. Choice Hotels are a leader in the value segment of the hotel industry. In the convenience-store industry, Alimentation Couche-Tard Inc., a large Quebec-based convenience store chain, operates a variety of stores under the following banners: Mac's, Beckers, Mike's Mart, Winks, and Daisy Mart. Couche-Tard is the dominant player in the convenience-store market in Canada.

Exploiting New Distribution Strategies

The identification and pursuit of new channels of distribution is now the battleground for companies wishing to expand. Several other practices are changing the nature of distribution strategy. These include the sale of products through direct marketing and electronic marketing techniques, multi-level marketing techniques and contract marketing, which guarantees exclusive availability of a product line in a particular establishment. Let us examine each of these practices.

THE MOVE TO DIRECT MARKETING AND ELECTRONIC MARKETING

In the pharmaceutical market, Glaxo, a prominent manufacturer, launched a 1-800 information line for migraine sufferers to call and request helpful information about Imitrex, its migraine medication. To fuel sales, it wants to plant information with the ultimate user who will request it when consulting a doctor. Pfizer Canada Inc. has done the same thing with Viagra, a drug designed to cure male impotence. Their print and television ads encourage men to talk to their doctor about the problem. Both companies feel that if consumers ask for the product, doctors will prescribe it. Another example of direct marketing in the pharmaceutical industry involves the distribution of prescription drugs through mail order pharmacies or from online pharmacies. In such a channel, it is possible to bypass traditional retail pharmacies and offer consumers lower prices.

Advancing technology makes marketing by mail, telephone, and the Internet very efficient. In all cases, the traditional channel of distribution is bypassed. For example, Amazon.com buys books from publishers and markets them directly to consumers. No brick and mortar stores are needed. Dell computer has built its entire business around direct marketing, first by telephone and now by the Internet and telephone. Orders received online by Dell now account for about half of the total business. In both cases, consumers are opting for convenience when buying online, an important factor that manufacturers must consider when developing a marketing strategy.

The issues of direct marketing and electronic marketing are discussed in detail in Chapters 15 and 17.

MULTI-LEVEL MARKETING

multi-level marketing, or network marketing

Multi-level marketing or network marketing, as it is often referred to, is a distribution system in which distributors are stacked on top of each other in a shape resembling a pyramid. Multi-level marketing companies depend on direct selling and a word-of-mouth distribution system. Friends tell friends about the company and its products, with each person getting a commission from sales by those distributors below them. Pyramid selling, which offers compensation for recruitment, is prohibited in Canada under the Competition Act, while multi-level marketing is legal.

Consumers are often approached about joining a multi-level marketing company. Many who join are successful, while others fail miserably. In assessing whether or not to get involved with such a practice, a consumer should be aware of exaggerated claims of earning potential, the nature of inventory management expectations (e.g., how much an individual has to stock), product return policies, and required purchases as a condition of entry into the system. According to recent laws, measures can be taken against companies that set up unreal expectations of earning potential, and if claims are made, they must be the average of all participants.

Amway Corp. is one of the oldest, most reputable, and most profitable multi-level marketing companies, selling home and personal care products worldwide since the 1950s. Their success is based largely on customer loyalty. Other organizations that have survived include the Fuller Brush Company and Watkins Inc. Some organizations in the multi-level marketing arena seem more concerned with making a quick buck. These firms reflect negatively on the entire direct selling industry.

CONTRACT MARKETING

In business-to-business marketing, selling via a contract is normal practice. A typical contractual agreement covers price policies, conditions of sale, territorial rights, service responsibilities, and contract length and termination conditions. More specifically, a supplier agrees to provide goods at certain prices or with certain discounts, and at a quality level that is guaranteed. Further, policies and procedures for returned merchandise are established. If geographical area of operation is an issue, that too must be established (e.g., exclusive territories for a Harvey's or KFC franchise). Usually, the buyer limits the duration of such a contract in order to maintain control. They also specify conditions that could lead to the termination of the contract.

Progressive companies with the desire to expand are breaking ground by using contract selling as a means to enter non-traditional channels or to steal business away from competitors in an existing channel of distribution. Alcan Aluminum Limited did just that when it signed an aluminum supply agreement with Ford Motor Co. Alcan will supply one-half of Ford's aluminum body sheet requirements and one-quarter of its wheel alloy needs. The deal is worth billions over the life of the contract.[11]

Exclusive distribution agreements can give one company a distinct advantage over a competitor. To illustrate, Coca-Cola Beverages has a five-year fountain sales agreement (1999–2002) with Prime Restaurants. Prime operates over 100 casual dining restaurants that include East Side Mario's, Casey's Grillhouse, Pat and Marios, Prime Pubs, and Red Devil Barbecue & Tavern. The complete line of soft drinks (Coca-Cola Classic, Diet Coke, Sprite, and Barq's), juices (Fruitopia and Minute Maid), and iced teas (Nestea) will be the only non-alcoholic beverages available in the restaurants.[12] Coca-Cola also has an exclusive distribution agreement with McDonald's.

Physical Distribution and Logistics Management

5.
Explain the various components of logistics management.

physical distribution, or logistics management

order processing

Physical distribution or logistics management involves planning, implementing, and controlling the physical flow of materials, finished goods, and related information from points of origin to points of consumption to meet customer requirements at a profit.[13] The components of a physical distribution system include order processing, warehousing, inventory management, transportation and transportation coordination, and customer service (Figure 12.8).

ORDER PROCESSING

Essentially, **order processing** involves four activities: a credit check of the customer placing the order (new customer); recording the sale (e.g., assigning it to a sales representative for commission purposes); making the necessary accounting entries; and then locating the item and shipping it. Inventories are adjusted once the four-step cycle is complete.

Components of Logistics Management

Figure 12.8

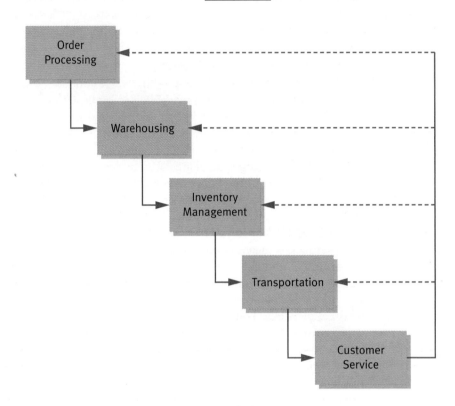

Good customer service affects all aspects of a logistics management system.

Sometimes, not all items that a customer orders are available for shipment. This situation is referred to as a **stockout**. Customers must be advised of stockout situations so that they will know if the item will be shipped automatically at a later date or if a new order must be placed for the item. In today's operating environment much of the ordering and billing processes is fully automated, if not completely done electronically between buyers and sellers.

stockout

WAREHOUSING

warehouse

storage warehouse

The role of a **warehouse** is to receive, sort, and re-distribute merchandise to customers. There are two types of warehouses: storage warehouses and distribution warehouses. A **storage warehouse** holds products for long periods of time in an attempt to balance supply and demand for producers and purchasers. Generally, these facilities are not specialized; they handle a variety of items, such as tires, equipment, appliances and other hard goods, and case goods. Very often, a storage warehouse stores manufacturer inventory that the manufacturer cannot handle in its own storage facilities.

distribution warehouse, or distribution centre

A **distribution warehouse, or distribution centre**, assembles and redistributes merchandise, usually in smaller quantities and in shorter periods of time. A variety of goods ordered by a customer are assembled into a truckload by the distribution centre for shipment to the customer. Sobey's warehouses, for example, receive shipments from a variety of manufacturers (see Figure 12.3). These warehouses store, assemble, and re-distribute the same merchandise in smaller quantities to their retail locations. The success of many organizations, including Wal-Mart and Canadian Tire, has been built on the efficiency of their distribution centres.

Modern warehousing operations are very sophisticated; some are fully automated, with orders being placed electronically. The use of hand-held scanners to place orders is commonplace in many retail operations. Orders are then processed from a fully automated warehouse that can read computerized orders, determine the correct quantity of each product, and move them in desired sequence to the loading dock. The automated system then determines how much stock is needed from producers. Automated warehouses are extremely expensive, but in the long term, they provide for cost efficiency in large-volume distributors, such as grocery and hardware chains.

INVENTORY MANAGEMENT

inventory management

Inventory management is a system that ensures a continuous flow of needed goods by matching the quantity of goods in inventory to sales demand so that neither too little nor too much stock is carried. It is the system of balancing supply with demand in such a way that the costs of carrying inventory are kept to a minimum, while enough inventory is maintained to meet the demands of customers.

just-in-time (JIT) inventory system

Many firms in Canada and the United States have adopted a system that is of Japanese origin called **just-in-time (JIT) inventory system**, the objective of which is to reduce the amount of inventory on hand by ordering small quantities frequently. Past practice involved ordering large quantities at low costs to save money in purchasing rather than in storing. A JIT inventory system is more feasible than ever, considering the use of computer technology in inventory planning and in other forms of business planning. The system is now referred to as **electronic data interchange (EDI)**. With EDI, companies in the channel of distribution exchange vital information electronically. The goal is to reduce inventory costs and ensure efficient transportation of goods to customers. All three North American automakers—General Motors, Ford, and Chrysler—as well as durable-goods and high-technology companies, such as General Electric and IBM, use such systems. Electronically exchanging data between companies online is becoming more commonplace.

electronic data interchange (EDI)

Retailers such as Canadian Tire and manufacturers such as General Motors have taken JIT a step further by having suppliers electronically linked to inventory databases. Such a practice is part of the relationship marketing concept that is popular in business today. General Motors formed a relationship with Formet, a manufacturing division of Magna International Inc. The Formet facility uses cutting-edge software and hardware and integrates every aspect of the supply chain process. It is the sole producer of GM truck frames in North America. Robots are linked to wireless equipment and a complex planning system that coordinates production, supply, purchasing, finance, and human resources through 300 000 transactions a day. The plant churns out 5000 frames a day—1.3 million a year. If it shuts down, production at all GM truck assembly plants shuts down.[14]

Magna International Inc.
www.magnaint.com

Canadian Tire is another company that has taken advantage of EDI. Canadian Tire now shares information with suppliers that it never did before—sales forecasts and point-of-sale information. Now, Canadian Tire buyers do not have to worry about calculating required inventory. Instead, buyers can focus on buying the correct merchandise, determining product mixes, and keeping up with the latest trends in the marketplace.

TRANSPORTATION

Transportation tends to be the most costly item in physical distribution. The goal of a transportation system is to be efficient so that the producer has a competitive advantage. Hence, a logistics manager evaluates the basic modes of transportation available for the delivery of goods and the location of the customer, and then selects the most efficient. The modes of transportation are truck, rail, air, and waterways.

Trucks are used to make small shipments over short distances. Deliveries within a local area or a certain region are made by truck. Truck transportation is also used for very long hauls, when time is not a consideration. The main advantages of truck delivery are that it can serve a number of locations, particularly distant and remote locations that other modes cannot reach. On the negative side, damages to goods do occur when using trucks. Truck transport is significant. Approximately 70 percent of Canada's two-way merchandise trade with the United States moves by truck (80 percent export and 60 percent import).[15]

Railways are the most efficient mode of transporting bulky items over long distances (e.g., farm equipment, machinery, steel, and grain). From Ontario and Quebec, new automobiles are shipped to destinations all over Canada and the United States. Trains can carry a wide range of products, and they serve a large number of locations. The frequency of shipments is, however, low.

Air carriers commonly carry expensive items that can absorb the high freight costs (e.g., technical instruments and machinery). It is also common to ship perishable goods and urgently needed goods by air. The appeal of this method lies in its speed and in the number of markets it serves, particularly major urban markets in Canada and around the world. Its high cost is its major disadvantage.

Shipping by **waterways** involves moving goods by ocean tankers and inland freighters. In Canada, waterway shipping through the St. Lawrence Seaway and the Great Lakes is common. The use of water transportation is widespread for bulky items, such as coal, iron ore, grain, chemicals, and petroleum products. High-value finished goods from overseas are also shipped by water. For example, automobiles from Japan and South Korea arrive in Vancouver by water carrier.

Water transportation is attractive because it allows a wide range of products to be moved at low cost, with only a small amount of loss or damage. On the other hand, movement by water is slow; water carriers can only reach certain places; and shipments tend to be infrequent.

TRANSPORTATION COORDINATION

To increase efficiency, more and more firms are employing a combination of transportation modes to ship their products. When several modes of transportation are used, containerization plays a key role. **Containerization** entails the grouping of individual items into an economical shipping quantity that is sealed in a protective container for intermodal transportation to a final customer. These loads are easily transferred from one mode of transportation to another as they reach different destinations (e.g., air to truck or rail to truck).

containerization

piggybacking

The most common form of intermodal transportation is piggybacking. **Piggybacking** is a system in which the entire load of a truck trailer is placed in a rail flatcar for movement from one place to another. The railway performs the long haul, and the truck performs the local pick-up and delivery. Other combinations for intermodal transportation are possible, such as the combination of trucking and water. For example, ferries are used to transport goods from Vancouver Island to the mainland, and trucks are used to complete the delivery of goods.

The combination of air and truck transportation is common for cargo carriers, such as UPS (United Parcel Service), Federal Express, and Air Canada Cargo. These companies combine truck fleets for ground travel with air cargo for overnight delivery to distant locations. Due to the growth of online marketing, business has been booming for third-party cargo carriers, such as UPS. Companies that have embraced the Internet as a means of marketing goods require the specialized services that UPS and others provide. As well, courier companies are now very active in larger shipments reflecting the just-in-time demands of today's supply chain-smaller, more frequent shipments that have helped eliminate inventory, and in many cases, entire warehouses from the distribution system.

freight forwarder

Freight forwarders are used when only small quantities of goods are to be shipped. A **freight forwarder** is a firm that consolidates small shipments—shipments that form less than a carload or truckload—from small companies. Freight forwarders are essential to firms that do not meet the minimum requirements of such traditional carriers as railways and trucks. The forwarders prosper because the common carrier charges them the carload or truckload rate, while they, in turn, charge their customers a higher rate to pay for their services and to generate a profit.

Ryder Integrated Logistics
www.ryder.com

Coordinating the transportation activities of a large company is a challenge, and sophisticated electronic technology is changing the way in which transportation alternatives are evaluated. Consequently, many firms are now looking at outsourcing their logistics management systems. It seems that companies would prefer to spend more time on what they do best, which is the manufacture and marketing of a product. Distribution and related issues are left to experts such as Ryder Integrated Logistics, a full-service trucking operation that specializes in just-in-time delivery.

CUSTOMER SERVICE

Determining how much customer service to provide and how much to spend on this service are the major considerations for a company that is developing a physical distribution strategy. To provide good service, suppliers of goods develop an order-processing system designed to maximize frequency (how often orders are received), speed (the time it takes to process orders), and consistency (the correct and punctual filling of orders). They also provide warehousing when necessary and develop emergency shipping policies.

In providing good distribution service, a firm evaluates costs against opportunities. Usually, the alternatives with the lowest costs are preferable to the organization, but not to the customer. Therefore, to encourage sales, firms may choose higher cost options. To illustrate, a producer might want to ship by rail, but loading and unloading at various points might slow down delivery. The customer might want prompt, direct shipment by truck transport, a method that could cost the producer more. To meet the service needs and expectations of customers, the firm may decide to ship by truck, despite the extra expense.

Summary

Distribution planning entails making decisions regarding the physical movement of merchandise and its transfer between producers and consumers. A channel of distribution comprises organizations known as intermediaries, middlemen, or channel members. The role of such intermediaries as wholesalers, agents, brokers, and retailers is to facilitate the transfer of merchandise in an efficient, economical manner.

Since manufacturers ship large quantities, while retailers and consumers purchase in small quantities, wholesalers provide a sorting function. Sorting refers to the accumulation, allocation, classification, and assorting of merchandise.

Channels of distribution are either direct (short) or indirect (long). Short channels are commonly used to distribute expensive capital goods under circumstances in which communications between the producer and buyer are crucial. For goods that are less valuable and purchased more frequently, long channels of distribution are used. The elements a firm considers when designing channel strategy include customer location, product characteristics, competition, company resources, and the stage in the product life cycle. Usually, a company that wants to maintain control over marketing programs and customer contact will use direct channels. Companies that are more flexible about control will use indirect channels. Throughout the life cycle of a product, a firm seeks new distribution alternatives to ensure that the product is readily available to customers.

Channel length refers to the number or levels of intermediaries in the channel of distribution. Channel width is the number of middlemen at any one level of the channel. Usually, a channel becomes wider as the product moves towards the point of purchase (i.e., the retail level where consumers buy). Distribution can be intensive, selective, or exclusive, depending on the marketing objectives of the producing firm.

Within any channel, conflict between members may occur. Conflict can be horizontal (i.e., between similar members at the same level) or vertical (i.e., between members at different levels). The channel captain implements strategies that encourage cooperation between channel members. These strategies include providing good service, fair pricing policies, advertising and promotional support, sales training programs, and the adoption of relationship marketing principles.

Integrated marketing systems are a means of gaining increased control over channel operations. Basically, two types of integrated marketing systems exist. In a vertical marketing system, a manufacturer, wholesaler, or retailer could be in control. These vertical systems are (1) administered, in which case the member with the most economic influence holds control; (2) contractual, in which case control is maintained through a legal agreement; and (3) corporate, in which case one company operates at each level of the channel. In a horizontal marketing system, one firm has many members at one level of the channel.

The pursuit of new channels of distribution is now a hotly contested battleground among competing companies wanting to expand sales. Both manufacturers and retailers are adding direct marketing and Internet strategies as a means of serving consumers whose shopping habits are changing. Other popular alternatives include multi-level marketing systems and contract marketing.

Physical distribution refers to the activities involved in the delivery of merchandise. The major components of physical distribution include customer service, transportation, warehousing, inventory management, and order processing. Advancing computer and communication technologies are changing the nature of logistics management. Progressive companies interested in cost savings are implementing electronic data interchange systems that facilitate the transfer of goods in the channel of distribution. Another cost-savings alternative is the outsourcing of transportation to third-party delivery companies.

Key Terms

accumulation 316
administered VMS 332
allocation 316
assorting 317
backward integration 333
channel captain 326
channel length 322
channel width 322
containerization 338
corporate VMS 333
direct channel 317
distribution 315
distribution planning 315
distribution warehouse (distribution centre) 337
electronic data interchange (EDI) 337
exclusive distribution 324
forward integration 333
franchise agreement 333
freight forwarder 339
horizontal conflict 325
horizontal marketing system 333
indirect channel 317

intensive distribution 324
intermediary 315
inventory management 337
just-in-time (JIT) inventory system 337
multi-level marketing (network marketing) 334
multiple channel 323
order processing 335
physical distribution (logistics management) 335
piggybacking 339
retail cooperatives 332
selective distribution 324
sorting 317
sorting process 315
stockout 336
storage warehouse 336
supply chain 329
supply chain management 329
vertical conflict 325
vertical marketing system (VMS) 332
voluntary chain 332
warehouse 336

Review Questions

1. What is the basic role of intermediaries in the channel of distribution?

2. What is the role of the sorting process in the distribution of goods? Briefly describe the basic elements of the sorting process.

3. What is the difference between a direct channel and an indirect channel? Under what conditions would a company select one option or the other?

4. Briefly describe the factors a firm considers when designing a channel of distribution.

5. What is the difference between channel length and channel width?

6. Under what conditions are the following types of distribution appropriate?
   a) Intensive
   b) Selective
   c) Exclusive

7. What is the difference between horizontal conflict and vertical conflict in the channel of distribution?

8. What is a channel captain, and what role does the channel captain play in the distribution channel?

9. Identify the factors that encourage cooperation among members of a channel of distribution.

10. What are vertical integration and horizontal integration? Provide a new example of each concept.

11. Briefly describe the various functions of physical distribution.

Discussion and Application Questions

1. What type of channel of distribution would you recommend for:
   a) A daily newspaper
   b) Cellular telephone
   c) A Rolex watch

2. What degree of distribution intensity is appropriate for each of the following?
   a) *Maclean's* magazine
   b) Toyota Lexus car
   c) Calvin Klein blue jeans
   d) Lever 2000 soap
   e) Rolex watches

3. Review the Marketing in Action vignette "Should Suppliers Be Retailers?" Examine the facts presented in the vignette and answer the question posed in the title. Is competition from the manufacturer fair to the existing dealer network? Conduct some additional research on this issue before arriving at a conclusion.

4. Review the Marketing in Action vignette "War and Peace Between Ford, Ford Dealers." Are there other distribution strategies that Ford should be implementing? Discuss potential opportunities and provide appropriate rationales for their inclusion.

5. Conduct some secondary research on contract marketing (contract distribution) in North America. Identify some markets and companies that have been successful in implementing this strategy. Is it fair to block out competition in this manner? What is your opinion?

6. Assume you are going to open a coffee shop in your local market. Would you pursue a franchise opportunity, or would you open up your own independent shop? For cost details on franchises you may wish to consult the *Franchise Annual*, which should be available in the reference section of your school library. If you were contemplating buying a franchise, which one would you select? Defend your selection.

E-Assignment

In this assignment, you will assess the channel strategy being employed by Chapters bookstores. Chapters traditionally sold books in "big box"-style stores that are located in major Canadian cities. More recently, Chapters opened Chapters Online to capitalize on the trend of online book buying. Amazon.com from the United States was doing a brisk business in Canada. Conduct some Web-based research to determine the success of Chapters' online venture. In the long term, what effect will the online business have on Chapters' bricks-and-mortar business? Are multiple channels the route for Chapters to follow? Are there other distribution strategies Chapters should be considering in the short term and long term?

Endnotes

1. Joel Evans and Barry Berman, *Marketing*, 3rd Edition (New York: MacMillan Publishing Company. 1987). p. 234.

2. Michael Dell, "Growing with the Internet: Worldwide and Direct" (speech), November 3, 2000, www.dell.com/us/gen/corporate/speech.

3. William Band, "Successful Distribution Strategies," *Sales & Marketing Management in Canada*, April 1987, pp. 11-12.

4. Mark Evans, "The push to pull buyers online," *Globe and Mail*, August 19, 1999, pp. T1, T2.

5. "Retail foodservices on the rise," *Ontario Restaurant News*, May 1999, p. 20.

6. Suzanne Bidlake, "Coffee shops perk up Nestle's U.K. ambitions," *Advertising Age*, October 9, 1999, p. 9.

7. "United Airlines customers to experience the joy of Pepsi," press release, March 25, 2002,www.pepsico.com/press.

8. Marina Strauss and Showwei Chu, "IBM Canada to shut stores as result of shrinking sales, *Globe and Mail*, March 1, 2002, p. B3.

9. Scott Gardiner, "A wall of silence around retailers' growing clout," *Marketing*, May 28, 2000, p. 16.

10. Zena Olijnyk, "Giant retailers wielding enormous power: suppliers," *Financial Post*, February 7, 2000, pp. C1, C9.

11. Allan Robinson, "Alcan clinches a 5-year deal to supply Ford with aluminum," *Globe and Mail*, January 25, 2000, p. B2.

12. Mark De Wolf, "Coke signs prime deal," *Strategy*, May 25, 1998, p. 5.

13. Philip Kotler, Gary Armstrong, Peggy Cunningham, and Robert Warren, *Principles of Marketing*, 3rd Canadian Edition (Toronto, ON: Prentice-Hall Canada Inc., 1997), p. 437.

14. Keith Kalawsky, "No hands," *Canadian Business*, November 26, 1999, pp. 149, 150.

15. "Quick facts about trade and trucking," advertising supplement in *Canadian Business*, February 2002.

Sun Media Corp.

Wholesaling and Retailing

> Learning Objectives

After studying this chapter, you will be able to

1. Define wholesaling and identify its functions.
2. Characterize the three main categories of wholesaling and the types of wholesaling firms that operate in each category.
3. Explain what retailing is and what its functions are.
4. Describe the different types of retailing operations categorized by ownership, marketing strategy, and method of operation.
5. Outline the major elements of retail planning.

Wholesaling and Its Functions

1.
Define wholesaling and identify its functions.

wholesaling

Wholesaling is the process of buying or handling merchandise and subsequently reselling it to organizational users, other wholesalers, and retailers. It is big business in Canada. In 2001, the total value of transactions by wholesalers across all trade groups was $396 billion. The largest categories of wholesalers are motor vehicles ($78 billion) and food products ($66 billion).[1] As discussed in the previous chapter, the wholesaling role is performed either by manufacturers themselves or by independent channel members. Not all independent wholesalers, however, perform every wholesaling function, so when wholesalers are required, a company will select one that meets its needs. The following list describes the basic functions performed by wholesalers.[2]

1. *Covering the Market* Manufacturers produce and market their goods from one or a few locations, or goods could be imported and stored in a distribution warehouse. Since customers tend to be geographically dispersed, a wholesaler provides the means to efficiently reach them. The wholesaler takes possession of the goods for redistribution to retail customers. In distributing goods, a wholesaler's sales force can complement a manufacturer's own sales force.

2. *Holding Inventory* In many cases, the title to the merchandise is transferred to the wholesaler, who then holds the goods in inventory. For the manufacturer, this reduces the financial burden of carrying inventory and improves its cash flow to other operational costs.

3. *Order-Processing* Wholesalers represent many manufacturers of similar products. Unlike manufacturers, wholesalers ship small quantities of a variety of merchandise to their customers. Not only do wholesalers process orders for the manufacturers' products, they also spread the costs of the order processing across all the manufacturers' products that they represent.

4. *Performing Market Intelligence* Since wholesalers are in frequent contact with their customers, they have a good understanding of customer needs (e.g., product requirements, service expectations, price). This information is passed on to manufacturers to assist in improving marketing strategies.

5. *Providing Service* After goods have been transferred to the next level in the channel—to another wholesaler, retailer, or organizational customer—the wholesaler can address any problems that arise. Such service takes the form of returns or

exchanges, installations, adjustments, general repairs, technical assistance, and training users in how to use equipment.

6. ***Providing Assortment*** Wholesalers carry a wide variety of manufacturers' products. The amassing of various items is called assortment. The assortment function simplifies customers' ordering tasks. In certain cases, customers can order from one wholesaler instead of many. A few general-line wholesalers can provide customers with most of the products they need.

breaking bulk

7. ***Breaking Bulk*** Breaking bulk refers to the delivery of small quantities to customers. Very often, customers do not meet the minimum-shipping-weight requirement established by the transportation companies that deliver the goods. Therefore, wholesalers buy in large quantities from manufacturers and break the "bulk" orders into small quantities so that their customers may buy in the quantities they need.

Types of Wholesalers

2.
Characterize the three main categories of wholesaling and the types of wholesaling firms that operate in each category.

Within Canadian industries, wholesalers belong to one of three main categories: manufacturer wholesaling; merchant wholesaling; and agents, brokers, and commission merchants (Figure 13.1).

MANUFACTURER WHOLESALING

manufacturer wholesaling

In the case of **manufacturer wholesaling**, the producer undertakes the wholesaling function because the firm feels that it can reach customers (retailers and organizational customers) effectively and efficiently through direct contact. Direct contact may be necessary due to the fact that the product requires complex installation or servicing. Examples of such firms include technology-based companies such as IBM and Xerox, that may ship directly to other organizational customers; and snack-food and beverage manufacturers, such as Hostess Frito-Lay and Pepsi-Cola, that use their own delivery trucks to ship directly to retailers. In each case, the manufacturer itself stores the merchandise in a warehouse and delivers it directly to retail customers.

branch office

sales office

Manufacturers often conduct wholesaling activities through a branch office or a sales office. Let us distinguish them from one another. A **branch office** is a company office in a specified geographic area, which usually includes a warehouse facility, from which goods are delivered to customers in the area. For example, the prairie provinces may be served by a branch office (e.g., located in Regina) of a national company. A sales office is usually located near the customers, but it does not carry inventory. A **sales office** accepts orders that are processed elsewhere (e.g., a branch office or regional warehouse). In Canada, it is quite common for a manufacturer, such as Procter & Gamble or General Mills, to have centralized production and warehousing facilities and regional sales offices in key areas, such as the Atlantic Provinces, Quebec, Ontario, the Prairies, and British Columbia.

MERCHANT WHOLESALING

merchant wholesalers

Merchant wholesalers perform the traditional functions of wholesaling. They buy goods and take both title to and possession of them, then resell them to other customers in the channel. The two classifications of merchant wholesalers are full-service wholesalers

Types of Wholesalers

Figure 13.1

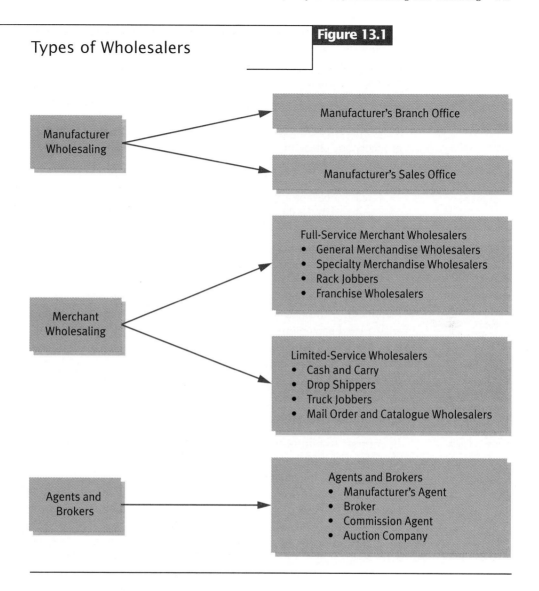

and limited-service wholesalers. The difference between the two classifications lies in the number and extent of services each provides.

Full-Service Merchant Wholesalers

full-service merchant wholesaler

Full-service merchant wholesalers assemble an assortment of products in a central warehouse and offer their customers a full range of services, including delivery, storage, credit, and support in merchandising and promotion and in research and planning. They usually employ their own sales force that calls regularly on retail customers. Full-service merchant wholesalers, who work closely with the manufacturers they represent, are common in certain industries: apparel and dry goods, plumbing and heating equipment, farm machinery and supplies, drug and tobacco products and hardware supplies.

general-merchandise wholesaler

There are many varieties of full-service merchant wholesalers. A **general-merchandise wholesaler** carries a full line or wide assortment of merchandise that serves virtually all its customers' needs. Such wholesalers can be found in such industries as automotive parts, electrical, plumbing, and hardware supplies. AutoSense, for example, is a 160-store national chain supplying auto parts to repair shops and consumers through a distribution centre located in Mississauga, Ontario.

specialty-merchandise wholesaler

A **specialty-merchandise wholesaler** carries a limited number or a narrow line of products but offers an extensive assortment within these lines (i.e., a wide selection of colours, sizes, features, and price ranges). Specialty wholesaling, for instance, is used in the grocery industry.

rack jobber

Rack jobbers are responsible for stocking merchandise-display racks, which they own and which display the products they carry. Rack jobbers typically supply non-food items to the supermarket trade, such as health and beauty aids, cosmetics, magazines, and stationery supplies. Rack jobbers sell on a consignment basis, that is, the retailer pays the jobber after the items are sold, and the jobber takes back unsold merchandise.

franchise wholesaler, or wholesale-sponsored voluntary chain

Franchise wholesalers, or **wholesale-sponsored voluntary chains**, are developed when retailers affiliate with an existing wholesaling operation and agree to purchase merchandise through it. The operation of the affiliates is standardized in accordance with a legal agreement: the franchises operate under a certain name, use the same purchasing system, have similar store designs, and advertise cooperatively. Drug Trading Co. follows a system of franchise wholesaling. It supplies products to drugstores operating under the IDA, Guardian, RxCentral, and Community Drug Mart retail banners.

AutoSense, Inc.
www.autosense.ca

Limited-Service Merchant Wholesalers

limited-service merchant wholesaler

In contrast to full-service wholesalers, **limited-service merchant wholesalers** are selective about the functions they perform. They exist in numerous forms: cash-and-carry outlets, drop shippers, and truck jobbers.

cash-and-carry outlet

A **cash-and-carry outlet** serves small independent retailers, such as convenience stores, corner grocery stores, and hardware stores, who come to the wholesaler to purchase small quantities of goods. These establishments do not provide credit, delivery, promotion support, or selling assistance. In grocery distribution, cash-and-carry outlets serve small independent grocers and variety stores.

drop shipper

A **drop shipper** purchases goods from manufacturers but does not take possession of them. It buys the item and leaves it with the manufacturer. Then it contacts customers and puts together carload quantities that can be delivered economically. Drop shippers are prevalent in markets where goods are heavy and freight costs are high (e.g., raw-materials, such as coal, lumber, and building supplies).

truck jobber

A **truck jobber** is a specialty wholesaler operating mainly in the food distribution industry. The jobber distributes well-known brands of semi-perishable goods and perishable goods, such as breads, dairy products, and snack foods. Voortman Cookies and Betty Bread deliver fresh product to its retail customers by means of a local delivery truck jobber. In each case, the truck jobber sells and delivers merchandise during the same sales call, supplying the retailer with fresh product on short notice.

AGENTS AND BROKERS

Agents and *brokers* perform a variety of wholesaling functions but do not take title to the goods that are sold. They represent the seller in the transaction and work for commissions paid by the selling organization. The main difference between an agent and a broker is in the relationship with the seller. An agent is more likely to be used on a permanent basis, whereas a broker is usually used on a temporary basis. The main types of agents and brokers are manufacturers' agents, brokers, commission merchants, and auction companies.

Manufacturers' Agents

manufacturer's agent

A **manufacturer's agent** carries and sells similar products for non-competing manufacturers in an exclusive territory. Such agents are commonly associated with particular industries: electronics, automotive parts, clothing, and food. The commission arrangements for these wholesalers are attractive to small manufacturers, who cannot afford the cost of directly contacting the same customers themselves. The agents' primary task is selling, and they do so on the basis of pricing policies established by the manufacturers they represent.

Brokers

broker

A **broker** plays a key role in the negotiations between buyers and sellers. Depending on the industry and the nature of the selling situation, the broker's relationship with the supply organization can be permanent or temporary. Brokers are common in the financial services industry and the food industry. In financial services, licensed stockbrokers advise business clients and buy and sell stocks on their behalf. Food brokers represent suppliers (usually small manufacturers) to the wholesale and retail food trade. In both these markets, the relationship between the broker and client is usually a long-term one. Food brokers are paid a commission (5 percent is common), and their agreement with the supplier is usually outlined in a contract that clearly defines the length and terms of the arrangement.

Temporary relationships are commonly found in the real estate industry, where brokers are used for individual transactions. The broker may represent many different vendors (sellers) at any one time, but the relationship with each one ends when the sales transaction is complete. Canadian firms wishing to do business in foreign markets frequently employ the services of an export broker.

Commission Merchants

commission merchant

A **commission merchant** works with small manufacturers or suppliers that require representation to reach customers in centralized markets. The merchant receives and sells goods on consignment. Typically, the supplier lacks marketing resources, so the commission merchant arranges shipment of the product to a market, completes the sale, and returns the collected funds (less the commission earned) to the supplier. Dairy and produce farmers rely on merchants to sell their products in urban markets, since the farmer cannot accompany each shipment of goods to the city.

Auction Companies

auction company

An **auction company** brings buyers and sellers together at a central location to complete a transaction. The supply and demand for the merchandise at auction time determines the selling price. Auctions play a key role in markets, such as those for livestock, tobacco,

Sotheby's Auction House
www.sothebys.com

and used automobiles. In Canada, one of the more famous auction companies is the British-based Sotheby's, which specializes in Canadian art and related products. Auction companies are usually paid a flat fee or a commission for the service provided.

Retailing and Its Functions

3.
Explain what retailing is and what its functions are.

retailing

Retailing refers to those activities involved in the sale of goods and services to final consumers for personal, family, or household use. It is the last stage in the channel of distribution. In Canada, overall retail sales have increased steadily. Between 1998 and 2001, retail sales increased from $246.6 billion to $289.1 billion, an average annual increase of approximately 3.9 percent.[3] During this time, the nature of the retailing landscape changed significantly. Stores such as Wal-Mart and Costco that offer better value in terms of price (lower prices generally) and quality became more attractive to consumers. Traditional department stores such as the Bay and Sears lost business to discount department stores and specialty stores. Now, all traditional bricks-and-mortar retailers face competition in the form of electronic retailers (e-tailers). See Figure 13.2 for information on market share trends among department stores.

Generally, retailers perform four main functions (Figure 13.3):

1. Retailers are part of the sorting process: the store buys an assortment of goods and services from a variety of suppliers and offers them for sale.

2. They provide *information* to consumers through advertising, promotion, and personal selling.

3. They *market* goods by storing merchandise, establishing selling prices, and placing items on the sales floor.

Department Store Market Shares

Figure 13.2

Store	1996	2000	2001
Wal-Mart	24	28	31
Sears	18	31*	30*
Zellers	23	26	25
Bay	15	15	14
Eaton's	12		
Kmart	8		

*Includes Eaton's, which was acquired by Sears in 2000. Kmart is out of business in Canada.

Source: "Report on market shares," *Marketing*, May 27, 2002, p. 10. Reprinted with permission from *Marketing Magazine*, Rogers Publishing.

The Functions of a Retailer

Figure 13.3

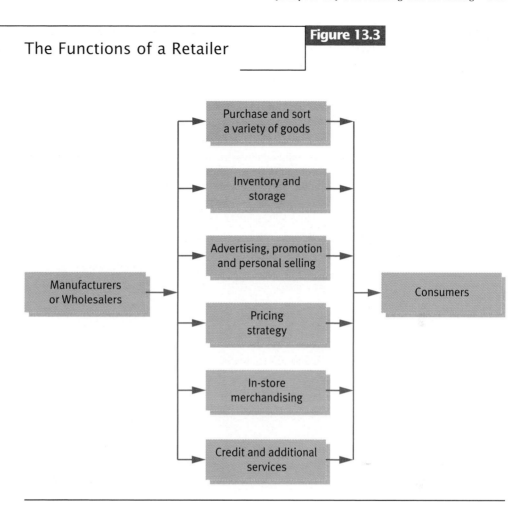

4. They complete a *transaction* by offering credit terms, convenient hours, and store locations, and other services, such as debit card and credit card purchasing and delivery.

When shopping for goods at retail, the consumer usually has a number of retailers to choose from. A retail store is chosen on the basis of such factors as store image, hours of operation, availability of parking, quality of products carried, additional services provided, store location, and the environment of the store.

In planning a strategy, retailers consider the factors listed above and develop a **retailing mix** (retail version of a marketing mix) to attract customers to the store. Retailers are discovering that the behaviour of shoppers is changing. It is more important now to understand and respond to their specific needs regarding merchandise, quality, value, and customer service, while not trying to be all things to all people (see Figure 13.4). The growth of discount retailing illustrates the changing value systems of shoppers today. A retailer must also understand how and when customers buy products. For example, time-pressed shoppers now view the Internet as an acceptable alternative to

retailing mix

Understanding Consumers Pinpoints Strategic Focus for Retailers

Figure 13.4

In a changing retail environment the companies that will succeed are those that understand consumer needs and realize they can't be all things to all people.

Successful retailers are the ones that focus on only a few core strengths. All consumer transactions can be reduced to five elements—**price, product, service, access,** and **experience.** The best retailers understand this and devote their resources to the one or two elements where they feel they can compete. Here are a few examples:

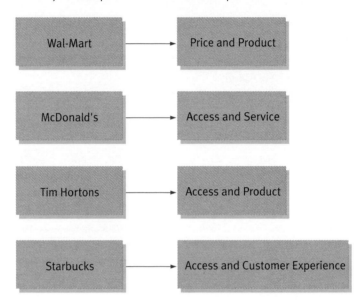

Wal-Mart	Price and Product
McDonald's	Access and Service
Tim Hortons	Access and Product
Starbucks	Access and Customer Experience

Source: Adapted from Elizabeth Church, "Retailers don't listen, consumer study says," *Globe and Mail,* August 16, 2001, p. B3.

personal shopping. Smart Canadian retailers, therefore, are implementing e-buying sites to take advantage of new opportunities.

Canadian Tire is the most-shopped retailer in the country, attracting more than 90 percent of consumers at one time or another.[4] Facing stiff competition from large American chains such as Wal-Mart and Home Depot, Canadian Tire moved away from a strategy of being all things to all people, and decided to focus on three specific product categories: sports and leisure, auto parts, and home products. Its goal was to become the destination of choice for all three.

Canadian Tire also embarked on an expansion and renovation program that included bigger stores, wider aisles, improved displays, brighter lighting, and in-store boutiques for sporting goods. Female shoppers were identified as a priority target—they make up a growing proportion of hardware shoppers, and they form a significant customer base in their stores. Canadian Tire introduced a line of Martha Stewart paints in an attempt to draw in more female shoppers. The changes have worked. Canadian Tire remains the leader in the hardware store segment of the market and is a very profitable company.

Retailer Classifications

4.
Describe the different types of retailing operations categorized by ownership, marketing strategy, and method of operation.

Canadian retailers are classified into groups according to form of ownership, marketing mix strategy (e.g., products and services offered), and method of operation. The different types of stores have different characteristics and, therefore, diverse marketing strategies.

In terms of ownership, there are three prevalent forms: chain stores, independent retailers, and retail franchises.

CHAIN STORES

retail chain store

Sport Chek
www.sportchek.ca

A **retail chain store** is an organization operating four or more retail stores in the same kind of business under the same legal ownership. Chain stores are a dominant and growing presence in the Canadian retail marketplace. Examples of large chain stores include specialty stores, such as Sport Chek (sports products and leisure wear), The Brick (consumer electronics), Safeway and Sobeys (supermarkets), and Sears and Wal-Mart (department stores).

As mentioned earlier, the trend in shopping behaviour is towards discount department stores, warehouse outlets, and price clubs, and away from traditional chain stores. Costco, for example, a relatively new price club operation, has annual sales of $3.4 billion, and is the country's fourth largest merchandiser (Figure 13.5).[5] That is a lot of money taken away from traditional retailers, such as the Bay, Sears, and Canadian Tire. Let us distinguish between these new types of retail outlets.

warehouse outlet

price club

Warehouse outlets are no-frills, cash-and-carry outlets that offer consumers name-brand merchandise at discount prices. Examples of warehouse outlets include Brico (building supply stores in Quebec) and Home Depot (building supply stores in other regions). **Price clubs** are essentially the same as warehouse outlets, except consumers must pay an annual fee (usually $35.00–$45.00) for the privilege of shopping there. The only price club in Canada is Costco.

Warehouse outlets and price clubs are somewhat hybrid operations; they actually perform many wholesaling and retailing functions in one operation, since their size and buying power allow them to buy in large volume, and manufacturers deliver directly to each outlet. They carry anything from Mont Blanc pens to Pirelli tires to Bounty paper towels, so they are competing with all kinds of traditional retailers. In response, some supermarkets and merchandisers, such as Canadian Tire, are opening their own warehouse stores. Warehouse stores are part of a major transformation under way in wholesale and retail distribution that will affect a wide variety of consumer goods, from food to hardware to electronics to building supplies.

INDEPENDENT RETAIL STORES

independent retailer

An **independent retailer** is a retailer operating one to three stores, even if the stores are affiliated with a large retail organization. Independent retailing is dominant among dealers of domestic and imported cars, pharmacies, automotive parts dealers, and locally owned food stores.

Canada's Top Merchandisers, Food and Drug Stores

Figure 13.5

Rank	Company	Revenues ($000)
Top Merchandisers		
1	Hudson's Bay Co.	7 445 813
2	Costco Canada	6 726 400
3	Sears Canada	5 374 759
4	Canadian Tire Corp.	5 374 759
5	Liquor Control Board of Ontario	2 734 937
Food and Drug Stores		
1	Loblaw Cos. Ltd.	21 486 000
2	Empire Co. Ltd.	11 538 600
3	Canada Safeway Ltd.	5 338 600
4	METRO Inc.	4 868 900
5	Shoppers Drug Mart	3 634 567

Wal-Mart revenue figures are not separated from Wal-Mart U.S. in the *National Post* rankings of companies, so they do not appear on the list above.

Source: "Financial Post Industry Leaders," *National Post Business*, 2002 Edition, pp. 138, 140.

Independent retailers contrast greatly with chain stores. Competing with large chains is difficult. The chain store is a large-scale operation, and because it buys in large quantities, it can offer customers lower prices than the independent retailer can (although chains do not always choose to offer low prices). The risk of financial loss is also spread across many stores in a chain operation; successful stores compensate for the unsuccessful. To survive as an independent, adequate financial resources and good management skills are required.

RETAIL FRANCHISING

retail franchise

A **retail franchise** is a contractual agreement (a franchise) between a franchiser (a manufacturer, wholesaler, or service sponsor) and a franchisee (the independent business person). In a franchising arrangement, the franchisee purchases the right to own and operate a certain line or brand of business from the franchiser for a specific location. Further, the franchisee agrees to subscribe to a certain set of rules and business practices—a franchiser requires that the product be prepared in a certain way; and management practices and accounting systems must be consistent among all franchisees.

The typical franchise arrangement involves an initial franchise fee and a percentage of sales (a royalty) to be returned to the franchiser. Franchisees also contribute to a pool of advertising funds, which is spent by the franchiser in markets where franchises exist. To illustrate, a Dairy Queen franchise in Canada requires an initial investment of

$200 000 minimum; a Burger King franchise requires a $350 000 minimum. At Dairy Queen, royalty fees are 4 percent of sales, and advertising fees are 3 percent.[6]

Through franchising, the marketing and economic base of a business is broadened by the cooperative efforts of the franchiser and the franchisee. For the franchisee, the primary benefit is the purchase of risk reduction. The risks are much lower, compared with starting up an independent business, because the trial-and-error process is eliminated. It is estimated that the chances for success for a new independent business are approximately 20 percent; the success rate for franchises is about 80 to 90 percent.[7]

The advantages of owning and operating a franchise are similar to those associated with being part of a large chain. Franchises have a great buying capability, and each franchisee benefits from the image of the total franchise system. Knowing when to enter into a franchise agreement is crucial. There are risks associated with joining a new franchise early. A large investment could be wasted. Also, in a franchise there is little scope for innovation for the franchisee.

In Canada, some of the more common names in franchising include Canadian Tire, McDonald's, Boston Pizza, Golden Griddle, Tim Hortons, Choice Hotels Canada (Comfort, Quality, Clarion, and Sleep Inns), Midas, and Uniglobe.

Tricon Global, Inc.
www.triconglobal.com

piggybacking, or co-branding

A fairly recent trend in franchising is **piggybacking**, or **co-branding**. This involves two or more separate franchise operations in one facility. In theory, co-branding works best when stores offer complementary products. The strength of Wendy's lunch and dinner menu, for instance, works well with Tim Hortons' coffee and donut offerings. Tricon Global, the master franchiser in Canada for Pizza Hut, Taco Bell, and KFC, is now putting all three restaurants under one roof.

MARKETING MIX STRATEGY

To classify retail stores by their marketing mix strategy requires a look at the product lines offered and the services provided to customers.

self-serve store

There are two types of services offered: self-service and full service. In a **self-serve store**, the retailer provides minimum services. The stores rely heavily on in-store displays, merchandising, and reasonable prices to attract customers. Warehouse stores, such as Costco, are self-serve operations, as are supermarkets, hardware stores, and drugstores. In contrast, a **full-serve store** offers customer assistance and a greater variety of in-store service that include fitting rooms, delivery, installations, and alterations, as part of the product mix. Traditional department stores, such as the Bay and Sears, and specialty stores, such as Holt-Renfrew and Harry Rosen, are full-serve stores. Discount stores, such as Zellers and Wal-Mart, offer some personal services, but their goal is to keep services minimal so that they can maintain lower prices for shoppers. Stores like these can be classified as **limited-service stores**.

full-serve store

limited-service store

specialty store

Stores classified by product line are determined by the variety of different items they carry and the assortment of each item. A **specialty store** carries a variety of products for a single product line; for example, Bata carries shoes, and Bluenotes and Old Navy carry casual clothing. A **limited-line store** carries a large assortment of one product line or a few related lines of goods (e.g., Athlete's World sells a variety of sporting goods equipment and a variety of leisure sportswear; IKEA sells home furnishings and housewares).

limited-line store

big box, or category killer

A more recent phenomenon in limited-line retailing is the growth of stores offering a huge selection of low-priced merchandise for a single product line. Referred to as **big box** stores or **category killers**, these stores have severely affected traditional retailers that have weak distribution and merchandising strategies. Prominent category killers have taken hold of numerous product categories—Toys "R" Us (toys and children's accessories), Staples Business Depot (office equipment and supplies, and Home Depot (home renovation and repairs). Shoppers Drug Mart recently announced it would build big box stores (twice the size of a typical Shoppers store) in order to appeal to consumers' needs for one-stop shopping and to fend off competition from Costco, Loblaws, Wal-Mart, and Zellers.[8]

general-merchandise store

Finally, a **general-merchandise store** offers a wide variety of product lines, and a selection of brand names within these product lines. Stores such as Sears and the Bay fall into this classification.

Within each of these categories of stores are different types of stores. Common terms to describe these stores include convenience stores, supermarkets, superstores, variety stores, department stores, and discount department stores. Descriptions such as these suggest the nature of products carried and services offered. For a description of these stores and a few examples refer to Figure 13.6.

Stores by Type of Operation

Figure 13.6

Type of Store	Description	Example
Convenience	Small, food-oriented stores in local communities	Mac's, 7-Eleven, Bonisoir
Supermarket	Departmentalized food stores (dairy, meat, produce, frozen and packaged food)	Safeway, Sobeys, A&P
Discount Supermarket	Limited-line supermarket offering fewer services and lower prices	Save-On, No Frills
Superstores	Diversified supermarkets carrying a broad range of products	SuperCentres, Real Atlantic Food Stores
Specialty Stores	Stores selling a single line or limited line of merchandise	Radio Shack, Bata Shoes, Athlete's World, Ikea
Variety Stores	Stores carrying a wide range of staple merchandise	Bi-Way, Metropolitan
Department Stores	General-line retailers offering a variety of products in many price ranges	Bay, Sears
Discount Department Stores	Stores carrying a full line of products at popular prices (fewer services than department stores)	Wal-Mart, Zellers

Source: "Financial Post Industry Leaders," *National Post Business*, 2002 Edition, pp. 138, 140.

As indicated earlier in the chapter the Canadian retail market is changing rapidly. The influx of American-owned chain stores and the rapid growth among big-box stores is placing added pressure on existing Canadian retailers. The competition is forcing Canadian retailers to sharpen their focus and develop strategies that are in tune with the times. Those retailers that have not adapted to the new marketplace are out of business—Eaton's, Kmart, Marks & Spencer, to name a few. Others have adapted and are more successful than ever. Loblaws, for example, continues to stay relevant. For insight into why they are successful, read the Marketing in Action vignette **Loblaws Scrambles for Growth**.

METHOD OF OPERATION

The previous sections described retailing in the traditional sense, that is, the purchase of goods in retail stores. There are other ways a retailer can market goods to consumers. In today's market, there is a trend toward marketing to consumers directly. Such retailing includes vending machines, direct home retailing, direct marketing, and electronic retailing (e-tailing).

Vending Machines and Automated Merchandising

We do not usually think of a vending machine as a form of retailing, but it is. Vending machines often sell cigarettes, soft drinks, and confectionery products. These machines generate annual sales of approximately $460 million (2001) each year.[9] The machines are usually owned and operated by the retail stores, restaurants, and service stations, where they are located. In other arrangements, space in retail locations may be leased by vending machine operators, or the retailer and vending machine operator may strike a deal to share profits in return for the space granted by the retailer.

Vending operators are expanding their traditional lineup of chocolate bars, hot and cold drinks, and other snack foods. Specialty coffees, such as cappuccino and espresso, have been added to the vending menu. Manufacturers are looking at vending machines as a way of increasing market penetration and brand recognition. Ault Foods, for example, sells Drumstick, Oreo Cookie, and Haagen-Dazs ice cream treats through its own vending machines while Nestlé Canada uses vending machines to sell some of its top-selling brands (Nescafé coffee, Stouffer's entrees, Kit Kat, and Smarties).

Automatic banking machines (ABMs) are a form of vending that has proven to be an overwhelming success for financial institutions and are capable of offering many more services in the future. In the next few years, financial institutions will introduce terminals that will allow customers to apply for loans and mortgages.

Direct Home Retailing

direct home retailing

cold canvas

Direct home retailing is the selling of merchandise by personal contact in the home of the customer. Several variations of direct home selling exist, covering a wide variety of product lines from cosmetics to vacuum cleaners, newspapers, and toys. Some of the selling alternatives include cold canvas, referrals, and party selling. When the **cold canvas** technique is used, a salesperson in search of customers knocks without notice on doors in a neighbourhood. Electrolux and other vacuum cleaners are sold in this manner. *Telemarketing* campaigns such as those conducted by Bell Canada to sell additional services are another form of cold canvas selling.

Marketing in Action

Loblaws Scrambles for Growth

A local newspaper contains a colouful flyer showcasing summer clothes, garden tools, and toys. Must be from Zellers or Wal-Mart you think. No, it's from Loblaws, Canada's newest "department" store.

Loblaws is broadening its horizons with the promise of one-stop shopping for busy mothers and time-strapped professionals, and in the process is starting to compete more directly with the likes of Costco and Wal-Mart. "One of our overall strategies is to be the supplier of consumers' everyday household needs," says Geoffrey Wilson, vice-president, industry and investor relations at Loblaws.

Loblaws is expanding its housewares section, with kitchenware, bed and bath things, seasonal items, cooking and tableware items, small furniture, televisions, and stereos. While these items don't all fit into a shopping cart, it's hoped that the popularity of Loblaws' well-known private label food items will entice customers to the higher-priced merchandise.

To accommodate the household items, Loblaws is building huge stores (100 000 square feet plus) and adding space to existing stores where possible. It's becoming a complete shopping experience under one roof. Boutique-style operations in a shop-in-shop format include Photolab and PC Financial. There are new sections for office supplies, cosmetics, skin care products, and electronics. The really big stores include a complete pharmacy.

Loblaws is becoming a model for success. "They consistently reinvest every dollar of cash flow so they have beautiful stores. They spend more on capital spending than the rest of the industry combined, on an annual basis," says Cynthia Rose-Martel, a retail analyst. "They're just damn good merchants— probably one of the best in the world. Literally, they build a better mousetrap."

Loblaws doesn't fear made-in-the-USA competition. It has size. With annual sales revenue of $20 billion compared to Wal-Mart's $16 billion and Sobeys $11 billion, Loblaws is capable of protecting its turf. However, Wal-Mart will be opening full-scale Supercentres to sell groceries. In the not-too-distant future Loblaws and Wal-Mart will compete head-to-head.

Loblaws may have the edge because of the strength of its private label products. People will trust their expansion into other items and be comfortable with it. Loblaws also offers a much different shopping experience. The stores feature softer-lit, roomier interiors to attract sophisticated, value-conscious consumers, compared to the bright lights and prominent signage in Wal-Mart or Costco. The ambience extends into in-store marketing, with section banners using attractive colour photographs of fruit and vegetables, and white umbrellas hanging over cosmetics displays.

Next on the horizon is gasoline. John Lederer, president of Loblaws, says, "Gasoline is a natural. Twenty-five thousand customers drive to our large stores everyday. Gasoline is an everyday product. We continue to expand our definition of everyday household needs."

Clearly, Loblaws is a company that is evolving in order to meet consumers' needs and to stay a step ahead of the competition—a classic case of the marketing concept in action. They are focused on the consumer, not on any one competitor. It's not coincidence, however, that Wal-Mart sells groceries and gasoline. The battle lines are drawn!

Adapted from Oliver Bertin, "Loblaws set to provide more products," *Globe and Mail*, May 2, 2002, p. B3; and Sarah Smith, "Checking out the new Loblaws," *Marketing*, April 29, 2002, pp. 10-11.

Dick Hemingway

referrals

If **referrals** are used, visits with customers are planned. A salesperson secures names of potential customers from satisfied customers and makes an initial contact by telephone to arrange a time for a face-to-face meeting. A company such as Avon or Amway operates in this way.

party selling

In a **party selling** situation, one person acts as a host and invites friends to his or her home for a sales demonstration. Tupperware products are the merchandise best known for being sold on a party-plan basis, though Tupperware has expanded into mail order and telemarketing programs more recently.

Direct Marketing and Catalogue Marketing

direct marketing

In the case of **direct marketing**, a sales message reaches consumers through the media—television, radio, newspaper, magazine, and computer—or consumers are contacted directly by telephone or mail. In delivering merchandise to consumers, the supplier ships them directly (i.e., the normal channel of distribution is bypassed). The operating costs of direct marketing are low for manufacturers, and companies can use it to reach a geographically dispersed consumer market efficiently. In Canada, Sears is probably the largest direct marketing organization, selling goods directly through the Sears Catalogue. Other successful direct marketing retailers include L. L. Bean, Victoria's Secret, and J. Crew. Revenues generated from catalogue sales and various forms of direct response advertising average about $3.5 billion annually in Canada.[10]

E-Tailing

The retailing experiment with perhaps the best promise-and surely the most hype-is selling on the Internet. Presently, the Internet only generates about 1 percent of all retail sales, but as consumers immerse themselves in technology, this figure will rise significantly. Canadian consumers continue to grapple with the decision to buy online mainly due to online security concerns and the lack of Canadian retailers on the Internet. A recent study by Deloitte & Touche revealed that Canadians want to buy online and they would prefer to buy from Canadian e-tailers.[11]

Sears
www.sears.ca
Roots
www.roots.com

The transition to electronic retailing has been relatively easy for Sears. Sears was an established catalogue retailer, so selling online was an extension of an existing infrastructure that included an automated warehouse and delivery system. Sears expected to reach sales of $350 million online by the end of 2001.[12] Sears.ca is consistently one of the top sites in Canada for online traffic. For that reason Sears refers to itself as "Canada's online merchant."[13] Sears is also developing an online strategy that will result in the creation of a separate shopping portal on which other retailers can buy space. With this strategy, Sears will warehouse and distribute the goods for third-party retailers. Roots Canada is one company that has opted to work directly with Sears in terms of fulfilling orders. The Roots Web site is designed to build brand image and display goods offered for sale at their stores.[14]

Many Canadian retailers have entered and exited the online commerce world already. They found it very difficult to make a profit. Despite the potential the Internet offers, the "how to" of Internet commerce has yet to be written. Chapters Online, a division of Indigo Books, for example, is online and is perceived by Canadians to be a trailblazer in electronic commerce. Being a leading e-tail brand has come at a cost. For every dollar in revenue generated from online sales, the cost to the company has been $2. This places a financial hardship on overall operations.[15]

It seems that the ingredients for success online are essentially the same as they are for bricks and mortar stores. Where many e-tailers came up short is in the area of customer service and delivery (fast delivery). Since online buying is becoming a normal way of buying for many shoppers, online retailers are finding that the selling-buying process is a game of relationships, and relationships only develop if good service is provided. In this day and age, nobody can afford to lose customers. For more insight into online retailing in Canada read the Marketing in Action Vignette **Blazing the "E" Trail**.

Direct marketing and online marketing are increasing in importance as a marketing strategy among retailers and business-to-business marketing organizations. These topics are discussed in detail in Chapters 15 and 17.

Elements of Retail Planning

5.
Outline the major elements of retail planning.

The major considerations in retail planning are location, brand identity, atmosphere, merchandise assortment, merchandise control, and marketing strategy (Figure 13.7).

LOCATION
Many experts suggest that two factors contribute to the success of a retail operation: *location* and *location*! Traditional thinking suggests that a good location in a high-traffic area gets people into a store. Once they are inside, the quality of the product and the

Elements of Retail Planning

Figure 13.7

Subject	Concerns
Site Location	Where to locate (e.g., in the central business district, regional shopping mall, strip mall, power mall, or in the inner city or the suburbs)
Brand Identity	Presentation of brand banner (logo) in association with other marketing strategies affects consumers' perceptions of a store
Atmosphere	Physical characteristics required to establish and maintain the store image desired (e.g., store exterior, sign, layout of store, in-store displays)
Merchandise Assortment	Determining the breadth and depth of product selection, the relationships between product lines and stock balance
Merchandise Control	Implementing controls that measure the correspondence between actual performance and planned performance (e.g., analyzing stock turnover)
Marketing the Establishment	Keeping abreast of changes in consumer buying behaviour and other trends in the market so that strategies can be planned to encourage loyalty

Marketing in Action

Blazing the "E" Trail

While the "how to" of electronic retailing has yet to be written, some recent experiences among retailers show that the fundamental principles of "bricks-and-mortar" retailing also apply to online shopping. Essential ingredients include good service, a pleasant shopping experience, and a marketing strategy that will attract shoppers to the Web site.

Considering the length of time it had taken a true e-player like Amazon.com to turn a profit (5 years of online activity), and considering that countless stand-alone e-tailers went belly up in the dot-com bust of 2001, one can hardly blame traditional retailers for treading slowly with e-commerce programs. Traditional retailers see tremendous costs and problems associated with marketing, warehousing, and delivery.

Lingerie retailer La Senza is actively involved in e-tailing. Lawrence Lewin, president of La Senza, says "Handling orders is not a stress for the company. Consumers know they can trust our brand. We have 200 shops in Canada and 80 more in other countries. People will visit other sites but they don't know who they are or what they are. They will gravitate toward companies that have substance (like La Senza), not ethereal presences floating through cyberspace."

Lewin may be right. A recent study conducted by Deloitte & Touche observed that Canadian e-shoppers want to buy Canadian. In fact, 80 percent of those asked said they'd prefer to buy products online from Canadian sites if possible. Such a response bodes well for the state of Canada's burgeoning e-tail industry.

Not surprisingly, the same survey shows that in the eyes of the public Canada's top e-tailers are also some of our top retailers. Topping the list were Sears (sears.ca), Chapters (chapters.ca), Staples Business Depot (staples.ca/business depot.com), and Future Shop (futureshop.ca). These sites are all "e-tail Blazers," e-businesses that aren't just successful online stores, but a hit with online shoppers who keep coming back for more.

Many consumers are reluctant to shop online. A survey conducted by consulting firm KPMG among 2100 North American consumers found that 74 percent of respondents worry about divulging credit card information online, and 62 percent are uncomfortable doing business with an organization that can only be reached online. The latter statistic substantiates the opinion of La Senza's president, expressed earlier.

What then should retailers be doing about an online presence? Perhaps the best advice is to proceed with caution. They should establish a Web site that will at least help drive customers into stores, improve brand image and product knowledge among potential customers, and expand the store's range.

While retailers may not be jumping on the e-tail bandwagon, some successful e-tailers are launching retail stores. Justwhiteshirts.com, originally created as an e-commerce and catalogue operation, has expanded its product line to include dress pants, ties, colognes, and shaving cream under the brand name "Just." The multi-channel model composed of mail order, online, and now retail gives the company a way to cross sell and promote. Look out Harry Rosen!

Adapted from Chris Daniels, "Justwhiteshirts.com to open stores," *Marketing*, January 7, 2002, p. 2; "Where are Canada's e-tail blazers?" press release, Retail Council of Canada, www.retailcouncil.org/press/pr20001003; and Mary Gooderham, "Uneasy state of evolution makes e-tailing risky play," *Globe and Mail*, December 20, 2000, p. B13.

service will determine whether and how often the customers will return. Consumers today, however, are willing to travel greater distances to obtain better value for their shopping dollar. The popularity of warehouse stores in industrial areas of large cities is testament to this notion as are mega-malls that attract customers from hundreds of miles away. The ability to buy online from anywhere in the world is another factor that suggests location will be less important in the future.

central business district

The **central business district** is normally the hub of retailing activity in the heart of the downtown core (i.e., in the main street and busy cross-streets of a central area). The area usually contains the major financial, cultural, entertainment, and retailing facilities of the city. In Toronto, Bloor Street between Yonge Street and Avenue Road is now considered one of the great shopping avenues in the world. It is a street where those with money can find something to spend it on. The Eaton Centre in Toronto, Rideau Centre in Ottawa, and Pacific Centre in Vancouver, all downtown malls, are among the busiest shopping centres in their respective markets. The downtown location is a deterrent for many shoppers, though—the traffic congestion and lack of parking keep them away.

suburban mall

A **suburban mall** is located in built-up areas beyond the core of a city. In Toronto, for example, malls are geographically dispersed. In the east end of the city, there is the Scarborough Town Centre, and the west end has Sherway Gardens and Woodbine Centre. Yorkdale Mall, which is more centrally located in suburban Toronto, was the first indoor mall developed in North America. These malls draw most of their customers from those who work or live in the immediate area.

Malls located in the central business district or in suburbia contain as many as 100 or more stores and several large department stores. The stores carry shopping goods and include established retail specialty chains, such as HMV, Athlete's World, Northern Reflections, Bata, and Radio Shack. Department stores usually anchor the mall.

mega-mall

The latest trend in regional malls is the super shopping mall or **mega-mall**. The West Edmonton Mall, one of the world's largest indoor malls, helps set the standard for competing malls in this size range. The mall has an area equivalent of 115 football fields, and includes over 800 stores and services, 110 eating establishments, and 5 amusement areas, including a wave pool and rides for the children, a hockey rink, and many other attractions. A similar mall (The Mall of America) is located in Minneapolis, Minnesota. Both malls are, in fact, marketed as travel destinations.

These types of malls are growing in popularity. A new mega-mall called Vaughan Mills is scheduled to open just north of Toronto in 2004. It will be the largest mall in the region and has a potential customer base of 5 million people within 40 miles of the site. Touted as "the next generation of retailing," Vaughan Mills will be the first destination-oriented entertainment and value-oriented retail outlet centre in Canada. There will be 200 stores, mega-size theatre complexes, and other entertainment facilities. Approximately half of the tenants will be US-based stores new to the Greater Toronto Area.[16]

strip mall

A **strip mall** is usually a small cluster of stores that serve the convenience needs of the immediate residential area. Such a shopping district is generally composed of a supermarket, a drug store, a variety store, a dry cleaner, a bank, a hair stylist, and other similar service operations.

freestanding store

A **freestanding store** is an isolated store usually located on a busy street or highway. The nature of the business often influences the location of such a store. Consumers will travel beyond their immediate area for the products and services these stores provide. Examples include factory outlets, garden supply centres, discount department stores (e.g., Wal-Mart), and category killers (such as Home Depot and Staples Business Depot). The problem facing these types of retailers is that they must attract their customers without assistance from other retailers.

power mall, or power centre

A **power mall or power centre** is a mall that houses a number of category-killer superstores in one area. It is a concept that capitalizes on consumers' expressed interest in shopping in superstores where value is perceived to be greater. Stores that frequently locate in power malls include Home Depot (household products), Future Shop (electronics), Sears Home Furnishings (furniture, appliances and bedding) and Sport Chek (sporting goods).

Suburban and regional malls are being battered by the combination of power malls and consumer indifference. Research surveys indicate that people are shopping at the more traditional-style malls less frequently (2.6 visits a month in 1994, compared with 1.9 visits in 1998). Many people perceive malls to be too expensive and too crowded and admit they do not have as much time to shop anymore.[17] Given that consumers of today are working longer hours (so there is less time for shopping), and considering the dramatic growth in the development of power malls on the outskirts of urban areas, the traditional-style mall will continue to lose ground. In fact, many retail analysts predict that today's malls will be extinct within the next 10 years.

BRAND IDENTITY

In today's marketplace, a retailer must think more like a brand marketer. Effective branding strategies will affect the perceptions of the retailer held by consumers. For example, applying a store banner to a premium-quality program will enforce a premium image for the store. To demonstrate, Harry Rosen is not just another menswear retailer. Successful marketing strategies have separated Harry Rosen from its competitors. Their brand name suggests such attributes as quality, reputation, contemporary fashion, and personalized service. This shows that a powerful brand identity can be a retailer's most valuable asset.

The brand name and how it is presented to consumers is the one visual element that, without exception, must be consistently applied to all packaging, advertising, and promotions. To illustrate, one of Canada's hottest retailers is La Senza, a lingerie retailer operating under the names La Senza and Silk & Satin. The brand is the store and the store is the brand. La Senza is one of a chosen few retailers—think Gap and Roots—to have a brand that customers immediately identify and understand. La Senza is not a Canadian version of Victoria's Secret. It is a store that walks a fine line between how men see lingerie—racy and exotic—and the way women view it, as something that should be pretty but comfortable. La Senza is successful at selling lingerie in a boutique setting. The name La Senza roughly translates from Italian into "little nothings," an appropriate expression for what they sell.[18]

ATMOSPHERE

atmosphere

In retailing, **atmosphere** refers to the physical characteristics of a retail store or of a group of stores that are used to develop an image and attract customers. The image of a store has an impact on the type of customer who shops there, so retailers give their stores looks that will attract the sort of patrons they want. Image is created by a combination of elements: exterior appearance, interior appearance, store layout, and interior merchandising and display practices.

To demonstrate, the image and merchandising activity of a discounter, such as Wal-Mart, is quite different from a specialty retailer like La Senza. Wal-Mart uses bin displays to promote specials and industrial-style shelving upon which inventory can be stored on the higher shelves); lots of colourful signs that focus on price; centrally located cash registers at exits; shopping carts; and minimal personal service. On the other hand, La Senza uses the latest in merchandising display racks: store surroundings are elegant (sort of an upscale bedroom effect); well-trained and plentiful sales staff serve the customer (e.g., male customers buying gifts) discreetly; and customers pay for goods at the back of the store.

boutique, or shop-in-shop

A recent innovation to improve the atmosphere of department stores is the introduction of the boutique. A **boutique**, also referred to as **shop-in-shop**, is a store-within-a-store, a scaled down version of a freestanding store within a larger department store. Fashion boutiques for clothing lines, such as Ralph Lauren, Tommy Hilfiger, and Nautica, are found in the Bay and other department stores.

Sony recently adopted the shop-in-shop concept by striking a deal with the Bay. Building an entire Sony shop in Bay stores is a response to the consumers' desire to see leading-edge technology in a dedicated environment. Each shop features high-end consumer electronics products sold by Sony. According to John McCarter, corporate communications director at Sony, "We are always looking for new ways to expand distribution. We have carved out a niche by consistently seeking out ways of targeting lifestyle needs of consumers."[19]

MERCHANDISE ASSORTMENT

merchandise assortment

Merchandise assortment refers to the product mix; it is the total assortment of products a retailer carries. To ensure that an adequate supply of goods is available to meet customer demands, retailers take into account three merchandising components: breadth and depth of selection, assortment consistency, and stock balance.

breadth of selection

The **breadth of selection** concerns the number of goods classifications a store carries. For example, a department store carries fashion apparel, furniture, appliances, toys, sporting goods, home furnishings, fashions for men and women, linens, dry goods, and many more sorts of goods. A drugstore stocks cough and cold remedies, personal care products, cosmetics, confectionery goods, and a mixture of general merchandise.

depth of selection

The **depth of selection** is the number of brands and styles carried within each classification. A drugstore sells numerous brands of toothpaste in a variety of sizes (50, 100, 150 ml) and flavours (regular, mint, gel). The type of retailer an operation is (e.g., department store, convenience store, or variety store) and the needs of the customers it serves determine the breadth and depth of product assortment.

assortment consistency

Assortment consistency refers to product lines that can be used in conjunction with one another or that relate to the same sorts of activities and needs. An example of such consistency is a store such as Sport Chek that carries various lines of sporting-goods—baseball, hockey, basketball, and running, for example—as well as clothing and accessories to complement these sports.

scrambled merchandising

Some retailers adopt a strategy of assortment inconsistency. Called **scrambled merchandising**, it arises when a retailer begins to carry products and product lines that seem unrelated to the products it already carries. Supermarkets, such as Loblaws, have now added large pharmacy sections and general merchandise sections, and discount stores, such as Wal-Mart, are adding grocery sections. The distinctions between competitors in today's marketplace are now blurred. Such a practice stemmed from consumers' growing demand for convenience. The demand led to a one-stop shopping concept. The benefit to the retailer is that scrambled merchandising can increase traffic and profit. The retailer does, however, face additional forms of competition. Refer back to the marketing in Action vignette **Loblaws Scrambles for Growth.**

stock balance

Stock balance is the practice of maintaining an adequate assortment of goods that will attract customers while keeping inventories of both high-demand and low-demand goods at reasonable levels. This is not an easy task, but such factors as profit margin, inventory costs, and stock turnover have a direct impact on cash flow and profitability. In addition, the retailer must know the market and tailor the product mix accordingly. Thus, decisions are made regarding what assortment of name brands and private-label brands to stock, what variety of price ranges to offer, and what mix of traditional (established) products and innovative (new) products to stock.

MERCHANDISE CONTROL

There is a direct link between merchandise planning and merchandise control. The best of plans can go awry if proper controls are not implemented to measure the relationship between actual performance and planned performance. The concept of stockturn or stock turnover is a key measure of retail control. **Stockturn** is the number of times during a specific time period that the average inventory is sold. The period for calculating stockturn is usually one year. Stockturn is calculated by dividing retail sales by the average inventory. Therefore, if sales were $100 000 and the average inventory was $20 000, the stockturn would be 5 ($100 000 divided by $20 000). If a retailer determined that this was a poor stockturn rate, new marketing strategies would be considered to try to improve the situation.

stockturn

Knowing the stockturn rate allows the retailer to plan inventory (i.e., to match supply with demand) effectively. It also enables the retailer to compare the current turnover with past turnovers, to compare one department with another, and to compare the turnover (performance) of different stores in a chain operation. Stockturn is a guideline for planning.

MARKETING STRATEGY FOR RETAILERS

A host of planning elements must be coordinated into a coherent marketing strategy if growth is the goal. Survival today depends on the retailer's ability to build brand loyalty because consumers are suffering from "time starvation" and shopping at fewer stores. Surveys show that shoppers are still making between 2.6 and 3.3 shopping trips a week, but they are going to fewer stores. Consumers are thinking of stores the way they do brands, so it follows that stores to which they are extremely loyal will succeed and stores for which they feel little loyalty will fail. In response to this trend, Canadian Tire's philosophy, for example, is to "think like a brand, act like a retailer." They are building bigger and better stores that provide consumers with a pleasant shopping experience.

To devise and implement a marketing strategy, it is important for the retailer to understand what the influencers are on where people shop. Several factors are important: price, convenience, and demographics. In the past, it was the product that determined where consumers shopped, but today there is so much overlap in the places where products can be purchased that consumers' shopping patterns have changed. For example, groceries were once the domain of supermarkets, but now they are readily available in warehouse outlets, combination stores, price clubs, and online delivery services. Successful retailers react to and evolve with change in the marketplace and typically, they have certain characteristics in common. See Figure 13.8 for details of these characteristics.

Characteristics of Successful Retailers

Figure 13.8

They deliver a customer-driven, superior retail value proposition (RVP)

In being superior, they examine a package of benefits involving four elements: selection, customer experience, price, and convenience.

They lead geographic markets, categories and channels

A position of strength (market share) provides a significant bottom line bonus. Leaders, such as Canadian Tire and Shoppers Drug Mart, demonstrate this in Canada. When Canadian Tire ventured into the vast waters of US retail, they floundered and were unprofitable there.

They execute better than competitors

Successful retailers implement successful loyalty programs, and they harness information technology for such things as merchandise selection, store planning, and controlling costs.

They don't rest on their laurels but lead change by re-inventing themselves

The rapid pace of change means that a winning strategy or RVP today may sink the company tomorrow. Loblaws' move to fresh foods in the meal replacement market and Shoppers Drug Mart's redesign of its stores to present a more appealing image show the necessity to change. Stand pat and you're dead.

Source: Adapted from Harvey Schacter, "Lessons to be learned from power retailers," *Globe and Mail,* September 29, 1999, p. M1.

One of the most successful retail organizations in Canada right now is the Forzani Group Limited. Forzani operates 345 stores across Canada under banners such as Sport Chek, Forzani's, Sport Mart, Sports Experts, and Coast Mountain Sports. Forzani is achieving sales growth averaging 8 to 9 percent annually in a retail market only growing by 3 to 4 percent.

Marketing strategy has played a key role in making Forzani the No. 1 sporting goods chain in Canada. In terms of products, the company sticks to what it does best—selling a variety of sporting goods equipment and leisure clothing at various price points. Some stores (e.g., Sport Chek) are competitively priced while others (e.g., Sport Mart) offer lower prices. A recent acquisition of Mountain Sports provided an entry into the fishing, hunting, and mountaineering markets, a specialized niche with attractive growth potential.

Being the largest sporting goods retailer in the country, Forzani has buying power. That power translates into better prices for consumers. Big box sports retailers that entered Canada in the mid 1990s were a threat to Forzani initially, but they have since retreated to the south. The Forzani Group spends about $20 million annually on advertising. The budget is directed almost exclusively at radio and print because they are the media that provide the best value, according to John Forzani, CEO of the company. Says Forzani, " We concentrate on telling people what we've got and what it costs."

The atmosphere of the stores is very important. All Sport Chek stores have been upgraded with new décor and lighting. Says Forzani, "We give our customers a pleasant shopping experience. Many of the stores have a boutique-style and feel." Finally, the Forzani Group is becoming Web-savvy. An investment of $10 to $15 million in the Internet is a clear indication that the company sees e-commerce as an important part of its future. More importantly, it is a vehicle to develop relationship marketing programs. Regarding the future, John Forzani doesn't know what to expect. "The important thing is to aggressively pursue opportunities and never stand still." This is a good lesson for any retailer to follow.[20]

Summary

This chapter introduces some of the key elements of wholesaling and retailing activities. Wholesaling involves buying and handling merchandise and reselling it to organizational users, to other wholesalers, and to retailers. The functions of a wholesaler include providing direct sales contact, holding inventory, processing orders, offering sales support, enabling assortment, and breaking bulk.

There are three main categories of wholesalers. In a manufacturer's wholesaling operation, product is sold directly to customers through branch offices and sales offices. Merchant wholesaling consists of full-service wholesalers and limited-service wholesalers. Full-service wholesalers include general-merchandise wholesalers, specialty-merchandise wholesalers, and franchise wholesalers. Cash-and-carry outlets, drop shippers, truck jobbers, and mail-order wholesalers are limited-service wholesalers. The agent and broker categories encompass manufacturers' agents, brokers, commission merchants, and auction companies.

Retailing is the activity involved in selling goods and services to final consumers. The primary function of a retailer is assortment (i.e., bringing together a wide selection of merchandise to one location to meet the needs of customers). Many types of retail operations exist in Canada, and the businesses fall into various classifications, depending on form of ownership, marketing mix strategy, and method of operation.

When classified according to the nature of their ownership, stores are categorized as retail chain stores, independent stores, or retail franchise stores. When classified according to marketing mix strategy, stores are classified as self-serve, full-serve, and limited-serve. The types of stores in this category include convenience stores, supermarkets, discount supermarkets, superstores, specialty stores, variety stores, department stores, discount department stores, boutiques, and catalogue showrooms. Non-store retailing includes the use of vending machines, direct home retailing, and direct marketing. An emerging trend affecting traditional retailing is the growth of warehouse outlets, price clubs, and big box stores (category killers).

The diversity of competition facing today's retailers is creating new challenges. The biggest challenge is how and when to enter the world of electronic commerce. Many retailers are launching Web sites that will help build brand image and drive shoppers to retail locations. Others are integrating e-commerce directly with bricks-and-mortar stores.

Planning in retailing operations centres on store location. When assessing location, a retailer considers the central business district, suburban or regional shopping malls, power malls, and a variety of smaller mall alternatives. Other factors crucial to retail planning are brand identity, atmosphere, merchandise assortment, breadth and depth of selection, assortment consistency, and the creation of a marketing strategy that will encourage customer loyalty.

Key Terms

assortment consistency 364

atmosphere 363

auction company 349

big box or category killer 355

boutique (shop-in-shop) 364

branch office 346

breadth of selection 364

breaking bulk 346

broker 349

cash-and-carry outlet 348

central business district 362

cold canvas 357

commission merchant 349

depth of selection 364

direct home retailing 357

direct marketing 359

drop shipper 348

franchise wholesaler (wholesale-sponsored voluntary chain) 348

freestanding store 362

full-serve store 355

full-service merchant wholesaler 347

general-merchandise store 356

general-merchandise wholesaler 348

independent retailer 353

limited-line store 355

limited-service merchant wholesaler 348

limited-service store 355

manufacturer wholesaling 346

manufacturer's agent 349

mega-mall 362

merchandise assortment 364

merchant wholesaler 346

party selling 359

piggybacking (co-branding) 355

power mall (power centre) 363

price club 353

rack jobber 348

referrals 359

retail chain store 353

retail franchise 354

retailing 350

retailing mix 351

sales office 346

scrambled merchandising 364

self-serve store 355

specialty store 355

specialty-merchandise wholesaler 348

stock balance 365

stockturn 365

strip mall 362

suburban mall 362

truck jobber 348

warehouse outlet 353

wholesaling 345

Review Questions

1. Describe the basic functions associated with wholesaling.

2. What is the difference between a manufacturer wholesaling system and a merchant wholesaling system?

3. Identify and briefly describe the types of full-service merchant wholesalers.

4. Identify and briefly describe the types of limited-service merchant wholesalers.

5. Under what circumstances are agents and brokers likely to be used by a manufacturing organization?

6. What are the basic functions of a retailer?

7. In the context of retail franchising, what is "piggybacking"?

8. What is a category killer?

9. Briefly describe the difference between a power mall and a mega-mall.

10. Contrast the characteristics and composition of a suburban or regional mall with a strip mall.

11. What is scrambled merchandising?

12. Explain the importance of stockturn for a retailer.

Discussion and Application Questions

1. Provide a few examples of each of the following types of retailers. Do not include examples mentioned in the textbook.

   a) Discount supermarket

   b) Convenience store

   c) Specialty store

   d) Chain store

   e) Retail franchise

   f) Discount department store

   g) Category killer

2. Visit a department store in your local market, then present a brief analysis of your perception of the store's image as conveyed by the atmosphere considerations discussed in this chapter. Do the same analysis for a category killer.

3. What is the best location for the following types of stores in the market nearest your college or university? Explain your choice.

   a) Photography equipment and supply store

   b) Leisure sportswear store

   c) Upscale specialty dress shop

   d) Japanese car dealership

4. Considering the trends in retailing that were presented in this chapter, what is your assessment of the future direction of retailing? For example, will consumers opt for convenience and flock to warehouse outlets, power malls and the Internet, or will they retreat to neighbourhood shops, where personalized service is more important? What is your opinion?

5. Review the vignette "Loblaws Scrambles for Growth." Does it make sense for Loblaws to add all kinds of general merchandise lines and to compete directly with Wal-Mart and Costco? Should they stick to what they know best—groceries? What is your opinion of Loblaws strategy to add unrelated goods to their merchandise mix?

6. Select a retailer in your local market or a national chain retailer operating in your market. Conduct some secondary research on that retailer to determine the nature of its marketing strategy. What elements of the retail marketing mix are given priority? Are there any areas the retailer could improve upon?

E-Assignment

Visit the Web site of a few of the retailers mentioned below. Compare and contrast the Web sites for their ability to build image and market goods and services. Are some sites easier to navigate than others? Is it easier to buy on some sites than others? What are the characteristics of a good retail Web site? Some Web sites to visit include:
Canadian Tire
Sears
Hudson's Bay
La Senza
Mark's Work Wearhouse

Endnotes

1. www.statcan.ca/daily/English/020419/d020419a.htm.

2. Adapted from Bert Rosenbloom, *Marketing Channels: A Management View*, 3rd Edition (New York: Dryden Press, 1987), pp. 44-46.

3. www.statcan.ca/english/Pgdb/Economy/Communications/trade15.htm.

4. "State of the retail industry," *Marketing*, August 24/31, 1998, p. 34.

5. "FP500 Industry Leaders, *National Post Business*, June 2001, p. 162.

6. *Canadian Business Franchise Directory 2002*, pp. 114, 116.

7. *Canadian Franchise Annual*, 1999, p. 115.

8. "Shoppers plans big boxes," *Marketing*, May 27, 2002, p. 1.

9. *Market Research Handbook*, 2001 Edition, Statistics Canada, p. 179, annual growth rate of 4% added to 1996 data.

10. *Market Research Handbook*, 2001 Edition, Statistics Canada, p. 178.

11. "Who are Canada's e-tail blazers?" www.retailcouncil.org/press/pr20001002.

12. Sean Silcoff, "Winners take everything," *Canadian Business*, September 24, 1999, pp. 47-50.

13. Philip Quinn, "All in favour of online shopping, say 'I'" *Financial Post*, May 23, 2001, p. E2.

14. Ian Austen, "Beaver fever," *Canadian Business*, April 15, 2002, pp. 46-50.

15. Marina Strauss, "Soaring sales fail to stem Chapters red ink," *Globe and Mail*, May 25, 2000, p. B3.

16. "Megamall update: Vaughan Mills to open in 2004," www.city.vaughan.on.ca/html/cityhall/news02-01.

17. "Malls losing popularity with shoppers," *Marketing News*, May 26, 1998, p. 10.

18. Zena Olijnyk, "Va va va boom," *Canadian Business*, May 13, 2002, pp. 49-52.

19. Lucy Sadddleton, "Sony expands shop-in-shop," *Strategy*, August 27, 2001, p. 4.

20. Norma Ramage, "Forzani sticks to offence," *Marketing*, October 9, 2000, p. 23 and Hollie Shaw, "Forzani earnings soar 64%," *Financial Post*, March 23, 2002, p. FP3.

Integrated Marketing Communications

This section examines the role of the various elements of the integrated marketing communications mix. Integrated marketing communications embrace numerous forms of communication: advertising, public relations, sales promotion, personal selling, event marketing and sponsorships, direct response, and interactive communications. Chapter 14 initially describes the various elements of the marketing communications mix and then discusses in detail two elements of that mix: advertising and public relations. Advertising is examined from the point of view of how messages are created and delivered. The chapter ends with a discussion of public relations and its role in the communications mix.

Chapter 15 focuses on direct forms of communication by discussing various forms of direct response and interactive advertising opportunities.

Chapter 16 discusses related elements of the communications mix: sales promotion, personal selling, and event marketing and sponsorships.

Canadian Breast Cancer Foundation. CIBC Run for the Cure.

THINK PINK!

CIBC RUN
for the CURE
.com

seven

Integrated Marketing Communications: Advertising and Public Relations

After studying this chapter, you will be able to

1. Describe the marketing communications process and the role of the various elements of the integrated marketing communications mix.

2. Identify the factors that influence the size of a marketing budget and list the methods for determining a budget.

3. Characterize the various forms of consumer and business-to-business advertising.

4. Identify the types of creative strategies commonly used in advertising.

5. Describe the roles media planning has in the advertising process.

6. Describe the various types of public relations activities.

7. Explain what role public relations has in the communications process.

8. Assess the usefulness of a variety of public relations tools.

The Integrated Marketing Communications Mix

1.
Describe the marketing communications process and the role of the various elements of the integrated marketing communications mix.

integrated marketing communications

integrated marketing communications mix

Integrated marketing communications is the process of building and reinforcing mutually profitable relationships with customers and the general public by developing and coordinating a strategic communications program that enables them to make constructive contact with the company or brand through a variety of media.[1]

The **integrated marketing communications mix** comprises seven main elements: advertising, public relations, sales promotion, personal selling, event marketing and sponsorships, direct response advertising, and interactive communications (see Figure 14.1). This chapter focuses on two of these elements: advertising and public relations. Prior to examining each element of marketing communications, the reader should have an understanding of marketing communications and how the various elements of the mix are integrated so that they will have an impact on consumers.

The influence of technology and change in consumer media habits has forced managers to view and utilize communications alternatives differently. The traditional mass communications alternatives—television, radio, magazines, newspaper, and outdoor advertising—play key roles, but technological change has introduced more specialized media into the mix. For example, direct response television (DRTV), direct mail, public relations, and the Internet now play more prominent roles.

The development of integrated marketing communications starts with an analysis of the customer. Information is gathered on media consumption patterns, the relevance of a company's message to customers, and when customers are most receptive to messages. This information is combined with demographic and psychographic information, purchase data, and possibly attitudinal information about brands and products. Armed with such information, a marketer can develop plans to reach customers effectively and efficiently. Since organizations tend to operate with scarce resources for communications, they recognize that an integrated effort across all communications programs encourages synergy, which in turn, should have a stronger impact on the target audience.

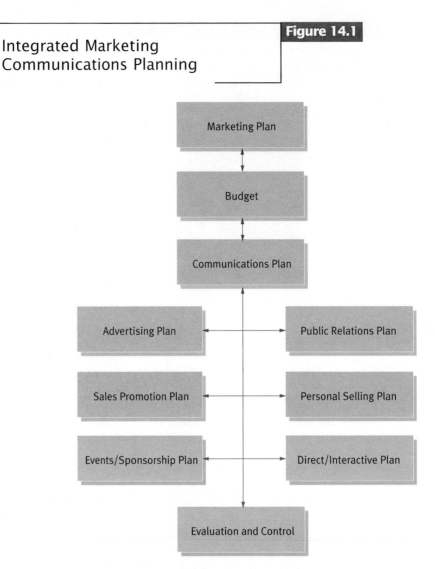

Integrated Marketing Communications Planning

Figure 14.1

The marketing communications mix is like a toolbox—the organization selects the appropriate tools that will blend together to achieve the marketing objectives of the organization. The funds available for marketing communications influence the tools that are selected.

Marketing Communications Planning

marketing communications planning

Marketing communications planning is the process of making systematic decisions regarding which elements of the communications mix to use in marketing communications. In doing so, objectives and strategies for the plan are outlined (Figure 14.1). A company develops its marketing communications plans in accordance with the direction provided by corporate plans and marketing plans. The marketing communications plan complements other marketing mix plans, such as those for pricing, product, and distribution, and together they form the company's marketing plan or a plan for a specific product or service.

MARKETING COMMUNICATIONS OBJECTIVES

Like other elements of the marketing mix, communications activity must complement the total marketing effort. Thus, each element of the mix is assigned a goal on the basis of what it is capable of contributing to the overall plans. Some typical marketing communications goals might be:

- To create, maintain, or build a company or brand image
- To position or reposition the perception of a product in the customer's mind
- To stimulate trial purchase of a product
- To create a perception of competitive advantage
- To diffuse a potentially damaging situation
- To illustrate how objectives at various levels of planning within an organization are linked together, refer to Figure 14.2.

MARKETING COMMUNICATIONS STRATEGY

Strategy is the battle plan that outlines the means of achieving the objectives. While objectives state what is to be accomplished, strategy describes how it is to be accomplished. There are two basic types of marketing communications strategy: push and pull.

Figure 14.2

The Relationships of Objectives at Different Levels of Planning

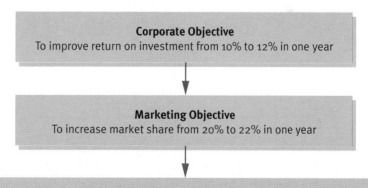

Corporate Objective
To improve return on investment from 10% to 12% in one year

Marketing Objective
To increase market share from 20% to 22% in one year

Marketing Communications Objectives

Advertising Objective
To achieve an awareness level of 60% among the 18–25-year-old segment of the market

Sales Promotion Objective
To secure trial purchase with 25% of 18–25-year-old market segment

Sales Objective
To secure distribution in 75% of key customer accounts in the first year of sales

Public Relations Objective
To generate local market media support through distribution of press releases and product samples

Push Strategy

push strategy

In a **push strategy**, the organization creates demand for a product by directing its efforts at distributor intermediaries, who, in turn, advertise and promote the product among consumers. Push strategies tend to rely on a mixture of personal selling and sales promotion techniques to create demand. The use of trade discounts and performance allowances are the foundation of push strategies (see chapters 11 and 16 for more details on specific discounts and trade promotions).

Pull Strategy

pull strategy

In a **pull strategy**, the organization creates demand by directing its efforts at consumers or final users of a product (i.e., at the business user or buyer in an organization). Pull strategies tend to rely on mass media advertising, public relations, consumer promotion activities, and event marketing and sponsorships. These activities cause consumers to search for the product in stores; by asking for the product, they put pressure on the retailer to carry it. This strategy "pulls" the product through the channel.

Most firms feel that attention must be given to both channel customers and final users; thus, it is very common for firms to combine push and pull strategies. Such companies as Nike, Coca-Cola, Kraft Canada, and Microsoft advertise their product heavily to end users, while their sales forces sell the products among business customers or channel members, using a combination of trade promotion and pricing incentives. Refer to Figure 14.3 for a visual illustration of push and pull strategies.

MARKETING COMMUNICATIONS BUDGETS

In order to develop a marketing communications budget, the manager responsible analyzes several factors, each of which has an impact on the amount of funds required.

The Flow of Push and Pull Marketing Strategies

Figure 14.3

Pull
- Activity is directed at consumers, who, in turn, request the product from distributors, and pull the product through the channel

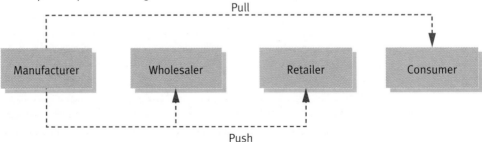

Push
- Activity is directed at distributors, who resell the product and push the product through the channel

2.
Identify the factors that influence the size of a marketing budget and list the methods for determining a budget.

The Customer

Managers must consider what type of customer is targeted when they decide on the nature of the communications activity and the size of the marketing budget. In consumer goods marketing, products directed at a wide cross-section of the population rely on advertising. In contrast, business-to-business marketing involves products with a more narrowly defined and geographically centred audience. Consequently, personal selling, sales promotion, and event marketing (e.g., trade shows) play more prominent roles in the purchase decision process. Budgets are allocated for activities when a company determines the most effective means of reaching its targets.

Degree of Competition

Crest
www.sparkle-city.com

A firm monitors the amount of money its competitors invest in communications programs as well as the effectiveness of these investments. How much its competitors spend provides a useful guideline when a firm is planning a budget. Firms that do not keep pace with others risk a loss in sales. For instance, in markets where two products or two firms dominate (Crest versus Colgate toothpaste or Coca-Cola versus Pepsi-Cola soft drinks), industry analysts project that the battle for market share between the rivals could be won or lost by the amount of communications support they offer. Competitive pressure, therefore, causes brands like Coca-Cola and Pepsi-Cola to advertise heavily to protect and build market share.

Stages in the Product Life Cycle

The amount of money required for support varies with each stage of the product life cycle. In the *introductory stage*, the objective is to create demand along with product and brand awareness. In relation to sales, the investment in marketing communications will be extremely high. Since the objective is brand development, it is common for a budget to exceed the projected return in sales. Initial losses on a brand are tolerated, as long as the brand is expected to provide adequate profit in the long-term.

In the *growth stage*, competition is present, so the competitors' budgets enter the picture. A manager is concerned about two objectives now: continuing to build awareness, and creating brand preference in the customer's mind. Accomplishing both objectives costs money. Building market share in a competitive environment is challenging and requires a budget that will attract users of competitive brands. Consequently, the brand may wind up spending more on communications in this stage than it would like to. The battle to build market share among PDAs (personal digital assistants) for brands such as Palm, BlackBerry, and Sony involve communications designed to encourage brand preference.

The focus in the *mature stage* shifts from brand development to profit maximization. Rather than spending money on communications, there is a conscious effort to preserve money wherever possible. A brand at this stage is in a maintenance position, so the budget should be just enough to sustain market share position while maximizing bottom-line profit. If life cycle extension strategies such as product modifications, new packaging and new varieties occur, the level of communication support could increase in the short-term (e.g., to create awareness during part of a year).

In the *decline stage*, profit motives take priority. Since new products have taken over the market, marketing budgets for old products are cut significantly or withdrawn entirely. Profits that are generated from brands in this stage are allocated to brands that are in their developmental stages.

BUDGETING METHODS

An organization can use a variety of budgeting methods: percentage of sales, industry averages, arbitrary allocation, and task or objective.

Percentage of Sales

percentage-of-sales method

For the **percentage-of-sales method**, the usual procedure is to forecast sales volume in dollars for the forthcoming year and allocate a predetermined percentage of those sales to marketing. This predetermined percentage may be a figure traditionally used by the organization. The shortcoming of this system is obvious—the philosophy underlying the method is that communications result *from* sales, whereas the wise manager prefers to believe that communications result *in* sales. The popularity of this method is due to its simplicity and to the fact that it at least connects expenditures with sales.

Industry Averages

industry average

Some marketing organizations try to base their marketing communications budgets on the **industry average** (e.g., the average of what all competitors spend). Depending on the performance objectives established for a product, the company decides to lag behind, to be equal to, or to exceed the spending of competitors. Using average historical expenditures for the industry as a starting point, companies attempt to forecast competitive spending for the next year and then position their budget accordingly. For example, if an industry historically spends from 5 to 10 percent of their sales on marketing communications, such a figure would be a good one to start with. However, the influence of other planning objectives, such as the desire to grow or build market share, often forces the firm to modify this "starting point" budget.

Arbitrary Allocation

arbitrary-allocation method

The **arbitrary-allocation method** is popular with small firms that lack the resources for much promotional support and do not have a formal budgeting process. Relying on his or her own knowledge and experience, the owner or manager analyzes cost and profit trends and then assigns an arbitrary amount to cover promotion expenses. Because the amount allocated is an arbitrary one, the effects of communications as a marketing stimulus are not considered in the case of this method.

Task (Objective)

task method

The budgeting methods discussed so far fail to acknowledge that communications is a means of achieving marketing objectives. The **task method**, on the other hand, assumes that promotion has an impact on sales. There are a few basic steps to this method: determine the task, determine the type and quantity of communications activity needed (e.g., how to employ each element of the marketing communications mix), and determine the cost of the various recommendations. The sum of these costs becomes the budget.

Advertising and Its Role

advertising

Advertising is a paid form of nonpersonal message communicated through the media by an identified sponsor.[2] Advertising is persuasive and informational, and is designed to influence the thought patterns of the target audience in a favourable manner. Once a favourable attitude develops, the role of advertising is to motivate purchase of a specific brand of product.

Prior to discussing advertising, it is imperative the reader understand the nature of communications process (see Figure 14.4). The process begins with a sender (the advertiser) who develops a message to be transmitted by the media (TV, radio, Internet, magazine, newspaper, etc.) to a receiver (the consumer or business customer).

In the communications process, competing products also send messages to the same target market; meanwhile the target market may be doing things that distract them from all messages being sent to them. Such distractions are referred to as **noise**. Advertisers take steps to try and break through the clutter of competitive advertising and make an impact on consumers. Typically, breakthrough messages produce positive attitudes and higher rates of purchase (a form of positive feedback). Dull messages or misunderstood messages that don't break through the clutter do not influence attitudes, so purchase rates are low (a form of negative feedback).

When deciding what products to buy, a consumer passes through a series of behaviour stages, and advertising can influence each stage. One such model refers to the various stages as AIDA, an acronym for *awareness, interest, desire,* and *action*. Another model is ACCA, an acronym for *awareness, comprehension, conviction,* and *action*.

It is difficult to directly link advertising to sales; what *can* be measured is how well the message communicates (e.g., in generating awareness and interest) and whether consumers like or dislike the message and the way it is presented. If an ad grabs attention and stimulates interest and preference (e.g., the message influences behaviour), there is a stronger likelihood that the desired action will occur. A description of each behaviour stage is provided below.

1. *Awareness* In this stage, the customer *learns of something for the first time*. Obviously, the learning can occur only if he or she is exposed to a new advertisement. Awareness

The Communications Process

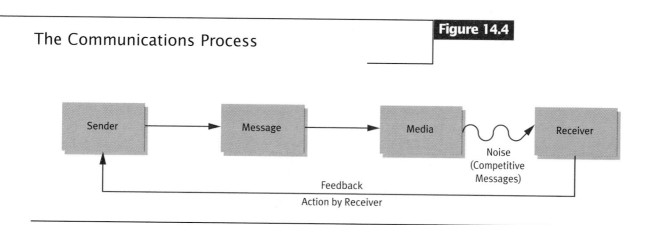

Figure 14.4

can also come from word of mouth, a situation that is beyond the control of the organization.

2. **Comprehension** By this stage, *interest* has been created. The individual perceives the message as relevant, and the product, judged from the information presented, is considered useful. The product becomes part of the customer's frame of reference.

3. **Conviction** The customer evaluates the product benefits presented in the advertising. The product is viewed as satisfactory, and has gained *preference* in the customer's mind. The customer may be sufficiently motivated to buy it when needed.

4. **Action** In this stage, the desired active *response* occurs. For example, a car advertisement motivates a customer to visit a dealer or a Web site; a coupon motivates a reader to clip it for use in an initial purchase.

Simply stated, the goal of advertising is to link the benefits of a product to the needs of a target market. By doing so, an advertiser can start to influence customer perceptions and hopefully create preference over competitive alternatives. Apple Computers Inc., for example, positions the iMac computer as something that is fun and easy to use (Figure 14.5). For first-time buyers who may be somewhat afraid of technology, the iMac might be just the computer they are looking for.

Apple Canada
www.apple.ca

The Forms of Advertising

3.
Characterize the various forms of consumer and business-to-business advertising.

Advertising is classified into two broad categories: consumer advertising and business-to-business advertising.

CONSUMER ADVERTISING

Consumer advertising can be further subdivided into four types.

national advertising

National advertising is the advertising of a trademarked product or service wherever the product or service is available. The term "national" here refers to the brand name rather than to a geographic area. National advertising messages identify a brand name, the benefits offered, and the availability of the product or service. The advertising messages for such products as Coca-Cola, Campbell's Soup, Nissan cars, and the Royal Bank are examples of national advertising. The ads displayed throughout this chapter fall into this category.

retail advertising

Retail advertising refers to advertising by a retail operation to communicate image, store sales, and the variety of merchandise carried. Retail advertising is one of the largest categories of advertising in Canada and includes advertisers such as the Bay, Wal-Mart, The Hudson's Bay Company (the Bay and Zellers), and Sears. Specialty store retailers such as Harry Rosen (men's fashions) and Roots (active leisure fashions) are also in this category.

end-product advertising

End-product advertising is advertising that promotes an ingredient of a finished product. Advertising of this nature encourages consumers to look for a particular component when buying a final product. For example, a consumer takes his or her film to a retailer to get it processed into a picture (the finished product). Kodak encourages consumers to visit a shop that displays the Kodak paper sign (the customer's guarantee of quality prints). Kodak paper is part of that finished product.

direct-response advertising

Direct-response advertising involves advertising directly to consumers and bypassing traditional channels of distribution (wholesalers and retailers) in the delivery of the

A Clear and Convincing Message
to Differentiate Apple from Other
Personal Computers

Figure 14.5

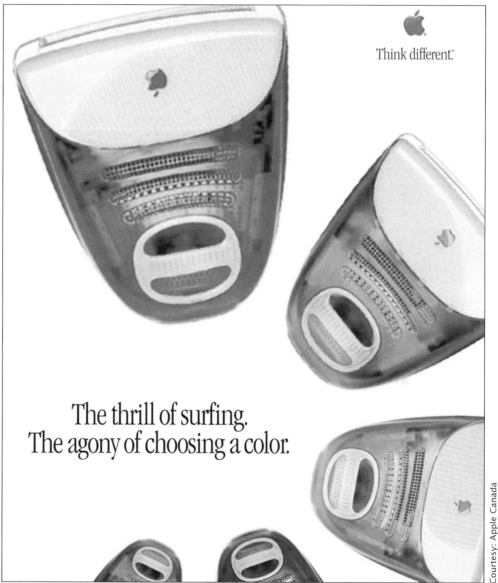

Think different.

The thrill of surfing.
The agony of choosing a color.

Courtesy: Apple Canada

product. Such advertising includes infomercials that are shown on television, direct-mail offers, and banner advertising on the Internet. Ads in these media include information on how to order goods or services directly.

BUSINESS-TO-BUSINESS ADVERTISING

business-to-business advertising

Business-to-business advertising occurs when a business advertises its products, its services, or itself to other business organizations. Among the major types of business-to-business advertising are trade advertising, industrial advertising, service industry advertising, and corporate advertising.

trade advertising

Hardware Merchandising www. hardwaremerch.com **Canadian Packaging** www. canadianpackaging. com

industrial (business) advertising

service industry advertising

Trade advertising originates from a source supplier, such as a manufacturer, and is directed at members of a channel of distribution. The goal of trade advertising is to encourage distributors to carry and resell a product. The message is communicated to distributors in trade publications, such as *Canadian Grocer* (food distribution trade), *Hardware Merchandising* (building-supply and related retail trade), and *Foodservice and Hospitality* (food-service and restaurant trade).

Industrial (business) advertising is advertising by industrial suppliers directed at industrial buyers. For raw materials, processed materials, and accessory equipment, advertising generally conveys two messages: one to create initial product awareness, and the other to develop sales leads. Specialized magazines aimed at specific industries such as *Heavy Construction News, Canadian Packaging,* and *Materials Management and Distribution* provide a vehicle for industrial advertising. Leads are developed when prospects exposed to messages take action (e.g., responding to a toll-free number, returning a reply card, or interacting with a Web site).

Service industry advertising is a type of advertising that increases awareness and communicates detailed information about products and services. Drug manufacturers, for example, address the medical profession through a number of publications, including *The Medical Post* and *Canadian Family Physician*. The legal profession can be reached through such magazines as *Canadian Lawyer* and *The Lawyer's Weekly*. Marketers to the legal profession include producers of accounting systems, legal software systems, and business equipment.

Creating the Advertising Message

advertising agencies

The task of developing an advertising campaign is usually handled by an advertising agency. **Advertising agencies** are organizations responsible for creating, planning, producing, and placing advertising messages for clients (the advertisers). The development of an advertising campaign can be divided into two basic parts: creative (message) and media.

copywriter

art director

In an advertising agency, the creative department develops advertising ideas and concepts. A **copywriter** converts marketing information into a persuasive sales message composed of a headline, body copy, and slogan, while the **art director** develops a visual presentation that works with the copy in gaining an interested response from the target audience. Copywriters and art directors usually work as a team, collaborating on client assignments to impart a certain continuity and consistency to the advertising effort.

CREATIVE OBJECTIVES

creative objectives

key benefit statement

support-claims statement

Setting creative objectives is the first stage in developing an advertising message. **Creative objectives** state what information is to be communicated to a target audience. They usually contain a **key benefit statement**, which conveys the basic idea, service, or benefit the advertiser is promising the consumer, and a **support-claims statement**, which verifies or provides proof of the promise. To illustrate the use of promise and support claims statements, refer to the illustration in Figure 14.6. The benefit that Sony promises for its flat screen TV is the elimination of distortion and reflections, and crisp and clear colour. Copy statements such as "pioneers in flat screen technology," "digital reality creation (DRC)," and "high precision deflection yoke" provide the proof of

Sony Presents the Key Benefit (Promise and Support Claims) with a Graphic Visual Demonstration

Figure 14.6

Courtesy: Sony Canada

promise. Showing the message as it would appear on a regular TV (an art direction decision) helps substantiate the promise. Sony summarizes its message with the slogan, "Everything Looks Better On A Wega." Wega is pronounced VAY-guh.

CREATIVE STRATEGY

The **creative strategy** specifies how a message is to be communicated to the target audience. It pinpoints the personality and image that an agency should strive to create for its client's products and services through the mood, tone, and style of the advertising. For example, the ad for a perfume may appeal to a customer on the basis of sex or love; one may use humour to dramatize a household cleaner's effectiveness; and the ad for a food product may use a taste comparison with a competitor to show superior taste benefit. For more details, see the section titled Types of Advertisements.

CREATIVE EXECUTION

creative execution

Creative execution refers to the formation of more precisely defined strategies for presenting the message. In this stage, strategies are converted into a physical presentation that expresses the desired image, mood, and personality. The goal is to find the best or most convincing way to present a product so that the customer will be motivated to take the desired action.

To illustrate, consider a TV spot aired by General Motors to communicate its contribution to driver safety. The spot, called "What If," was shot in black and white and used slow-motion imagery of a car crash shown in reverse. The effect on viewers was captivating and sometimes chilling. The creative team opted for black and white (unusual for television) because the creative team wanted the spot to be more graphic and dramatic.[3] Refer to Figure 14.7 for a visual impression of the spot.

TYPES OF ADVERTISEMENTS

This section examines some of the common strategic and execution techniques used in advertising today.

Humorous

In humorous advertisements, the promise and proof are presented in a light-hearted manner. One such example is the television commercial for Danone La Creme yogurt. The commercial opens with a scantily clad maid (short black skirt, black hosiery, and low-cut blouse to expose some cleavage) apparently serving the male master of the house. The two characters interact and laugh together as she serves and he enjoys the yogurt. The maid then sits on the man's lap. Just then, a young girl enters the room with a friend unexpectedly. Looking disgusted, she says, "My parents are so weird." The mother responds, "You're home early."

Humour is an effective advertising technique. In a recent poll of Canadian viewers one-third of respondents said humour in a commercial is the one thing that can make it more appealing than another commercial.[4]

Comparative

In comparative advertisements, the promise and proof are shown by means of comparing the attributes of a given product with those of competing products—attributes that are

A Car Crash Shown in Black and White Slow-Motion Reverse Increases the Impact of a General Motors Commercial

Figure 14.7

1 – A wrecked car rests at a telephone pole after an accident.

2 – The car begins to move backwards, retracing the accident's path. Dents and scratches vanish as the film moves in reverse.

3 – The car continues moving backwards to the point where it left the road. More dents and scratches vanish, the broken windshield reconstructs.

4 – The car continues retracing its path to the point where it swerved to avoid an 18-wheeler truck.

5 – The car moves in reverse away from the truck and down the road. The car is in perfect condition.

6 – The car parks and the film stops moving in reverse. With the film now moving forward, the driver gets out and walks away.

Courtesy: General Motors of Canada and MacLaren McCann

important to the target market, usually the primary reason why they buy the product. Comparisons can be direct (e.g., the other brand is mentioned) or indirect (e.g., there is reference to another brand but it is not identified). Dove soap, a Lever Ponds brand, compares itself to Oil of Olay soap, a Procter & Gamble brand, on the basis of mildness.

Comparative campaigns present an element of risk for the initiator, usually the number two brand in a market. If the brand leader fights back, financial commitment is required in order to extend the comparison battle. Further, any claims of superiority must be supported by marketing research data. The brand that initiates the comparison cannot mislead the public with any false claims. If they do, the competitor is likely to instigate legal proceedings to force the offending brand to offer proof of its claims.

Emotional

Emotional advertisements concentrate on creating a mood and conveying the message in a manner that arouses the feelings of the audience or shows that psychological satisfaction is gained by using the product.

One of the best examples of an emotional message is the ad for De Beers diamonds which has been on television for years. In the spot, there are shadows of a man and woman, darting, swirling, and touching to the soaring intensity of an original orchestral firestorm, the glowing diamond being slipped onto her finger, the shadows kissing deeply. The commercial was shot in black and white with a Cape Cod beach house as the backdrop. By the time the voice-over positions the diamond as being worth two months' salary, you're saying, "Is that all?"[5]

Lifestyle

Some advertisers attempt to associate their brand with the lifestyle of a certain target audience. This type of appeal is demonstrated in the "Just Do it" campaign for Nike. Nike's ads embody courage, glory, dedication, attitude, and superhuman achievement. So powerful are the messages that Nike received thousands of letters from people all over North America, who claimed the campaign gave them the inspiration or courage to "just do" all kinds of things: to get fit, to go back to school, to change careers. That is the spirit of Nike, and that is the meaning the company drives into the brand.[6]

Porsche Motor Cars
www.porsche.com

Lifestyle appeals are becoming increasingly popular, owing to the greater availability of psychographic information on Canadian consumers. For example, Labatt Blue uses lifestyle appeals extensively in its "Out of the Blue" campaign. Here, active young people are shown enjoying a particular lifestyle. The imagery in the ads along with the catchy slogan reinforce the lifestyle association, while the core message is intended to reflect the attitude of Blue's target market. Automobile marketers also rely on lifestyle appeals, particularly for top-end brands. The Porsche ad in Figure 14.8 appeals to an upscale lifestyle.

Testimonial

In the case of testimonial advertising, a typical user of the product or an apparently objective third party describes the benefits of the item. Such a tactic is quite common in automobile advertising, where comments about a car by an influential car magazine are incorporated into an ad. In the toothpaste market, Colgate Total incorporates the phrase "Colgate Total is the only dentifrice to earn the Canadian Dental Association seal of approval for gingivitis reduction and for the prevention of tooth decay." Such an endorsement by a third party enhances the credibility of its message (see Figure 14.9). Colgate is the leading brand of toothpaste in Canada.

An Advertisement Appealing to an Upscale Lifestyle

©2000 Porsche Cars North America, Inc. Porsche recommends seat belt usage and observance of all traffic laws at all times. Specifications for comparison only.

Boxster S, Sunflower field, Route 59, CO.

What a dog feels when the leash breaks.

Instant freedom, courtesy of the Boxster S. The 250 horsepower boxer engine launches you forward with its distinctive growl. Any memory of life on a leash evaporates in the wind rushing overhead. It's time to run free. Contact us at 1-800-PORSCHE or porsche.com.

PORSCHE

PORSCHE, BOXSTER and the Porsche Crest are registered trademarks and the distinctive shapes of PORSCHE automobiles are trade dress of Dr. Ing, h.c.F. Porsche AG. Used with permission of Porsche Cars North America, Inc. Copyrighted by Porsche Cars North America, Inc.

Celebrity Endorsements

An endorsement is a testimonial by a celebrity or "star," whose popularity the advertiser attempts to capitalize on. Stars from television, movies, music, and sports form the

Figure 14.9

The Endorsement by an Independent Third Party Enhances Credibility

The choice of today's dentists.

At your next check-up, ask your dentist about Colgate Total, the only toothpaste that goes beyond fighting cavities to provide long-lasting protection against plaque, tartar, and gingivitis. Colgate Total's unique formula actually works to protect you between brushings.

Recently, the Canadian Dental Association awarded Colgate Total its coveted Seal of Recognition. Colgate Total is the first and only toothpaste recognized by the CDA for both helping to prevent tooth decay and for reducing gingivitis. That's why it's the choice of today's dentists.

®Registered Trademark of Colgate-Palmolive Canada Inc.

nucleus of celebrity endorsers. Tiger Woods appears frequently in television ads for Buick automobiles and American Express.

Advertisers must be careful about whom they select to present the product. Among the techniques deemed unbelievable by consumers, endorsements rank the highest (72 percent of respondents in a recent survey).[7] Despite this fact, star power attracts advertisers. No sooner did Jamie Salé and David Pelletier win their silver medal (upgraded to a gold medal due to an international judging controversy) at the Salt Lake City Olympic Games than the duo appeared in ads for Crest Whitestrips, a product that whitens teeth. The image of Salé and Pelletier—the "all-Canadian couple"—was a perfect fit for the brand. Compared to professional athletes however, Olympic athletes can fade from the public's radar screen fast. Advertisers beware!

Character Presenters

What character is closely associated with Kellogg's Frosted Flakes? You are right if you said Tony the Tiger. Character presenters help differentiate one brand from another and play a leading roll in producing a positive image for a brand. Over time, there have been many popular brand icons, among them: the Pillsbury Doughboy, the Energizer Bunny, and the A&W Root Bear. They may also be human characters like the idle Maytag Repairman and the Man from Glad.

In many cases, the history of these characters have become so neatly woven into the social fabric—witness Ronald McDonald or Tony the Tiger—they are destined to live forever. Characters can be creatively limiting because they lock a brand into a campaign for an extended period of time. Their personalities cannot change, for then they wouldn't be the same character. At A&W for example, the Root Bear is traditionally depicted ambling in his slow, bumbling style. When A&W tried to put him in unusual or unbelievable situations the results were disastrous. Since the bear has never spoken, he will never speak.[8] See the illustrations in Figure 14.10.

Advertising Icons

Figure 14.10

Energizer Bunny courtesy of Eveready Battery Company Inc.; Ronald McDonald used with permission from McDonald's Corporation.

In Canada, a group of characters known as the Tetley tea folk have played a significant role in building the Tetley brand of tea. Very recently, Tetley added a new character to the family—Aunt Welly. The new character helped launch a line of specialty teas and updated the brand's image among the 35- to 54-year-old target market.[9]

Sexual Appeal

The use of sexual appeal in certain product categories has become increasingly popular in recent years. For such product categories as cosmetics, perfumes, and lingerie, sex is used as an effective motivator. As long as core customers don't find the use of sex offensive, an advertiser may be onto something.

Generally speaking the use of sex in an ad should fit the product and the lifestyle of the target market. In recent years Carlsberg beer has used sexual themes to its advantage. One ad featured a man and woman lustily groping each other in a motel doorway (the room number: 69). The punch line to the ad was that the couple was actually married. A more recent ad for Carlsberg features a woman discussing a new boyfriend with two other women. Using a subtle downward hand gesture, her friend alludes to his prowess at giving oral pleasure. "I don't even have to ask," the woman murmurs unbelievingly. When the man joins the group a moment later, he is greeted by approving glances all around. As one veteran creative said, "It's a whole new twist on the tired old beer phrase, 'It goes down great.'"[10]

Product Demonstrations

The use of a demonstration is quite common in advertising centred on product performance. Several execution options are available. For example, a "before-and-after" scenario is common for diet-related products and exercise equipment, where the message implies usage by the presenter. A second strategy is to simply show the product at work—a technique commonly used in advertising for household products, such as paper towels, cleaners, and floor wax. Remember Bounty towels—the quicker picker-upper!

Another technique is to portray the *brand as a hero*—it solves those really big or messy problems—as in the case of a laundry detergent getting things really clean. See Figure 14.11 for an illustration. Taking a demonstration to extremes (e.g., exaggerated punishment for the product) is referred to as a *torture test*. The Timex watch campaign, "Takes a licking and keeps on ticking" is perhaps the classic case of the use of torture testing.

For more insight into the nature of advertising messages and how the ideas for ads are developed, refer to the Marketing in Action vignette **Flashy Ads Aren't Tim Hortons' Cup of Coffee**.

VIRTUAL ADVERTISING

virtual advertising

Advancing electronic technology has created a new form of advertising called virtual advertising. **Virtual advertising** involves the insertion of electronic images such as signs, logos, and even product packages into live or taped television programs. The computer-generated ads are sufficiently life-like that viewers see them as real even though they are anything but.

So far, virtual advertising has been a novelty in live sports programs (e.g., racing cars driving by make-believe billboards, or make-believe signs behind home plate at a

A Simple Message that Demonstrates the Brand-As-Hero Technique

Figure 14.11

First for every disaster.

S.O.S
Steel wool soap pads

Courtesy: The Clorox Company of Canada Inc.

Blockbuster Video
www.blockbuster.ca

baseball game), but mainstream programs are now moving in that direction. Advertisers are now paying fees to have images of their products inserted after show production is completed. Blockbuster, Coca-Cola, and Evian are a few advertisers that are experimenting with virtual advertising.[11] Critics of virtual advertising claim the technique deceives consumers. Marketing managers claim it is a useful technique to reach channel surfers who flip around during commercial breaks.

Marketing in Action

Flashy Ads Aren't Tim Hortons' Cup of Coffee

For many advertising agencies, winning advertising awards is a sign of success. It gets the agency into the business news, improves their image, and attracts new clients. But is that what good advertising is about? Do award-winning advertising campaigns produce the desired business results—do they increase market share or sales?

Sometimes when an ad, particularly a television ad, gets too creative, the original objective of the ad gets lost. The end result is an ad that may be great to watch, but doesn't make an impact. Did it deliver a message that was understood by the audience? It could be a waste of money! Tim Hortons and its advertising agency, Enterprise Creative Selling, agreed on an approach of sticking to the basics, and by doing so produce results—they sell a whack of coffee, donuts, and bagels.

Tim Hortons' advertising has helped build the company into a Canadian icon (over $2 billion in sales revenue)—proving that advertising doesn't have to be flashy to work. "We'd love to win awards, but it's just not our driving force," says Alison Simpson, general manager of Enterprise. And Tim Hortons is quite happy about that. In fact, Tim Hortons and Enterprise have been business partners for 11 years, a considerably long time for an industry where clients and agencies play musical chairs frequently.

Churning out ads that work consistently is a challenge for Enterprise. In 1996 Enterprise only produced 8 commercials; in 2001 it produced 22 commercials, not counting original creative developed for French-language markets. With so much work on their plate, keeping the ads simple, just like the products they promote, makes sense. To be sophisticated would alienate Tim Hortons' core customers.

At times there is some flare and a bit of goofiness. Think of the guy at the border butchering the "RRRollup the rim to win" slogan. And how about Shorty Jenkins—the old dude with a pink cowboy hat and superior rink flooding skills—almost a national hero after appearing in a TV ad. The same can be said about Lilian, an elderly woman with a walking cane who walks half way across town every day for a large Tim Hortons coffee. These ads were part of Tim Hortons' "True Stories" campaign.

The strength of Tim Hortons' advertising is its simplicity; the focus is always on the product. Another strength is variety—the ads change constantly in order to promote new or different products like coffee cake, or to rejuvenate interest in old standbys—such as selling a box of Tim Bits for 99 cents. The TV spots are a true reflection of the experience of visiting a Tim Hortons. According to Ken Wong, marketing professor at Queen's University, "Their advertising is not brilliant, but it's disciplined." And perhaps that is a good lesson for all advertisers to learn. Doing what's best for the client is always best for the advertising agency. If an award or two happens to come along, then it's icing on the cake!

Adapted from John Heinzl, "Enterprise finds that hokey sells," *Globe and Mail*, March 15, 2002, p. B7.

Dick Hemingway

Media Planning

5.
Describe the roles media planning has in the advertising process.

The media department of an advertising agency is responsible for planning and arranging the placement of advertisements; it schedules and buys advertising time (broadcast media) and space (print media). The media department prepares a document that shows all the details of how a client's budget is spent to achieve advertising objectives. In scheduling, they strive to achieve maximum exposure at the lowest possible cost.

MEDIA OBJECTIVES

media planning

Media planning begins with a precise outline of media objectives, a media strategy, and the media execution and culminates in a media plan that recommends how advertising funds should be spent to achieve the previously established advertising objectives.

media objectives

In defining **media objectives**, media planners consider how, when, where, and to whom the message will be sent. The first consideration is the target market. The target market is defined in terms of demographic, psychographic, and geographic variables. The desired physical presentation of the message (whether in print or by broadcast) influences the actual medium (newspaper, magazine, billboards, radio, or television) that is selected to communicate with the target. Next, geographic market priorities are established, a selection process usually influenced by the size of the media budget. The final thing to be considered is the best time to reach the target: the best time of day, day of week, or period of weeks during the year.

MEDIA STRATEGY

media strategy

A **media strategy** describes how the media objectives will be accomplished: how many advertisements or commercials will run, how often, and for what length of time they will appear. A media strategy presents recommendations regarding what media to use and details why certain media are selected and others rejected.

Matching the Target Market

Essentially, the task of an advertising agency's media department is to match the advertised product's target-market profile with a compatible media profile, such as the readership profile of a magazine or newspaper, or the listenership of a radio station. Three common target-market media strategies are as follows:

profile matching

1. In the case of **profile matching**, the advertising message is placed in media where the profile of readers, listeners, or viewers is reasonably close to that of the product's target market. For example, advertising in the *Globe and Mail's Report on Business* reaches one type of person; an advertisement in *Hockey News* reaches another.

shotgun strategy

2. In the case of a **shotgun strategy**, general-interest media are selected to reach a broad cross-section of a market population. For example, television may be chosen to make contact with diverse age groups, from young children to teens to adults (e.g., an NHL game); newspapers may be used to gain access to a broad cross-section of adult age groups.

rifle strategy

3. In the case of a **rifle strategy**, the target market is defined by a common characteristic, such as employment in a certain industry or participation in a leisure activity. Media that appeal specifically to this common characteristic are then used. For example, *Ski Canada* magazine is used to reach skiers and *Hotel & Restaurant* magazine to reach people in the hospitality industry.

Reach, Frequency, and Continuity

reach

During the development of a media strategy, the organization must decide on the reach, frequency, and continuity needed to fulfill the media objectives for an advertising message. These factors interact with one another. **Reach** refers to the total audience potentially exposed, one or more times, to an advertiser's schedule of messages in a given period, usually a week. It is expressed as a percentage of the target population in a geographically defined area. Assume a television station is seen by 30 000 households in a geographic area of 150 000 households. The reach would be 20 percent (30 000 divided by 150 000).

frequency

Frequency refers to the average number of times an audience is exposed to an advertising message over a period, usually a week. The airing of a television commercial three times on a station during a week would represent its frequency. In media planning, a balance must be struck between reach and frequency. A common dilemma faced by a media planner is whether to recommend more reach at the expense of frequency, or vice versa.

continuity

Continuity refers to the length of time required to ensure a particular medium affects a target market. For example, an advertiser may schedule television commercials in eight-week flights three times a year, thus covering a total of 24 weeks of the calendar year. A **flight,** or **flighting**, refers to the purchase of media time and space in planned intervals, separated by periods of inactivity.

flight or **flighting**

impressions

The combination of reach, frequency, and continuity is expressed in terms of impressions made on a target audience. **Impressions** refer to the total audience delivered by a media plan. Impressions are calculated by multiplying the number of people reached by the average number of times they are reached in the total schedule.

Market Coverage

coverage

Coverage refers to the number of geographic markets where the advertising is to occur for the duration of a media plan. In deciding the extent of coverage, the advertiser could select national, regional, or particular urban markets, depending on its marketing and advertising objectives. Such factors as budget, sales volume by area, and level of distribution by area affect the selection.

Timing

In determining the best time to reach a target market, marketers may focus on the time of the day, the week, or the year. The best time to advertise a product or service is the time at which it will have the most impact on the consumer's buying decision. For example, the decision to buy a snowmobile is probably made in the fall. Therefore, if advertising is scheduled for the winter, the message will be delivered too late. Sometimes an advertiser plans its advertising in bursts. A **blitz strategy**, for example, involves spending a large amount of money in a short space of time and then tapering off considerably. In contrast, a **build-up strategy** starts out slowly and gradually builds over a longer period of time. Both alternatives are appropriate for launching new products.

blitz strategy

build-up strategy

Assessing Media Alternatives

In conjunction with other strategic factors, the advantages and disadvantages of the various media are considered (Figure 14.12). An advertiser can rarely use all the media.

Media Selection Considerations

Figure 14.12

Media Alternatives

Advantages	Disadvantages
Television	
1. Impact—sight, sound, and motion; demonstration	1. Cost—high cost of time and commercial production
2. Reach—very high among all age groups	2. Clutter—commercials are clustered together, reducing impact
	3. Fragmentation—audience has many stations to choose from
Radio	
1. Targeting—reaches a selective audience based on type of music	1. Retention—short, single-sense messages
2. Reach and Frequency—reaches the same audience frequently	2. Fragmentation—many stations in large markets reduces impact
Newspaper	
1. Coverage—good local market reach	1. Life Span—short, a one-day medium
2. Flexibility—the message can be inserted quickly and altered quickly	2. Target Market—reaches a broad cross-section; not specific target
Magazine	
1. Target Marketing—specialized magazines reach defined demographic groups	1. Clutter—each issue contains too many advertisements
2. Environment—quality of editorial content enhances the advertising message	2. Frequency—low message frequency (monthly publication)
Outdoor and Transit	
1. Reach and Frequency—frequent message sent to same target audience (based on daily travel patterns)	1. Message—small size in transit; short messages in outdoor
2. Coverage—available on a market-by-market basis	2. Targeting—reaches the broad cross-section of a market's population
Direct Marketing	
1. Targeting—reaches a preselected and defined audience	1. Image—low (e.g., junk mail) image; hard-sell approach required to solicit orders
2. Control—expenditure can be evaluated directly for effectiveness	
Internet	
1. Targeting—reaches a specific audience (tracking capabilities of medium)	1. Reach—low penetration of medium so far
2. Interactive—two-way communication of detailed content	2. Behaviour—surfers avoid ads (low click rates)

traditional mass media

Specific media are chosen in keeping with budget constraints and in consideration of the habits of the target market and of such variables as reach, frequency, and continuity. Television, newspaper, magazine, radio, and transit and billboard advertising are among the **traditional mass media**. Automobile advertising, for example, is concentrated in television and print (magazines and newspapers). Television creates awareness and a sense of excitement about an automobile, while print creates awareness and gives readers more specific details about the automobile.

In addition, a marketing organization can send messages by unique vehicles. Among these vehicles are: sports and stadium advertising, theatre-screen advertising, mural advertising (hand-painted messages covering the entire sides of buildings), and elevator advertising.

sponsor integration

Smart marketers are now looking at alternative ways of getting a brand message in front of their target audience. Recognizing that television viewing is declining somewhat and that the public is literally bombarded with messages each day, they ask what is the likelihood of being noticed and remembered? The solution is to mesh brand advertising with program content, a concept called **sponsor integration**. TSN was an innovator in this area. The prime advantage of sponsor integration is obvious—the ad is part of the editorial content, ensuring that people aren't looking away and flipping channels. During the NHL playoffs (2002) TSN promoted a segment called "Molson Canadian Playoff Breakdown," a fast-paced commentary on games featuring Gord Miller (host), Bob MacKenzie (analyst) and Pierre McGuire (analyst).

MEDIA EXECUTION

media execution

Media execution is the final stage of media planning. It is the process of fine-tuning media strategy into specific action plans. Such action plans are divided into the following areas: evaluating cost comparisons so that one particular medium may be selected over another; scheduling specific media in a planning format (i.e., establishing a media calendar of activity); and developing budget summaries that show how advertising funds are to be spent. For example, if magazines are the chosen medium, the decision regarding which magazines to use and how often advertisements will appear in the magazines is made. To reach a business executive, an advertiser, such as Mercedes-Benz or Jaguar, may decide to use a combination of magazines, such as the *National Post's Business* magazine, the *Globe and Mail's Report on Business* magazine, or *Canadian Business*. Depending on the budget available, these advertisers could use all or any combination of the magazine alternatives.

CPM (cost per thousand)

The selection decisions just described are made on the basis of which medium is the most cost efficient in reaching the target audience. Each magazine mentioned above would be compared on the basis of CPM. **CPM (cost per thousand)** is the cost incurred in delivering a message to 1000 individuals. It is calculated by dividing the cost of the ad by the circulation of the publication in thousands. Therefore, if an ad cost $30 000 and the circulation was 750 000, the CPM would be $40 ($30 000 divided by 750). The publication with the lowest CPM is the most efficient at reaching the target.

Public Relations

public relations

Public relations consists of a variety of activities and communications that organizations undertake to monitor, evaluate, and influence the attitudes, opinions, and behaviours of groups or individuals who constitute their publics. There are two differ-

6.

Describe the various types of public relations activities.

internal publics
external publics

ent publics: *internal publics* and *external publics*. **Internal publics** involve those who the organization communicates with regularly. These parties are close to the day-to-day operations of the organization and include employees, distributors, suppliers, shareholders, and regular customers. **External publics** are not close to the organization and are usually communicated with infrequently. They include the media, governments (all levels), prospective shareholders, the financial community, and community groups.

The word "*relations*" is important, for it signifies the organization is involved in a relationship with its publics, and that relationship should be a positive one. Positive relations are the result of open, honest, and forthcoming communications with an organizations' publics.

It is important to understand the difference between advertising and public relations. Advertising is usually concerned with brand image. In contrast, public relations is usually more concerned with corporate image. Public relations spreads good news about an organization and helps remedy problem situations when they arise. Advertising is bought and paid for by an organization so it controls the content of the message. In contrast, public relations is controlled by the media; it is not paid for by the sponsoring organization. Organizations, however, can and often do include paid advertising as part of their public relations activity.

The Role of Public Relations

7.

Explain what role public relations has in the communications process.

The role of public relations is varied but generally falls into six key areas: corporate communications, reputation management, publicity generation, developing sound relationships with the media, developing positive relationships with the community, and fund raising by not-for-profit organizations.

CORPORATE COMMUNICATIONS

As suggested earlier, public relations can play a vital role in building and protecting the image of a company. It doesn't take much for a company's image to come tumbling down if a crisis situation is handled improperly.

issue management

On the positive side of the ledger, an organization takes a stand on issues that directly or indirectly affect its operations. Referred to as **issue management**, activities deliver to the public a message that shows exactly where the company stands on a particular issue. For example, a company's stance on environmental issues may be of utmost importance. Is the company taking a pro-active stance on protecting the environment? If they are, then a loud and clear message should be sent to the public.

corporate advertising

These kinds of messages can be delivered to the public by paid advertising or through public relations. **Corporate advertising** is advertising designed to convey a favourable image of a company among its various publics (consumers, shareholders, business customers, suppliers, and so on). It may attempt to create or improve a company image by showing how the resources a firm has solves customers' problems, by promoting goodwill, or by demonstrating a sense of social responsibility. **Social responsibility** is an attitude of corporate conscience that anticipates and responds to social problems. Shell Canada Limited advertises how it integrates economic progress with environmental issues. Refer back to Chapter 1 (Figure 1.8) for an illustration).

social responsibility

advocacy advertising

Another alternative is advocacy advertising. **Advocacy advertising** is any kind of public communication, paid for by an identified sponsor, that presents information or a point of view on a publicly recognized, controversial issue. The objective is to influence public opinion (see Figure 14.13 for an illustration). The Ontario attorney general initiated a campaign to stop drinking and driving to reduce the number of accidents caused by people driving while under the influence of alcohol.

REPUTATION MANAGEMENT

Public relations is a vital form of communication for a company during a crisis. The final outcome of such a crisis often depends on how effectively a firm manages its public relations activity. For instance, a drug manufacturer may face an angry public when a drug it markets is linked to certain unexpected health problems. When the press gets a hold of such a story and informs the public, a company has to be instantly ready to go into crisis management mode.

Figure 14.13

An Illustration of Advocacy Advertising

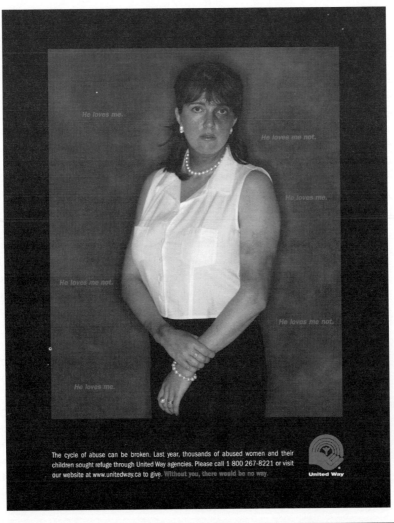

Courtesy: United Way of Greater Toronto

A much publicized public relations disaster in recent years was the Bridgestone/Firestone tire scandal. Bridgestone did not manage the crisis effectively. The company mishandled concerns about tire safety by not addressing consumer questions and requests for replacement tires quickly enough. The tires were linked to more than 100 deaths and as many as 6.5 million tires were eventually recalled. The fatal mistake made by Bridgestone/Firestone was in not taking action before being forced to by the US government. When action was taken it was merely a reaction.

To add fuel to the fire, Bridgestone tried to implicate the Ford Motor Company by attacking safety problems associated with the Ford Explorer. Passing the buck doesn't cut it with angry customers! If there is any doubt that public relations plays a role in marketing communications, this case proves it. In 2000, Bridgestone's earnings dropped 80 percent and its stock value dropped in value by 50 percent.[12]

As a safety valve, companies must be prepared for crisis situations. Senior executives must be prepared to act quickly and show that they have control of the situation. They must take control of the communications agenda early and ensure that messages are credible and based on fact from the outset. Company presidents and high-level executives must be ready to meet the demands of a more sophisticated and more demanding consumer audience, or suffer the consequences of its wrath.

PRODUCT PUBLICITY

publicity

Publicity is news about a person, product, or service that appears in the print or broadcast media. Essentially, publicity must be newsworthy. Unfortunately, what seems like news to a company may not be news to the media. Opportunities to communicate newsworthy information include the launch of a new product, revealing new information based on research evidence (e.g., a discovery), securing a significant contract that will generate new jobs, and achieving significant sales and profit results.

The greatest success of a prescription drug ever was driven solely by publicity. In March 1998, Pfizer Inc. launched Viagra, a scientific breakthrough for male impotence, via a news conference and satellite video news releases to stations in every TV market. The company fielded more than 1000 media calls from news organizations and scientific and medical media. Viagra became an instant headline around the globe. A week later pharmacists were filling 20 000 prescriptions a day. Within six weeks more than a million prescriptions were filled. The rush to Viagra was fuelled entirely by massive coverage in the news media. A previously taboo subject was being discussed openly on shows such as *20/20* and *Prime Time Live*. Viagra later launched a national advertising campaign that encouraged readers to "ask their doctor" for more information.[13]

PRODUCT PLACEMENT AND PRODUCT SEEDING

product placement

Product placement is the insertion of brand logos or branded merchandise into movies and television shows and is another tactic for generating publicity. Since television viewers have a tendency to channel surf during commercial breaks, product placement has become increasingly popular with many companies. In fact, product placement is now so blatant that the brand is integrated right into the script of the show or movie. *Castaway*, starring Tom Hanks, was nothing more than an extended commercial for FedEx. In addition to featuring countless FedEx packages and logos, the film even managed to accommodate a brief history of the courier's corporate rise. *Survivor*, the popular reality-TV show, featured brands such as Reebok, Mountain Dew, Budweiser, and Doritos.[14] So much for roughing it in the outback!

product seeding   A more recent phenomenon to generate publicity is seeding. **Product seeding** involves placing a new product with a group of trendsetters who in turn influence others to purchase the new product. For more insight into the effectiveness of product placement and product seeding see the Marketing in Action vignette **Creating Buzz**.

Creating Buzz

One of the latest trends in marketing is a thing called buzz marketing. Loosely defined, buzz is using the power of word-of-mouth communications to create excitement and awareness, and stimulate sales of a product.

Some very prominent companies and brands have literally been built on buzz: The Body Shop, Tropicana, and Krispie Kreme to name a few. Strategic programs and events can catapult brands onto the front pages of newspapers and into the national spotlight of TV news—as was the case when Guy Lafleur (once a famous hockey player) did a public service announcement about erectile difficulties, paid for by Pfizer Canada, the maker of Viagra.

In the wake of changing demographic trends, consumer preferences, and lifestyles, brand marketers are shifting their way of thinking in order to be relevant to consumers. Consumers are spending less time with the media (they are time-poor) so public relations and buzz are taking on a new role in building and protecting a brand.

Consider what Reebok Canada did when it launched of the new U-Shuffle DMX shoe for women. The shoe is a laceless black and red sneaker, a trendy kind of style. The company gave 90 young women from across Canada a free pair ($150 value) and asked them to wear them around town. A classic case of product seeding. Reebok's goal was to get the funky cross-trainer on the feet of suburban trendsetters, who in turn would influence others to purchase the new product. It worked! The trendsetters were asked all kinds of questions about the shoes and women wanted to know where they could buy them.

Buzz marketing offers several advantages. The biggest advantage is the low cost—it's nowhere near the cost of an ad campaign to launch a new product.

It also has the capability of reaching a narrowly defined target, as in the case of Reebok. Reebok carefully screened 1000 women in Toronto, Montreal, and Vancouver to select the right 90 people for the seeding. If the seeding works it will attract the attention of the media and next thing you know there is a complete story in the newspaper!

Does buzz marketing and word-of-mouth communications really work? The jury is still out on this issue but one thing is certain. It is gaining in popularity because consumers are more connected than ever due to cell phones and the Internet—word can spread really fast! Reebok is a true believer. According to Micki Rivers, marketing manager for Reebok Canada, "The seeding strategy got the shoes off to a running start. The new Urban Training collection line that includes the U-Shuffle DMX, was the most successful women's launch in recent history."

Other marketing factors also played a role in the success of the new shoe. For that reason it is difficult to identify the true impact of seeding and a word-of-mouth strategy. Consequently, many marketing managers remain skeptical about its effectiveness.

Adapted from Judy Lewis, "Building buzz," *Marketing*, January 28, 2002, p. 17; and John Heinzl, "If the shoe fits, sell it," *Globe and Mail*, September 7, 2001, p. M1.

A.Inden/Zefa/MaXx Images

MEDIA RELATIONS

media relations

Media relations specialists are employed by public relations companies, and their primary responsibility is to develop unique and effective relationships with the media that cover the particular industry in which they specialize (e.g., financial information, computer hardware and software, automobiles, retailing). Their role is to get industry analysts on board so they will communicate favourable information about a company or brand. The relationship between a media relations specialist and a reporter is important and is something that develops over time. It is predicated on characteristics such as respect, honesty, accuracy, and professionalism.

COMMUNITY RELATIONS AND PUBLIC AFFAIRS

In an era of social responsibility, companies are placing high value on programs that foster a good public image in the communities in which they operate. Many companies encourage their employees to give back to the community; some even provide a few hours of work time each week to get involved. Sponsoring community events and teams is part of being a good corporate citizen. Tim Hortons is involved with numerous community programs: it supplies team jerseys to local soccer and hockey teams, free ice skating for families in local communities during the Christmas holidays, and sends thousands of children to camp each year through the Tim Hortons Children's Foundation.[15]

public affairs
lobbying

Public affairs involves strategies to deal with governments. To communicate with governments involves lobbying. **Lobbying** involves activities and practices that are designed to influence policy decisions of governments. Naturally, a company or an industry wants government policy to conform to what's best for business. Governments, however, must balance economic well-being with social and environmental well-being, and therein lies the conflict between business, governments and special interest groups (e.g., groups that attack companies on the basis of their handling of environmental issues or labour practices).

FUND RAISING

In the not-for-profit market sector, public relations plays a key role in fundraising. A national organization like the United Way faces a huge challenge each year. Some people perceive the organization to be a big "money hole," and wonder where all of the donations go. To change this perception, public relations is used to educate the public about how the funds are used, to predispose people to give, to solicit commitment, and to make people feel good about giving. The goal of the United Way's campaign (or any other similar campaign) is to create a positive image and secure support by sending a message to the public that clearly states what the organization is all about.

The Tools of the Trade

8.
Assess the usefulness of a variety of public relations tools.

The tools available to execute public relations programs are diverse. There are those that are used routinely to communicate newsworthy information and those that are used periodically or on special occasions only. This section discusses those vehicles that are used routinely. Refer to Figure 14.14 for some information about some unique and periodically used vehicles.

	Figure 14.14
Some Unique and Innovative Public Relations Tools	

Here are some tactical suggestions for getting the media and the public to take notice of a brand or company.

Awards	Brand or company-sponsored awards that support brand positioning and leadership (e.g., Imperial Oil Awards for Achievement for minor hockey players in Canada).
CEOs	The top executive should be the company's most effective media spokesperson (e.g., Bill Gates at Microsoft and Steve Jobs at Apple).
Road Shows	The brand hits the road with a decorated vehicle as a means of attracting attention. Product samples may be given away at each stop. Red Rose Tea reshaped a Volkswagen Beetle to look like a teapot (handle on the back hood and spout on the front hood).
Trade Shows	Shows are the ideal launching pad for new products. Be where your customers are (e.g., Comdex shows display the latest gadgetry in computers and telecommunications; auto shows display new cars and concept cars for the future).

PRESS RELEASE

press release

A **press release** (news release) is a document containing all of the essential elements of the story (who, what, when, where, and why). Editors make quick decisions on what to use and what to discard. Copies of the release are mailed to a list of preferred editors (e.g., established and reliable contacts based on past relationships) and it can also be distributed by a national newswire service and posted on the company Web site. News releases are distributed at news conferences or sent to the media directly by mail, fax, and e-mail.

PRESS CONFERENCE

press conference

A **press conference** is a gathering of news reporters invited to witness the release of important information about a company or product. Because the conference is time consuming for the media representatives, it is usually reserved for only the most important announcements. Handing a crisis situation, for example, is usually handled by a

press kit

press conference. A press kit is usually distributed at a conference. The **press kit** includes a schedule of conference events, a list of company participants including biographical information, a press release, photographs, copies of speeches, videos, and any other relevant information.

PUBLICATIONS

house organ

A publication or **house organ** is a document that outlines news and events about the organization and its employees. It can be distributed internally to employees or externally to suppliers, distributors, shareholders, and alumni, etc. A house organ can be in the form of a newsletter, newspaper, or magazine. The objective of the house organ is to generate goodwill and build positive public opinion about the organization. Most colleges and universities have an alumni publication that is well received by former students. They like to know what's going on at the alma mater.

POSTERS AND DISPLAYS

Posters and displays are a common form of internal employee communications. They communicate vital information regarding safety, security, employee benefits, and special events. Displays and exhibits are a portable and mobile form of communications. An exhibit typically provides a history of an organization, product displays and information, and future plans (e.g., plant expansion, new product innovations, etc.). Exhibits are appropriate for shopping malls, colleges, and universities. Internally, bulletin boards are a useful vehicle for keeping employees informed about news and events. E-mail is now a quick and convenient way to communicate important information to employees.

WEB SITES

Since the purpose of the Web site is to communicate information about a company it can be an effective public relations tool. Visitors to a Web site quickly form an impression about a company based on the experience they have at the site. Therefore, the site must download quickly and be easy to navigate. Providing some kind of entertainment or interactive activity also enhances the visit. The Web site provides an opportunity to inform the public of an organization's latest happenings. Content can vary from financial information to product information to games and contests. It is now quite common to post all press releases about the company on the corporate Web site.

Summary

Marketing communications is any means of communication used by marketing organizations to inform, persuade, or remind potential buyers about a product or service. To fulfill these tasks, an organization employs an integrated marketing communications mix comprising advertising, public relations, sales promotion, personal selling, event marketing and sponsorship, direct response advertising, and Internet communications. Integrated marketing communications is a process of building and reinforcing mutually profitable relationships with customers and the general public by developing and coordinating a strategic communications program that enables them to make constructive contact with the company or brand through a variety of media. A company can use two types of communications strategy: push and pull. In the case of a push strategy, the firm directs its efforts at the channel members or intermediaries; with a push strategy it directs efforts at final business users or consumers. Often, a firm will use a combination of push and pull strategies.

In developing a budget, a business considers many factors, including the characteristics of the customers and the activities that motivate their purchase decisions, the degree of competition that exists, and the stage of the product life cycle the product has reached. Several different methods of determining the actual size of a budget are available to the firm.

The primary role of advertising is to influence the behaviour of a target market in such a way that its members view the product, service, or idea favourably. In developing print and broadcast messages, the creative team (copywriter and art director) considers the behavioural stages an individual passes through prior to making a purchase decision. These behaviour stages are awareness, comprehension, conviction, and action.

In advertising planning, there is a clear division between creative and media functions. On the creative side, creative objectives (what to communicate) are established, and a creative strategy (how to communicate) is developed. In communicating messages, a company uses a variety of techniques, including humour, comparisons, testimonials, celebrity endorsements, character presenters, demonstrations, and sexual, emotional, and lifestyle appeals. The media plan is divided into three sections: media objectives, media strategy, and media execution. A well-conceived media plan will use the right media to gain maximum exposure for the message developed by the creative department. The media plan will consider such factors as reach, frequency, continuity, market coverage, timing, and which medium is appropriate for delivering the message. All media decisions are influenced by the amount of budget available. Since budgets tend to be scarce, new alternatives such as sponsor integration are being added to the media mix.

Public relations refers to the communications a firm has with its various publics. Controlled by the media, it is a form of communication for which the organization does not pay, but it is based on information supplied by the organization. Public relations plays a role in developing an organization's image and is an important means of communication in times of crisis. At the product level, publicity and product placement are strategies used to promote brands.

The key areas of public relations are corporate communications, reputation management, product publicity, product placement and seeding, media relations, community relations and public affairs, and fund raising.

The most commonly used tools of the public relations trade include press releases, press conferences, publications, posters and displays, and Web Sites.

Key Terms

advertising 379

advertising agencies 382

advocacy advertising 397

arbitrary-allocation method 378

art director 382

blitz strategy 394

build-up strategy 394

business-to-business advertising 382

continuity 394

copywriter 382

corporate advertising 397

coverage 394

CPM (cost per thousand) 396

creative execution 384

creative objectives 382

creative strategy 384

direct-response advertising 380

end-product advertising 380

external publics 397

flight (flighting) 394

frequency 394

house organ 403

impressions 394

industrial (business) advertising 382

industry average 378

integrated marketing communications 373

diff {

Review Questions

1. Briefly describe the elements that comprise the integrated marketing communications mix.

2. Briefly explain the difference between a push strategy and a pull strategy.

3. When devising an advertising budget, what factors must a manager evaluate?

4. Explain the difference between percentage of sales budgeting and industry average budgeting.

5. Explain the significance of the following behaviour stages in terms of developing an advertising message: awareness, comprehension, conviction, and action.

6. What is the difference between a key benefit statement and a support claims statement?

7. In the context of message development, what is the difference between creative strategy and creative execution?

8. What is virtual advertising?

9. In what situations would the following target market media strategies be used: shotgun strategy, profile matching strategy, and rifle strategy?

10. Explain the following media strategy concepts: reach, frequency, and continuity.

11. Briefly explain the concept of "sponsorship integration" in television programming.

12. Identify and briefly explain two different roles of public relations.

13. What is the difference between product placement and product seeding?

14. What is the difference between a press release and a press conference?

Discussion and Application Questions

1. Provide examples of commercials or campaigns that use the following creative appeals:

    a) Humour

    b) Emotion

    c) Lifestyle

    d) Testimonial

    e) Comparison

    f) Sex

2. Is virtual advertising a distortion of the truth? Does it breach any ethical advertising standards?

3. Assume you are the marketing manager for Powerade, and you are considering using a celebrity to present your product in advertising. What type of celebrity would you select? Would you select a rising star or an established star? Justify the position you take.

4. Which media are best suited to a profile-matching strategy, e.g., a shotgun strategy? Provide some specific examples.

5. Assume you are responsible for devising a media plan for the Apple iMac computer or a Harley-Davidson motorcycle. Define the primary target market and then identify the primary medium you would recommend to reach the target. Provide justification.

E-Assignment

1. Your task is to conduct an Internet-based secondary research investigation to find information that will verify the effectiveness or ineffectiveness of a particular creative strategy. Pick a strategy from among the following: humour, comparison, emotion, lifestyle, testimonial, celebrity endorsement, character presenter, sex, and product demonstration. Prepare a brief report based on your findings.

2. Visit the Web site for a few of the following companies (or others you may visit frequently). Evaluate the site as a vehicle for public relations activity. Does the site provide worthwhile information that will create goodwill for the company? Does it present a positive image? Make appropriate recommendations for changes where necessary. Prepare a brief report for each company you select.

Volkswagen	vw.com
The Body Shop	the-body-shop.com
Levi Strauss	levi.com
Apple	apple.com
Disney	disney.com

Endnotes

1. William F. Arens, *Contemporary Advertising*, 6th Edition (Chicago, IL: Richard D. Irwin, 1996), p. 198.

2. Betsy-Ann Toffler and Jane Imber, *Dictionary of Marketing Terms*, Barron's Business Guides, 1994, p. 13.

3. Lesley Young, "Grace under fire," *Marketing*, Create Supplement, Spring 2002, p. 5.

4. Marc Leger and Dave Scholz, "The last laugh," *Marketing*, April 15, 2002, p. 12.

5. Barry Base, "Staying power measure of a great campaign," *Strategy*, November 9, 1999, p. 18.

6. Eric Young, "Harnessing the power of the brand," *Marketing*, May 8, 1995, p. 37.

7. Jo Marney, "Credibility and advertising," *Marketing*, June 3, 1998, p. 22.

8. Sinclair Stewart and Paul Brent, "Off with their heads!" *Financial Post*, August 28, 2000, pp, C1, C5.

9. Lisa D'Innocenzo, "New character, updated message round out Tetley ads," *Strategy*, January 14, 2002, p. 7.

10. Wendy Cuthbert, "Racy ads pushing the boundaries," *Strategy*, September 25, 2000, p. 20.

11. David Carr, "TV advertising goes virtual," *Marketing*, March 22, 1999, p. 20.

12. "Crisis," *Strategy*, Special Report on Public Relations, April 9, 2001, p. 18.

13. Thomas L. Harris, *Value-Added Public Relations*, (Chicago: NTP Publications, 1998), p. 63.

14. Sinclair Stewart, "On-screen products create credibility gap," *Financial Post*, March 26, 2001, p. C5.

15. www.timhortons.com.

First Light

seven

Direct Response and Interactive Communications

> Learning Objectives

After studying this chapter, you will be able to

1. Describe the various types of direct response advertising.
2. Explain the advantages and disadvantages of various forms of direct response advertising.
3. Assess the strategies for delivering effective messages via direct response techniques.
4. Describe the various elements of Internet communications.
5. Evaluate the various online advertising models available to marketing organizations.
6. Assess the potential of the Internet as an advertising medium.

Direct response advertising is a form of media advertising that communicates messages directly to marketing prospects. Direct mail is the most common means of delivering these messages, but other forms of direct communication such as telemarketing, direct response television, and catalogues now play a more significant role. The Internet allows organizations to reach prospects in their own environment with a message that is active and interactive in nature compared to passive, traditional forms of advertising. The Internet is a different medium so marketing managers must evaluate new strategies for communicating with customers if the Internet is to be part of the communications mix.

Direct Response Advertising

1.
Describe the various types of direct response advertising.

Direct response is rapidly becoming a vital component of the integrated marketing communications mix and it plays a key role in influencing buying behaviour. A recent study among Canadian companies conducted by the Canadian Marketing Association (CMA) indicates that within 5 years (2005) direct response will experience 38 percent growth. That would mean spending of $12.9 billion in 2005, up from 9.4 billion in 2000. Overall sales as a result of this investment are expected to reach $81.7 billion, up from $51.2 billion in 2000. John Gustavson, president of the CMA, says this huge increase in direct response is a strong indication of Canadian companies' increasing recognition of its effectiveness.[1]

Currently, direct mail advertising amounts to $1.2 billion or 14 percent of net advertising revenues (for time and space only) in Canada. As an advertising medium, direct mail ranks third, just behind newspapers (18 percent of net advertising revenue) and television (26 percent of net advertising revenue).[2] Presently, Canadians only spend about one-third the amount that an American does making purchases through direct response communications vehicles.[3] Such a low figure supports the premise that there is tremendous potential for direct response initiatives in Canada.

In Canada, direct marketing will continue to grow. Some of the reasons for this include companies' desire for immediate returns on advertising dollars spent, which direct response advertising offers, the trend toward niche marketing, and the availability of database marketing techniques. As well, advances in computer software technology are fuelling high interest in database marketing techniques and customer relationship marketing programs. Very simply, firms can now design and develop programs that reach customers individually and efficiently. Finally, the growing costs associated with mass media such as television and newspapers has forced companies to search for more efficient methods to communicate with customers.

Prior to discussing some of the direct response communications techniques, some distinctions should be made between the following marketing terms, which are often confused with each other. Students should first recognize that direct response advertising is a subset of direct marketing. Second, students should understand that the objective of direct response communications is to encourage action immediately. Direct response communications delivers an offer to customers.

direct marketing

1. **Direct Marketing** is a marketing system, fully controlled by the marketer, that develops products, promotes them directly to the final consumer through a variety of media options, accepts direct orders from consumers, and distributes products directly to the consumer.

direct response advertising

2. **Direct Response Advertising** is advertising through any medium designed to generate a response by any means (such as mail, television, telephone, or fax) that is measurable. If traditional mass media is used, the message will include a 1-800 telephone number, mailing address, or Web site address where more information can be secured.

The major forms of direct response advertising are direct mail, direct response television (DRTV), telemarketing, and catalogues. Direct mail is currently the primary medium for delivering direct response advertising messages; however, due to advancing electronic technology, it is expected that direct response television will play a much stronger role in the communications mix in the future.

Direct Mail

direct mail

2.
Explain the advantages and disadvantages of various forms of direct response advertising.

Direct mail is a form of advertising communicated to prospects via the postal service. The use of mail is widespread due to its ability to personalize the message (the name can be included in the mailing), the need to send lengthy messages (e.g., copy-oriented sales messages along with reply cards and contracts that are returned by prospects), and its ability to provide a high degree of geographic coverage economically (e.g., the mailing can be distributed to designated postal codes anywhere in Canada). There are numerous options available.

Sales Letters

letter

The most common form of direct mail, the **letter**, is typeset, printed, and delivered to household occupants or to specific individuals at personal or business addresses. Letters are usually the primary communication in a mailing package, which typically includes a brochure, reply card, and postage-paid return envelope.

Leaflets and Flyers

leaflets and **flyers**

Leaflets and **flyers** are usually standard letter-sized pages (8.5" x 11") that offer relevant information and accompany a letter. Leaflets expand on the information contained in the letter and generate a response (i.e., the recipient takes action).

Folders

folders

Folders are sales messages printed on heavier paper, and often include photographs or illustrations. They are usually folded, and are frequently designed in such a way that they can be mailed without an envelope. **Postage-paid reply cards** are an important component of a folder. See Figure 15.1 for an illustration.

postage-paid reply cards

Statement Stuffers

bounce backs

Statement stuffers, or **bounce backs** as they are often called, are advertisements distributed via monthly charge-account statements (such as those one receives from Sears, the Bay, or VISA). Capitalizing on the ease of purchasing by credit, such mailings make it very convenient to take action. In this case, one order leads to another, and the prospect is reached at very low cost. Usually, the credit card number is the only information the seller requires.

A Folder With a Postage-Paid Reply Card Makes It Easy to Respond to an Offer

Figure 15.1

Videocassettes and CD-ROMS

Organizations now send serious prospects information by more sophisticated means. Videos are popular for demonstrating how a product works, how nice a resort destination looks, how well an automobile performs. In business-to-business markets the CD-ROM is useful for presentation purposes (when combined with personal selling practices) and for letting customers review things on their own time. Both videocassettes and CD-ROM aptly portray how a product works. As well, technical information about a product that is hard to communicate in hard copy is easily accessed on a CD-ROM. These are but a few applications for these media. They can be part of a direct mail campaign or a follow-up to a direct mail campaign (e.g., for those who requested more information from the original mailing).

DIRECT MAIL STRATEGY

Essentially, an organization has the option of delivering a mail piece by itself and absorbing all of the costs associated with such a mailing, or delivering an offer as part of a package that includes offers from other companies. The latter option is far less costly. This is the difference between solo direct mail and cooperative direct mail.

Solo Direct Mail

solo direct mail, or selective direct mail

Solo direct mail or **selective direct mail** refers to specialized or individually prepared direct mail offers sent directly to prospects. Solo direct mail pieces are commonly employed in business-to-business communications, supplementing the messages frequently communicated via traditional business publications. Due to the degree of personalization, response rates to this type of mailing tend to be much higher than for a co-operative mailing. Refer to Figure 15.2 for an illustration of a solo direct mail piece.

Cooperative Direct Mail

co-operative direct mail

Co-operative direct mail refers to envelopes containing special offers from non-competing products. Consumer-goods marketers commonly employed this method. A typical mailing would contain coupons for a variety of grocery, drug, and related products, magazine subscription offers, pre-printed envelopes offering discounted rates for film processing, and so on. The Val-Pak envelope—distributed nationally, but contains ads for local businesses—is an example of a cooperative direct mailing. Co-operative direct mailings are frequently used by marketing organizations to achieve trial purchase of a good.

Direct mail marketing has been around for a long time but it was an activity that traditional advertisers such as packaged goods companies, banks and financial institutions, and automobile manufacturers avoided for a long time. These industries were turned off by the negative images that were associated with direct marketing techniques. Now, these very industries and the leading companies within them are among the largest users of direct mail. Clearly, the advantages of direct mail are an attraction to companies wanting to deliver messages to customers one-on-one.

For a summary of the advantages and disadvantages of direct mail as an advertising medium refer to Figure 15.3.

Contents of a Typical Direct Mail Campaign

Figure 15.2

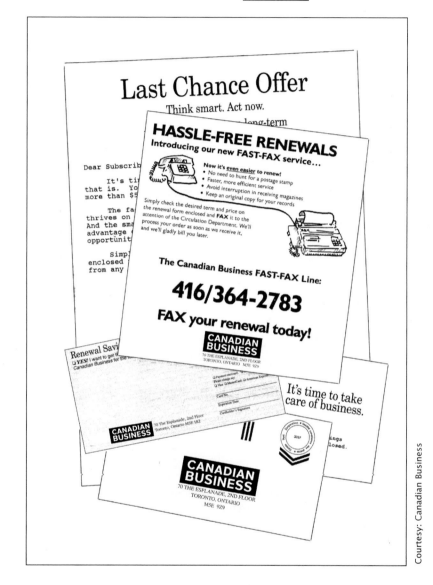

Courtesy: Canadian Business

Included in this campaign are a cover letter, a pamphlet outlining benefits, a response card or order form, and a postage-paid return envelope.

Information Is Key to Success

3.
Assess the strategies for delivering effective messages via direct response techniques.

Embarking upon a direct mail marketing campaign involves three basic steps: obtaining a proper prospect list, conceiving and producing the mailing piece, and distributing the final version.

Advantages and Disadvantages of Direct Mail Advertising

Figure 15.3

Advantages	Disadvantages
Audience Selectivity	**High Cost per Exposure**
Precise targets can be reached in terms of demographic and geographic variables. House lists are a good starting point, along with lists from brokers.	Costs can be higher than other print alternatives when costs of producing the mailing, renting lists, mailing, and fulfilling orders are considered.
Message Flexibility	**Absence of Editorial Support**
There is an opportunity to include a lengthy message (tell more, sell more) and incentives to stimulate action.	Direct mail stands alone; it must grab the receiver's attention quickly.
Exclusivity	**Image**
Mail does not compete with other media when it arrives in a household.	Consumers perceive it to be "junk" mail, so it may be promptly discarded.
Measurability	**Delivery Delays**
Based on historical conversion patterns, sales results can be accurately forecast. Traditional media can only measure for awareness and interest.	Relying on the postal service and third class mail could result in delivery delays; timing of a delivery may be important.

OBTAINING DIRECT MAIL LISTS

The direct mail list is the backbone of the entire campaign. Both the accuracy and definition of the list can have a significant bearing on the success or failure of a campaign. Companies recognize that it costs about six times as much to acquire a new customer as it does to keep an existing one.[4] As a result, companies are compiling databases to keep track of existing customers and are forming relationships with them through the mail and electronic means. Lists are secured from two sources: internal sources and external sources.

INTERNAL SOURCES

There is no better prospect than a current customer. Therefore, a company's internal database must be monitored and updated routinely. For example, Canadian Tire accumulates considerable data on customers through its own credit card. As well, Hudson's Bay Company collects a mountain of data from its Hudson's Bay Rewards program card. Data mining techniques allow these companies to determine who their heavy customers are, what they buy, how much they buy, and how often they buy. For companies placing value on repeat business, this information can be used to develop new offers that will be of interest to current customers. Today, banks and financial institutions are the most frequent users of internal database-driven, direct mail techniques. In direct mail terms, an internal customer list is referred to as a **house list**.

house list

As an alternative, companies can take steps to form lists of potential customers. Such customers are referred to as prospects. As Figure 15.4 illustrates, DaimlerChrysler is collecting information about customers that they can use in the future. This information-oriented postcard appeared in a national magazine with a full-page ad for a Chrysler automobile.

EXTERNAL SOURCES

People that have a history of responding to mail offers tend to be attractive prospects for new offers. Buying by mail is part of their behaviour. Therefore, the challenge is to find prospects that have a demographic profile, and perhaps a psychgraphic profile, that mirror the profile of current customers. A **list broker** can assist in finding these prospects. The buyer provides the broker with the profile of the target customer, and the

list broker

Figure 15.4

A Reply Card That Collects Valuable Information about Potential Customers

☑ Please send me more information on 2001 Chrysler Town & Country

(Please print)

Please circle one: Mr. Mrs. Ms. Miss Date of Birth____

First Name____ Middle Initial____ Last Name____

Mailing Address____

City ____ Province ____ Postal Code____

Work Phone____ Extension____ Home Phone____

E-mail Address____

1. Do you have a preferred retailer? Yes ☐ No ☐ Retailer Name____
2. Language Preference: English ☐ French ☐
3. What vehicle(s) do you currently own?
   Year____ Make____
   Model ____ Own ☐ Lease ☐
   Year____ Make____
   Model ____ Own ☐ Lease ☐
4. What other vehicle are you considering?
   Year____ Make____
   Model ____

By completing this form, you recognize that DaimlerChrysler Canada has a serious and legitimate interest in collecting personal information for the purpose of operating its business. You acknowledge and give your consent to DaimlerChrysler Canada to collect, use, store, disclose and distribute your personal information for the purpose of receiving more information about its products and/or marketing programs, and to share this information with its affiliates, agents and financial institution for any legitimate commercial purpose.

Your file will be maintained in Windsor, Ontario, and you may, upon written request, have access to it. You may also request that your personal information be corrected or that your consent to maintain and disclose your information be withdrawn, except where otherwise required by law.

5. When do you plan to acquire your next vehicle?
   ☐ Less than 2 months ☐ 2-3 months ☐ 4-6 months
   ☐ 7-12 months ☐ 1 year +
6. Do you plan to purchase or lease your next vehicle?
   ☐ Purchase ☐ Lease ☐ Undecided
7. How often do you acquire a new vehicle?
   ☐ Every 1-3 years ☐ Every 4-7 years ☐ 7 years +
8. What are the three most important deciding factors when making your new vehicle purchase? ☐ Styling ☐ Comfort ☐ Safety ☐ Performance and Handling ☐ Passenger Capacity ☐ Quality and Workmanship ☐ Price/Monthly Payment

CHRYSLER

MA MCLETC 0102001

Courtesy: DaimlerChrysler Corporation

merge/purge

broker supplies a list of possible prospects on a cost-per-name basis. Generally, a high-quality list is developed through a **merge/purge** process on a computer, whereby numerous lists are purchased, combined, and stripped of duplicate names. Names are typically purchased on a CPM (cost per thousand basis). As the quality of a list becomes more sophisticated or specialized (e.g., more demographic or geographic factors are added), the rate per thousand increases.

Canada Post also supplies information vital to the accurate targeting of messages. For example, a postal code can isolate a small geographic area—say, a city block—and can then be combined with census data to provide relevant statistics regarding the ages and incomes of homeowners in the area, and whether children are present in the households.

A few types of lists are available: response lists, circulation lists, and compiled lists.

Response Lists

response list

A **response list** is a list of proven mail-order buyers. Such lists include book-of-the-month-club buyers, tape and CD music buyers, or people who order from cooperative direct mailing firms. Because these lists include proven mail order buyers they tend to cost more. For example, customers of Time Life Products (an established direct mail marketing company) rent a list for $365/M ($365 for each 1000 names). The list includes buyers of books, videos, and children's products. A minimum purchase of 5000 names is required.[5]

Circulation Lists

circulation lists

Cornerstone Group
www.cstonecanada.
com

Circulation lists are magazine subscription lists that target potential customers by an interest or activity. A publishing company, for example, sells its list of subscribers to any other business that is interested in a similar target. Cornerstone List Management (a list brokerage) is responsible for managing and renting all Rogers Media consumer publication lists which include *Chatelaine*, *Flare*, *Maclean's*, *Profit*, *Canadian Business*, *L'actualité*, and *Money Sense*. A total of about 1 million names are available at a base cost of $125/M.[6]

PC Magazine, a leading publication for trends and information about computer hardware and software, makes its list available to marketing organizations. By renting a portion of the *PC Magazine* list, an advertiser can deliver a specific message by mail in an uncluttered environment. The magazine has over 900 000 active subscribers and 80 percent of them have purchased technology products online.[7]

Compiled Lists

compiled lists

Canadian Medical
Association
www.cma.ca

Compiled lists are prepared from government, census, telephone, warranty, and other publication information. These are the least expensive of the lists and are not always personalized. For example, a business firm may be identified on the list but not the appropriate contact person within the firm. Names of business prospects are compiled from print sources such as the Standard Industrial Classification (SIC), *Fraser's Canadian Trade Index*, or *Scott's Industrial Index*. Provincial and national associations such as the Canadian Medical Association commonly provide mailing lists of their physicians, or, in the case of other associations, lawyers, teachers, and accountants.

Direct Response Television

**direct response
television (DRTV)**

infomercial

Direct response television (DRTV) is a sales-oriented commercial that encourages viewers to buy immediately. There are essentially three forms of direct response television: 60-second or longer commercials that typically appear on cable channels, infomercials, and direct home shopping channels. In all cases, the use of 1-800 numbers and credit cards make the purchase more convenient for the viewer. An **infomercial** is usually a 30-minute commercial that presents, in great detail, the benefits of a product or service. The range of products employing this technique is endless (e.g., exercise equipment to financial investment opportunities).

Direct response television commercials are classified into two categories:

Traditional An infomercial that stresses the "buy now, limited time offer." It tries to sell as much as possible at the lowest cost per order.

Corporate/Brand An infomercial that establishes leads, drives retail traffic, launches new products, creates awareness, and protects and enhances the brand image.

The nature of direct response television advertising has changed over time. Once regarded as schlock, direct response advertising was associated with "O-matic" types of products. Today, DRTV is redefining itself. Infomercials no longer exclusively revolve around get-rich-quick concepts or flashy gadgets; in fact, highly informative, well-produced commercials have been created for many blue-chip companies in the pharmaceutical, banking, and not-for-profit sectors. In Canada some of our mightiest mainstream marketing organizations such as Ford, Bell, and TD Bank have embraced direct response television.

**direct home
shopping**

Direct home shopping is a service provided by cable television through The Shopping Channel (TSC). This network offers products for sale by broadcast message. Messages to prospects are presented in the form of close-up shots of the product, or in the case of clothes and accessories, by models wearing the goods. George Foreman, once the heavyweight boxing champion, pitches his cooking grill on The Shopping Channel. The Shopping Channel has annual sales of $150 million and has sold 90 000 Foreman grills over a two-year period.[8] Now that's effective marketing communications!

A study conducted by the Gallup organization in the US found that 30 percent of those surveyed purchased a direct response product. Of those who bought products, 8 percent purchased from home shopping shows, 6 percent from direct response commercials, and 5 percent from infomercials.[9]

For more insight into the benefits derived from direct mail and direct response television communications see the Marketing in Action vignette **Direct Response Works for ING Direct and ClubLink**.

Catalogues

catalogues

Catalogues are reference publications, usually annual, distributed by large retail chains and other direct marketing organizations. Typically, catalogues would be mailed to current customers-customers whose names are stored in a company database. A catalogue can be general in nature, as is the case of the Sears catalogue and the Canadian Tire catalogue, or it may contain specialized merchandise that is targeted at a specific audience based on some kind of interest (e.g., sporting goods, leisure sportswear, or computers and computer accessories). At the present time, Sears is the largest catalogue marketing organization in Canada with direct sales approaching $1.5 billion annually.

Marketing in Action

Direct Response Works for ING Direct and ClubLink

What do the ING Direct bank and ClubLink have in common? Not much other than both companies offer a service that is ideally suited to the use of direct response advertising. And of course, you may need a loan from the bank to pay for the golf club membership! The cost of entry into ClubLink is a cool $23 000, and then of course, there is an annual fee.

ING Direct bank was initially skeptical about using direct response television ads fearing they would erode some of the brand equity that traditional television ads have built up. In hindsight, however, "had we realized the power in them we would have started them sooner," says Stacey Grant-Thompson, senior vice-president marketing with ING Direct. The bank presently has some 500 000 clients and $5 billion in deposits.

Their first direct response TV ad ran in the summer of 2001. The results, when compared with the traditional branding campaign, were surprising. "We more than doubled our qualified leads and nearly doubled the clients we acquired. As a result, 2001 was a year in which ING was able to grow business much more quickly than we had been, and we spent much less per client (about half the cost of acquiring clients by more traditional advertising techniques)."

Since its inception in Canada in 1997, ING had been using 30-second TV spots featuring a straight-talking Dutchman who invited Canadians to consider ING as an alternative to traditional banks. That campaign did achieve awareness objectives and a good many new customers. Direct response has focused more on converting prospects into customers. As Grant-Thompson tells it, "TV ads builds awareness, direct response television ads generate customers."

ClubLink definitely broke par with its direct mail campaign. In conjunction with creative prepared by Sharpe Blackmore Euro RSCG, ClubLink identified 75 000 elite prospects in the Greater Toronto Area and surrounding bedroom communities where many of their golf courses are located. A solo direct mail drop to 75 000 prospects resulted in 90 paid members. Low numbers you say. Quite right! But let's examine the economics of the situation.

The cost of a membership is $23 000. This fee gives a member access to any of the luxurious and challenging golf courses owned by the company—and there are many throughout Ontario and Quebec. The cost of the direct mail campaign was $150 000 ($2 per mailing). Therefore, ClubLink realized a $2 million return on a $150 000 investment. That's effective marketing communications!

Such success clearly proved a point to the non-believers in direct mail at ClubLink. Previously, the company had relied solely on mass advertising in print, radio, and television to build an image for the chain of golf resorts. Given this kind of result, ClubLink is rethinking how it allocates the communications budget and has decided to invest as much as 20 percent of its budget into direct response. Bi-annual direct mail efforts along with e-mail and postcard promotions to promote more new memberships are on the horizon.

Adapted from Susan Heinrich, "ING finds success in direct response television advertising," *Financial Post*, March 18, 2002, p. FP6; and Craig Saunders, "P.S. postscript," *Strategy Direct + Interactive*, October 9, 2000, p. D12.

The Sears catalogue is distributed to more than four million Canadian households. Each year Sears publishes 2 general catalogues (Spring and Summer/Fall and Winter), 2 seasonal catalogues (e.g., Christmas and Back to School), and 14 sale catalogues (see Figure 15.5). Sears is now a fully integrated marketing and marketing communications organization. They accept orders by fax, e-mail, and through its Web site. Its 1-800 number is the most frequently called toll-free number in Canada.[10]

Figure 15.5

Sears Integrates Catalogue Buying with Online Buying

Canadian Tire is moving full scale into catalogue marketing and online marketing. Says Mark Foote, president of Canadian Tire's retail division, "We make sure virtually every Canadian household has a catalogue. Eight out of ten Canadians keep it for a full year, until the new one arrives."[11] Each form of communication (catalogue and online) feeds off the other.

Sears and Canadian Tire recognize that catalogue and online activities will cannibalize some sales at stores, but the shift is necessary because they have to respond to customers' wants, and ordering items for home delivery is one of them. Customers are into multi-channel shopping.

Sears
www.sears.ca
Canadian Tire
www.canadiantire.ca

Telemarketing

telemarketing

Telemarketing involves the use of telecommunications to deliver a sales message. Communications via telemarketing is a booming business in North America. Much of the telemarketing activity is conducted at call centres, of which there are over 6000 in Canada. A **call centre** is a central operation from which a company operates its inbound

call centre

and outbound telemarketing programs. According to a study conducted by the provincial government of British Columbia, the call centre industry is worth $60 billion in North America and is a $15 billion industry in Canada—a quarter of the total.[12] Canadian-based call centres are the focal point of North American operations for many companies.

inbound tele-marketing

outbound tele-marketing

Delta Hotels
www.deltahotels.com

There are two types of telemarketing: inbound and outbound. **Inbound telemarketing** refers to the reception of calls by the order desk, customer inquiry, and direct response calls often generated through the use of toll-free 1-800 or 888 numbers. **Outbound telemarketing**, on the other hand, refers to calls that a company makes to customers in order to develop new accounts, generate sales leads, and even close a sale.

Call centre operations are expected to expand in the future for several reasons. First, companies are aggressively mining their databases for opportunities, and the telephone is an efficient way of tapping these opportunities. As well, development of database software and phone system technology makes it cost-effective for companies to link their database to the phone. Delta Hotels, for example, established a call centre in New Brunswick to service its North American operations. It receives an average of 2000 calls a day. In addition to taking reservations, the call centre provides additional services such as servicing its Privilege Card members, handling consumer complaints, and supporting the sales efforts of its business accounts.[13]

The primary advantage of telemarketing is that it can complete a sale for less cost than is needed to complete a sale using such techniques as face-to-face sales calls or mass advertising. However, to be effective, proper training and preparation of telemarketing representatives needs to be as comprehensive as it is for personal selling. Planning the message is as important as the medium itself.

A drawback to telemarketing is the fact that consumers react negatively to it. A survey conducted by Ernst & Young concluded that 75 percent of Canadians consider marketing calls unwelcome and intrusive; they are ranked as one of the least desirable sales techniques. Further, 51 percent of people think there are too many calls and the same number of people react to them by hanging up.[14] Despite this behaviour, organizations see advantages such as call reach and frequency, and cost-efficiency outweighing the disadvantages.

Interactive Advertising

In the 1950s, media planners faced the problem of determining how television would fit into the advertising world. There it was, a brand-new medium that would upset the status quo for radio, newspaper, and magazines. Existing media survived the onslaught, but their share of the advertising pie would change forever. Now, advancing technology has thrust upon us another medium that is revolutionizing how companies look at advertising, and certainly how they allocate money between the various media.

Companies are exploring new forms of advertising made available by the Internet, and in many cases, adding an online component to their traditional media advertising. These new media are providing progressive companies with a means of reaching what was once thought to be an unattainable goal: a personal, one-to-one relationship with customers involving continuous interaction in the pre-transaction, transaction, and post-transaction phase of a purchase. The Internet seems to offer unlimited communications potential.

"The Internet is substantially different. It's a bit of direct response, it's a bit of broadcast, it's a bit of print, and it's a bit of technology."[15] Some things do appear certain, however. First, like television in the 1950s, it will eventually play a major role in communicating information about goods and services, and such communications will result in more electronic purchasing by customers. Second, like television, the Internet will not replace existing media. Instead, they will complement the communications programs that are implemented in the mass media.

The Internet

Internet

World Wide Web

The **Internet** is a network of computer networks linked together to act as one. It works just like a global mail system in which independent authorities collaborate in moving and delivering information. The **World Wide Web** is the collection of Web sites on the Internet. Organizations that use the Internet set up a site on the World Wide Web. They use the site to distribute information or they can place ads on other sites that are linked to their own Web site. Internet users actively go to a Web site that interests them and browse the material for as long as they like.

Most Web sites on the Internet are commercial in nature. For example, a company Web site delivers important information about the company and/or its products to visitors. It also provides a means of collecting information about visitors (e.g., through contests and surveys). If managed properly, the Internet is one component of a database management system. The information collected at a Web site can be used to identify prospects and better market products in the future.

ELEMENTS OF THE INTERNET

4.
Describe the various elements of Internet communications.

e-mail

In terms of residential commercial use, the two most popular applications are e-mail and the World Wide Web.

1. **E-Mail** Through **e-mail**, an individual or organization can communicate with anyone else who has an e-mail account (usually available from an Internet provider for a monthly charge). E-mail can reach recipients anywhere, anytime. In terms of advertising communications it offers an organization a cost-effective way of delivering messages to existing customers and prospects (it costs much less than regular direct mail and any form of mass advertising).

2. **World Wide Web** A Web site is a location on the Internet or World Wide Web. It refers to an encompassing body of information as a whole, for a particular domain name. A Web site provides an organization with creative latitude as words, display graphics, video clips, and audio clips can be integrated into the site. Each site has a unique address (i.e., www.kjt.com). When an Internet user visits a site, the first thing he or she sees is a **home page**. The home page sets the tone for the company. If the home page looks interesting, further browsing may occur. The primary advantage of a Web site is its interactive capability. It can generate sales leads by requesting information from visitors, and it can distribute product information and investor information requested by visitors.

home page

ONLINE ADVERTISING

The Internet provides access to customers all over the world and delivers information in ways that traditional print and broadcast media cannot. Traditional media are passive

5.

Evaluate the various online advertising models available to marketing organizations.

by nature. In contrast, communications on the Internet goes both ways—it is an interactive medium. The potential offered by the Internet in terms of communication leaves little doubt that it will become an important medium among advertisers looking to reach large numbers of people in a cost-effective manner.

As an advertising medium, however, the Internet has been slow to take off. As of 2000, Canadian advertisers only spent $56 million in online advertising, just 0.26 percent of total ad spending in Canada.[16] At this level of spending the Internet is not a threat to traditional forms of media advertising—at least not yet. It seems that consumers do their best to ignore ads that appear online; they find them more of a nuisance than anything.

online advertising

Online advertising is defined as the placement of electronic communication on a Web site, in e-mail, or over personal communications devices (e.g., personal digital assistants and cell phones) connected to the Internet. While the ultimate goal of most forms of advertising is to motivate the purchase of a brand, online advertising is useful for:

- Creating brand awareness
- Stimulating interest and preference
- Providing a means to make a purchase
- Providing a means to contact an advertiser
- Acquiring data about real/potential consumers

Based on these objectives, the essential role of the Internet is to communicate vital information about a company and its products. When a company quotes a Web site address in other forms of communications, it finds that interested buyers start to visit its site for new information. Such behaviour could eventually translate into a purchase. Therefore, organizations shouldn't neglect traditional forms of advertising. Very often, the best way to advertise a Web-based company is through traditional media.

Prior to examining the various online advertising alternatives some basic terminology should be understood. All terms relate to how Internet ads are measured for effectiveness:

impressions

Impressions This refers to the number of times a banner image is downloaded to a page being viewed by a visitor. This is the standard way of determining exposure for an ad on the Web.

clicks (click-throughs)

Clicks (Clickthroughs) This refers to the number of times that users click on any banner ad. Such a measurement allows an advertiser to judge the response to an ad. When the viewer clicks the ad they are transferred to the advertiser's Web site or to a special page where they are encouraged to respond in some way to the ad.

clickthrough rate

Clickthrough Rate The *clickthrough rate* indicates the success of an advertiser in attracting visitors to click on their ad. For example, if during one million impressions, there are 20 000 clicks on the banner, the clickthrough rate is 2 percent. The formula is clicks divided by ad impressions.

visitor

Visitor A visitor is one single user who comes to a Web site.

visit

Visit A visit is a sequence of page requests made by a visitor at a Web site. A visit is also referred to as a *session* or *browsing period*.

A site's activity is described in terms of visits and visitors, the former always being larger than the latter, because of repeat visitors. A site that can report, for example, that it had 8 million page views, 100 000 visitors, and 800 000 visits last month would be doing very well. It means that the average visitor returns to the site 8 times each month, and views 10 pages on each visit. That's incredible "stickiness"(most sites don't do that well)!

TYPES OF ONLINE ADVERTISING

There are presently five choices available to online advertisers: banner advertising, interstitials, rich media, sponsorships, Web sites, and e-mail advertising.

Banner Advertising

banner ad

A **banner ad** usually refers to third party advertising on a Web site. In terms of design it stretches across a page in a narrow band. Its appearance is much like that of an outdoor poster or a banner ad that stretches across the bottom of a newspaper page. This style of banner is static in nature and the content is minimal. Smaller versions of the banner **buttons** (e.g., one half the width, smaller rectangles, and squares) are referred to as **buttons**. Since banners have not been very successful, the industry has introduced larger sizes and integrated new technologies to make the ads more interactive—and more tempting to click on!

skyscraper

rectangle

New formats include skyscrapers, rectangles, animated banners, and interactive banners. A **skyscraper** is a tall, skinny oblong that appears at the side of a Web page. The **rectangle** is a larger box. It is not as wide as a banner but offers more depth. The thinking behind these sizes is quite simple: the bigger the better. The sheer size of the ad provides an opportunity for advertisers to be more creative with their ads—they will be able to integrate some animation that will attract more attention. Refer to Figure 15.6 for an illustration.

animated banners

Animated banners are the type that spin or have some form of action. It is a series of frames shown repeatedly on the screen. Animated banners are now quite popular and their click-through rates are much higher than banners without animation.

interactive banners or **rich media banners**

Interactive banners, or **rich media banners**, engage the viewer (e.g., playing a game, answering a question or providing information). As indicated earlier, consumers want to be entertained online. The interactive banner helps satisfy this need.

Banner advertising presently accounts for about 65 percent of all ad revenue.[17] Unfortunately, results achieved from banner ads have been short of expectations and as a result, advertisers are looking more seriously at sponsorships and e-mail advertising.

Interstitials

interstitial

An **interstitial** is an ad that pops onto the screen and interrupts users. It is often referred to as a "pop-up." This type of ad comes in different sizes and has varying levels of interactivity, from static to animated productions. Since there is no warning when it will appear (e.g., any time during a visit to a particular site), it does grab the user's attention. A potential disadvantage of the interstitial is its intrusiveness. Since it is not asked for, the user might object to receiving it and view the brand negatively. Advertisers must remember that the Internet started out as a commercial-free environment.

Rich Media

rich media

The latest craze is the rich media banner. **Rich media** generally allows for greater use of interaction with animation, audio, and video. To view such banners usually requires

Figure 15.6

An Illustration of a Standard Size Banner Ad and a Larger Rectangular Ad

Reproduced with permission of Yahoo! Inc. 2002. Yahoo! and the Yahoo! Logo are trademarks of Yahoo! Inc.

superstitial

special software such as Flash, Shockwave or Javascript. Ads that embrace these technologies are sometimes referred to as a **superstitial** and are the Internet's version of a television commercial—they resemble a TV commercial.

The inclusion of audio and full motion video is referred to as *streaming media*. If, for example, Flash software is used, the audio and video content is streamed to you. That means you don't first download them and you don't save them on your local computer, you just view or listen to them as they are streaming. Streaming media is used extensively by radio station Web sites and sites like cbc.ca.

For more insight into online advertising and the role of Web sites to communicate information read the Marketing in Action vignette **Inescapable Ads**.

Marketing in Action

Inescapable Ads

D o you pay attention to advertising when surfing the Internet? Probably not! More than anything the ads probably frustrate you when you are doing something important. Those nagging pop-up-style ads for example, are bound to bother anyone. Truth be known, Internet users are going to have to accept advertising in one form or another in the near future. Otherwise, the Internet as we know it will change. Having so much free access to information can't go on forever.

It's like a battle between banks and bank robbers. One side has to stay a step ahead of the other. With regard to the Internet, online advertising is becoming more intrusive as marketers vie for surfers' attention with a new generation of catchy ads. Typically, it is easy for a surfer to ignore a banner ad or click past a pop-up ad. But they often have no choice but to watch new ads that stream across their screens or block out portions of the Web pages they are trying to view. These ads don't leave the screen until they are viewed. Now that's technology!

There are several new types of ads: floating or flash ads, also known as vokens (short for virtual tokens), which feature animation; interstitials which are full-page billboards that pop up without the user requesting them; and full page commercials. On the US-based *Playboy* site, for example, viewers must watch a 25-second ad for Jack Daniels whiskey before they can enter the site. This technique is referred to as a roadblock.

Some advertisers see the fact that their ads are inescapable as a real advantage, says Simon Jennings, director of sales at Yahoo! Canada, a Web portal that features voken-style campaigns. "We are interested in pushing the envelope but we are very

aware of the piss-off factor," he says. "We don't want to do that to users but there are advertisers who, if they had their way, would take it further than most sites now allow."

CHUM Ltd.'s MuchMusic station site uses the new breed of ads. The station realizes that some visitors will get frustrated and they may perceive the ads to be a bit of an intrusion. But, says Heather Gordon, sales manager for ChumCity Interactive, "Our audience understands the relationship between ads and content so we do our best to keep their frustrations to a minimum."

The new ads seem to be grabbing attention. On the MuchMusic site, up to 15 percent of visitors click on the floating ads, compared with just 0.3 percent of banner ads. The technology allows MuchMusic to offer more to its advertisers, and more leading edge content to its visitors. That should keep both advertisers and visitors to the site happy. It also reinforces the "cool" factor at MuchMusic.

Adapted from Randy Ray, "Online advertisers learn to create captive audience," *Globe and Mail*, April 5, 2002, p. B11.

Courtesy: Monster

Sponsorships

sponsorship

Callaway Golf
www.callawaygolf.
com

Sponsorships are the second most popular advertising tool (14 percent of advertising revenue in 2000) and are projected to grow in popularity. With a **sponsorship**, an advertiser commits to an extended relationship with another Web site. For example, a skin care product might sponsor a weather site. Chapstick, a product associated with both hot and cold weather, does just that. In effect, sponsorships usually target the content, rather than the audience. For example, Callaway (makers of golf clubs and balls) might purchase a sponsorship on a golf news or golf booking Web site. They are targeting the content, and assuming that the audience comes to that Web site because they are golfers.

Web Sites

The nature of the information communicated will vary from one organization to another. For example, news and information organizations such as the *Globe and Mail*, *Maclean's*, CNN, and others use the Internet to disseminate information. *Maclean's* magazine is now available online at the *Maclean's* magazine Web site (www.macleans.ca). Entertainment companies like Disney and Universal Studios build pre-release excitement for new movies through online promotions and giveaways and by broadcasting movie trailers at their Web sites. Using the Internet in this manner can create demand in a less expensive way than using traditional forms of advertising.

A Web site provides companies with an opportunity to really "tell a story." A company cannot tell or show as much through traditional media as inexpensively as it can on the Internet. Advertising in the traditional media should always provide a Web site address and encourage customers to contact the site for additional information. While this practice is becoming commonplace, research shows that 60 percent of Web site visitors are there because the site was mentioned in a print ad (53 percent because of a television ad).[18]

Figure 15.7, the home page and a subsequent page for Shoppers Drug Mart, clearly demonstrates the diversity of information that can be communicated. Health information is a primary category and the site provides information about basic health concerns along with specific information for certain targets: children, women, men, and seniors. Other categories include diseases and conditions, and herbs and supplements.

E-Mail Advertising

permission-based e-mail

sponsored e-mail

One of the most promising applications in online advertising doesn't use flashy graphics or oversized banners. **Permission-based e-mail**, in which a user chooses to receive messages from a particular advertiser, is growing quickly. Other commonly used terms for permission-based e-mail include *direct e-mail* and *e-mail marketing*. This form of advertising is relatively inexpensive, response rates are easy to measure, and it is targeted at people who want information about certain goods and services (see Figure 15.8). An offshoot of e-mail advertising is **sponsored e-mail**. Many Internet sites that mail information to subscribers now include a short message from a sponsor, along with a link to its Web site.

E-mail advertising is very similar to direct mail advertising in terms of how it operates. The difference though, is that e-mail advertising is generating higher response rates. Unlike banner advertising in its various forms, sending sales messages by e-mail seems quite acceptable to Internet users since they agree to accept the messages (e.g., a

Detailed Health Information by Topic is Available at the Shoppers Drug Mart Web Site

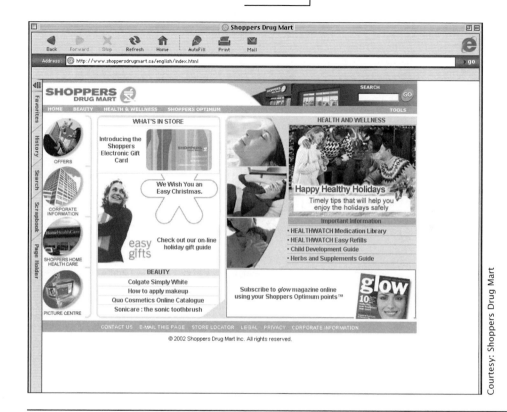

user can subscribe and unsubscribe to e-mail advertising as they wish). A recent survey reveals that 79 percent of Canadian Internet users agree to receive e-mail advertising from an average of 5.2 Web sites.[19]

As with direct mail, the success of an e-mail ad campaign depends on the quality of the list. There are two kinds of lists: a rented e-mail list and an in-house list. The **rented list** is usually obtained from a list broker. Typically, these lists include "opt-in" names and addresses. **Opt-in** means the people on the list have agreed to receive direct e-mail. Sending e-mail advertisements to lists that are not opt-in is spam. **Spam** refers to the inappropriate use of a mailing list to deliver a message—it is unsolicited "junk" e-mail.

In the age of database marketing, the compilation of an in-house list is essential. Since all forms of advertising should invite people to visit a Web site, the site should include a section where people can sign up for e-mail newsletters or e-mail updates that may announce the introduction of new products. Sending e-mail to customers and prospects that specifically request the mail will almost always work better than using a rented list. In accordance with Internet etiquette, in-house lists should not be rented to another organization—"permission rented is permission lost." The concern for privacy is always an issue in Internet marketing.

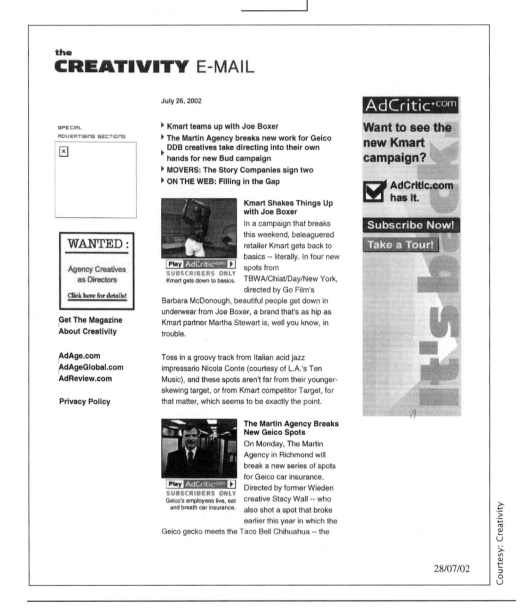

Figure 15.8

A Sample of Permission-Based E-Mail

Courtesy: Creativity

ONLINE ADVERTISING AND THE COMMUNICATIONS MIX

6.
Assess the potential of the Internet as an advertising medium.

The Web is more accurate at capturing measurement information than any other medium largely due to the technology that is built into it. The owner of a Web site can quickly assess the traffic the site generates and the time a visitor spends at the site. Such information can be used to improve the quality of content on the site or the navigability of the site. Further, the interactive potential of online advertising kind of separates it from traditional media that are passive in nature.

Thus far, the Internet has failed to meet high expectations, but being a new medium, part of the problem has been lack of experience with the medium among advertisers. For this reason many organizations have not invested in Web-based advertising campaigns. As time progresses and advertisers gain more experience with the medium, the true benefits of the medium will be realized.

What is known is that younger target audiences spend considerable time online (e.g., the 15- to 24-year-old age group). Since this is a hard-to-reach target through any medium, the Internet represents a welcome opportunity to reach them. Some companies often put their latest TV spots on their Web sites. Other companies have created a buzz around TV ads with an Internet component. Levi Strauss, for example, generated a lot of publicity for a new television campaign by putting three new ads on its Web site and asking people to vote for their favourite. The most popular spot, *Crazy Legs*, then made its debut on the 2002 Super Bowl. By then people were already talking about the ads and the actor who demonstrates his crazy legs dance moves in the spot. Says Julie Klee, marketing director for Levi Strauss, "With kids today it's hard to get to them. The media they are influenced by are fragmented so it really takes a multi-dimensional approach. For us, the Web site extends the company's reach."[20]

For a summary of the advantages and disadvantages of online advertising refer to Figure 15.9.

Advantages and Disadvantages of Online Advertising

Figure 15.9

Advantages

Targeting Capability

Technology in the form of cookies (electronic identification tags) allows ads to be targeted to Web site visitors based on their browsing behaviour. Database information enhances the quality of the online advertising effort.

Timing

The Internet is a 24/7 operation so ads are delivered anytime, anywhere. Content of the message can be changed quickly if need be.

Interactivity and Action

There is an opportunity to interact and develop a relationship with visitors to a Web site. Sufficient information and proper interaction can motivate a customer to take action.

Disadvantages

Effectiveness Is Low

While more than half of Canadians have access to the Internet, a majority of users do not perceive it to be an advertising medium. Consequently, ads are avoided or simply go unnoticed.

Selective Reach

In terms of reaching prospects at home, the Internet remains the domain of middle to upper class target markets. The cost of participation for consumers is high.

Privacy Concerns

Consumers are concerned about how information collected about them is used. Consumers are concerned about the intrusiveness of advertising (some ads can't be avoided). Their privacy is being invaded.

Summary

Direct response advertising is one of the largest advertising media in Canada. The major forms of direct response advertising are direct mail, catalogues, direct response television, and telemarketing.

Direct mail is the most prominent form of direct response advertising. A direct mailing usually includes a sales letter, leaflet or flyer, folder, and statement stuffer. Advertisers choose between solo direct mail and cooperative direct mail. Solo distribution is much more expensive than cooperative distribution.

The primary advantages of direct mail for advertisers are its audience selectivity, high reach potential, and geographic flexibility. Disadvantages include the absence of editorial support and poor image. The success of any direct mail campaign largely depends on the quality of the list the advertiser uses. Lists are available from list brokers on a cost per thousand cost basis, and other secondary sources such as directories and trade indexes.

The catalogue industry in Canada is underdeveloped and is largely controlled by Sears. Catalogues do cannibalize sales from stores, but in today's market customers are demanding alternative and convenient ways to shop. Consequently, retailers like Sears and Canadian Tire are establishing a catalogue and online presence.

Advancing technology has spurred growth in direct response television and telemarketing. Whether it's a 60-second direct response commercial or a 30-minute infomercial, direct response commercials are becoming popular with traditional advertisers. They are used to establish leads, build image, and launch new products. They are effective in communicating information that involves a lot of details.

Companies are attracted to telemarketing (inbound and outbound) because of the relatively low cost. Quite simply, telemarketing is far less expensive than face-to-face communications or mass advertising. A drawback is the negative perceptions people have about this communications technique.

The Internet appears to be a strong media alternative in the future. The key elements of the Internet are e-mail and World Wide Web sites. Both are efficient ways to communicate information. Currently, the Internet is widely used for information purposes, but commercialization of the Net is occurring. Internet users tend to be younger, highly educated, and earn above-average incomes. These demographics make them an attractive target for advertisers.

Internet users behave differently from traditional media users. The Net has a culture of its own, a culture where commercialism is shunned. Consequently, advertisers must tread carefully so as to not offend users. Unlike traditional media, the challenge for advertisers is to create interesting interactive communications without alienating users. Information is somewhat of a loss leader but the provision of good information will create goodwill and brand interest.

In terms of advertising, organizations purchase banner ads on various Web sites. They may also take advantage of sponsorship opportunities or advertising on third-party sites. The intent of a banner ad is to stimulate just enough interest so that the viewer clicks the ad for more information. When clicked, the viewer is transferred to the advertiser's Web site for more details. Banners have changed significantly since their introduction and are now available in larger and interactive formats (interstitials and superstitials). Permission-based e-mail represents significant opportunities for advertisers. Using rented lists or lists generated from in-house databases, e-mail represents a cost-effective way to reach prospects and current customers.

As an advertising medium, the Internet offers targeting capability at a very reasonable cost and tracking capabilities that measure effectiveness of campaigns in a variety of ways (clicks, leads, and purchases). Some drawbacks of the Internet include selective reach (higher educated and higher income groups are the main users) and the perception among users that advertisers are invading their privacy.

Key Terms

animated banner 423
banner ad 423
bounce back 411
button 423
call centre 419
catalogues 417
circulation list 416
clicks (clickthroughs) 422
clickthrough rate 422
compiled list 416
cooperative direct mail 412
direct home shopping 417
direct mail 410
direct marketing 410
direct response advertising 410
direct response television (DRTV) 417
e-mail 421
folder 411
home page 421
house list 415
impressions 422
inbound telemarketing 420
infomercial 417
interactive banner (rich media banner) 423

Internet 421
interstitial 423
leaflet (flyer) 410
list broker 415
merge/purge 416
online advertising 422
opt-in 427
outbound telemarketing 420
permission-based e-mail 426
postage-paid reply card 411
rectangle 423
rented list 427
response list 416
rich media 423
skyscraper 423
solo direct mail 412
spam 427
sponsored e-mail 426
sponsorship (online) 426
superstitial 424
telemarketing 419
visit 422
visitor 422
World Wide Web 421

Review Questions

1. What are the major forms of direct response advertising?

2. What is the difference between direct marketing and direct response advertising?

3. What is the difference between a solo direct mail campaign and a co-operative direct mail campaign?

4. What are the advantages and disadvantages of direct mail advertising for a business-product advertiser (e.g., a manufacturer of business equipment)?

5. Explain the differences between a response list, circulation list and a compiled list.

6. Explain the following terms as they relate to direct response advertising:

   a) bounce backs

   b) house list

c) list broker

d) merge/purge

e) infomercial

f) inbound telemarketing versus outbound telemarketing

7. In terms of communications what is the primary role of the Internet? What strategies should a potential advertiser apply when communicating with an Internet user?

8. Explain the following terms as they relate to advertising on the Internet:

a) click

b) clickthrough rate

c) impression

d) visit

9. What is banner advertising and how does it work?

10. Identify and briefly explain the various types of banner ads.

11. Briefly explain how an online advertising sponsorship works.

12. Briefly explain the following Internet communications terms:

a) Permission-based e-mail

b) Opt-in

c) Spam

13. What is a cookie and how does it work?

14. Identify and briefly explain two advantages and two disadvantages of Internet-based advertising.

Discussion and Application Questions

1. "The dollars an advertiser invests in direct mail advertising are wasted owing to the poor image of the medium." Discuss.

2. Catalogues seem to be the reserve of big retail organizations such as Sears and Canadian Tire. How should smaller retail organizations, with less financial resources, compete with bigger retailers? What direct response strategies should they adopt and why?

3. What is your opinion about advertising on a Web site? Will it play an expanding role in the communications mix in the future? If so, what media will suffer? Defend your position.

4. "Persistent invasions of consumer privacy will be the undoing of Internet-

based advertising." True or false? Conduct some online secondary research to update the status of this issue. Report on your findings.

5. "Direct response television will play a more prominent role in future television advertising campaigns for traditional advertisers such as banks, automobile manufacturers, and insurance companies." Is this statement true or false? Discuss.

6. Conduct some secondary research on the DRTV business. Has the image of DRTV really changed? What companies are using this technique and how successful have they been with it?

E-Assignment

Take 10 minutes to do some surfing on the Internet using the MSN or Yahoo search engines (Yahoo.com or msn.com). Identify the industries and companies that appear frequently in banner ads or pop-up ads. Do the ads change frequently while you are surfing or do the same ads appear repeatedly? Are the ads targeted in any way?

Visit the Yahoo Web site and type in a few key words in the search box. Use general terms such as finance, hockey, books, music. Do the different key words trigger different banner ads? Do the ads seem targeted in any way?

Endnotes

1. "Direct response spending expected to go nuts," *Marketing Direct*, February 12, 2001, p. 15.

2. Canadian Media Directors' Council Media Digest, 2001-2002, p. 9.

3. Kara Kuryllowicz, "How entrepreneurs can boost business by using direct mail," *Financial Post*, n.d.

4. Franzi Weinstein, "Short, sweet and smarter creative," *Marketing*, April 29, 1996, p. 17.

5. Based on costs obtained from Accountable List Brokers. www.listbroker.com, direct responders Time Life.

6. "Cornerstone List Management wins Rogers Media's consumer list business," press release, www.cstonecanada.com, August 2001.

7. www.worldata.com/ziffdavis/dcards.htm.

8. Paul Brent, "Brawn + brains = bucks," *Financial Post*, March 29, 1999, pp. C1, C7.

9. "Öand their impact on viewers," *Marketing*, May 15, 1995, p. 34.

10. "Sears Canada This Year's Directors' Choice," *Strategy Direct Response*, November 22, 1999, p. 10.

11. Stephen Theobald, "Canadian Tire's flyer grows up," *Toronto Star*, March 15, 2001, p. E1.

12. Eve Lazarus, " The new call centre Mecca," *Marketing Direct*, February 12, 2001, p. 24.

13. "Comprehensive efforts for Delta," *Strategy*, February 19, 1996, p. 18.

14. Mary Gooderham, " Level of antipathy a wake-up call for telemarketers," *Globe and Mail*, May 7, 1997, p. C11.

15. Bernadette Johnson, "Advertisers revisiting the Web: Study," *Strategy*, February 12, 2001, pp. 1, 14.

16. "Canadian Internet Advertisng 2000: A Message for the Medium," a report published by the Internet Advertising Bureau of Canada and Multimediator Strategy Group Inc., 2000, p. 19.

17. Internet Advertising Bureau, www.iabcanada.com.

18. "Information still killer app on the Internet," *Advertising Age*, October 6, 1977, p. 48.

19. "Canadians open to e-mail," *Marketing*, April 8, 2002, p. 4.

20. Susan Heinrich, "Lipton Brisk commercial gets more bang for the buck with Internet site," *Financial Post*, April 8, 2002, p. FP6.

Dick Hemingway

Marketing Communications: Sales Promotion, Personal Selling, Event Marketing, and Sponsorships

seven

>> Learning Objectives

After studying this chapter, you will be able to

1. Describe the various types of consumer and trade promotion activities.
2. Describe the roles of sales representatives and the types of selling that occur in a business organization.
3. Outline the steps in the selling process.
4. Explain the importance that event marketing and sponsorships have in contemporary marketing.
5. List the unique considerations involved in planning event marketing programs.

This chapter examines three elements of the marketing communications mix: sales promotion, personal selling, and event marketing and sponsorships. These activities, along with advertising, public relations, and direct response and Internet communications, complement one another and work together to help achieve the marketing and business objectives.

Sales Promotion

1.
Describe the various types of consumer and trade promotion activities.

Sales promotion is any activity that provides special incentives to bring about immediate action from consumers, distributors, and an organization's sales force; in other words, it encourages the decision to buy. The expression "advertising appeals to the heart, and sales promotion to the wallet" shows the distinction between the two types of activity. For instance, advertising tells us why we should buy a product, whereas sales promotion offers financial or other incentives (e.g., a cents-off coupon, a free sample, or a sale price) to purchase a product.

Sales promotion is an important factor affecting product sales. A study published by the *Journal of Advertising Research* reports that consumer promotion alone accounts for 80 percent of the total effect on sales, while advertising alone accounts for only 13 percent of the total effect on sales.[1]

Two principal kinds of sales promotion exist: consumer promotion and trade promotion.

sales promotion

**Journal of
Advertising Research**
www.arfsite.org/
Webpages/JAR_pages/
jarhome.htm

**consumer
promotion**

CONSUMER PROMOTION

Consumer promotion is any activity that promotes extra brand sales by offering the consumer an incentive over and above the product's inherent benefits. These promotions are designed to pull the product through the channel of distribution by motivating consumers to make an immediate purchase. The objectives of consumer promotions are as follows:

1. *Trial Purchase* When introducing a new product, marketers want customers to make a first purchase right away so that product acceptance can be secured quickly. Something as simple as a coupon will accomplish this goal.

2. *Repeat Purchases* Marketers protect loyalty to an established product by offering incentives for consumers to buy the item repeatedly. Including coupons with a

product that can be redeemed on the next purchase of the product is a way of holding loyalty, as are loyalty cards where points are accumulated for future use.

3. **Multiple Purchases** Promotions of this nature "load the consumer up." For example, a contest may be run to spur many entries and purchases, or cash refunds may offer savings that increase with each additional purchase of an item. For instance, a $1.00 refund may be available on one purchase and a $3.00 refund on two purchases.

The major types of consumer promotion are coupons, free samples, contests, cash refunds, premiums, frequent-buyer programs, and delayed payment incentives.

Coupons

coupon

The first major type of consumer promotion is the coupon. A **coupon** is a price-saving incentive to stimulate quicker purchase of a designated product. In Canada, coupons are distributed in mass quantity. As of 2001, the total number of coupons distributed by packaged goods manufacturers amounted to 2.67 billion, of which 122 million were redeemed (Figure 16.1). With the average face value of coupons distributed being $1.25, consumers saved a $128 million on purchases.[2]

redemption rate

The effectiveness of a coupon campaign is determined by the **redemption rate**, or the number of coupons returned to an organization expressed as a percentage of the total number of coupons in distribution for a particular coupon offer. Figure 16.2 shows the average redemption figures for different kinds of coupons. Coupons are delivered to consumers in many different ways: by the product, the media, including electronic distribution online, and at the point of purchase.

product-delivered coupons

Product-delivered coupons appear in or on the package. One kind of product-delivered coupon, the **in-pack self-coupon**, is redeemable on the next purchase of the same product. The package is usually "flagged" somehow to draw attention to the

---

Coupons Distributed and Redeemed in Canada

Figure 16.1

Direct-to-Consumer Coupons	1999	2000	2001
Quantity distributed	2.5 billion	2.52 billion	2.67 billion
Quantity redeemed	115.0 million	112.0 million	122.0 million
Average face value of coupon redeemed	$0.97	$1.08	$1.25
Consumer savings	$115.0 million	$120.0 million	$128.0 million

Source: Wayne Mouland, "Coupon Usage Grows in 2001," press release, Watts NCH Promotional Services Ltd., February 2002.

	Figure 16.2

Average Redemption Rates by Method of Distribution, 2001

Media	Range	Average
Freestanding Insert (FSI)	0.1– 4.1%	0.5%
In-store—all methods	0.1–89.8%	9.2%
In-store: ad pad	2.0–36.9%	12.0%
In/on package	0.6–42.5%	5.9%
Direct mail	0.1–52.3%	4.2%
Charity	0.2–34.2%	12.7%
Magazine/Newspaper	0.1– 2.8%	1.0%
Other	0.1–22.8%	1.2%

Source: Wayne Mouland, "Coupon Usage Grows in 2001," press release, Watts NCH Promotional Services Ltd., February 2002.

coupon included inside the package. An ***on-pack self-coupon*** usually appears on the back or side panel of the package and is valid for a future purchase of the same product. An ***instantly redeemable coupon*** is valid when the product carrying the coupon is bought and the coupon is removed from the package. Another variation is the **cross-ruff** (or cross-promotion), an in-pack or on-pack coupon valid on the purchase of a different product. Such coupons encourage the consumer to buy complementary products. For example, a tea or coffee brand may carry coupons for a brand of cookies and vice versa.

cross-ruff

Media-delivered coupons are coupons distributed through newspaper, magazines, cooperative direct-mail packages, and online through various Web sites. The Carole Martin envelope or the Val-Pak envelope received by households are examples of a cooperative direct-mail package; they are delivered numerous times each year and contain coupons for a range of non-competing products.

media-delivered coupons

Among media-delivered coupons, the free-standing insert is the most popular method of placing coupons directly in the homes of consumers. A **free-standing insert (FSI)** is a pre-printed advertisement in single- or multiple-page form that is inserted loose into newspapers. Distribution statistics reveal that 55 percent of all direct-to-consumer coupons that are distributed annually are in FSIs (Figure 16.3).[3] Free-standing inserts are marketed by distribution organizations that use such names as "The Coupon Clipper" and "Shop and Save."

free-standing insert (FSI)

Savvy shoppers now look to online sources for valuable money-saving coupons. A consumer can select specific goods and services, survey the discounts offered, and then print the coupons off. Save.ca and Coupons.com offer marketers the opportunity to provide coupons online. According to Wayne Mouland, vice-president of NCH

Share of Coupons Distributed by Method of Delivery

Figure 16.3

Distribution Method	1999	2000	2001
Freestanding insert	52%	55%	55%
In-store	17%	17%	16%
In/on package	16%	13%	12%
Direct mail	8%	5%	5%
Magazine/Newspaper	2%	5%	6%
Charity	2%	2%	2%
Other	3%	3%	4%

Source: Wayne Mouland, "Coupon Usage Grows in 2001," press release, Watts NCH Promotional Services Ltd., February 2002.

Promotional Services and a leading expert on coupon trends in Canada and their redemption, "Online coupons (e-coupons) are the fastest growing method of coupon distribution and the redemption rates are much higher than their regular counterparts, a testament to their popularity."[4] Save.ca claims redemption rates in the 15 to 20 percent range.[5] See Figure 16.4 for an illustration.

in-store-delivered coupons

In-store-delivered coupons include coupons distributed by in-store display centres and dispensing machines, usually located near the store entrance; are available on the shelves from shelf pads (the consumer tears off a coupon that can be redeemed instantly); or are distributed by handout, as the customer enters the store.

electronic coupons (e-coupons)

In recent years, **electronic coupons** distributed by supermarket loyalty cards have increased in popularity with leading chain stores. Such coupons eliminate the need for consumers to clip coupons and, because the discounts are registered by the swipe of a card, consumers don't even think about the discounts they are getting. Such coupons negate the purposes of a coupon, which are to generate excitement and competition among brands, encourage new consumers to buy, or re-interest those who have gone to another brand.

A benefit of electronic coupon cards is that retailers and manufacturers know who the customer is (the customer signed up for the card), so a database is developed that can be used in future relationship marketing programs.

The objectives of a coupon promotion affect the way that the coupons will be delivered. These objectives are often related to the stage in the product life cycle that the item has reached. In the introduction and growth stages, a key objective is to get the target audience to try the product. Therefore, coupons delivered by the media are common. As a product moves into maturity, coupons are frequently distributed in or on products because prompting current consumers to continue purchasing is vital to pre-

Sample of an Online Generated Coupon

Figure 16.4

Courtesy: SAVE.CA Inc.

These coupons were requested online at the Save.ca Web site. Save.ca mails the coupons to the person requesting them.

serving market share. When the objective is to make competitive users switch to one's own brand, regardless of the stage of the life cycle, delivering coupons through the media is effective.

Free Sample

free sample

A **free sample** is a free product distributed to potential users, either in a small trial size or in its regular size. Sampling is commonly practised when a company is introducing a new product, a line extension of a new product, or a product improvement, such as a new flavour, taste, blend, or scent. It is an effective way of getting trial usage because it eliminates the financial risk of a purchase. In comparison to coupons, the sample is less efficient in converting trial users to regular users, and it is an expensive proposition because of the costs of the product and its packaging and distribution.[6]

The most frequently used method of sample distribution is in-store. There are several variations of in-store sampling: product demonstrations and sampling, saleable sample sizes (small replica pack sizes of the actual product), and cross-sampling. Samples distributed in stores are an attempt to influence the consumer's decision at the point of purchase. Packaged-goods companies, such as Kraft and General Mills, frequently employ this type of sampling, as do retailers who promote their private label brands. **cross-sampling** **Cross-sampling** refers to an arrangement whereby one product carries a sample of another product (e.g., a regular-sized box of Cheerios cereal carries a small sample package of Count Chocula cereal).

Other alternatives for delivering free samples include co-operative direct mail (provided the sample is small and light enough to be accommodated by the mailing envelope), home delivery by private organizations, theatre and event sampling, and finally, street level sampling. Lady Speed Stick, for example, offered free samples at busy Toronto intersections. Two female rollerbladers dressed in black actually demonstrated the product and how it wouldn't mark clothing, prior to handing out samples.

A recent survey shows that consumers perceive sampling programs favourably: 94 percent of respondents view sampling as a risk-free way of trying a new product and 83 percent see a demonstration as a way of increasing the comfort level when buying the product.[7]

Sampling programs tend to be an expensive proposition for a marketing organization because of the product, package, and distribution costs. In spite of these costs, sample promotions rank second in popularity among marketers, so clearly the long-term benefits outweigh the short-term costs. Further, sampling combined with a coupon is the best way to achieve a first purchase by a new customer. On the downside, a sample is the fastest way to kill an inferior product.[8] See Figure 16.5 for an illustration of a product sample offer.

The Internet has spawned another form of sampling. Software suppliers can now download demonstration copies of their programs directly to interested customers for a trial period of 30 to 60 days. If satisfied, the customer can order the complete version at the end of the trial period and download it directly over the Internet.

Contests

Contests are designed to create short-term excitement about a product. A contest usually provides an incentive to buy an item, requiring, for example, the submission of a product label or symbol and an entry form that is included with the product. Consumers are encouraged to enter often and thereby improve their chances of winning a prize. This results in many purchases. While contests tend to attract the current users of a product, they are less effective in inducing trial purchases than are coupons and samples. Consequently, contests are most appropriate in the mature stage of the product life cycle, when the aim is to retain the present market share. Sweepstakes and instant wins are two major types of contests.

sweepstakes   A **sweepstakes** contest is a chance promotion involving the giveaway of products and services of value to randomly selected participants who have submitted qualified

A Free Sample Offer

Figure 16.5

Courtesy: Reckitt Benckiser

entries. Prizes, such as cash, cars, homes, and vacations, are given away. Consumers enter contests by filling in a blank entry form, usually available at the point of purchase or through print advertising, and submitting it along with a proof of purchase to a central location where a draw is held to determine the winners.

game (or instant-win) contest

A **game** (or **instant-win**) **contest** is a promotion vehicle that includes a number of pre-determined, pre-seeded winning tickets, in the overall, fixed universe of tickets. Packages containing winning certificates are redeemed for prizes. Variations of this type of contest include collect-and-wins, match-and-wins, and small-prize instant-wins combined with a grand-prize contest.

In the age of database marketing, companies have integrated contests into their Web sites. Potential customers are encouraged to visit sites through traditional forms of advertising, but when they arrive there they want to be entertained. A contest is one way of doing that. It also provides an opportunity to collect valuable demographic information about the potential customer.

Contests are governed by laws and regulations and any company that runs one must publish certain information: how, where and when to enter; who is eligible to enter the contest; the prize structure, value, and number of prizes; the odds of winning and the selection procedure; and conditions that must be met before a prize is awarded (e.g., a skill-testing question must be answered).

Tim Hortons has one of the most popular and ongoing contest promotions in Canada. For insight into their promotion activities, read the Marketing in Action vignette **RRRoll Up the Rim**.

Cash Refunds (Rebates)

cash refund or **rebate**

A **cash refund**, or **rebate**, as it is often called, is a predetermined amount of money returned directly to the consumer by the manufacturer after the purchase has been made. For companies in the packaged-goods industry, cash refunds are useful promotion techniques in the mature stage of the product's life cycle, for such activity reinforces loyalty. The most common type of refund is the single-purchase refund in which consumers receive a portion of their money back for the purchase of a specified product. However, refunds are designed to achieve different objectives; hence, they can be offered in different formats. Refunds encourage consumers to make multiple purchases and stock their pantries. For example, the value of the refund may escalate as the numbers of items purchased increases. An offer could be structured as follows:

- Buy one and get $1.00 back
- Buy two and get $2.50 back
- Buy three and get $5.00 back

slippage

In this case, the refund is greatest when the consumer takes maximum advantage of the offer. In refund offers where multiple purchases are necessary, slippage generally occurs. **Slippage** happens when a consumer starts collecting proofs of purchase for a refund offer but neglects to follow through and submit a request for the refund. In effect, the manufacturer does not pay for the purchases induced by the promotion. Slippage is a significant factor. In a survey of grocery shoppers, it was found that one-half of all refund participants sometimes neglect to submit a request for a refund even after they have bought the product with the intention of using the refund offer.[9]

Marketing in Action

RRRoll Up the Rim

How do you know when you have a successful promotion? Perhaps it is when the Royal Canadian Air Farce comedy troupe spoofs the idea on television. This is proof that you have worked your way into the cultural fabric of Canada. And that is what happened with Tim Hortons' "Roll up the Rim" promotion. Like the call of the loon, "rrroll up the rim to win" has hit the airwaves for 15 consecutive springs.

The promotion began in 1987 as a way to boost coffee sales during the summer, but it has evolved into a national obsession that draws customers to the donut shops year after year, win or lose. Customers are powerless to resist the temptation of winning something as small as a donut or muffin or as large as a colour television, bicycle, or automobile.

According to Ron Buist, director of marketing services at TDL Group (the corporate name for Tim Hortons), one of the keys to success is the KISS principle: "Keep it simple and, whenever possible, silly, too. We want it to be fun, and most of all we want it to be easy to play." This promotion proves that a simple idea coupled with a memorable advertising slogan can generate a huge payoff for a company. The company will not discuss sales figures, but one Ontario franchisee says business climbs by 10 to 15 percent during the roll up promotion.

In looking at the history of the promotion, it was a radio spot developed in 1993, featuring an actor with a thick Scottish accent rolling the letter R in the slogan that really got the ball rolling (pardon the pun). The ad drew a few complaints about how it was stereotyping Scots, but it also launched the slogan into the psyches of consumers. The Scottish accent has been dropped, but the rolling R remains in all forms of advertising.

The "Rrroll up the rim" promotion demonstrates the application of some important planning variables. To have a chance at being successful, a promotion contest should be easy to play, deliver a consistent theme, and include a catchy and memorable phrase. The advantage of having this kind of long-running promotion is self-evident. It becomes less of a promotion than a brand unto itself. "Roll up the Rim" has become recognized as its own entity, much as a product would.

There's an expression "Imitation is the best form of flattery." Tim Hortons' competitors (Country Style Donuts and Coffee Time) have experimented with their own versions of Roll up the Rim. Why invent something when you can simply copy it!

Adapted from Laura Pratt, "Roll up the Rim major player for Tim Hortons," *Strategy*, May 22, 2000, p. 22; Liza Finlay, "Perpetual promos," *Marketing*, May 31, 1999, pp. 11-12; John Heinzl, "Tim Hortons rrrolls up a winner," *Globe and Mail*, March 24, 1999, p. B29.

Courtesy: The TDL Group

Rebates are now popular among manufacturers of durable goods like cars and major household appliances. Offers of $1000 or $2000 back are quite common in the automobile industry when the economy takes a bit of a downturn and new cars aren't selling.

Premium Offers

A **premium** is an item offered free or at a bargain price to consumers who buy another specific item or make a minimum purchase. The goal of a premium offer is to provide added value to new and repeat purchasers. McDonald's and other fast food restaurants consistently use premiums, because they are effective with its primary target (families), and they reinforce the company's goal of offering value to consumers. Recently, fast-food restaurants have focused their premium efforts on characters from popular movies. McDonald's, for example, has a 10-year promotion agreement with Disney to distribute toy characters.

Premiums are usually offered to consumers in three ways: either as a mail-in (e.g., send in proofs of purchase and the item will be returned by mail), as an in-pack or on-pack promotion (e.g., an item is placed inside a package or attached to a package), or by a coupon offer distributed by in-store shelf talkers. Distributing a premium with a product is popular, as it provides instant gratification. General Mills recently launched a series of popular Hasbro CD-ROM games (Clue, Monopoly, Junior Yahtzee, and others) with boxes of Cheerios, Honey Nut Cheerios, and Frosted Cheerios. According to General Mills, the CD-ROM promotion has been their best ever. In the dry cereal category the name of the game is to break through the clutter (the category is a poster child for advertising clutter) and that's just what the promotion did.[10]

The use of premiums achieves several objectives: they increase the quantity of brand purchases made by consumers; they help to retain current users; and they provide a merchandising tool to encourage display activity in stores.

Loyalty (Frequent-Buyer) Programs

Canadian retailers and a variety of service industries, such as airlines and hotels, have made loyalty or frequent-buyer programs popular. In fact, almost two-thirds of Canadians have at least one loyalty card in their wallet or purse.[11] A **loyalty (frequent buyer) program** offers the consumer a small bonus, such as points or "play money," when they make a purchase. The bonus accumulates with each new purchase. The goal of such an offer is to encourage loyalty, and that's what a program like Shoppers Drug Mart's Optimum rewards program does. In this program shoppers accumulate points that are redeemable on future purchases. The card is an integral component of Shoppers' new customer relationship management program. Shoppers can electronically cross-reference transaction data and tailor offers and services to specific customers in-store or by e-mail. The company already has over one million names in its database.[12]

Canadian Tire's program is, perhaps, the best-known and longest-running (over 40 years) frequent-buyer program in Canada. It has become engrained as Canada's second currency. It rewards regular shoppers who pay for merchandise with cash or a Canadian Tire credit card with Canadian Tire "money" worth up to 5 percent of the value of the purchase. Canadian Tire now allows customers to collect virtual money on the company's house credit card, its Web site, and its affiliate MasterCard. Canadian Tire money captures the essence of a rewards program because customers really can purchase something for free. With a program like Air Miles, it takes a considerable length of time before rewards kick in.

Delayed-Payment Incentives

In a **delayed-payment incentive** promotion, a consumer is granted a grace period during which no interest or principal is paid for the item purchased. Once the purchase is made from the retailer, a finance company assumes the agreement and charges interest if full payment is not made by the agreed-upon date.

Leon's Furniture pioneered the delayed-payment concept in Canada under promotions called the "Don't Pay a Cent Event" and the "No Money Miracle." According to Terry Leon, executive vice-president of Leon's, "Consumers need more incentives than ever to spend, and credit arrangements are merely part of an overall package that includes good value, good prices, and a wide selection. The 'Don't Pay a Cent' promotion accounts for 40 to 60 percent of the company's business, depending on the time of year."[13] This innovative technique has spread to other hard goods retailers in the household furnishings and consumer electronics markets.

Combination Offers

In order to maximize the effectiveness of a promotion, marketers often combine the consumer promotion techniques discussed in this chapter. For example, when a free trial sample is given away in a store or distributed through a direct mailing, it is common to include a coupon. Assuming the consumer is satisfied with the trial usage, the coupon provides an added incentive to make the first official purchase of the product. Coupons and contests are another frequent combination. The coupon attracts the user for the initial purchase, and the contest encourages additional purchases. See Figure 16.6 for an illustration.

Figure 16.6

A Promotion Offer That Combines a Coupon With a Contest

Courtesy: Scott Paper Ltd.

TRADE PROMOTION

trade promotion

Trade promotion is promotional activity directed at distributors to push a product through the channel of distribution; it is designed to increase the volume purchased and encourage merchandising support for a manufacturer's product. Along with trade discounts and performance allowances (discussed in Chapter 11), the most commonly used trade promotion activities are cooperative advertising, in-ad coupons, dealer premiums, collateral materials, dealer display materials, and trade shows.

Cooperative Advertising

cooperative advertising

In the case of **cooperative advertising**, manufacturers allocate allowances to pay a portion of a retailer's advertising. The advertisements by major supermarket chains showing weekly specials, for example, are partially paid for by the manufacturers participating in the advertisements in any given week. In some cases, the manufacturer may agree to pay half of the retailer's cost of advertising, and frequently, the manufacturer provides advertising illustrations and artwork that are integrated into the retailer's advertising message.

Performance Allowances

performance allowance

A **performance allowance** is an additional discount (over and above a trade allowance) offered by manufacturers to encourage retailers to perform specific merchandising functions (e.g., display the product at retail, provide an advertising mention in a flyer, or offer a lower price for a period of time). Before paying the allowance, the manufacturer requires proof of performance from the retailer.

Retail In-Ad Coupons

retail in-ad coupon

A **retail in-ad coupon** is a coupon printed in a retailer's weekly advertising, either in the newspaper or in supplements inserted in the newspaper. These coupons are redeemable on national brands and are usually paid for by the manufacturer. Retailers pay for coupons redeemable on private label brands. The programs for national brand products are negotiated between manufacturers' sales representatives and retail buyers. Usually, the funds to cover such coupons are derived from a trade-promotion budget; thus, they are included as a trade-promotion activity.

Dealer Premiums

dealer premium

A **dealer premium** or dealer loader is an incentive offered to a distributor by a manufacturer to encourage a special purchase (e.g., a specified volume of merchandise) or to secure additional merchandising support from a distributor. Premiums are usually offered in the form of merchandise (e.g., a set of golf clubs, or other forms of leisure goods or sporting goods); the value of the premium increases with the amount of product purchased by the retailer.

Their use is often controversial. Some distributors forbid their buyers to accept premiums because they feel only the individual buyer, rather than the organization, benefits. Such a situation, often referred to as "payola," may lead the buyer to make unnecessary purchases and ignore the objectives of the distributor. The other side of the argument is that the purchase of the goods at significant savings (through allowances and premiums) offers direct, tangible benefit to the buying organization. These practices are perceived by many to be unethical, and they should not occur. Nonetheless, some dealings do happen under the table, so students should be aware of it.

Collateral Material

collateral materials

To help itself in the personal-selling process, the sales force uses **collateral materials** supplied by the manufacturer to provide information to customers. These materials include price lists, catalogues, sales brochures, pamphlets, specification sheets, product manuals, and audio-visual sales aids prepared by the manufacturer. Web sites are now very popular for communicating lengthy and complex information.

Dealer-Display Material

dealer-display material or **point-of-purchase material**

Dealer-display material, or **point-of-purchase material**, consists of self-contained, custom-designed merchandising units, either permanent or temporary, that display a manufacturer's product. It includes posters, shelf extenders (tray-like extensions that project outward from the shelf to extend shelf display), shelf talkers (small posters that hang from shelves), channel strips (narrow strips containing a brief message attached to the channel face of a shelf), advertising pads or tear pads (tear-off sheets that usually explain details of a consumer promotion offer), display shippers (shipping cases that convert to display bins or stands when opened), and permanent display racks. The use of such displays and materials is at the discretion of retailers, whose space they occupy. The role of a manufacturer's sales representative is to convince the retailer of the merits of using the display.

Trade Shows

Trade shows are typically organized by an industry association each year to demonstrate the latest products of member manufacturers. There are, for example, toy shows, automobile shows, computer shows, and appliance shows. Trade shows are the fastest way to reach a large number of targeted customers in a fixed time frame where you can talk, show, and impress them with the latest wizardry while getting leads for the future.

A recent research study shows the value of trade show participation. The average cost to close a lead (make a sale) obtained through field sales is $1140 versus $705 to close a lead from a trade show.[14] Trade shows are a cost-effective way of doing business.

Personal Selling

personal selling

Personal selling is a personalized form of communication that involves a seller presenting the features and benefits of a product or service to a buyer for the purpose of making a sale. It is an integral component of the marketing communications mix, for it is the activity that in many cases clinches a deal. Advertising and sales promotion creates awareness and interest for a product. Personal selling creates desire and action. In creating that desire and action, the interaction between the seller and buyer is crucial. While the purpose of selling is to make the sale, the role of the sales representative goes beyond this task.

THE ROLE OF THE CONTEMPORARY SALESPERSON

Gathering Market Intelligence

2.
Describe the roles of sales representatives and the types of selling that occur in a business organization.

In a competitive marketplace, salespeople must be attuned to the trends in their industry. They must be alert to what the competitor is doing, to its new product projects, and to its advertising and promotion plans, and they must listen to feedback from customers regarding their own products' performance. Competitive knowledge is important when the salesperson faces questions involving product comparisons. Data collected by a salesperson can be reported electronically to the company's head office. Managers can retrieve the information and use it appropriately at a later date.

Problem Solving

The only way a salesperson can make a sale is to listen to what a customer wants and ask questions to determine his or her real needs. Asking, listening, and providing information and advice that is in the best interests of the customer is what consultative selling is all about. In performing this task the seller must demonstrate a sincere concern for the customer and his or her company's problems.

Locating and Maintaining Customers

Salespeople who locate new customers play a key role in a company's growth. A company cannot be satisfied with its present list of customers because aggressive competitors attempt to lure them away. To prevent shrinkage and to increase sales, salespeople actively pursue new accounts. Their time is divided between finding new accounts and selling and servicing current accounts.

Follow-Up Service

In the eyes of the customer, the salesperson is the company, as he or she is the first point of contact should anything go wrong or should more information be required. Maintenance of customers is crucial, and very often, it is the quality of follow-up service that determines if a customer will remain a customer. Since the salespeople are the company's direct link to the customer, it cannot be stressed enough how important their handling of customer service is. The sale is never over. Once a deal has been closed, numerous tasks arise: arranging for delivery, providing technical assistance, providing customer training, and being readily available to handle any customer problems that emerge during and after delivery. The personalized role of the sales representative is instrumental in building relationships.

TYPES OF SELLING

Business-to-Business Selling

Xerox Canada
www.xerox.ca

Business-to-business salespeople either sell products for use in the production and sale of other products, or sell products to channel members who in turn resell them. For example: a Xerox sales representative sells photocopiers to another business for use in its daily operations; a representative from Nike may sell a new line of running shoes to the head office of a group of specialty retailers, such as Foot Locker or Athlete's World, who, in turn, distribute the running shoes through their retail locations.

Thoroughly trained and adequately prepared sales representatives are crucial in the examples mentioned above. Investment in other forms of marketing communications could be all for naught if the personal selling execution is weak.

Retail Selling

Retail selling is the sale of merchandise or services to final customers for personal use. These salespeople are often referred to as sales clerks or associates and are employed by department stores, specialty stores, and other types of retailing firms. Wal-Mart, for example, uses the term "associates" for its sales and service employees. Anyone employed by these types of stores and who is in contact with a customer has a direct or indirect influence on the sale of merchandise or the level of customer satisfaction and, therefore, should have some basic training in sales and customer service.

A trend in retailing is to reduce the number of employees responsible for selling. Many retailers are shifting towards self-service and a reliance on visual merchandising and price promotions to make the sale. This approach is risky as it can lead to customer dissatisfaction when proper service is not available. An unhappy customer will not return. All of Canada's big retailers such as the Bay, Sears, Wal-Mart, and Canadian Tire are experimenting with varying degrees of self-service.

Direct Selling

in-home selling

There are several types of direct selling. **In-home selling** uses a network of local people to sell products in their communities, often at home "parties." These selling practices take advantage of the social environment of a home party, and as such, there is less pressure to buy. Companies that operate in this way include Mary Kay (cosmetics), Avon (perfumes, cosmetics, and a variety of personal-care products), and Tupperware (plastic goods for the household).

telemarketing

Telemarketing involves the use of a telephone as an interactive medium for marketing response. It employs highly trained people and database marketing techniques to seek and serve new customers. Telemarketing improves productivity because it reduces direct-selling costs. Telemarketing is useful for screening and qualifying incoming leads, generating leads from directories and mailing lists, and calling current customers to secure orders, offer additional services, sell products to new customers, or determine the level of customer satisfaction. Telemarketing is discussed in greater detail in Chapter 15.

online selling

Online selling refers to the use of Internet Web sites as a vehicle for conducting business transactions. Consumers who are looking for convenience as part of their shopping experience now look to the Internet for a solution. Web sites are capable of accepting and processing orders, receiving payment, and delivering goods and services directly to businesses and consumers. Since all transactions are electronically recorded, companies are accumulating huge databases of information that can be used for marketing purposes in the longer term.

TYPES OF SALESPEOPLE

Salespeople are classified by the nature of the tasks they perform, including processing orders and being creative sellers and missionary sellers.

Order Processors

Order processing is common at the wholesaling and retailing levels and is essential in maintaining current customers. In wholesaling, the order taker processes an order over the telephone or from mail orders. Such a job is a good training position, as it is a good means of learning about a company and its products and how to deal with customers. In retailing, the order taker is the retail clerk, a person responsible for responding to customers' questions, preparing invoices, checking credit, handling complaints, and completing the sale.

Creative Sellers

When selling creatively, the primary responsibility is to pursue an order aggressively. This requires extensive knowledge about the product, competing products, and the sales-communication process. It is a process in which the seller makes the customer recognize that the product being sold will resolve a problem. Success depends on the salesperson's ability to solve problems and counsel customers. This is a challenging type of selling that involves all of the steps in the selling process (discussed in the following section). Creative sellers play an essential role in business-to-business marketing environments and in building customer relationships.

Missionary Sellers

missionary selling

Missionary selling is an indirect activity dedicated to selling the goodwill of a company. It is a supplement to creative selling. For example, a missionary, or merchandiser, as they are often referred to, will contact retailers to check stocks, arrange displays, and provide basic information about new products. Many leading packaged-goods companies, such as Procter & Gamble, Nestle, and Neilson Cadbury, have added merchandisers and reduced the number of sales representatives in their sales forces. This combination results in lower customer contact costs and gives the sales representative more time to concentrate on selling. In an industrial environment, a missionary is responsible for technical assistance or training to ensure that customers get maximum usage from the products or services they have purchased.

THE STEPS IN THE SELLING PROCESS

Prospecting

prospecting

3.
Outline the steps in the selling process.

Seven steps are commonly associated with personal selling (Figure 16.7). The first step is **prospecting**, which is a systematic procedure for developing sales leads. If salespeople do not allocate enough time to finding new customers, they risk causing a decline in sales for their company. If their income is geared to the value of the business they produce, they risk the loss of personal compensation as well. Potential customers, or prospects, are identified by means of published lists and directories, such as *Scott's Industrial Directory*, *Fraser's Canadian Trade Directory*, and *Canadian Key Business Directory*. The salesperson also seeks referrals from satisfied customers or tries to find new customers by cold canvass, the process of calling on people or organizations without appointments or advance knowledge of them.

Steps in the Selling Process

Figure 16.7

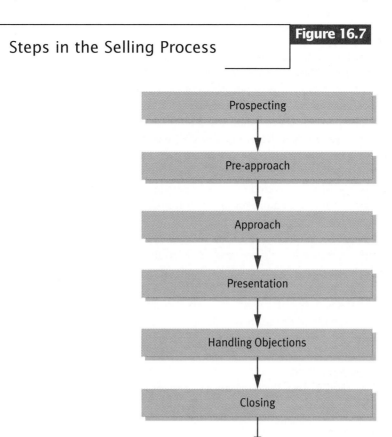

Prospecting

Pre-approach

Approach

Presentation

Handling Objections

Closing

Follow-up

Pre-approach

pre-approach

qualifying

The **pre-approach** involves gathering information about potential customers before actually making sales contact. During the pre-approach stage, customers are qualified. **Qualifying** a customer is the procedure for determining if a prospect needs the product, has the authority to buy it, and has the ability to pay for it. There is little sense in pursuing customers who lack the financial resources or have no need to make the business relationship successful. The seller also gains insights into the customer that can be used in the sales presentation: information such as the buyer's likes and dislikes, personal interests and hobbies, buying procedures, and special needs and problems.

Approach

approach

The **approach** is the initial contact with the prospect, usually a face-to-face selling situation. Since buyers are usually busy, little time should be wasted in the approach. In the first few minutes of a sales interview, the salesperson must capture the attention and interest of the buyer so that an effective environment is created for the presentation of the product's benefits.

Presentation

presentation

The actual sales **presentation** consists of a persuasive delivery and demonstration of a product's benefits. An effective sales presentation shows the buyer how the benefits of the product satisfy his or her needs or help resolve a particular problem. In doing so, the seller focuses on the benefits that are most important to the buyer. Critical elements usually focus on lower price, the durability of the product, the dependability of supply, the performance of the product, and the availability of follow-up service.

It is at this stage that asking proper questions and listening attentively are most important. A salesperson listens to and analyzes what buyers are saying, then uses what he or she has discovered when presenting the appropriate benefits. Being flexible and making changes to a presentation in mid-stream could be the difference between making a sale and not making a sale.

Laptop computers and changing technology now allow for multimedia presentations. Sellers rely on PowerPoint or equivalent software presentations; video can be integrated into the presentation to demonstrate the product. While technology helps put the spotlight on the product, it is important not to get carried away with presentation technology—the content of the presentation is what is most important. A useful tactic in the presentation is to let the buyer handle the product and the materials relevant to it. This action results in a feeling of ownership and helps in the decision-making process.

As a supplement to a presentation, electronic catalogues (CD-ROM format) that show photos of products along with prices and specifications can be left with the customer. Lengthy and complex information should be available on a Web site for customer reference at any time.

Handling Objections

objection

An **objection** is an obstacle that the salesperson must confront and resolve if the sales transaction is to be completed. Prospects almost always express resistance when contemplating the purchase of a product. An objection is a cue for more information. The buyer is suggesting that the presentation of a product has not revealed how the product will satisfy a particular need. The objection, therefore, is feedback that should be analyzed and used. It may enable the salesperson to discover another benefit in the product, a benefit that can then be presented to the buyer.

Typical objections involve issues related to price, quality, level of service, and technical assistance. The salesperson must remain calm and not take these objections personally, recognizing that they are the normal reactions of a buyer. Instead, the salesperson should ask questions of the buyer to confirm his or her understanding of the situation, then answer the objection, and then move on to the next benefit or attempt to close the sale.

Closing

closing

Does the buyer voluntarily say "Yes, I'll buy it"? The answer is, no! Getting the buyer to say "yes" is the entire purpose of the sales interview, but this task is only accomplished if the salesperson asks for the order. **Closing** consists of asking for the order, and it is the most difficult step in the process of selling. Salespeople are reluctant to ask the big question, even though it is the logical sequel to a good presentation and demonstration. In

trial close

fact, a good salesperson attempts a close whenever a point of agreement is made with the buyer. If the buyer says "no," the close is referred to as a **trial close**, or an attempt to close that failed. The salesperson simply moves on to the next point in the presentation.

Timing a close is a matter of judgment. Good salespeople know when to close—it is often referred to as the "sixth sense" of selling. The salesperson assesses the buyer's verbal and non-verbal responses in an effort to judge when he or she has become receptive, and at the right moment, asks the big question. When the time to close arrives, the seller may employ one of these commonly used techniques:

1. *Assumptive Close* In the case of this close, the salesperson assumes the prospect has already decided to buy. The representative makes a statement, such as, "I will have this model delivered by Friday," or asks a question, such as, "What is the best day for delivery?" An agreement or answer confirms the assumption that the customer has chosen to buy.

2. *Alternative-Choice Close* Here the seller also assumes that the sale has been made and simply inquires which option is preferable. For example, the representative may ask, "Would you prefer the metallic blue or cherry red colour?"

3. *Summary-of-Benefits Close* The salesperson using this close summarizes the key benefits that the buyer acknowledged during the presentation, such as the favourable credit terms, the dependability of the product, the availability of frequent service, and the prompt delivery. When the summary is complete, the representative then poses a direct closing question, such as "Do we have a deal?" or "When would you like delivery?"

4. *T-Account Close* In this case, the prospect evaluates the pros and cons of the purchase. The salesperson lists the positive and negative points in a manner suggesting that the positive points outweigh the negative. In doing so, he or she leads the prospect to the decision that now is the time to buy.

Follow-up

follow-up

There is an old saying: "The sale never ends." There is truth to this statement, for a new sale is nothing more than the start of a new relationship. Keeping current customers satisfied is the key to success. Effective salespeople make a point of providing **follow-up**; that is, they keep in touch with customers to ensure that the delivery and installation of the goods are satisfactory, that promises are kept, and that, generally, the expectations of the buyer are met. When problems do occur, the salesperson is ready to take action to resolve the situation.

To be successful in selling requires dedication, determination, and discipline. What separates the successful salesperson from the unsuccessful one usually boils down to how well an individual follows an established set of principles. While the wording of these principles may vary from one source to another, the intent behind them is consistent. See Figure 16.8 for some pointers on what separates the professionals from the average salespeople.

SELLING IN A CHANGING BUSINESS ENVIRONMENT

The nature of selling is changing rapidly. To be successful in the future, a salesperson and his or her company must consider the importance of teamwork in communicating with customers (another aspect of integration), the importance of building long-term

Tips for Successful Selling

Figure 16.8

Tips for Successful Selling

1. Selling Is a Skill, not a Talent

Successful salespeople develop skills in asking questions, listening attentively, identifying customer needs, and developing product benefits that satisfy those needs. Knowledge of the product, the customer, and the competition is essential.

2. You Are the Most Important Product of All

Successful salespeople sell themselves. If the customer isn't sold on you, he or she won't buy your product.

3. Relationships, Emotions, and Feeling Are Important

Successful salespeople not only have all the facts, they also have the ability to create positive emotions about themselves and their products.

4. Effective Prospecting Is Crucial

Organizing and managing your time when not selling is important. Discipline is required to contact prospects to request appointments. Proper follow-up is essential to keep a customer.

5. A Sales Call Is a Performance

Be prepared! Begin with a bang that will get the prospect's attention and interest. Encourage participation so the customer discovers the benefits for himself or herself.

6. Develop Negotiation Skills

A successful salesperson closes a profitable sale by developing and using negotiation skills. It is important to package together all points of agreement and use them to your advantage.

7. Use Objections to Advantage

A successful salesperson encourages the prospect to raise concerns. Solving those concerns leads to agreement and opportunities to close the sale.

8. Always Be Closing

Closing begins at the start of a presentation. The challenge is to build agreement and help the prospect decide how to buy, not whether to buy. When the prospect agrees, ask for the order!

relationships, and the importance of adapting to technologies that directly influence the selling process.

Selling Is a Team Effort

Traditionally, selling has been thought of as an individual effort (e.g., the salesperson calling on the customer and presenting a product one-on-one or to a committee of buyers). Today, selling is a team effort involving everyone in an organization, spearheaded by the salesperson. For example, selling sophisticated technical equipment in a business-to-business environment requires a team of experts, including research and design specialists, engineers, accountants, and other marketing personnel, in addition to the salesperson. They all bring different expertise to the presentation and make the customer feel more at ease with the decision-making process.

Companies Sell Relationships, Not Products

Organizations abiding by contemporary corporate culture—that is, those that believe in relationship marketing—actively pursue relationships in the selling process. Making a sale, or getting the order, is simply one step in the sales continuum. It symbolizes the start of a new relationship or solidification of an existing relationship.

The key for the seller is to determine how his or her company's resources can give the customer an edge. It is a consultative process in which the seller proves to the buyer that there is an advantage in doing business together. The search for a good fit between sellers (suppliers) and buyers stems from customers' relentless search for value in everything they purchase.

Impact of Technology

The nature of selling is changing in many industries due to the advances in communications technology. Members of a channel of distribution that include raw material suppliers, manufacturers, wholesalers and retailers, and end users, are working cooperatively on supply chain management programs. By electronically transferring information between participants in the supply chain, basic buying decisions are automated. Therefore, the challenge facing creative sellers is how to get their products into such a system. The practice of online marketing is a threat to the traditional way of selling.

Firms are also increasing their investment in direct response and online marketing techniques because of the cost savings associated with these practices. As a consequence, the role of personal sellers is changing. They are spending less time with personal contact and more time with electronic contact. They are also scouring databases for the best possible prospects and are spending much more time providing customer service in order to retain present customers. Companies using technology to help market goods and services are finding that geographical boundaries are being eliminated, as buyers search for the best value in what they require.

SALES MANAGEMENT

The sales manager is the link between the sales force and the company. Sales managers are responsible for numerous managerial functions, including recruitment and selection, training, organization, supervision, motivation, compensation, and evaluation and control. Typically, a company will have a national sales manager, who is ultimately responsible for the activities and performance of all the salespeople. Below the national manager may be a group of regional sales managers, each responsible for a different geographic area (e.g., Maritimes, Quebec, Ontario, Prairies, and British Columbia). The sales manager represents the needs of the customers and the sales representatives to senior management.

In some markets, particularly, business-to-business markets, sales management functions are allocated by industry or market segment. As discussed in the chapter on business-to-business marketing, companies are altering their organizational structures so that they can reach and serve those segments with the greatest sales potential more efficiently. By focusing on specific industries, marketing and sales programs can be tailored to industry specific needs.

Event Marketing and Sponsorships

4.
Explain the importance that event marketing and sponsorships have in contemporary marketing.

event marketing

event sponsorship

Molson Indy
www.molsonindy.
com

Event marketing and sponsorships are fast becoming important elements of the marketing communications mix. **Event marketing** is the process, planned by a sponsoring organization, of integrating a variety of communication elements behind an event theme (e.g., Molson's coordination of advertising, public relations, and sales promotion activities for the Molson Indy car race).

Event sponsorship is the financial support of an event (e.g., an auto race, theatre production, or a marathon road-race) by a sponsor, in return for advertising privileges associated with the event. Usually, an event marketer offers sponsorships on a tiered basis. For instance, a lead sponsor or sponsors would pay a maximum amount and receive maximum privileges. Other sponsors would pay less and receive fewer privileges.

Event marketing is big business! According to IEG Consulting, a Chicago-based sponsorship measurement firm, the North American sponsorship market is valued at $9.5 billion and the annual rate of growth is in the 10 percent-range. Sports events attract the lion's share (about 70 percent) of sponsorship revenue.[15] Sponsorships in Canada could be worth as much as $950 million annually.

Investment in event marketing and sponsorships is mainly divided between three areas: sports, entertainment, and cultural events. VISA, for example, is involved in all three areas—it sponsors the Olympic Games, the Visa Triple Crown (a series of thoroughbred horse races), Canadian film festivals, and the Dubai Shopping Festival, among many other sponsorships.

Royal Bank of Canada
www.royalbank.com

SPORTS SPONSORSHIP

Sports sponsorship occurs at amateur and professional levels and can be subdivided into classifications from local events to global events (Figure 16.9). Sports sponsorships tend to be dominated by certain industries and manufacturers. For example, the automobile industry is well represented by General Motors and Ford, the brewing industry by Molson and Labatt, and the financial industry by Royal Bank and Bank of Montreal, and VISA and MasterCard.

ambush marketing

A recent phenomenon associated with event marketing is the practice of ambush marketing. **Ambush marketing** is a strategy used by non-sponsors to capitalize on the prestige and popularity of an event by giving the false impression they are sponsors. Such a strategy works because people are often confused about who the real sponsors are. In the recent 2002 Winter Olympic Games, Labatt was a major advertising sponsor on the CBC network (the broadcast rights holder in Canada). During the Olympic period, Molson placed Olympic-themed television ads (ads showing Canada's Olympic hockey opponents as being afraid to face our national team) on competing networks—a classic case of ambush marketing.[16]

venue marketing
or venue
sponsorship

Venue marketing, or **venue sponsorship,** is another form of event marketing. Here, a company or brand is linked to a physical site such as a stadium, arena, or theatre. In Canada, there is the Corel Centre in Ottawa (Ottawa Senators play there), the Air

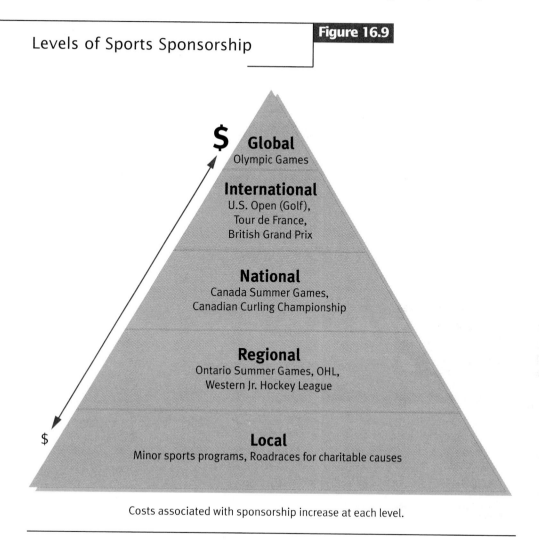

Figure 16.9

Levels of Sports Sponsorship

$ **Global**
Olympic Games

International
U.S. Open (Golf),
Tour de France,
British Grand Prix

National
Canada Summer Games,
Canadian Curling Championship

Regional
Ontario Summer Games, OHL,
Western Jr. Hockey League

$

Local
Minor sports programs, Roadraces for charitable causes

Costs associated with sponsorship increase at each level.

Canada Centre (Leafs and Raptors), and GM Place (Vancouver Canucks). Inside the Air Canada Centre, there's the Sears Theatre and inside GM Place there's the Air Canada Club. Pre-eminent title positions like these break through the clutter of other forms of advertising but this does come at a cost. Air Canada spent $20 million on a 20-year agreement for the naming rights to the Toronto Maple Leaf's home rink. Hummingbird, a software development company, paid a flat fee of $5 million to have their name on a performing arts theatre in Toronto.[17]

Organizations that are contemplating sports sponsorships can do so at much lower costs if they consider **grassroots** participation. Local participation at much lower cost can produce attractive results. Sunlight detergent, for example, is actively involved with children's soccer leagues across Canada. Muddy soccer uniforms fit like a glove with Sunlight's "Go ahead. Get dirty." positioning strategy. Other companies involved with the Canadian Soccer Association include MasterCard, McDonald's, Sunny Delight, and Adidas.[18]

How effective is investment in sports sponsorship? A key indicator of success is awareness and association. For example, which beer company is closely associated with *Hockey Night in Canada*? If you cannot answer this question, the sponsors have a problem. Presently, Labatt is the exclusive beer sponsor of *HNIC*, but that's about to change. Labatt did not renew its exclusive rights deal with the CBC so as of the 2003–04 season, Molson beer advertising will also be part of HNIC—a showdown between Canadian and Blue is brewing! Labatt had paid the CBC $80 million for its present exclusive arrangement. Such an investment is now deemed too expensive.[19]

The grandest of sports sponsorships is for the Olympic Games. The Olympics present an attractive yet expensive opportunity for corporate sponsors. Financial support for the Canadian Olympic Association (COA) gives a company the right to run advertising and sales promotion programs in the years and months that precede the event. For insight into the benefits and drawbacks of Olympic sponsorship programs see the Marketing in Action vignette **Sponsoring The Big One!**

Marketing in Action

Sponsoring the Big One!

Is sponsoring the Olympics a wise investment? A select group of global companies including McDonald's, Coca-Cola, Visa, and Canadian companies like Labatt and Bell make a point of closely associating themselves with the Games. They go out of their way to create original advertising and sponsor athletes. Others, such as Air Canada and IBM have had enough. After 40 years as an Olympic sponsor, IBM did not participate in the Salt Lake Winter Games in 2002.

So what's the scoop? In evaluating a sponsorship property, advertisers take into account not only quantifiable audience data but also such intangibles as what an audience thinks of the property. Clearly an event revered for its purity and dedication to excellence, as the Olympics once were, is going to generate more interest than one held in contempt, as the Olympics increasingly are. But, despite bribery allegations against officials, drug scandals among athletes, and tainted judging, people continue to watch the Olympics in droves. That fact brings the advertisers back for more.

According to Nick Marrone, Canadian Olympic Association director of marketing, "The Olympics are still the most powerful sports brand in the world." In spite of recent problems the wholesome image still sells. "The value system the Olympics aspire to are the values we'd like our children to have," says McDonald's chief marketing officer Rem Langan. "It's a great fit for a family restaurant."

Another reason the Olympics are popular with advertisers is that they appeal to all age groups. For two straight weeks the Olympic Games are viewed by entire families, a rarity in television advertising.

For every Olympics the Canadian Olympic Association signs its own slate of sponsors. General Mills quickly signed on for the 2002 Winter Games. General Mills launched a national, on-pack program featuring six Canadian Olympic hopefuls: long track speed skater Catriona Le May Doan, women's hockey player Cassie Campbell, men's hockey players Steve Yzerman and Martin Brodeur, and figure skaters Jamie Salé and David Pelletier—great selections as they all won gold! Leading up to the Games, pictures and biographies of the athletes appeared on the boxes of Cheerios, Golden Grahams, and Nut Chex cereals.

Eric Lucas, General Mill's vice-president, marketing, said he wants Canadians to see the company as "part of the support system for Canadian Olympic athletes. Just as friends and families play a role, so do

ENTERTAINMENT SPONSORSHIPS

Canadian corporations invest huge amounts of money to sponsor concerts and secure endorsements from high-profile personalities in the hope that the celebrity–company relationship will pay off in the long run. Companies such as Molson, Coca-Cola, and Pepsi-Cola, which are interested in targeting youth and young adult segments, use entertainment sponsorship as a vehicle for developing pop-music and youth-lifestyle marketing strategies. According to Dave Perkins, vice-president marketing at Molson, "Sponsorships are part of Molson's commitment to provide our consumers with the best in sports and entertainment." By plastering the Molson banner on tickets and publicity, the company hopes to attract the young drinker on the verge of forming lifelong brand loyalties.[20]

Teens and young adults are a difficult target to reach, but MuchMusic plays right into the hands of sponsors who want to reach this demographic. An entertainment event called SnowJob (an annual event for the past 10 years) encourages anyone with a ski

---

corporations." General Mills is associating itself with the "Olympic values of partnership and excellence." The payoff, if consumers begin to make the association of brand with event, as is the case with Roots and the Olympics, is potentially huge, according to Lucas.

Roots' participation in the Olympics has been a financial bonanza. Outfitting Canadian teams with trendy styles is becoming the talk of the Games. For the 2002 Winter Games, Roots clothed the American team as well. People flocked to their Olympic village store for Canadian and American hats, berets, and other items. Says Michael Budman, co-founder of Roots, "Demand for our product is unprecedented. On some items we have had to limit the number people can buy." That limit actually created a black market for hats—$20 hats were being resold for as much as $300.

The scope of the Olympics equates to huge costs for sponsors. Worldwide rights for global sponsors like Coca-Cola, Samsung, and Xerox were in the $50-million range for the 2002 Winter Olympics. Air Canada, a long time sponsor of the COA, bowed out of the Winter Olympics citing "prohibitive" costs. IBM was looking for a better return on investment in a climate of flat or slashed marketing budgets. IBM re-evaluated its entire sponsorship portfolio and generally sees less emphasis on sports sponsorship in its future. According to Rick Singer, director, worldwide sponsorship marketing, "Our business strategies are shifting,

and we need to pick the right properties to reflect that. Taking a more cautious approach to sponsorship, each event must generate real stories of how problems are solved for IBM customers."

So, you be the judge. The costs are high but the potential payoff could be even higher. Is it a wise investment or a waste of money?

Adapted from Jim Byers, "Toronto-based clothier reaps gold at Winter Olympics," *Toronto Star*, February 20, 2002, pp. E1, E12; Patrick Allossery, "Will sponsors start keeping a distance from the Olympics?" *Financial Post*, February 18, 2002, p. FP7; Chris Zelkovich, "Corporations love Games," *Toronto Star*, January 23, 2002, p. C6; and Patrick Allosssery, "The biggest game going," *Financial Post*, January 14, 2002, p. FP6.

Courtesy: Adrian Wyld/CP Photo Archive

pass to travel up a mountain to watch the music and other activities during the six days the event takes place. Around 200 000 skiers and snowboarders and 25 contest winners check out the event; the resulting footage fills hours of time on MuchMusic in the month of March. Over half the audience is 12- to 17-year-olds. The event attracts sponsors like Nike, Pantene, and Sprite.[21]

CULTURAL EVENT SPONSORSHIPS

Arts and cultural event opportunities embrace dance, film, literature, music, painting, sculpture, and theatre. What separates cultural events from sports and entertainment events is the audience size. Depending on the sponsor, this is an advantage or a disadvantage. A company such as Molson prefers the mass audience reach of a sports event, whereas Infiniti or BMW may prefer to reach a more selective and upscale audience through an arts event. Perhaps only 2500 people attend the cultural event, but those people can be powerful. Typically, their education level would be above average, as would their income. Such an audience profile would be a good match for promoting a new luxury car.

Bell Canada
www.bell.ca

The primary benefit these companies gain by sponsoring the arts is goodwill from the public. Most firms view this type of investment as part of their corporate citizenship objectives (e.g., they are perceived as a good, contributing member of society). Bell has always invested in the communities it serves and has a varied sponsorship portfolio that includes major cultural and sporting events that enable it to be present in the community throughout the year. An illustration of their commitment appears in Figure 16.10. Some of the cultural events sponsored by Bell include the Stratford Festival, Shaw Festival, International Film Festivals in Toronto and Vancouver, and the *Just for Laughs Festival* in Montreal.

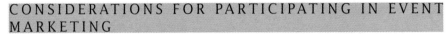

CONSIDERATIONS FOR PARTICIPATING IN EVENT MARKETING

5.
List the unique considerations involved in planning event marketing programs.

Companies enter into sponsorships in an effort to create a favourable impression with their customers and target groups. For this to be accomplished, the "fit" between the event and the sponsor must be a good one. For instance, Nike sponsors national and international track and field events as well as community-based events, such as fun runs. Much of the company's success has been based on event sponsorship and the distribution of merchandise that bears Nike's trademark logo—the swoosh. Generally, event sponsorship is a vehicle for enhancing the reputation of a company and the customer's awareness of a brand. The most effective sponsors adhere to the following principles when considering participation in event marketing.

1. ***Select Events Offering Exclusivity*** The need for companies to be differentiated within events they sponsor calls for exclusivity, meaning that direct competitors are blocked from sponsorship. Also, a concern among sponsors is the clutter of lower-level sponsors in non-competing categories that reduce the overall impact of the primary sponsor.

2. ***Use Sponsorships to Complement Other Promotional Activity*** The role that advertising and promotion will play in the sponsorship must be determined first. Sponsorship of the proper event will complement that company's other promotional activity. For example, FedEx sponsors drivers' baseball caps and tiny logos on the Championship Auto Racing Teams or CART circuit. They have corporate banners

A Corporate Ad That Communicates Bell's Commitment to the Community

Figure 16.10

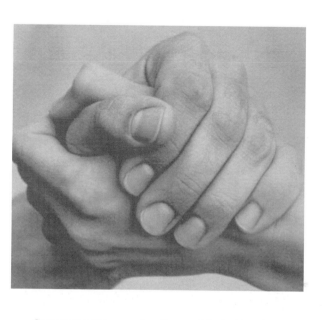

Communication makes the world a better place.

At Bell we are committed to enriching the lives of Canadians and the communities we live in. One of the ways we do this is by contributing millions of dollars each year to support charitable programs that connect people, technology and knowledge in new ways. Because we believe in the power of communication to change the world.

Imagine A Caring Company

Bell

Courtesy: Bell Canada

at the site, their trucks do pace laps, and uniformed employees present trophies.[22] Is there a better angle for a speedy delivery company than race cars? Their message in traditional media advertising emphasizes speed of delivery.

3. ***Choose the Target Carefully*** Events reach specific targets. For example, while rock concerts attract youth, symphonies tend to reach audiences that are older, urbane, and upscale. As suggested earlier, it is the fit, or matching, of targets, that is crucial.

4. ***Select an Event with an Image That Sells*** The sponsor must capitalize on the image of the event and perhaps the prestige or status associated with it. Sponsorship works best when the attraction to a brand is affected by such irrational considerations. A luxury car, such as the Mercedes M-Class Sport Utility Vehicle, may be a suitable sponsor for a significant arts or cultural event or a major national golf championship (e.g., the Mercedes Open in Hawaii). The prestigious image and status of such events have an impact on the sale of products that project a comparable image (in this example, the image and status that come with ownership of a Mercedes-Benz automobile).

5. ***Establish Selection Criteria*** In addition to using the criteria cited above, companies evaluating potential events for sponsorship should consider the long-term benefit such sponsorship offers compared with the costs in the short term. For example, being associated with an event that is ongoing, popular, and successful is wise, as there is less risk for the sponsor. Before committing financial resources to an event, a company should also consider whether it is likely to receive communications exposure through unpaid media sources. Before committing financial resources to an event, a company should also consider whether it is likely to receive exposure through unpaid media sources and whether it will be able to administer the event efficiently. The organization must establish objectives in terms of awareness and association scores, image improvement, and sales so that proper evaluation of the activity can be undertaken.

MEASURING THE BENEFITS OF SPONSORSHIP

One reason many companies are reluctant to enter into sponsorship programs is that results are difficult to measure. Large sums of money are spent at one time for a benefit that may be short lived. The basic appeal of event marketing is that it provides an opportunity to communicate with consumers in an environment in which they are already emotionally involved. Beyond this, companies conduct marketing research in order to determine the impact that sponsorship association has. The following indicators, many of which are obtained from research, are used to measure the benefits of sponsorship.

1. ***Awareness*** How much awareness of the event within each target group is there, and how well do people recall the brand or product name that sponsored the event?

2. ***Image*** What change in image and what increase in the consumer perception of leadership or credibility result from the sponsorship? For additional details regarding image enhancement, refer to the Marketing in Action Olympics vignette **Sponsoring The Big One!**

3. ***New Clients*** How many new clients were generated as a result of the company's sponsoring an event? Entertaining prospective clients in a luxury box at an event goes a considerable way in building a relationship.

4. ***Sales*** Do increases in sales or market share occur during post-event periods? Be aware that the real sales benefit may take years—it takes time for a sponsor to become closely associated with an event.

5. ***Specific Target Reach*** Do the events deliver constituency? Carefully selected events reach specific targets that are difficult to reach by conventional communications. For example, pre-teens and teens are difficult to reach through conventional media but can be reached effectively through sponsorship of rock concerts and music tours.

6. ***Media Coverage*** What value was derived from editorial coverage? Did the sponsorship result in free publicity for the sponsor? The industry benchmark for sports sponsorship is currently 4:1, meaning $4 in exposure (e.g., free air time) for every $1 spent on sponsorship and its marketing support.

For sponsorships to be successful, they must be integrated into corporate marketing and marketing communications plans seamlessly. All forms of communications must be complementary. The organization must leverage the use of its Web site and incorporate the sponsorship into public relations campaigns; it must also run thematic promotions to get all customer groups (trade and consumers) involved. Above all, the organization has to make a financial commitment above and beyond the rights fees. A general ratio for spending should be three-to-one. In other words, for every dollar spent on securing the rights, $3 should be spent to promote the relationship to the event.[23]

Summary

Sales promotion plays a key role in influencing purchase behaviour. Sales promotion activity can be divided into two categories. The first is consumer promotions. These are designed to pull the product through the channel of distribution and prompt purchases (trial, repeat, or multiple) of the product. Such promotions may take the form of coupons, free samples, contests, cash refunds, premiums, frequent-buyer programs, and delayed-payment incentives.

Trade promotions, the second kind of sales promotion, are designed to push the product through the channel of distribution and secure product listings among distributors, build sales volume, and gain merchandising support. Trade discounts, performance allowances, cooperative advertising, retail in-ad coupons, dealer premiums, collateral materials, point-of-purchase (or dealer) displays, and trade shows are among the types of trade promotion that occur.

Personal selling refers to personal communication between sellers and buyers. The role of the salesperson is to locate customers whose needs can be satisfied or whose problems can be resolved through the use of a company's products or services. The selling process involves seven distinct steps: prospecting, pre-approach, approach, presentation, handling objections, closing, and follow-up. The nature of personal selling today relies on direct communications and the establishment of enduring relationships between buyers and sellers. If partnerships are formed between the two organizations or between the organization and final consumer, both will prosper financially. Technology is changing the nature of the creative salesperson. Less time is now spent on personal content, while more time is devoted to electronic contact and activities designed to service and retain customers.

Event marketing and sponsorship programs are now an important element of a firm's marketing communications mix, particularly among large Canadian corporations. Sponsorship is concentrated in three popular areas, namely, cultural events, sports, and entertainment. Sports attract the lion's share of the sponsorship pie. Prior to getting involved with sponsorships an organization should establish specific criteria for participation. Factors to consider include product category exclusivity, relationships with other marketing communications programs, and the image-building potential offered by an event. Once a sponsor has established an association with an event, the expectations turn to improving image, attracting new clients, and building sales.

Key Terms

ambush marketing 456
approach 451
cash refund (rebate) 442
closing 452
collateral materials 447
consumer promotion 435
cooperative advertising 446
coupon 436
cross-ruff 437
cross-sampling 440
dealer premium 446
dealer-display material (point-of-purchase material) 447
delayed-payment incentive 444
e-coupon 438
event marketing 456
event sponsorship 456
follow-up 453
free sample 440
free-standing insert (FSI) 437
game (instant win) contest 442
in-home selling 449
in-store-delivered coupon 438

loyalty (frequent-buyer) program 444
media-delivered coupon 437
missionary selling 450
objection 452
online selling 449
performance allowance 446
personal selling 447
pre-approach 451
premium 444
presentation 452
product-delivered coupons 437
prospecting 450
qualifying 451
redemption rate 436
retail in-ad coupon 446
sales promotion 435
slippage 442
sweepstakes 441
telemarketing 449
trade promotion 446
trial close 453
venue marketing 456

Review Questions

1. What are the objectives of consumer promotions and trade promotions?

2. Explain how the product life cycle affects the use of media-delivered coupons and product-delivered coupons.

3. What are the basic marketing benefits of e-coupons for the manufacturer distributing them?

4. Briefly explain the nature of a loyalty (frequent buyer) program.

5. How is cooperative advertising different from other forms of advertising?

6. List and briefly describe the seven steps in the selling process.

7. What is telemarketing, and what functions can telemarketing perform for a marketing organization?

8. What is the difference between event marketing and event sponsorship?

9. What is ambush marketing? Briefly explain.

10. Briefly describe the main benefits of event marketing participation.

11. What are the basic factors an organization should consider prior to participating in event marketing and sponsorships?

Discussion and Application Questions

1. Identify which consumer promotion activities are best suited to meet the following marketing objectives:
   a) Trial purchase
   b) Brand loyalty
   c) Multiple purchase

2. "The use of dealer premiums is an unethical practice in contemporary marketing." Discuss this statement.

3. If you were the marketing manager for Nike or BMW, what events would you sponsor? What benefits would you derive from these sponsorships? Be specific.

4. Assume you are the marketing manager for Apple Computers in Canada. Your market share is about 4 percent and you rank as the number 6 brand. Hewlett-Packard with 6.5 percent share and Toshiba with 5 percent share are just ahead of you. Your goal is to move ahead of at least one of these brands. What promotion recommendations do you have to build Apple's market share? Justify your recommendations. Conduct some secondary research on the computer market to familiarize yourself with competitive activity.

5. Assume you are a brand manager for Nabob coffee (a mature brand leader). The primary marketing objective is to encourage brand loyalty. What promotion recommendations do you have? Be specific, and justify your recommendations.

6. "Advances in communications technology will dramatically change the role and nature of selling." Discuss and provide examples of changes that are already having an influence on selling strategies.

7. Read the vignette, "Sponsoring the Big One!" Is Olympic sponsorship a wise investment or a waste of money? Present a case for or against such an effort.

E-Assignment

Select an actual contest campaign (visit a supermarket or drugstore for ideas) that is being advertised in the mass media (television, radio, newspaper, and magazines) or on packages and point-of-purchase material. Visit the Web site for the company or brand and evaluate how the Internet was integrated into the campaign. Is the Internet a viable vehicle for implementing sales promotion activities?

Endnotes

1. Hy Haberman, "Enough is enough: Promotion is strategic," *Strategy*, August 30, 1999.

2. Wayne Mouland, "Coupon usage grows in 2001," press release, *Watts NCH Promotional Services*, February 2002.

3. Ibid.

4. Wayne Mouland, "Clip your coupons here," press release, *Watts NCH Promotional Services*, June 2001.

5. Marina Strauss, "Smart shoppers find it's hip to clip," *Globe and Mail*, January 25, 2002, p. B9.

6. Jo Marney, "The basics of promotion," *Marketing*, February 6, 1989, p. 28.

7. Geoff Dennis, "Sampling growth spurs creativity," *Strategy*, May 20, 2002, p. 1.

8. "A special presentation on coupon promotion fundamentals," *NCH Promotional Services* Ltd., 1998.

9. NCH Promotional Services, *A Marketer's Guide to Consumer Promotion*, 1990, p. C4.

10. James Careless, "Cereal killer," *Marketing*, May 14, 2001, p. 24.

11. Danny Kucharsky, "Consumers drawn to loyalty rewards," *Marketing*, May 6, 2002, p. 3.

12. "Shoppers launches creative loyalty program," *Marketing*, December 18/25, 2000, p. 21.

13. Daniel Girard, "Rarity in rugged retail field Leon's keeps profits rising," *Toronto Star*, June 12, 1993, pp. C1-C2.

14. Barry Suskind, "Trade shows work—it's all in the numbers," *Small Business Canada Magazine*, March/April 2002, p. 43.

15. Mark Donnison, "Using equity to make your sponsorship soar," *Strategy*, March 12, 2001, p. B9.

16. Chris Zelkovich, "Corporations love Games," *Toronto Star*, January 23, 2002, p. C6.

17. "Your name here," *R.O.B. Magazine*, May 2002, p. 31.

18. Carrie Toane, "Soccer's new game," *Marketing*, August 21, 2001, p. 12.

19. John Heinzl, "Labatt scales back sponsorship," *Globe and Mail*, February 15, 2001, pp. B1, B6.

20. Mark Evans, "Brewers cheer concert boom," *Financial Post*, July 6, 1992, p. S25.

21. Michael Gillings, "Edgy SnowJob helps sponsors reach youth," *Strategy*, March 12, 2001, p. B8.

22. Bob Weeks, "New name coming to Brier," *The Globe and Mail*, March 9, 2001, p. S1.

23. Wendy Cuthbert, "Sponsors pump ROI with experimental approach," *Strategy*, March 12, 2001, p. B7.

Emerging Directions in Marketing

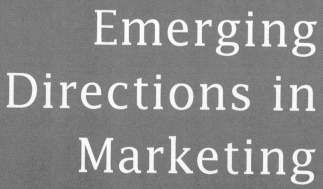

The marketplace is constantly changing, and the practice of marketing must change right along with it. This section presents some of the emerging areas of contemporary marketing, along with the special marketing considerations necessary for its success.

Chapter 17 presents the fundamental activities associated with online marketing. The chapter describes the role of online marketing and examines how this new and exciting way of doing business will improve the effectiveness and efficiency of business operations.

Chapter 18 examines the unique characteristics of the services and not-for-profit marketing sectors, and shows how marketing strategies are adapted to serve customers in these markets.

Chapter 19 emphasizes the importance of analyzing global market opportunities and strategies for pursuing global markets.

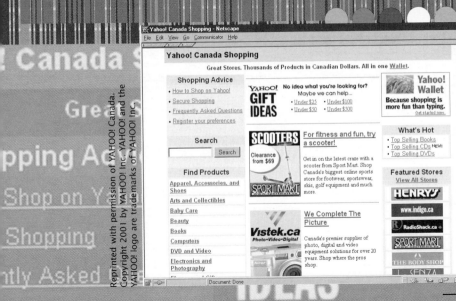

C H A P T E R

17

Internet Marketing

eight

> Learning Objectives

After studying this chapter, you will be able to

1. Describe the fundamental activities associated with online marketing.
2. Describe the role and importance of online marketing today and in the future.
3. Explain the opportunities for marketing, sales, and customer service presented by the Internet.
4. Describe the role the Internet can play in marketing research.
5. Demonstrate how the various elements of the marketing mix apply to Internet marketing.

Introduction to E-Commerce

1.
Describe the fundamental activities associated with online marketing.

Today's business climate can be summed up in three words: everything has changed. And much of that change is directly related to technology. "Technology is like a steamroller. You are either on top of it or under it." This expression sums up the rapid pace of Internet growth. Compared with any other form of communications technology, the Internet has been accepted more quickly. To reach 50 million households in North America, it took television 13 years, telephones 38 years, and VCRs 9 years. It took the Internet only 5 years to reach the same number of households, and the Internet is growing 5 times faster than television.[1] Given this rate of acceptance, it is clear that the Internet will play a more prominent role in an organization's marketing strategy in the future.

The growth and acceptance of electronic business practices have fuelled organizational interest in electronic marketing. Prior to getting into a discussion of Internet marketing, a few basic business terms should be clarified. **E-business** is defined as conducting business transactions, and business activities associated with those transactions, over the Internet. It embraces activities such as the electronic transfer of information between companies in order to facilitate the production and distribution of goods, and billing and payment processes in a virtual environment. **E-commerce** refers to selling goods online (e.g., Amazon.ca selling a consumer a book online). The growth of electronic business and electronic commerce is like an ocean rising. Each day more and more companies recognize the benefits that can be gained by integrating electronic business practices with traditional business and marketing practices. Those benefits include reaching new customers more efficiently, expanding market reach around the globe, and reducing process costs. On the other hand, many organizations perceive the Internet to be a risky business investment and point to the dot.com crash as a reason why.

The latest figures available (2001) reveal that the total value of electronic business in Canada is $10.4 billion, of which $8.1 billion are business-to-business transactions and $2.3 billion are retail sales.[2]

e-business

e-commerce

Internet Penetration and Adoption

INTERNET USER PROFILE

2.

Describe the role and importance of online marketing today and in the future.

Presently, a little more than 50 percent of households in Canada have Internet access, one of the highest penetration rates in the world.[3] That figure bodes well for the long-term future of Internet marketing.

All kinds of studies by numerous marketing research companies have been conducted to determine the profile of Internet users. Needless to say, the profiles vary and they are constantly changing. Keeping track of Internet usage is like following a moving target. The most recent survey from Statistics Canada reveals that males and females use the Internet equally; that younger people in higher-income households use the Net more frequently than lower-income households and older households; and that geographic location influences usage. For example, people in Western Canada and Ontario use the Internet more frequently than people in Quebec and Atlantic Canada. Overall, 53 percent of Canadians were online in 2000.[4] For a complete profile of Internet usage, see Figure 17.1.

The Statistics Canada survey shows the Internet to be an ideal medium for reaching a target market described as male and female between the ages of 15 and 44, college or university educated, with a household income of $40 000 plus, and having a slightly urban skew. Since it reaches a very desirable target market, it should play a vital role in future marketing activity.

The teen market is a priority market for many companies. The amount of time spent online by teens (12 to 15 hours per week) must be factored into a company's marketing communications strategy. Among teens, 85 percent use the Internet regularly, and 33 percent say they spent less time with television, magazines, and radio.[5] Given this trend, companies aiming at teens will have to reassess their media strategies and integrate the Internet if they are to reach teens in a cost-efficient manner.

On the horizon is the full-scale emergence of wireless communications. Small hand-held devices that are being developed by such companies as Nokia, RIM, and Motorola will make wireless communications in all forms the preferred method to connect to the Internet in the longer-term. Wireless networks will enable consumers to shop anytime and anywhere.

INTERNET CULTURE AND BEHAVIOUR

Trends indicate that Internet usage is increasing each year. As of 2001, Canadians at home spent 15.5 hours on the Net compared to 8.5 hours a year earlier. In fact, Canadians spent more time online than people from any other country.[6] The primary activities for Internet users are e-mail and searching for information via the Web. One of the main activities consumers perform online is to research purchase decisions. See Figure 17.2 for details.

The Internet user wants information. Therefore, the primary purpose of an organization's Web site should be the transfer of important company and product information. It must provide information that people will benefit from and perceive to be valuable.

People on the Internet seem to act and respond differently from typical consumers. They are information-oriented and more demanding by nature. They expect instant

A Profile of Canadian Internet Users

Figure 17.1

	Canada 2000 %
Gender	
Male	56.1
Female	49.6
Age Group	
15–24	84.5
25–34	66.1
35–44	60.3
45–54	50.7
55+	18.7
Education	
University degree	79.3
College diploma	57.5
Some university or college	69.4
High school diploma	41.2
Less than high school	30.9
Household Income	
Less than $30,000	32.8
$30,000–$49,999	49.9
$50,000–$79,900	65.5
$80,000+	80.5
Language	
English only	58.5
French only	43.9
Other	40.0
Urban/Rural	
Urban	55.0
Rural	44.9

Source: Statistics Canada "A Profile of Canadian Internet Users," adapted from the Statistics Canada publication *Overview: Access to and Use of Information Technology*, Catalogue number 56-5-5-XIE, Table 2, March 2001.

information, lower prices, and incentives such as free shipping. Details are attractive while commercialism is not. Organizations, therefore, must provide information on the assumption it will create goodwill, brand interest, and, in the future, some form of purchase. To survive, the Internet as we know it has to be an ongoing profitable venture for the organizations providing the information. Thus far, many companies are providing added value for customers but are not necessarily making money while doing so.

Figure 17.2

Uses of the Internet

The prime activities for Internet users continue to be e-mail and searching for informa-tion via the Web. One of the main purposes of online information gathering is now to inform purchasing decisions.

Use	Percentage*
E-mail	80.8
Download software	46.5
Research travel	43.0
Research products	42.6
Research companies/industries	41.9
Research cultural resources	36.9
Other research	33.8
Chat/Discussion groups	27.8
Research financial services	25.5
Purchase products/services	21.2
Training and education courses	16.3

* The chart shows the percentage of users performing each of the various activities.

Source: "Canadian Internet Usage 2000: A Message for the Medium," a report published by MultiMediator Strategy Group, March 2000, www.multimediator.com/mmsg. Courtesy of Delvinia.

E-Business Market Segments

B2B e-commerce

B2C e-commerce

There are two primary segments of e-business: business-to-business (B2B) and business-to-consumer (B2C). **B2B e-commerce** embraces the online communications and trans-actions between two or more businesses (e.g., it may involve procurement systems that secure multiple bids, issue payment orders, and make payments). **B2C e-commerce** is the retailing component in which online retailers sell their goods and services to con-sumers on the Internet.

It is the B2B segment that is propelling the growth of online marketing. As of 2001, transactions in the B2B segment accounted for 78 percent ($8.1 billion) of all Internet business in Canada. The B2C segment accounted for 22 percent ($2.3 billion). All together, customer orders over the Internet totalled $10.4 billion, a 43.4 percent increase over 2000. Despite such a significant gain, the number of businesses selling online grew only slightly, to 7 percent of those surveyed compared to 6 percent a year earlier. For every four firms that stopped selling online, five started.

To put the present role of the Internet into perspective, consider that the total sales of $10.1 billion only represents 0.5 percent of operating revenue in Canada. On a more positive note, 29 percent of businesses—accounting for 81 percent of all business income-operate a Web site.[7]

The transition to electronic business is well under way as large established companies in traditional industries, such as steel, forestry, and automobile manufacturing, are taking advantage of the online world. At the same time, new upstart companies are aggressively trying to dislodge the old order. Amazon was one such company. As one of the first Internet retailers, they had a dramatic and negative effect on bricks-and-mortar book retailers.

The B2C market has experienced much less growth largely due to the behaviour of Internet users discussed earlier. Many prominent companies who sell everyday types of products in a bricks-and-mortar environment have embraced the Internet and are conducting transactions with consumers. Among them are Canadian Tire, Sears, Wal-Mart and Chapters-Indigo. Others have tried the Internet and failed. Holt Renfrew, for example, an upscale fashion retailer for women, tried selling through a Web site but gave up. Many retailers resist the temptation to go online for fear they will cannibalize their own in-store sales. In the end, they will have to go online and eat their own business before a competitor does it for them.

Amazon.com
www.amazon.com
Wal-Mart
www.walmart.com
Chapters.Indigo.ca
www.chapters.
indigo.ca

The Internet Presents Marketing Opportunities

3.
Explain the opportunities for marketing, sales, and customer service presented by the Internet.

The marketing concept states that if you provide the consumer with something they want and do it better than the competition, sales and profits will grow. The Internet is facilitating this concept.

The Internet offers three significant opportunities. First, it will be the medium of choice for communicating detailed information about goods and services. Many businesses, including newspapers and magazines, specialize in the delivery of information. As well, companies that have embraced the Internet publish all kinds of information about themselves so that customers can make more informed buying decisions.

The second opportunity is the capability to sell goods online. Online storefronts, such as those for Sears and Canadian Tire fall into this category, as do the electronic communications systems established among business-to-business buyers and sellers.

mass customization

The third opportunity deals with the concept of mass customization. **Mass customization** refers to creating systems that can personalize messages and ultimately products to a target audience of one. Dell Computer Inc., for example, builds a computer to customer specifications once the order is received online.

As one of the leading makers of desktop and laptop computers, Dell's business was founded on the basis of direct marketing techniques. The transition to online marketing was smooth for Dell (see their Web site in Figure 17.3). Today, Dell operates one of the highest volume e-commerce sites in the world. Dell's Web site receives 840 million page requests per quarter at 82 country sites in 21 languages and conducts their transactions in 40 currencies. Dell understands how the Internet can impact a business. Of the $33 billion of revenue generated in the US, $20 billion is transacted online.[8]

For more insight into Dell's Internet success, read the Marketing in Action vignette **Dell Leads the Way**.

Figure 17.3

The Dell Web Site Is One of the Busiest Commercial Sites on the Internet

The Internet Marketing Model

The challenge for marketing organizations is to determine how the Internet fits in with traditional marketing models. The Internet is not a replacement for traditional activities but rather an additional tool that can assist the organization in achieving its marketing objectives. The success of Internet activities still relies on traditional marketing techniques, such as advertising, promotion, and public relations, for these activities draw attention to a company's Internet operations. More importantly, the Internet is used as a vehicle for most traditional marketing activities: advertising, sales promotions (e.g., delivering coupons), public relations, and pre- and post-sale customer service. Some of the key marketing functions the Internet can perform include:

1. *Creating Company and Brand Awareness* Through a company Web site essential information can be communicated about the company and its brands. Such information may have a financial orientation to help attract potential investors, or it may focus on the unique features and benefits of its product lines. In contrast to traditional media, online communications can be much more detailed. An organization can also place advertising in a variety of forms on other Internet sites. (Refer to Chapter 15 for additional details).

Marketing in Action

Dell Leads the Way

Michael Dell is a very rich man. He is presently ranked as the 18th richest man in the world with about $11 billion (US) in assets. Not bad for a guy who started making and selling personal computers in a college dormitory. He never did finish college.

Today, at only 37 years of age, Michael Dell is the chief executive of the world's largest personal computer company. He was recently asked what he thought of the giant merger between two of his competitors—Compaq and Hewlett-Packard. "Whether they merge, whether there's one company, two companies, or three companies—whatever. Our competitive advantage is quite strong and growing and expanding into more areas." He cited Canada as an illustration. Sales of Compaq computers are down 38 percent over one year. Sales of Dell are up 4 percent. The gap, he says, is a sign that competitors' customers are fleeing.

So what is Dell's competitive advantage? It has to do with the way the company makes and markets personal computers. Unlike all of its competitors, Dell was built on direct marketing techniques, so integrating the Internet into the direct model was a natural extension of its way of doing business.

What Dell does well is cut out the middleman. To buy a Dell you pick up the telephone or visit the company's Web site. It doesn't matter if you are buying one computer or a thousand computers. Dell doesn't need stores, so it doesn't pay any rent. The company doesn't retain a large inventory because computers are not manufactured until they have been sold. It doesn't need resellers and distributors, so the price tag doesn't swell. Dell is a unique company!

Michael Dell used the direct mail model back at college. The same direct marketing concept exists today but it is supported by an advanced made-to-order system and order-placement through the Internet. Today the company sells about half of all its computers over the Web.

Dell started out in 1984. In the first 8 years the company grew by 80 percent annually; in the next 6 years by 60 percent annually; and in the past 3 years by 40 percent annually. This business model is really about direct relationships with customers—big corporations, governments, or individual consumers. Dell's business model provides accountability, higher quality, more responsive support, and certainly lower cost.

Dell understands how the Internet can impact a business. In fact, while GDP in North America is only about 3 to 4 percent online, the GDP for Dell is about 50 percent online. Over $40 million (US) of sales in a seven-day week occur online and of the roughly $33 billion (US) of revenue generated in the latest year, about 20 billion (US) will be transacted online.

Dell's climb to market leadership is the result of a persistent focus on delivering the best possible customer experience by directly selling products and services based on industry-standard technology and by introducing relevant technology more quickly than competitors.

The question has to be asked. Why can't other companies duplicate what Dell is doing? Isn't Dell's direct marketing model adaptable to other industries and products?

Adapted from Tyler Hamilton, "That $18 billion smile," *Toronto Star*, April 2, 2002, pp. C1, C13; www.dell.com/us/en/gen/corporate/factpack; and www.dell.com/us/gen/corporate/speech/speech_2000-04-07-tor.

2. ***Branding and Image Building*** Branding is the responsibility of marketing communications activities. The intent is to have the public perceive a brand in a positive manner. Since consumers actively seek information about products at company Web sites, it is important that the site project an image that is in keeping with the overall company image. Therefore, the appearance and style of communications should be consistent between the traditional media and online media. Any advertising that is done online (e.g., at another Web site) should also project a similar look and image about the company or brand being advertised.

3. ***Offering Incentives*** Many sites offer discounts for purchasing online. Electronic coupons, bonus offers, and contests are now quite common. Such offers are intended to stimulate immediate purchase before a visitor leaves a Web site and encourage repeat visits. Canadian Tire offers special deals online as a means of getting people comfortable with online buying. Companies can also distribute online coupons to consumers. Save.ca identifies offers that are available, takes requests for the coupons from consumers online, and then mails the coupons to consumers.

4. ***Lead Generation*** The Internet is an interactive medium. Visitors to a site leave useful information behind when they fill in boxes requesting more information (e.g., name, address, telephone number, and e-mail address). A site may also ask for demographic information that can be added to the company's database. Such information forms the basis for efficient market segmentation and the development of customer relationship management programs.

5. ***Customer Service and Relationship Management*** In any form of marketing, customer service is important. Satisfied customers hold positive attitudes about a company and are apt to return to buy more goods. The Internet can perform a host of customer service activities but it is perceived to be a weak link in the marketing loop. E-commerce and e-marketing are more than just a Web site. Successful online businesses won't forget that a human component must back up the online activities. They must pay close attention to customer service, inbound sales, order tracking, order problems, out-of-stock issues, deliveries, and returns. All of these activities are part of a good customer relationship management program.

6. ***E-Mail Marketing*** Firms retain visitor information in a database. E-mailing useful and relevant information to prospects and customers helps build stronger relationships. As discussed in Chapter 15, permission-based e-mail is quite acceptable to Internet users. Other mail applications include distributing information about promotional offers, customer newsletters, and viral marketing techniques (encouraging customers to forward the e-mail to a friend).

7. ***Selling Online*** Presently, the business-to-business market is booming with business transactions. Firms in the supply chain are linking together to form what's called a B2B exchange. The goal of the exchange is to achieve efficiencies in the buying-selling process. For example, the Hudson's Bay Company links hundreds of the Bay, Zellers, and Home Outfitters vendors to buying groups for the interchange of electronic procurement documents.

Save.ca
www.save.ca

Consumer behaviour trends indicate the Internet will increasingly become more of a medium that consumers use to conduct research about a product. So, if the consumer does not buy online, the Internet will play an influencing role in purchases that are made in stores. The Internet will drive sales in traditional channels. As an example, Autobytel.com bridges the gap between the Internet and real-world buying by giving consumers a way of researching the prices of various makes and models of cars. When the search is complete Autobytel refers the consumer to the nearest dealer.[9] Car manufacturers such as Ford and General Motors also offer their cars for sale online but involve the dealers at the end of the consumer search process.

Marketing Research Applications

4.
Describe the role the Internet can play in marketing research.

As discussed in Chapter 3, marketing organizations access data to make more informed marketing decisions. The Internet facilitates the collection of information as it is now used for collecting secondary data and primary data. Secondary data on the Internet are usually more current because the medium does not face the long lead times associated with the print media. The data can be accessed quickly and inexpensively. Primary data are collected primarily through online e-mail and Internet surveys.

SECONDARY DATA COLLECTION

The primary advantage of Internet information is the speed at which the information is available. Data are readily accessible 24 hours a day, 7 days a week, from all over the world, and in a matter of seconds. Secondary information can be gathered from public and private sources. The major weakness of the data secured is similar to that of other secondary sources—it rarely solves an organization's specific marketing problems and it can become outdated rather quickly. Sites such as Hoovers.com, for example, provide useful financial information about a company along with links to a company's primary competitors. Therefore, another company could quickly develop a profile of industry participants by visiting such a site.

Marketing organizations conduct online and offline investigations to ensure they stay on top of trends that will affect the direction of marketing strategies. Updated information on demographic trends, social and cultural trends, lifestyle trends, technological trends, and competitor activity trends is essential. The Statistics Canada Web site (www.statcan.ca) is a good source of information on social, demographic, and economic trends.

Research organizations, such as Angus Reid, and consulting companies, such as Deloitte & Touche, often publish the results of their surveys on the Internet. Company Web sites are another source of information—very often, a good source of information for students doing marketing projects! It is now common practice for a company to publish their annual report online along with press releases that contain the latest news about the company.

PRIMARY DATA COLLECTION

The most common types of online research include focus groups, observations, and online surveys.

1. *Focus Groups* A traditional focus group collects qualitative data from 10 to 12 participants who are brought together at a central location. Unlike traditional focus groups, the online focus group brings people together in a virtual environment from diverse geographic areas. Participants respond to questions independently and as a result are less intimidated by others while expressing their views (a factor that influences regular focus group opinion). The advantage of online focus groups is that they are quicker and less expensive to operate than traditional groups. There are

several drawbacks: body language of the participants cannot be observed; and the authenticity of the respondent can be questionable (e.g., a teenager could pose as a 35-year-old adult and vice versa).

2. **Online Observations** The technology is available to observe visitor behaviour automatically. The most common form of observation is to record and analyze viewing patterns at a Web site. A visitor's entry point, clicks, and time on a page are recorded in a log file. Periodically, the log file is analyzed to determine the most popular aspects of the site. It allows managers to adjust the arrangement of the site in order to best serve the customer. At a site such as Amazon.com (a seller of books and music) where a user registers before using the site, data about purchases are captured in a database. Based on historical ordering of items, Amazon can make recommendations to customers by sending e-mail to them at a later date.

3. **Online Surveys** In an online survey, respondents usually click on choices to indicate their response (e.g., from a drop-down list, checking in a box, or clicking a button). Online surveys offer several advantages: they are fast and inexpensive, compared with traditional survey methodologies (e.g., personal interview, mail); participants respond immediately, and there are no fees for personal contact or return mailings; and no data entry errors occur—the respondent fills in the information and it is fed directly to a database with no possibility of coding or input errors. Finally, some researchers have discovered that respondents answer questions more openly and honestly when an interviewer is not present.

The primary disadvantage of online surveys is their inability to draw a probability sample. Researchers do not have access to the multitude of predetermined lists that are commonly used in other forms of quantitative research. Yet, e-commerce companies are in the process of developing lists from the database techniques they are employing. For now, it is common for respondents to come to the researcher. Because of this bias, an organization must be careful when interpreting data. Another disadvantage is the concern mentioned above about respondent authenticity. People can disguise themselves very easily on the Internet. Children can pose as adults, men can pose as women, and so on. These situations bias the survey results.

Online Marketing Strategies

How an organization integrates the potential offered by Internet marketing with the traditional forms of marketing is a challenge that all companies now face. Due to the newness and uncertainty of the Internet, some companies have chosen to take bold steps and are excelling, while others are moving slowly and perhaps failing. Others yet jumped in immediately and are now out of business. There is a learning curve associated with Internet marketing along with a lot of experimentation to figure out what does and doesn't work.

How a company uses technology seems to be the key to success. Scanning devices at the point of sale and the electronic observation techniques employed online are producing gold mines of data. As mentioned in the chapter on marketing research, organizations have to invest in data mining activities if they are to exploit the full business potential of the Internet.

This section briefly examines the components of the marketing mix: product, price, distribution, and marketing communications in the context of online marketing strategy.

PRODUCT STRATEGIES

The Internet is proving to be a viable means of creating awareness and securing orders for a variety of products. However, some products are more suited for Internet marketing than others. To market a product successfully on the Internet, an organization's Web site plays a key role. Such attributes as effective Web site navigation, quick download speed, site organization and attractiveness, secure transactions, and user privacy must be considered. User-friendliness is probably the most important attribute a Web site can offer.

J. Crew
www.jcrew.com

Some goods and services lend themselves to online marketing and sales while others do not. Personal computers are among the products that sell easily, while more complicated products requiring individual tailoring, sell poorly. Clothes are difficult to sell online for bricks and mortar retailers. Among the few exceptions that have experienced success is J. Crew, a prominent US-based catalogue sales company. It was well positioned to take advantage of the Internet because its customers were familiar with their sizes and accustomed to buying clothes without actually seeing or feeling them.[10]

The Internet has changed how some products get into the hands of consumers. For example, media companies have had to re-examine the way they distribute information. Since Internet usage is increasing each year (e.g., hours spent per day or week on the Internet), people are spending less time with traditional media. Therefore, traditional media, such as newspapers, magazines, radio, and television, have established their own Web sites. All the important news stories from *The Globe and Mail* or CBC are readily available at their respective Web sites. To many people, the physical product (e.g., going out and buying the newspaper) is redundant. Refer to Figure 17.4 for an illustration.

When the sales of online products are analyzed, it can be seen that successful online products share certain attributes that make them attractive for online sales.[11] Popular sellers online tend to be:

1. **Nonperishable** The items can be shipped by common carrier without spoiling in transit. They are classified as shopping goods and include such items as toys, books, music, and information. They tend to be "low touch" products and can be sampled directly online before purchase.

2. **Of High Relative Value** Computers and software tend to be expensive. These items are a serious purchase, and information is usually collected about the product before making a decision. Computer software is a natural for online selling because the product is delivered electronically.

3. **Information Intensive** The items require research before making a purchase decision, and that research can be conducted online. For example, people will research extensively when planning a vacation or when making an investment decision online.

4. **High-Tech in Nature** The Internet's current users have a strong interest in technical products, so as a market segment, the purchase of computer hardware, consumer electronics products, and conducting online banking transactions is a popular practice. In fact, 16 percent of respondents in a survey conducted by the Canadian Bankers Association said they did most of their banking using the Internet. In 2000, the figure was only 8 percent.[12]

Refer to Figure 17.5 from additional details about products sold online.

An Illustration of Traditional Media Adapting to a New Technology

Figure 17.4

BRANDING STRATEGIES

In a traditional marketing environment, companies use family brand names or individual brand names along with symbols to create an image for the brand in the minds of customers. Names, such as Tim Hortons and Coca-Cola, and symbols, such as the classic shape of the Coke bottle, become registered trademarks of the company and are

Where North Americans Spend Their E-Tail Dollars

Figure 17.5

Merchandise	Total Online Sales %
Computer hardware/software and consumer electronics	49
Banking/Financial fees	15
Non-food home consumables	12
Entertainment	8
Books and magazines	8
Food	2
Other	2
Cards/gifts and flowers	1
Travel	1

Source: Adapted from Alexandra Eadie, "The Consumer: Ready or Not for E-tail?" *Globe and Mail*, November 10, 2000, p. E12.

legally protected from imitation. A good brand name and symbol often create a deep emotional bond with consumers.

In an online environment there are new branding issues that must be dealt with. For example, Amazon broadened its scope into new product categories, but it is still considered a bookstore by most people. Says Jeff Bezos, chairman of Amazon, "Brands to a certain degree are like quick-drying cement; when they're young, they are stretchable and pliant, but over time they become more and more associated with a particular thing and harder to stretch."[13]

Nike
www.nike.ca
Dell
www.dell.ca

Companies going online face numerous brand decisions. What domain name should be used on the site? Should the name be an existing brand name or should new brand names apply if the product is new? Popular brands, such as Nike or Dell, use their corporate name as the domain name, for the products and company are one and the same. Customers searching for specific information can browse through these sites once they arrive at the home page. In the case of a packaged goods company like Procter & Gamble or Colgate Palmolive the company name is the domain name. There are specific brand pages at the company site. Popular brands such as Tide (a P&G brand) have a standalone Web site.

Other companies use acronyms or shortened versions of their company name as part of their domain name. Such use presumes widespread awareness of the acronym. Canadian Pacific, Canadian National, and the Canadian Broadcasting Corporation are

Canadian Pacific
www.cp.ca
Canadian National
www.cn.ca
Canadian Broadcasting Corporation
www.cbc.ca

examples of this strategy. These companies' site names already have a meaning to consumers based on marketing activity that has preceded Web-based marketing. For example, people refer to the Canadian Broadcasting Corporation as the CBC.

Interbrew, the world's second largest brewer and owner of Labatt in Canada, opted for a unique name for its Web site. Rather than using the company name or a brand name it chose beer.com. This was chosen because the site was to be beer specific, not brand specific. This is a global beer site so certain efficiencies prevail and it is full of content of interest to beer drinkers: sub-pages are under the headings of beer, sex, music, and fun. The site is loaded with interactivity through countless games and contests.[14] Such a name will attract a lot of unintentional consumers who will learn more about the company and its brands.

Choosing the right domain name is important because it can influence the amount of traffic at a Web site. The length of the name is another factor to consider. Names that are too long can be misspelled, and the user will never find the site. Whatever the decision, the name should be consistent with the company or brand's marketing communications strategy. As mentioned earlier, domain names should always appear in all other forms of marketing communications to increase awareness of the Web site.

The image a brand projects online should be identical to the image it projects offline. Brand names, symbols, and slogans that appear in print and television advertising should play a role in online advertising and on company or brand Web sites. With reference to Figure 17.6, note that the design and layout of the home page of the Delta Hotels Web site is the same as what appears in print advertising. The packaging of information at a Web site plays a role in creating and enhancing an image in the browsing public's mind.

A confusing branding issue for consumers is the use of .com (a United States designation) and .ca (a Canadian designation) in domain names. There is a tendency for browsers to automatically include the .com designation. If incorrect, an unknown host message appears on the screen. To confuse matters more, not-for-profit organizations use the.org designation. The proliferation of domain names and the addition of new designations (e.g., .biz, and .info) will keep this aspect of branding confusing.

PRICING STRATEGIES

In business-to-consumer transactions, intermediaries, such as wholesalers and retailers, are eliminated in the distribution of goods. In traditional channels, when intermediaries are eliminated, there are fewer markups to be taken in the channel, so prices to consumers are lower. Initially, it was perceived that a similar situation would occur on the Internet because traditional distributors were eliminated. In practice, however, new intermediaries were added, so prices have not been lowered that much. The consumer perception that you will get a better price online is simply not true.

When marketing online, there are several factors that tend to increase prices and several factors that decrease prices. Things tend to balance out. Factors that have a tendency to increase online prices include the following:

1. **Direct Distribution** Online retailers have to ship to each customer individually. Therefore, the costs of shipping are added to the price of the product, and shown in the total price quoted to customers. Though all reputable online retailers disclose shipping costs upfront, customers usually don't think about shipping costs until they see them added to their total at the end of the checkout process. At that point, many

Figure 17.6

An Illustration of Consistent
Design between Traditional
Advertising and Web Site

customers decide that shipping costs may outweigh the other benefits of shopping online.

2. **Auctions** In an auction, prospective customers bid on items they wish to buy. Items are posted on a Web page and a time for the auction is set. Interested customers can return to the auction page at any time to monitor the progress of their item. The winner of the item is notified by e-mail, and put in contact with the seller. In some cases, bidding can drive the price higher than fair market value (similar to a traditional auction) or it could be lower—it's a function of supply and demand. Customers should be aware of fair market value before entering into an auction.

3. **Web Site Development** Establishing and maintaining a site is expensive. Development costs range anywhere from $10 000 to $100 000 plus, and then, a company incurs hardware, software, and Internet connection costs to maintain the site. Because of the cost, small businesses have the option of outsourcing. There are services available that allow them to have a Web site for under $5000 for a year.

4. **Marketing Costs** The costs of directing Internet traffic to a site is very high. A Boston Consulting Group survey found that 43 percent of online retail revenue goes toward marketing and advertising a new online company. For bricks-and-mortar retailers with established brand names, the investment is only 14 percent when they go online. If the Web site name is different from the bricks-and-mortar name, there are additional costs associated with creating awareness for the domain name. According to consulting firm McKinsey & Co., the average e-commerce company spends $250 US on marketing and advertising to acquire one customer. Customer relationship management programs have to be implemented to ensure repeat business from that customer, and there are additional costs associated with that.[15] There are also new costs associated with 24/7 service and the development of customized products for customers.

Factors that have a downward influence on price include the following:

1. **Competition** Consumers can search the Internet worldwide (global rather than local sourcing) for the best possible price. Therefore, the identification and knowledge of competitors is not as clear as it once was. Knowing that consumers will conduct product searches to compare prices, it is important to keep prices as low as possible. There are Internet businesses that specialize in price searches, and they post comparative prices for the shopper.

2. **Product Life Cycles** The rate of change is so rapid that life cycles of products in some categories are not that long. Therefore, the high price that is usually associated with first entry advantage does not last very long, either.

3. **Streamlined Order Processing** In business-to-business situations where partnerships have been formed in the channel of distribution, automatic reordering and delivery systems save money for all partners. Savings can be passed on to customers. Customer relationship management programs involving channel members encourages efficiency in purchasing goods so that all members benefit from lower prices.

4. **Location** Online retailers such as Amazon who do not operate traditional stores do not need to rent expensive retail space in high-traffic locations. Their inventory can be stored in warehouses that are located in low-rent and low-tax areas. The result is lower prices for the products they sell. In contrast, retailers such as Chapters-Indigo, Future Shop, and Canadian Tire are divisions of a bricks-and-mortar operation that have much higher overhead costs.

Online firms are struggling with their pricing strategies. They are under pressure from customers to offer lower prices online than offline, yet in consumer products with razor-thin margins, such as books, it becomes nearly impossible for the company to turn a profit. Lower distribution costs ease the situation somewhat, but the fact remains that a lot of online companies are losing money.

PRICING ALTERNATIVES

Online pricing strategies are different from those in offline markets. In an era of value consciousness, consumers tend to shop for the best possible deals. Value pricing is popular in a bricks-and-mortar environment so why should it be any different online? It seems as though customers have been conditioned—possibly because of Amazon.com, the first online retailer—to believe that prices must be cheaper. Given the consumers' perceptions about the direct nature of the distribution channel that was discussed earlier, a price skimming strategy does not seem appropriate. On the Internet, even time-pressed consumers have time for comparison shopping, thus forcing prices down and ultimately making them less important as a differentiator.

The objective for an online company is to be competitive while offering value to potential customers. The perception of added value (e.g., convenience of ordering and delivery) offers a company some leeway in increasing prices.

penetration strategy

Grocery Gateway
www.grocerygate-way.com

A **penetration strategy** involves charging a low price for a good or service for the purpose of gaining market share. It is an appropriate strategy to get someone to try something for the first time. This strategy is an appropriate one for Internet marketers. To illustrate, consider what Grocery Gateway is doing. Grocery Gateway takes orders and delivers dry goods groceries, fresh produce, meat, and frozen food to households from an online menu of goods. A $6 delivery fee is added to each order. Gateway does not promise lower prices all the time but on the average bill the savings are in the 5 percent range compared to retail grocery stores. While pricing is a draw, it is not the major draw—convenience is.[16] The combination of time-pressed consumers, good pricing providing marginal savings, and efficient delivery is a successful one.

price leadership

Price leadership is generally an issue in offline marketing and it usually refers to the brand with the highest price—typically the brand leader in a market. On the Internet, **price leadership** refers to the company charging the lowest price. As discussed in the previous section, such a strategy is only feasible if costs are kept as low as possible. In an offline environment, the largest producer usually has the economies of scale and the lowest prices. On the Internet, however, small companies may have much lower operating costs, so ultimately the small company could have the lowest price and be the price leader. Theoretically, the playing field is more level on the Internet. Small firms can compete better with big firms, at least on price—a definite argument for small businesses to start marketing online.

Distribution Strategies

The traditional functions of distribution were discussed in Chapters 12 and 13. The value of the various functions change when they become Internet based. This section briefly examines the influence of the Internet on distribution functions.

In terms of performing a *marketing intelligence* function, information is obtained in a more timely fashion (e.g. from a computer in an office). In general, collecting information from distributors and consumers online saves an organization time and money and allows a company to react faster to changes in the environment.

Marketing communications with channel members and consumers is performed quickly—information is sent directly to literally millions of people simply by hitting a "send" button. Assuming the information is sent only to those who requested it, or who subscribed to receive updates, it will be well received. In comparison to traditional methods, such as direct mail (which requires paper, envelopes, and postage), the cost of delivering an online message is lower.

The Internet provides an additional means of **buyer contact**. Unlike traditional forms of advertising, a dimension of interactivity is added. Teens, especially, are moving toward interactivity in their daily communications with friends through such software programs as ICQ. Interactivity adds value since information can be targeted directly (e.g., it can be customized for each individual). Further, people can access Web sites for information any time or any day of the week.

Matching products to suit consumers' needs is easier on the Internet. Comparison shopping sites such as www.pricescan.com allow consumers and companies to compare prices and features in product categories. By altering price or feature requirements while visiting this site, the consumer can identify a product source where value is the greatest. Some of the more well established online retailers use filtering software to analyze what combinations of products people buy, then use this data to "suggest" to customers what product they might like. Amazon is one company using this technology. In doing so, Amazon provides value-added opportunities that create a pleasant shopping experience for customers.

On the Internet, **physical distribution** is replaced by electronic distribution for some products. It is an ideal medium for distributing text, graphics, and audio and video content. Unfortunately, this has created a nightmare for the music industry, as people can download music from a variety of sites. On the positive side of things, newspapers (www.globeandmail.com), news (www.cbc.ca), and sports reports (www.tsn.ca) are available online.

For goods that require physical delivery, existing specialists can play a key role. Sears, for example, has an established warehousing and distribution system for its catalogue operations. The same system is used for online marketing and distribution activities. Sears offers their facilities and expertise to other companies that want to go online but do not have the expertise or financial resources to build their own infrastructure. Companies working with Sears are then capable of offering their customers the convenience of online shopping. Sears is now handling the online business for Roots, starting with a Roots boutique within the Sears.ca site.[17]

Receive goods directly, pay for them directly—that is the mantra of the Internet. In the business-to-business market, where cooperative working relationships have been established between buyers and sellers, the *financing* aspect of e-commerce transactions has been widely accepted. Many consumers perceive things differently and worry about providing credit card information online. These consumers must be made aware that providing credit card information online is no more dangerous that providing it elsewhere (e.g., leaving a copy of a receipt in a restaurant or giving it out over the telephone). Views on this issue change once the initial online purchase is made and the financial transaction is complete.

As mentioned in the pricing strategy section, **price negotiation** is available to online shoppers. Submitting bids at auction sites is a form of price negotiation. Consumers can select products from a wide cross-section of suppliers and bid for the goods that are available. In theory, a wide supply of products should produce lower prices for bidders. In business-to-business markets, online buying groups are better able to negotiate lower prices due to the high volume the group purchases.

CHANNEL STRATEGIES

Any form of direct marketing, such as direct mail, telemarketing, and online marketing, involves a direct or short channel of distribution. In traditional or longer channels, intermediaries provide specialized services and functions that are beyond the capability of the source manufacturer.

On the Internet, some intermediaries have disappeared, but their functions have not. The Internet has gone through a process of disintermediation and reintermediation. Refer to Figure 17.7 for an illustration. **Disintermediation** refers to the disappearance of intermediaries in the channel of distribution. As intermediaries disappear, costs are reduced, so theoretically, prices of goods and services bought by consumers should

disintermediation

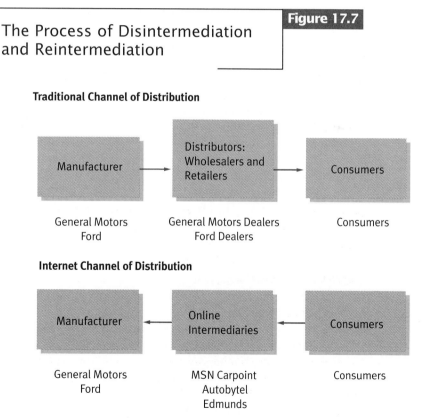

Figure 17.7

The Process of Disintermediation and Reintermediation

Traditional Channel of Distribution

Manufacturer → Distributors: Wholesalers and Retailers → Consumers

General Motors
Ford

General Motors Dealers
Ford Dealers

Consumers

Internet Channel of Distribution

Manufacturer ← Online Intermediaries ← Consumers

General Motors
Ford

MSN Carpoint
Autobytel
Edmunds

Consumers

In an online market, traditional distributors, such as car dealers, are eliminated (disintermediation). They are replaced by new intermediaries. These intermediaries will provide information to consumers, search the market for consumers for the best deals, and conduct transactions with consumers (reintermediation).

be lower. Initially, it was thought that disintermediation would take hold on the Internet. Granted, traditional channel members, such as wholesaling specialists and retailers, have been eliminated, but in many cases, they have been replaced by Internet equivalents.

The replacement of old intermediaries with new and different intermediaries is referred to as **reintermediation**. For example, online distributors such as Cars4U.com and MSN CarPoint are supplanting the role of bricks-and-mortar car dealers. MSN Carpoint is the most visited American online car-buying service, reaching more than 6 million consumers a month. MSN, which is owned by Microsoft Corp., opened a Canadian site in June 2000.[18] These online companies allow consumers to compare models with various features and prices, and then refer the customer to the nearest dealer if they want to buy the car.

Let us examine the disintermediation and reintermediation process from a consumer's perspective. Assume that you are going to buy a new set of golf clubs. In a traditional marketing environment, you would buy the item in a retail store. The retailer would have purchased a quantity of sets of clubs from a wholesaler or directly from the manufacturer. This is the typical channel of distribution.

In the online environment, you may be able to buy the clubs directly from the manufacturer, or you could visit a Web site, such as mySimon.com, which will search through the online merchant market and indicate where you can buy the clubs and at what price. Traditional channel members are eliminated, so this is disintermediation.

A delivery specialist such as FedEx or UPS ships the golf clubs directly to you from the manufacturer's warehouse or the online merchant's warehouse. These warehouses have replaced wholesalers and retailers, and the delivery specialists have replaced truck and rail transporters who formerly delivered to wholesalers and retailers. This is reintermediation.

In the disintermediation and reintermediation process, costs have not been reduced very much. In fact, the manufacturer of the golf clubs must absorb inventory costs that did not exist before. As well, you will pay for shipping charges that were once buried in the channel of distribution. If goods are purchased in the United States and delivered to Canada, appropriate taxes and duty fees are added. All things considered, potential cost savings disappear. Therefore, marketing organizations must invest resources into activities that will change consumers' perceptions about the advantages and disadvantages of buying online.

CHANNEL CONTROL

In Canada, powerful retailers control the channel of distribution (e.g., in grocery retailing and general merchandise retailing). Wal-Mart and Canadian Tire, for example, gained control when they introduced electronic reorder systems that simply advised suppliers how much merchandise they required. Suppliers who thought they were in control of the buying-and-selling situation had to adjust to a new way of thinking.

The Internet is customer centric, and despite the fact that markets are broadened, the availability of information and the ability to search shifts a lot of the power advantage to the consumer. Also, the advent of shopping agents who rank sources of supply by price on spreadsheets gives buyers a lot of flexibility as to where and who they buy from.

In business-to-business situations, the Internet has facilitated further use of EDI systems. **Electronic data interchange (EDI)** refers to computerized transfer of information among business partners. Such an automated system produces efficiency in the ordering

reintermediation

MSN CarPoint Canada
en.msn.carpoint.ca

electronic data interchange (EDI)

and delivery systems among partners in a distribution channel. EDI systems are expensive to install since all partners had to be linked in order to share data.

On the Internet, EDI has changed. Most organizations have an intranet. An **intranet** is an internal Web site that only employees can access. An intranet facilitates the transfer and manipulation of company information internally. In the context of distribution, EDI is referred to as an extranet. An **extranet** is a system that connects the intranets of individual companies together. Therefore, all partners in a supply chain or channel of distribution can be connected by an extranet, a completely paperless environment.

intranet

extranet

Grand & Toy, one of Canada's leading business supply companies recently introduced an Internet-based strategy to serve its business-to-business customers. For insight into how their system operates, read the Marketing in Action vignette **Grand & Toy's B2B Net Strategy.**

Grand & Toy's B2B Net Strategy

One of Canada's foremost suppliers of business products recently launched a full-fledged Internet strategy to better serve its business customers. Previous Net efforts focused on G&T's larger customers but the new model is designed for all customers regardless of size.

The new site allows business customers the ability to do catalogue searches, receive real-time inventory information, and receive customer-specific pricing (based on the amount of business they buy, a customer may qualify for certain discounts). This type of site is important since 80 percent of G&T's total revenue is generated from commercial enterprise; the remaining 20 percent comes from retail sales.

In a B2B environment, communications with a customer is similar to communications with a consumer—the information has to be tailored to their specific needs to make it simpler for them to place orders. While G&T has three distinct market segments (small, medium, and large sizes), this single medium (the Web site) allows different individuals to access different information that is centrally placed.

G&T has been an active database marketer and they have leveraged that strength to their Net strategy. Customer segmentation, customer promotions and personalization features are incorporated into the site to help convert existing customers to the e-commerce

environment. They have made it easy for customers to transact with them, but many customers still voice the usual objections, like lack of security.

The site also features opt-in, permission-based e-mail marketing, and to grease the wheel the company launched an online newsletter to provide customers information on subjects to help them with their daily office routines—everything from ergonomics to nutrition.

G&T has big plans for its Internet strategy. According to Mike Duggan, director of commercial marketing and e-commerce at Grand & Toy, "G&T hopes to expand its overall volume of business with its online presence and the goal is to derive 50 percent of its business through the Internet by 2003. Presently, 25 percent or $100 million worth of business is transacted online."

Adapted from Bernadette Johnson, "Grand & Toy forges ahead with full-fledged Net strategy," *Strategy Direct + Interactive,* January 29, 2001, pp. D1, D14.

Courtesy: Grand & Toy

MARKETING COMMUNICATIONS STRATEGIES

5.
Demonstrate how the various elements of the marketing mix apply to Internet marketing.

The nature of Internet-based marketing communications was presented in Chapter 15, as it is an important component of integrated marketing communications strategies. Therefore, this section will simply review some of the important communications concepts.

The Internet seems to offer unlimited communications potential. It is a medium that reaches vast numbers of potential customers in a cost-effective manner, so it will play a more prominent role in a company's comprehensive marketing strategy in the future.

The objective of online and offline advertising is to get the viewer to the company or product Web site where detailed information is provided. The Internet must be seen as a supplement to traditional forms of advertising; it is by no means a replacement. In fact, generating traffic to a company's Web site involves advertising the existence of the site in all media, including the Internet.

ONLINE COMMUNICATIONS

All aspects of marketing communications can be implemented online. The most common alternatives include online advertising in a variety of formats, public relations, sponsorships, sales promotions, and Web sites.

Response rates for standard banner ads are now in the .03 percent range, reflecting a very low click rate. Advertisers have started using more advanced banners that include animation and video. As well, some ads, referred to as pop-ups, simply appear on a computer screen. While users do not like such an intrusion, the ads do grab the users attention, and that's the first thing an ad must do. Some ads will not disappear until they are viewed.

The Internet's strength in terms of advertising is its direct response capability. Interactive two-way communications combined with online transaction capabilities at a Web site means a user can complete the entire purchase decision cycle simply by clicking on an ad. Assuming a high level of satisfaction when a user visits a site, there is an opportunity to make the sale. The gap between grabbing one's attention and generating action can be closed quickly.

Sponsorships

sponsorship

An Internet **sponsorship** occurs when an advertiser commits to an extended relationship with another Web site. To illustrate, Colgate-Palmolive, the makers of Mennen Speed Stick, uses a hockey pool (a seasonal sponsorship and contest promotion) operating on the Canoe Web site (www.canoe.ca) to leverage Mennen Speed Stick (the official deodorant of the NHL) among its target audience of men aged 16 to 29. The interactive format of the pool is popular with participants and the long hockey season allows for a more extensive branding effort than a banner campaign. The sponsorship fee paid by Colgate-Palmolive is absolutely cheap for the degree of exposure the brand will gain on the World Wide Web.[19]

E-mail Advertising

Using e-mail to deliver an advertising message is the equivalent of direct mail in traditional mass advertising. The most effective way to communicate with customers is to encourage them to subscribe to receive information. When a customer asks to receive product information, the rate of conversion increases. Usually an incentive of some kind (e.g., free information, a free sample, or a discount on the first purchase) must be offered in exchange for the customer's registration. Once a company has a list of subscribers it can begin to send offers by e-mail. There are software systems that can be used to send messages, monitor responses and failures, track whether the recipient clicked on a link in a message, and even reply automatically.

permission-based e-mail

In accordance with present day netiquette, online visitors accept e-mail as long as they have agreed to receive it. This is referred to as **permission-based e-mail**. Typically, they agree to receive information about things they are interested in (e.g., investment information, recreation information, business information, etc.). If, for example, Microsoft develops a new version of a software package, it is likely that current users of Microsoft would want to know about it. After all, the consumer can download the new version almost immediately on release. All e-mail is not promotion-oriented. Many companies provide information to consumers via e-mail newsletters that are sent to subscribers by permission. Many magazines for example, e-mail to subscribers newsletters containing headlines of stories that will appear in their publication. By clicking on the headline, the consumer can read the article in advance of the magazine (hard copy) going into distribution.

SALES PROMOTION

The Internet is capable of distributing coupons and samples to prospective customers. Retailers such as Canadian Tire distribute e-coupons through their e-flyer, which is available online. There are also some independent coupon sites such as coupons.com that distribute coupons on behalf of national manufacturers of all kinds of goods and services.

Some sites allow users to sample their products prior to purchase. This has become an essential aspect of Web marketing for packaged goods companies. For the cost of delivering a sample, a company like Kraft or Colgate-Palmolive secures a wealth of information about a customer (e.g., demographic, psychographic, and geographic information) from an online survey. Consumers tend to provide such information more freely online than they would by other means. The information is used to develop longer-term marketing strategies.

Many software companies allow a free download of a demonstration version of their software. Once the demonstration period expires (30 to 60 days), a timer built into the download displays a message that you must purchase the software, and instructs you how to do so.

Contests have proven to be another effective online tool for creating interest in a brand. Wrigley's Excel gum recently ran an integrated marketing campaign to help launch the new Cherry Chill flavour. As part of the campaign, advertising was purchased on Canada.com. Customers could visit the site and guess what day would be the coldest day of the year (The Weather Network would verify the coldest day). A grand prize of $20 000 was awarded to the winner.[20]

The example of Mennen Speed Stick presented in the sponsorship section also shows how various elements of the communications mix can be combined in order to have greater impact on a target market.

PUBLIC RELATIONS

An organization can use the Internet to communicate information to a variety of publics in a timely and inexpensive manner. Many different publics will visit a corporate site: shareholders, prospective employees, suppliers, customers, and the media, to name just a few.

The information provided must be meaningful and representative of what the company is about. One of the primary objectives of public relations is to improve the image of the company and its products. The mere existence of the Internet encourages people to seek out information about a company. Therefore, a person's visit to a company Web site should be an enjoyable experience. They should be able to navigate the site quickly, and the information should be presented in an interesting and interactive format. Information should always be kept up to date and all recent press releases about the company should be readily available. Including colourful pictures and detailed information in the form of an annual report helps build interest and credibility with the public that visits the site.

THE WEB SITE

The Internet provides a new and exciting means of gaining additional exposure for a company. The Web site should deliver qualified leads because visitors are expressing interest simply by being there. In effect, the Web site is lining up qualified buyers at an electronic showroom and giving them enough relevant information to make a buying decision. Therefore, it is not the quantity of people attracted to a site that is important but rather the quality of the experience while interacting at the site that counts. A small number of loyal customers is much more valuable than millions of hits by people who will not return.

The Web site educates the customer through information transfer, and it can generate a sale. A vast quantity of information is made available and at low cost. It is nothing like an expensive television commercial that is only on for 30 seconds or an ad buried deep in a daily newspaper—here one day and gone the next. On the Web site, the information is always there. The Internet, then, is a less expensive and more expansive medium than the mass media.

flow

As suggested above, a person's experience at a site is important. Some experts describe the experience in terms of **flow**. They say the experience should integrate the active and the passive to absorb and immerse the customer in a memorable and enjoyable experience that makes them want to come back again and again.[21] A consumer who faces frustration in securing information or in placing an order will find another site to shop at. Additional ways of getting visitors back to a site is to provide health tips, recipes, contests, and news. Incentives offered depend on the nature of the site and why people visit the site in the first place.

Customer Relationship Management

Online customer service strategies go well beyond post-sale activities. The Internet provides a vehicle for a company to develop a true customer relationship management program. Online marketers must be able to do three things well. They must predict changing needs, wants, behaviours, and expectations of e-consumers; pursue an e-marketing strategy that is relevant to each e-consumer; and, identify high value e-consumers and repeatedly satisfy them better than competitors can.

Organizations must acknowledge that the Internet is a "product pull" individual-user medium, not a "product push" mass-marketing medium. Therefore, if the 80/20 rule of business applies to the Internet, 20 percent of customers will be in the high-value category and will generate 80 percent of profits. These high-value and tech-savvy customers must be part of an effective and efficient customer relationship management program. If they are not, they will do business with other companies.

When FedEx first put up its Web site in 1995 they estimated they would save $1 million per day, because customers would be able to check the status of their package online, rather than having to call. Today, "chat" is a technology that allows customer service representatives to speak to customers in real time over the Web. It seems that the opportunities for companies to better serve their customers, to reduce costs, and to build relationships is one of the most important uses of the Internet to marketing.

Summary

Due to the rapid pace of change in technology and the growing willingness by businesses and consumers to conduct transactions electronically, organizations are integrating e-marketing techniques into their marketing strategies. Presently, the business-to-business segment of e-commerce is much larger than the business-to-consumer segment.

The typical Internet user has a higher than average level of education and household income. Future growth of online commerce between companies and consumers is dependent on technology being more readily available to and accepted by lower-income households.

For marketers, the Internet offers three opportunities: it is a medium to communicate with customers, it allows a company to conduct transactions online, and it permits mass customization. Online marketing complements other marketing strategies, as it can help build awareness and image, offer incentives to stimulate sales, generate leads, improve customer service, and conduct transactions without the use of intermediaries. If programs are implemented effectively, cost efficiencies in distributing goods are achieved and prices are lowered for consumers.

The Internet is an effective medium for conducting marketing research. Consumers and companies can access secondary data and information quickly and conveniently. Online primary research in the form of focus groups, electronic observation, and surveys also provides a lower cost, accurate, and speedier means of collecting information from consumers. Certain research biases such as sample misrepresentation can influence the credibility of information collected.

Consumers shopping online do so based on the perception that prices are lower than offline prices. For a variety of reasons including the cost of developing and maintaining a Web site and the cost associated with marketing strategies to attract visitors to the site, that is not the case. Unlike the offline environment, small companies can compete effectively with large companies online. Since their overhead costs are lower, theoretically, they should be able to offer lower prices to consumers.

The Internet performs all distribution functions, but in a different manner. The primary benefit for online companies is their ability to communicate with channel members and consumers in an interactive manner. As well, some goods can be delivered directly online. The response time between ordering a product and having it delivered by an independent carrier is shortened due to the directness of the channel. Although the Internet is still in its infancy, the distribution channel has already gone through a process of disintermediation and reintermediation. New distributors in the online market have replaced distributors that are key members of the channel in the offline market.

In terms of marketing communications, the Internet provides a new and effective means of reaching consumers and business customers. In addition to a variety of forms of banner advertising, companies can pursue sponsorship opportunities online along with e-mail marketing strategies. Permission-based e-mail marketing programs are proving to be very effective. The Internet also presents opportunities to offer sales promotion incentives that attract visitors and develop loyalty (return visits). As a public relations tool, a company Web site is an ideal medium to communicate information about a company and to build goodwill that will directly or indirectly provide benefits in the long-term. The quality and quantity of information that can be delivered by a Web site is far beyond that of the traditional media.

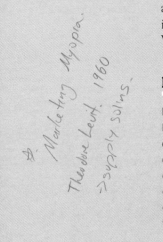

Key Terms

B2B e-commerce 472
B2C e-commerce 472
disintermediation 487
e-business 469
e-commerce 469
electronic data interchange (EDI) 488
extranet 489
flow 492

intranet 489
mass customization 473
penetration strategy 485
permission-based e-mail 491
price leadership 485
reintermediation 488
sponsorship 490

Review Questions

1. What is the difference between e-business and e-commerce?

2. The Internet has presented three significant opportunities for business organizations. What are those opportunities?

3. Explain the concept of mass customization. Provide an Internet illustration of this concept.

4. Identify and briefly explain some of the key marketing functions that can be conducted on the Internet.

5. Briefly explain how primary marketing research can be conducted online.

6. Assess the benefits and drawbacks of conducting focus groups and surveys in an online environment.

7. Identify the profile of successful products marketed on the Internet.

8. Identify the basic elements that contribute to a successful online branding strategy.

9. Identify and briefly explain two factors that tend to increase the price of merchandise bought online, and two factors that tend to decrease the price.

10. In the context of online marketing, what does "price leadership" mean?

11. In the context of online marketing, explain the concepts of disintermediation and reintermediation.

12. What is the difference between an intranet and an extranet? What impact have extranets had on electronic data interchange (EDI)?

Discussion and Application Questions

1. What is your assessment of Internet marketing over the next 5 to 10 years? Will it be as significant as industry forecasters believe it will be?

2. Is consumers' concern for security and privacy valid? Conduct some online secondary research and present an opinion on these issues.

3. Conduct some Internet-based research to determine the extent to which small business is adopting e-commerce business and marketing models. Is there positive movement in terms of adoption? Are small businesses successful when they adopt e-commerce? Cite specific examples.

E-Assignment

Review the Marketing in Action vignette "Grand & Toy's B2B Net Strategy" and then visit the Web site to further evaluate what the company is doing. Based on what you know about Grand & Toy's Internet strategy, have they done enough to defend themselves against Staples Business Depot? Visit the Canadian Staples Web site before drawing any conclusions. Should Grand & Toy be doing more?

Visit the mySimon.com Web site and conduct a search for the purchase of an item of your choosing. What is your assessment of the effectiveness of mySimon's service? Are you satisfied with the results of the search, or are there better deals to be had offline?

Visit the Ford.ca Web site and spec out a car of your choice (e.g., select a make, model, options packages, etc.). What is your opinion of this process? Are you satisfied with the information provided? Would you buy a car online? Why or why not?

Endnotes

1. Judy Strauss and Raymond Frost, *Marketing on the Internet* (Upper Saddle River, NJ: Prentice-Hall, 1999), pp. 49-50.

2. www.strategis.gc.ca, 2002-04-07.

3. Joe Greene, "The state of the Canadian e-commerce nation," supplement to *Canadian Business*, 2001.

4. Patrick Brethour, "Women narrow Internet gender gap," *Globe and Mail*, March 27, 2002, pp. B1, B2.

5. Daniel Mchardie, "Web surfing teens turn off TV," *Globe and Mail*, May 24, 2000, pp. A1, A5.

6. Patrick Brethour, "Women narrow Internet gender gap," *Globe and Mail*, March 27, 2002, pp. B1, B2.

7. www.statcan.ca/Daily/English/020402.

8. Michael Dell, "*Leadership in the Internet economy,*" address to the Canadian Club of Canada, April 7, 2000, www.dell.com/us/en/corporate/speech_2000-04-07.

9. Mark Evans, "Net future as a research tool: Study," *Globe and Mail*, May 16, 2000, p. B6.

10. Kate MacNamara, "Web sales surge 43 percent," *Financial Post*, April 3, 2002, p. FP5.

11. Judy Strauss and Raymond Frost, *Marketing on the Internet*, pp. 138-139.

12. "Online banking continues to grow," *Marketing*, July 22, 2002, p. 18.

13. Frank Feather, *Future Consumer.com*, (Toronto, ON: Warwick Publishing, 2000), p. 272.

14. Terrence Belford, "Labatt's beer.com builds repeat traffic," *Financial Post*, April 3, 2000, p. E3.

15. Troy Young, "Delivering customer service online," *Business Sense*, January/February 2001, p. 38.

16. Patrick Brethour, "E-biz of the week," *Globe and Mail*, March 1, 2001, p. T3.

17. Sean Hart, "Canadian retailers piggyback smaller players," *Strategy Direct + Interactive*, May 21, 2001, p. D5.

18. David Steinhart, "Microsoft plans online car-buying service," *Financial Post*, June 6, 2000, p. C6.

19. Fawzia Sheikh, "Putting it in the Net," *Digital Marketing*, July 13, 1998, pp. 13-14.

20. Sarah Smith, "Wrigley plays on Canada's famous cold weather," *Digital Marketing*, March 2002, p. 11.

21. Frank Feather, p. 23.

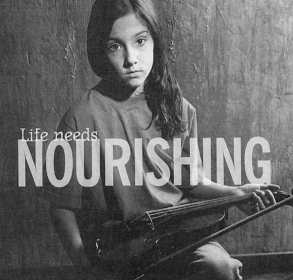
Services and Not-for-Profit Marketing

eight

> Learning Objectives

After studying this chapter, you will be able to

1. Identify the factors that have contributed to the growth of services marketing.
2. Outline the characteristics of services marketing and distinguish between service and product marketing.
3. Describe the elements of the services marketing mix.
4. Explain the nature, scope, and characteristics of not-for-profit marketing.
5. Describe the types of not-for-profit marketing and the role of the marketing mix in not-for-profit environments.

Services Marketing

The service industry in Canada is divided into four primary categories: leisure and personal services; food and beverage services; accommodation; and business services. The services industry includes some of Canada's largest employers as it embraces banks and other financial service companies, telecommunications companies, professional firms of accountants and management consultants, real estate companies, advertising agencies, and hotel and food-service businesses.

In Canada, the period since the Second World War has been marked by a steady shift away from the production of goods towards more emphasis on services. More than 7 out of 10 employed Canadians now work in the service industry. Much of Canada's employment growth in the past decade has come from the service industries, and this trend is expected to continue in the next decade as we move further into the technology and information era. Because of the high-tech nature of certain service sectors, growth in services will more than compensate for declines in the manufacturing sector.

FACTORS CONTRIBUTING TO GROWTH IN SERVICES

1.
Identify the factors that have contributed to the growth of services marketing.

Several factors have influenced growth in services. Among them are technology, the adoption of a marketing orientation by service providers, changing characteristics of consumers, and outsourcing.

Technology

Technological developments have spurred the service sector. Advancing technology and the shift to online business models has actually created a new industry, that of online consulting. Traditional companies wishing to go online require the expertise of such companies. Technology both creates and erases jobs. The introduction of automatic teller machines and online banking has eliminated clerical positions, and the use of robotics in automobile assembly plants has eliminated manufacturing jobs. In both cases, however, the lost jobs are offset to some extent by the creation of service jobs that are needed to operate, service, and support technology.

Marketing and Customer Service Orientation

Professionals in the service sector have become aware of the usefulness of marketing. In order to differentiate themselves from competitors, service providers, such as accountants, lawyers, and management consultants, are adopting a marketing philosophy to attract new business (Figure 18.1). The quality of service provided by a professional then determines how well they retain those clients.

Changing Consumer Characteristics

In the consumer market, the key issue is time. Dual-income households are time-pressed to even do the smallest of chores. Consequently, there is a rising demand for a variety

An Ad for a Consulting Firm Stressing a Unique Area of Specialization

Figure 18.1

Courtesy of Accenture

of household services, such as maid and cleaning services, lawn and garden care, and home decorating and renovations. The emergence of online grocery services, such as GroceryGateway.com, that deliver goods directly to households is a natural to capitalize on this trend. The whole concept of online shopping for virtually all goods and services will have a dramatic and negative impact on traditional bricks-and-mortar retailers.

Outsourcing

Manufacturing firms have been going through the rationalization process (e.g., the process of downsizing and the search for cost-saving strategies), and many have decided to contract out services previously done in-house. Advertising, legal, payroll, and computer systems services, among others, fall into this category. Such a transfer of responsibility has contributed to growth in the service business sector.

CHARACTERISTICS OF SERVICES

A **service** is defined as work done by one person (organization) that benefits another. In a business-to-business context, one business sells assistance and experience rather than a tangible product.[1] There are four characteristics that distinguish services from products: intangibility, inseparability, quality variability, and perishability of demand.

Intangibility

Intangibility is the quality of not being perceivable by the senses (i.e., a service cannot be seen, heard, tasted, smelled, or touched). For example, a life insurance policy may be worth $500 000, but its true benefit is the security it imparts, and security cannot be seen or touched. This type of product is quite different from something like coffee, whose aroma can be smelled and whose flavour can be tasted.

Intangibility is something of a problem for marketers of services. To deal with it, marketers attempt to express the value of the service in tangible terms. In this regard, advertising plays a key role. Messages for a parcel express service such as FedEx or UPS frequently show the extent to which those firms will go to deliver a package—the images shown portray a level of service a customer can always count on. Brand names help establish images that convey the material effects of a service. Such names as Budget Rent-A-Car and Discount Car and Truck Rentals suggest price savings that are not offered by competitors.

Budget Rent A Car
www.budget.ca
Discount Car and Truck Rentals
www.discountcar.
com

Inseparability

Inseparability refers to the equating of the provider of the service with the service itself. People feel this way about their doctor, their financial planner, or even their hairstylist. While apparent substitutes are available, the buyer feels more comfortable with his or her preferred and regular source of supply. A close relationship, or inseparability, exists between the service and the supplier.

To operate efficiently, a business organization must reduce the tendency to identify a service with a particular person. To do so, the organization trains people to perform the service at the desired level; in other words, the business standardizes the performance of many individuals at a desired level of service. Such is the nature of a call centre operation, where customer complaints are handled, and where technical problems incurred by customers are resolved. Hotels implement training programs dealing with guest satisfaction—a crucial aspect of achieving repeat business from a customer. Once the desired level of service is in place it must be communicated to the customer. In the Metropolitan Hotel advertisement (Figure 18.2), the unique selling point is the special services provided by the hotel to business guests. For new customers who cannot judge the quality of service prior to purchase, corporate advertising promoting image, reputation, and value-added services is helpful.

Figure 18.2

An Ad Stressing Value-Added Services to Attract Business Customers

Reprinted courtesy of Metropolitan Hotels

Quality Variability

quality variability

To customers, a quality service is one that meets their expectations, is available when needed, and is administered in a consistent manner. Can a services provider meet this challenge? **Quality variability** refers to the variations in services offered by different individuals, even within the same organization. For example, all Sun Life insurance agents perform the same service, but they each approach and deal with their customers differently, and some are much more attentive to their clients' needs than others. This is a challenge for marketers.

Like inseparability, quality variability can be controlled through standardization programs. The growth of franchises and their acceptance by consumers is a result of their ability to offer uniform quality throughout the franchise system. McDonald's motto of quality, service, and value and the intensive training program that all its employees and managers must undergo demonstrate how food can be prepared and delivered in a standardized way. The quality of service offered in franchise operations can be monitored via customer feedback surveys.

Perishability of Demand

perishability of demand

Services suffer from a high degree of **perishability of demand**, that is, demand for them varies over a given period. Demand for a service may diminish, but the facilities offering the unwanted service still remain. To understand the concept of uneven demand, consider that hotel rooms sit idle during weekends, when business travel is less frequent, and that theatre seats are often vacant on weekdays and full on weekends. In both cases, the building must be large enough, or have sufficient rooms or seats, to accommodate the crowds during peak demand.

Hoteliers, for example, counter perishability of demand by offering reduced rates for hotel rooms on weekends (typically a hotel is busier during the week with business travellers). A phone company offers discounted phone rates in non-business hours. Such measures encourage the use of services during times of low demand.

BUYING BEHAVIOUR IN SERVICES

In marketing services, an organization should be aware that there are some differences in consumer behaviour between services and goods. Differences exist in attitudes, needs and motives, and basic decision-making behaviour.

Attitudes

When deciding whether to purchase a good or a service, customers are obviously influenced by their own attitudes. Since services are intangible, the impression that a customer has of the service and of the supplier is a strong influence on his or her decision to purchase the service. It is also much easier for a customer to express dissatisfaction with a service because of the personal nature of a service offering.

Canadian Transportation Agency
www.cta-otc.gc.ca/index_e.html

Canada's airline industry has numerous problems in this area. In fact, the Canada Transportation Agency's Air Travel Complaints Commissioner, Bruce Hood, identifies attitude as the major area of concern. In his recent report about the industry he said, "Air Canada staff were hostile, rude, indifferent, and particularly disdainful of passengers who pay low fares."[2] He is expressing a consumers' point of view. Since new customers often rely on the views of others who have tried a service, this is not the kind of news that Air Canada would want the media or its customers to publicize, but it is a situation they have created for themselves. Providers of a service must ensure that customers are satisfied.

Needs and Motives

Both goods and services satisfy needs and motives, often the same ones. Thus, one could satisfy the need to repair a roof either by buying shingles and laying them oneself or by hiring a contractor to provide and lay the shingles. Purchasing the goods and purchasing the service both address the same requirement. The provider of the service offers the customer convenience and expertise in getting the task performed. Yet, in addition to satisfying the need for a repaired roof, the service could also cater to another need of the customer—the need for personal attention. People often feel that the personal touch is lacking in their hurried, hectic lives. Customizing the service for individual customers with unique needs gives them the satisfaction of receiving personal attention.

Purchase Behaviour

A customer must decide what to buy, when to buy it, and whom to buy it from. The purchase of many services is seasonal. Household improvements are commonly made in the spring and summer; retirement plans sell heavily in the winter, and vacation travel peaks in the summer months. Whatever the time of year, selecting a service takes longer than choosing goods because it is difficult for a buyer to assess the quality and value of a service due to its intangibility.

Buyers of services are influenced more by information provided by potential suppliers. They pay more attention to advertising and surf the Internet for detailed information and visuals that aptly portray the service. Buyers of services also value the opinions of other people—be they friends, neighbours, or relatives—than are buyers of tangible goods. To illustrate, consider a family planning a summer or winter vacation at a resort. Once the information search is complete (e.g., pamphlets, brochures, and Internet search) and potential destinations are identified, a person will then seek references from acquaintances that have used the facilities. Then, a decision is made.

THE SERVICES MARKETING MIX

Services as a Product

3.
Describe the elements of the services marketing mix.

The elements of the marketing mix for services are the same elements as those found in the mix for tangible goods. As a "product," however, a service differs from other products because the selling attributes are intangible (Figure 18.3). With services, the customer is less interested in ownership or physical qualities and more interested in certain conveniences, such as timing, availability, and consistency. Following is a list of some of the intangible qualities that sell a service:

1. **Consistency** UPS Canada uses the slogan "Moving at the Speed of Your Business" in its advertising. Their television commercials show the physical lengths to which its couriers will go to deliver a package on time. As such, it is a good illustration of how a company offers consistency—in this case parcel delivery on time, all the time.

The Services Marketing Mix

Figure 18.3

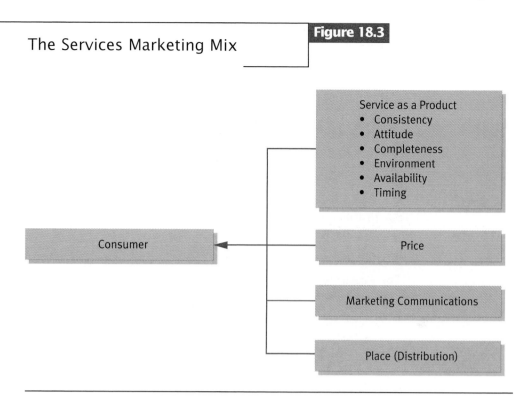

2. **Attitude** The attitude of those providing the service may be a selling point. Equally important is the degree of personalization between the supplier and the customer. Taking a personal approach and addressing key customers by name and then asking if the quality of the service they received was satisfactory leads to the formation of a relationship with the customer.

3. **Completeness** Some organizations provide a range of conveniences to attract customers. For business travellers a hotel may offer an express check-in/check-out service and fully stocked rooms with online capabilities to meet the needs of business travellers. A VISA card offers consumers numerous conveniences, but a VISA Gold Card offers an enhanced list of benefits, such as a higher spending limit, a personal line of credit, and travel insurance. As VISA says, it is "All you need."

4. **Environment** Clean rooms in a hotel, non-smoking rooms and floors in a hotel, and non-smoking sections in restaurants are environmental attributes that customers look for.

5. **Availability and Timing** An airline or bus line that offers frequent and convenient departure times, or ease of entry and accessibility for the disabled, is selling availability. Being available at the time it is needed is a selling attribute for a service. For example, a cleaning service may be prepared to assist during emergencies in a hotel. Availability and timing (e.g., the promise of next day delivery) are crucial product service elements in the parcel delivery business.

6. **Supplementary Services** A company will often market a primary service and then supplement the basic offering with peripheral services.[3] For example, the primary

service supplied by a luxury hotel is clean lodging. Yet a hotel can distinguish itself from competitors by offering toll-free reservation service, free parking, recreation facilities, bathrobes, and other amenities within rooms, as well as free transportation to and from airports. For business travellers, Metropolitan Hotels provide an array of business services (e.g., broadband connectivity, laser printers, and fax in rooms.) See Figure 18.2 for details.

The addition of peripheral services does increase the amount that a firm must invest in its operations; however, consumers like to choose among services that are clearly differentiated, just as they do with tangible products. Differentiating the service through the service mix can ensure that the service attracts its target market. In the case of the hotel, consumers can compare room rates and additional services before selecting the one that meets their needs.

Pricing

The various types of services require various pricing strategies from the supplier. Prices can be determined by regulation, tradition, or negotiation.

1. ***Regulated Pricing*** In the case of utilities, telephone service, and cable television, the services provided are regulated by government agencies. The suppliers of the service must present and defend rate increases to the agency prior to changing prices.

2. ***Traditional Pricing*** Some services have prices that are established or have become traditional. It could be an established hourly rate for a service provided by an auto mechanic, electrician, or plumber, or a set rate of commission for a real estate agent or financial planning broker.

3. ***Negotiated Pricing*** Fees for the services of lawyers and marketing research and management consultants are often negotiated. Typically, these companies will submit bids based on specifications supplied by the client. The client then selects a supplier from among the bids, often after further decreases in price have been negotiated.

A buyer's ability to negotiate is often critical and can save a company considerable sums of money. For example, corporations negotiate room rates with hotel chains for executive and business-related travel. Rates are usually pegged to the number of room nights a company reserves in a one-year period. Traditionally, corporate discounts for hotel rooms are in the 20 to 25 percent range, but sharp negotiation skills can earn a company higher discounts. Consumers can also negotiate a better room rate if they possess the right negotiation skills. Don't accept the first rate that is quoted to you!

In the Internet world, where auctions take place, service companies do accept low price bids. Through Priceline.com, for example, customers submit prices (lower than normal prices) for unfilled airline seats. The airline can either accept or reject the bid. The airline weighs the incremental cost of filling the seat against the potential revenue when making such a decision.

Distribution

In the service sector, where the relationship between the supplier and the client is close, the distribution channels tend to be direct. Because services are intangible and cannot be stored, there is often no need for intermediaries. Even if intermediaries are used, and in some businesses they commonly are (e.g., numerous small insurance companies are represented by independent insurance agents), their role is to create demand rather than perform the traditional functions of a distributor.

At one time, it was generally thought that personal contact was the key to marketing services, particularly in such industries as insurance, financial investments, and travel planning. The acceptance of online marketing by consumers has changed this way of thinking and these and other industries have had to react. Stockbrokers are being eliminated by discount brokers, or e-brokerages, such as E*trade. Tech-savvy investors are making their own investment decisions instead of listening to the advice of their former stockbrokers. Traditional travel agents (bricks and mortar) have lost considerable business to online travel sites such as travelocity.com and Webflyer.com. The financial industry is now doing a lot of business directly online. See Figure 18.4 for an illustration.

E*Trade Canada
www.etrade.ca

Marketing Communications

Marketing communications strategies focus on the primary service, detailing what it is and what it does for the customer. In today's competitive market, it is imperative that service companies use all elements of the communications mix. Financial institutions and card marketers, such as VISA and MasterCard, spend a great deal of money on advertising to create awareness and interest for the services they provide. To secure new business, they also employ personal selling and direct response techniques. Information-rich Web sites reinforce messages from the mass media and provide the details that help convert a prospect into a customer.

Service companies in the technology sector have a difficult time communicating the nature of their services because they are restricted by the space and time parameters of the traditional media. How does a software development company, for example, communicate essential information to get a traditional business ready for online marketing? They rely on their Web site. Mass advertising creates awareness of their service and gets potential clients to visit the Web site for complete details.

For more insight into the changing nature of services marketing and the need to keep pace with change, read the Marketing in Action vignette **Relationship Building Crucial for Hotels**.

Not-for-Profit Marketing

not-for-profit marketing

Not-for-profit marketing refers to the marketing effort and activity of not-for-profit organizations. These organizations operate in the best interests of the public or champion a particular idea or cause, and they do so without seeking financial profit. The goals and objectives of these groups are quite different from those of profit-based enterprises.

NATURE AND SCOPE OF NOT-FOR-PROFIT MARKETING

4.
Explain the nature, scope, and characteristics of not-for-profit marketing.

social marketing

Not only do not-for-profit organizations market goods and services, but they also market people, places, ideas, and organizations. One major goal of not-for-profit marketing is to promote a social consciousness. The use of marketing to increase the acceptability of social ideas is referred to as **social marketing**. Examples of social marketing include programs dealing with ecological concerns, recycling, the preservation and conservation of natural resources, and spousal abuse, to name a few. Many of these issues are financially supported and promoted by profit-based organizations. For an illustration, refer to Figure 18.5.

Figure 18.4

Services Provided by an Insurance
Company Are Available Online

manulifeone.com
1-877-MANU111

manulifeone.com

5 minutes could save you 5 years in mortgage payments.

Visit the Manulife one Web site
and you'll find a new and better
way to pay off your mortgage
years earlier — without paying more.

Prove it to yourself. Use our
unique calculator to plug in
your own numbers and see how
Manulife one can save you
thousands of dollars in interest.

In just 5 minutes you'll discover
how Manulife one can make
you mortgage-free faster.
Visit www.manulifeone.com,
or call your financial advisor.

It's different. Switch to Manulife one.

Manulife Financial
Helping You Make Better Financial Decisions™

Manulife one and the one logo are Trademarks of The Manufacturers Life Insurance Company.

Courtesy of Manulife Financial

Marketing in Action

Relationship Building Crucial for Hotels

Hotels do their best to establish one-to-one relationships with clients. They know it's the key to success. In the past, personal service combined with a splash of mass advertising and a dash of direct response was the formula for success. No longer however. In the post 9/11 era things have changed for the hotel industry.

In the past year business travellers were cutting way back. Hotels in Canada encountered a 10 percent drop in occupancy rates, the equivalent of about $300 million in lost revenue. Then, as business travellers started travelling again their behaviour was different—they were looking for better deals—in marketing terms they were trading down.

One of the quickest ways to start building back a business is to cater to "best customers" needs. And that's what many hotel chains did. Suddenly, hotels were placing a priority on database marketing. They delved into their databases, developed programs that targeted special needs of their most loyal customers, and tailored promotions directly to them. Direct mail and e-mail were the media of choice.

Out of necessity budget and mid-priced hotels caught the attention of business travellers. Choice Hotels, for example, who operate under the banners Comfort, Quality, Sleep, and Econo Lodge quickly took advantage of the trading down trend among business travellers. While some mid- to upper-end hotels were actually cutting travel agency commissions to save money, Choice upped commissions from 10 to 15 percent. Travel agents responded in kind with more bookings.

With rates starting at around $85 per night, Choice was well positioned to take advantage of current corporate travel needs. Among their regular corporate clients are companies such as General Motors, Nortel Networks, Sears Canada, Home Hardware, and Wendy's.

In the long-term, rewards programs are another technique for fostering a relationship. Travelodge, a pioneer in rewards (20 years and counting) allows its guests to collect 10 travel miles for every lodging dollar spent. The miles can also be redeemed for merchandise at several prominent Canadian merchants. The rewards program is enhanced through co-marketing agreements with Hudson's Bay Rewards programs and CIBC. CIBC Entourage Business American Express customers get preferred rates at Travelodge and Thriftlodge in addition to regular rewards perks.

At Travelodge, loyalty club members account for 30 percent of the business and 70 percent of the members are corporate business travellers who stay 80 to 100 nights a year. Customers in this category have to be satisfied! According to Dorothy Dowling, president and COO of Travelodge Canada, "The hotel business is quite different from other industries—the relationship we have is a very personal one. While our customers appreciate information about specials, discounts and programs, the true customer relationship is really one that exists with the front desk agent, and through loyalty programs."

Adapted from "Frequent traveler: Back to business," Advertising Supplement, *Maclean's*, May 13, 2002; "Hotels step up direct marketing tactics," *Strategy*, March 25, 2002, pp. D1, D6; and Anne Kerr, "Hotels roll out the red carpet," *Globe and Mail*, March 14, 2002, pp. T1, T5.

Dick Hemingway

An Illustration of Social Marketing

Figure 18.5

Reproduced courtesy of CN

Canadian Forces
www.dnd.ca
Humane Society
www.humanesociety.
com
**Canadian Cancer
Society**
www.cancer.ca
YMCA Canada
www.ymca.ca

Not-for-profit organizations that use marketing strategies effectively include colleges and universities, political parties and politicians, the Canadian Armed Forces, the Humane Society, the Canadian Cancer Society, and the YMCA of Canada. This brief cross-section of organizations indicates that marketing achieves different objectives. It is used to recruit personnel, to raise funds to support causes, and to encourage the public to volunteer time and to make other contributions to worthwhile causes.

CHARACTERISTICS OF NOT-FOR-PROFIT MARKETING

There are many similarities between marketing in a not-for-profit environment and marketing in a profit-oriented environment. In both situations, the customer must choose between competing organizations. A person must decide which charitable groups to support and how much support to give, just as he or she must determine which car to buy and how much to pay for it. People also experience varying levels of satisfaction or dissatisfaction with the activities and performance of both types of organizations.

However, there are some differences between not-for-profit and profit-based marketing, especially in the areas of philosophy, exchange (what is exchanged), objectives, benefits, and target groups.

Philosophy

Not-for-profit marketing is concerned with the promotion and support of people, causes, ideas, and organizations. It raises funds to support a cause or promote a concept. In the case of profit-based marketing, the goal is to generate a financial return on investment. An illustration of the not-for-profit philosophy is included in Figure 18.6.

Figure 18.6

An Advertisement Encouraging Support of a Worthwhile Cause

United Way of Greater Toronto

Exchange

In profit-based marketing, money is exchanged between buyers and sellers for the goods or services provided. While money may exchange hands in not-for-profit marketing, it does so under different circumstances. What people receive for their money cannot be quantified; they give, for example, for the psychological satisfaction of supporting a cause they believe in. In the political arena, the exchange may take the form of a vote given in return for the promise of a better government.

Objectives of the Organization

Profit-oriented companies establish objectives in terms of sales, profit, return on investment, and market share. In not-for-profit organizations, the objectives are not always quantifiable and measurable. They establish targets for fund-raising, but these are subordinate to other non-financial objectives. The Canadian Cancer Society attempts to find a cure for a disease, as do similar organizations. Other groups like MADD—Mothers Against Drunk Driving—attempt to change the public's attitudes or to get the public to agree with a certain position.

Benefits Derived

In an exchange made for profit, a buyer benefits directly from the good or service supplied by the selling firm. In a not-for-profit environment, only a small portion of "buyers," or supporters, ever receive any material benefits from the supported association or institution. For instance, funds to aid health organizations are solicited from the general population, but only a relatively small number of people contract a particular disease and use the services of any given health clinic each year.

Targets

Not-for-profit organizations must serve two groups: clients and donors. Clients are those to whom the service is provided. Donors are those from whom the resources are received. The resources they donate may be in the form either of money or of time. Donors are concerned about the availability of goods and services, about whether or not the resources they provide are spent well in the provision of service, and, generally, about receiving recognition for their contribution.

TYPES OF NOT-FOR-PROFIT MARKETING

5.
Describe the types of not-for-profit marketing and the role of the marketing mix in not-for-profit environments.

There are four categories of not-for-profit marketing: organization marketing, people marketing, place marketing, and idea marketing.[4]

Organization Marketing

organization marketing

Organization marketing is marketing that seeks to gain or maintain acceptance of an organization's objectives and services. Colleges and universities engage in such marketing; they turn to fundraising campaigns as a survival tactic in the wake of government restraints on funds for education. The organizations not only want the public to accept their goals but also to use their services. Colleges and universities promote the concept of life-long learning, and they seek to have organizations use their facilities for business training, seminars, and conferences.

People Marketing

people marketing

People marketing refers to a process of marketing an individual or a group of people in order to create a favourable impression of that individual or group (e.g., politicians, political parties, sports and entertainment celebrities).

To illustrate, consider what process must take place before a celebrity appears in an advertising campaign for a commercial product or a not-for-profit cause. Celebrities employ agents and marketing consultants who seek and secure contracts for them. One of Canada's best known and widely used endorser is Wayne Gretzky. His imprint on a product or service or support of a worthy cause has a dramatic impact on how the public perceives and supports that cause. While Gretzky's exploits in the commercial world are well known, his contribution to worthwhile causes is less known. He recently worked with TransAlta Corp., an Alberta-based company, on its Project Planet Challenge, a contest for school kids to create projects to improve the environment.[5]

Politicians, aware that their career is created or destroyed by their image, call upon image-makers to fine-tune their personal and presentation style. In preparing for political debates on television, all participants are carefully prepared by consultants, so that their strengths, and not their weaknesses, will show in the heat of battle.

The objective of people marketing is to create or maintain a positive impression or image of an individual among a target group. A person can be said to have made an impression if people are aware of, and hold certain attitudes about, that person. For more insight into the role that celebrities play in cause marketing situations, read the Marketing in Action vignette **Celebrities Pave the Way**.

Place Marketing

place marketing

Place marketing draws attention to and creates a favourable attitude towards a particular place, be it a country, province, region, or city. Places are marketed in much the same way as products. The benefits and advantages of the location are the focal points of advertising and promotion campaigns. Themes and slogans are developed for long-term use to provide continuity in advertising (see Figure 18.7). Provincial governments, for example, use catchy slogans such as "A World Away" (Newfoundland), "More to Discover" (Ontario), and "Super, Natural" (British Columbia). In place marketing, advertising is the principal strategy, for it creates the image for the destination. Specific details that are essential for planning vacations and travel are available on information-rich Web sites.

Idea Marketing

idea marketing

Idea marketing encourages the public to accept and agree with certain issues and causes. The campaigns aimed at convincing people of the need to wear seatbelts, to avoid drinking and driving, and to exercise regularly are instances of idea marketing. Idea marketing is social marketing, and its ultimate objective is to induce the majority of the population to accept a given idea, cause, or way of thinking (refer to Figures 18.5 and 18.6).

advocacy advertising

Advocacy advertising is a form of idea marketing practised by corporations and associations that are concerned about issues or legislation that affect them. It is designed to communicate a company's position on a particular issue. A pulp and paper company may use this form of advertising to tell the public what it is doing about restoring forests, for example. It is common for consumer groups who disagree with a corporation's position to advertise the opposite point of view.

Marketing in Action

Celebrities Pave the Way

Every disease imaginable has a foundation that raises funds annually. From the Cancer Society to the Heart Fund to the Parkinson Foundation, the goal is the same: find a cure. Most foundations use the same tactics to raise funds—a combination of public service announcements in the print and broadcast media followed by rounds of direct response mail and telephone calls. The monotony of such a regimen almost defeats the purpose of the calls.

More recently, celebrities are volunteering their services to support causes that are dear to them. Tragedy, it seems, can strike anyone regardless of stature and age. Michael J. Fox, for example, is lending his famous name to the Parkinson Foundation. The actor is the best-known Canadian to struggle with Parkinson's disease. As the top-billed star of the hit comedy serial "Spin City," Fox holds great power to raise awareness about the disease and raise funds for research into its causes and potential treatments. Fox departed from "Spin City" at the height of his career to further the cause of Parkinson's disease research.

Parkinson's disease is the degeneration of certain brain cells that control electrical impulses to the rest of the body. It causes tremors and impedes movement, and, in some cases, causes personality changes and memory loss. Other famous people with the disease include Muhammad Ali and Johnny Cash.

The power of celebrity to help fund raising and research is well established, especially by film and sport stars. Rock Hudson and Magic Johnson brought international attention to AIDS, and Christopher Reeves has raised millions for spinal cord research. Muhammad Ali is the official spokesperson for Parkinson's disease in the United States. His carrying the Olympic torch at the 1996 Atlanta Games drew immediate attention to the disease. One year later, Ali appeared before a committee of the US House of Representatives and was the driving force behind the passing of a bill to allocate $100 million for Parkinson's disease research.

Michael J. Fox will continue to carry the torch on behalf of all Parkinson's disease sufferers.

Adapted from Charlie Gillis, "Celebrity spokesmen can raise the funds that allow doctors to continue vital research," *Financial Post*, November 27, 1998, p. A6.

Maybe I was supposed to get Parkinson's.

Make a donation today. Visit www.michaeljfox.org or call 1-800-708-7644.

Chelsea Piers, Pier 62 New York, New York, 10011

MARKETING STRATEGY IN A NOT-FOR-PROFIT ORGANIZATION

A comprehensive marketing strategy is crucial to the success of any not-for-profit group today. As suggested earlier, communications plays a prominent role, but all elements of the mix are given due consideration. This section briefly examines the contribution of product, price, distribution, and marketing communications to the strategic market planning of not-for-profit organizations.

Figure 18.7

Vivid Pictures and Catchy Slogans Promote Tourism in Canada

Canadian Tourism Association

Product

Product strategy in a not-for-profit organization is virtually the opposite of the strategy employed by a firm driven by the profit motive. Profit-based organizations start by trying to discover what needs the consumer has and then formulating a concept—a product or a service—to satisfy those needs. Not-for-profit bodies, on the other hand, believe from the start that they provide what the public needs. Very often, they feel that others only have to be made aware of a certain viewpoint regarding an idea, cause, person, or place, for it to become widely accepted. Campaigns for such causes as the Heart Fund or the Alzheimer's Society exemplify this strategy. Contemporary not-for-profit organizations are like companies that operate for a profit, in that they find it effective to develop a product mix that includes identification (e.g., logos), a package (membership cards to acknowledge contribution), and other product variables.

Price

In a not-for-profit organization, money is not necessarily the only form of exchange. Sometimes no money changes hands; instead, time or expertise is volunteered in return for the psychological satisfaction of helping others or the knowledge that society will be made better. Even if money is involved, the nature of the exchange is different from an exchange made for material profit. While long-term profit is the goal of the profit-based organization, a short-term gain is all a not-for-profit organization seeks. Special events are frequently a means of generating revenue for not-for-profit organizations.

Distribution

Because not-for-profit entities deal in intangibles, channels tend to be direct, that is, the organization tends to work directly with the donors. If intermediaries—professional fund-raisers, for example—are used, they act on behalf of the organization. They do not assume any responsibility or control.

Marketing Communications

Communications is the most visible aspect of not-for-profit marketing. Advertising and various direct response techniques, including the mail and telephone, form the nucleus of an organization's effort, particularly for fundraising programs (refer back to Figures 18.5 and 18.6). Public service announcements, a low-cost form of advertising, may be used to point out the benefits of contributing to a cause or charitable foundation.

Mass advertising plays a bigger role in people marketing. Think of all those ads you see in a federal election campaign. Their role is to create and maintain an image for a person or party. Very often, a charitable organization will use a known personality as its spokesperson. As indicated in the vignette "Celebrities Pave the Way," Michael J. Fox is a primary spokesperson for the Parkinson Foundation, a disease that afflicts him.

Personal selling is common: the Heart Fund, and many other worthwhile causes, use local residents to solicit funds door-to-door in their own neighbourhoods. Such campaigns are undertaken annually and are supported with advertising to build awareness of the fund-raising project.

Summary

The service sector in Canada is a rapidly growing segment of the economy and includes many large corporations in a cross-section of markets. Advancing technology, the use of modern marketing strategies by service companies, and the growing number of time-starved consumers have contributed to the expansion of this sector.

Services have certain characteristics that distinguish them from products. A service is intangible; it cannot be seen, heard, or touched. It is inseparable from the source of supply, since each supplier is unique, despite competitive attempts to imitate a service. The quality of a service also varies, even within a single organization, where different people perform the same service in different ways. Finally, demand for certain services is perishable; in other words, demand is uneven, in some cases seasonal, and this creates a problem for marketers of services.

Since services are intangible, their price is derived more from the value they provide consumers than from direct costs. The channels of distribution are direct, and promotional efforts are aimed directly at the final user. Service marketers do employ all elements of the marketing mix, but the main planning concern is that the firm understands exactly what it is that the customer is buying. Once it establishes what the primary service is, a firm develops a complete service mix. A service mix includes those additional elements that differentiate one service from another in the minds of consumers.

Not-for-profit marketing is used by organizations whose goals do not centre on financial gain. Such organizations operate in the best interests of the public or advocate a particular idea or cause. Not-for-profit groups have unique characteristics and different objectives. Their objectives are to promote (1) people, by fostering certain attitudes towards particular persons; (2) ideas, by gaining acceptance for a way of thinking; (3) places, by encouraging visits to a country, province, or city; and (4) organizations, by raising funds, cultivating an image, or persuading people to use the facilities. Rather than aiming for financial targets, not-for-profit bodies attempt to change attitudes. In doing so, they must consider two distinct targets: the clients who use and derive the benefits of the organization and the donors who provide the organization with resources.

A strategic marketing focus that embraces all elements of the marketing mix is now used in the not-for-profit sector so that organizations can achieve their goals.

Key Terms

advocacy advertising 511	people marketing 510
idea marketing 511	perishability of demand 501
inseparability 499	place marketing 510
intangibility 499	quality variability 501
not-for-profit marketing 505	service 499
organization marketing 510	social marketing 505

Review Questions

1. What factors have contributed to the growth of the service economy in Canada?

2. Briefly describe the basic characteristics of services.

3. How important a role do customers' attitudes play in their decisions to purchase services?

4. "A service is an attribute or series of attributes offered to consumers." What does this statement mean?

5. How is pricing a service different from pricing a tangible product? What are the different pricing strategies used in services marketing?

6. Briefly describe the various types of not-for-profit marketing.

7. Describe the basic differences between marketing for profit-oriented and not-for-profit organizations.

Discussion and Application Questions

1. If you were in the home-decorating business (painting and wallpapering), how would you convince do-it-yourselfers to use the service?

2. Review the concept of perishability of demand in the service industry. If you were in charge of marketing for the following businesses, what strategies would you recommend to overcome perishability of demand?
   a) Air Canada Centre (or any other major arena)
   b) Holiday Inn Hotels

3. Assume you are in charge of marketing for the following companies. Describe the quality of service offerings that would be given priority in order to attract and maintain customers.
   a) Air Canada
   b) Budget Rent-A-Car
   c) McDonald's
   d) Cineplex Odeon Theatres
   e) Tripeze.com

4. You are the Director of Marketing for the Toronto Blue Jays. The average attendance at games is in the 15 000 to 20 000 range in a stadium that seats about 50 000. These seats used to be filled. What do you do to resurrect interest in this troubled baseball franchise, to get people back into those seats?

E-Assignment

1. Visit the Web site for a popular hotel chain (e.g., Sheraton, Holiday Inn, Delta, or another of your choice). On the basis of the information you gather from the site, analyze the hotel's primary services in terms of the various characteristics of services: intangibility, inseparability, quality variability, and perishability of demand. What influences will these characteristics have on the marketing strategies employed by the hotel? Discuss.

2. Assume you are booking an airline flight to a popular destination in the United States. Visit the Web site for Air Canada and one of its American competitors (e.g., Delta, Continental, or American Airlines) and go through the process of finding the best price for a return trip to that destination. Evaluate the pricing strategies of the two airlines. Will your decision to pick one airline over the other be based solely on price, or will other elements of the marketing mix have an influence? Discuss.

Endnotes

1. *Dictionary of Marketing Terms*, Barron's Business Guides, 1994, p. 479.

2. www.cbc.ca/stories/2002/04/18/Consumers/travelcomplaints.

3. J. Evans and J. Berman, *Marketing*, 3rd Edition (New York: Macmillan Publishing Company, 1987), p. 623.

4. Philip Kotler, *Marketing for Nonprofit Organizations*, (Englewood Cliffs, NJ: Prentice-Hall, 1982), p. 26.

5. Carol Howes, "Still scoring in ad game," *Financial Post*, June 5, 2000, pp. C1, C14.

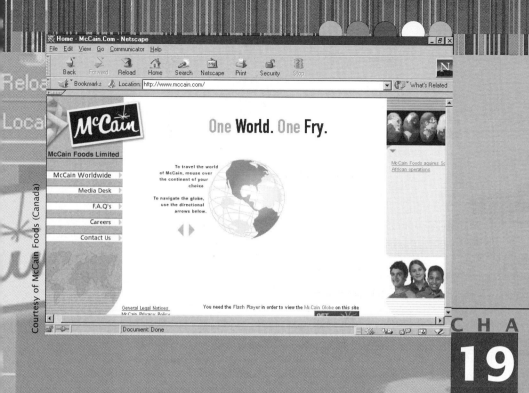

Global Marketing

After studying this chapter, you will be able to

1. Outline the importance of international trade for Canada and Canadian companies.
2. Describe the reasons why a growing number of firms are active in seeking global market opportunities.
3. Outline the factors that an organization considers when planning to enter foreign markets.
4. Describe the business strategies commonly used by firms entering foreign markets.
5. Describe the nature of marketing strategies used by firms seeking global market opportunities.

The first decade of the 21st century will be a challenging one for Canada and Canadian businesses as a new era of global marketing beckons. Domestically, many prominent companies operate in industries where growth potential is flat or marginal at best. Consequently, these companies look at expansion in foreign countries as a viable alternative for growth. Several prominent Canadian retail chains are examining opportunities in the United States, a market long seen as too competitive for Canadian companies. Among them is Montreal-based Aldo Group (seller of shoes under the Aldo, Pegabo, Simard, Calderone, Globo, Transit, and Feet First banners). Presently, the US market comprised of 120 stores generates one-third of its revenue (about $200 million annually). Aldo is looking at expansion into the Middle East, continental Europe, and Asia.[1]

The companies that will succeed will be those with the capability to standardize global manufacturing and technologies while tailoring products and services to meet local preferences. In attempting to meet this challenge, Canadian organizations will look for potential growth in four key regions: North America (through the North American Free Trade Agreement, or NAFTA); the European Union; Eastern Europe and Russia; and the Pacific Rim (China, Japan, Malaysia, Indonesia, and Thailand, among others).

Canada has many world-class marketing organizations. Nortel Networks is a world leader in telecommunications technology (95 percent of sales are outside of Canada); Seagram is a noted distiller of spirits and wine (97 percent of sales outside Canada); Bombardier is a worldwide manufacturer and exporter of aircraft and mass transit parts and vehicles (90 percent of sales outside Canada); and Alcan Aluminum (93 percent of sales outside Canada).[2]

Canadian International Trade

1.
Outline the importance of international trade for Canada and Canadian companies.

For Canada, the importance of international trade is significant. In 2000, exports to foreign countries amounted to $412 billion, while imports were $357 billion, for a positive trade balance of $55 billion. By far, Canada's largest trading partner is the United States, which accounts for 87 percent of exports and 64 percent of imports.[3]

While Canada enjoys a positive trade balance overall with our neighbour to the south, we have a negative balance with some countries. Thus, exports to the United States are an important contributor to Canada's overall positive balance. For example, Canada imports many more goods from Europe and the Far East than it exports. Refer to Figure 19.1 for statistical information on Canada's international trade position.

Canada's five leading merchandise exports are automotive products, machinery and equipment, industrial goods, forestry products, and agricultural and fishing products. In true trading fashion, Canada's leading imports are similar and include machinery and equipment, automotive products, industrial goods, consumer goods, and agricultural and fishing products. Clearly, the health of the Canadian automobile industry has a significant impact on the economy.

The World Trade Organization (WTO) governs international trade. The WTO has six basic functions: administering WTO agreements, handling trade disputes, being a forum for trade negotiations, monitoring national trade policies, providing technical assistance and training for the developing countries, and cooperation with other international organizations. Its primary objective is to ensure that trade flows as smoothly, predictably, and freely as possible between nations. At the heart of the WTO system are the basic ground-rules for international commerce. Essentially, they are contracts guaranteeing member countries important trade rights. They also bind countries to keep their trade policies within agreed upon limits, to everybody's benefit.[4]

International trade is very important to the well-being of Canada. Among the factors that show the importance of trade are the following:

World Trade Organization
www.wto.org

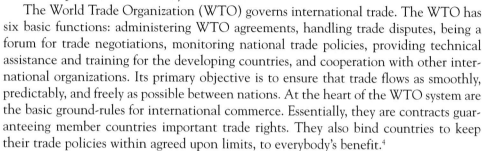

Canada's Major Trading Partners— 2001

Figure 19.1

Country	Exports $ Million	Exports %	Imports $ Million	Imports %
United States	351 085	85.0	255 087	72.8
Japan	9 363	2.3	10 585	3.0
United Kingdtom	6 454	1.5	11 830	3.4
European Countries	25 749	6.2	41 822	11.9
Other Countries	20 458	5.0	31 178	9.9
Total	**413 108**	**100.0**	**350 502**	**100.0**

European countries include members and non-members of the European Economic Community. These are the latest available statistics.

Source: Adapted from the Statistics Canada CANSIM II database <http://cansim2.statcan.ca/cgi-win/CNSMCGI.EXE>, tables 228-0001, 228-0002, and 228-0003.

1. One-quarter of our national wealth is derived from international trade.
2. One-third of our jobs depend on international trade.
3. Nine thousand new jobs result from every $1 billion of additional exports.
4. Nearly half of Canada's manufacturing output is exported.

The Movement to Global Markets

2.
Describe the reasons why a growing number of firms are active in seeking global market opportunities.

There are several reasons why companies are moving towards global marketing. First, most opportunities have been exhausted in domestic markets. Molson, for example, owns 45 percent of the Canadian beer market, a market characterized by flat growth from year to year. Molson is expanding in the United States, Brazil, and China in order to grow. Second, the formation of common markets or trading blocks has influenced how companies approach world trade. In the next decade NAFTA, which encourages open trade between Canada, the United States, and Mexico, will affect other countries and companies wanting to trade with these three nations.

European countries have combined forces to form the European Community, a trading union that features a common currency known as the Euro. This union presents challenges for North American companies wanting to trade there. Other areas of opportunity include the Pacific Rim and Eastern Europe. Presently, the Asia-Pacific region represents 60 percent of the world's population, 50 percent of the world's production, and 40 percent of the world's consumption. China and Japan are the countries that marketing organizations will be targeting.

When deciding to market in a foreign country, certain advantages must exist. These are described as absolute advantage and comparative advantage.

ABSOLUTE ADVANTAGE

absolute advantage

Absolute advantage occurs when only one country provides a good or service, or when one country produces a product, at significantly lower cost than others. Asian countries, for example, have labour rates much lower than in North America (some critics say they are so low that North American companies are simply exploiting the workers). These countries manufacture products such as toys, clothing, and electronic goods much less expensively than in North America. As a result, goods can be sold in North America at prices lower than those of similar, domestically produced products.

COMPARATIVE ADVANTAGE

comparative advantage

Comparative advantage occurs when a country can produce and market an item more efficiently or abundantly, as well as more cheaply, than other countries. Such an advantage could be based on the resources available, specialization, technology, and geography (e.g., climate). Countries attempt to exchange goods in which they have an advantage for those in which they have a disadvantage.

Canada, for example, is a market leader in forestry products because of its comparative advantage (plentiful resources) in this natural resource-based industry. Canada is also a leader in telecommunications and aerospace technology. Some Canadian companies that are international leaders in their respective fields include Nortel Networks (telecommunications), Quebecor Inc. (multimedia), Alcan Aluminum (mining and metals), and Bombardier Inc. (high-tech manufacturing).[5] Japan and the United States are leaders in technology; hence, both enjoy comparative advantage in certain markets: computers, automobiles, electronics, and aircraft.

NORTH AMERICAN FREE TRADE AGREEMENT

The North American Free Trade Agreement has been in existence since 1989. Originally, the agreement was only between Canada and the United States, but in 1992, it became a trilateral agreement when Mexico joined in. The agreement changed the competitive environment in North America and presented new opportunities for Canadian and American firms to gain competitive advantage. On the basis of trade patterns between the three countries, it is anticipated that Mexico will replace Canada as the largest trading partner with the United States.[6] In fact, Mexico will pass Canada in automobile production within the next two years. The cost of labour and manufacturing is much less in Mexico. Jobs in this industry will be lost in Canada.

North American Free Trade Agreement Secretariat
www.nafta-sec-alena.org

The open North American market has encouraged Canadian business to expand manufacturing facilities and improve the efficiency of their operations in order to supply the volume of products necessary to meet the needs of a much larger market. The elimination of tariffs presents an opportunity for companies to increase their market share. The positive trade balances that Canada has with its partners in this agreement suggest that free trade has been helpful in spurring Canada's economy. (See Figure 19.1 for data.) The agreement has encouraged American-based businesses to make further investments in their Canadian operations so that these operations can be expanded to serve the North American market.

The full implications of the North American Free Trade Agreement remain uncertain at this time. What *is* certain, however, is that Canadian and American companies will continue to rationalize operations and make decisions that will have both positive and negative effects on employment in Canada. General Motors, for example, has closed American and Canadian manufacturing facilities in favour of production in Mexico. The boom and bust cycles of the technology sector also play havoc with labour. After rapid expansion in the late 1990s (job gains due to the move into information technology), there were massive layoffs associated with the dot-com bust in 2001.

Analyzing Global Marketing Opportunities

3.
Outline the factors that an organization considers when planning to enter foreign markets.

When a firm is determining if it should enter a foreign market, it analyzes the same set of external environments as it does in the case of domestic markets. These environments are economy, culture and language, consumer behaviour, politics and legal regulations, competition, and technology.

ECONOMIC ENVIRONMENT

From nation to nation, economies vary considerably. The economic character of any country is shaped by variables that include its natural resources, population, income distribution, employment, systems of education, and by the way its goods are marketed. There are four basic types of economies: subsistence, raw material exporting, industrializing, and industrialized.[7]

1. *Subsistence Economy* A subsistence economy is based on land and agriculture and consumes most of what it produces, a circumstance that leaves the country few opportunities for trade. A number of nations in Africa and Asia are in this category.

countertrading or **bartering**

The level of literacy and technology in such countries usually is low. What is available after satisfying its own needs is generally used for countertrading or bartering. **Countertrading**, or **bartering**, is a system of exchange whereby something other than currency or credit is used as a form of payment.

2. *Raw-Material Exporting Economy* Countries with this sort of economy usually have one rich natural resource or a few natural resources that can be exported, but lack many manufacturing industries. These economies are attractive to companies that export equipment, technology, and transportation and communications expertise—all products that can be used in the extraction of the natural resource. Examples of resource-based nations include Saudi Arabia (oil), Columbia (coffee), and Cuba (sugar).

3. *Industrializing Economy* These countries have a skilled or semi-skilled work force and a growing manufacturing base. Education and technology are rising and labour rates are lower than industrialized nations. Their populations are shifting into middle and upper classes. Several Latin American countries, the Philippines, and Mexico have economies of this kind. Such countries import the goods and services needed to facilitate their industrial development.

4. *Industrialized Economy* These countries have a highly skilled work force and a strong manufacturing and technological base. They export manufactured goods, services, and investment funds. Their extremely large middle class makes them a good target for imported consumer goods. Canada, the United States, Japan, Australia, and members of the European Community are all industrialized nations.

The European Community (Austria, Belgium, Denmark, Finland, France, Germany, Greece, Ireland, Italy, Luxembourg, the Netherlands, Portugal, Spain, Sweden, and the United Kingdom of Great Britain and Northern Ireland) is now a desired target for North American goods. Comprising 290 million people, it is almost the same size as the United States. Its adoption of a single currency will allow companies selling goods between countries to devote more energy to marketing their products, as they will be freed from the headache of trying to beat exchange rates.

CONSUMER ENVIRONMENT

In assessing the consumer environment, a company will look at how culture, language, and differences in needs and motivation will affect the development of global marketing strategies. Needless to say, there are significant variations from one part of the world to another. How a company interprets these differences is another matter.

Culture

Segmenting markets on the basis of culture is important in global marketing, since the values and beliefs held by people vary from nation to nation. While businesses must think globally, they must act locally. Failing to recognize cultural differences has resulted in marketing blunders by even the biggest corporations.

It is critical that a marketer understand an audience's values, norms, and customs. These can be as obvious as avoiding certain farm animals in ads that target Muslim or Jewish communities or so subtle that only an insider would know the influences. In Japan, for instance, there is a reluctance to market anything in groups of four because the Japanese word for four, *shi*, also means death. A Chinese clothing manufacturer encountered dismal sales of an underwear line in the United States. Only after speaking to some Americans did the Chinese company learn the brand name, *Pansy*, was not ideal for male undergarments.[8]

Marketing communications strategies must be adapted to local customs and preferences if the company is to be successful in a foreign country. Benetton, a retailer known for controversial advertising, once ran a print ad in the United States showing two hands cuffed together, one white and one black. There was an immediate outcry as American people jumped to the conclusion that the photograph was one of a white man arresting a black man. The same ad in Canada received no such complaints. These brand and communications examples clearly point out the need for consumer research prior to entering a foreign country.

The challenge for marketers, however, is knowing when to adapt to local conditions and when not to. In this regard, they try to identify as many similarities as possible.

Language

Language is the most obvious barrier to a global marketing program. A product name chosen to appeal to an English-speaking market must be replaced with something that will have greater effect in non-English-speaking countries. In North America, for example, Lever markets a fabric softener under the brand name Snuggle. The brand name has connotations that Lever wanted to carry over into other markets. For this reason, the brand name has been changed to Fa Fa in Japan, and Cajoline in France. The packaging, the positioning, and the teddy bear mascot remain the same everywhere.

Very simple mistakes in judgment, however, or carelessness in checking out local interpretations of names and phrases has proven costly for many firms. Volkswagen's Vento went over well in Germany, but in Italy it had people holding their noses. To them, Vento means fart. During the summer Olympics in Sydney, Australians giggled at the Roots apparel worn by Canadian athletes. In Aussie slang, to root is to have sexual intercourse.[9] Roots would have to deal with brand name issues if it ever expands to Australia.

Needs and Motivation

Differences in consumers' needs and motivation for buying products make it difficult to establish marketing strategies that work globally. For example, Kellogg is the recognized international leader in the ready-to-eat cereal market, but it has struggled in Asia. In Asia, the concept of "cereal flakes—be it bran, oat, or corn" is not well established. Asia is a rice market. As well, Asians are more accustomed to cooked rice breakfasts; the ready-to-eat bowl of bran flakes was not what Asians needed.[10] In contrast, numerous North American fast food restaurants have been readily accepted in Far Eastern countries. Among them are McDonald's, KFC, and Pizza Hut.

The Kellogg example suggests that differences in behaviour determine how people think about products and the needs they have in relation to those products. The trick, therefore, is to give local needs priority over global needs. Tricon Global, operators of KFC, Taco Bell, and Pizza Hut do this. KFC, for example, sells tempura crispy strips in Japan and potato-and-onion croquettes in the Netherlands.[11]

Rarely can a product be positioned uniformly around the world. Perhaps the Gillette Sensor razor is one of the exceptions (see Figure 19.2). Gillette Sensor has followed a common positioning strategy that emphasizes the technical features of the product (e.g.,

Global Advertising Strategy for the Gillette Sensor Razor

Figure 19.2

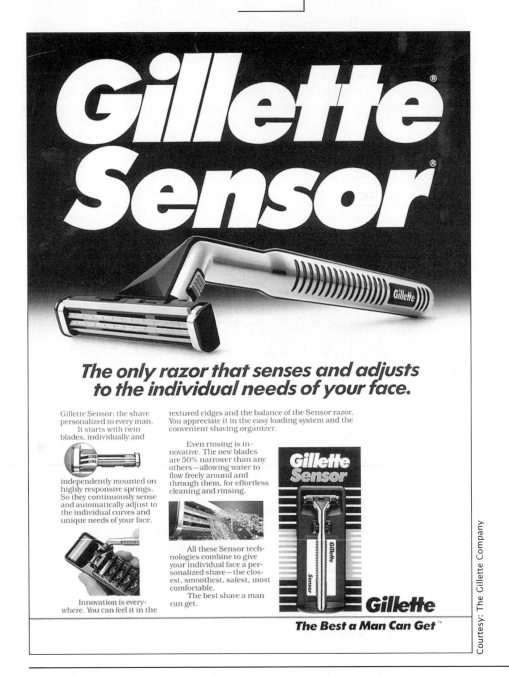

the razor senses and adjusts to the contours of an individual's face, providing a safe, comfortable shave). That should be important to men everywhere.

For additional details and idiosyncrasies about the culture, language, and needs of global consumers, see Figure 19.3.

Some Facts and Oddities About
Global Marketing

Figure 19.3

Market Segmentation

Heineken beer is positioned everywhere in the world (except Holland) as a premium-priced, high-quality brew. In its home market, it is a popular-priced brand and is perceived to be "just another beer" by beer drinkers.

Product and Package

In Britain, you can buy cold milk in cans in vending machines. Do you think that canned milk (other than evaporated milk) would sell in Canada?

Psychographics and Demographics

In most countries, psychographic analysis can be more revealing than demographics. Lifestyle-based research provides valuable insights into target market opportunities. For example, Volvo designed a small, sporty coupe, specifically for the European career woman. Is Canada ready for a sporty Volvo? Is this your image of Volvo?

Quality, Quality, and More Quality

Consumers around the world rate goods made in Japan, Germany, and the United States tops in quality, in that order. Canada ranks sixth behind both France and Britain. The poll among 20 000 consumers suggests the existence of "nation equity" or the perceived quality that countries' goods enjoy. (Source: Gallup Worldwide Poll, 1994)

Making Generalizations

Marketers cannot generalize about the Asia-Pacific region. Even within a country, consumers are not alike. In China, there are 60 different ethnic groups and 300 different dialects spoken. The northern Chinese tend to be taller and have long faces. Southern Chinese tend to be shorter and have rounder, fuller faces.

Know Your Customer

Doing business in China revolves around personal relationships. Getting to know your customer means getting to know them personally. Without a personal relationship, there is no business relationship.

POLITICAL ENVIRONMENT

The political environment in foreign countries can shape trading policy and have a dramatic impact on a company's profitability. For example, a change in government could alter how a North American company operates in a foreign country. Such was the case for Coca-Cola in India in the late 1970s. A new government ordered Coca-Cola to dilute its investment in its Indian subsidiary and to turn over its secret formula. It was unthinkable that Coke would reveal its formula! Coke pulled up its stakes and quit India. One of its Indian bottlers then developed a cola-type product and called it Thums Up. It caught on immediately and became the leading seller in India.

In 1993, when the Indian government liberalized its economy and encouraged foreign investment, Coke returned and gained a commanding lead in the market by buying up Thums Up. Coca-Cola was re-introduced in India as well, but Thums Up outsells it by a four to one margin.[12] Coke has tried everything to re-establish itself in India but realizes that a generation of consumers has grown up without the product. It could be said that politics destroyed the Coca-Cola brand in India.

Trade Barriers

trade barrier

The purpose of a **trade barrier** is to protect a country from too much foreign competition within its borders. Canada and the United States, for example, believe that the automobile industry needs some form of protection. Consequently, only so many foreign-produced cars are allowed into these countries each year. Such a belief protects employment domestically. **Protectionism** is a belief that foreign trade should be restricted so that domestic industries can be preserved. The World Trade Organization (WTO) disagrees with North America's view on protectionism as it applies to the automobile industry. Several cases are presently before international courts.

protectionism

Even Canada and the United States have their trade disagreements in spite of the free trade agreement. The dispute between the two nations regarding Canadian softwood lumber shipments is a good example. Believing that Canadian government subsidies have lowered the price of our lumber below that of the United States, the US government imposed a tariff (27.2 percent) on our exports to the US. Says Prime Minister Jean Chrétien about the dispute, "If we're in a free trade agreement, we have to be free traders."[13] He has a point!

To restrict trade, governments use tariffs, quotas, embargoes, and local content laws.

tariff

A **tariff** is a tax or duty imposed on imported goods. In Canada, prices for domestically produced goods and services tend to be high, due to the high costs of labour, raw materials, and parts. In comparison, goods from Asian countries in such markets as toys, clothing, and electronics are produced at a much lower cost. To balance the price differences between imported and domestic products in these industries, Canada imposes a tariff on incoming foreign goods. The advantage of a tariff is that it can be specific in nature and protect particular industries, when needed (for example, see the Canada-US dispute about software lumber described above).

quota

A **quota** is a specific limit on the amount of goods that may be imported into a country. In Canada, precise quotas are placed on Japanese automobiles each year to restrict their penetration of the domestic market. In the late 1980s, several Japanese producers built Canadian production facilities as a means of circumventing quotas. Canada reacted and introduced local content laws. A **local content law** is another way of protecting local industry and employment. In this case, a foreign-based manufacturer is required to use a specified amount of locally produced components (car parts). Such a law could spur employment in the domestic auto parts industry.

local content law

An **embargo** disallows entry of specified products into a country. Concerns related to politics, health, and morality are frequently cited as the reasons for imposing embargoes. Canada Customs is responsible for screening various products—pharmaceutical, chemical, food, and many others—as they enter the country. Products that do not meet standards are rejected. For example, toys from abroad that do not meet Canadian safety standards are rejected at the border.

Some items are placed under an embargo because the majority of the population or its government finds them morally objectionable. The Canadian government does not allow the entry of sexually explicit materials, for example, though what is acceptable and unacceptable is often the focus of debate among citizens and governments.

Non-governmental organizations and groups can also impose embargoes in the form of a boycott. A **boycott** is an organized refusal to buy a specific product. The Body Shop became the first business to back a consumer boycott of Esso stations in the UK, pledging to distribute leaflets in its stores and banning its fleet of trucks from filling up at Esso stations. The boycott was originally launched by an alliance of green groups including Greenpeace and Friends of the Earth. These groups claim Exxon Mobil (Esso's parent company) has been instrumental in helping to derail the Kyoto Protocol by funding organizations like the Global Climate Coalition. They also claim the company hasn't spent a cent on renewable energy resources in recent years. In short, they claim Exxon Mobil is not a good corporate citizen.[14]

boycott

The Body Shop
www.bodyshop.
com
Exxon Mobil
www.exxon.com

LEGAL AND REGULATORY ENVIRONMENT

Marketing organizations must know what they can and cannot do with a product in a foreign country. Awareness of local laws and regulations for packaging and advertising is crucial. In the Middle East, for example, advertisements can only show the product; in Austria, children cannot be used in advertisements.

Canada and the United States have their own idiosyncrasies that foreign marketers must deal with or that apply when the two countries are trading with each other. For instance, packaging in Canada must be bilingual. A firm manufacturing in the United States must develop separate packaging if it wishes to pursue the Canadian market. Canadian food companies must have separate packaging if they sell their products in the United States. The regulations that govern ingredient lists and nutritional guides vary in each country. Marketing a product over the border in either direction is not as easy as simply shipping a product across the border.

TECHNOLOGICAL ENVIRONMENT

The technological environment in a country is influenced by the type of economy it has. For instance, a company that plans to organize a technologically based manufacturing operation in a non-industrialized country must do so with caution, for the available work force may not have the education and skills required to run it. The foreign firm may have to commit to extensive training and development, which adds to the cost of operations. When the Japanese and South Korean automobile manufacturers built facilities in Canada, they had to deal with this situation to a certain extent. While Canada was knowledgeable in automobile manufacturing and its labour force was skilled, the foreign firms had to educate their Canadian employees in their management style and their way of doing business. Such integration of Canadian and foreign influence allowed the foreign organization to learn about Canadian culture, trade, consumers, and ways of doing business.

Of concern to Canadian companies is the increasing sophistication of technology, the speed at which technology is developed, and the fact that new technology, like competition, can originate from many places. Technology advancements in the Far East tend to be ahead of North America, so these countries will have a significant impact on Canada as we move further into the 21st century. To illustrate, a large majority of

Japanese consumers presently use hand-held personal digital assistants (multi-purpose devices) whereas Canadians and Americans are only at the infancy stage with this technology. Japan is well ahead of North America in moving to a wireless communications world.

COMPETITIVE ENVIRONMENT

Firms that market globally are aware of the developments that affect the global economy generally. These influences include cartels, orderly market agreements, and common markets.

cartel

Organization Of Petroleum Exporting Countries
www.opec.org

A **cartel** is a group of firms or countries that band together to conduct trade in a manner similar to a monopoly. The purpose of a cartel is to improve the bargaining position of its members in the world market. One of the world's most influential cartels in recent times is the Organization of Petroleum Exporting Countries (OPEC), which comprises 13 oil-producing nations from around the world. OPEC countries can restrict the supply of oil, a resource that is in high demand in other nations, thereby forcing the price up. The higher prices affect the economy of an importing country because any increase in oil price is added to the cost of manufacturing in that country. This means that consumers ultimately pay more for the products they purchase.

orderly market agreement

An **orderly market agreement** is an agreement by which nations share a market, eliminating the trade barriers between them. The free trade agreement between Canada, the United States, and Mexico (NAFTA) is an example of an orderly market agreement because it allows the markets to become open to industries on both sides of the border.

common market

A **common market** is a regional or geographical group of countries that agree to limit trade barriers among its members and apply a common tariff to goods from non-member countries. The European Union referred to earlier in this chapter is an example of a common market. Gradually, the trade barriers that had existed between its members were removed and all countries have agreed to a common currency—the Euro. New marketing strategies will be needed for Canadian companies wanting to do business in this region.

Strategies for Entering Global Markets

4.
Describe the business strategies commonly used by firms entering foreign markets.

Companies pursuing international opportunities must decide how to enter the various markets. Some of the strategies for doing so include direct investments and acquisitions, joint ventures, and exports (Figure 19.4).

DIRECT INVESTMENT AND ACQUISITIONS

direct investment

Direct investment refers to a company's financial commitment in a foreign country whereby the investing company owns and operates, in whole or in part, the manufacturing or retailing facility in that foreign country.

Wal-Mart's global expansion has been largely based on direct investment. In Canada, it purchased Woolco and reconfigured all stores to the Wal-Mart format (Wal-Mart is now the undisputed leading department store in Canada); in Britain it purchased Asda Group PLC, a leading supermarket chain; and more recently it purchased a two-thirds interest in Seiya, a leading Japanese department store retailer. This acquisition gives Wal-Mart access to the world's second-richest consumer market. Both Seiya and Wal-Mart brands will be available in the stores, a practice Wal-Mart followed with its Asda acquisition in Britain.[15] Wal-Mart is presently the largest company in the world with revenues of $218-billion US and counting.

Strategies for Entering Global Markets

Figure 19.4

Risk, commitment, and control increase as a marketing organization moves from simply exporting goods to a foreign country to actually manufacturing the goods in a foreign country.

Molson Inc., now a pure brewing player since it sold the Montreal Canadiens and the Molson Centre, recently acquired two brewing interests in Brazil. The initial acquisition involved the Bavaria brand that controlled about five percent of the market. That was followed with the acquisition of Kaiser beer. Brazil is the fourth largest beer market in the world and these acquisitions immediately made Molson the second largest brewer in Brazil.[16]

Acquisition strategies allow a firm quick entry into a foreign market. As well, a company will avoid the cost of developing new products and the need to invest heavily in marketing to create an awareness of new products in that country.

JOINT VENTURES

joint venture

In a global context, a **joint venture** is a partnership between a domestic company and a foreign company. Such an arrangement allows a company to produce and market in a foreign country at a lower cost and with less risk to itself than would be the case if it undertook a venture on its own. Even the largest of companies are pursuing joint ventures to reduce the costs of expansion. The partnership of General Motors and Toyota, producing small cars in a California production facility, is an instance of a joint venture between two large multinational corporations. The foreign partner, in this case Toyota, can take advantage of the domestic company's knowledge of the country's culture, lifestyles, and business practices.

On the cost side of the marketing equation, companies in related industries are forming consortiums as a means of slashing purchasing costs. One recently formed consortium includes the global organizations Nortel Networks, IBM, Toshiba, Hitachi, Matsushita, LG Electronics, Seagate Technology, and Solectron. The online procurement site called e2open.com allows participants to buy and sell such equipment as semiconductors and displays among themselves.[17] The launch of this site suggests the electronics and communications industries are changing the ways they do business.

Relationship marketing practices are playing a key role on the road to growth and development for companies such as these.

Coca-Cola recently struck an agreement with Nestlé SA to jointly develop and market coffees and teas. Coke will also join forces with Walt Disney Co. to market children's beverages around the world, a move that fits Coke's aim of moving actively beyond fizzy drinks and Disney's aim to extend its brand more strongly into areas such as food and beverage.[18]

Other options for shared enterprises are licensing, franchising, and contract manufacturing.

Licensing

Licensing is the granting of a temporary agreement allowing a company (the licensee) to use the trademark, patent, copyright, or manufacturing process of another company (the licenser). In this type of agreement, the licensee assumes most of the financial risk. In return for the license, the source company is paid a royalty. Designer-clothing firms use this strategy to gain access to foreign markets. Firms such as Levi Strauss, Ralph Lauren, and Calvin Klein license their products in many countries. While the investment risk is minimal for licensers that adopt this strategy, they lack control over local operations. Sometimes the lack of control poses problems for the owner of the brand. Often issues arise regarding how the brand is marketed by the licensee.

International Franchising

International franchising is the same as domestic market franchising, except that it is done in other countries. Major fast food chains, such as McDonald's, Burger King, and Wendy's, have franchise networks in many nations. In many cases, the products have to be adapted to conform to local tastes if the company is to be successful. In other cases, the consumers in foreign countries gradually accept the taste of the original food. The Asian market is poised to be the next mecca for North American franchise operations. Tricon Global Restaurants, the company that owns KFC, Pizza Hut, and Taco Bell, is actively pursuing opportunities in the Far East.

For insight into how a Calgary-based bakery expanded into Asia, read the Marketing in Action vignette **Cinnzeo Heads East, Far East**.

Contract Manufacturing

Contract manufacturing occurs when a manufacturer stops producing a good domestically, preferring to find a foreign country that can produce the good according to its specifications. Typically, the original firm will seek a nation where labour and raw material costs are lower. In most cases, such initiatives are taken because the costs of manufacturing in the domestic country are too high. Even though the good is produced elsewhere, the same brand name appears on the product. Nike, for example, is a prominent American company that produces its goods in the Far East. Often accused of sweatshop production practices, Nike has had to defend its position on where and how goods are produced via public relations programs.

The contract manufacturing option saves the company money. It avoids any direct investment in the producing nation, while capitalizing on, for example, its low labour rates.

Marketing in Action

Cinnzeo Heads East, Far East

The likelihood of a Calgary-based bakery becoming an International franchise operation seems improbable if not impossible. But that's just what happened to Cinnaroll Bakeries Ltd., a company that operates 25 Cinnzeo outlets in Western Canada. The product: fresh-baked cinnamon buns.

Currently, Cinnzeo has 10 franchises in the Philippines with 30 more to open before the end of 2002. There are plans for 50 more in Southeast Asia. How did it all happen?

Co-owners Barry Latham and Barry Wolton owned 18 franchises of another chain called Cinnabon. Seeing significant potential in terms of expansion, they sold out and opened their own chain called Cinnzeo. Once established in the West, the plan was to gradually move eastward, in Canada, that is.

Out of the blue came a letter from a group of Filipino businessmen who had seen a franchise in Vancouver. So impressed were they with what they saw, they wanted the franchise rights for the Philippines. Skeptical at fist, the two Barrys trekked east and soon discovered a country of 68 million people with the world's largest middle class—an opportunity they couldn't pass up. Other franchise food businesses were flourishing there. In fact another Canadian bakery, Saint Cinnamons, was already there.

In negotiating a franchise deal, the Filipino partners wanted a different look for the stores. In Canada the indoor mall locations called for a small, functional design and a rather spartan look. In the Philippines it would be street-front locations, a Starbuck's café environment, and a design and look that would include comfortable seating and piped-in music. The product would remain the same.

Today, Cinnzeo is the leading cinnamon bun maker in the Philippines. Latham credits its strategy of "adapting its franchise to local market needs" for its success. In terms of marketing, they haven't done much—they have relied on word-of-mouth and its Web site. The company Web site is linked to dozens of franchise-related sites.

Working with other Asian partners, Cinnzeo now has plans for franchises in China, Singapore, Brunei, Hong Kong, Thailand, and Malaysia. Franchise inquiries are coming from all over the world—a sure sign of success!

Adapted from Norma Ramage, "Canadian cinnamon buns savoured in Asia," *Marketing*, May 15, 2001, p. 6.

Courtesy: Cinnaroll Bakeries Limited

INDIRECT AND DIRECT EXPORTING

indirect exporting

There are two forms of exporting available to a company: direct and indirect. The difference is in the distribution strategy each form entails. A company using **indirect exporting** employs an intermediary or trading company that specializes in international marketing to establish a distribution system for its goods in the foreign country. Generally, the intermediary works for a commission. In terms of control, the foreign company has very little. This is usually an attractive option for firms that are new to the global market scene.

direct exporting

A company using **direct exporting** usually strikes agreements directly with local market companies, which would be responsible for distribution in that country. Basically, the company itself performs the role of the intermediary. An export division or export sales force often becomes part of an organization's structure and is responsible for developing the distribution network. The foreign company faces a greater risk than does a company pursuing indirect exporting, but it has greater control over the distribution process.

Global Marketing Strategy

5.
Describe the nature of marketing strategies used by firms seeking global market opportunities.

Does a firm develop specific strategies for each country, or does it use a common strategy in all countries where its products are available? In the past, the tendency was to specialize by giving consideration to the unique characteristics and tendencies of local markets. Then, in the 1980s and 1990s, there was a movement towards the use of global marketing strategies, a trend that is expected to continue.

global marketing strategy

In its purest sense, **global marketing strategy** is taking one brand and marketing it exactly the same way around the world. The growing popularity of global marketing strategies suggests that advancing technology in communications and distribution has created markets for standardized products; everyone everywhere wants the same things. The global approach enables a company to enjoy economies of scale in production and marketing expenditures, particularly in the areas of advertising, distribution, and management. BMW (luxury automobiles), and Nike (sporting goods and accessories), for example, are global brands because they stand for the same things in every country.

country-centred strategy

If a firm uses a **country-centred strategy**, it develops a unique marketing strategy for each foreign market it enters. It does so because of the unique needs, values, and beliefs of consumers in that market. Such an approach does add to the marketing costs of an organization.

glocalization

A more common practice is referred to as **glocalization**—the creation of products and services intended for the global market but customized to suit a local culture. In other words, it does not completely use one marketing strategy or the other. McDonald's has been a leader in glocalization in its quest to conquer the fast food world. Once the advocate of standardization, McDonald's now allows for local autonomy. The name and the arches remain but in France they serve wine, in India they serve lamb, and in South Korea they serve kimchi (cabbage-based) burgers. Coca-Cola's formula is a secret but there are about a dozen versions of it around the world. Did you know that the Canadian formula is seven calories sweeter than the US version?[19]

When determining which strategy to use, answers are required for three basic questions:

1. How does market development differ from one country to another?

2. Do the needs of consumers vary from country to country?

3. Are the characteristics of the target market profile different?

The Kellogg's experience with bran flakes serves as an example to show the importance of these questions. Kellogg's attempt to market bran flakes in Asia was a futile one because the customer expects to have rice-based products for breakfast. As well, hot cereal is preferred over cold cereal. Kellogg had not considered the needs and values of the Chinese market.

In contrast, Starbucks has been a huge success in Asia—it has 250 stores in 10 countries—countries that, traditionally, are better known for tea drinking. The Starbucks' brand carries a cachet of wealth, success, and status that is attractive to an emerging Asian middle class willing to pay a premium price for a cup of coffee. The chain's chic interiors and sturdy wooden tables—the decor is nearly identical to that in North America—is a sharp contrast to familiar tea stalls and smoky cafés.[20]

The Marketing in Action vignette **Four Seasons Hotels: A Canadian Global Success Story** provides insights into how a luxury hotel markets itself around the world.

PRODUCT

When it comes to global product strategy, a company has three options: to market a standardized product in all markets, to adapt the product to suit local markets, or to develop a new product.

Using *standardized products* in all markets can be a successful strategy. Polaroid cameras (the film-developing process is uniform) and John Deere farm equipment (farm equipment is farm equipment) are examples of successfully marketed standardized products.

Adapting a product to local tastes and preferences is common in the fast food industry. Different ingredients may be used to make a fairly uniform product more attractive to local customers. Fast food companies alter their products somewhat, since taste preferences vary from country to country. Manchu WOK, a Canadian-based food retailer, operates 103 restaurants in US malls and 84 in Canada. According to Julie Brennen, marketing manager at Manchu WOK, "Our three required combo meals are different from the US to Canada. We make allowances for different tastes from region to region. In Florida, seafood dishes wouldn't do, because they can't get seafood fresh."[21]

The final alternative, *developing a new product,* is the most costly. A company only employs such a strategy when its market analysis indicates the existence of a sizable market opportunity. This strategy presents a high degree of risk because the company may not fully understand the needs and customs of the local market in different countries. The assistance of local marketing consultants is essential to ensure that development heads in the right direction.

In the packaged goods arena the cost of building a brand is very high, so the value of an existing brand name is important. If a brand can be extended to foreign markets, the development and marketing costs are spread over a larger market. Strong brands should be used in as many markets as possible, and weak brands should be replaced if a stronger name is available. In Canada, for example, PepsiCo recently eliminated the Hostess potato chip brand in favour of its Frito-Lay brand name, one that is popular in the United States and other countries. Procter & Gamble eliminated the Canadian brand name Royale (paper products) in Canada in favour of Charmin (toilet paper) and Puffs (paper towels), both prominent brand names in the US.[22] For more insight into what constitutes a truly global brand name refer to Figure 19.5.

PRICE

McCain Foods Limited
www.mccain.com

dumping

Among the factors affecting price are local competition, dumping, tariffs, and the value of currency. McCain Foods Limited of Florenceville, New Brunswick, the world's biggest producer of frozen french fries, found that it had to lower prices in order to penetrate the American market. The sheer size and reputation of McCain's meant nothing to food service customers.

Dumping is the practice of selling goods in a foreign market at a price lower than they are sold for in the domestic market. Used as a means of penetrating foreign markets, it is judged by most countries to be an unfair practice, since it can undermine

Marketing in Action

Four Seasons Hotels: A Canadian Global Success Story

Provide personalized service, charge a premium price, offer only exclusive locations, and keep communication with customers low key and informative. Sounds simple, but that's the Four Seasons formula for success.

It's hardly surprising that foreigners question the origin of the Four Seasons since Canada is not known as a source of luxury leadership. But make no mistake about it—Four Seasons has grown to become the world's largest provider of upscale lodging for the rich and famous. Here's what the *Gallivanter's Guide* says about Four Seasons: "Celebrities like it when Four Seasons treats them as ordinary people, and ordinary people like it when Four Seasons treats them like celebrities." Tom Cruise stayed at Four Seasons in Toronto while promoting his movie *Vanilla Sky*.

Product-wise, Four Seasons is about personalized service—good service is a cornerstone belief of founder Isadore Sharp. Sharp's goal was to create a group of medium-sized hotels with exceptional quality; he certainly succeeded. The brand today stands for luxury by offering consistently exclusive services regardless of location around the world.

Consistency has enabled Four Seasons to become the world's largest hotel brand. From small beginnings, the company now operates 56 hotels in 25 countries and there are 20 new properties currently in development stages in choice locations around the world. How good are they? In last year's Readers' Choice Awards issue of *Condé Nast Traveler* magazine, five of the world's top ten hotels were Four Seasons locations. The customers are quite happy!

The company's marketing communications programs solidly support the brand. Advertising for a particular location matches the actual experience the guest receives. There are no surprises, just elegant luxury. Four Seasons is focused on making its guests feel comfortable in the environment they happen to be in, whether it's for business or leisure.

Distribution decisions have played a key role in success. Years ago Four Seasons decided to look overseas for opportunity. It had reached a peak in terms of major market coverage in North America and didn't want to get into secondary markets where room rates would be lower. Concerned that lower prices would harm the image Four Seasons had established, the decision to go overseas made perfect business sense.

To build overseas requires investment from local investors and given Four Seasons reputation, money is not hard to come by. According to Osman Berkman, chairman of the investment company that owns the Four Seasons Hotel Istanbul, "Four Seasons is the best-known hotel chain in the world. They sell rooms at higher rates than other comparable hotels."

On the issue of price, they never drop it. Even in the post 9/11 era when they and all other hotels were suffering low occupancy rates due to reduced business travel by companies, Four Seasons kept their prices high. Competitors like the Ritz-Carlton slashed room rates to acquire business. Four Seasons refused to engage in a price war. According to Susan Helstab, vice-president of marketing, "It's important to protect market share, but not by discounting the product or by compromising the level of service."

Analysts applauded such a strategy for its forward thinking. "They are sacrificing volume to protect their brand. When the business travellers do return, Four Seasons will be firmly positioned to serve them while others will have a difficult time raising their prices."

Adapted from Chris Daniels, "A room for all seasons," *Marketing*, February 4, 2002, pp. 6, 7; and Elena Cherney, "Four Seasons dreams of faraway places," *Globe and Mail*, October 30, 2000, p. B7.

Courtesy: Four Seasons Hotels and Resorts

Characteristics of Truly Global Brands

Figure 19.5

THE GLOBAL BRAND SCOREBOARD—TOP 10 BRANDS

Rank and Brand	2001 Brand Value US$ billions	Country of Ownership
1. Coca-Cola	$68.95	U.S.
2. Microsoft	$65.07	U.S.
3. IBM	$52.75	U.S.
4. GE	$42.40	U.S.
5. Nokia	$35.04	Finland
6. Intel	$34.67	U.S.
7. Disney	$32.59	U.S.
8. Ford	$30.09	U.S.
9. McDonald's	$25.29	U.S.
10. AT&T	$22.83	U.S.

The characteristics of a great global brand are many. Here are a few of the key characteristics. A strong global brand

- has leadership at home
- is associated with its country of origin
- has a compelling platform that propels it beyond domestic borders
- is ever-renewing and is tailored to local markets
- is obsessed with innovation
- makes money

Source: Adapted from Jeffrey Swystun, "Canada's reticent brands," *Marketing*, September 17, 2001, pp. 15, 17.

domestic companies and the work force they employ. To protect themselves against such undermining and to maintain a reasonable level of competition between foreign and domestic marketers, countries impose tariffs (see earlier discussion).

The value of the Canadian dollar in relation to foreign currencies also has an impact on the level of demand for Canadian goods. When its value is low in relation to the American dollar, the prices for our goods are more attractive to American buyers; therefore, demand for Canadian goods increases, and exports to the United States increase. Conversely, if the Canadian dollar rises in relation to the American dollar, the prices of our goods are less attractive than those of American products or other foreign products; therefore, demand for Canadian goods decreases. The present value of the Canadian dollar in relation to the American dollar has a significant impact on our positive trade balance with the United States.

Mars Inc. used a unique pricing strategy when it entered the Russian market. The disintegration of the Soviet Union threw open a vast Russian market hungry for consumer goods. Without government subsidies, Russian factories sat idle, and there was no production of chocolate at all. Despite a volatile political landscape, Mars forged ahead into Russia with Mars Bars, Milky Way, and Snickers. While many Western companies offer goods only for hard currency, Mars sold its products for rubles. Each bar cost about 300 rubles (30 cents US). For Russians, they were among the most affordable Western status symbols.

MARKETING COMMUNICATIONS

While a product may be suited for worldwide distribution, it is very difficult to promote it in a uniform manner everywhere. In similar markets, such as the Canadian and American markets, a uniform promotion can be successfully implemented, but regional differences will often dictate that alternative strategies be used. Since organizations like to protect their brand image, it is common for standard communications to be made available for foreign markets. Manchu WOK, referred to earlier in the product section, provides bus shelter, and mall posters, and coupons for newspapers and flyers to all of its franchisees in the US. Generic artwork is provided but the franchisee can customize their header, food combo, and price. Unique local material will also be provided if the franchisee requests it.[23]

On a more worldly scale, marketing communications is not that simple. Because of the differences in language and culture around the world, companies often adapt a communications strategy to meet local tastes. Standardized advertising is only effective if consumers think, act, and buy in the same manner.

Language poses the main challenge to global advertising. When KFC entered China it wanted to use the famous slogan "Finger-lickin' good. When translated to Chinese it read as "So good you will eat your fingers off." Ouch! Perdue Chickens, entering the Mexican market, attempted to translate the phrase "It takes a tough man to make a tender chicken." The result: "It takes a virile man to make a chicken aroused." So much for that idea![24]

The Parker pen ad in Figure 19.6 illustrates global marketing communications strategy. Gillette's Parker brand ads stress functional craftsmanship with product close-ups and the tagline, "A Parker Is In The Details." According to Gillette, this strategy has universal appeal. North America only represents 20 percent of Parker sales, so success in this global communications strategy is crucial to the brand's success.[25]

Today, there is a movement towards globalization in the advertising industry, since most large advertising firms now have offices or subsidiaries around the world to help multinational clients adapt their advertising to local ways. Appropriateness is the key element of the global advertising equation.

DISTRIBUTION

Firms generally secure distribution in international markets in two ways. They either use existing channels employing middlemen, or they introduce new channels; their choice depends on the needs of the marketing organization. If it chooses existing channels, a firm may employ a trading company in the home country, making it responsible for distributing goods to other distributors and to final users in the foreign country. Wal-Mart's expansion into Hong Kong, China, and Japan would not have happened had it not formed a partnership agreement with a trading company in Hong Kong and existing department stores in China and Japan.

A company may also decide to use a specialized sales force of its own that sells directly to existing foreign-market agents, distributors, or final users (Figure 19.7). On the

Figure 19.6

Global Advertising Strategy: The Functional Craftsmanship of a Parker Pen Appeals to a Global Audience

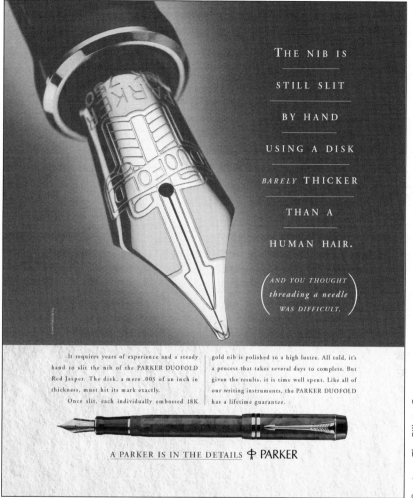

THE NIB IS STILL SLIT BY HAND USING A DISK *BARELY* THICKER THAN A HUMAN HAIR.

(AND YOU THOUGHT threading a needle WAS DIFFICULT.)

It requires years of experience and a steady hand to slit the nib of the PARKER DUOFOLD Red Jasper. The disk, a mere .005 of an inch in thickness, must hit its mark exactly.

Once slit, each individually embossed 18K gold nib is polished to a high lustre. All told, it's a process that takes several days to complete. But given the results, it is time well spent. Like all of our writing instruments, the PARKER DUOFOLD has a lifetime guarantee.

A PARKER IS IN THE DETAILS ✿ PARKER

other hand, new channels of distribution can be developed. To illustrate, two North American fast food outlets, McDonald's and KFC, have successfully extended their distribution strategies into the European and Asian markets. The acceptance of superstores (stores selling groceries and general merchandise under one roof) in the United States and Canada is an example of European distribution systems working in North America.

Since shipping overseas involves water transportation, the port facilities of foreign-market destinations are an important consideration in distribution planning. For instance, some ports are unequipped to load and unload containerized ships, a circumstance that makes water transportation impractical for some countries. Distribution capabilities must be evaluated when a company is considering marketing products in other countries.

Global Distribution Channels

Figure 19.7

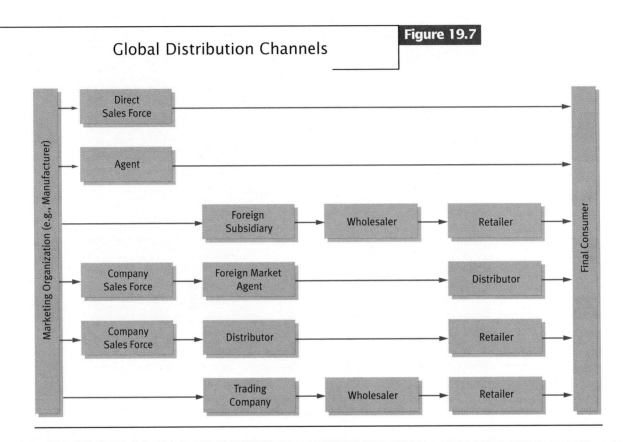

Summary

As Canada and Canadian businesses move into the next century, more and more emphasis will be placed on regional marketing and global marketing. Such factors as the North American Free Trade Agreement, the European Union, and the development in Pacific Rim countries represent new challenges for Canadian marketing organizations.

To analyze global market opportunities, a marketing organization considers a host of factors, including the economy, culture, language barriers, varying consumer needs, politics, laws and regulations, technology, and competition in countries where potential markets exist. Before entering a foreign market, a firm must understand that market if it is to develop appropriate marketing strategies for penetrating it.

Several options are available to a firm that is going into an international market. Among the more common strategies are direct investment and acquisition, and such joint ventures as partnerships, licensing agreements, franchising, and contract manufacturing. Exporting goods indirectly through middlemen or directly by the company are other options.

As it does in domestic marketing, a company that is developing a marketing strategy for a foreign market employs the elements of the marketing mix: product, price, marketing communications, and distribution. The company can either use a global strategy, that is, a standardized product is marketed in a uniform manner in all markets where it is available, or a country-centred strategy, in which case the marketing mix is tailored to the specific needs of individual countries. Often, a firm combines the best elements of both and implements a strategy referred to as glocalization.

Key Terms

absolute advantage 520
— boycott 527
— cartel 528 – diamonds.
common market 528
comparative advantage 520
— contract manufacturing 530
countertrading (bartering) 522
country-centred strategy 532
direct exporting 532
direct investment 528
— dumping 535
— embargo 526

global marketing strategy 532
glocalization 532
indirect exporting 532
joint venture 529
licensing 530
local content law 526
orderly market agreement 528
— protectionism 526
— quota 526
— tariff 526
— trade barrier 526

Review Questions

1. What is the difference between an absolute advantage and a comparative advantage?

2. How does knowledge of a nation's stage of economic development assist a global marketer?

3. Why do countries impose trade barriers?

4. What is the difference between the following trade barriers?

   a) Tariff

   b) Quota

   c) Embargo

5. What is the difference between a cartel and an orderly market agreement?

6. What is a joint venture, and what benefits does it provide participants?

7. Distinguish between licensing and contract manufacturing as strategies for pursuing global market opportunities.

8. What is the difference between a global marketing strategy and a country-centred marketing strategy?

9. What does glocalization refer to? Briefly explain.

Discussion and Application Questions

1. "Because of the cultural differences that exist from nation to nation, marketing communications strategies must be tailored to each country." Discuss the validity of this statement.

2. Are Canadian corporations likely targets for takeover by foreign-based companies? Conduct some secondary research about acquisition strategies by foreign companies prior to reaching any conclusions. Present your views on this statement.

3. If you were marketing a soft drink, such as Pepsi-Cola or 7-Up, in Latin America, what factors would you consider when developing a marketing strategy?

E-Assignment

In this exercise, you will conduct a Web-based secondary investigation to determine the market potential of entering a foreign country.

Situation: You are the brand manager for a specific product (conduct some research and pick one) at one of the following Canadian companies:

McCain Foods
Roots
Maple Leaf Foods

Your first task is to identify relevant aspects of the marketing strategy used in Canada. In other words, develop a brief profile for product strategy, price strategy, marketing communications strategy, and distribution strategy. Also identify what the primary target market is.

The second task is to conduct appropriate secondary research to assess the potential of marketing your product in a foreign country (a country of your choice). You must identify the challenges and opportunities that exist and then identify relevant factors that will influence your marketing strategy. What elements of the Canadian marketing strategy will be retained, and what elements will have to change? Present your findings in a brief report.

Endnotes

1. Danny Kucharsky, "Aldo Steps Out," *Marketing*, January 21, 2001, p. 7.

2. "Canada's 500 largest corporations," *National Post Business*, June 2001, p. 112.

3. "Top 10 country exports from Canada/imports to Canada," *National Post Business*, August 2001, p. 38.

4. www.wto.org/wto/inbrief.

5. *National Post Business*, June 2001, p. 112.

6. "Mexico eyes No. 1 trade spot with US," *Globe and Mail*, May 29, 2000, p. B3.

7. Philip Kotler, Gordon McDougal, and Gary Armstrong, *Marketing*, Canadian Edition (Toronto: Prentice-Hall Canada Inc., 1988), p. 424.

8. Wendy Cuthbert, "No-go marketing," *Financial Post*, February 5, 2001, p. C12.

9. John Heinzl, "Brand names that can't cross the border," *Globe and Mail*, December 22, 2000, p. B12.

10. "Navigating the global route," *Marketing*, April 6, 1992, pp. 1, 3.

11. "Building a global brand," *Marketing*, December 31, 2001, p. 30.

12. Nikhil Deogun and Jonathan Karp, "Coke gives Thums Up to Indian version of cola," *Ottawa Citizen*, April 30, 1998, p. C6.

13. Allan Freeman and Steven Chase, "PM tells Bush Canada is tired of tariffs," *Globe and Mail*, May 29, 2002, p. B4.

14. Stefano Ambrogi, "Body Shop's boycott support rubs Esso wrong way," *Financial Post*, July 5, 2001, p. C12.

15. Yuri, Kageyama, "Wal-Mart goes to Japan," *Toronto Star*, May 24, 2002, p. E6.

16. Claudia Penteado, "The Kaiser role," *AdAgeglobal*, April 2002, p. 8.

17. Danile McHardie and Lawrence Surtees, "Nortel joins online market," *The Globe and Mail*, June 12, 2000, p. B1.

18. Betsy Mckay, "Coke determined to think local," *Globe and Mail*, March 1, 2001, p. B12.

19. Murray Campbell, "Asterix promoting Mcburgers in France," *Toronto Star*, January 24, 2002, p. A3.

20. Ginny Parker, "Starbucks finds Asia a vast, thirsty market," *Globe and Mail*, May 29, 2000, p. B6.

21. Lisa D'Innocenzo, "Niche marketing key to successful stateside retail expansion," *Strategy*, March 11, 2002, pp. 1, 10.

22. Angela Kryhul, "Global where possible, local where necessary," *Marketing*, October 21, 2001, p. 8.

23. Lisa D'Innocenzo, pp. 1, 10.

24. John Heinzl, p. B12.

25. Rebecca Fannin, "Gillette out to differentiate premium pens," *Advertising Age*, November 18, 1996, p. 20.

The Financial Implications of Marketing Practice

The objective of this appendix is to illustrate the financial implications of marketing decisions. The readers must recognize that marketing actions and results are measured quantitatively. It can be said that marketing actions directly affect the financial well being of an organization.

This appendix presents some of the key financial areas for marketing managers, namely, the operating statement and the balance sheet (plus the various ratios obtained from these) and markups and markdowns.

Operating Statement

One of the major financial statements of an organization is the operating statement, often referred to as an income statement or a profit-and-loss statement. It shows whether a business achieved its primary objective—earning a profit. A profit or net income is earned when revenues exceed expenses (losses occur when expenses exceed revenues).

Revenues are inflows of cash or other properties received in exchange for goods or services provided to customers. Expenses are goods and services consumed in operating a business. From the various figures included in an operating statement, ratios are calculated and reviewed so that the financial performance of the firm can be assessed. For the purposes of analysis and control, the marketer can relate each component of an operating statement to sales. Operating statements are used for comparative purposes. For example, the ratios on the latest statement can be compared with past ratios or with planned ratios for a given period. The analysis of ratios indicates problems that management may try to correct through marketing and financial decisions.

IMPORTANT COMPONENTS OF THE OPERATING STATEMENT

Sales

The top line of any operating statement is sales; in the sample statement for KJT Enterprises, the top lines are gross sales and net sales. The level of sales is influenced by numerous marketing decisions, such as pricing strategy and the budget allocated to generate sales. Returns and allowances must be deducted from gross revenues, as net sales are the actual revenues received by the firm. Returns and allowances include returned merchandise (i.e., faulty or damaged products) and partial refunds or rebates to the customer. Since customer service is an important element of the marketing process, an organization should not view returns and allowances negatively. How product returns are handled has a direct impact on the level of customer satisfaction.

Cost of Goods Sold

The cost of goods sold in a manufacturing organization includes the costs of work in process and the inventory costs of raw materials and finished goods. In a retailing environment, cost of goods sold refers to the value of inventory offered for sale. Firms attempt to minimize the cost of goods sold, wherever possible. The lower the cost of goods sold, the higher is the gross profit.

Operating Expenses

These expenses are costs other than the merchandise costs and inventory costs cited in the cost-of-goods-sold explanation. Typically, operating expenses include marketing or selling expenses (advertising, sales expenses, and other related expenses), general expenses (rent, salaries, utilities, telephone, and so on) and interest expense. The objective of the firm is to control such expenses as much as possible, thereby improving profitability.

Let us assume that the operating statement for KJT Enterprises, Inc. is as follows:

Operating Statement
as at December 31, 200X

	$ Value	% of Net Sales
Gross Sales	820 000	102.5
Less: Returns and Allowances	20 000	2.5
Net Sales	800 000	100.0
Less: Cost of Goods Sold	480 000	60.0
Gross Profit	320 000	40.0
Less: Operating Expenses	200 000	25.0
Net Profit before Tax	120 000	15.0
Income Tax	40 000	5.0
Net Profit after Tax	80 000	10.0

THE OPERATING STATEMENT AND RATIO ANALYSIS

These ratios are worthy of explanation:

1. **Gross Profit Percentage** This percentage indicates the average profit margin on all merchandise sold during a period. Such information can be compared with past results, with a plan for the year, or with industry averages, if such information is known. If margins are too far above or below industry averages, it may indicate a cost problem or a pricing problem in the firm.

2. **Operating Expense Ratio** This ratio is needed to control individual expense categories and to evaluate performance. Ratios in this area have a direct relation to market-

ing activity, since marketing budgets are included in operating expenses. The challenge for managers is to minimize operating expenses (lower the ratio) while maximizing sales.

3. **Net Profit Percentage** This is a ratio that takes into account prices, costs, and all other expenses and is, therefore, a reflection of the firm's bottom-line profit. Since the bottom-line profit is often used to determine the objectives of the firm, it is a figure scrutinized very closely by managers, shareholders, and potential investors. The net profit percentage clearly relates the quality of a firm's decisions to the revenue it generates. Decisions that reduce costs and expenses while maintaining or increasing sales revenue have a positive effect on the net profit percentage.

The ratios for the sample operating statement for KJT Enterprises are calculated by means of the following formula:

$$\text{Operating ratio} = \frac{\$\text{Value of Component}}{\text{Net Sales}} \times 100\%$$

Each ratio compares a particular component with sales, the actual amount of revenue received by KJT Enterprises.

Therefore,

$$\text{Cost of Goods Sold} = \frac{\text{Cost of Goods Sold}}{\text{Net Sales}} \times 100\%$$

$$= \frac{480\ 000}{800\ 000} \times 100\%$$

$$= 60\%$$

$$\text{and, Gross Profit} = \frac{\text{Gross Profit}}{\text{Net Sales}} \times 100\%$$

$$= \frac{320\ 000}{800\ 000} \times 100\%$$

$$= 40\%$$

$$\text{and, Operating Expenses} = \frac{\text{Operating Expenses}}{\text{Net Sales}} \times 100\%$$

$$= \frac{200\ 000}{800\ 000} \times 100\%$$

$$= 25\%$$

$$\text{and, Net Profit before Tax} = \frac{\text{Net Profit before Tax}}{\text{Net Sales}} \times 100\%$$

$$= \frac{120\ 000}{800\ 000} \times 100\%$$

$$= 15\%$$

$$\text{and, Net Profit after Tax} = \frac{\text{Net Profit after Tax}}{\text{Net Sales}} \times 100\%$$

$$= \frac{80\ 000}{800\ 000} \times 100\%$$

$$= 10\%$$

KJT Enterprises would compare the above ratios with those of a plan or those of past years to determine if the financial results are satisfactory.

Balance Sheet

The purpose of a balance sheet is to show the financial position of a business on a specific date. The financial position is shown by listing the assets of the business, its liabilities or debts, and the equity of the owners. The balance sheet of an organization allows an organization to evaluate its earnings in a given period against the amount of money invested in the organization. Managers, therefore, assess ratios from both the profit-and-loss statement and the balance sheet.

Assume that the balance sheet for KJT Enterprises is as follows:

BALANCE SHEET
as at December 31, 200X

Assets	
Cash	$200 000
Accounts Receivable	100 000
Inventory	100 000
Facilities	200 000
Equipment	50 000
Total Assets	650 000
Liabilities	
Accounts Payable	120 000
Long-term Liabilities	100 000
Total Liabilities	220 000
Owner's Equity	
Capital	330 000
Retained Earnings	100 000
Total Owner's Equity	430 000
Total Liabilities and Owner's Equity	650 000

THE BALANCE SHEET AND RATIO ANALYSIS

Return on Investment (ROI)

This ratio compares earnings directly against investment in a particular year. Return on investment is calculated using the formula:

$$\text{ROI} \quad = \quad \frac{\text{Net Profit (Net Income)}}{\text{Average Assets}} \times 100\%$$

Therefore, following the sample statements of KJT Enterprises, Inc., the calculation would be:

$$\text{ROI} \quad = \quad \frac{120\,000}{650\,000} \times 100\%$$

$$= \quad 18.5\%$$

For the purposes of this calculation, the net profit before taxes was compared with the value of the firm's assets at the end of the period. Another way to look at the 18.5 percent ROI percentage is to say that for every dollar of assets held by the firm, there was a return of 18.5 cents. These figures, like those derived from the operating statement, can be compared with past years, plans, or industry averages.

Return on Equity (ROE)

This ratio compares the firm's earnings directly with the amount of money an owner has invested in the business, an amount called owner's equity. Return on equity is calculated using the formula:

$$\text{ROE} \quad = \quad \frac{\text{Net Profit}}{\text{Owner's Equity}} \times 100\%$$

Therefore, using the sample statements of KJT Enterprises, Inc., the calculation would be:

$$\text{ROE} \quad = \quad \frac{120\,000}{430\,000} \times 100\%$$

$$= \quad 27.9\%$$

This figure can be used by the organization to assess the worth of the investment. If the return on equity is below that of potential returns on bank deposits and certificates, the firm would question the value of being in business. On the other hand, if the ratio is very high, effort could be put into growth and expansion plans for the business.

Markups and Markdowns

Markups and markdowns are a form of financial analysis commonly used by members of a channel of distribution (wholesalers and retailers).

MARKUPS

A markup involves adding a predetermined amount to the cost of a product to determine a selling price. If a product costs $10.00 and sells for $14.00, the difference between the two prices is the markup. Markup is the difference between selling price and the cost. Markups can be expressed as:

$$\text{Markup} = \text{Retail Price} - \text{Cost}$$
$$\text{or}$$
$$\text{Cost} + \text{Markup} = \text{Retail Price}$$

Markups should be high enough to cover operating expenses and desired profit. The percentage markup can be computed in two ways (i.e., by markup on cost or by markup on sales).

$$\text{Markup (MU) on Cost} = \frac{\text{Dollar Markup}}{\text{Purchase Cost}} \times 100\%$$

$$\text{Markup (MU) on Sales} = \frac{\text{Dollar Markup}}{\text{Selling Price}} \times 100\%$$

To illustrate these formulae, let us assume the following figures. The product has a cost of $200.00 and the desired profit is $80.00. Therefore,

$$\text{Markup (MU) on Cost} = \frac{80}{200} \times 100\%$$

$$= 40\%$$

$$\text{and, Markup (MU) on Sales} = \frac{80}{280} \times 100\%$$

$$= 28.6\%$$

Both these figures are used in many ways by wholesalers and retailers. Markup on cost is a method of setting prices. In the example above, the cost was $200.00 and the desired markup was $80.00, resulting in a selling price of $280.00.

MARKDOWNS

A markdown refers to a downward adjustment in selling price. For example, if a $30.00 jacket is marked down $5.00, the new selling price is $25.00. Retailers express the markdown as a percent of the new selling price. To compute the markdown percent, the following formula is used:

$$\frac{\text{Markdown}}{\text{New Selling Price}} = \text{Markdown Percentage}$$

$$\frac{\$5.00}{25.00} = 20\%$$

When a retailer offers a price reduction (e.g., for an item on sale), the markdown is expressed as a percentage of the original selling price for the consumer's benefit. The markdown formula in this case would be:

$$\frac{\text{Markdown}}{\text{Old Selling Price}} = \text{Markdown Percentage}$$

$$\frac{\$5.00}{30.00} = 16.66\%$$

Internally, the markdown is usually based on a net sales figure rather than the original sales figure. To illustrate the offset of markdowns on a larger scale, consider an example where the total value of the markdowns is $60 000. The calculation for markdown would be as follows:

$$\text{Markdown Percentage} \quad = \quad \frac{\text{Markdown on \$}}{\text{Net Sales}} \times 100\%$$

Therefore, if net sales are $240 000 and the markdown in dollars is $60 000, the calculation would be:

$$\text{Markdown Percentage} \quad = \quad \frac{60\ 000}{240\ 000} \times 100\%$$

$$= \quad 25\%$$

In the example, the markdown represents 25 percent of net sales. Wholesalers and retailers frequently use markdowns to promote sale items, to reduce inventories of certain goods, or to balance out sales volume over a period. The results of such marketing decisions can be viewed in light of previous years' activities.

Canadian Marketing Cases

These cases can be found in the Instructor's Manual and on the Canadian Marketing Cases Web site at **www.pearsoned.ca/tuckwell**. For your reference, a complete list is shown below.

Part 1—Marketing Today
1. McDonald's Restaurants
2. Cineplex Odeon Theatres

Part 2—Inputs for Marketing Planning
3. Molson: The Plastic Beer bottle
4. Beiresdorf Inc.: Nivea for Men

Part 3—Marketing Planning
5. Country Style Food Services, Inc.
6. Hudson's Bay Company

Part 4—Product
7. Campbell's Soup Company
8. *National Post*

Part 5—Price
9. Western Trail Company
10. Fit for Life

Part 6—Distribution
11. QuikBlade®
12. Levi Strauss & Company: GWG Jeans

Part 7—Integrated Marketing Communications
13. Labatt 50
14. Lincoln Navigator

Part 8—Emerging Directions in Marketing
15. Toronto Blue Jays
16. The Running Room

Glossary

• **Absolute advantage** A situation in global marketing when only one country provides a good or service or when one country produces a product at significantly lower cost than others.

• **Accessory equipment** Items that are usually not part of a finished product.

• **Accumulation** The purchase by wholesalers of quantities of goods from many producers for re-distribution in smaller quantities to retailers they serve.

• **Acquisition strategy** A corporate strategy in which a company decides to acquire other companies that represent attractive financial opportunities.

• **Adoption** A series of stages a consumer passes through on the way to purchasing a product on a regular basis.

• **Advertising** Any paid form of non-personal message communicated through the media by an identified sponsor.

• **Advertising agencies** Service organizations responsible for creating, planning, producing, and placing advertising messages for clients.

• **Advocacy advertising** Any kind of public communication, paid for by an identified sponsor, that presents information or a point of view on a publicly recognized, controversial issue.

• **Allocation** The division of available goods from a producer among the various wholesale and retail customers.

• **Ambush marketing** A situation whereby non-sponsors of an event give a false impression through marketing communications that they are sponsors of an event.

• **Animated banner** A form of online banner advertising that includes movement or action.

• **Approach** The initial contact with the prospect, usually a face-to-face selling encounter.

• **Assorting** Making sure that the merchandise is available to consumers in an adequate variety of brand names, price ranges, and features.

• **Assortment** The variety of products that meet a retailer's target market needs.

• **Assortment consistency** Product lines that can be used in conjunction with one another or that all relate to the same sorts of activities and needs.

• **Atmosphere** The physical characteristics of a retail store or group of stores that are used to develop an image and attract customers.

• **Attitudes** An individual's feelings, favourable or unfavourable, toward an idea or object.

• **Auction (online)** A method of sale, whereby an object for sale is secured by the highest bidder.

• **Auction company** A commission merchant who brings together sellers and buyers at a central location to complete a transaction.

• **B2B e-commerce** Online communications and business transactions between two or more organizations.

• **B2C e-commerce** The retailing component of online selling; retailers selling their goods online to consumers.

• **Backward integration** A situation in which retailers have control of the channel.

• **Bait and switch** A situation in which a company advertises a bargain price for a product that is not available in reasonable quantity; when customers arrive at the store they are directed to another product, often more highly priced than the product advertised.

• **Banner ad** A rectangular ad in the shape of a narrow band that stretches across a portion of a page on an Internet site.

• **Bartering** The practice of exchanging goods and services for other goods and services rather than for money.

• **Behaviour response segmentation** The division of buyers into groups according to their occasion for using a product, the benefits they require in a product, the frequency of use, and their degree of brand loyalty.

• **Beliefs** The strongly held convictions on which an individual's actions are based.

• **Bid** A written tender submitted in a sealed envelope by a specific deadline.

• **Big box (category killer)** A product-specific mega store that offers a huge selection of low-priced merchandise.

• **Bill-back** A discount in which the manufacturer records sales volume purchased by a customer and then pays the customer the total accumulated discount at the end of a deal period.

• **Blended family** A family structure created by separation or divorce; two separate families merge into a single household as spouses remarry.

• **Blitz strategy** A media strategy in which there is a heavy concentration of spending in a short period of time.

• **Bounce back** An offer that rides along with a product shipment or with an invoice from a previous order.

• **Boutique** A store-within-a-store concept (e.g., designer label boutiques in large department stores).

• **Boycott** An organized refusal to buy a specific product.

• **Branch office** A company office in a specified geographical area, which usually includes a warehouse facility from which goods are delivered to customers in the area.

• **Brand** A name, term, symbol, or design, or some combination of them, that identifies the goods and services of an organization.

• **Brand acceptance wall (BAW)** A barrier that stops most products from further consumer acceptance.

• **Brand equity** The value a consumer derives from a product over and above the value derived from the physical attributes.

• **Brand insistence** At this stage, a consumer will search the market extensively for the brand he or she wants.

• **Brand loyalty** The degree of consumer attachment to a particular brand, product, or service.

• **Brand manager** An individual assigned responsibility for the development and implementation of effective and efficient marketing programs for a specific product or group of products.

• **Brand name** That part of a brand that can be vocalized.

• **Brand preference** The stage of a product's life at which it is an acceptable alternative and will be purchased if it is available when needed.

• **Brand recognition** Customer awareness of the brand name and package.

• **Brandmark (logo)** That part of a brand identified by a symbol or design.

• **Breadth of selection** The number of goods classifications a store carries.

• **Break-even analysis** Determining the sales in units or dollars that are necessary for total revenue to equal total costs at a certain price.

• **Breaking bulk** The delivery of small quantities, usually below the weight requirement established by transportation companies, to customers.

• **Broker** A sales agent who represents suppliers, usually small manufacturers, to the wholesale and retail trade in a particular industry.

• **Build-up strategy** A media strategy where the spending pattern or intensity of media weight gradually builds over a period of time.

• **Business analysis** A formal review of some of the ideas accepted in the screening stage, the purpose of which is again to rank potential ideas and eliminate those judged to have low financial promise.

• **Business goods** Products purchased by business, government, institutions, and industries that facilitate the operations of an organization.

• **Business-to-business advertising** A business advertising its products, services, or itself to other businesses.

• **Business-to-business market** Individuals in an organization who are responsible for purchasing goods and services that the organization needs to produce a product or service, promote an idea, or produce an income.

• **Button** A small circle, square, or rectangular-shaped banner ad.

• **Buying centre** An informal purchasing process in which individuals in an organization perform particular roles but may not have direct responsibility for the actual decision.

• **Buying committee** A formal purchasing process involving members from across a business organization who share responsibility for making a purchase decision.

• **Call centre** A central operation from which a company operates its inbound and outbound telemarketing programs.

• **Canadian Marketing Association (CMA)** A not-for-profit association comprising a cross-section of industry members.

• **Cannibalization (rate)** The rate at which a new product reduces the sales of an existing product.

• **Capital items** Expensive goods with a long lifespan that are used directly in the production of another good or service.

• **Cartel** A group of firms or countries that band together and conduct trade in a manner similar to a monopoly.

• **Cash discounts** Discounts granted for prompt payment within a stated period.

• **Cash refund** Pre-determined amount of money returned directly to the consumer by the manufacturer after the purchase has been made.

• **Cash-and-carry outlet** A limited-service merchant wholesaler who serves small independent retailers who come to the wholesaler to purchase small quantities of goods.

• **Catalogue** A reference publication distributed by large retail chains and other direct marketing organizations that promote the sale of goods.

• **Catalogue showroom** A form of discount retailer that lists its merchandise in catalogues and displays selected lines of merchandise in a showroom where customers come to place their orders.

• **Category killer (Big box)** A product-specific mega-store that offers a huge selection of low-priced merchandise.

• **Category manager** An individual assigned the responsibility for developing and implementing marketing activity for a group of related products or product lines.

• **Cause marketing** See Social marketing.

• **Census Metropolitan Area (CMA)** An area that encompasses all rural and urban areas that are linked to a city's urban core, either socially or economically.

• **Central business district** Normally, it is the hub of retailing activity in the heart of the downtown core (i.e., the main street and busy cross-streets in a centralized area).

• **Chain store (retail chain store)** An organization operating four or more retail stores in the same kind of business under the same legal ownership.

• **Chain-markup pricing** In this method, the firm considers the profit margins of its distributors.

• **Channel captain** A leader that integrates and coordinates the objectives and policies of all other members.

• **Channel length** Refers to the number of intermediaries or levels in the channel of distribution.

• **Channel width** Refers to the number of intermediaries at any one level of the channel of distribution.

• **Circulation lists** Moderately priced magazine subscription lists that target potential customers by an interest or activity.

• **Clicks (clickthroughs)** In Internet marketing, the number of times that users click on any banner ad.

• **Clickthrough rate** A calculation that determines the effectiveness of an ad in generating clicks; clicks divided by impressions is the clickthrough rate.

• **Closed bid** A written, sealed bid submitted by a supplier for review and evaluation by the purchaser on a particular date.

• **Closed-end lease** An agreement in which the lessor (leasing company) assumes financial responsibility for the difference between the depreciated value of the item and its actual cash value at the end of the lease.

• **Closing** The point in the sales presentation when the seller asks for the order.

• **Co-branding** Occurs when a company uses the equity in another brand name to help market its own brand-name product or service (two brand names on a product). This term also applies to two organizations sharing common facilities for marketing purposes (e.g., two restaurants in one location).

- **Cognitive dissonance** An individual's unsettled state of mind after an action he or she has taken.

- **Cold canvass** A type of selling where a sales representative in search of customers knocks on doors without notice.

- **Collateral material** Literature and promotional materials used by a company's sales force to help sell a product (e.g., pamphlets, bulletins, price lists, and specifications sheets).

- **Commercialization** The full-scale production and marketing plan for launching a product on a regional or national basis.

- **Commission merchant** A wholesaling merchant who receives and sells goods for suppliers in centralized markets on consignment.

- **Common market** A regional or geographical group of countries that agree to limit trade barriers among their members and apply a common tariff to goods from non-member countries.

- **Community shopping mall** A medium-sized mall that serves an immediate geographic area; a community shopping mall contains convenience goods as well as shopping goods operations.

- **Comparative advantage** A situation in global marketing in which one country produces and markets an item more efficiently or abundantly, as well as more cheaply, than other countries.

- **Comparative testing** Used in direct marketing, it is the altering of one component of the proposed campaign to judge the effect of the change on the acceptability of the offer.

- **Competition Act** Replaced the original Consumer and Corporate Affairs Act; it has three purposes.

- **Competitive bidding** A situation in which two or more firms submit written price quotations to a purchaser on the basis of specifications established by the purchaser.

- **Competitive pricing** Placing of prices above, equal to, or below those of competitors.

- **Compiled lists** Lists prepared from public sources of information.

- **Component parts** Goods used in the production of another product but which do not change form as a result of the manufacturing process.

- **Concept test** The presentation of a product idea in some visual form, with a description of the basic product characteristics and benefits, in order to get customers' reactions to it.

- **Consultative selling** In personal selling, the process of asking questions, listening attentively, and providing information and advice that is in the best interests of the customer.

- **Consumer analysis** The monitoring of consumer behaviour changes (tastes, preferences, lifestyles) so that marketing strategies can be adjusted accordingly.

- **Consumer behaviour** The acts of individuals in obtaining goods and services, including the decision processes that precede and determine these acts.

- **Consumer goods** Products and services ultimately purchased for personal use.

- **Consumer promotion** Activity promoting extra brand sales by offering the consumer an incentive over and above the product's inherent benefits.

- **Consumerism** A social force within the environment designed to aid and protect the consumer by exerting legal, moral, and economic pressure on businesses.

- **Containerization** The grouping of individual items into an economical shipping quantity that is sealed in a protective container for intermodal transportation to a final customer.

- **Contingency plan** The identification of alternative courses of action that can be used to modify an original plan if and when new circumstances arise.

- **Continuity** The length of time required to create an impact on a target market through a particular medium.

- **Contract manufacturing** A situation when a manufacturer stops producing a good domestically, preferring to find a foreign country that can produce the good according to its specifications.

- **Convenience goods** Those goods that consumers purchase frequently, with a minimum of effort and evaluation.

- **Convenience store** A food and general merchandise store, situated in a busy area of a community, selling limited numbers of lines over long hours.

- **Cookie** An electronic identification tag sent from a Web server to a browser to track a person's surfing patterns.

- **Cooperative advertising** Funds allocated by a manufacturer to pay for a portion of a retailer's advertising.

- **Cooperative direct mail** Mail envelopes containing special offers from non-competing products.

- **Copyright** The exclusive right to reproduce, sell, or publish the matter and form of a dramatic, literary, musical, or artistic work.

- **Corporate advertising** Advertising designed to convey a favourable image of a company among its various publics.

- **Corporate barter company** A company that takes possession of goods and redistributes them among barter exchange members.

- **Corporate culture** The values, norms, and practices shared by all the employees of an organization.

- **Corporate objectives** Statements of a company's overall goals.

- **Corporate plan** Identifies the corporate objectives to be achieved over a specific period.

- **Corporate planning** Planning done by top management that includes three variables: a mission statement, a statement of corporate objectives, and a statement of corporate strategies.

- **Corporate strategies** Plans outlining how the objectives are to be achieved.

- **Cost reductions** Reductions of the costs involved in the production process.

- **Cost-based pricing** A type of pricing whereby a company calculates its total costs and then adds a desired profit margin to arrive at a list price for a product.

- **Cost-benefit analysis** Used in the evaluation of price by a customer in a purchase situation, it is a procedure whereby all associated costs of the product are measured against the benefits of the product.

- **Countertrading (bartering)** A system of exchange in which something other than currency or credit is used as a form of payment.

- **Country-centred strategy** The development of unique marketing strategies for each country a product is marketed in.

- **Coupons** Price-saving incentives offered to consumers by manufacturers and retailers to stimulate purchase of a specified product.

• **Coverage** The number of geographic markets where advertising is to occur for the duration of a media plan.

• **CPM (cost per thousand)** The cost of reaching 1000 people with a message; it is a quantitative measure for comparing the effectiveness of media alternatives.

• **Creative boutiques** Specialist advertising agencies that concentrate on the design and development of advertising messages.

• **Creative execution** The formation of more precisely defined strategies for presenting a message to a target market.

• **Creative objectives** Statements of what information is to be communicated to a target market.

• **Creative strategy** Statements outlining how a message is to be communicated to a target market.

• **Cross-elasticity of demand** The degree to which the quantity demanded of one product will increase or decrease in response to changes in the price of another product.

• **Cross-marketing** A strategy in which two independent organizations share facilities and/or resources to market their goods and services to similar customers. Also referred to as co-branding.

• **Cross-ruff** An in-pack or on-pack coupon valid on the purchase of a different product.

• **Cross-sampling** Distribution of free samples by using another product as the means of distributing them.

• **Cross-tabulation** Comparison and contrast of the answers of various sub-groups or of particular sub-groups and the total response group.

• **Cult brand** A brand that captures the imagination of a small group who spread the word, make converts, and help turn a fringe brand into a mainstream brand.

• **Culture** Behaviour learned from external sources, which influences the formation of value systems that hold strong sway over every individual.

• **Customary pricing** The strategy of matching prices to a buyer's expectations: the price reflects tradition or is a price that people are accustomed to paying.

• **Customer relationship management (CRM)** The partnering of manufacturers with members of a channel of distribution to produce efficient operations so that all partners benefit.

• **Cyberspace** The world of online computer networks.

• **Damage control techniques** Sales support systems that companies employ to ensure that a customer remains a customer, such as toll-free 1-800 numbers, recall notices, liberal refund policies, intensive staff training, training of customer service personnel, warranties and extended warranties, and repair and maintenance reminders.

• **Data analysis** The evaluation, in market research, of responses on a question-by-question basis, a process that gives meaning to the data.

• **Data interpretation** Relating accumulated data to the problem under review and to the objectives and hypotheses of the research study.

• **Data mining** The analysis of information so that relationships are established between pieces of information and more effective marketing strategies can be identified and implemented.

• **Data transfer** a process whereby data from a marketing research questionnaire is transferred to a computer.

• **Database** A customer information file that is continuously updated by a company.

• **Database management system (DMS)** See Management Information System (MIS).

• **Database marketing** The process of analyzing customer and prospect data contained in a database to identify new markets and selling opportunities and to prepare marketing programs targeted to people most likely to buy.

• **Dealer premium** An incentive offered to a distributor by a manufacturer to encourage a special purchase (i.e., a specified volume of merchandise) or to secure additional merchandising support.

• **Dealer-display material** See point-of-purchase material.

• **Decision support system** An interactive, personalized marketing information system, designed to be initiated and controlled by individual decision makers.

• **Decline stage** At this stage in the product's life cycle, sales begin to drop rapidly, and profits are eroded.

• **Delayed-payment incentive** Incentive allowing the consumer a grace period during which no interest or principal is paid for the item purchased.

• **Demand-based pricing** A pricing strategy whereby the firm calculates the markup needed to cover selling expenses and profits and determines the maximum it can spend to produce the product; the calculations work backwards, since they initially consider the price the consumer will pay.

• **Demand-minus (backward) pricing** An organization determines the optimum retail selling price that consumers will accept and then subtracts the desired profit margin and marketing expenses to arrive at the cost at which the product should be produced.

• **Demarketing** Reducing demand to a level that can be reasonably supplied.

• **Demographic segmentation** The division of a large market into smaller segments that are based on combinations of age, gender, income, occupation, education, marital status, household formation, and ethnic background.

• **Demographics** The study of the characteristics of a population.

• **Department store** A large general-product line retailer that sells a variety of merchandise in a variety of price ranges.

• **Depth of selection** The number of brands and styles carried by a store in each product classification.

• **Derived demand** Demand for products sold in the business-to-business market is actually derived from consumer demand.

• **Differential advantages** The unique attributes of a product.

• **Diffusion** The manner in which different market segments accept and purchase a product between the stages of introduction and market saturation.

• **Diffusion of innovation** The gradual acceptance of a product from its introduction to market saturation.

• **Direct channel** A short channel of distribution.

• **Direct competition** Competition from alternative products and services that satisfy the needs of a common market.

• **Direct exporting** A form of international distribution whereby the exporting company itself strikes agreements with local market companies that would be responsible for distribution in the foreign country.

• **Direct home retailing** The selling of merchandise by personal contact in the home of the consumer.

• **Direct home shopping** A shopping service provided by cable television stations, whereby products are offered for sale by broadcast message (e.g., Canadian Home Shopping Network).

• **Direct investment** A company's financial commitment in a foreign country, whereby the investing company owns and operates, in whole or in part, the facility in that country.

• **Direct mail** A form of direct advertising communicated to prospects through the postal service.

• **Direct marketing** An interactive marketing system, fully controlled by the marketer, who develops products, promotes them directly to customers through a variety of media, accepts orders directly from customers, and distributes products directly to consumers.

• **Directory database** A commercial database that provides quick information about a company (e.g., size, sales, location, and number of employees).

• **Direct-response advertising** Messages that prompt immediate action, such as advertisements containing clipout coupons, response cards, and order forms; such advertising goes directly to customers and bypasses traditional channels of distribution.

• **Direct-response television (DRTV)** A sales-oriented television commercial message that encourages people to buy right away, usually through 1-800 telephone numbers.

• **Discount (junior) department store** A store that carries a full line of merchandise at low prices while offering consumers limited customer service.

• **Discount supermarket (or warehouse store)** A supermarket offering limited lines, a limited assortment of brands, few services, low margins, and low prices.

• **Disintermediation** In an Internet marketing context, the disappearance of intermediaries in the channel of distribution.

• **Disposable income** Actual income after taxes and other expenses; it is income available for optional purchases.

• **Distribution planning** A systematic decision-making process regarding the physical movement and transfer of ownership of goods and services from producers to consumers.

• **Distribution strategy** The selection and management of marketing channels and the physical distribution of products.

• **Distribution warehouse** A warehouse, or distribution centre, that assembles and re-distributes merchandise, usually in smaller quantities and in shorter periods of time.

• **Diversification strategy (corporate)** A situation where a company invests its resources in a totally new direction (e.g., a new industry or market).

• **Divestment strategy** Removal of an entire division of a company through sale or liquidation.

• **Double targeting** Devising a single marketing strategy for both sexes.

• **Double ticketing** A situation in which more than one price tag appears on an item.

• **Drop shipper** A merchant wholesaler who purchases goods from manufacturers, then contacts customers and puts together carload quantities of goods that can be delivered economically.

• **Dumping** The practice of selling goods in a foreign market at a lower price than they are sold in the domestic market.

• **Durable goods** Tangible goods that survive many uses.

• **Early adopters** A large group of opinion leaders who like to try new products when they are new.

• **Early majority** A group of consumers representing the initial phase of mass market acceptance of a product.

• **E-commerce** The conducting of business transactions, and the business activities associated with those transactions, in a virtual environment.

• **Economic order quantity (EOQ)** The size of an order of goods that will strike the best balance between the cost of ordering goods and the cost of carrying goods in inventory.

• **E-coupon (electronic coupon)** Coupons that are printed directly from Web sites for use by consumers.

• **Editing** In marketing research, a stage where completed questionnaires are reviewed for consistency and completeness.

• **Elastic demand** A situation in which a small change in price results in a large change in volume.

• **Electronic data interchange (EDI)** The computerized transfer of information among business partners in order to facilitate efficient transfer of goods.

• **Embargo** A trade restriction that disallows entry of specified products into a country.

• **Emergency goods** Goods purchased immediately when a crisis or urgency arises.

• **Encryption** A set of complex algorithmic codes that ensure network privacy; in online business transactions, messages are encrypted in both directions.

• **End-product advertising** Advertising that promotes an ingredient of a finished product.

• **E-procurement** An Internet-based business-to-business marketplace through which participants are able to purchases goods from each other.

• **Event marketing** The process, planned by a sponsoring organization, of integrating a variety of communication elements behind an event theme.

• **Event sponsorship** A situation in which a sponsor agrees to support an event financially in return for advertising privileges associated with the event.

• **Evoked set** A group of brands that a person would consider acceptable among competing brands in a class of product.

• **Exchange** The transfer of something of value from an organization in return for something from the customer so that both parties are satisfied.

• **Exclusive distribution** The availability of a product in only one outlet in a geographic area.

• **Execution (tactics)** Action plan that outlines in specific detail how strategies are to be implemented.

• **Experimental research** Research in which one or more factors are manipulated under controlled conditions, while other elements remain constant, so that respondents' reactions can be evaluated.

Exploratory research A preliminary form of research that clarifies the nature of a problem.

• **Extranet** A system that connects the intranets of individual companies together.

• **F.O.B. destination pricing** A geographic pricing strategy, whereby the seller agrees to pay freight charges between point of origin and point of destination (title does not transfer to the buyer until the goods arrive at their destination).

• **F.O.B. origin pricing** A geographic pricing strategy, whereby the price quoted by the seller does not include freight charges (the buyer assumes title when the goods are loaded onto a common carrier).

• **Fact gathering** The compilation of already discovered data, originally published for reasons that have nothing to do with the specific problem under investigation.

• **Fad** A product that has a reasonably short selling season, perhaps one or a few financially successful seasons.

• **Family brand** The use of the same brand name for a group of related products.

• **Family life cycle** A series of stages a person undergoes, starting with being a young single adult, progressing to marriage and parenthood, and ending as an older single individual.

• **Fashion** A cycle for a product that recurs through many selling seasons.

• **Fixed costs** Costs that do not vary with different quantities of output.

• **Fixed-response questioning** Questionnaire used for a large sample that contains pre-determined questions and a selection of answers that are easily filled in by the respondent or interviewer.

• **Flexible pricing** Charging different customers different prices.

• **Flight (flighting)** The purchase of media time and space in planned intervals, separated by periods of inactivity.

• **Focus group** A small group of 8 to 12 people with common characteristics, brought together to discuss issues related to the marketing of a product or service.

• **Folders** A direct response sales message printed on heavier stock paper; typically, they can be mailed without an envelope.

• **Follow-up** An activity that keeps salespeople in touch with customers after the sale has been made, to ensure that the customer is satisfied.

• **Forward buying** The practice of buying deal merchandise in quantities sufficient enough to carry a retailer through to the next deal period offered by the manufacturer.

• **Forward integration** A situation in which manufacturers have control of the channel.

• **Franchise agreement** A franchisee (retailer) conducts business using the franchiser's name and operating methods in exchange for a fee.

• **Franchise wholesaler** Retailers affiliate with an existing wholesaling operation and agree to purchase merchandise through it.

• **Freestanding insert (FSI)** A pre-printed advertisement in single- or multiple-page form that is inserted loose into newspapers.

• **Freestanding store** An isolated store usually located on a busy street or highway.

• **Freight forwarder** A firm that consolidates small shipments—shipments that form less than a carload or truckload—from small companies.

• **Frequency** The average number of times an audience is exposed to an advertising message over a given period, usually a week.

• **Frequency distribution** In a survey, the number of times each answer was chosen for a question.

• **Frequent-buyer program** Offers the consumer a small bonus when a purchase is made.

• **Full pay-out lease** A type of lease where the lessor recovers the full value of the goods leased to a customer.

• **Full-cost pricing** A desired profit margin is added to the full cost of producing a product.

• **Full-serve store** A retailer that carries a variety of shopping goods that require sales assistance and a variety of services to facilitate the sale of the goods (such services may include fitting rooms, delivery, and installations).

• **Full-service agencies** Advertising agencies that offer a complete range of services to their clients.

• **Full-service merchant wholesalers** Wholesalers who assemble an assortment of products in a central warehouse and offer their customers a full range of services, including delivery, storage, credit, support in merchandising, promotion, and in research and planning.

• **Full-text database** A database that contains the complete text of a source document making up the database.

• **Funnelling** The dividing of a subject into manageable variables so that specifically directed research can be conducted.

• **Funnelling (of questions)** Using general questions initially, then progressing to more specific questions.

• **Game (or instant-win) contest** Promotion vehicle that includes a number of pre-determined, pre-seeded winning tickets in the overall, fixed universe of tickets. Packages containing winning certificates are redeemed for prizes.

• **General merchandise store** A store offering a wide variety of product lines, and selection of brand names within those product lines (e.g., a department store).

• **General merchandise wholesaler** A wholesaler who carries a full line or wide assortment of merchandise that serves virtually all of its customers' needs.

• **Generic brand** A product without a brand name or identifying features.

• **Geodemographic segmentation** The isolation of dwelling areas through a combination of geographic and demographic information, based on the assumption that people seek out residential neighbourhoods in which to cluster with their lifestyle peers.

• **Geographic pricing** Pricing strategy based on the question, "Who is paying the freight?"

- **Geographic segmentation** The division of a large geographic market into smaller geographic or regional units.

- **Global marketing strategy** A marketing strategy whereby a product is marketed in essentially the same way, whatever the country, though some modification to particular elements of the marketing mix is often necessary.

- **Globalization** The idea that the world as a marketplace is becoming smaller and progressive-minded companies are pursuing opportunities for growth, wherever possible.

- **Glocalization** The creation of products and services intended for the global market but customized to suit local needs.

- **Grey market** A market segment based on age and lifestyles of people who are over the age of 65 years.

- **Gross Domestic Product (GDP)** The total value of goods and services produced in a country on an annual basis.

- **Growth stage** The period of rapid consumer acceptance.

- **Head-on positioning** A marketing strategy in which one brand is presented as an equal or better alternative than a competing brand.

- **Hierarchy of needs** The classification of consumers' needs in an ascending order from lower level needs to higher level needs.

- **Horizontal conflict** Conflict between similar organizations at the same level in the channel of distribution.

- **Horizontal marketing system** A situation in which many channel members at one level in the channel have the same owner.

- **House list** An internal listing of customers.

- **House organ** An internal communications document that outlines news and events about an organization to employees.

- **Hypotheses** Statements of predicted outcomes.

- **Idea marketing** Encouraging the public to accept and agree with certain issues and causes.

- **Impressions** The total audience delivered by a media plan.

- **Impressions (page views)** The number of times a banner image is downloaded to a page being viewed by a visitor.

- **Impulse goods** Goods bought on the spur of the moment, or out of habit when supplies are low.

- **Inbound telemarketing** The reception of calls by an order desk, customer-service enquiry, and direct-response calls, often generated through toll-free telephone numbers.

- **Independent retailer** A retailer operating one to three stores, even if the stores are affiliated with a large retail organization.

- **Indirect channel** A long channel of distribution.

- **Indirect competition** Competition from substitute products that offer customers the same benefit.

- **Indirect exporting** A form of international distribution where a company employs a middleman or trading company to establish a distribution network in a foreign country.

- **Individual brand** The identification of each product in a company's product mix with its own name.

- **Industrial (business) advertising** Advertising by industrial suppliers directed at industrial buyers.

- **Industrial (business) goods** Products and services purchased to be used directly or indirectly in the production of other goods for resale.

- **Inelastic demand** A situation in which a change in price does not have a significant impact on the quantity purchased.

- **Inflation** The rising price level for goods and services that results in reduced purchasing power.

- **Infomercial** Typically a 30-minute commercial that presents in more detail the benefits of a product or service.

- **In-home selling** A form of personal selling whereby an individual uses a network of local people to sell products in their communities, often at home parties.

- **Innovators** The first group of consumers to accept a product.

- **In-pack or on-pack premium** A free item placed inside the package or attached to a package and overwrapped for protection and security.

- **Inseparability** The equating of the provider of the service with the service itself.

- **Installations** Major capital items used directly in the production of another product.

- **Instant bust** A product that a firm had high expectations of but that, for whatever reasons, was rejected by consumers very quickly.

- **Instant wins** See Game contest.

- **In-store delivered coupons** Coupons distributed by in-store display centres and dispensing machines usually located near the store entrance, or on the shelves from shelf pads.

- **Intangibility** The quality of not being perceivable by the senses.

- **Integrated marketing communications (IMC)** The process of building and reinforcing mutually profitable relationships with customers and the general public by developing and coordinating a strategic communications program that enables them to make constructive contact with the company or brand through a variety of media.

- **Intensive distribution** The availability of a product in the widest possible channel of distribution.

- **Interactive banner (rich media banner)** A banner ad that engages the viewer in some kind of activity (e.g., a game, or providing information).

- **Intermediary** Offers producers of goods and services the advantage of being able to make goods and services readily available to target markets.

- **Internet** A network of computers linked together to act as one in the communication of information.

- **Interstitial** An online ad that pops onto a computer screen and interrupts users.

- **Intranet** An internal Web site that employees can access; a private network on the Internet in which companies can communicate with one another.

- **Introduction stage** The period after the product is introduced into the marketplace and before significant growth begins.

- **Inventory management** A system that ensures continuous flow of needed goods by matching the quantity of goods in inventory to sales demand so that neither too little nor too much stock is carried.

• **Issue management** Public relations messages that deliver a message showing where a company stands on a particular issue.

• **Joint or shared demand** A situation in which industrial products can only be used in conjunction with others, when the production and marketing of one product is dependent on another.

• **Joint venture** In a global marketing situation, a partnership between a domestic company and a foreign company.

• **Just-in-time (JIT) inventory system** A system that reduces inventory on hand by ordering small quantities frequently.

• **Knock-offs** Look-alike products that are often a copy of a patented product.

• **Labels** Printed sheets of information affixed to a package container.

• **Laggards** The last group of people to purchase a product.

• **Late majority** A group of consumers representing the latter phase of mass market acceptance of a product.

• **Law of demand** States that consumers purchase greater quantities at lower prices.

• **Law of supply and demand** An abundant supply and low demand lead to a low price, while a high demand and limited supply lead to a high price.

• **Leaflets (flyers)** Standard letter-sized pages that offer relevant information about a direct mail offer; they expand on information contained in a letter.

• **Lease** A contractual agreement, whereby a lessor, for a fee, agrees to rent an item to a lessee over a specified period.

• **Licensed brand** Occurs when a brand name or trademark is used by a licensee.

• **Licensing** One firm legally allowing another firm to use its patent, copyright, brand name, or manufacturing process, for a certain period.

• **Lifestyle** A person's pattern of living as expressed in his or her activities, interests, opinions, and values.

• **Limited edition brand** A brand that is only on the market for a short period; it capitalizes on the popularity of an individual or event.

• **Limited-line store** A store that carries a large assortment of one product line or a few related product lines.

• **Limited-service merchant wholesalers** Wholesalers that are selective in the functions they perform.

• **Limited-service store** A type of retailer that only offers a small range of services in order to keep operating costs to a minimum.

• **Line extension** The introduction of a different version of an existing product (e.g., a new flavour, scent, or size) under the same brand name.

• **List broker** A specialist who makes all the arrangements for one company to use the lists of another company.

• **List price** The rate normally quoted to potential buyers.

• **Lobbying** A public relations activity designed to influence policy decisions of government.

• **Local content law** A way of protecting local industry and employment by requiring a foreign-based manufacturer to use a specified amount of locally produced components.

• **Loss leaders** Products offered for sale at or slightly below cost.

• **Mail-in premiums** Items offered free or at a bargain price to consumers who send away for them.

• **Mail-order wholesaler** A wholesaler who relies on catalogues instead of a sales force to contact customers.

• **Management information system (MIS)** People and equipment organized to provide a continuous, orderly collection and exchange of information needed in a firm's decision-making process.

• **Manufacturer wholesaling** When a producer undertakes the wholesaling function, feeling that it can reach customers effectively and efficiently through direct contact.

• **Manufacturer's agent** A sales agent who carries and sells similar products for non-competing manufacturers in an exclusive territory.

• **Manufacturer's suggested list price** The price manufacturers suggest retailers should charge for a product.

• **Market** A group of people who have a similar need for a product or service, the resources to purchase it, and the willingness and ability to buy it.

• **Market analysis** The collection of appropriate information (i.e., information regarding demand, sales volume potential, production capabilities, and resources necessary to produce and market a given product) to determine if a market is worth pursuing.

• **Market challenger** Firm or firms attempting to gain market leadership through aggressive marketing efforts.

• **Market development** A strategy whereby a company attempts to market existing products to new target markets.

• **Market differentiation** Targeting several market segments with several different products and marketing plans.

• **Market follower** A company that is generally satisfied with its market share position.

• **Market integration** Expansion from a single segment into other similar segments.

• **Market leader** The largest firm in the industry and the leader in strategic action.

• **Market nicher** A firm that concentrates resources on one or more distinguishable market segments.

• **Market penetration** A strategy whereby a company attempts to improve the market position of existing products in existing markets.

• **Market planning** The analysis, planning, implementation, evaluation, and control of marketing initiatives to satisfy target market needs and achieve the organization's objectives.

• **Market segmentation** The division of a large market (mass market) into smaller homogeneous markets (targets) on the basis of common needs and/or similar lifestyles.

• **Market share** The sales volume of one competing product or company expressed as a percentage of total market sales volume.

• **Marketing** The process of planning the conception, pricing, promotion, and distribution of ideas, goods, and services to create exchanges that satisfy individual and organized objectives.

• **Marketing audit** A systematic, critical, and unbiased review and appraisal of the basic objectives and policies of the marketing department and of the organization, methods, procedures, and people employed to implement the policies.

• **Marketing channel** A series of firms or individuals that participate in the flow of goods and services from producer to final users or customers.

• **Marketing communications planning** The process of making systematic decisions about which elements of the marketing communications mix to use.

• **Marketing communications strategy** The blending of advertising, sales promotion, event marketing and sponsorship, personal selling, and public relations to present a consistent and persuasive message about a product or service.

• **Marketing concept** The process of determining the needs and wants of a target market and delivering a set of desired satisfactions to that target market more effectively than the competition does.

• **Marketing control** The process of measuring and evaluating the results of marketing strategies and plans and taking corrective action to ensure that marketing objectives are attained.

• **Marketing execution** Planning that focuses on specific program details that stem directly from the strategy section of the plan.

• **Marketing management** The directing of marketing activity on the basis of geography, type of customer, product line, or category of product, depending on the nature of the organization.

• **Marketing mix** The four strategic elements of product, price, distribution, and marketing communications.

• **Marketing objectives** Statement outlining what a product or service will accomplish in one year, usually expressed in terms of sales volume, market share, or profit.

• **Marketing planning** The analysis, planning, implementation, evaluation, and control of marketing initiatives in order to satisfy target market needs and organizational objectives.

• **Marketing plans** Plans that are short-term, specific, and combine both strategy and tactics.

• **Marketing research** A function that links the consumer, customer, and public to the marketer through information—information used to define marketing opportunities and problems; to generate, refine, and evaluate marketing actions; to monitor marketing performance; and to improve understanding of marketing as a process.

• **Marketing strategies** Identify target markets and satisfy the needs of those targets with a combination of marketing mix elements within budget constraints.

• **Maslow's hierarchy of needs** This theory states that needs can be classified in an ascending order.

• **Mass customization** The creation of systems that can personalize messages to a target audience of one.

• **Mass marketing** The use of one basic marketing strategy to appeal to a broad range of consumers without addressing any distinct characteristics among them.

• **Mature stage** The stage of a product's life cycle when it has been widely adopted by consumers; sales growth slows and eventually slightly declines.

• **Media objectives** Media planning statements that consider the target market, the presentation of the message, geographic market

priorities, the best time to reach the target, and the budget available to accomplish stated goals.

• **Media planning** A precise outline of media objectives, media strategies, and the media execution, culminating in a media plan that recommends how funds should be spent to achieve the previously established advertising objectives.

• **Media strategy** Statements that outline how media objectives will be accomplished; typically, they outline what media will be used and why certain media were selected and others rejected.

• **Media-buying service** A specialist advertising agency that concentrates on planning and purchasing the most cost-efficient time and space in the media for their clients.

• **Media-delivered coupons** Coupons distributed by advertisers through newspapers and magazines.

• **Mega-mall** A destination mall characterized by its incredibly large size and diversity of stores and services; they include amusements and other attractions that entertain shoppers.

• **Merchandise assortment** The total assortment of products a retailer carries.

• **Merge / purge** A procedure in which duplicate names are eliminated from lists that are going to be used for direct mail purposes.

• **Micro-marketing** The development of marketing strategies on a regional basis, giving consideration to the unique needs and geodemographics of different regions.

• **Mission statement** A statement of purpose for an organization reflecting the operating philosophy and direction the organization is to take.

• **Missionary selling** A form of selling that focuses on building goodwill; missionaries contact retailers to check stocks, arrange displays and provide basic information about products.

• **Modified rebuy** The purchase by an organization of a medium-priced product on an infrequent basis.

• **Monopolistic competition** A market in which there are many competitors, each offering a unique marketing mix based on price and other variables.

• **Monopoly** A market where there is a single seller of a particular good or service for which there are no close substitutes.

• **Motives** The conditions that prompt the action necessary to satisfy a need.

• **Multibrand strategy** The use of a different brand name for each item a company offers in the same product category.

• **Multi-level marketing** A distribution system in which distributors are stacked on top of each other in a shape resembling a pyramid. Distributors higher up in the pyramid receive commissions from the sale of merchandise by distributors situated below them.

• **Multinational corporation** A firm that operates in several countries and usually has a substantial share of its total assets, sales, and labour force in foreign subsidiaries.

• **Multiple channel** A type of distribution for which different kinds of intermediaries are used at the same level in the channel of distribution.

• **Multiple-unit pricing** Offering items for sale in multiples, usually at a price below the combined regular price of each item.

• **National advertising** Advertising of a trademarked product or service wherever the product or service is available.

• **Nationalization** A form of expropriation, whereby the government of a country takes control of the operation of a foreign company operating there.

• **Need** A state of deprivation or the absence of something useful.

• **Need description** In business-to-business marketing, a stage where a buying organization identifies the general characteristics of the items and services it requires.

• **Needs assessment** The initial stage of marketing planning in which a company collects appropriate information to determine if a market is worth pursuing.

• **Neighbourhood shopping mall** This type of mall contains a row or strip of stores, mainly selling convenience items and services. It typically houses a drugstore, a variety store, a hardware store, a bake shop, a hair stylist, and a convenience store.

• **Network marketing** A distribution system in which distributors are stacked on top of each other in the shape of a pyramid. Distributors higher up in the pyramid receive commissions from the sale of merchandise by distributors below them.

• **New product** A product that is truly unique and that meets needs that have been previously unsatisfied.

• **New product strategy** A corporate strategy that calls for significant investment in research and development to develop innovative products.

• **New task purchase** The purchase of an expensive product by a business for the first time.

• **Niche marketing** Targeting a product line to one particular segment and committing all marketing resources to the satisfaction of that segment.

• **Nondurable goods** Tangible goods normally consumed after one or a few uses.

• **Non-probability sample** The respondents have an unknown chance of selection, and their being chosen is based on such factors as convenience for the researcher or the judgment of the researcher.

• **Not-for-profit marketing** The marketing effort and activity of not-for-profit organizations.

• **Objection** An obstacle that the salesperson must confront and resolve if the sales transaction is to be completed.

• **Objectives** Statements that outline what is to be accomplished in a corporate plan or marketing plan.

• **Observation research** A form of research in which the behaviour of the respondent is observed and recorded.

• **Odd-even pricing** A psychological pricing strategy that capitalizes on setting prices below even-dollar amounts.

• **Off-invoice allowance** A temporary allowance that is deducted from the invoice at the time of customer billing.

• **Oligopoly** A market situation in which a few large firms control the market.

• **One-on-one interview** An in-depth face-to-face interview between a moderator and a respondent.

• **Online advertising** The placement of a commercial message on a Web site, in e-mail, or over personal communications devices.

• **Online database** A public information database accessible to anyone with proper communications facilities.

• **Online selling** The use of Internet Web sites as a vehicle for conducting business transactions.

• **Open bid** An informal submission by a potential supplier of a price quotation in written or verbal form.

• **Open-end lease** An agreement in which the lessee (customer) assumes financial responsibility for the difference between the estimated wholesale value of the item and the proceeds of its sale at the end of the lease.

• **Operating lease** A short-term lease involving monthly payments for use of equipment, which is returned to the lessor.

• **Order and reorder routine** In business-to-business marketing, the placing of an order and the establishment of a repeat order process with a supplier.

• **Order processing** A distribution activity that involves checking credit ratings of customers, recording a sale, making the necessary accounting entries, and then locating the item for shipment.

• **Orderly market agreement** An agreement by which nations share a market, eliminating the trade barriers between them.

• **Organization marketing** Marketing that seeks to gain or maintain acceptance of an organization's objectives and services.

• **Organizational buying** The decision-making process that firms follow to establish what products they need to purchase, and then identify, evaluate, and select a brand and a supplier for those products.

• **Outbound telemarketing** The calls a company makes to a customer in order to develop new accounts, generate sales leads, qualify prospects, and close a deal.

• **Outsourcing** The contracting out of services or functions previously done in-house (e.g., a firm contracts out its computer services function).

• **Packaging** Those activities related to the design and production of the container or wrapper of a product.

• **Partnering** See Relationship marketing.

• **Parts and materials** Less expensive goods that directly enter another manufacturer's production process.

• **Party selling** A form of selling where a person (a host) invites friends to his or her home for a sales demonstration.

• **Patent** A provision that gives a manufacturer the sole right to develop and market a new product, process, or material.

• **Penetration strategy (corporate)** A corporate strategy that calls for aggressive and progressive action on the part of an organization—growth is achieved by investing in existing businesses.

• **People marketing** The marketing of an individual or group of people to create a favourable impression of that individual or group.

• **Perceived risk** Closely associated with attitudes and beliefs, this risk factor is generally higher for first-time purchases or when the price of any purchase increases.

• **Perception** How individuals receive and interpret messages.

• **Perceptual map** In the context of product positioning, a grid-like diagram in which competing brands are plotted according to certain product characteristics.

• **Performance allowance** Discount offered by a manufacturer to a distributor who performs a promotional function on the manufacturer's behalf.

• **Performance evaluation** Process that determines the effectiveness of a marketing strategy or marketing mix activity and therefore acts as a control mechanism.

• **Perishability of demand** Demand for services varies over a given period.

• **Permission-based e-mail** A situation where consumers agree to accept online messages from commercial sources.

• **Personal selling** Face-to-face communication involving the presentation of features and benefits of a product or service to a buyer for the purpose of making a sale.

• **Personality** Distinguishing psychological characteristics of a person that produce relatively consistent and enduring responses to the environment in which that person lives.

• **Phantom freight** The amount by which average transportation charges exceed the actual cost of shipping for customers near the source of supply.

• **Physical distribution (logistics management)** The range of activities involved in the flow of materials, finished goods, and related information from points of origin to points of consumption to meet customer requirements at a profit.

• **Piggybacking** A system in which the entire load of a truck trailer is placed in a rail flatcar for movement from one place to another. In retailing, piggybacking also means the sharing of facilities for marketing purposes (see also Twinning and Co-branding).

• **Place marketing** Drawing attention to and creating a favourable attitude toward a particular place, be it a country, province, region, or city.

• **Planning** The process of anticipating the future business environment and determining the courses of action a firm will take in that environment.

• **Point-of-purchase material** Self-contained, custom-designed merchandising units that either temporarily or permanently display a manufacturer's product.

• **Population** A group of people with certain specific age, gender, and geodemographic characteristics.

• **Portfolio analysis** A process of reviewing the business categories or market segments that a firm operates in, based on the fact that the total company can be divided into strategic units.

• **Positioning** Designing and marketing a product to meet the needs of a target market and creating the appropriate appeals to make the product stand out from the competition in the minds of customers.

• **Post-testing** The evaluation of an advertisement, commercial, or campaign, during or after its implementation.

• **Power mall (power centre)** A mall that houses a number of category-killer superstores in one enclosed space.

• **Pre-approach** Gathering information about potential customers before actually making sales contact.

• **Predatory pricing** A situation in which a large firm sets an extremely low price in an attempt to undercut all other competitors, thus placing them in a difficult financial position.

• **Premium** An item offered free or at a bargain price to customers who buy another specific item or make a minimum purchase.

• **Presentation** The persuasive delivery and demonstration of a product's benefits.

• **Press conference** A gathering of news reporters invited to a location to witness the release of important information.

• **Press kit** The assembly of relevant public relations information into a package (press releases, photographs, schedules, etc.) that is distributed to the media for publication or broadcast.

• **Press release** A document prepared by an organization containing public relations information that is sent to the media for publication or broadcast.

• **Prestige pricing** A situation in the sale of luxury goods in which a high price contributes to the image of a product and to the status of the buyer.

• **Pre-testing** The evaluation of an advertisement, commercial, or campaign to determine the strengths and weaknesses of the message prior to a final creative production.

• **Price** The exchange value of a good or service in the marketplace.

• **Price clubs** Essentially the same as warehouse outlets, except customers must pay a fee (usually $25.00) to shop there.

• **Price elasticity of demand** Measures the effect a price change has on the volume purchased.

• **Price fixing** Competitors banding together to raise, lower, or stabilize prices.

• **Price lining** The adoption of price points for the various lines of merchandise a retailer carries.

• **Price penetration** Establishing a low entry price in order to gain wide market acceptance quickly.

• **Price planning** Developing a strategy that provides reasonable profit for the firm while making the product or service attractive to the customer.

• **Price skimming** Establishing a high entry price so that a firm can maximize its revenue early.

• **Price strategy** The development of a pricing structure that is fair and equitable for consumers and still profitable for the organization.

• **Primary package** The package containing the actual product (e.g., the jar that contains the jam).

• **Primary research** Data collected and recorded for the first time to resolve a specific problem.

• **Private label brand** A brand produced to the specifications of the distributor, usually by national brand manufacturers that make similar products under their own brand names.

• **Probability sample** The respondents have a known or equal chance of selection and are randomly selected from across the country.

• **Problem awareness** Attempting to specify the nature of the difficulty in the marketing research process.

• **Problem recognition** In the consumer buying process, a stage where a consumer discovers a need or an unfulfilled desire.

• **Processed materials** Materials used in the production of another product but which are not readily identifiable with the product.

• **Product** A bundle of tangible and intangible benefits that a buyer receives in exchange for money and other considerations.

• **Product development** A strategy whereby a company markets new products or modified existing products to current customers.

• **Product differentiation** A strategy that focuses on the unique attributes or benefits of a product that distinguish it from another product.

• **Product item** A unique product offered for sale by an organization.

• **Product life cycle** The stages a product goes through from its introduction to the market to its eventual withdrawal.

• **Product line** A grouping of product items that have major attributes in common but may differ in size, form, or flavour.

• **Product line depth** Number of lines in the mix.

• **Product line width** Number of items in the line.

• **Product manager** See Brand manager.

• **Product mix** The total range of products offered for sale by a company.

• **Product placement** In public relations, the placement of a product in a movie or television show so that the product is exposed to the viewing audience (e.g., the branded product is a prop in the show).

• **Product planning** Organizations examine ways to design products in line with consumers' expectations.

• **Product seeding** Placing a new product with a group of trendsetters who in turn influence others to purchase the product.

• **Product strategy** Making decisions about such variables as product quality, product features, brand names, packaging, customer service, guarantees, and warranties.

• **Product stretching** The sequential addition of products to a product line to increase its depth or width.

• **Product testing** In direct marketing, the testing of the viability of a product or service to see how acceptable it is to the target market.

• **Product-delivered coupons** Coupons that appear in or on the package.

• **Profile matching** A media strategy whereby the advertising message is placed in those media where the profile of readers, listeners, or viewers is reasonably close to that of the product's target market.

• **Profit maximization** To achieve this, an organization sets some type of measurable and attainable profit objective on the basis of its situation in the market.

• **Promotion (performance) allowance** A rebate or discount offered by a manufacturer or its agent to a distributor who agrees to promote the product purchased under allowance.

• **Promotion mix** The combination of five promotional elements: advertising, sales promotion, personal selling, public relations, and event marketing and sponsorships.

• **Promotion planning** A systematic decision-making process regarding the use of various elements of the promotion mix in marketing communications, the process by which objectives and strategies are outlined.

• **Promotion strategy** The blending of advertising, sales promotion, event marketing and sponsorship, personal selling, and public relations activity to present a consistent and persuasive message about a product or service.

• **Promotional pricing** The temporary lowering of prices to attract customers.

• **Proposal solicitation** A situation where a buying organization seeks and evaluates written proposals from acceptable suppliers.

• **Prospecting** A systematic procedure for developing sales leads.

• **Protectionism** A belief that foreign trade should be restricted so that domestic industry can be preserved.

• **Prototype** A physical version of a potential product, that is, of a product designed and developed to meet the needs of potential customers; it is developmental in nature and refined according to feedback from consumer research.

• **Psychographic segmentation** Market segmentation based on the activities, interests, and opinions of consumers.

• **Psychological pricing** Pricing strategies that appeal to tendencies in consumer behaviour other than rational ones.

• **Public affairs** A form of communications strategy in which communications activities are focused on various levels of governments.

• **Public image** The reputation that a product, service, or company has among its various publics.

• **Public relations** A variety of activities and communications that organizations undertake to monitor, evaluate, influence, and adapt to the attitudes, opinions, and behaviours of their publics.

• **Publicity** The communication of newsworthy information about a product, service, company, or idea, usually in the form of a press release.

• **Pull strategy** Creating demand by directing promotional efforts at consumers or final users of a product, who, in turn, put pressure on the retailers to carry it.

• **Pure competition** A market in which many small firms market similar products.

• **Push strategy** Creating demand for a product by directing promotional efforts at middlemen, who, in turn, promote the product among consumers.

• **Qualifying** The procedure for determining if a prospect needs the product, has the authority to buy it, and has the ability to pay for it.

• **Qualitative data** Collected from small samples in a controlled environment, the data result from questions concerned with "why" and from in-depth probing of the participants.

• **Qualitative variability** The variations in services offered by different individuals, even within the same organization.

• **Quantitative data** Collected using a structured procedure and a large sample, the data provide answers to questions concerned with "what," "when," "who," "how many," and "how often."

• **Quantity discount** Offered on the basis of volume purchased in units or dollars.

• **Quota** A specific limit imposed on the amount of goods that may be imported into a country.

• **Quotation** A written document, usually from a sales representative, which states the terms of the price quoted.

• **Rack jobbers** Wholesalers responsible for stocking merchandise-display racks that they own and that display the products they carry.

• **Rain cheque** A guarantee by a retailer to provide an original product or one of comparable quality to a consumer within a reasonable time.

• **Rationalization** The restructuring, downsizing, and, if necessary, the closing of operations that are not economically justified.

• **Raw materials** Farm goods and other materials derived directly from natural resources.

• **Reach** The total audience potentially exposed, one or more times, to an advertiser's schedule of messages in a given period, usually a week.

• **Real income** Income adjusted for inflation over time.

• **Rebate** A temporary price discount in the form of a cash return made directly to the consumer, usually by a manufacturer.

• **Recall test** A message-effectiveness test that measures consumers' comprehension following exposure to a message.

• **Recognition test** A message-effectiveness test that determines the level of consumer awareness of an advertisement.

• **Rectangle** An oversized rectangular-shaped banner ad.

• **Redemption rate** The number of coupons returned to an organization expressed as a percentage of the total number of coupons in distribution for a particular coupon offer.

• **Reference group** A group of people with a common interest that influences the members' attitudes and behaviour.

• **Refund** See Cash refund.

• **Regional shopping mall** This is a large mall containing as many as 100 or more stores and several large department stores.

• **Reintermediation** The replacement of old intermediaries with new and different intermediaries in a channel of distribution.

• **Relationship marketing** The formation of integrated ties between customers and suppliers in a channel of distribution so that all parties derive mutual benefit. Also called partnering or database marketing.

• **Reliability (of data)** Refers to similar results being achieved if another research study were undertaken under similar circumstances.

• **Reorder point** An inventory level at which new orders must be placed if normal production operations are to be maintained or demand for finished products to be satisfied.

• **Repositioning** Changing the place a product occupies in the consumer's mind, relative to competitive products.

• **Research objectives** Statements that outline what the research is to accomplish.

• **Response list** A purchasable list that identifies mail order buyers.

• **Retail advertising** Advertising by a retail operation to communicate image, store sales, and the variety of merchandise carried.

• **Retail barter exchange** A buying-selling situation where small companies band together through an exchange agent who facilitates transactions among members for a fee.

• **Retail chain store** See Chain store.

• **Retail cooperatives** Retailers that join together to establish a distribution centre that performs the role of the wholesaler in the channel.

• **Retail franchise** A contractual agreement between a franchiser and a franchisee.

• **Retail in-ad coupon** A coupon printed in a retailer's weekly advertising, either in the newspaper or in supplements inserted in the newspaper.

• **Retailing** Activities involved in the sale of goods and services to final consumers for personal, family, or household use.

• **Retailing mix** The plan a retailer uses to attract customers.

• **Reverse marketing** In business-to-business marketing, an effort by an organizational buyer to build relationships that shape a suppliers goods and services to fit the buyer's needs and those of its customers.

• **Reversification** A corporate strategy in which a company sells off unprofitable divisions and retreats to its core areas where profit potential is greater.

• **Rich media** A form of online advertising that incorporates greater use of, and interaction with, animation, audio, and video.

• **Rifle strategy** The selection of media that appeal to a common interest of a particular target market.

• **Sales office** A company that is usually located near the customers but does not carry inventory.

• **Sales promotion** Activity that provides special incentives to bring about immediate action from consumers, distributors, and an organization's sales force.

• **Sales volume maximization** A firm strives for growth in sales that exceeds the growth in the size of the total market so that its market share increases.

• **Sample (free sample)** A free product distributed to potential users either in a small trial size or in its regular size.

• **Sample population** A representative portion of an entire population used to obtain information about that population.

• **Sampling frame** A listing that can be used to access a population for research purposes.

• **Sandwich generation** A generation of parents who are simultaneously caring for children and aging relatives.

• **Scanner** A device that reads the UPC codes on products and produces instantaneous information on sales.

• **Scrambled merchandising** The addition, in retailing, of unrelated products and product lines to original products.

• **Screening** An early stage in the new product development process where new ideas are quickly eliminated.

• **Seasonal discounts** Discounts that apply to off-season or pre-season purchases.

• **Secondary data** Data that have been compiled and published for purposes other than that of solving the specific problem under investigation.

• **Secondary package** An outer wrapper that protects the product, often discarded once the product is used the first time.

• **Selective distribution** The availability of a product in only a few outlets in a particular market.

• **Selective exposure** Only noticing information that is of interest.

• **Selective perception** Screening out information and messages that are in conflict with previously learned attitudes and beliefs.

• **Selective retention** Remembering only what you want to remember.

• **Self-concept theory** States that the self has four components: real self, self-image, looking-glass self, and ideal self.

• **Self-liquidating premium** A premium offer in which the full cost of the premium is recovered by the purchase price of the offer.

• **Self-regulation** A form of regulation whereby an industry sets standards and guidelines for its members to follow.

• **Self-serve store** A store that is characterized by the limited number of services offered. Such a store tends to rely on in-store displays and merchandising to sell products.

• **Semantic differential** Use of opposite descriptions of the attributes of a product or service to describe product or service attributes.

• **Service mix** The particular combination of all services that a supplier offers.

• **Service quality** The expected and perceived quality of a service offering.

• **Services** The activity and benefits provided by an organization that satisfy the buyer's needs without conferring ownership of tangible goods; also, intangible offerings required to operate a business efficiently (e.g., repair or maintenance services).

• **Shopping goods** Goods that the consumer compares on such bases as suitability, quality, price, and style before making a selection.

• **Shopping mall** A centrally owned, managed, planned, and operated shopping facility comprising a balanced mix of retail tenants and adequate parking for customers.

• **Shotgun strategy** The selection of general-interest media to reach a broad cross-section of a market population.

• **Situation analysis** Collecting of information from knowledgeable people inside and outside the organization and from secondary sources.

• **Skyscraper** A tall, oblong-shaped banner ad that usually appears at the side of a Web page.

• **Slippage** A situation in which a consumer starts collecting proofs of purchase for a refund offer but neglects to follow through and submit a request for the refund.

• **Slotting allowance** Discount offered by a supplier to a retail distributor, for the purpose of securing shelf space in retail outlets; such allowances are commonly associated with product introductions.

• **Social class** The division of people into ordered groups on the basis of similar values, lifestyles, and social history.

• **Social marketing** Marketing activity that increases the acceptability of social ideas.

• **Social responsibility** An attitude of corporate conscience that anticipates and responds to social problems.

• **Socially responsible marketing** The notion that business should conduct itself in the best interests of consumers and society.

• **Solo direct mail** Specialized or individually prepared envelopes containing offers sent directly to prospects.

• **Sorting** Separating merchandise into grades, colours, and sizes.

• **Sorting process** The accumulation, allocation, sorting, and assorting of merchandise.

• **Source list** A list maintained by the Ministry of Supply and Services that includes the names, products, and services of all companies that have expressed an interest in dealing with the federal government.

• **Spam** The inappropriate use of an online mailing list to deliver a message; it is unsolicited junk mail.

• **Specialty goods** Goods that consumers will make an effort to find and purchase because the goods possess some unique or important characteristic.

• **Specialty store** A store selling a single line or limited line of merchandise.

• **Specialty-merchandise wholesaler** A wholesaler that carries a limited number or narrow line of products but offers an extensive assortment within these lines.

• **Sponsored e-mail** The inclusion of a second message (from a sponsor) when a Web site mails information to a subscriber.

• **Sponsorship (online)** An advertiser committing to an extended relationship with a Web site unrelated to the company's own site.

• **Standard industrial classification (SIC)** A numbering system that allows a supplier to track down customers who can use its goods and services within an industry category.

• **Staple goods** Products that are needed or used on a regular basis.

• **Stock balance** The practice of maintaining an adequate assortment of goods that will attract customers while keeping inventories of both high-demand and low-demand goods at reasonable levels.

• **Stockout** Items that are not available when a customer's order is shipped.

• **Stockton** The number of times during a specific period that the average inventory of a store is sold.

• **Storage warehouse** A warehouse that holds products for long periods of time in an attempt to balance supply and demand for producers and purchasers.

• **Straight (or full) rebuy** The purchase of inexpensive items on a regular basis by an organization.

• **Strategic alliance** A partnering process whereby two firms combine resources in a marketing venture for the purpose of satisfying the customers they share; the firms have strengths in different areas.

• **Strategic business unit (SBU)** A unit of a company that has a separate mission and objective and that can be planned independently of other company business.

• **Strategic control** Long-term control measure common in multiproduct, multi-division companies.

• **Strategic planning** The process of determining objectives and identifying strategies and tactics within the framework of the business environment that will contribute to the achievement of objectives.

- **Strategies** Statements that outline how objectives will be achieved.

- **Strip mall** A collection of stores attached together in a neighbourhood plaza.

- **Subculture** A subgroup of a culture that has a distinctive mode of behaviour.

- **Supermarket** A departmentalized food store, selling packaged grocery products, produce, dairy, meat, frozen food, and general merchandise.

- **Superstitial** Online ads that include animation, audio, and video; they resemble a television commercial.

- **Superstore** A diversified supermarket that sells a broad range of food and non-food items.

- **Supplier search** A stage in the business-to-business buying process where a buyer looks for potential suppliers.

- **Supplier selection** The stage in the business-to-business buying process where the buying organization evaluates the proposals from various suppliers and selects the one that matches its needs.

- **Supplies** Standardized products that are routinely purchased with a minimum of effort.

- **Supplies and services** Goods purchased by business and industry that do not enter the production process but facilitate other operations of the organization.

- **Supply chain** A sequence of companies that perform activities related to the creation and delivery of a good or service to consumers or business customers.

- **Supply chain management** The integration of information among members of a supply chain to facilitate efficient production and distribution of goods to customers.

- **Survey research** Data that is collected systematically through some form of communication with a representative sample by means of a questionnaire.

- **Sweepstakes** A type of contest in which large prizes, such as cash, cars, homes, and vacations, are given away to randomly selected participants.

- **SWOT analysis** The examination of critical factors that have an impact on the nature and direction of a marketing strategy (strengths, weaknesses, opportunities, and threats).

- **Tabulation** Counting the various responses for each question and arriving at a frequency distribution.

- **Target market** A group of customers who have certain characteristics in common.

- **Target pricing** A pricing strategy designed to generate a desirable rate of return on investment and based on the full costs of producing a product.

- **Tariff** A tax or duty imposed on imported goods.

- **Telemarketing** The use of telecommunications to promote the products and services of a business.

- **Test marketing** Placing a product for sale in one or more representative markets to observe performance under a proposed marketing plan.

- **Total product concept** The package of benefits a buyer receives when he or she purchases a product.

- **Trade advertising** Advertising directed at channel members by a source supplier, such as a manufacturer.

- **Trade fair** A periodic show or exhibition at which manufacturers in a particular industry gather to display merchandise to prospective wholesalers and retailers.

- **Trade promotion** Promotional activity directed at distributors that is designed to increase the volume they purchase and encourage merchandising support for a manufacturer's product.

- **Trade-in allowance** Price reduction granted for a new product when a similar used product is turned in.

- **Trademark** That part of a brand granted legal protection so that only the owner can use it.

- **Trading bloc** Economic alliance between countries in the same area of the world.

- **Trial close** An attempt to close that failed.

- **Truck jobber** A specialty wholesaler operating mainly in the food distribution industry, who sells and delivers goods to retail customers during the same sales call.

- **Twinning** Offering two or more different brands at the same location or adjoining locations (e.g., two restaurants under one roof). See also Piggybacking and Co-branding.

- **Uniform delivered pricing** A geographic pricing strategy that includes an average freight charge for all customers regardless of their location.

- **Unique selling point (USP)** The primary benefit of a product or service, the one feature that distinguishes a product from competing products.

- **Unit pricing** The expression of price in terms of a unit of measurement (e.g., cost per gram or cost per millilitre).

- **Unsought goods** Goods which consumers are unaware they need or about which they lack knowledge.

- **Validity (of data)** Refers to a research procedure's ability to actually measure what it is intended to.

- **Value pricing (EDLP)** The establishment of a fair everyday price that is attractive to consumers and profitable for the company (often referred to as everyday low pricing).

- **Variable costs** Costs that change according to the level of output.

- **Variety store** A store selling a wide range of staple merchandise at low or popular prices.

- **Vendor analysis** An evaluation of potential suppliers based on an assessment of their technological ability, consistency in meeting product specifications, quantity, delivery, and their ability to provide needed quantity.

- **Venue marketing** The linking of a brand name (company name) to a physical site such as a theatre, stadium or arena.

- **Vertical conflict** Conflict that occurs when a channel member feels that another member at a different level is engaging in inappropriate conduct.

- **Vertical integration strategy** A corporate strategy where a company owns and operates businesses at different levels of the channel of distribution.

- **Vertical marketing system (VMS)** The linking of channel members at different levels in the marketing process to form a centrally controlled marketing system in which one member dominates the channel.

• **Video brochure** A video presentation of a product.

• **Virtual advertising** The electronic placement of an advertising image into television programs, both live and taped.

• **Vision statement** A statement that defines plans for the future, what the company is and does, and where it is headed.

• **Visit** A sequence of page requests made by a visitor at a Web site.

• **Visitor** A unique user who comes to a Web site.

• **Voluntary chain** A wholesaler-initiated organization consisting of a group of independent retailers who agree to buy from a designated wholesaler.

• **Warehouse** a distribution centre that receives, sorts, and redistributes merchandise to customers.

• **Warehouse outlets** No-frills, cash-and-carry outlets that offer customers name-brand merchandise at discount prices.

• **Web browser** A software program that allows a user to navigate the World Wide Web.

• **Web site** An encompassing body of online information for a particular domain name (e.g., an organization or business).

• **Wholesaling** Buying or handling merchandise and subsequently reselling it to organizational users, other wholesalers, and retailers.

• **World Wide Web** A collection of Web sites linked together on the Internet.

• **Zone pricing** The division of a market into geographic zones and the establishment of a uniform delivered price for each zone.

Index

Note: Key terms are boldface.